Advances

in COMPUTERS
VOLUME 53

Advances in
COMPUTERS
Emphasizing Distributed Systems

EDITED BY

MARVIN V. ZELKOWITZ

Department of Computer Science
and Institute for Advanced Computer Studies
University of Maryland
College Park, Maryland

VOLUME 53

ACADEMIC PRESS

A Harcourt Science and Technology Company

San Diego   San Francisco   New York   Boston
London   Sydney   Tokyo

Academic Press
A Harcourt Science and Technology Company
525 B Street, Suite 1900, San Diego, California 92101-4495, USA
http://www.academicpress.com

Academic Press
A Harcourt Science and Technology Company
32 Jamestown Road, London NW1 7BY, UK
http://www.academicpress.com

ISBN 0-12-012153-0

A catalogue for this book is available from the British Library

Typeset by Mathematical Composition Setters Ltd, Salisbury, UK
Printed and bound in the United Kingdom
Transfered to Digital Printing, 2011

Contents

Shared-Memory Multiprocessing: Current State and Future Directions

Per Stenström, Erik Hagersten, David J. Lilja, Margaret Martonosi, and Madan Venugopal

Shared Memory and Distributed Shared Memory Systems: A Survey

Krishna Kavi, Hyong-Shik Kim, Ben Lee, and A. R. Hurson

Resource-Aware Meta-Computing

Jeffrey K. Hollingsworth, Peter J. Keleher, and Kyung D. Ryu

Knowledge Management

William W. Agresti

A Methodology for Evaluating Predictive Metrics

Jarrett Rosenberg

An Empirical Review of Software Process Assessments

Khaled El Emam and Dennis R. Goldenson

State of the Art in Electronic Payment Systems

N. Asokan, P. Janson, M. Steiner, and M. Waidner

Defective Software: An Overview of Legal Remedies and Technical Measures Available to Consumers

Colleen Kotyk Vossler and Jeffrey Voas

CONTENTS

Contributors

William W. Agresti is Chief Scientist in the Systems Technology Center at Mitretek Systems, Inc., in McLean, Virginia, providing software engineering technology support across the corporation. He recently returned from the National Science Foundation where he was Program Director for Experimental Software Systems. His research interests are in empirical software engineering and information technology measurement. He previously held positions with the MITRE Corporation, and with Computer Sciences Corporation, where he led software development and applied research projects for the Software Engineering Laboratory at NASA's Goddard Space Flight Center. He was technical manager of the NASA/CSC team that pioneered the use of object-oriented design and Ada for flight dynamics mission support. Earlier he was a Professor and Associate Dean of Engineering. He received his PhD from New York University.

N. Asokan is a senior research engineer at the communication systems laboratory at Nokia Research center, Helsinki, Finland. He is interested in security issues in various domains including internetworking, mobile computing, and electronic commerce. He received his BTech in computer science and engineering from the Indian Institute of Technology at Kharagpur, MS in computer science from Syracuse University, and PhD in computer science from the University of Waterloo.

Khaled El Emam is currently at the National Research Council in Ottawa. He is co-editor of ISO's project to develop an international standard defining the software measurement process, and knowledge area specialist for the software engineering process in the IEEE's project to define the Software Engineering Body of Knowledge. He has also co-edited two books on software process. Previously, he worked in both small and large research and development projects for organizations such as Toshiba International Company, Yokogawa Electric, and Honeywell Control Systems. Khaled El Emam obtained his PhD from the Department of Electrical and Electronics Engineering, King's College, the University of London (UK) in 1994. He was previously the head of the Quantitative Methods Group at the Fraunhofer Institute for Experimental Software Engineering in Germany, a research scientist at the Centre de recherche informatique de Montreal (CRIM) in Canada, and a researcher in the software engineering laboratory at McGill University.

Dennis R. Goldenson is a member of the technical staff in the software engineering measurement and analysis group at the Software Engineering Institute. His work focuses on the impact of software process improvement and other software engineering practices. Related interests are in tools to support collaborative processes, survey research, and experimental design. Other recent work has included evaluation of distance learning and the acquisition of software intensive systems. He also served for several years as Secretary-Treasurer of the Foundation for the Empirical Studies of Programmers. Dr. Goldenson came to the SEI in 1990 after teaching at Carnegie Mellon University since 1982. He began working on software development over 35 years ago, initially as a research programmer for custom statistical software, then as a lead programmer/designer for an early decision support system. Immediately prior to coming to the SEI, he was co-principal investigator of a large National Science Foundation funded project for the development and evaluation of integrated programming environments.

Erik Hagersten received an MS in electrical engineering and a PhD in computer science, both from the Royal Institute of Technology (KTH), Stockholm, Sweden. He was recently appointed a professor in computer architecture at Uppsala University. Before that, he was the Chief Architect for the High-End Server Engineering Group, Sun Microsystems, Inc., Menlo Park, CA, since it joined Sun from Thinking Machines in 1994. He has previous experience from high-end CPU design and large fault-tolerant systems at Ericsson and from applied computer architecture research in the Multiprocessor Emulation Facility Project at Massachusetts Institute of Technology (MIT). During his 5 years in academia, he introduced the new architecture ideas of cache-only memory architecture (COMA) and simple COMA (S-COMA), while managing the computer system's research group at the Swedish Institute of Computer Science (SICS). He is the author of more than 25 academic papers and has filed more than 50 patents.

Jeffrey Hollingsworth is an assistant professor in the Computer Science Department at the University of Maryland, College Park, and affiliated with the Department of Electrical Engineering and the University of Maryland Institute for Advanced Computer Studies. His research interests include performance measurement tools for parallel computing, high performance distributed computing, and computer networks. He received his PhD and MS degrees in computer science from the University of Wisconsin in 1994 and 1990 respectively. He earned his BS in Electrical Engineering from the University of California at Berkeley in 1988. Dr. Hollingsworth is a member of the IEEE Computer Society and ACM.

A. R. Hurson is a member of the Computer Science and Engineering Faculty at the Pennsylvania State University. His research for the past 17 years has been directed toward the design and analysis of general as well as special purpose computer architectures. He has published over 170 technical papers in areas including computer architecture, parallel and distributed processing, dataflow architectures, cache memory, database systems, multi-databases, object oriented databases, Global Information Sharing process, and VLSI algorithms. Dr. Hurson served as the Guest Co-Editor of special issues of the *IEEE Proceedings* on supercomputing technology, the *Journal of Parallel and Distributed Computing* on load balancing and scheduling, and the *Journal of Integrated Computer-Aided Engineering* on multidatabase and interoperable systems. He is also the co-founder of the IEEE Symposium on Parallel and Distributed Processing (currently IPDPS). He has served as a member of the IEEE Computer Society Press Editorial Board and an IEEE Distinguished speaker. Currently, he is serving in the IEEE/ACM Computer Sciences Accreditation Board, as the editor of *IEEE Transactions on Computers*, and as an ACM lecturer.

Phil Janson is the manager of the applied computer science department at the IBM Zurich Research Laboratory. His research interests include operating systems, distributed systems, computer communication, and security. He has written several papers and holds several patents in these fields and is the author of a text book on operating systems. He received a BS in electrical engineering from the University of Brussels and an MS, an EE, and a PhD in computer science from the Massachusetts Institute of Technology.

Krishna Kavi is Professor and Eminent Scholar in the Department of Electrical and Computer Engineering at the University of Alabama in Huntsville. He received a BS in electrical engineering from the Indian Institute of Science in 1976 and a PhD in computer science and engineering from Southern Methodist University in Dallas, Texas in 1980. Previously he was a program manager at the National Science Foundation in Washington, DC, with the University of Texas at Arlington, and the University of Southwestern Louisiana. His research interests are in dataflow and multithreaded systems.

Peter J. Keleher is an Assistant Professor in the Computer Science Department at the University of Maryland, College Park. His research interests lie primarily in the field of distributed computing. The two primary thrusts of his current work are in consistency management in mobile databases and object stores, and in global resource management in large-scale systems. The work on consistency management is aimed at developing lightweight protocols that communicate via epidemic algorithms and commit updates in an entirely decentralized fashion, without requiring any server to have complete knowledge of system membership. The resource management work encompasses a large number of issues involved in executing parallel applications in large-scale, non-dedicated, possibly heterogeneous environments.

Hyong-Shik Kim, before returning to Korea, was a post-doctoral researcher at the University of Alabama in Huntsville during 1997–1999. His research interests include multithreaded processing, computer systems architecture, parallel processing, performance measurement, scheduling and load balancing, and design automation. He received his BSE, MSE and PhD degrees in Computer Engineering from the Seoul National University, Seoul, Korea. He is a member of the IEEE Computer Society, the ACM and the Korea Information Science Society.

Ben Lee received a BE in Electrical Engineering in 1984 from the Department of Electrical Engineering at State University of New York at Stony Brook, and a PhD in Computer Engineering in 1991 from the Department of Electrical and Computer Engineering, The Pennsylvania State University. He is currently an Associate Professor in the Department of Electrical and Computer Engineering at Oregon State University. His research interests include parallel processing, computer architecture, program partitioning and scheduling, multithreading and thread-level speculation, and network computing. Professor Lee is a member of the IEEE Computer Society.

David J. Lilja received his PhD and MS degrees, both in Electrical Engineering, from the University of Illinois at Urbana-Champaign, and a BS in Computer Engineering from Iowa State University in Ames. He is currently an Associate Professor in the Department of Electrical and Computer Engineering, and a Fellow of the Minnesota Supercomputing Institute, at the University of Minnesota in Minneapolis. He also is a member of the graduate faculty in the program in Computer Science and the program in Scientific Computation, and was the founding Director of Graduate Studies for the program in Computer Engineering. Previously, he worked as a research assistant at the Center for Supercomputing Research and Development at the University of Illinois, and as a processor development engineer at Tandem Computers (now a division of Compaq) in Cupertino, California. He is an associate editor for the *IEEE Transactions on Computers*, and is a distinguished visitor of the IEEE Computer Society. In 1994, he was awarded a McKnight Land-Grant Professorship by the Board of Regents of the University of Minnesota. His main research interests include high-performance computer architecture, parallel processing, and computer systems performance analysis, with a special emphasis on the interaction of software and compilers with the architecture. He is a senior member of the IEEE Computer Society, a member of the ACM, and a registered Professional Engineer.

Margaret Martonosi has been an Assistant Professor of Electrical Engineering at Princeton University since 1994. Prior to that, Dr. Martonosi received MS and PhD degrees from Stanford University and a BS degree with distinction from Cornell University. Her research interests lie at the hardware–software interface and most recently have focused on performance analysis techniques and their application to adaptive execution. She was a 1995 recipient of the NSF Career Award and a 1998 recipient of Princeton's Howard B. Wentz Award. She is a member of ACM and a senior member of IEEE.

Jarrett Rosenberg is a statistician and quality engineer at Sun Microsystems. He obtained his doctorate from the University of California at Berkeley, and he worked at Xerox and Hewlett-Packard Laboratories before joining Sun in 1990. He is a member of the ACM, the American Statistical Association, and the American Society for Quality, and is an ASQ Certified Quality Engineer, Reliability Engineer, and Software Quality Engineer.

Kyung D. Ryu is a PhD student and Graduate Research Assistant in the Computer Science Department, University of Maryland, College Park. He received his BS and MS in Computer Engineering from Seoul National University in 1993 and 1995, respectively. He has another MS in Computer Science from University of Maryland in 1997.

Michael Steiner is a research scientist at the Department of Computer Science, Universität des Saarlandes, Saarbrücken and in the network security research group at the IBM Zurich Research Laboratory. His interests include secure and reliable systems as well as cryptography. He received a Diplom in computer science from the Swiss Federal Institute of Technology (ETH) in 1992 and expects to receive a doctorate in computer science from the Universität des Saarlandes, Saarbrücken.

Per Stenström is a Professor of Computer Engineering and a Vice-Dean at the School of Electrical and Computer Engineering at Chalmers University of Technology with responsibility for the PhD programme. He received an MSc in Electrical Engineering and a PhD in Computer Engineering from Lund University in 1981 and 1990, respectively. His research interests are in computer architecture and real-time systems with an emphasis on design principles and design methods for computer systems in applications with challenging performance requirements. He has authored or co-authored two textbooks and more than 70 papers in international conferences and journals and has also been a visiting scientist/professor and participated in computer architecture projects at Carnegie-Mellon, Stanford, and the University of Southern California. He is also an associate editor of the *Journal of Parallel and Distributed Computing* (JPDC) and has guest edited special issues on multiprocessing in *IEEE Computer* and *Proceedings of the IEEE*. Dr. Stenstrom is a Senior member of the IEEE and a member of the IEEE Computer Society.

Madan Venugopal is Manager, Strategic Marketing at S3 Incorporated. He has previously worked for SGI, Digital Equipment Corporation, Alliant Computer Systems, and Multiflow Computer in technical and marketing positions. His experience covers a wide range of shared and distributed memory parallel systems using RISC, VLIW, and vector processors. His research interests include computational mechanics, parallel processing, and multimedia computing. He received a BTech in Naval Architecture and Shipbuilding from the University of Cochin, an MASc in Mechanical Engineering from the University of British Columbia and an SM and PhD in Ocean Engineering from the Massachusetts Institute of Technology. He is a member of the IEEE Computer Society.

Jeffrey Voas is a Co-founder and Vice-President of Reliable Software Technologies (RST). In 1999, RST was named to the WashTech-50, identifying it as one of the 50 fastest growing high-tech companies in the Washington, DC area. Also in 1999, RST was ranked as the fifth fastest-growing technology company in Virginia. Dr Voas has coauthored two Wiley books: *Software Assessment: Reliability, Safety, Testability* (1995), and *Software Fault Injection: Inoculating Programs Against Errors* (1998). He was the General Chair for COMPASS'97, was the Program Chair for ISSRE'99, and Program Co-Chair for ICSM 2000. Dr Voas received a PhD in computer science from the College of William & Mary in 1990, is a Senior Member of the IEEE, and in 1999 was named Young Engineer of the Year by the District of Columbia Council of Engineering and Architectural Societies. He is an adjunct professor at West Virginia University.

Colleen Kotyk Vossler is an associate in the technology practice group of Shaw Pittman, a law firm based in Washington, DC, where she focuses on Internet issues, including e-commerce. Ms. Vossler's experience includes preparation of computer maintenance, end-user licensing, operating, employment, and escrow agreements. She has assisted technology, real estate and corporate clients with the complexities of digital and electronic signature laws and the applicability of trade secret laws to Internet sales.

Ms. Vossler is admitted to practice in Maryland. She received her JD from William & Mary School of Law in 1998 and her AB cum laude in Government at Harvard College in 1993.

Michael Waidner is the manager of the network security and cryptography research group at the IBM Zurich Research Laboratory. His research interests include cryptography, security, and all aspects of dependability in distributed systems. He has co-authored numerous publications in these fields. Dr. Waidner received his diploma and doctorate in computer science from the University of Karlsruhe, Germany.

Preface

As the computer industry moves into the 21st century, the long-running *Advances in Computers* series is ready to tackle the challenges of the new century with insightful articles on new technology, just as it has chronicled the advances in computer technology of the 20th century since 1960. As the longest-running continuing series on computers, *Advances in Computers* presents those technologies that will affect the industry in the years to come.

In this volume, the 53rd in the series, we present eight relevant topics. The first three represent a common theme on distributed computing systems—using more than one processor to allow for parallel execution, and hence completion of a complex computing task in a minimal amount of time. The other five chapters describe other relevant advances from the late 1990s.

The first chapter "Shared-memory multiprocessing: current state and future directions," by P. Stenstrom, E. Hagersten, D. Lilja, M. Martonosi, and M. Venugopal, presents an overview of shared-memory research. The goal of this approach is to allow multiple processors, with access to a common memory, to use this common memory to switch among the relevant programs in a timely manner. The chapter discusses various approaches to this problem, from new hardware architectural designs to programming language solutions to the problem.

The second chapter, "Shared memory and distributed shared memory systems: A survey," by K. Kavi, H. Kim, B. Lee, and A. Hurson, presents similar material from a different perspective. They have extended the concept of a distributed memory system from Chapter 1 by allowing for distributed memory systems where each processor does not have access to all of the available memory and a message-passing scheme has to be employed.

Chapter 3, "Resource-aware meta-computing," by J. Hollingsworth, P. Keleher, and K. Ryu, uses a specific method to achieve the distributed-memory computing discussed in the two previous chapters. They define "meta-computing" as the simultaneous and coordinated use of semi-autonomous computing resources in physically separate locations and use their Harmony system as an example of such a system.

Chapter 4, "Knowledge Management," by William Agresti, is the first chapter in the second part of his book, Other Advances in Computing. His chapter addresses the increasingly important topic of knowledge management systems which turn the computerized data files of a corporation into business assets. How one is able to understand, file, retrieve, and synthesize various computer data assets into information for business decisions has a major impact on the "bottom line" of large corporations.

Chapter 5, "A methodology for evaluating predictive metrics," by Jarrett Rosenberg, addresses an important software engineering issue. There is great interest in collecting data from software development projects, but how does one collect such data, how does one analyze it, and what does it mean? Software engineers often lack the appropriate background in statistics required to address those questions. In this chapter, Dr. Rosenberg presents an approach toward data collection and analysis applicable to the software development domain.

One of the major topics in software development today is the concept of software process improvement and assessment. Everyone agrees that software development practices can be improved; the issue is how? Concepts such as the Capability Maturity Model, ISO 9001 and others have been proposed as approaches to force organizations to improve their development practices and as ways to measure that improvement. In Chapter 6, "An empirical review of software process assessments," K. El Eman and D. Goldenson present an overview of the software process improvement area and present data applicable to understanding the benefits and pitfalls of using such assessments in an organization.

As the world wide web continues to expand, more and more companies are using the web as a means for conducting business. The secure transfer of funds is crucial if the web is to be an effective vehicle for conducting such commerce. In Chapter 7, "State of the art in electronic payment systems," by N. Asokan, P. Jansen, M. Steiner, and M. Waidner, the authors discuss the security requirements needed for e-commerce to survive.

In the final chapter, "Defective software: An overview of legal remedies and technical measures available to consumers," by C. Vossler and J. Voas, the authors present information of vital importance to developers and consumers alike – how to deal with the legal issues involved in defective software. For the most part, software companies have relied on the "shrink-wrap" legalese saying "buyer beware." However, as computers take over more and more processes in our everyday lives, such legal protection is likely to fail. Companies have to become more aware of their legal requirements and how they can protect themselves in order to develop good software products.

I hope you find these topics stimulating and useful in your professional lives. If you have any ideas for future topics, please let me know at mvz@cs.umd.edu.

Marvin V. Zelkowitz
College Park, Maryland

Shared-Memory Multiprocessing: Current State and Future Directions

PER STENSTRÖM

Department of Computer Engineering
Chalmers University of Technology
SE-412 96 Gothenburg
Sweden
pers@ce.chalmers.se

ERIK HAGERSTEN

Department of Information Technology
Uppsala University
SE-751 05 Uppsala
Sweden
eh@docs.uu.se

DAVID J. LILJA

Department of Electrical Engineering
University of Minnesota
Minneapolis, MN 55455
USA
lilja@ece.umn.edu

MARGARET MARTONOSI

Department of Electrical Engineering
Princeton University
Princeton, NJ 08544-5263
USA
martonosi@ee.princeton.edu

MADAN VENUGOPAL

S3 Inc.
2841 Mission College Blvd
Santa Clara, CA 95052
USA
email: madan@alum.mit.edu

ADVANCES IN COMPUTERS, VOL. 53
ISBN 0-12-012153-0

1

Abstract

Progress in shared-memory multiprocessing research over the last several decades has led to its industrial recognition as a key technology for a variety of performance-demanding application domains. In this chapter, we summarize the current state of this technology including system architectures, programming interfaces, and compiler and tool technology offered to the application writer. We then identify important issues for future research in relation to technology and application trends. We particularly focus on research directions in machine architectures, programming interfaces, and parallelization methodologies.

1. Introduction

For several decades, performance improvements in the computer industry have been fueled by the combined push–pull effects of significant technology and architectural improvements and ever-increasing application needs. Although uniprocessor performance has improved at an impressive rate of roughly 50% per year, there are still important application domains whose considerable computational needs are not met by current uniprocessors. These include not only scientific computations, but also other increasingly important application areas enabled by the global information infrastructure such as various forms of information and multimedia processing.

Parallel computers, especially shared-memory multiprocessors, have recently been recognized as a commercially viable technology to respond to these needs, after several decades of active research [1]. The major reason for the particular success of shared-memory multiprocessors is their attractive programming and resource sharing model that has made it possible to port standard operating systems and parallelized database software from independent software vendors. This has made shared-memory multiprocessors a key technology for applications beyond the traditional high-performance computing (HPC) domain.

Shared-memory multiprocessors grew naturally out of technologies used for designing high-end single-processor machines. As a result, they are built from a number of high-performance processors that share the same address space, thus making it possible to run software designed for single-processor systems. Moreover, since a shared address-space model is offered to the programmer, the task of developing parallel software, or converting serial code for parallel execution, is simplified. The first generation of shared-memory multiprocessor servers implemented a shared address-space by physically sharing a number of memory modules between processors. Although such machines only scale to typically fewer than a hundred processors, this scale happens to coincide with the sweet spot of the market which is dominated by medium-scale servers for database applications and not by large-scale servers typically required for HPC applications. Nevertheless, this style of building shared-memory multiprocessors faces a scalability limit that has been overcome by distributed-memory machines in which interprocess communication is supported with explicit message exchanges between processing nodes with private memories.

Like multiprocessors, distributed-memory machines interconnect high-end single-processor nodes to fairly large configurations. Unlike multiprocessors, however, they do not support a shared address-space. As a result, it is the responsibility of the parallel software developer, sometimes with the help from the programming system, to establish sharing to support interprocess communication. Recently, we have seen a unification between shared-memory and distributed-memory machine organizations. In designing large-scale systems, it is possible to support a shared address-space. The unifying model is called a *distributed shared-memory system* (DSM) and has recently been implemented in many commercial systems.

The overall goal of this chapter is to provide an overview of the major innovations that have led to the current state of multiprocessor technology, considering not only the architectural evolution but also the developments in terms of infrastructures to develop highly efficient codes for these machines. A secondary goal is to identify issues which are important in order to make multiprocessors an easy-to-use technology for high-performance application development, taking into account current trends in application and technology.

Because representative applications play a key driving role in computer technology developments, the first section deals with the application domains that have driven the technology and expected future trends. We then focus on the major advances behind the current state of machine architecture, programming interfaces, and parallelization and tool technology in Sections 3–6. Each section concludes with what we believe are the most pressing issues to address in making shared-memory multiprocessing a productive technology for future high-performance applications. Finally, Section 7 provides some concluding remarks on where the technology is headed.

2. Application Trends for Shared-Memory Multiprocessors

Scientific applications have traditionally been the key drivers of parallel computers. In the early 1970s when the first parallel computer architecture research projects were initiated, scientific problems based on matrix computations played a key role in the developments. Owing to their regular nature, it was reasonable to first adopt the SIMD paradigm in which multiple simple processors, or functional units, were fed by the same instruction stream. In response to the significant efforts needed to adopt algorithms to SIMD architectures, the general MIMD paradigm became an active research topic in the late 1970s.

Another key development was the emergence of relational database technology in the 1970s. Relational databases afford significant degrees of parallelism, in terms both of executing a single query and of parallelism between the execution of multiple queries. Not surprisingly, when the first database engines based on relational database algebra became commercially widespread in the 1980s, they were adopted for MIMD machines.

In general, two forms of parallelism are possible: intra-as well as inter-application parallelism. Intra-application parallelism can potentially reduce the response time as well as the throughput, whereas inter-application parallelism can improve the throughput only. Many other applications can benefit from the latter form of parallelism. With the emergence of distributed computing facilities comes the need to coordinate common resources, such as shared files and email. The throughput can be greatly improved by implementing such resources as parallel servers. We now consider how these applications position themselves on the server market.

2.1 Dominant Application Domains

We have made an attempt to enumerate important applications for shared-memory multiprocessors based on generated revenue, starting with the most important ones. See Table I for detailed statistics. The applications can be roughly sorted into two bins: *data intensive* (DI) and *numerically intensive* (NI).

- *Operating system.* This is of course not thought of as an application, but nevertheless is the most important piece of software for a shared-memory machine. Most operating systems have been ported to shared address-space machines, e.g., various dialects of Unix and Windows/NT.
- *Database (DI).* Database applications come in two major flavors: *on-line transaction processing* (OLTP) such as airline reservation systems and *decision support systems* (DSS) such as the selection of addresses for a targeted direct-mail campaign. Database vendors typically support both shared address-space and distributed-memory machine versions of their products.
- *File servers (DI).* Many servers are used as a file server servicing a large number of workstations or PCs. Apart from performance of the basic platform, I/O performance is of particular concern.
- *Scientific and engineering applications (NI).* Scientific and engineering programs were among the earliest examples of parallel applications, and today shared address-space servers are often employed as compute servers for such codes. Even when run on a shared address-space

TABLE I

MARKET VOLUME TRENDS FOR SERVERS DIVIDED INTO DIFFERENT APPLICATION DOMAINS

Application domain	Factory revenue 1995 ($M)	Factory revenue 2000 ($M)	Annual growth 1995–2000 (%)
Database	7774 (32%)	19 195 (39%)	20
File server	7549 (32%)	12 048 (25%)	10
Scientific and engineering	3887 (16%)	6624 (14%)	11
Print server	2079 (9%)	3564 (7%)	11
Media and email	1383 (6%)	3964 (8%)	23
Others	1289 (5%)	3193 (7%)	20
Total	23 961	48 588	15 (average)

Source: Dataquest 1995

architecture, these applications typically use a message-passing programming models based on PVM and MPI (see section 5).

- *Media/email server (DI)*. Few can be unaware of the new and emerging application field of media/email servers, such as web servers. Here, the task is to service a large number of accesses, or hits, to a widely-available pool of information.
- *Other shared-memory applications (DI/NI)*. Even though the shared address-space programming paradigm is regarded as simpler than the message-passing one, it is still far from an easy model to manage. This is largely due to the lack of appropriate programming tools (see section 6).

    From Table I, we can make two key observations

- data intensive applications are the dominant drivers of the server market
- the market share of data intensive applications is increasing.

This makes it clear that the needs of data intensive applications should be a key concern in designing future shared address-space multiprocessors.

All applications need high performance either to cut the response time or to increase throughput, but they also have other needs. Data intensive applications are often critical components in corporate management of information. Apart from performance, the cost associated with the downtime of such systems imposes strong requirements on reliability, availability, and serviceability.

Why the above-mentioned applications are well matched to the properties of multiprocessor machines is an interesting question. Apart from the simple programming model, the shared address-space model also provides a simple performance and resource-sharing model for processors, memory, and I/O. Although such properties may matter less for some regular and easily partitionable numerically intensive applications, flexible resource sharing is crucial to many of the less predictable commercial data intensive applications with widely shifting demands for resources.

The reason why resource sharing is greatly simplified can be illustrated through a couple of examples.

- First, a shared address-space machine does not require data and code to be placed in any special node, nor does it need any special configure-to-fit hardware organization for an application to run well. Popular code and data structures are easily shared by all the CPUs. A suspended process may be rescheduled on any processor.
- Second, managing the memory is also easier: any free physical memory can be utilized when any processor needs more memory

allocated. Imagine a hypothetical case of two parallel tasks, one needing 1 GB of memory and 1 CPU, and another task requiring 100 MB of memory and 4 CPUs. In order to run the two tasks in parallel, a distributed-memory machine built from five identical one-CPU nodes will need 1 GB memory in each node; i.e., a total of 5 GB, of which 3.9 GB will not be utilized, in order to run well. On the other hand, a shared-memory machine with only 1.1 GB of total memory and at least 5 CPUs will run these two tasks well in parallel. As long as the total number of resources in a shared address-space machine matches the total requirements of the two tasks, that architecture will fit.

Clearly, a challenge for the architects is how to realize this simple resource sharing model at a reasonable cost and how to make it scale to large numbers of processors. We review the major innovations behind this in section 3.

An additional attractive property of shared address-space machines is the creation of a seamless family of scalable architectures. The workstation with 2 CPUs, the work-group server with 4 CPUs and the supercomputer with 64 CPUs can all have the same programming model and be binary-compatible with each other. A last, but rarely discussed, issue is the complexity involved in the management of the large-scale systems. Adding and removing resources from a shared address-space machine does not change its being a single system running one operating system—a shared address-space machine comes up and down and gets upgraded like a single system. Consequently, adding resources to a shared address-space machine does not add complexity at the same rate. The same cannot be said about distributed-memory machines such as a network of workstations, where an increased number of nodes increases the number of systems to manage and adds substantially to management complexity.

Although HPC applications have typically pushed scalability to its limits, the success of computer vendors has traditionally been dictated by what size of machines the biggest fraction of the market requires. The market volume for different sizes of machines is shown in Table II. One observation is that 79% of the server market is covered by relatively small machines with a price below $250k. This translates to shared address-space architectures with less than 16 processors. The dominance of these small and medium-size machines conforms to the observation that data intensive applications represent a larger market share than numerically intensive HPC applications. The dominance of this size of machines has also been affected by other factors, such as cost, high-availability requirements, and/or lack of program scalability.

TABLE II

MARKET VOLUME FOR SERVERS OF DIFFERENT SIZE USED IN DIFFERENT APPLICATION
DOMAINS 1995. THE ANNUAL GROWTH FIGURE HINTS AT FUTURE DEVELOPMENTS

Machine price	Scientific & engineering ($M)	Commercial ($M)	All applications ($M)	Annual growth rate (1995–2000)
< $10k	260 (1%)	4436 (19%)	4696 (20%)	19%
< $50k	1259 (5%)	5971 (25%)	7230 (30%)	48%
< $250k	1170 (5%)	5740 (24%)	6910 (29%)	33%
< $1M	460 (2%)	2085 (9%)	2545 (11%)	33%
> $1M	750 (3%)	1836 (8%)	2586 (11%)	14%
Total	3899 (16%)	20 068 (85%)	23 967 (100%)	31%

Source: Dataquest 1995

2.2 Future Trends

Predicting the future in computer development has proved to be a difficult task. From Table II it appears that the trend is a continued dominance for small and medium-sized machines. Table I shows that the predicted application trend for the year 2000 is a lower annual growth for scientific/engineering applications than for data intensive applications, especially database and media applications.

In contrast to these observations, shared-memory multiprocessing research has focused on the requirements of HPC applications. As a consequence, scalability issues for large number of processors has played a key role. Moreover, other issues such as reliability and availability have not been seriously addressed. Although pushing the scalability in this area is an interesting problem, which is far from solved, it is not very representative of how servers are used today. Table II shows that above the $1M price point, servers used for scientific and engineering applications represent only 3% of the entire server market revenue. Between 1993 and 1995 the annual revenue growth for this size of servers grew only 14% yearly—a smaller increase than all the other server-price categories.

The global information infrastructure will most likely change the application requirements. Although database applications will grow in importance, new applications will emerge. One such new application area is enterprise resource planning (ERP) software, such as software from SAP, Baan, and Peoplesoft.

Visualization and virtual reality are other applications of growing importance. These applications have a lot of inherent parallelism that can be exploited naturally. Therefore, research into virtually any aspect of shared-memory multiprocessing should reflect the requirements of such future applications.

3. Current State of Shared-Memory Architectures

In this section, we focus on the key innovations behind contemporary shared-memory multiprocessor systems. We do this in an evolutionary manner. We first consider the evolution behind small-scale symmetric multiprocessors in section 3.1. Then we consider scalable system designs in sections 3.2 and 3.3. Finally, in section 3.4, we review the methodologies developed and used to evaluate the performance of architectural design alternatives.

3.1 Symmetric Multiprocessors

With the emergence of microprocessors at the beginning of the 1970s, many recognized the vision of designing cost-effective parallel machines by interconnecting several of them. The major concern of multiprocessor research efforts quickly became how to implement a shared address-space without suffering from devastating serialization to the physically shared memory. An early example of such a project is the C.mmp system at Carnegie-Mellon University in the late 1970s.

C.mmp advocated the use of a crossbar switch. A crossbar connects N units of one type (e.g., processors) to N units of another type (e.g., memory modules). One desirable property is that N processors can communicate with N memory modules with no interference as long as all processors access different memory modules. Early crossbars had the disadvantage that their complexity scaled $O(N^2)$, which made a common bus more attractive.

Bus-based multiprocessor systems quickly became the norm and spurred several research projects as well as early commercial attempts [2] in the 1980s. In such systems, all processors can access all memory modules by sending requests across the bus. Given the limited bandwidth of the bus, the main issue became how many processors a bus could accommodate before saturating. Because the capacitive load and the length of the bus increases when the number of modules connected to it is increased, the available bandwidth will actually decrease as the number of processors increases. Moreover, in light of the steady performance growth of processors, the sense was that bus-based multiprocessors would soon become impractical as the saturation point would be reached for very few processors. However, this has not yet happened, as a result of two developments whose impact was not fully understood: snoopy cache protocols and high-bandwidth bus and switch technologies.

Attaching a cache with each processor reduces the average memory access time as well as the memory-bus bandwidth needed. For example, assuming a hit rate of 90%, the bandwidth needed will be cut by an order of magnitude. However, attaching caches to processors allows multiple copies of a memory block to exist. Inconsistency among the multiple copies may violate the notion of a single address-space. This is the well-known *cache coherence problem* which became a focal point of many research efforts in the 1980s. Solutions to this problem aim at implementing the model that each memory request atomically accesses a single memory location regardless of the physical distribution of copies of that location (see, e.g., [3, 4]).

The key mechanism used in bus-based systems is called *snoopy cache protocols* and basically come in two flavors: write–update and write–invalidate. Under write–update, a write causes the local cache to broadcast the value so that potential copies of the same location in other caches can be updated. This scheme seems intuitive and attractive, but it suffers from a performance problem; all writes will cause global actions regardless of whether other processors will consume the new value. Because bus bandwidth is a scarce resource, write–update has not been a popular choice. Instead, most machines have adopted the write–invalidate approach which implements coherence as follows. When a processor writes to a location, all other copies are erased before the local cache copy is updated by broadcasting invalidate requests to all other caches. This can save bus-bandwidth because subsequent writes from one processor, with no intervening reads from other processors, result in a single bus transaction. However, a subsequent read access to this location by another processor will cause a cache miss, called a *coherence miss*, which is serviced by the cache attached to the processor that most recently modified the location. Coherence is maintained, but at the cost of a higher cache miss ratio. Clearly, although this protocol increases the miss ratio, it does not suffer from the bandwidth consumption problems of write–update. An example of write–update protocol is the Firefly protocol; examples of write–invalidate protocols are the write–once, Berkeley SPUR, and Illinois protocols [3].

These initial research efforts eventually led to the commercial emergence of bus-based multiprocessors in the early 1990s. They are often referred to as *uniform memory access* (UMA) machines because the access time to any memory module is about the same for all processors. Another widely used term is *symmetric multiprocessors* (SMPs). The term "symmetric" points to the fact that the performance model of the machine is such that the software does not have to bother about differences in access times. Therefore, SMP and UMA have so far been equivalent terms.

For a long time it was felt that SMP implementations could not scale to large configurations. The major reason for limited scalability is that snoopy cache protocols implemented on shared buses rely on broadcast. It was also thought that the UMA model itself imposed an inherent scalability problem; a shared address-space implies physical sharing of data. However, SMP implementations have moved to more scalable technologies, such as the crossbar switch-based UMA protocol of Sun's E10000 [5] containing 64 processors and HP's V9000 v2500 containing 32 processors.

3.2 Distributed Shared-Memory Machines

Despite the successful design of UMA machines that scale to about 100 processors, most architectural research has targeted the issue of how to scale shared-memory multiprocessors beyond 100 processors. Three critical design approaches have been taken to allow for more scalable solutions: non-uniform memory access (NUMA) organizations, interconnects with scalable bandwidths using general (non-bus) topologies, and scalable cache coherence solutions.

In *NUMA machines*, the memory modules are distributed across the processing nodes, where a node could be a single processor or a whole SMP. If the code and data structures of the programs can be mapped to the memory modules so that a vast majority of the memory references from each processor are serviced by the local memory module, a NUMA machine can scale to a large number of processors. The first NUMA machine was the CM at Carnegie Mellon. Subsequently, RP3 was designed at IBM Yorktown Heights [6]. An early commercial effort was the BBN Butterfly [7].

The performance of NUMA machines is obviously sensitive to per-processor memory locality – the *NUMA problem*. One way to deal with this problem is to map data structures on a page granularity across the memory modules in a way that maximizes the access frequency from the local processor to its associated memory. Significant research on page-based mapping algorithms has been carried out (see, e.g., references contained in [8]). Among the approaches that have been investigated are initial page placement, page migration, and replication. At one extreme, the programmer could guide page placement through annotations that pin a particular data structure to the memory attached to the processor where the process accessing this data structure is run. At the other extreme, a fully automatic approach is to dynamically measure reference locality and migrate the data structure in page-sized chunks to the processor that has the highest access frequency to each page. This approach is called *dynamic page migration*. Competitive algorithms, meaning algorithms with a performance that is guaranteed to be within a certain bound compared to the performance of an optimal off-line algorithm, have been proposed and evaluated by Black *et al.* [9]. Overall, although these algorithms are effective if locality can be exploited at the page level, they do not work well if processes allocated to different nodes access the same page with similar access frequencies.

In order to make NUMA machines less sensitive to page placement, a common approach is to use coherent caches. An obvious approach would then be to adopt snoopy cache protocols. Unfortunately, snoopy cache protocols broadcast invalidations and updates to all nodes, which severely limits scalability. In the late 1980s, this triggered an interest in scalable cache coherence solutions. Interestingly, one of the first published cache coherence protocols had the desirable property of not relying on broadcast. This protocol, the directory-based protocol [10], keeps track of which nodes have copies of a memory block in a directory associated with each memory module. Using this information, invalidations or updates can be selectively sent only to those nodes having copies, which drastically reduces the bandwidth needed and thus improves scalability. A drawback of the initial attempts to design directory protocols is that the memory overhead associated with the directory grows linearly with the number of nodes. Alternative designs that cut down the memory overhead have been proposed; among them are the *scalable coherent interface* [11] and various protocols that keep track of nodes having a copy of a memory block using a tree structure [12]. Other attempts have traded memory overhead for protocol execution overhead by implementing parts of the hard-wired protocol engines by software handlers. Some approaches along these lines are the LimitLESS protocol [13], cooperative shared memory [14], and software-only directory protocols [15].

Two notable projects, the Stanford DASH [16] and the MIT Alewife [17], aimed to demonstrate that NUMA machines with coherent caches, referred to as cache coherent NUMA (CC-NUMA) machines, could be built with reasonable engineering efforts. Shortly after their successful completion, the CC-NUMA concept impacted in industry through several commercial efforts. The general class of shared-memory machines with a distributed memory organization is often referred to as *distributed shared-memory machines* (DSM). DSM implemented across several enclosures where each enclosure takes the form of a small or medium-scale SMP can enable shared-memory implementations beyond the amount of hardware that one can fit into one enclosure. Currently, SGI supports up to 256 CPU DSM [18], and Sequent can build DSMs up to 252 CPUs [19]. Both these architectures are implementations with NUMA, very similar to earlier research machines such as the Stanford Dash [16]. The ratio between local memory and remote memory for these architectures is between 3 and 20, depending on the size of the system.

3.3 COMA machines

Despite the potential scalability of CC-NUMA machines, they are more sensitive to cache performance and placement of data and code than UMA machines. Locality-aware application optimizations, such as the page-based policies discussed above, are often needed in order to provide good scalability [20].

A more aggressive approach to avoid the NUMA problem, known as *cache-only memory architectures* (COMA), is represented by two proposals dating from the late 1980s: the experimental Data Diffusion Machine [21] and the commercial Kendall Square Research machine [22]. The hardware organization of COMA is similar to distributed memory machines in that the memory is distributed between many nodes. In contrast, all the memory in COMA is used to implement giant caches. The contents of the caches are kept coherent with a mechanism similar to the directory protocols discussed above and the application is presented with a view of a single address-space. This has the advantage that data will be automatically migrated and/or replicated by hardware mechanisms according to their usage. Unlike NUMA policies, which apply migration and replication of data on page-sized chunks, COMA systems use finer block-sized chunks. Although it promised better scalability than the CC-NUMA systems, the lack of market focus and some technical problems forced KSR out of the market in the mid 1990s. The COMA concept deviated too much from the commercial building-blocks available to be competitive. In particular, in comparison with CC-NUMA machines, COMA cache protocols are more complex and the memory overhead required in order to convert memory modules into caches is higher.

An alternative to COMA is to extend a CC-NUMA machine with a giant cache aimed at caching data from remote memory modules. Such remote access caches are used in the Sequent NUMA-Q [19] machine. Architectural evaluations have shown that this approach can achieve nearly identical performance as a COMA at comparable memory sizes [23].

Another alternative to COMA is the *Simple COMA* architecture [24]. Simple COMA is a combined software/hardware approach that allows for a simpler hardware implementation than the traditional COMA architecture. The hardware simplifications stem from using the virtual memory support to manage the allocation of blocks in the memory modules, thus eliminating hardware mechanisms needed to convert memory into a cache. Simple COMA allows for replication to take place in the memory of fairly conventional DSM nodes. Replication memory is allocated by the operating system at page granularity. The replicated memory is kept coherent on a cache-line granularity by a fairly conventional DSM cache coherence protocol. The driving force behind Simple COMA is to provide a DSM that automatically replicates and migrates data across the memory modules rather than to push scalability beyond that of CC-NUMAs. This approach has been used in the experimental WildFire system from Sun Microsystems [25], which has demonstrated a UMA-like performance when running database code optimized for UMA systems.

In summary, research into shared-memory multiprocessor architectures ranging from small-scale bus-based SMPs to larger-scale DSM machines has led to successful commercial systems. Overall, the fundamental problem is related to achieving a high memory-system performance across applications that represent usage. The next issue we treat is how architects evaluate and compare design alternatives.

3.4 Architecture Evaluation Methodologies

A prevalent way of evaluating and comparing different architectural approaches is through benchmarking. The ultimate performance measure is either the execution time of an application or the throughput of applications. For existing systems, the running time of a set of benchmark programs is typically recorded. In order to identify and understand what limits performance, many machines today provide instrumentation in terms of hardware counters to measure events at the hardware level that have a dramatic impact on performance such as cache misses. This is discussed further in section 6.2.

Two fundamental issues must be addressed to fully understand performance consequences of design alternatives. One issue is related to the workloads that drive the analysis. This workload should represent usage in order to provide useful performance indications. The second issue is how to fully understand how the complex interaction between hardware and software subsystems affects the performance. Such interaction virtually takes place between all system layers including the application, the system software (OS), and the underlying hardware platform. Ultimately, one must be able to fully observe all system events that affect the performance.

As for finding a representative workload, research into parallel computers has traditionally been driven by numerically intensive workloads typically used at universities and national research laboratories. Although benchmarking naturally has a longer history for single-processor systems, it was seriously applied to multiprocessor systems in the early 1990s. The starting point was the SPLASH suite [26] from Stanford, which consists of a handful of parallel applications containing scientific simulations and VLSI-CAD as well as computer graphics applications. The applications have been parallelized by hand using shared-memory programming directives (see section 5) and performance-tuned for CC-NUMA machines.

In terms of evaluating the performance of architectural design alternatives, another major breakthrough has been the availability of highly efficient simulation methodologies such as Tango-Lite [27] and CacheMire [28]. The basic approach is to execute parallel code either on top of the host processor or on a simulation model of a processor and then drive memory-system simulators with the memory traces in a way that preserves the timing of the entire system. These simulators can be fully instrumented, which unlike hardware-monitoring mechanisms (such as hardware counters), which are further discussed in section 6, enables complete performance observability in terms of events that have a significant impact on the performance.

The availability of a suite of programs for shared-memory machines in combination with the simulation methodology has been the prevailing tool-set for architectural research into design principles of shared-memory multiprocessors. It has been possible to compare results objectively, and knowledge has been gained in terms of understanding performance issues related to scalable shared-memory architectures as discussed above.

Since simulation models cannot execute programs at full speed, a severe limitation has been that system simplifications have to be made. One such limitation is that many studies have not taken operating system interactions into account. Secondly, the problem sets of the applications have been small in comparison to the problems one would like to run on real machines. This has forced researchers to carefully address the impact of problem scaling on performance [29].

4.   Future Directions of Architecture Research

The two driving forces behind progress in architecture are application and technology trends. In section 4.1 we first consider some of the application requirements that need attention. Two technology trends are particularly important in terms of future directions for architecture research. One is related to the fact that the performance growth of high-end microprocessors is expected to continue. Therefore, in section 4.2 we review the key approaches being considered today in the area of processor architecture in light of application trends. Performance growth of microprocessors has been quite substantial, but the pace at which memory-system performance has increased has been more modest. Since the speed-gap between the processor and the memory is particularly devastating for multiprocessors, we end this section by focusing on directions of architectural improvements of memory systems for multiprocessors. This is the theme of section 4.3.

4.1 Impact of Application Trends

Considering that architectural research has been driven by the demands of numerically intensive applications, the key question is whether their machine interactions reflect those of the data intensive applications that dominate the market and seem to grow in importance. Unfortunately, many recent studies provide empirical data demonstrating that this is not the case. For example, in a study by Maynard *et al.* [30], characteristics of database applications that have a strong impact on many architectural tradeoffs are observed. Data intensive applications, such as databases, have typically much larger data sets, which obviously have a strong influence on the design of the memory system. Moreover, database applications also interact with processor architectural tradeoffs in a different manner than numerically intensive applications. The code rarely contains floating-point operations and the branch behavior is not as easily predicted as in typical loops in numerically intensive applications. Although numerically intensive applications interact with the operating system very little or virtually not at all, the performance of data intensive applications relies heavily on the performance of the operating system as well as on the I/O subsystem.

In order to address these differences, benchmark suites should be extended to focus on a reasonable mix of data intensive and numerically intensive applications. Some progress in this direction has been made in architecture research targeting single-processor systems. For example, emerging SPEC benchmark suites are gradually reflecting the growing importance of data intensive workloads. However, no such effort has materialized for shared-memory multiprocessors. An unbiased investigation of benchmarks for shared-memory multiprocessors would be a worthwhile effort. These should cover a broad class of applications likely to be of interest for future shared-memory multiprocessors.

Given a benchmark suite for multiprocessors that reflects future usage, there are other obstacles to be addressed. First, getting the source-code for a commercial database is next to impossible. Second, even if the code were available, running standard database benchmarks such as the TPC-B, C, or D, is a very complex task that requires a great insight into the structuring of the database. Finally, most database companies prevent the publication of any performance data. Nevertheless, some empirical data useful for the architecture research community has been reported [31, 32]. Another obstacle is associated with modeling the complex interaction between data intensive applications, operating systems, and the underlying computing platform. The previous generation of simulation methods was too slow to make modeling of even a fraction of a second of such a system feasible. Recent advances in simulation techniques, as exemplified by the SimICS [33] and SimOS systems [34] have made it possible to get some insights into the machine interactions of these complex codes, but significant progress in evaluation methodologies is needed to help designers make architectural tradeoffs for such applications. An important goal is to be able to understand particularly how problem scaling impacts on the performance interaction. The performance impact of problem scaling has so far only targeted numerically intensive applications [29].

Simulation-based methodologies are likely to be too slow to study the performance impact of the size of problems one would like to run on real machines; they must be complemented by other approaches. One approach might be to use analytical models driven by synthetic workloads that aim to mimic the interactions in real systems at full problem sizes. Of course, it then becomes important to validate such approaches against real systems and workloads.

4.2   Directions in Processor Architecture Research

Changes in processor technology and applications are having a significant impact on the architecture of the processors that comprise the individual compute nodes of a shared-memory system. The new applications discussed in section 2 share several characteristics that make them very difficult to parallelize using traditional approaches. For example, these programs typically contain many loops with early exit conditions, such as *do-while* loops. Parallelizing these loops requires architectural and compiler support for thread-level speculative execution. Small granularity loops with low trip counts, which are common in these applications, can be efficiently parallelized only when the system provides fast communication and synchronization. Parallelizing programs with extensive memory aliasing, which occurs often when using pointers, requires hardware support for data speculation or runtime dependence checking between threads. None of these features are provided in current systems at the level required to support these difficult-to-parallelize application programs.

In addition to the challenges in parallelizing these irregular applications, changes in processor technology will affect the design of future shared-memory multiprocessors. Designers of high-performance microprocessors in the past have had the luxury of borrowing architectural ideas originally developed for mainframe and supercomputer systems. As a result, almost all microprocessors available today use such techniques as out-of-order execution, register renaming, branch prediction, and multiple instruction issue per cycle to provide high single-processor performance. Unfortunately, this "grab-bag" of performance enhancement tricks is now essentially empty.

It is reasonable to predict, however, that, within the next decade, it will be possible to integrate a billion transistors on a single component, as pointed out in the September 1997 issue of *Computer*. The problem then is to determine how these huge numbers of transistors should be exploited to most effectively deliver high performance. Should system designers continue to follow current design trends and simply construct an entire shared-memory multiprocessor system on a chip? Or should these transistors be used to construct uniprocessors with giant caches that will become the compute nodes in a shared-memory system? Or should the main memory be integrated on the same die as the processor? Or do these advances in transistor density allow more innovative solutions to be developed?

These processor technology and application changes are driving computer architects to develop radically new approaches for improving the performance of the individual compute nodes of the multiprocessor. Several of these approaches are summarized below.

4.2.1   Wide-issue uniprocessor

Perhaps the most straightforward approach to exploiting additional parallelism within the compute nodes is simply to increase the width of a superscalar processor's issue logic. This approach allows more instructions to be executed simultaneously from a single stream of control; i.e., from a sequence of instructions accessed using a single program counter. One of the fundamental design issues with this approach is how the processor's functionality should be partitioned [35]. As the processor's cycle time decreases, communication latency within a single chip becomes a limiting performance factor. The need to limit intrachip communication delays, combined with the need to find enough instruction-level parallelism to feed the very wide compute core, leads to a need for very aggressive branch prediction [36] and complex control structures.

The trace processor [37], for instance, proposes a hierarchical control structure that uses very aggressive control and data speculation to expose more parallel instructions to be issued in a very wide superscalar-like configuration. This approach appears to be very effective for improving instruction-level parallelism within the single thread of execution within a single compute node.

Very long instruction word (VLIW) processors [38] also attempt to issue multiple instructions in a single cycle. This approach reduces the complexity of the processor's control logic compared to a very wide issue superscalar processor by moving the task of finding independent instructions to issue simultaneously into the compiler [39, 40].

4.2.2 Multithreading

Multithreaded processor architectures execute multiple independent threads of execution within a single processor. It is useful to distinguish between two types of multithreading.

- In the *context switching* form of multithreading, a fast context switch mechanism allows a single processor to efficiently alternate between several concurrent tasks. This approach has traditionally been used to increase the system throughput.

- With the *concurrent multithreading* type, on the other hand, the processor, which must include multiple thread execution units, can exploit instruction-level parallelism from several separate instruction windows simultaneously. The aggregate size of the windows, and the total number of instructions issued in one cycle from all concurrent threads, can be comparable to that of a very large window in a single-threaded wide-issue processor. This form of multithreading can be thought of as a hybrid between a wide-issue uniprocessor and a very tightly-coupled multiprocessor on a single chip. It can be used to reduce the execution time of a single application as well as improve the overall throughput by executing threads from multiple tasks.

4.2.1.1 Multithreading to increase throughput
The fast task switching type of multithreading has been shown to be particularly effective in improving throughput in applications with a high frequency of stalls owing to memory and I/O transactions [41, 42]. If more than one thread resides in a processor, and the thread switching overhead is sufficiently low, the time a processor would be stalled can instead be used by otherwise idle threads. Typically, each thread corresponds to an independent process from, for instance, a single transaction or the independent iterations from a parallel loop.

Note that with this type of multithreading, a single processor is rapidly switching between independent tasks which may not be from the same application. Thus, the goal with this type of multithreading is to increase the overall number of instructions executed per cycle (i.e., throughput), but not necessarily to reduce the execution time of any specific application. The *simultaneous multithreading* (SMT) processor [43], for instance, allows instructions from multiple threads to be fetched and interleaved arbitrarily in the pipeline of a superscalar processor. The thread fetch policy attempts to fetch instructions from threads that have a low probability of stalling the processor, such as those with the fewest outstanding cache misses or unresolved branches [44].

4.2.1.2 Concurrent multithreading to reduce execution time

One shortcoming of the fast context switching type of multithreading can arise when a single task must be completed quickly. For example, a task that holds a heavily contended lock should process the protected code as quickly as possible to prevent other tasks from idling while they wait for access to the lock. The extra resources devoted to supporting multiple concurrent tasks in the SMT type of multithreading model are not helpful in improving the execution of a single task, however. In contrast, *concurrent multithreading* [45–48] and the related single-chip multiprocessor [49], allow the processor to execute independent tasks from a single parallel application using both instruction-level and thread-level parallelism.

The *superthreaded* [48] and *multiscalar* [47] processor architectures, for example, have multiple thread execution units, each with their own program counter and instruction execution data path. Each of these thread units can fetch and execute instructions from multiple program locations simultaneously. A special memory buffer holds the temporary thread context needed for both control speculation and runtime resolution of data dependences. The program must be partitioned into threads either dynamically at runtime or statically at compile-time where each thread corresponds to a specific portion of the control flow graph of a single application. For instance, a thread could be one or several iterations of a loop, or a procedure body. For loops with bounds that are unknown at compile-time, such as *do-while* loops, a thread can fork its successor threads with control speculation. In this case, the thread performing the fork must later verify all of the speculated dependences. If any of these speculated dependences are false, the thread must abort all of its successor threads.

4.2.3 Raw processors

The *raw processor* architecture [50] replicates very simple processors, called *tiles*, on to a single die with all of the low-level details exposed to the compiler. The compiler then programs the tiles to match the needs of a specific application. For example, if the compiler determines that an application would benefit from a certain systolic array organization, for instance, it programs the tiles into this configuration specifically for the execution of that single application.

4.2.4 Integration of processor and memory (PAM)

One of the primary factors limiting the performance of both uniprocessor and multiprocessor systems is the delay required to retrieve data values from memory. The *PAM* concept (also called PIM, IRAM, embedded RAM, etc.) [51, 52] attempts to alleviate this memory bottleneck by incorporating the processor directly within the dynamic RAM (DRAM) memory structure itself. Since intrachip communication delays are substantially lower than interchip communication delays, this approach can provide a direct high-bandwidth connection between the processor and the large main memory. It further improves memory performance by eliminating the need to copy data between the on-chip processor cache and the external DRAM, as is needed in conventional memory hierarchies. One of the main difficulties of this approach is to incorporate the processor's high-speed logic design into the process technology used to produce DRAM devices. The electrical noise produced by the fast switching of the processor logic, for example, can corrupt the values stored in the DRAM. These types of problems may be overcome, but this will require new process technologies and design methodologies.

To summarize, in order to keep up with the current pace of performance improvements, future processor architectures will continue to exploit more parallelism. Whether the parallelism exploited will be at the instruction level or the thread-level, or a combination of the two, is still to be seen. In any case, future multiprocessors will use these processors as essential building blocks to reach much higher performance levels.

4.2.5 Metasystems

Many of these architectural enhancements can substantially improve the performance of a single processor which can then help improve the overall system performance when they are used within the individual compute nodes of a shared-memory multiprocessor system. Furthermore, trends in distributed computing systems are to interconnect multiple heterogeneous systems using standardized data communication networks, such as ATM, Fibre Channel, and HiPPI. These networks provide sufficiently high bandwidth and low latency to allow the collection of systems to be viewed as a single, large *metasystem* [53, 54] on which very large applications can be executed.

These complex systems provide multiple levels of parallelism for enhancing the performance of large application programs. For instance, an application's instruction-level parallelism can be exploited within the superscalar-style processing units of a single thread's execution unit, while the first level of loop parallelism can be exploited across the thread processing units on a single chip. A second level of loop parallelism then can be distributed across the nodes within the shared-memory configuration. Finally, very coarse-grained parallelism, most likely using a message-passing programming model, could be exploited across the systems comprising the overall metasystem.

Of course, these complex hierarchies of parallelism severely complicate the tasks of the compiler and the application programmer. Increasing the power of the individual compute nodes will also put additional stress on the memory system and the interconnection network, further exacerbating the problems due to memory delays. Nevertheless, the tremendous opportunities for increasing performance provided by these complex systems will force system architects and software designers to develop new strategies for exploiting them.

4.3   Directions in Shared-Memory Architecture Research

Multiprocessors leverage on high-performance processors and thus take advantage of all the innovations that are expected in the processor architecture area, as discussed in the previous section. However, since the speed gap between processors and memories is expected to increase, multiprocessors in particular will rely on effective strategies to manage their memory systems. Therefore, research into high-performance memory systems will be even more important, especially given the increased emphasis on data intensive applications discussed in section 4.1.

Since research into memory systems for shared-memory multiprocessors has so far been driven by the characteristics of numerically intensive applications, we argue that it is presently unclear whether proposed techniques will be adequate for future systems. Let us therefore review proposed techniques in the light of the requirements for data intensive applications.

The UMA model is intuitively appealing in that it offers a simple performance model to the software; how data is mapped to the memories is not an issue. A challenge then is how far scalability can be pushed. Current systems scale to about 100 processors [5]. Research into scalable multi-processor designs has focused on distributed shared-memory (DSM) systems that employ a NUMA model and has almost completely overlooked the possibility of further pushing the UMA model. A key issue is how to make cache protocols scale to larger configurations in the context of UMA systems. Directory-based protocols are an obvious alternative, but they introduce devastating miss penalties that snoopy cache protocols do not suffer from. Low-latency, scalable solutions to the cache coherence problem in UMA systems are an important topic for future research that has been only partly addressed [55].

In scaling multiprocessors beyond what the UMA model can offer, it is natural to use SMP nodes as building blocks for larger configurations, as demonstrated by many contemporary designs [19, 25, 56]. They implement the NUMA model and thus introduce a more complex performance model to the software. Although the COMA concept used in the WildFire system [25] can potentially migrate and replicate data on a fine granularity across the memory modules in an automatic fashion, the COMA concept is of no help in attacking the memory access penalties for coherence actions. The only remedy is then to tolerate the latencies associated with these actions. We next review latency reducing and tolerating techniques.

4.3.1 Latency reducing techniques

One approach to reduce memory access latency in NUMA systems is to dynamically replicate or migrate page-sized chunks using the virtual memory support in each node as discussed in section 3.2. Although NUMA policies have proved effective for some numerically intensive applications [20], they do not work well in applications where accesses from several processors are colocated on the same page. NUMA policies have only been studied in the context of numerically intensive parallel applications [8]. There is a need to review how effective page-based policies are for data intensive applications.

Increasing the cache space in each SMP compute node can also be effective in reducing average memory latencies, although it is not clear how big the caches need to be. In a study focusing on applications from the SPLASH suite [57] it was shown that fairly small caches suffice to keep the working sets because the most performance-sensitive working sets in these applications typically grow slowly with the problem size. Since the SPLASH benchmark suite emphasizes numerically intensive applications, it is unclear whether these observations extend to data intensive applications such as OLTP and DSS.

Multiprocessors as well as single-processor systems rely on effective caching strategies. An additional hurdle in multiprocessors is coherence maintenance. Since most multiprocessors rely on write–invalidate protocols, as discussed in section 3.1, another source of cache misses is caused by coherence actions. Coherence actions may introduce severe memory access penalties, especially in DSM systems, because the latencies involved in invalidating and servicing coherence misses can be several hundred processor cycles. Methods that track coherence actions and eliminate them are therefore important. Some strides have been taken in the past to eliminate the impact of coherence actions on performance. Two particular program behaviors that cause predictable sequences of coherence actions are *migratory* and *producer/consumer* sharing [58]. Migratory sharing shows up when a shared variable is read and modified by several processors in turn. This sharing behavior is particularly common when data is modified within critical sections. In producer-consumer sharing, on the other hand, one set of processors modify data that is read by another set of processors. Both these sharing patterns can result in severe invalidation and cache miss penalties.

Techniques that aim at reducing the impact of these sharing patterns on access penalties for coherence maintenance have been proposed in the past (see, e.g., [59] and the references contained therein). Notable examples of migratory sharing optimizations are [60–62]. If migratory data is detected, it is possible to eliminate the need for invalidations because data will be modified by the same processor that reads it into its cache. The approach taken by these techniques is to detect, either statically or dynamically, a migratory shared-memory block and then bring in an exclusive copy of the block in anticipation of a later modification of the same block. Write–update cache policies seem a better tradeoff than write–invalidate for producer/consumer-shared memory blocks. A protocol that dynamically detects such sharing patterns and switch to write–update has been proposed and evaluated by Grahn and Stenstrom [63]. However, although these techniques showed quite significant performance improvement of cache coherent (CC)- CC-NUMA machines for numerically intensive parallel codes, few studies so far have considered data intensive benchmarks.

It is time to reconsider what kind of program behaviors cause devastating coherence interactions in the kind of workloads that we anticipate in the future. In some recent work, it has been observed that migratory sharing is common in OLTP workloads [64]. A recent study has evaluated the effectiveness of optimizations for migratory data on OLTP workloads [65].

4.3.2 Latency tolerating techniques

When latency cannot be reduced, e.g., by using bigger caches, improving data placement, or eliminating coherence actions, tolerating latency by overlapping computation with communication is the only alternative. Latency tolerating techniques aim at exploiting parallelism between application execution and costly memory-system events such as cache misses. The key to success is finding computations independent of memory-system events so that the latency can be overlapped.

In the framework of DSM machines using a write–invalidate cache coherence mechanism, cache misses will force the processor to stall eventually when the data is needed. What is less intuitive is that also write–accesses that cause invalidations may have to force the processor to stall in order to enforce correctness. This correctness criterion has its root in the semantics of a shared address–space model that programmers often assume and that is referred to as the *memory consistency model* [66].

Programmers often view a shared address–space machine as a monolithic memory that is accessed by all processors so that the order of memory requests from each processor is preserved by handling them one at a time. This model is the same as if all processes were executed in a pseudo-parallel fashion on a single-processor system. Leslie Lamport formalized this semantic view in the sequential consistency model (see, e.g., [66]) which states that

> the result of any [parallel] execution is the same as if the [memory operations] of all the processors were executed in some sequential order and the [memory operations] of each individual processor occur in this sequence in the order specified by its program.

Because of the concurrency in a typical memory system of a multi-processor that is caused by allowing multiple copies of data, this simple model can be violated if processors are allowed to issue memory operations without waiting for them to complete. For example, if a processor issues two writes destined to different memory blocks, the invalidations that they cause can be carried out in an order opposite to the program order, which then may violate sequential consistency. A straightforward remedy is to stall the processor when the first write is issued until the associated invalidation is carried out. Clearly, coherence misses as well as invalidation requests can cause severe penalties. We will now discuss the most important approaches that have been studied to tolerate the latencies associated with invalidations and cache misses. These include relaxation of the memory consistency model, prefetching, and multithreading [67].

In programs that use synchronizations to impose serial access to shared data, sequential consistency is overly restrictive. As long as synchronizations are handled correctly, accesses to shared data between two consecutive synchronizations do not have to stall the processor. Models that relax access ordering by still respecting synchronizations are called *relaxed memory consistency models* (see references contained in [66]). Again, the performance improvements obtained from relaxed memory consistency models have been studied using numerically intensive parallel benchmarks, e.g., SPLASH. Although these models allow latencies associated with invalidations to be tolerated, they also require that the programs are designed so that the correctness relies on explicit synchronizations that can be detected at the hardware level. There has been a concern that software systems originally designed for single-processor systems, such as operating systems and database engines, which have been ported to multiprocessors, may lack explicit synchronizations and may therefore not work correctly under these models. Therefore, the performance improvements obtained from these models may not be worthwhile. Moreover, since much of the latency can be tolerated by support for speculative execution which has begun to be used seriously in high-performance microprocessors, the benefit of relaxed memory consistency models is further questioned [68]. Yet, no evaluation that targets data intensive workloads has been reported.

The second approach to tolerate access latencies is prefetching. The idea is to bring into cache (or more aggressively into registers) data that is predicted to be used in the future so as to hide the latency with useful computation. Cache prefetching techniques come in two flavors: software-and hardware-controlled prefetching. In *software-controlled prefetching*, the user or the compiler inserts special prefetch instructions sufficiently far ahead of a load instruction that is expected to miss in the cache so that the latency of the miss can be completely hidden. Clearly, it is a non-trivial task for the compiler to figure out where to insert prefetch instructions, and this has been successfully demonstrated only for fairly regular numerically intensive codes [69].

Hardware-controlled prefetching, on the other hand, aims at predicting future cache misses based on heuristics and automatically launch prefetches with no involvement from the software. Key approaches that have been taken include sequential and stride prefetching that typically target regular access patterns such as vector accesses with constant strides (see [70] and references contained therein).

Although prefetching techniques for multiprocessors have gained significant attention, they have proved promising only for applications with regular access patterns such as vector accesses with constant strides that occur in numerically intensive codes. In database applications, for example, index-based searching does not necessarily result in such regular access patterns. Even worse, they may result in chains of data-dependent loads, called pointer-chasing, which are very hard to attack with known prefetch techniques [71]. Thus, prefetching techniques should be revisited in the light of emerging data intensive applications. Some advances have been made in attacking pointer-chasing in database codes [72], but there is still room for improvement.

Finally, as discussed in section 4.2, one form of multithreading switches between independent threads when a long-latency operation is encountered. This approach requires hardware support for fast thread switches and extra program concurrency to be effective. Three trends can make multithreading a useful weapon against memory access penalties:

● The speed gap between processors and memories increases, thread-switch overhead will be less of a concern [42].

- The difficulty of extracting more instruction-level parallelism at an affordable complexity level may eventually lead to the breakthrough of multithreaded architectures [45, 47, 73, 74].

- Unlike current prefetch approaches, multithreading does not make any particular assumption regarding the access pattern caused by the workload.

5. Programming Interfaces

In discussing parallel programming models, it is important to distinguish the architecture of the machine from the model presented to the programmer. The *programming model* is the interface between the programmer and the machine; the *architecture* is the underlying structure of the machine itself. The choice of a specific programming model determines how a programmer views the machine, independent of its actual structure. For instance, distributed shared-memory architectures, such as the Stanford DASH [16] and the SGI Origin [18], have the memory physically distributed among the processors. Messages are passed automatically by the hardware to provide the illusion of a single shared global address space to the programmer These messages also provide automatic cache coherence for improved performance. As a result, every processor uses the same name to refer to the same global location in memory, which makes sharing data among processors relatively simple.

In a message-passing programming model, on the other hand, each processor has its own private address space. Any sharing of data requires the programmer to include explicit *send* and *receive* statements in the source code.

Although there may be performance advantages to having the programming model match the underlying architecture, it is possible to implement a message-passing model on top of a shared-memory architecture, or to implement a shared-memory model on top of a message-passing architecture [75].

Far too often, however, when an application is designed for coarse-grained parallelization and implemented using a portable message-passing approach, the high scalability obtained is attributed to the new message-passing version of the code rather than to the extensive algorithmic changes that could have been implemented at least as efficiently with a shared-memory model. Further, there is an equivalence between shared-memory parallelism and message-passing [75, 76]. As a result, an implementation of a message-passing model on a shared-memory machine can provide both good performance and portability [77, 78].

5.1   Shared-Memory Programming Interface

The shared-memory programming model is usually viewed as a compiler-based programming model. Applications are parallelized by inserting compiler directives to demarcate parallel regions.

The following example illustrates a parallelized matrix multiply using typical compiler directives [79]:

```
C$DOACROSS share(A,B,C,L,N,M), local(I,J,K)
          DO K = 1, L
            DO I = 1, N
              DO J = 1, M
                C(I,K) = C(I,K) + B(I, J) * A(J,K)
          ENDDO
```

The `C$DOACROSS` directive identifies the outer `DO` loop as a parallel region. It also forces different iterations of the loop to be executed on different processors. The `share` and `local` directives identify which of the variables in the parallel region are to be treated as shared and which of them are to be treated as local to each processor. The example shown is in Fortran, but there are equivalent constructs for C and C++.

The above example is only intended to illustrate the programming model and does not imply that the granularity of the code in the parallel region is sufficient to generate a good parallel performance. Also not considered are the issues of blocking of memory references to optimize cache accesses and load balance.

The above segment of code has different performance characteristics based on the size of the arrays referenced and the architecture of the shared memory system it is run on. For example, on a system with vector processors, if the array sizes are above a certain minimum corresponding to the number of vector registers on the processor, the performance of the segment of code improves asymptotically to close to the theoretical peak of the processor with increasing vector lengths. However, on a cache-based system, both the uniprocessor and multiprocessor performance can drastically be affected if the data being operated on does not fit into the cache local to the processor. This is due to the hierarchical memory architecture of such systems. Performance can be improved on such systems by reconfiguring the arrays to maximize cache reuse. Such performance optimization is termed *cache blocking* and can dramatically improve the single processor and parallel performance of applications on cache-based shared memory parallel systems [89].

Load balancing refers to the distribution of the parallel work among the available processors. There are various schemes by which this can be done, statically or dynamically. The choice usually depends on the parallel application and the architecture of the shared memory parallel system and the performance characteristics of the processors used in the system.

Both of the above factors can significantly affect the delivered performance. Most modern parallel compilers provide additional directives to control these factors. These factors are strongly affected by the underlying architecture of the parallel machine and the operating system it happens to be running. The list of directives available on a state-of-the-art shared-memory parallel computer is very rich, covering parallelization, scheduling, and a variety of other important factors. On CC-NUMA architectures, this list is enhanced to provide control over the placement of data in the parallel region to thereby control the locality of memory accesses.

One basic issue that can affect portability of code from one parallel machine to another is whether all variables are assumed local or shared by default. In the above example, the local and shared variables are specified explicitly. This approach becomes increasingly cumbersome when the parallel regions contain many unique variable names. Consequently, compilers make default assumptions about variables. On shared-memory systems, such as the SGI Power Challenge [79] and the KSR-1 [80], all variables in a parallel region were assumed to be shared unless explicitly declared local. On shared-memory parallel computers such as the Alliant FX/2800, in contrast, all variables in a parallel region were assumed to be local unless explicitly declared otherwise. There are good arguments for either choice. However, the choice of one or the other on different systems affects the portability of parallelized applications. Many of the parallel systems manufacturers provide excellent documentation covering parallel programming on their systems and several papers and texts also provide excellent coverage of programming on shared-memory parallel computers [79, 81, 82, 83].

Shared memory programming has undergone considerable evolution since the time of the Cray vector supercomputers and IBM mainframes. The Cray X-MP was introduced in 1983 and supported shared-memory parallel processing [84, 85] using compiler directives. The next generation of shared-memory parallel systems was the minisupercomputers introduced in the late 1980s and early 1990s, such as the Convex C210 and the Alliant FX/80 and FX/2800. These systems supported a shared-memory programming model also based on compiler directives. The Alliant FX/2800 had a Unix operating system and could also support task parallelism by allocating shared regions in memory and spawning parallel tasks with operating system calls. The KSR-1, which was the first commercial shared-memory parallel system with physically distributed memory, also supported a shared-memory programming model using compiler directives [80]. In addition to the shared-memory programming model, the Alliant FX/2800 and the KSR-1 also supported message-passing using the PVM, p4, TCGMSG and PARMACS message-passing libraries. The message passing libraries were usually implemented using KSR's native pthreads library.

The current generation of shared-memory parallel systems is based on commodity microprocessors. The operating systems range from proprietary versions of Unix and Microsoft's Windows/NT to the open-systems Linux. The latest release of Linux, for instance, includes multiprocessing support [86]. Compaq, HP, Sun, SGI and many other vendors also offer shared-memory systems. In most cases, they support both the compiler-based shared-memory programming model and a message-passing programming model. With the rapid proliferation of low-cost shared-memory parallel systems, more and more applications are being written with parallelism in mind. This produces a demand for a more uniform shared-memory programming interface.

Much of the early demand for parallel processing was driven by the performance requirements of computationally intensive scientific applications. As a result, the earlier parallel machines were targeted for these types of applications. The most popular parallel programming languages for applications were Fortran and C, simply because many of the large scientific applications were written in these languages. Typically, compiler support on shared-memory systems was directed at loop-level parallelism using directives, since this was the least disruptive method of parallelizing existing applications. However, the use of these directives did not lead to the most efficient methods of extracting parallelism. Since compilers still are not capable of completely parallelizing large applications, many of the computer systems manufacturers hand-parallelized the most important applications using their special compiler directives.

An advantage of the shared-memory model is that it enables incremental parallelization at varying levels of granularity. This feature has resulted in parallel ports of large legacy serial applications. Although much less than ideal scalability often results, the performance enhancements and resulting speedups made possible are of great importance to the many users of these applications and increases the popularity of shared-memory parallelism [87, 88].

It has also been shown that good scalability can be achieved with the shared-memory model. For example, consider the following results from the implementation of a commercial CFD application, GASP, on the Silicon Graphics Origin 2000 system. The parallel implementation of this application on a bus-based shared-memory machine [89] was also used for the Origin 2000 system. Table III shows the compute time and the speedup for 10 time steps for a $321 \times 321 \times 101$ grid size problem (10.4 million grid

TABLE III

PARALLEL GASP ON THE SGI ORIGIN 2000 SYSTEM

Number of processors	CPU user time (h:min:s)	Parallel speed up
1	03:28:28	1
2	01:44:49	1.99
16	00:14:14	14.65
32	00:07:24	28.17
64	00:03:52	53.91
128	00:02:20	89.34

points) with 512 zones when executed on an SGI Origin system with 128 processors, 4 Mb caches, and 16 Gb of memory. This problem requires about 2.8 GB of memory and about 1 GB of disk. The startup overhead due to the first step has been removed, and the CPU times are as reported from within GASP. We note that the same algorithm could have been implemented using message-passing. However, by using the shared-memory directives, the parallel version of the code closely resembles the original sequential version so that only small modifications were necessary to express the available parallelism.

As the number of parallel applications and system vendors increased, there was a natural desire for a more uniform shared-memory programming model. This led to the formation of the emerging OpenMP standard for shared-memory parallelism [90–92]. OpenMP, like its predecessors ANSI X3H5 and the Parallel Computing Forum, is an attempt to standardize the directives for shared-memory parallelism. However, unlike its predecessors, it appears to enjoy broad industry support. Owing to a consolidation in the mainframe and mini-supercomputer world, the largest number of shared-memory parallel systems currently are based on commodity processors. Further, some of the system vendors no longer have the luxury of using their own native compilers and operating systems. These trends have led to increasingly broad support for standards such as OpenMP.

Although shared-memory architectures can scale well for scientific applications, it was thought that massively parallel MPP message-passing systems would be more scalable than shared-memory architectures for database applications. However, published TPC-D results demonstrate that shared-memory implementations can perform quite well. The good performance of this architecture can be explained by their system properties [93]. Since the huge common memory and the I/O are uniformly shared by all processors, there is no limitation on how the database must be partitioned, or "striped", across disks to obtain good performance. On an MPP, on the other hand, the specific striping used can limit performance and scalability since the optimum striping tends to be different for different queries. Furthermore, the striping may need to change when additional processors are added. These architectural features make it clear that shared-memory systems are a very competitive and scalable alternative for large DSS databases.

5.2   Distributed Memory Programming Interfaces

Programming for distributed memory systems has been largely based on message-passing. Applications for these systems were typically written from scratch using this model owing to the underlying architecture of these systems. As a result, distributed memory parallel systems have had a smaller base of high-performance applications than comparable shared-memory parallel systems. In contrast, since shared-memory parallel applications were typically based on extensions to existing code for uniprocessor systems, they tended to show poorer parallelism. In part, this led to a perception that the shared memory programming model was limited in performance and scalability.

At a fundamental level, though, the programming models are inter-changeable. For example, on a shared-memory machine, the same program could be implemented using message-passing or the shared-memory programming model with comparable performance, as discussed earlier [78, 75, 76, 77].

With the rapid proliferation of distributed memory systems in the late 1980s and early 1990s, there was a desire for portability of applications among various systems. The iPSC-2 was one of the earliest commercially available message-passing systems. It used a native message-passing library called NX. Successors to the iPSC-2 included the ipSC-860, the Touchstone Delta and the Intel Paragon systems, all of which used the NX message-passing library. The iPSC systems used a hypercube interconnect topology, while the Delta and Paragon used mesh topologies. The IBM SP1 and SP2 are massively parallel distributed memory systems which use a native message-passing library called MPL. The Thinking Machines CM-5 was a distributed memory parallel system which used a message-passing library called CMMD. NCUBE also had a series of hypercube-based systems which used its own message-passing library [94]. The Cray T3D and T3E systems are physically distributed memory systems which support several message-passing libraries in addition to a shared-memory access library called shmem. Using networks of uniprocessor workstations as a distributed-memory parallel computer also has become popular for a relatively small number of latency tolerant applications [95].

Since there were a relatively small number of applications for these systems, there was a desire for portability among the various distributed memory computers. The lack of commercial success of the distributed memory computers accentuated the desire for portability. Initially, this desire led to a wide variety of message-passing libraries, such as PVM, p4, TCGMSG, PICL, PARMACS, Zipcode, and others [96]. This proliferation of incompatible libraries, however, actually accentuated the original portability problem [97]. To address this portability issue, a cross-industry group formulated the *message-passing interface* (MPI) in 1994 [96, 98]. The resulting standard did receive broad acceptance in the industry and is now available as a message-passing programming interface on almost all distributed-memory systems, including clusters of workstations and shared-memory systems.

In a typical message-passing library, system calls are available for the initialization of the system, the exchange of point-to-point and broadcast messages (i.e., `send` and `receive`, the identification of the number of processes, the self-identification of a process, and synchronization). MPI, for example, has a subset of 6 calls that can be used to write functional programs. It also has a larger set of over 100 calls to program increasingly complex applications. Gropp *et al.* [96] provide excellent examples of message-passing applications using MPI, as well as methods for porting applications written for other message-passing libraries to MPI.

There are also examples of programming interfaces that enable programs parallelized for shared-memory systems using compiler directives to be transparently ported to distributed memory systems, such as clusters of workstations [99, 100]. However, in these cases, the application has to be sufficiently latency tolerant to accommodate the higher latencies inherent in such a distributed memory system.

Clusters of shared-memory parallel systems can be programmed using a combination of shared-memory and distributed-memory models [78].

However, the applications must be tolerant of the mix of latencies and bandwidths inherent in such systems. Although few applications exist with sufficient hierarchical parallelism available to deliver good performance on clusters of shared-memory parallel systems, there are some interesting examples of applications in computational chemistry, finite element analysis, seismic processing and computational fluid dynamics (CFD), which have been programmed using MPI, OpenMP and various combinations of the two [78]. The applications are particularly interesting in that they show an increasing trend towards the use of standards-based parallel programming using both message-passing and shared-memory models on parallel computing platforms constructed of commodity processing components.

5.3. Trends in Programming Interfaces

Independent of the system architecture, the desired features of any programming model are to provide high performance while being easy to use. It is relatively easy to quantify performance using a program's total execution time, but comparing the relative ease-of-use of different programming models is inherently more subjective. A recent study [101] does suggest, however, that programming with a message-passing model is consistently more complex than programming with a shared-memory model, although the differences, as measured by the complexity of the programs' control flow, are typically not large. These results also suggest that there is a weak inverse relationship between parallel program complexity and performance. For instance, the high-level abstractions provided by the implicitly parallel HPF programming language provide a degree of hardware independence and programming simplicity, but often with a consequent loss in performance.

There is a growing disconnect between current parallel programming models and emerging hardware technology. Although most hardware trends indicate a growing and widespread acceptance of scalable shared-memory systems, the commonly adopted message-passing programming model is best supported by a previous generation of distributed-memory hardware. One issue that hinders the acceptance of shared-memory programming models is confusion between parallel algorithms, the particular programming model by which these algorithms are implemented, and the system architecture. Another issue is the lack of standards to facilitate the portability of applications between shared-memory systems from different hardware vendors. The latter issue is being addressed by emerging standards such as OpenMP [90].

Applications that are written from scratch for a particular architecture can often be designed to be insensitive to the variability of memory access delays. However, writing applications for specific architectures is a time-consuming task and, in some sense, defeats the ease of use that comes with the shared-memory model. Estimating the effects of the variability of access costs for existing parallel applications requires good models, which are currently lacking. These models would enable users to predict performance levels achievable when parallelizing applications. For system designers, these models will suggest the required balance between processor performance and memory latencies and bandwidths. These issues will become increasingly important since, as discussed in section 4, processor technology is changing very rapidly, while memory hierarchies continue to become even more complex.

Misconceptions about shared-memory scalability will continue until a separation of algorithm, implementation, and architecture issues is presented when reporting parallel results. Performance studies comparing the two models on similar algorithms, e.g., [75, 101], are required to clarify the distinction between the algorithm and the programming model. These studies, combined with a widely adopted standard for shared memory parallel programming, would naturally lead to a much more widespread use of the shared-memory model in the software development community.

Processors based on the Intel X86 architecture vastly outnumber any other processor family in computer systems today [102]. SMP systems based on such processors are rapidly proliferating in the market for use as file and web servers, for instance, and for a wide variety of other applications, including computationally intensive applications. A recent report discusses porting commercial scientific applications from Unix systems to Intel/ Windows NT systems using OpenMP [103], for instance. These systems are currently based on small numbers of processors, typically fewer than 32 with 4–8 being the most common.

However, one issue which is not easily addressed, even with standards such as OpenMP, is the concept of performance portability when migrating parallel applications between SMP, DSM, and COMA architectures. Such portability is probably more an issue of good parallel algorithm design. Issues such as granularity of the parallelism, architecture, latency, and bandwidth of the system all have to be considered. If the parallel algorithm is flexible enough to deal with variations of all or most of the above parameters, there is a reasonable chance of performance portability in addition to functional portability.

As discussed earlier, an increasing number of applications are being programmed using industry-standard programming interfaces. OpenMP shows some promise in addressing the need for a standard for shared-memory parallel programming. The widespread availability of low-cost commodity multiprocessor systems along with shared-memory multiprocessing support from the dominant and emerging server operating systems and environments such as Windows NT and Linux will surely advance the popularity of shared-memory parallel processing.

6. Compilers and Tools

The holy grail of parallel computation is a model in which programmers can be blissfully unaware of the fact that their programs will indeed run on a parallel machine. That is, we would ultimately like compilers to automatically parallelize the code for the targeted parallel architecture in a programmer-invisible way.

The difficulty in achieving this ideal has always been that it is nearly impossible for the compiler to discern the inherent parallelism of the code, without programmer hints. The key stumbling blocks have long been data and control dependences. Control dependences are instances in which the execution path of the program depends on the outcome of a conditional branch. Programs with irregular control flow are difficult for compilers to analyze and parallelize.

Data dependences are instances in which parallelization is impeded because one computation depends on the data produced by another computation. True data dependences often reflect a lack of parallelism in the application itself. On the other hand, compilers need to be conservative in their analysis of *potential* data dependences. This conservatism is particularly vexing in pointer-based codes, where hard-to-know pointer values can make it difficult to find sufficient parallelism.

Automated compiler parallelization in highly-regular, loop-based scientific codes has reached a level of significant maturity. In such codes, the control flow is easy to discern, and data dependences among the array accesses can also be detected with good accuracy. Speedups of $12\times$ or more on machines with 16 processors are now achievable on many full programs (not just kernels). The SUIF parallelizing compiler framework has posted some of the world's best SPECfp results through aggressive automatic parallelization [104]. Other commercial parallelizing compiler efforts have come from Silicon graphics [105], the KAP compiler [106], and others.

In many cases, however, compiler parallelization is impeded by overly conservative assumptions about data dependences. In such cases, performance can be improved via an interactive framework in which the user can point out instances where apparent dependences can be safely ignored by the compiler. For example, the ParaScope tool developed at Rice allows for interactive user editing of a program dependence list [107].

Dependence analysis in pointer-based codes has also made some moderate strides in recent years. In particular, recent work on pointer disambiguation in C code [108] and on memory allocation for the RAW architecture [109] has improved the formerly bleak prospects in this difficult research area.

Until automatic parallelization is made effective on a broader range of architectures and programs, hand parallelization, and performance tuning will inevitably be needed to help achieve the needed performance levels. It is hoped that performance tools can assist programmers in these efforts. In [110] the authors describe their real-life experiences in tuning a parallel disk-to-disk sorting program. Although their efforts led to world-record sort speeds, it is sobering to note that they used no formal "parallel performance tools" to achieve these results. Tools continue to be the topic of intense research, but there has not yet been sufficient convergence of platforms and programming environments to lead to a convergence of tools and tuning strategies.

None the less, interesting tools and monitoring strategies have been developed and convergence in the shared-memory multiprocessor market is likely to encourage their acceptance. Examples can be categorized according to the type and overhead of performance monitoring implemented. When fairly general performance information is desired from actual program runs, then traditional tools like prof or SpeedShop can be used to gather performance numbers. In some cases, slightly more detailed information, such as synchronization performance, may be required. In such cases, a number of performance tools are available which gather synchronization traces and offer summaries or timelines of parallel thread performance [111–113]. This information can be generated with relatively low monitoring overheads [111]. When extensive detail on memory or communication behavior is desired, the tools will either be software-based with fairly high overheads, or will reduce overheads by relying on some hardware support. For example, recent research has included specialized hardware performance monitors for communication observation [114]. Other approaches have embedded performance monitoring code into hardware already used by the multiprocessor for other purposes. These include the FlashPoint tool embedded into the MAGIC chip of the Stanford FLASH system [115] and a similar tool embedded in the firmware of a Myrinet LANai processor used as part of a Myrinet-based SHRIMP system [116].

6.1   Trends in Compilers

Explicit hand-parallelization remains the most common means for exploiting parallelism today, but automatic compiler parallelization is a natural goal, and is moving closer to reality. Compilers are now reaching a point where they can parallelize many interesting scientific codes [117, 118]. Although they are not always successful, there is a growing class of applications in which parallelism can be automatically identified. Significant challenges remain for parallelizing compilers at this point, as discussed in the following paragraphs.

6.1.1   Identifying Parallelism: Moving Beyond Loop-Oriented Code

Parallelism can be automatically identified in many loop-oriented scientific codes [117, 118]. Difficulties ensue, however, with commercial programs; such codes are often much larger (with perhaps hundreds of thousands of lines of code) and more complex. Further, there are large classes of applications such as database, telecommunications, GIS, graphics, and stock and option trading which are run sequentially today on shared-memory parallel machines. Some of these do not possess the advantages of structure which scientific applications have. Parallelizing them may therefore be much more challenging. However, they may also be more rewarding in terms of the payback from parallelization. Key challenges for parallelizing compilers have included memory accesses through pointers where data dependences are difficult to analyze, and parallelism that spans procedure boundaries.

In particular, pointer analysis and memory disambiguation remains the most pressing issue preventing full identification of program parallelism. Some strides have been made in analyzing C programs with pointers [108], but loops with very dynamic access patterns remain unparallelized. In such cases, interactive parallelization techniques may be one promising tack. Here, compilers query users for higher-level program information that may aid them in identifying parallelism or deducing when perceived dependencies need not impede parallelization.

Parallelism spanning procedure boundaries has also been attacked in some experimental and commercial compilers by applying compiler analysis passes interprocedurally. In conjunction with techniques such as array privatization, interprocedural analysis can help to identify much coarser-grained parallelism in the code. On many shared-memory multiprocessors, coarse-grained parallelism is desirable because it can reduce both synchronization and memory costs for the code [119, 120].

One parallelization method used by applications experts is *algorithm recognition and substitution*. For example, many linear algebra algorithms have interesting parallel variants. Compilers can often do some of the simpler cases of "recognize and substitute" such as optimizing sum reductions. The compiler community should consider the next few examples of "recognize and substitute" to be attempted by compilers. This question clearly need not be restricted to scientific computing.

6.1.2 Managing Parallelism

In many cases, compilers can successfully identify sufficient parallelism in major program loops. Some automatically parallelized programs exhibit excellent speedups, but often other programs have properties that limit speedup even after parallelism has been identified at compile-time.

For example, memory behavior is one key performance-limiting factor for many compiler-parallelized codes. One reason for this is that parallelizing compilers often aggressively parallelize as many loops as possible. Such aggressiveness can cause fine-grained loops to be parallelized in ways that lead to extreme true or false sharing. In some cases, these parallelized loops with sharing problems perform much worse than executing the loop sequentially would have [119, 120]. Better memory analysis and combinations of communication and computation analysis [121] could limit the cases where poor parallelization choices are made. Finally, in some cases, the memory behavior can be adequately analyzed by the compiler, but insufficient memory hierarchy control is afforded to the compiler. Instruction-set architectures that allow for compiler hints regarding cache control could improve memory behavior somewhat orthogonally to the parallelism deduced.

Whether memory behavior or other hard-to-analyze factors are limiting performance, the upshot is that while parallelizing compilers have become quite good at *identifying* parallelism, they are less adept at pre-determining the *degree* of parallelism. As a result, a compiler-parallelized application may execute its computation on more processors than it can effectively use, not only wasting processors that could be applied to other useful work, but in some cases even slowing down the computation itself. This waste of computational resources becomes more acute as the number of processors increases, particularly for parallel computers used as multiprogrammed compute servers.

Perhaps the most straightforward technique for sharing the processors of a shared-memory multiprocessor among several competing parallel application programs is to *time-share* them [122]. With this approach, the operating system maintains a single queue of tasks that are ready to be executed. Whenever a processor becomes idle, the next available task, which is the one at the head of the queue, is assigned to that processor. The task then is allowed to run for a fixed period of time, called the *quantum* or *time slice*. When this time expires, the task is evicted from the processor and placed at the end of the ready queue. The next available task is then assigned to the processor for execution.

Multiplexing a single processor among many different tasks using this time-sharing technique is effective in maintaining high system utilization. However, the use of time-sharing to control the allocation of processor resources to parallel tasks can substantially reduce the performance of each individual parallel application [123–125]. The time required to perform the actual context switch is relatively small, on the order of tens of microseconds in typical operating systems available today. Thus, the performance impact due to the context switching overhead itself is relatively small. However, switching a process out of a processor corrupts the caches and can lead to excessive synchronization overhead.

In particular, when a process is swapped out of a processor, the data and instructions it had stored in the caches will be overwritten by the next process that executes on the processor. When the first process is again assigned to a processor for execution, it must completely rebuild its working set. The performance impact of this cache corruption has been measured to be as high as 23% [123]. Another problem occurs when a process that holds a synchronization lock is swapped out owing to the expiration of its time slice [125]. Any other processes that are waiting for this lock will be unable to continue their execution until the process holding the lock again rises to the top of the ready queue. These waiting processes will consume processor resources while doing nothing more than busy-waiting on a lock that may not become available for a long time.

Several solutions to the problem of active processes waiting for locks held by inactive processes have been developed. One obvious approach is to have the scheduler check to see if a process holds an active lock before deallocating it from the processor and returning it to the ready queue [126]. A complementary approach is to force any processes that are waiting for a lock to give up the processor by putting them back on the ready queue [127]. Both of these approaches can increase the context switching rate, however. Additionally, they can substantially reduce the performance of the parallel application by severely limiting the time each of its tasks is allowed to execute.

Coscheduling [125] and *gang-scheduling* [128] address the process thrashing and the inefficient locking and synchronization problems by scheduling all of the tasks from a parallel application as a single group. This approach forces parallel tasks that interact heavily to all run at the same time. Thus, if one of the tasks must wait for another task to release a lock, it is guaranteed that the task with the lock will be scheduled to run at the same time. This approach can improve the performance of a parallel application by reducing process thrashing, but its primary disadvantage is that, if a single task from the group is not ready to run, none of the tasks will be allowed to run. Furthermore, processor resources can be wasted when a gang does not need all of the available processors. If the next available gang that is ready to run requires more than the number of available processors, it will not be scheduled. As a result, the available processors will remain idle until the time slice of the currently executing gang expires. Gang scheduling also does not address the cache corruption problem since context switching must still occur and there is no assurance that a task will always run on the same processor.

Another processor allocation strategy statically partitions the processors in the system into completely independent groups. Each parallel application is then assigned to its own partition where it can run to completion with no interference from other applications. This approach completely eliminates the need for context switching and it eliminates the problem of tasks waiting on locks held by inactive processes. Since the tasks run uninterrupted on a single processor, the contents of the caches are preserved.

This *space-sharing* appears to solve all of the problems introduced by simple time-sharing, but it typically leads to very low overall system utilization. In particular, the number of processors needed by a parallel application tends to vary over the execution of the program. During some periods it may need all of the available processors; during other periods it may need only a single processor. Furthermore, the application is limited to using only the processors allocated to its partition, even though there may be idle processors in other partitions.

Dynamic partitioning, on the other hand, treats all of the processors in the system as one common pool of available resources. The number of processors allocated to each individual application program can then be varied over the program's total execution lifetime as its degree of parallelism varies [129, 130]. The *automatic self-allocating threads* (ASAT) mechanism [131], for example, dynamically adjusts the number of threads an application can use for its execution based on the system load. At fixed intervals, an application that uses the ASAT mechanism will indirectly estimate the current system load by measuring the time required to synchronize its threads. If it estimates that the load has increased since the last time it was measured, the application will reduce the number of processors on which it will run its threads. If the load has decreased, however, it will increase the number of processors it uses.

The *loop-level process control* (LLPC) mechanism [124] performs a similar dynamic reallocation of processors to parallel applications. In this case, the application determines the system load by examining a state variable maintained by the operating system. The number of threads used to execute a parallel region is adjusted at the start of each region to ensure that the total number of threads being used by all of the applications does not exceed the total number of processors in the system. Thus, each application is able to use as many processors as possible without overloading the system. In the worst case, each application will be able to create only a single thread. If the system is only lightly loaded, however, the application will be able to use all of the idle processors in the system. The Convex C-series system implements a similar dynamic scheduling approach, called *automatic self-allocating processors* (ASAP), directly in hardware. This mechanism allows an application to quickly create the appropriate number of threads at the start of each parallel region. All but one of the threads are automatically terminated at the end of the parallel region.

Most recently, research has shown the promise of adapting processing usage on a per-loop basis as the program runs [132]. The system described in this paper monitors, on a per-loop-nest basis, how efficiently the programs are using the processors assigned to them. When applications are achieving speedups much lower than ideal, i.e., much lower than the number of assigned processors, the processors are reallocated to other applications. This loop-based approach allows a time-sharing system with parallel programs to use processors more effectively than prior, generally-coarser-grained scheduling approaches. Overall, this work has led to 3× or more improvements in workload runtimes, compared to unmanaged program executions. Furthermore, because the monitoring and adaptive code is integrated into the compiler runtime system, the modifications are entirely programmer invisible. Key remaining research issues involve reducing the monitoring overhead of collecting such performance information, and refining management policies for the processor allocation.

6.1.3 Compiler feedback and ease of use

Given that the state of the art in compiler technology is such that automatic parallelization of large applications is not yet practical, it would be useful for compilers to provide feedback to the user to assist in hand parallelization. For example, the compiler gathers a lot of useful information regarding memory behavior and dependencies. Even if the compiler does not succeed in automatic parallelization, the information gathered during analysis may be useful to enable easier manual parallelization or optimization of the application. Formal mechanisms for conveying pertinent information derived from analysis would be useful.

Delivered parallel performance on applications and ease of use of shared memory parallel machines have the potential of dramatically improving the popularity of parallelism. Compilers have a dramatic effect on both of these issues.

Finally, standardization of compiler directives is an important issue which affects portability and ease of use. Even though there are several different shared memory machines in existence today, there is no standard for shared memory parallelization directives or compiler flags. Distributed memory machines have had more success with standards such as MPI. Standardization would greatly improve portability of applications.

6.1.3.1 Run-time dependence checking The ability of a compiler to find independent sections of a program that can be executed in parallel on multiple processors is often limited by the inherent incompleteness of the information available at compile-time. It is often the case that the information necessary for the compiler to prove independence between program statements depends on values that are not known until the program is actually executed. For example, the compiler must know the number of iterations of a loop that will be executed to be able to generate

appropriate code to execute the loop in parallel. Common program constructs, such as subscripted subscripts in array variables and the use of pointer indirection, can also obscure opportunities for parallelism. If the compiler cannot unambiguously determine that sections of a program are independent, the sections must be assumed to be dependent and, therefore, executed sequentially.

In many programs, this assumption proves to be overly conservative. When the program is actually executed, it may turn out that the program sections are, in fact, independent, and so could have been executed in parallel. *Run-time dependence checking* schemes attempt to compensate for the necessary conservatism of the compiler by checking whether dependences between program sections actually exist when the program is executed. This technique allows the compiler to assume that program dependences that are unknown at compile-time will not actually occur at runtime. It can then generate code that executes these sections in parallel, along with code that performs the appropriate dependence test at runtime.

These runtime dependence checking schemes have typically been targeted to the parallelization of loops that access one or more single-or multi-dimensional arrays. In these loops, the compiler must determine whether array locations accessed in different iterations are always unique, or whether one iteration may write to an element of the array while another iteration within the same loop reads the same element. In the former case, the iterations can be executed in parallel since the iterations can be executed in any order. In the latter case, however, the compiler must execute all of the iterations sequentially. The problem is that the compiler may not be able to *disambiguate* the array references to determine if there is a dependence. For example, if one iteration reads an array with an indirect reference, such as x[a[i]], while another iteration writes the array using a different subscript, such as x[b[i]], the compiler can be unable to determine if the different iterations reference the same array element since it lacks sufficient information to determine if a[i] == b[i].

When this type of memory referencing information cannot be determined at compile-time, the runtime dependence checking schemes attempt to determine if these two types of accesses actually do reference the same array element when the program is executed. These schemes typically execute the loop in two phases [133, 134]. The *inspector* phase first runs a modified version of the loop being tested. This modified loop does not perform any of the actual operations on the array elements accessed within the loop. Instead, it simply executes a stripped-down version of the loop that performs only the memory access operations. As it runs this memory access-only loop, it records information in *shadow variables* about which array elements are accessed by the loop, and the order in which they are accessed.

The *executor* phase then executes the loop iterations in parallel, but making sure that the iterations are executed in an order that does not violate any of the interloop iteration dependences found by the inspector stage.

One of the limitations of these basic inspector–executor schemes is that the inspector stage must be run before the executor, which adds to the total execution time of the loop. An alternative is to assume that dependences between the loop iterations are unlikely to actually occur at run-time. In this case, the executor stage can execute the loop iterations *speculatively* at the same time that the inspector is testing the memory accesses in the loop iterations [135]. If the inspector ultimately determines that the loop iterations cannot be executed in parallel, the values written by the executor phase in its speculative mode of operation must be discarded. The entire loop then must be re-executed sequentially. In the case where the inspector finds that the loop can be safely executed in parallel, however, many of the actual loop iterations will have already been completed. Thus, if the probability is high that there will be no interiteration dependences, this speculative mode of execution can substantially improve the overall performance.

To further reduce the inspector overhead, the runtime dependence checking can be assisted by special hardware [136]. With this hardware support, the loop iterations are initially assumed to be independent and so are speculatively executed in parallel. Extensions to the multiprocessor's cache coherence protocol are made to automatically detect any dependence violations. When such a dependence violation occurs, the loop's execution is immediately terminated and the memory is restored to its state before the loop began executing. The loop is then restarted and executed sequentially.

Although these inspector–executor schemes are effective in parallelizing array-based application programs, a compiler cannot normally parallelize the common *do-while* program control construct since a *do-while* loop executes an unknown number of iterations. Similarly, memory accesses specified using indirect pointers and linked lists are difficult for compilers to disambiguate, and so frustrate automatic parallelization efforts. The *coarse-grained thread pipelining* execution model [137] adapts the fine-grained thread pipelining model from the superthreaded processor architecture [48] to extend run-time dependence checking schemes to allow the parallelization of general-purpose program constructs.

6.2 Trends in Tools

When hand-parallelization is used, performance tools are essential to aggressive parallel programmers interested in hand-tuning their code. Despite the great importance of parallel performance analysis to good program speedups, parallel tools still require significant advances.

Many current program performance tools provide basic high-level information on the compute performance and the coarse-grained communication behavior of parallel programs. In shared-memory multiprocessors, interprocessor synchronization is relatively easy to monitor and display statistics about. The fine-grained user-level timers that have begun to appear on commercial multiprocessors are extremely helpful in providing accurate timing statistics as well.

Memory behavior, however, is still quite difficult to monitor. This is largely because software has traditionally been presented with the abstraction of a uniform high-speed memory. Unlike branch instructions—which observably alter control flow depending on which path is taken—loads and stores offer no direct mechanism for software to determine if a particular reference was a hit or a miss. Since shared-memory parallel programs communicate via shared data, statistics on memory accesses are crucial because they reveal much about the interprocessor communication behavior of the program being studied.

For these reasons, we advocate careful processor support for observing memory behavior. Recently, CPU designers have provided user-accessible memory event counters on-chip [138–141]. These counters offer good aggregate views of memory behavior, although it is difficult to use them to determine if a *particular* reference hits or misses in the cache. This requires reading the miss counter value just before and after each time that reference is executed, and these reads sequentialize the pipeline. Lightweight cache miss traps combined with performance counters in handler software may be a more general approach [142].

At the software level, tools have also been hobbled by the lack of standardization in programming interfaces. With so many parallel languages and programming environments available, tool interoperability is nearly impossible to achieve. As we reach consensus on a handful of common parallel programming models, it will become feasible to develop well-tested, widely used code for these models. Furthermore, we feel that integrating the tool infrastructure with a full programming and compilation environment will offer the best hope that performance tools are actively used as part of the standard program development cycle.

7. Concluding Remarks

In the past few years, research in shared-memory multiprocessing has clearly paid off commercially. Several vendors are now selling cost-effective commercial multiprocessors that improve the performance of many important applications. In spite of this clear progress, additional hurdles must be overcome in order for multiprocessing to offer even larger performance improvements on a wider variety of applications.

Most importantly, future research must facilitate parallel software development by improving automatic parallelization techniques, parallel programming performance tools, and standardized programming interfaces that improve portability. Throughout these software developments, researchers must retain a broad view of the application domains to be served; past research has focused heavily on scientific applications, sometimes to the detriment of other important domains. The final challenge may prove the most difficult: all these suggested developments face a moving hardware target. Thus, software improvements must be made in the midst of constant increases in the integration levels, on-chip parallelism, and memory hierarchy complexity that will characterize further architectural changes over the next decade.

ACKNOWLEDGMENTS

This article sprang out of creative discussions during a task force meeting in Maui, Hawaii in January 1997. The key driving force behind this meeting was Professor Yale Patt of University of Texas at Austin. We are deeply indebted to Yale for believing that we could focus our thoughts to produce a white paper that laid the ground for this contribution. Other people who have contributed their thoughts to this paper are Dr. Dan Lenoski, Dr. Brond Larson, Dr. Woody Lichtenstein, Dr. John McCalpin, and Dr. Jeff McDonald.

REFERENCES

[1] Culler, D., Singh, J. P., and Gupta, A. (1999). *Parallel Computer Architecture: A Hardware/Software Approach.* Morgan Kaufmann, San Francisco.

[2] Stenstrom, P. (1988). Reducing contention in shared-memory multiprocessors. *IEEE Computer,* **21**(11), 26–37.

[3] Stenstrom, P. (1990). A survey of cache coherence schemes for multiprocessors. *IEEE Computer,* **23**(6), 12–25.

[4] Lilja, D. J. (1993). Cache coherence in large-scale shared-memory multiprocessors: issues and comparisons. *ACM Computing Surveys,* **25**(3), 303–338.

[5] Arpaci-Dusseau, R. H. (1998). STARFIRE: Extending the SMP envelope. *IEEE Micro,* **18**, 39–49.

[6] Pfister, G. *et al.* (1985). The IBM research parallel processor prototype (RP3). *Proceedings of the 1985 International Conference on Parallel Processing,* pp. 764–771.

[7] Butterfly Parallel Processor (1986). Technical Report 6148, BBN Laboratory, Cambridge, MA.

[8] Verghese, B., Devine, S., Gupta, A. and Rosenblum, M. (1996). Operating system support for improving data locality on CC-NUMA compute servers. *Proceedings of the 7th International Conference on Architectural Support for Programming Languages and Operating Systems,* pp. 279–289.

[9] Black, D., Gupta, A. and Weber, W.-D. (1989). Competitive *management of distributed shared memory. Proceedings of the* COMP-CON, pp. 184–190.

10] Censier, L. and Feautrier, P. (1978). A New solution to coherence problems in multicache systems. *IEEE Trans. Computers*, **27**, 1112–1118, December.

11] James, D., Laundrie, A., Gjessing, S. and Sohi, G. (1990). Scalable coherent interface. *IEEE Computer*, **23**(6), 74–77.

12] Nilsson, H. and Stenstrom, P. (1992). The scalable tree protocol: a cache coherence approach for large-scale multiprocessors. *Proceedings of the 4th IEEE Symposium on Parallel and Distributed Processing*, pp. 498–506.

[13] Chaiken, D., Kubiatowics, J. and Agarwal, A. (1991). LimitLESS directories: A scalable cache coherence solution. *Proceedings of the 4th International Conference on Architectural Support for Programming Languages*, pp. 224–234.

[14] Larus, J., Reinhardt, S. K., Hill, M. and Wood. D. (1993). Cooperative shared memory: software and hardware for scalable multiprocessors. *ACM Transactions on Computer Systems*, **11**(4), 300–318, November.

[15] Grahn, H. and Stenstrom, P. (1995). Efficient strategies for software-only directory protocols in shared-memory multiprocessors. *Proceedings of the 22nd Annual International Symposium on Computer Architecture*, pp. 38–47.

[16] Lenoski, D., Laudon, J., Gharachorloo, K. *et al.* (1992). The Stanford DASH multiprocessor. *IEEE Computer*, pp. 63–79, March.

[17] Agarwal, A. *et al.* (1995). The MIT Alewife machine: architecture and performance. *Proceedings of the 22nd International Symposium on Computer Architecture*, pp. 2–13.

[18] Laudon, J. and Lenoski, D. (1997). The SGI Origin 2000: A CC-NUMA highly scalable server. *Proceedings of the 24th International Symposium on Computer Architecture*, pp. 241–251.

[19] Lovett, T. and Clapp, R. (1996). A CC-NUMA computer system for the commercial marketplace. *Proceedings of the 23rd International Symposium on Computer Architecture*, pp. 308–317.

[20] P. Stenstrom, T. Joe, and A. Gupta. (1992). Comparative performance evaluation of cache-coherent NUMA and COMA architectures. *Proceedings of the 19th Annual International Symposium on Computer Architecture*, pp. 80–91.

[21] Hagersten, E., Landin, A. and Haridi, S. (1992). DDM-A cache-only memory architecture. *IEEE Computer*, **25**(9), 44–54.

[22] Burkhardt, H. III, Frank, S., Knobe, B. and Rothnie, J. (1992). Overview of the KSR-1 computer system. Technical Report KSR-TR-9202001, Kendall Square Research, Boston, MA, February.

[23] Zhang, Z. and Torrellas, J. (1997). Reducing remote conflict misses: NUMA with remote cache versus COMA. *Proceedings of the 3rd International Conference on High-Performance Computer Architecture*, pp. 272–281.

[24] Hagersten, E., Saulsbury, A. and Landin. A. (1994). Simple COMA node implementations. *Proceedings of the 27th Hawaii International Conference on System Sciences*, pp. 522–533.

[25] Hagersten, E. and Koster, M. (1999). Wildfire. *Proceedings of the 5th International Conference on High-Performance Computer Architecture*, pp. 172–181.

[26] Singh, J. P., Weber, W.-D. and Gupta, A. (1992). SPLASH: Stanford Parallel applications for shared memory. *Computer Architecture News*, **20**(1), 5–44.

[27] Goldsmith, S. (1993). Simulation of multiprocessor: accuracy and performance. PhD thesis, Stanford University, June.

[28] Brorsson, M., Dahlgren, F., Nilsson, H. and Stenstrom, P. (1993). The CacheMire test bench a flexible and effective approach for simulation of multiprocessors. *Proceedings of the 26th IEEE Annual Simulation Symposium*, pp. 41–49.

[29] Woo, S. C., Ohara, M., Torrie, E. et al. (1995). The SPLASH-2 programs: characterization and methodological considerations. *22nd Annual International Symposium on Computer Architecture*, pp. 24–36.

[30] Grizzaffi Maynard, A. M. et al. (1994). Contrasting characteristics and cache performance of technical and multi-user commercial workload. *Proceedings of the 6th International Conference on Architectural Support for Programming Languages and Operating Systems*, October, pp. 145–155.

[31] Trancoso, P., Larriba-Pey, J.-L and Torrellas, J. (1997). The memory performance of DSS commercial workloads in shared-memory multiprocessors. *Proceedings of the 3rd International Conference on High-Performance Computer Architecture*, pp. 250–260.

[32] Barroso, L., Gharachorloo, K. and Bugnion, E. (1998). Memory system characterization of commercial workloads. *Proceedings of the 25th Annual International Symposium on Computer Architecture*, pp. 3–14.

[33] Magnusson, P. et al. (1998). SimICS/Sun4m: a virtual workstation. *Proceedings of the USENIX'98*, pp. 119–130.

[34] Rosenblum, M., Herrod, S., Witchel, E. and Gupta, A. (1995). Complete system simulation: the SimOS approach. *IEEE Parallel and Distributed Technology*, Fall.

[35] Patt, Y. N., Patel, S. J., Evers, M., Friendly, D. H. and Stark, J. (1997). One billion transistors, one uniprocessor, one chip. *IEEE Computer*, September, pp. 51–57.

[36] Yeh, Tse-Yu and Patt, Y. N. (1993). A comparison of dynamic branch predictors that use two levels of branch history. *Proceedings of the 20th Annual International Symposium on Computer Architecture*, pp. 257–266, 17–19 May.

[37] Smith, J. E. and Vajapeyam, S. (1997). Trace processors: moving to fourth-generation microarchitectures. *IEEE Computer*, **30**(9), 68–74.

[38] Colwell, R. P., Nix, R. P., O'Donnell, J. J. et al. (1987). A VLIW architecture for a trace scheduling compiler. *Proceedings of the Second International Conference on Architectural Support for Programming Languages and Operating Systems*, 5–8 October, pp. 180–192.

[39] Lam, M. (1988). Software pipelining: an effective scheduling technique for VLIW machines. *Proceedings of the SIGPLAN'88 Conference on Programming Language Design and Implementation*, 22–24 June, pp. 318–328.

[40] Moon, Soo-Mook and Ebcioglu, K. (1992). An efficient resource-constrained global scheduling technique for superscalar and VLIW processors. *25th Annual International Symposium on Microarchitecture*, 1–4 December, pp. 55–71.

[41] Eickemeyer, R. J., Johnson, R., Kunkel E. et al. (1996). Evaluation of multithreaded uniprocessors for commercial application environments. *International Symposium on Computer Architecture*, pp. 203–212.

[42] Lo, J. L., Barroso, L., Eggers, A. S. J. et al. (1998). An analysis of database workload performance on simultaneous multithreading processors. *International Symposium on Computer Architecture*, pp. 39–50.

[43] Tullsen, D. M., Eggers, S. J. and Levy, H. M. (1995). Simultaneous multithreading: maximizing on-chip parallelism. *Proceedings of the 22nd Annual International Symposium on Computer Architecture*, 22–24 June, pp. 392–403.

[44] Tullsen, D. M., Eggers, S. J., Emer, J. S. et al. (1996). Exploiting choice: instruction fetch and issue on an implementable simultaneous multithreading processor. *International Symposium on Computer Architecture*, pp. 191–202.

[45] Dubey, P. K., O'Brien, K., O'Brien, K. and Barton, C. (1995). Single-program speculative multithreading (SPSM) Architecture: compiler-assisted fine-grained multithreading. *Proceedings of the IFIP WG 10.3 Working Conference on Parallel Architectures and Compilation Techniques, PACT '95*, 27–29 June, pp. 109–121.

[46] Hirata, H., Kimura, K., Nagamine, S. *et al.* (1992). An elementary processor architecture with simultaneous instruction issuing from multiple threads. *Proceedings of the 19th Annual International Symposium on Computer Architecture*, 19–21 May, pp. 136–145.

[47] Sohi, G. S., Breach, S. E. and Vijaykumar, T. N. (1995). Multiscalar processors. *Proceedings of the 22nd Annual International Symposium on Computer Architecture*, 22–24 June, pp. 414–425.

[48] Tsai, Jenn-Yuan, Huang, Jian Amlo, C. *et al.* (1999). The superthreaded processor architecture. *IEEE Transactions on Computers, Special Issue on Multithreaded Architectures and Systems*, September, pp. 881–902.

[49] Hammond, L., Olukotun, K. and Nayfeh, B. A. (1997). A single-chip multiprocessor. *IEEE Computer*, September, 79–85.

[50] Waingold, E. *et al.* (1997). Baring it all to software: raw machines. *IEEE Computer*, September, 86–93.

[51] Saulsbury, A., Pong, F. and Nowatzyk, A. (1996). Missing the memory wall: the case for processor/memory integration. *Proceedings of the 23rd Annual International Symposium on Computer Architecture*, May, pp. 90–101.

[52] Patterson, D. *et al.* (1997). A case for intelligent RAM. *IEEE Micro*, **17**(2), 34–44.

[53] Smarr, L. and Catlett, Charles E. (1992). Metacomputing. *Communications of the ACM*, **35**(6), 45–52.

[54] Hollingsworth, J. K., Keleher, P. J. and Ryu, K. D. (1999). Resource-aware metacomputing. *Advances in Computing*, **53**. 110–171.

[55] Ender-Bilir, E. *et al.* (1999). Multicast snooping: a new coherence method using multicast address network. *Proceedings of the 26th Annual International Symposium on Computer Architecture*, May, pp. 294–304.

[56] Brewer, S. and Astfalk, T. (1997). The evolution of the HP/Convex exemplar. *Proceedings of COMPCON*.

[57] Rothberg, E., Singh, J. P. and Gupta, A. (1993). Working sets, cache sizes, and node granularity issues for large-scale multiprocessors. *Proceedings of the 20th Annual International Symposium on Computer Architecture*, pp. 14–25.

[58] Gupta, A. and Weber, W.-D. (1992). Cache invalidation patterns in shared-memory multiprocessors. IEEE *Transactions on Computers*, **41**(7), 794–810.

[59] Stenström, P. *et al.* (1997). Boosting the performance of shared memory multiprocessors. *IEEE Computer*, **30**(7), 63–70.

[60] Stenström, P., Brorsson, M. and Sandberg, L. (1993). An adaptive cache coherence protocol optimized for migratory sharing. *Proceedings of the 20th Annual International Symposium on Computer Architecture*, May, pp. 109–118,

[61] Cox, A. and Fowler, R. (1993). Adaptive cache coherency for detecting migratory shared data. *Proceedings of the 20th Annual International Symposium on Computer Architecture*, May, pp. 98–108.

[62] Skeppstedt, J. and Stenstrom, P. (1996). Using Dataflow analysis to reduce overhead in cache coherence protocols. *ACM Transactions on Programming Languagues and Systems*, **18**(6), 659–682.

[63] Grahn, H. and Stenstrom, P. (1996). Evaluation of an adaptive update-based cache protocol. *Journal of Parallel and Distributed Computing*, **39**(2), 168–180.

[64] Ranganathan, P., Gharachorloo, K. Adve, S. and Barroso, L. (1998). Performance of database workloads on shared-memory multiprocessors with out-of-order processors. *Proceedings of the 8th International Conference on Architectural Support for Programming Languages and Operating Systems*, November, pp. 307–318.

[65] Nilsson, J. and Dahlgren, F. (1999). Improving performance of load-store sequences for transaction processing work- loads on multiprocessors. *Proceedings of the 1999*

International Conference on Parallel Processing. IEEE Computer Society Press, 246–255.

[66] Adve, S. and Gharachorloo, K. (1996). Shared memory consistency models: a tutorial. *IEEE Computer,* **29**(12), 66–76.

[67] Gupta, A., Hennessy, J., Gharachorloo, K. *et al.* (1991). Comparative evaluation of latency-reducing and tolerating techniques. *Proceedings of the 18th Annual International Symposium on Computer Architecture,* May, pp. 254–263.

[68] M. Hill (1998). Multiprocessors should support simple memory consistency models. *IEEE Computer,* **31**(8).

[69] Mowry, T. (1994). Tolerating latency through software-controlled data prefetching. PhD thesis, Computer Systems Laboratory, Stanford University.

[70] Dahlgren, F. and Stenstrom, P. (1996). Evaluation of stride and sequential hardware-based prefetching in shared-memory multiprocessors. IEEE *Transactions on* Computers, **7**(4), 385–398.

[71] Luk, C-K. and Mowry, T. (1996). Compiler-based prefetching for recursive data structures. *Proceedings of the 7th International Conference on Architectural Support for Programming Languages,* October, pp. 222–233.

[72] Karlsson, M., Dahlgren, F. and Stenstrom, P. (2000). A prefetching technique for irregular accesses to linked data structures. *Proceedings of the 6th International Symposium on High-Performance Computer Architecture,* January, pp. 206–217.

[73] Tullsen, D., Eggers, S. and Levy, H. (1995). Simultaneous multithreading: maximizing on-chip parallelism. *Proceedings of the 22nd International Symposium on Computer Architecture,* pp. 392–403.

[74] Tsai, Jenn-Yuan and Yew, Pen-Chung (1996). The superthreaded architecture: thread pipelining with run-time data dependence checking and control speculation. *Proceedings of International Conference on Parallel Architectures and Compilation Techniques, PACT '96,* October 20–23, pp. 35–46.

[75] Cox, A. L., Dwardakas, S., Keleher, P. *et al.* (1994). *Software Versus Hardware Shared-Memory Implementation: A Case Study. International Symposium on Computer Architecture,* pp. 106–117.

[76] Shekhar, S., Ravada, S., Kumar, V. *et al.* (1996). Parallelizing a GIS on a shared address space architecture. *IEEE Computer,* 42–48.

[77] Fischer, P. F. and Venugopal, M. (1995). A commercial CFD application on a shared memory multiprocessor using MPI. *Proceedings of Parallel CFD '95,* pp. 231–238.

[78] Gabb, H., Bova, S. W., Breshears, C. P. *et al.* (1999). Parallel programming with message passing and directives. *SIAM News,* November, **32**(9), pp. 1 + 10–11.

[79] Chen, Wei (D.) (1994). Parallel programming on Silicon Graphics multiprocessor systems. Silicon Graphics Computer Systems, March.

[80] *KSR Fortran Programming* (1993). Kendall Square Research Corporation.

[81] Dowd, K. (1993). *High Performance Computing.* O'Reilly, Sebastopol, CA.

[82] Brawer, S. (1990). *Introduction to Parallel Programming.* Academic Press, New York.

[83] Bauer, B. E. (1992). *Practical Parallel Programming.* Academic Press, New York.

[84] Lenoski, D. E. and Weber, W.-D. (1995). *Scalable Shared-Memory Multiprocessing.* Morgan Kaufman, San Francisco.

[85] Dongarra, J. (1994). Performance of various computers using standard linear equation software. Technical Report CS-89–85, CS Department, University of Tennessee, July.

[86] Dietz, H. (1999). Parallel processing using Linux. *yara.ecn.purdue.edu/pplinux/,* April.

[87] Anderson, A. F. and Venugopal, M. (1995). A parallel implementation of ADAMS on a shared memory multiprocessor. *Proceedings of HPC-ASIA '95.*

[88] Schartz, P. J., Venugopal, M. and Bauer, J. L. (1996). Automotive modal analysis using CSA/Nastran on high performance computers. *Proceedings of the International Conference on High Performance Computing in Automotive Design, Engineering, and Manufacturing.*

[89] Venugopal, M., Slack, D. C. and Walters, R. F. (1995). A commercial CFD application on a shared memory multiprocessor. In *High Performance Computing*, Tata McGraw-Hill, New York, pp. 305–310.

[90] Throop, J. (1999). OpenMP: shared-memory parallelism from the ashes. *IEEE Computer*, May, pp. 108–109.

[91] OpenMP (1999). *www.OpenMP.org*, May.

[92] Kuhn, R. H. (1999). Software lab: developing parallel applications on IA/NT workstations. Intel Developer Forum presentation, February.

[93] Carlile, B. (1996). Seeking the balance: large SMP warehouses. *Database Programming Design*, August, pp. 44–48.

[94] Palmer, J. (1988). The nCUBE family of high performance parallel computer systems. *Proceedings of the 3rd Conference on Hypercube Concurrent Computers and Applications*, January, pp. 847–851.

[95] Arpaci-Dusseau, R. H. (1998). The Berkeley NOW project. *now.cs.berkeley.edu/*.

[96] Lusk, E., Gropp, W. and Skjellum, A. (1994). *Using MPI Portable Parallel Programming With The Message-Passing Interface*. MIT Press, Cambridge, MA.

[97] Boyle, J., Butler, R., Disz, T. *et al.* (1987). *Portable Programs for Parallel Processors*. Holt Rinehart and Winston, New York.

[98] MPI (1994). MPI: A message-passing interface standard. *International Journal of Supercomputing Applications*, **8**(3/4).

[99] Myrias Software Corporation (1999). PAMS—parallel application management system for Unix. *www.myrias.com/products/pams/*.

[100] Merkey, P. (1994). Beowulf project at CESDIS. *www.beowulf.org/*, March.

[101] VanderWiel, S., Nathanson, D. and Lilja, D. J. (1997). Complexity and performance in parallel programming languages. *International Workshop on High-Level Parallel Programming Models and Supportive Environments, International Parallel Processing Symposium*, April.

[102] Dataquest (1998). What does a company with 93% of the market do for an encore?, Table 6–2.

[103] Intel Corporation (1998). Case studies in moving multi-threaded workstation applications from RISC/UNIX to the Intel architecture. *www.intel.com/businesscomputing/wrkstn/pdf/ Moving Multithreaded Applications.pdf*, June, pp. 1–12.

[104] Hall, M. W., Anderson, J. M., Amarasinghe, S. P. *et al.* (1996). Maximizing multiprocessor performance with the SUIF compiler. *IEEE Computer*, **29**(12), 84–89.

[105] Silicon Graphics Inc. (1999). *Technical Publications: MIPSpro Compiling and Performance Tuning Guide*, May. Silicon Graphics Inc.

[106] Kuhn, B. and Stahlberg. E. (1997). Porting scientific software to Intel SMPs under Windows/NT. *Scientific Computing and Automation*, **14**(12).

[107] Hall, M. W., Harvey, T. J., Kennedy, K. *et al.* (1993). Experiences using the ParaScope Editor: An Interactive Parallel Programming Tool. *Proceeding of the 4th ACM SIGPLAN Symposium on Principles and Practice of Parallel Programming*, May.

[108] Wilson, R. P. and Lam, M. S. (1995). Efficient context-sensitive pointer analysis for C programs. *Proceedings of the ACM SIGPLAN Conference on Programming Language Design and Implementation*, June.

[109] Barua, R., Lee, Walter, Amarasinghe, S. and Agarwal, A. (1999). Maps: a compiler-managed memory system for raw machines. *Proceedings of the 26th Annual International Symposium on Computer Architecture*, May.

[110] Arpaci-Dusseau, A. C., Arpaci-Dusseau, R. H. *et al.* (1998). Searching for the sorting record: experiences in tuning NOW-SOrt. *Proceedings of the ACM SIGMETRICS Symposium on Parallel and Distributed Tools*, August.

[111] Miller, B. P., Clark, M., Hollingsworth, J. *et al.* (1990). IPS-2: the second generation of a parallel program measurement system. *IEEE Transactions on Parallel and Distributed Systems*, 1(2).

[112] Lehr, T., Segall, Z. *et al.* (1989). Visualizing performance debugging. *IEEE Computer*, October, pp. 38–51.

[113] Miller, B. (1988). DPM: a measurement system for distributed programs. IEEE *Transactions on Computers*, 37(2), 243–248.

[114] Martonosi, M., Clark, D. W. and Mesarina, M. (1996). The SHRIMP hardware performance monitor: design and applications. *Proceedings of the ACM SIGMETRICS Symposium on Parallel and Distributed Tools*, May.

[115] Martonosi, M., Ofelt, D. and Heinrich, M. (1996). Integrating performance monitoring and communication in parallel computers. *Proceedings of the ACM SIGMETRICS Conference on Measurement and Modeling of Computer Systems*, May.

[116] Liao, Cheng, Martonosi, M., and Clark, D. W. (1998). Performance monitoring in a Myrinet-connected SHRIMP cluster. *Proceedings of the ACM SIGMETRICS Symposium on Parallel and Distributed Tools*, August.

[117] Hall, M. W., Murphy, B. R. and Amarasinghe, S. P. (1995). Interprocedural parallelization analysis: A case study. *Proceedings of the 7th SIAM Conference on Parallel Processing for Scientific Computing*, San Francisco, February.

[118] Wilson, R. *et al.* (1994). SUIF: An infrastructure for research on parallelizing and optimizing compilers. *ACM SIGPLAN Notices*, 29(12), 31–37.

[119] Torrie, E., Martonosi, M., Hall, M. W. and Tseng, Chau Wen (1996). Memory referencing behavior in compiler-parallelized applications. Invited paper. *International Journal of Parallel Programming*, August.

[120] Torrie, E., Martonosi, M., Tseng, Chau Wen and Hall, M. W. (1996). Characterizing the memory behavior of compiler-parallelized applications. *IEEE Transactions on Parallel and Distributed Systems*, December.

[121] Anderson, J. and Lam, M. (1993). Global optimizations for parallelism and locality on scalable parallel machines. *Proceedings of the SIGPLAN '93 Conference on Programming Language Design and Implementation*, Albuquerque, NM, June.

[122] Bach, M. J. (1990). *The Design of the Unix Operating System.* Prentice-Hall, Englewood Cliffs, NJ.

[123] Tucker, A. (1993). Efficient scheduling on multiprogrammed shared-memory multi-processors. PhD thesis, Department of CS, Stanford University.

[124] Yue, K. K. and Lilja, D. J. (1996). Efficient execution of parallel applications in multiprogrammed multiprocessor systems. *International Parallel Processing Symposium*, April, pp. 448–456.

[125] Ousterhout, J. (1982). Scheduling techniques for concurrent systems. *Distributed Computer Systems Conference*, pp. 22–30.

[126] Leutenegger, S. and Vernon, M. (1990). The performance of multiprogrammed multiprocessor scheduling policies. *Conference on Measurement and Modeling of Computer Systems*, pp. 226–236.

[127] Natarajan, C., Sharma, S. and Iyer, R. (1994). Impact of loop granularity and self-preemption on the performance of loop parallel applications on a multiprogrammed shared-memory multiprocessor. *International Conference on Parallel Processing*, August, volume II, pp. 174–178.

[128] Barton, J. and Bitar, N. (1995). A scalable multi-discipline, multiple-processor scheduling framework for IRIX. In *Job Scheduling Stratetgies for Parallel Processing*, ed. D. Feitelson and L. Rudolph, Lecture Notes in Computer Science **949**, Springer-Verlag, New York, pp. 45–69.

[129] Naik, V. *et al.* (1993). Performance analysis of job scheduling policies in parallel supercomputing environments. *Proceedings of Supercomputing-93*, 824–833.

[130] Anderson, T., Bershad, B., Lazowska, E. and Levy, H. (1992). Schedular activations: Effective kernel support for user-level management of parallelism. *ACM Transactions on Computer Systems*, **10**(1), 53–79.

[131] Severance, C., Enbody, R., Wallach, S. and Funkhouser, B. (1995). Automatic self-allocating threads on the convex exemplar. *International Conference on Parallel Processing*, volume I, pp. 24–31.

[132] Hall, M. W. and Martonosi, M. (1998). Adaptive parallelism in compiler-parallelized code. *Concurrency: Practice and Experience*, **14**(10), 1235–1250.

[133] Chen, D. K., Yew, P.-C. and Torrellas, J. (1994). An efficient algorithm for the run-time parallelization of doacross loops. *Proceedings of Supercomputing '94*, November, pp. 518–527.

[134] Zhu, C. Q. and Yew, P.-C. (1987). A scheme to enforce data dependence on large multiprocessor systems. *IEEE Transactions on Software Engineering*, June, **13**, 726–739.

[135] Rauchwerger, L. and Padua, D. (1994). The privatizing doall test: a run-time technique for DOALL loop identification and array privatization. *SIGPLAN Conference on Supercomputing*, July, pp. 33–43.

[136] Zhang, Y., Rauchwerger, L. and Torrellas, J. (1998). Hardware for speculative run-time parallelization in distributed shared-memory multiprocessors. *International Symposium on High-Performance Computer Architecture*, February, pp. 162–173.

[137] Kazi, I. H. and Lilja, D. J. (1998). Coarse-grained speculative execution in shared-memory multiprocessors. *International Conference on Supercomputing*, July, pp. 93–100.

[138] Heinrich, J. (1995). *MIPS R10000 Microprocessor User's Manual*. SGI Corporation.

[139] Digital Equipment Corporation (1992). DECChip 21064 RISC Microprocessor Preliminary Data Sheet. Technical report, Digital Equipment Corporation.

[140] Edmonson, J. H., Rubenfeld, P. I., Bannon, P. J. *et al.* (1995). Internal organization of the Alpha 21164, a 300 MHz 64-bit Quad-issue CMOS RISC microprocessor. *Digital Technology Journal*, **7**(1), 119–135.

[141] Mathisen, T. (1994). Pentium secrets. *Byte*, July, pp. 191–192.

[142] Horowitz, M., Martonosi, M., Mowry, T. and Smith, M. D. (1998). Informing memory operations: memory performance feedback mechanisms and their applications. *ACM Transactions on Computer Systems*, May, **16**(7), 107–205.

Shared Memory and Distributed Shared Memory Systems: A Survey

KRISHNA KAVI, HYONG-SHIK KIM

Dept. of Electrical and Computer Engineering
University of Alabama in Huntsville
Huntsville
Alabama 35899
USA
kavi@ece.vah.edu

BEN LEE

Dept. of Electrical and Computer Engineering
Oregon State University
Corvallis
OR 97331
USA
benl@ece.orst.edu

A. R. HURSON

The Pennsylvania State University
201 Old Main
University Park
PA 16802
USA

ADVANCES IN COMPUTERS, VOL. 53
ISBN 0-12-012153-0

55

1. Introduction

Parallel and distributed processing have not lost their allure since their inception in 1960s; that allure lies in their ability to meet a wide range of price and performance. However, in many cases these advantages have not been realized owing to longer design times, limited scalability, increased semantic gap and lack of software support, and the ever-increasing performance/cost ratio of uniprocessors [1]. Historically, parallel processing systems were classified as single instruction multiple data (SIMD) or multiple instructions multiple data (MIMD) [2]. SIMD systems involved the use of a single control processor and a number of arithmetic processors. The array of arithmetic units executed identical instruction streams, but on different data items, in a lock-step fashion under the control of the control unit. Such systems were deemed to be ideal for data-parallel applications. Their appeal waned quickly since very few applications could achieve the performance required to justify their cost. More flexibility came in the form of multicomputers or multiprocessors that fall under the MIMD classification, relying on independent processors. They were able to address a broader range of applications than SIMD systems. One of the earliest MIMD system was the C.mmp [3], built at Carnegie Mellon University, which included 16 modified PDP-11/20 processors connected to 16 memory modules via a crossbar switch. This can be viewed as a symmetric multiprocessor (SMP) or a shared memory system. The next version of a multiprocessor system at CMU was known as Cm [4] and can be considered the first hardware-implemented distributed shared memory system. It consisted of a hierarchy of processing nodes; LSI-11 processors comprising clusters where processors of a single cluster were connected by a bus, and inter-cluster connections used specialized controllers to handle accesses to remote memory.

The next wave of multiprocessors relied on distributed memory, where processing nodes have access only to their local memory, and access to remote data is accomplished by request and reply messages. Numerous designs on how to interconnect the processing nodes and memory modules were published in the literature. Examples of such message-based systems included Intel Paragon, N-Cube, and IBM's SP systems. Distributed memory (or message-passing) systems can accommodate larger number of computing nodes than can shared memory systems. This scalability was expected to increase the utilization of message-passing architectures.

1.1   The Changing Nature of Parallel Processing

Parallel processing systems, particularly those based on the message-passing (or distributed memory) model, have been researched for decades, leading to the implementation of several large-scale computing systems and specialized supercomputers. But their use has been limited to very specialized applications. One of the major reasons for this is that most users have found the message-passing paradigm very hard to program— especially when they want to maintain a sequential version of a program (during development and debugging stages) as well as the message-passing version. Programmers often have to approach the two versions completely independently. In general, they felt more comfortable in viewing the data in a common global memory, hence programming on a shared-memory multiprocessor system (SMP) was considered easier. In a shared-memory paradigm, all processes (or threads of computation) share the same logical address space and access directly any part of the data structure in a parallel computation. A single address space enhances the programmability of a parallel machine by reducing the problems of data partitioning, migration, and load balancing. The shared memory also improves the capability of parallelizing compilers, standard operating systems, resource management, and incremental performance tuning of applications.

Even in commercial parallel processing applications, the trend has been towards the use of small clusters of SMP systems, often interconnected to address the needs of complex problems requiring the use of large number of processing nodes. Even when working with networked resources, programmers are relying on messaging standards such as MPI (and PVM), or relying on systems software to automatically generate message-passing code from user-defined shared-memory programs. The reliance on software support to provide a shared-memory programming model (i.e., distributed shared memory systems, DSMs) can be viewed as a logical evolution in parallel processing.

DSM systems aim to unify parallel processing systems that rely on message-passing with the shared-memory systems. The use of DSMs as (logically) shared memory systems addresses the major limitation of SMPs—scalability.

The growing interest in multithreaded programming and the availability of systems supporting multithreading (Pthreads, NT-Threads, Linux Threads, Java) further emphasizes the trend towards the SMP model. The formation of the OpenMP group and the specification of OpenMP Fortran [5] in October 1997 drove the final nail into the coffin of the message-passing paradigm. The new standard is designed for computers that use either the Unix or Windows NT operating systems and employ multiple micro-processors for parallel computing. OpenMP Fortran is designed for the development of portable parallel programs on shared-memory parallel computer systems. One effect of the OpenMP standard will be to increase the shift of complex scientific and engineering software development from the supercomputer world to high-end desktop workstations.

1.2 Programming Example

In order to appreciate the differences between the shared-memory and message-passing paradigms, consider the following code segments to compute the inner product. The first program (Example 1) was written using Pthreads (on shared memory), the second (Example 2) using MPI (for message passing systems). Both programs assume a master process and multiple worker processes, where each worker process is allocated equal amounts of work by the master. There are two major differences in the two implementations, related to how the work is distributed and how the worker processes access the needed data. The Pthreads version shows that each worker process is given the address of the data it needs for its work. In the MPI version, the actual data is sent to the worker processes. The worker processes of the Pthreads version access the needed data directly as if the data is local. It can also be seen that the worker processes directly accumulate their partial results in a single global variable (using mutual exclusion). The worker processes of the MPI program are supplied the actual data via messages, and they send their partial results back to the master for the purpose of accumulation.

Example 1 Code for shared memory using Pthreads.

```
pthread_mutex_t lock = PTHREAD_MUTEX_INITIALIZER;
double sum = 0.0;
typedef struct {        /* data structure used for work
                           distribution */
    int n;              /* number of elements */
```

```
  double *x;            /* address of the first element of
                        the 1st array */
  double *y;            /* address of the first element of
                        the 2nd array */
} arg_t;
static void *worker(arg_t *arg)        /* worker process
{                                      begins here */
  int i;
  int n = arg->n;
  double *x = arg->x;          /* takes data location */
  double *y = arg->y;          /* takes data location */
  double partial = 0.0;
for (i = 0; i < n; ++i)               /* calculation */
    partial += x[i]*y[i];
pthread_mutex_lock(&lock);        /* lock */
  sum += partial;          /* accumulate the partial sums */
pthread_mutex_unlock(&lock);     /* unlock */
return NULL;
}
main(int argc, char *argv[])
{
  double x[N_VEC], y[N_VEC];              /* input vectors */
  pthread_t thread[N_PROC];
  arg_t arg[N_PROC];
  int i, status;
generate(x, y);                 /* generates two vectors */
for (i = 0; i < N_PROC; i++) {              /* master process
    arg[i].n = SZ_WORK;                     distributes the
    arg[i].x = x + i*SZ_WORK;               work */
    arg[i].y = y + i*SZ_WORK;
    status = pthread_create(&thread[i], NULL,
                               (void*) worker, &arg[i]);
    if (status) exit(1);
}
for (i = 0; i < N_PROC; i++) {                  /* wait for
    status = pthread_join(thread[i], NULL); all worker
    if (status) exit(1);                    processes to
    }                                       complete */
printf("Inner product is %f\n", sum);
```

Example 2   Code for message-passing systems using MPI.

```
#define MASTER       0
#define FROM_MASTER  1
#define TO_MASTER    2
```

```
double sum = 0.0;

static double worker(int n, double *x, double *y)
{                              /* called by worker process */
  double partial = 0.0;
  int i;
for (i = 0; i < n; ++i)         /* calculation */
    partial += x[i]*y[i];
return partial;
}


main(int argc, char *argv[])
{
  double x[N_VEC], y[N_VEC];            /* input vectors */
  double x_partial[SZ_WORK], y_partial[SZ_WORK];
                              /* a chunk of each vector */
  double partial;
  int i, self, mtype, offset;
  MPI_Status status;
MPI_Init(&argc, &argv);        /* initialize MPI */
  MPI_Comm_rank(MPI_COMM_WORLD, &self);
if (self == MASTER) {         /* master process */
generate(x, y);        /* generates two vectors */
mtype = FROM_MASTER;
  offset = 0;
    for (i = 1; i < N_PROC; i++) {        /* send messages
                                             to workers */
      MPI_Send(&x[offset], SZ_WORK, MPI_DOUBLE, i, mtype,
          MPI_COMM_WORLD);
      MPI_Send(&y[offset], SZ_WORK, MPI_DOUBLE, i, mtype,
          MPI_COMM_WORLD);
      offset += SZ_WORK;
    }
    mtype = TO_MASTER;
    for (i = 1; i < N_PROC; i++) {    /* receive messages
                                         from workers */
      MPI_Recv(&partial, 1, MPI_DOUBLE, i, mtype,
          MPI_COMM_WORLD, &status);
      sum += partial;
    }
    printf("Inner product is %f\n", sum);
}
  else {                               /* worker process */
    mtype = FROM_MASTER;               /* receive a message
                                          from master */
```

```
MPI_Recv(x_partial, SZ_WORK, MPI_DOUBLE, MASTER, mtype,
    MPI_COMM_WORLD, &status);
MPI_Recv(y_partial, SZ_WORK, MPI_DOUBLE, MASTER, mtype,
    MPI_COMM_WORLD, &status);
partial = worker(SZ_WORK, x_partial, y_partial);
mtype = TO_MASTER;
MPI_Send(&partial, 1, MPI_DOUBLE, MASTER, mtype,
    MPI_COMM_WORLD);
}                           /* send result back to master */

    MPI_Finalize();
}
```

There is another important difference between the two models. In the Pthreads implementation, the user is not concerned with the data distribution, but in the MPI version the programmer must explicitly specify where the data should be sent to.

1.3   Distributed Shared Memory Systems

As mentioned previously, DSMs attempt to unify the message-passing and shared-memory programming models. Since DSMs span both physically shared and physically distributed memory systems, they are also concerned with the interconnection network that provide the data to the requesting processor in an efficient and timely fashion. Both the *bandwidth* (amount of data that can be supplied in a unit time) and *latency* (the time it takes to receive the first piece of requested data from the time the request is issued) are important to the design of DSMs. Because of the generally longer latencies encountered in large-scale DSMs, multithreading has received considerable attention in order to tolerate (or mask) memory latencies. In this chapter we will not address issues related to interconnection networks or latency tolerance techniques.

Given that the overall objective of DSMs is to provide cost-effective mechanisms to manage the extended memory space across multiple levels of hierarchy, the design space is huge. In this chapter we address some of the more important aspects of the design space. In this section we overview the major issues that face the design of DSMs. To start with, the management of large logical memory space involves moving data dynamically across the memory layers of a distributed system. This includes the mapping of the user data to the various memory modules. The data may be uniquely mapped to a physical address (as in cache coherent systems) or replicating the data to several physical addresses (as in reflective memory systems and, to some extent, in cache-only systems). Even in uniquely mapped systems, data may be replicated in lower levels of memories (i.e., caches). Replication, in turn, requires means for maintaining consistency. Directories are often the key to tracking the multiple copies and play a key role in coherence of replicated data. Hardware or software can maintain the coherence.

The granularity of the data that is shared and moved across memory hierarchies is another design consideration. The granularity can be based on objects without semantic meaning, based purely on a sequence of bytes (e.g., a memory word, a cache block, or a page) or it can be based on objects with semantic basis (e.g., variables, data structures, or objects in the sense of an object-oriented programming model). Hardware solutions often use finer-grained objects (often without semantic meaning) whereas software implementations rely on coarser-grained objects.

The design trade-off in managing shared memory, in hardware or software, depends on the freedom (or limitations) provided by the semantics of the programming model. This leads to issues such as the order in which memory accesses performed by individual processors to individual memory modules and their interactions with memory accesses performed by other processors. The most restrictive programming semantics (known as *sequential consistency*) requires that

- the memory accesses of each individual processor be executed in the order of the sequence defined by the program executed on the processor
- memory accesses of different processors be executed in some interleaved fashion.

In order to utilize modern processors as the building blocks in a DSM, the sequential consistency model is often not guaranteed by the underlying system, placing the onus on the programmer to maintain the necessary order of memory accesses. There has been considerable research into various memory consistency semantics and the trade-off between performance and programming complexity.

Synchronization and coordination among concurrent computations (i.e., processes or threads) in SMP rely on the use of mutual exclusion, critical sections, and barriers. Implementation of the mechanisms needed for mutual exclusion (often based on the use of locks) and barriers exploit the hardware instructions spanning design space (such as test-and-set, load-linked, and store-conditional instructions, fetch-and-operate, combining networks), spin locks (including the use of shadow locks), queue or array locks, sense-reversing barriers, and tree-barriers. These solutions explore trade-offs between the performance (in terms of latency, serialization, or network traffic) and scalability.

Resource management, particularly in terms of minimizing data migration, thread migration, and messages exchanged, is significant in achieving cost–performance ratios that will make DSM systems commercially viable contenders. In Section 2, we discuss issues related to data-coherence, memory consistency models, and the implementation of locks and barriers. Section 3 studies three classes of hardware DSM implementations: cache-coherent architectures, cache-only architectures, and reflective memories. Section 4 addresses software DSM implementations covering page-based, variable-based, and object-based data models. Section 5 concludes the chapter with a set of open issues and a prognosis on the commercial viability of DSMs, and alternatives to them.

2. Issues in Shared Memory Systems

In this section we concentrate on three main issues in the design of hardware- or software-based DSM systems: data coherence, memory consistency, and synchronization.

2.1 Data Coherence

The use of cache memories is so pervasive in today's computer systems that it is difficult to imagine processors without them. Cache memories, along with virtual memories and processor registers, form a continuum of memory hierarchies that rely on the principle of locality of reference. Most applications exhibit temporal and spatial localities among instructions and data. *Spatial locality* implies that memory locations that are spatially (address-wise) near the currently referenced address are likely to be referenced. *Temporal locality* implies that the currently referenced address will likely be referenced in the near future (time-wise). Memory hierarchies are designed to keep most likely referenced items in the fastest devices. This results in an effective reduction in access time.

2.1.1 Cache Coherence

The inconsistency that exists between main memory and (write-back) caches, in general, does not cause any problems in uniprocessor systems. In a multiprocessor system, however, techniques are needed to ensure that consistent data is available to all processors. Cache coherence can be maintained by either hardware techniques or software techniques. We first introduce hardware solutions.

2.1.1.1 Snoopy Protocols These protocols are applicable for small-scale multiprocessors systems where the processors are connected to memory via a common bus, making the shared memory equally accessible to all processors. They are also known as symmetric multiprocessor systems (SMP) or uniform memory access systems (uma). In addition to the shared memory, each processor contains a local cache memory (or multilevel caches). Since all processors and their cache memories (or the controller hardware) are connected to a common bus, the cache memories can *snoop* on the bus to maintain coherent data. Each cache line is associated with a state, and the cache controller will modify the states to track changes to cache lines made either locally or remotely. A hit on a read implies that the cache data is consistent with that in main memory and copies that may exist in other processors' caches. A read miss leads to a request for the data. This request can be satisfied by either the main memory (if no other cache has a copy of the data), or by another cache, which has a (possibly newer) copy of the data. Initially, when only one cache has a copy, the cache line is set to *Exclusive* state. However, when other caches request for a read copy, the state of the cache line (in all processors) is set to *Shared*.

Consider what happens when a processor attempts to write to a (local) cache line. On a hit, if the state of the local cache line is *Exclusive* (or *Modified*), the write can proceed without any delay, and state is changed to *Modified*. This is because *Exclusive* or *Modified* state guarantees that no copies of the data exist in other caches. If the local state is *Shared* (which implies the existence of copies of the data item in other processors) then an invalidation signal must be broadcast on the common bus, so that all other caches will set their cache lines to *Invalid*. Following the invalidation, the write can be completed in local cache, changing the state to *Modified*.

On a write miss, a request is placed on the common bus. If no other cache contains a copy, the data comes from memory, the processor can complete the write and the cache line is set to *Modified*. If other caches have the requested data in *Shared* state, the copies are invalidated and the write is complete with a single *Modified* copy. If a different processor has a *Modified* copy, the data is written back to main memory and the processor invalidates its copy. The write can now be completed, leading to a *Modified* line at the requesting processor. Such snoopy protocols are sometimes called MESI, denoting the names of states associated with cache lines: *Modified, Exclusive, Shared,* or *Invalid.* Many variations of the MESI protocol have been reported [6]. In general, the performance of a cache coherence protocol depends on the amount of sharing (i.e., number of shared cache blocks), number of copies, number of writers, and granularity of sharing.

Instead of invalidating shared copies on a write, it may be possible to provide updated copies to other processors [7]. It may be also possible, with appropriate hardware, to detect when other processors no longer share a cache line, hence eliminating update messages. The major trade-off between update and invalidation techniques lies in the amount of bus traffic resulting from the update messages that include data as compared to the cache misses subsequent to invalidation messages. Update protocols are better suited for applications with a single writer and multiple readers, whereas invalidation protocols are favored when multiple writers exist.

2.1.1.2 Directory Protocols   Snoopy protocols rely on the ability to listen to and broadcast invalidations on a common bus. However, the common bus places a limit on the number of processing nodes in an SMP system. Large-scale multiprocessor and distributed systems must use more complex interconnection mechanisms, such as multiple buses, N-dimensional grids, crossbar switches, and multistage interconnection networks. New techniques are needed to insure that invalidation messages are received (and acknowledged) by all caches with copies of the shared data. This is normally achieved by keeping a directory with main memory units. There exists one directory entry corresponding to each cache block, and the entry keeps track of shared copies, or the identification of the processor that contains modified data. On a read miss, a processor requests the memory unit for data. The request may go to a remote memory unit, depending on the address. If the data is not updated, a copy is sent to the requesting cache, and the directory entry is modified to reflect the existence of a shared copy. If a modified copy exists at another cache, the new data is written back to the memory, a copy of the data is provided to the requesting cache, and the directory is marked to reflect the existence of two shared copies.

In order to handle writes, it is necessary to maintain state information with each cache block at local caches, somewhat similar to the Snoopy protocols. On a write hit, the write can proceed immediately if the state of the cache line is *Modified*. Otherwise (i.e., the state is *Shared*), an invalidation message is communicated to the memory unit, which in turn sends invalidation signals to all caches with shared copies (and receives acknowledgements). Only after the completion of this process can the processor proceed with a write. The directory is marked to reflect the existence of a modified copy. A write miss is handled as a combination of a read miss and a write hit.

In the approach outlined here, the directory associated with each memory unit is responsible for tracking the shared copies and for sending invalidation signals. This is sometimes known as the $p+1$ directory to reflect the fact that each directory entry may need $p+1$ bits to track the existence of up to p read copies and one write copy. Allowing fewer copies (less than p), and using "pointers" to track copies to the processors containing copies can alleviate the memory requirements imposed by this directory method. Whether using $p+1$ bits or a fixed number of pointers, (centralized) directories associated with memory modules maintain copies of data items. We can consider distributing each directory entry as follows: On the first request for data, the memory unit (or the home memory unit) supplies the requested data, and marks the directory with a "pointer" to the requesting processor. Future read requests will be forwarded to the processor, which has the copy, and the requesting processors are linked together. In other words, the processors with copies of the data are thus linked, and track all shared copies. On a write request, an invalidation signal is sent along the linked list to all shared copies. The home memory unit can wait until invalidations are acknowledged before permitting the writer to proceed. The home memory unit can also send the identification of the writer so those acknowledgements to invalidations can be sent directly to the writer. The *scalable coherence interface* (SCI) standard uses a doubly linked list of shared copies. This permits a processor to remove itself from the linked list when it no longer contains a copy of the shared cache line.

Numerous variations have been proposed and implemented to improve the performance of directory-based protocols. Hybrid techniques that combine snoopy protocols with directory-based protocols have also been investigated in the Stanford DASH system [8, 9]. Such systems can be viewed as networks of clusters, where each cluster relies on bus snooping and use directories across clusters.

The performance of directory-based techniques depends on the number of shared blocks, the number of copies of individual shared blocks, and, if multicasting is available, the number of writers. The amount of memory needed for directories depends on the granularity of sharing, the number of processors (in $p+1$ directory), and the number of shared copies (in pointer-based methods).

2.1.2 Software-Based Coherence Techniques

Using large cache blocks can reduce certain types of overheads in maintaining coherence as well as reduce the overall cache miss rates. However, larger cache blocks increase the possibility of *false sharing*. This refers to the situation when two or more processors that do not really share any specific memory address, appear to share a cache line, since the variables (or addresses) accessed by the different processors fall to the same cache line. Compile-time analysis can detect and eliminate unnecessary invalidations in some false sharing cases.

Software can also help in improving the performance of the hardware-based coherence techniques described above. It is possible to detect when a processor no longer accesses a cache line (or variable), and *self-invalidation* can be used to eliminate unnecessary invalidation signals. In the simplest method (known as *indiscriminate invalidation*) [10], consider an indexed variable X being modified inside a loop. If we do not know how the loop iterations will be allocated to processors, we may require each processor to read the variable X at the start of each iteration and flush the variable back to memory at the end of the loop iteration (i.e., it is invalidated). However, this is unnecessary since not all values of X are accessed in each iteration, and it is also possible that several contiguous iterations may be assigned to the same processor.

In the *selective invalidation* technique [11], if static analysis reveals that a specific variable may be modified in a loop iteration then the variable will be marked with a *change bit*. This implies that at the end of the loop iteration, some processor may have modified the variable. The processor that actually modifies the variable resets the change bit since the processor already has an updated copy. All other processors will invalidate their copies of the variable.

A more complex technique [12] involves the use of version numbers with individual variables. Each variable is associated with a *current version number* (CVN). If static analysis determines that a variable may be modified (by any processor), all processors are required to increment the CVN associated with the variable. In addition, when a processor acquires a new copy of a variable, the variable will be associated with a *birth version number* (BVN) which is set to the current CVN. When a processor actually modifies a variable, the processor will set the BVN to the CVN + 1. If the BVN of a variable in a processor is greater than the CVN of that variable, the processor has the updated value; otherwise, the processor invalidates its copy of the variable.

Migration of processes or threads from one node to another can lead to poor cache performance since the migration can cause false sharing: the original node where the thread resided may falsely assume that cache lines are shared with the new node to which the thread migrated. Researchers have proposed some software techniques designed to selectively invalidate cache lines when threads migrate.

Software-aided prefetching of cache lines is often used to reduce cache misses. In shared memory systems, prefetching may actually increase misses, unless it is possible to predict whether a prefetched cache line will be invalidated before its use.

2.2   Memory Consistency

Whereas data coherence (or cache coherence) techniques aim at assuring that copies of individual data items (or cache blocks) are up to date (or copies will be invalid), a *consistent memory* implies that the view of the entire shared memory presented to all processors will be identical. This requirement can also be stated in terms of the order in which operations performed on shared memory are made visible to individual processors in a multiprocessor system. In order to understand the relationship between the ordering of memory operations and memory consistency, consider the following example with two processors *P1* and *P2*. *P1* performs a write to a shared variable X (operation-1) followed by a read of variable Y (operation-2); *P2* performs a read of variable X (operation-3) followed by a write to shared variable Y (operation-4). For each processor, we can potentially consider 4! different orders for the 4 operations. However, we expect that the order in which each processor executes the operations (i.e., program order) be preserved. This requires that operation-1 always be executed before operation-2; operation-3 before operation-4. Now we have only 6 possible orders in which the operations can appear (Table I).

Although it is possible for the two processors to see the operations in different order, intuition tells us that "correct" program behavior requires that all processors see the memory operations performed in the same order. These two requirements (that program order is preserved, and that all processors see the memory operations in the same order) are used to define a correct behavior of concurrent programs, which is known as *sequential consistency of memory*.

2.2.1   Sequential Consistency

Sequential consistency [13] may also be described as follows: In addition to preserving the program order of each concurrent program, the behavior should be the same as if the program were executed on a single processor by

TABLE I

POSSIBLE PERMUTATIONS OF OPERATIONS WHILE PRESERVING ORDER

Ordering-1	Ordering-2	Ordering-3	Ordering-4	Ordering-5	Ordering-6
P1: Write X	*P1*: Write X	*P1*: Write X	*P2*: Read X	*P2*: Read X	*P2*: Read X
P1: Read Y	*P2*: Read X	*P2*: Read X	*P1*: Write X	*P2*: Write Y	*P1*: Write X
P2: Read X	*P1*: Read Y	*P2*: Write Y	*P1*: Read Y	*P1*: Write X	*P2*: Write Y
P2: Write Y	*P2*: Write Y	*P1*: Read Y	*P2*: Write Y	*P1*: Read Y	*P1*: Read Y

interleaving the operations of the concurrent program segments. The order in which all memory operations appear to all processors is then given by the interleaved execution.

Although conceptually appealing, sequential consistency can result in very poor performance on modern processing systems, because some modern architectural features must be thwarted to guarantee sequential consistency. Consider processors with cache memories. In such systems, it is not only sufficient to make sure a write is completed (written to local cache and even to the main memory), but we need to make sure that this write is "seen" by all processors and they either update or invalidate their caches. To guarantee this, we need to wait for acknowledgement signals from all cache copies before assuming that a write was made visible to all processors. Such a requirement significantly affects the performance of write operations. Likewise, buffers cannot be used for writes if sequential consistency must be guaranteed.

In order to improve the performance of concurrent processing systems, the hardware may not be required to guarantee the second memory consistency requirement. It is no longer necessary to maintain a common ordering among memory operations that is seen by all processors, but sequential consistency should be assured by other means (e.g., programming constructs). Consider one such relaxation on hardware requirements. In process consistency, different processors of a parallel processing system may see different ordering among memory operations; however, the program order is still preserved. In our previous example, it is now possible for processors $P1$ and $P2$ to see different orderings among the four memory operations (say ordering 1 and ordering 5, respectively). This is troubling, because now $P1$ and $P2$ will obtain different values for X and Y. In order to assure a correct program (in terms of sequential consistency), it is now necessary to use programming constructs such as locks (or synchronization) before allowing a processor to modify shared memory. In other words, it is now the responsibility of the programmer to define a sequential order among memory accesses for shared variables. Defining critical sections and the use of mutual exclusion to enter critical sections normally does this.

2.2.2 Weak Ordering

The hardware requirements can be reduced if the programmer explicitly serializes accesses to shared variables. This is the basis of all weak consistency models that have been proposed in the literature [14], where:

- Accesses to synchronization variables are **sequentially consistent**.
- No access to a synchronization variable is allowed to be performed until all previous writes have been completed everywhere.

- No data access (read or write) is allowed to be performed until all previous accesses to synchronization variables are complete.

The first condition forces a global order on all synchronization variables. Since ordinary variables are accessed only in critical sections (after accessing synchronization variables), sequential consistency is assured even on ordinary variables. The second condition implies that before a synchronization variable is released (and subsequently obtained by a different processor), all accesses made to ordinary variables are made globally visible to all processors. The third condition requires that before a processor can access ordinary variables inside a critical section, accesses to synchronization variables must be globally visible. This implies mutual exclusion on synchronization variables and forces changes in previous critical sections to be globally visible.

2.2.3 Release Consistency

In weak ordering, a locking mechanism is normally associated with synchronization variables. When one acquires a shared variable, it will be locked. When a lock is released, updates to shared variables are made available to other processors. In another words, consistent data must be maintained only on a lock release and hence, memory consistency is not guaranteed until a lock is released [15]:

- Before an ordinary variable is accessed, all previous locks on shared variables performed by the processor must have been completed.
- Before a release on a synchronization variable is allowed, all previous reads and writes on ordinary variables performed by the processor must have been completed.
- The acquire and release accesses must be processor consistent.

Note that sequential consistency on acquires is no longer needed, since mutual exclusion on acquires are assumed. In short, program correctness is assured by explicit usage of acquires and releases in proper order and accessing ordinary variables in critical section. The performance of release consistency can be improved using *lazy* release, whereby the shared memory is made consistent only on being acquired by a different processor [16].

2.2.4 Entry and Scope Consistency

In both weak ordering and release consistency models, the shared memory is made consistent when any synchronization variable is released (or accessed). Performance can be improved if a set of shared variables is associated with each synchronization variable; as a result, consistency on a set of variables is maintained when the associated synchronization variable is released (or accessed). *Entry consistency* [17] requires that the program specify the association between shared variables and synchronization variables. *Scope consistency* [18] is similar to entry consistency, but the association between shared variables and synchronization variables is implicitly defined. As an example, consider Example 3 where lock-1 and lock-2 are synchronization variables and *A*, *B*, *C*, and *D* are ordinary shared variables.

Example 3 Entry and scope consistency.

```
P1                          P2
Lock lock-1
  A = 1
  Lock lock-2
    B = 1
  Unlock lock-2
Unlock lock-1

                  Lock lock-2
                  C = A     ----- may not see A=1
                  D = B
                  Unlock lock-2
```

A similar effect will be achieved in entry consistency by associating lock-1 with variable *A* and lock-2 with variables *A*, *B*, *C*, and *D*.

2.2.5 Hardware Prefetch and Speculative Loads

The aforementioned relaxed memory consistency models increase programming complexity by either requiring the programmer to carefully and correctly synchronizes processors, or requiring the compiler to insert necessary barrier instructions (e.g., memory barrier and write barrier) to assure program correctness. A recent study indicated that although it is difficult to outperform the performance of relaxed memory models, nevertheless, two mechanisms—hardware prefetch and speculative loads— can be used to substantially improve the performance of sequential consistency hardware models [3].

- *Hardware prefetch for write.* Here, a request for exclusive access to a cache block is issued even before the processor is ready to do a write; as a result, the time for invalidations and acknowledgements, needed to implement sequential consistency correctly, is overlapped with other computations. However, it should be noted that improper use of the prefetch may unnecessarily invalidate cache copies at other processors and this may increase cache misses.

●   *Speculative loads*. Here cache blocks for load are prefetched, without changing any exclusive accesses that are currently held by other processors. If the data is modified before it is actually used, the prefetched copies are invalidated.

In general, current multiprocessor systems support weak ordering in one way or another, where sequential consistency is assured either implicitly and transparently by software layers or by the programmer. In addition to improved performance, weak ordering may also offer more fault-tolerance to applications using DSM systems, in terms of the amount state information that must be checkpointed [20].

2.3   Support for Synchronization

In the previous section we assumed that the programmer relies on synchronization among the processors (or processes) while accessing shared memory to assure program correctness as defined by the sequential consistency model. The two fundamental synchronization constructs used by programmers are mutual exclusion locks and barriers. Only one processor at a time can acquire mutual exclusion locks, forcing a global sequential order on the locks. When barriers are used, a processor is forced to wait for its partners and proceed beyond the barrier only when all partners reach the barrier. In this section we describe how mutual exclusion locks and barriers can be supported in hardware or software, and discuss performance of various implementations.

2.3.1   Mutual Exclusion Locks

In the simplest implementation, mutual exclusion can be achieved using an atomic test-and-set instruction that checks and sets a flag if it is currently reset. Such a test-and-set instruction was implemented in many older machines that supported multitasking (or time-shared) operating systems. With the advent of cache memories (and associated re-ordering of memory accesses), it became extremely inefficient to implement atomic test-and-set instructions. Modern processors actually use two separate instructions to achieve atomicity. Consider Example 4, which uses *load linked* (LL) and *store conditional* (SC) instructions. Typically, LL stores the memory address in a special *link-register* that is compared with the memory address of a subsequent SC instruction. The link-register is reset, either by any other processor that makes a reference to the same memory location, or on a context switch of the current process. In a multiprocessor system, LL and SC can be implemented using cache coherence techniques previously discussed. For example, in snoopy systems, snooping on the shared bus resets the link-register.

Example 4 LL and SC instructions.

```
Try:  Move R3, R4        ; Move value to be exchanged
      LL R2, O(R1)       ; Load linked to memory
      SC R3, O(R1)       ; Store conditional to the same
                                       memory location
      BEQZ R3, Try       ; if unsuccessful, try again
      Move R4, R3
```

In Example 4, the value in R3 will be stored only if SC is successful and the value in R3 will be non-zero. Otherwise, SC will fail to change the value in memory and R3 will be set to zero. Note that in this example we are actually using *spin locks* where a processor is not blocked on an unsuccessful attempt to acquire a lock. Instead, the unsuccessful processor will repeat its attempt to acquire the lock.

2.3.1.1 *Shadow locks*

So far we have assumed that the coherence of mutual exclusion lock-variables is guaranteed. This can significantly reduce the performance of shared-memory systems—the repeated attempts to acquire a spin lock can lead to repeated invalidations of the lock-variable. In order to improve the performance, processors are required to spin on a *shadow lock*. All spinning processors try to acquire the lock by accessing the lock-variable in common memory. An unsuccessful processor will cache the "locked-value" in local caches and spin on local copies. The local copies are invalidated when the lock becomes available.

Consider the code segment in Example 5 for an implementation of the spin locks. Here the first branch (BNEZ) does the spin and the second branch is needed for atomicity.

Example 5 Spin lock implementation.

```
Lockit:   LL R2, O(R1)            ; Load Linked
          BNEZ R2, Lockit         ; not available, spin
          Load Immediate   R2, #1 ; locked value
          SC R2, O(R1)            ; store
          BEQZ R2, Lockit         ; branch if unsuccessful
```

2.3.1.2 *Other Variations*

Spinning on a single variable causes excessive network traffic since all unsuccessful processors attempt to acquire the lock as soon as it becomes available. *Exponential-back-off* techniques [21], whereby a processor uses different amounts of delays while attempting to acquire a lock, can be used to reduce network traffics. Alternatively, one can associate an array for lock-variables so that each processor spins on a different array element (*array-base queuing lock* [21, 22]). A similar effect can be achieved using *ticket locks*. Here, an integer (or ticket number) is assigned to each unsuccessful processor. The value of the ticket being serviced is incremented on each release of the lock, and a processor with a matching ticket number will then be allowed to acquire the lock. This technique is similar to how customers are assigned a service number and are serviced when the current number matches their number. Finally, *queue locks* and *granting locks* can be used to link unsuccessful processors together so that the current lock holder can release the lock to the next processor in the queue. Note that this technique is similar to the technique used in earlier systems where an unsuccessful process is blocked and queued on the lock by the operating system.

2.3.2 Barrier Synchronization

In addition to mutual exclusion, shared-memory parallel programming requires coordination among the current processes (or threads), whereby processes are required to rendezvous periodically before proceeding with computation. Such coordination is traditionally achieved using fork-and-join constructs. Before forking to parallel computations, an integer value indicating the number of concurrent processes is set in a join-variable. As processes complete their assigned work, they execute the join operation which atomically decrements the current value of the join-variable. A value of zero indicates that all concurrent processes have completed their tasks. Two mutual exclusion locks are used to implement such barriers (i.e., join construct)—one to decrement the counter and one to force processes to wait at the barrier. Consider the implementation shown in Example 6.

Example 6 Fork-and-join construct.

```
Lock (counter_lock);              /* to make sure updates
                                  /* are atomic
If (counter == p) release = 0;    /* first reset release
                                  /* to make sure that
                                  /* processes are forced
                                  /* to wait
counter = counter-1;
unlock(counter_lock);
```

```
If (counter ==0) {
        counter = p;             /* after all arrive,
                                 /* reset the counter
        release = 1; }           /* and release waiting
                                 /* processes
    else   spin (release = 1);   /* otherwise spin until
                                 /* release
```

The implementation in Example 6 is not adequate in applications containing several rendezvous points. Consider a situation where there are *p* processes joining at a barrier. Normally, these processes repeat the join again at a different point in computation. The process which arrives last at the barrier is context-switched out, while one of the released processes that has completed its next assigned task and returned to the next barrier resets the release flag. When the context-switched process is restarted, it is blocked since the release flag is reset, leading to a deadlock since only $p - 1$ processes join at the next barrier. A suggested remedy for this situation, known as a *sense-reversing barrier* [23], uses alternating values for the reset flag: 0 at one instant and 1 at the next instant to indicate a release status.

2.3.3 Tree-Structured and Other Variations of Barriers

To have several processors spinning on the same release variable causes a significant amount of network traffic. Even if shadow variables are used, the invalidations on a release can degrade performance. To reduce the number of messages, several researchers have proposed more complex alternatives to implementing barriers. Consider a tree-structured algorithm where processors (or processes) are required to spin on different variables (Fig. 1). Here, processors are divided into groups and each group spins on a separate variable. The last processor in each group to arrive at the barrier must "report" to a higher level barrier in the tree and spin on a new variable. Reaching the root of the tree indicates the completion of the barrier, which releases the children of the root. These children in turn release their children, propagating the release signal downward.

The tree-structured barrier approach is dynamic by its very nature, since it is not possible to statically determine on which variable a processor spins. This may result in performance degradation since locality on spin variables could be violated. Variations of the tree barriers (e.g., butterfly, dissemination [23] and tournament barriers [24]) have been proposed to overcome this limitation. In addition, a tree-structured barrier can result in serialization delays where the processor that is responsible for propagating the release signals downward is forced to wait until all its children are released. In a variation on the tree-

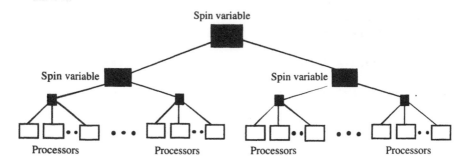

FIG. 1. Tree-structured barrier.

structured barrier [60], two separate trees with different fan-in and fan-out are considered; one for spinning and one for releasing processors. It is then possible to designate different processors as the roots in the two different trees. Smaller fan-outs for the release tree avoid long serialization delays.

3. Hardware Implementation of Distributed Shared Memory Systems

In this section, several distributed shared memory systems are examined. These systems were chosen because they use specialized hardware to support memory coherence, consistency, and synchronization. These systems can be classified as cache coherent NUMA (CC-NUMA) systems, cache-only (COMA) systems, and reflective memory systems.

- In *cache coherent systems*, the global memory is an aggregation of distributed-memory modules. Each processing node additionally has cache memories for keeping local copies of data. Typically, each datum is assigned a permanent "home memory" which is responsible for its maintenance.
- In a *cache-only (COMA) system*, data migrates with no permanent home. The (cache-only) memory is hierarchically organized and inclusive; as a result, higher-level memory nodes keep copies of the data contained in lower-level memory nodes. Data migration complicates "replacement" of cache blocks since there is no permanent home for data. Additionally, coherence maintenance may require longer latencies as requests and invalidation messages may have to travel across the hierarchy.
- *Reflective memories* are proposed as a means of constructing DSM systems with a small hardware overhead. In such systems, each node

designates a portion of its address space as part of global shared space. All such globally shared address spaces are logically mapped to represent the shared memory of the system. Each node is still responsible for maintaining its portion of the shared memory. Normally all write requests are sent to the home memory, thus simplifying the coherence process.

3.1 FLASH

The FLASH (Flexible Architecture for SHared memory) multiprocessor [26], a successor to DASH [9], supports both cache-coherent shared memory and low-overhead user-level message-passing (Fig. 2). This is accomplished by a custom node controller, the memory and general interconnect controller (MAGIC)—a highly integrated chip that implements data transfers, both within a processing node and between a processing node and the network. To offer high performance, the MAGIC chip contains a specialized datapath and an embedded processor (called TORCH) that updates the directory for cache coherence as well as effect the associated data transfers.

The programmable controller of MAGIC provides flexibility to implement different protocols. The on-chip instructions and data caches of MAGIC speed up accesses to frequently used protocol code and data residing in a dedicated portion of the node's main memory. The cache-coherence protocol uses a scalable directory and a set of handlers. Each 128-byte cache line of main memory has an associated 8-byte directory header to maintain the cache

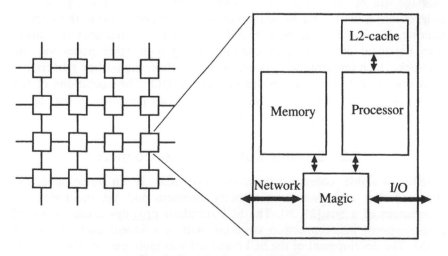

FIG. 2. Organization of the FLASH.

coherence protocol. Each directory header contains a flag field that defines whether that block has been shared, and a link field that points to a linked list of sharers.

The protocol divides all messages into requests and replies. Requests consist of read, read-exclusive, and invalidate; replies consist of data replies and invalidate acknowledgements. To insure deadlock avoidance, the protocol adheres to several requirements, including use of virtual channel support in the network routers—to transmit messages over separate logical networks—and constraints on all handlers to yield to the processor if they cannot run to completion. The latter requirement is met by having the scheduler not service an incoming message until the corresponding outgoing message space requirements are satisfied.

The internal organization of MAGIC is shown in Fig. 3 MAGIC accepts messages from the R10000 node processor, a network interface, or a PCI I/O interface. As messages arrive at the MAGIC chip, they are split into message headers and message data. Protocol independent data handling is done by the data transfer logic, and the control macro pipeline handles the protocol processing of the message headers.

The primary responsibility of the data transfer logic is to temporary buffer incoming data into one of the 16-entry data buffers, each containing a cache line, as it is forwarded from source to destination. The control macro pipeline, on the other hand, receives message headers from the processor (PI), network (NI), I/O, and forwards them to the protocol processor via the inbox. Figure 4 shows the internal organization of the control macro pipeline. The inbox basically decides which incoming queue the next message will be read from, then, using a portion of the message header, indexes into a jump table to determine the starting entry for in the suitable handler. Handler actions include updating machine state, communicating with the local processor, and communicating with other nodes via the network. Once the protocol processing is complete, the outbox performs a send operation to the appropriate PI, NI, or I/O. The operations of the inbox, the protocol processor, and the outbox are pipelined so that up to three messages can be processed concurrently.

3.2   Scalable Coherence Interconnect

IEEE scalable coherence interconnect (SCI) is an interconnection standard that addresses the scalability problem and yet maintains the advantages of a bus [27, 28]. The SCI standard provides a unidirectional point-to-point interconnection structure with a coherent cache image of DSM. The development of the SCI standard was motivated by the fact that scalability and low-latency communication can be achieved if interconnec-

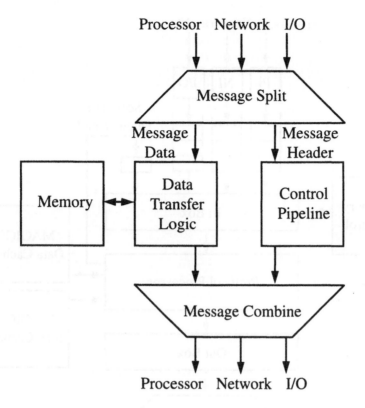

FIG. 3. Organization of MAGIC.

tion network is point-to-point and interfaced to the memory bus rather than the I/O bus. In order to provide these features, the SCI standard defines a number of requirements for interfacing nodes and interconnect, link and packet formats, and cache-coherence protocol.

Each node has an input link and an output link that are connected to form a *ringlet*. The ringlets are connected by switches to form larger networks. A SCI link is an 18-bit entity, called a *symbol*, containing 1 clock bit, 1 flag bit, and 16 data bits. SCI uses a split-transaction protocol based on packets. A packet contains a 14-byte header, a 2-byte CRC for error handling, and 0–256 bytes of data. At each SCI clock cycle, 1 symbol of a packet can be transmitted. Each SCI transaction consists of a request and a response. A request packet issued by a source node circulates in the ringlet until it reaches the destination node. At the destination node, the request is serviced and a response packet is formed and injected into the SCI ring.

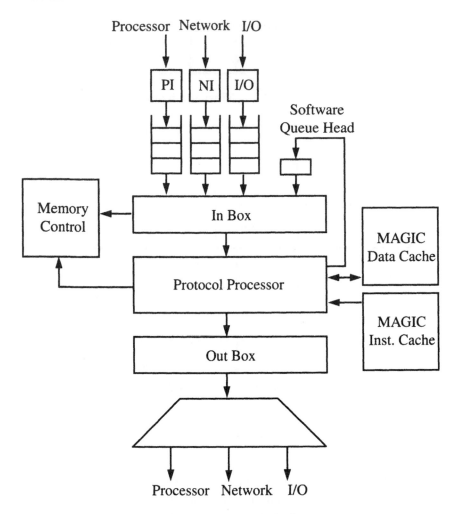

FIG. 4. Control Macro-pipeline.

The SCI coherence protocol defines three directory states, HOME, FRESH, and GONE. HOME means no remote cache in the system contains a copy of the block and the copy at the home is valid. FRESH indicates that one or more remote caches may have a read-only copy, and the copy in the memory is valid. GONE indicates that a remote cache contains a writable copy. The SCI directory structure is based on the flat, cache-based distributed doubly–linked directory scheme. In this scheme, each cache block has a linked list of sharers where the pointer to the head of this list is stored in the main memory of the home node. Each cached block is associated with a state indicating whether: it is modified and writable (DIRTY), unmodified but writable (CLEAN), data may be read but may not be writable until memory is informed (FRESH), unmodified and readable (COPY), etc. The state also indicates the relative location of the cache block within the shared-list: ONLY, HEAD, TAIL, or MID. The SCI standard allows three primitive operations on a distributed sharing list:

- adding a new sharer to the head of the list
- removing a node from a list
- purging or invalidating nodes by the head node.

Manipulation of a sharing list structure depends on the state of the requesting block in the home node and the request itself. For example, consider the sequence of operations that takes place in the event of a read request for a block in FRESH state at the home node (Fig. 5). Since the requesting block is FRESH, a sharing list already exists and the copy at home is valid. The home changes its head pointer to point to the requestor's cache block and sends back the cache block as well as the pointer to the previous head to the requestor (Fig. 5a). The requestor then sends a transaction asking a new head to be attached to the list (Fig. 5b). The previous head changes its state from HEAD_FRESH to MID_VALID and updates its backward pointer to point to the requestor's cache block and sends an acknowledgement back to the requesting node. When the requesting node receives the acknowledgement it sets its forward pointer to point to the previous head and changes its state from pending state to HEAD_FRESH (Fig. 5c).

For write requests, there are three possible cases—the requestor's cache block is:

- already at the head of the sharing list and there is at least one sharer
- not in the sharing list
- in the list but not at the head of it.

In the first case, the requestor first communicates with the home node to change the state of the block to GONE, then modifies that data in its own cache and purges or invalidates rest of the blocks in the sharing list. In the second case, the requestor must allocate space for and obtain a copy of the block, and then add itself to the list. For the final case, it must remove itself from the list and then add itself to the head. A number of commercial DSM systems have adopted the SCI specification [29, 30]. We now discuss one such system: sequent NUMA–Q.

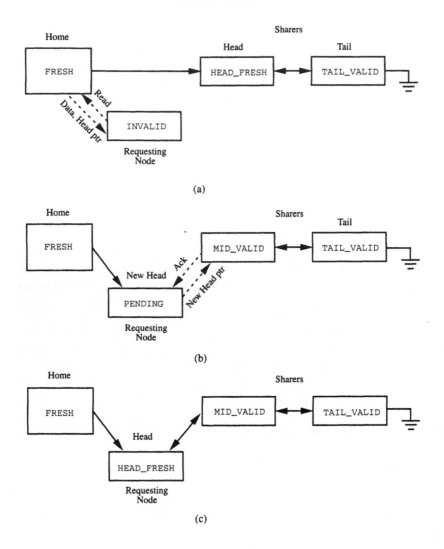

FIG. 5. An example of adding a new sharer to the list.

3.3 Sequent NUMA-Q

NUMA-Q is a collection of SMP nodes interconnected as a ring using high-speed links. Each node, called a *quad*, contains a modified off-the-shelf Intel SHV server board with four Pentium Pro processors (Fig. 6). Nodes are interconnected using IQ-Links based on the SCI standard.

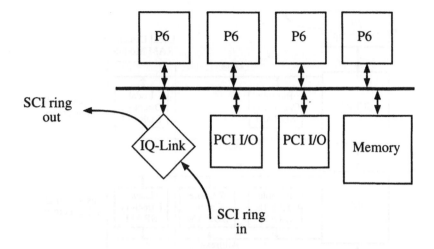

FIG. 6. Organization of a quad.

The IQ-Link is responsible for handling communication between quads and protocol processing (Fig. 7). It consists of the Orion bus interface controller (OBIC), the network interface (DataPump), the SCI link interface controller (SCLIC), and RAM modules. The OBIC, an ASIC developed by LSI logic, interfaces to the shared quad bus, and manages the remote cache data arrays as well as the bus snooping and requesting logic. The remote cache (32 Mbytes) maintains copies of blocks fetched from remote memories. The bus-side local directory contains two bits of state information for each block in the local quad memory. Directory state bits indicate three states for each cache line. The bus-side remote cache tags provides snooping information for the lines in the remote cache, indicating whether a given bus request to remote memory can be satisfied locally from the cache. Accesses to remote memories that miss the remote cache are passed to SCLIC.

SCLIC maintains the network-side local quad memory directory and the network-side remote cache tags used in the directory-based protocol. Each block in the local quad memory is represented in the network-side local directory by a 2-bit state field and a 6-bit list head pointer. For each block in the remote cache, the directory controller maintains a 7-bit state field, a 6-bit forward pointer, a 6-bit backward pointer, and a 13-bit address tag. All of the network-side directory and tag information is maintained in SDRAM storage.

The DataPump provides the link and the packet-level transport protocol of the SCI standard. The SCLIC—an interface between the OBIC and the

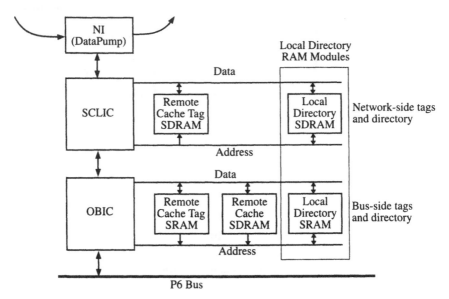

FIG. 7. Block diagram of IQ-Link.

DataPump—includes a programmable protocol processor and the directory tags which are used to manage the SCI coherence protocol. The DataPump, developed by Vitesse Semiconductor Corporation, provides the link and packet-level transport protocol for the SCI standard. DataPump operates at 500 MHz and drives a 1 GByte/s 18-bit wide SCI link. It can route and buffer the first symbol of a packet either to the current quad or the next quad in 16 ns and each additional symbol of the packet in 2 ns.

3.4 SGI Origin 2000

The Origin 2000 system is a highly scalable architecture that supports up to 512 nodes, each containing two R10000 processors [30] (Fig. 8). The nodes are interconnected using SGI SPIDER router chips and Craylinks to implement a hypercube topology for up to 32 nodes, and a hierarchical fat hypercube topology beyond 32 nodes.

Dual processors within a node are not kept coherent, as in other SMP-based nodes; instead, the SysAD bus that connects the processors is used to multiplex between the two processors. This sacrifices the potential advantage of cache-to-cache sharing found in other bus snooping systems. However, the designers found that the cache-to-cache sharing effect is minimal in two-processor systems, and the elimination of snooping overhead results is a performance advantage.

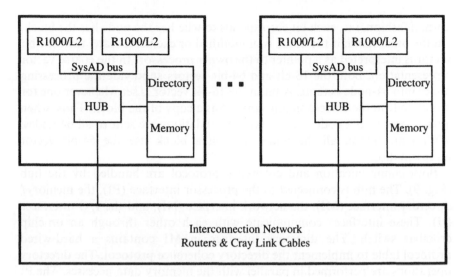

FIG. 8. Organization of the SGI Origin 2000.

The directory-based cache-coherence protocol used in Origin has three stable states and four transient states for a cache line: unowned, shared, and exclusive.

- *unowned* indicates no cached copies in the system
- *shared* indicates multiple read-only copies
- *exclusive* state indicates only one read-write cached copy in the system.

A number of enhancements to the basic directory protocol have been added to improve the performance; for example, *reply forwarding* (a read request is forwarded to the owner node) replies directly to the requestor node as well as sending a revision message to the home node. This eliminates the need for the home node to first send a response to the requesting node before another request from the requestor is sent to the owner node. The enhancement also supports *upgrade requests*, which move a block from shared to modified state without having to move memory data.

The directory structure used in Origin is based on a flat, memory-based directory scheme. However, unlike the full vector approach used in FLASH, Origin uses a scalable directory scheme to maintain coherence over 1024 processors. It uses 2 sizes of presence bit vectors: 16-bit and 64-bit. To overcome the obvious limitations of these bit vectors, the directory bit vector is interpreted differently depending on the system configuration. For example, if the block is in shared state, the bit vector is interpreted in the normal fashion, i.e., each bit corresponds to whether the node has the block. On the other hand, if the block is in modified or exclusive state, then the bit vector is interpreted as a pointer to the owner processor. In the coarse vector representation, both the 16-bit and 64-bit vectors subdivide the processing nodes into 64-node octants. A bit in the 16-bit vector is set whenever one (or more) node in the corresponding octant has a copy of the block. Thus, when a write occurs to a node in an octant, invalidations are sent to all 64 nodes. Within an octant, all the nodes sharing a block use the 64-bit vector representation.

Both communication and coherence protocol are handled by the hub (Fig. 9). The hub is connected to the processor interface (PI), the memory/directory interface (MI), the network interface (NI), and the I/O interfaces (II). These interfaces communicate with each other through an on-chip crossbar switch. The directory interface in MI contains a hard-wired protocol table to implement the directory coherence protocol. The directory operations are performed in parallel with the memory data accesses. The PI contains logic and buffers for keeping track of read and write requests initiated by a processor. These buffers, called coherent request buffers, also implement a portion of the coherence protocol. The NI sends and receives messages to or from the other three interfaces. It contains a routing table

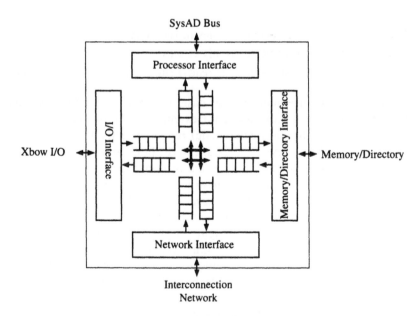

FIG. 9. Organization of the hub.

that is used to predetermine routing decisions based on source and destination nodes. It also handles generation of multiple invalidation messages due to a coherence operation.

3.5 Cache-Only Memory Architectures (COMA)

In a CC-NUMA machine, when a processor requests a remote cache block (i.e., home node), the cache block is brought in and stored in the requesting node's cache. This cache block, however, is not copied into the requesting processor's local memory. When the block is written back, the block has to be stored back to the local memory of the home node. To alleviate such write-back traffic, the operating system in CC-NUMA replicates or migrates a page to the local memory of the node where the page is referenced the most. The problem with this is that fetching a block from a remote node takes much longer than fetching a block from the local memory.

In COMA machines, a cache block does not have a home node initially assigned by the operating system. Instead, it uses a concept called *attraction memory*, where local memories are treated as caches, and the hardware takes care of the cache block replication and migration. For example, when a node requests a block from a remote node, the retrieved block is not only stored in the requesting node's cache but also into its local memory as well. This policy allows a node to gradually attract a large collection of cache lines, including its working set, into its local memory. In addition, since the granularity of replication and migration is a cache line, rather than a page, the likelihood of false sharing is reduced.

Since there is no home node for a block in a COMA machine, the source of directory information is not known a priori. Therefore, COMA machines use *hierarchical directory schemes*, where the directory information for each block is logically organized as a tree. Within it, the leaves represent the local memories, and non-leaf leaf nodes maintain directory information for the blocks. Thus, when a miss occurs, the nodes in the tree are traversed upward until a node is found that indicates its subtree has the block's state information.

The block replacement policy is also different from an ordinary cache. In a COMA, since blocks migrate, a given block does not have a fixed back-up location where it can be written back. Therefore, the system has to guarantee that at least one copy of the block remains in the system. For unmodified blocks, one of the multiple copies of the block is assumed to be the master copy. Thus, all other shared copies can be overwritten if replaced, and the master copy must always be relocated to another attraction memory. As a result of this policy, one has to decide how to relocate a master or a modified block. Alternatively, a node can be forced to accept the displaced block or displace the cache block to the node that caused the displacement in the first place. Naturally, automatic data migration and replication in COMA cause additional memory overhead. Thus, choosing an appropriate ratio between the application size and the total size of the attraction memories, called the *memory pressure*, is very important for performance. Joe and Hennessy [31] showed that as memory pressure increases, so does the relocation traffic and the number of attraction memory misses.

Important past projects in COMA are the Kendall Square Research KSR-1 [32, 33] and KSR2 [34], and the Data Diffusion Machine (DDM) [35]. KSR-1 is organized as a two-level hierarchy of slotted rings. The lower-level ring connects up to 32 nodes, each consisting of a processor, L1 and L2 cache, and a portion of the attraction memory (i.e., local memory) with a directory. The higher-level ring connects up to 43 lower-level rings. When a miss occurs, a request for the block is sent out to the lower-level ring. Each node on the ring checks its directory for the availability of the referenced block. A node that contains the block replies to the request either by sending a copy of the block for read or by migrating the block to the requestor for write. If no node in the lower-level ring has the block, the request is routed up to the higher-level ring.

3.6   Reflective Memory

The basic idea behind reflective memory is to provide a limited form of shared physical address space. This is done by establishing a connection between one virtual address page (transmit region) of one node to another virtual address page (receive region) in another node. When a data is written by a source node to its transmit region, the data is automatically transmitted, i.e., reflected, to the receive region in the destination node. Thus, shared memory is replicated on each node that accesses a location, and all writes to shared locations update all the other copies.

Reflective memory was first introduced in [36], and was adopted by DEC as part of their clustered workstation systems [37]. The most recent development is the incorporation of reflective memory technology into the DEC Memory Channel [38]. The Memory Channel a is dedicated interconnection network for DEC's TruCluster system, consisting of a collection of AlphaServer SMPs. The Memory Channel has a number of features for supporting shared-memory model. These include strict packet ordering and a fast, hardware-supported lock primitive.

3.7   The MIT Alewife

Based on the experiences gained in the design of the Stanford DASH and FLASH systems mentioned earlier, Alewife was tailored as a multiprocessor

system that can support both shared-memory and message-passing models
[39]. Each node in Alewife consists of a CPU (modified Sparc processors
known as Sparcle [40]), cache memory, and a custom device called CMMU
that supports data coherence and message communication among the nodes
of the system. Figure 10 depicts the overall structure of an Alewife node.

Shared memory support is provided via both hardware and software.
CMMU maintains directories similar to DASH, but software-based
coherence protocols (i.e., LimitLESS [41]) are used when appropriate to
improve the system performance. Message passing is achieved as a two-
phase operation:

- *describe*, which places the message and header in memory mapped
  network registers
- *launch*, which invokes network hardware operations to actually send
  the message.

Message receipt is handled using interrupts to quickly remove the message
from the network and place the message into user address space.
Synchronization support is based on J- and L-structures.

3.7.1 CMMU

As mentioned above, data coherence in Alewife is managed by a special
processor called the CMMU [42]. Each Alewife node can allocate 4 Mbytes

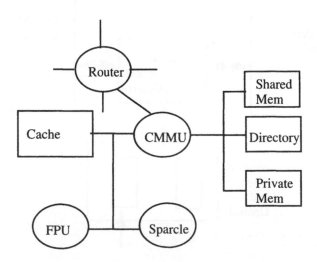

FIG. 10. A node in the Alewife system.

of its local memory to the distributed shared memory. In addition, a node can designate 2 Mbytes as private unshared memory. The memory is divided into 16-byte lines (the size of the cache line), and a directory entry is maintained for each cache line. Thus there can be as many as 512 K entries of 8 bytes each, for a total of 2 Mbytes of directory space. The overall structure of CMMU is shown in Fig. 11.

Figure 12 shows a directory entry maintained for each cache line. *State bits* (2 bits) are used to indicate if the data is shared, modified or unshared. *Metastate bits* (2 bits) define the following states:

- *normal*: directory entry is under hardware control
- *trap-on-write*: reads are handled by hardware, writes by software
- *write in progress*: directory is locked by software
- *trap-always*: all requests are handled by software.

As noted earlier, the system uses the LimitLESS protocol which combines hardware and software to maintain data coherence. The hardware directory

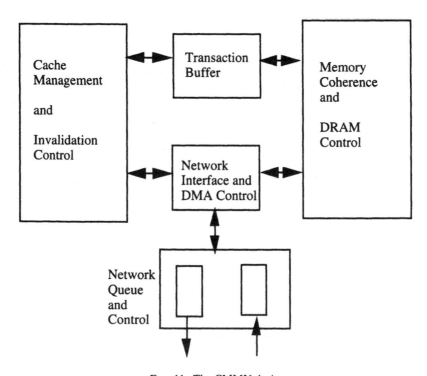

FIG. 11. The CMMU device.

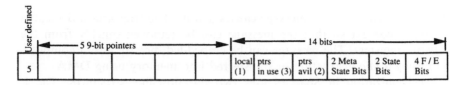

FIG. 12. Organization of an entry in the directory.

can only keep track of five shared copies (as shown by the five pointers). Additional pointers, when there are more than five copies, are stored in memory and managed by software.

A read request for a shared data is received by the CMMU hardware. If five copies of the data already exist, the request is sent to the local processor (software). The read requests can be processed concurrently by the CMMU hardware. Write requests, however, must be delayed until invalidations are sent to all copies by the software (as indicated by trap-on-write). The metastate *write-in-progress* is needed to prevent the hardware from making changes to the directory while the software is accessing the directory. The field in the directory entry called "pointers available" is used to indicate how many hardware pointers are available. Local bit assures that a hardware pointer will be given to the local node when it shares the data item.

On receiving a request for a remote data, the CMMU constructs a message and sends it to the network. When a response is received, the CMMU will supply the data to the processor. Finally, the transaction buffer (see Fig. 11) contains pending invalidations or other coherence-related requests, e.g., pre-fetched values and data that may be sent on the network in stages.

3.7.2 The SPARCLE processor

The processing at an Alewife node is performed by the Sparcle processor, which is a modified Sun Sparc processor [40]. The Sparcle was designed to support fine-grained computation, tolerate memory latencies, and integrate message-passing into the architecture. Fine-grained computation and latency tolerance is achieved by supporting fine-grained multithreading, fast context-switching using hardware contexts and instructions, and dataflow-like synchronization among threads using J and L structures. The register windows of the Sparc processor are modified to support four register contexts. Message-passing in Sparcle is achieved in two phases, describe and launch, as mentioned previously. The processor stores the message and header into memory-mapped network registers and issues a *stio* instruction. The CMMU launches the message in response to the *stio* instruction. Receipt of a message causes a trap. The trap uses a dedicated hardware context so that the message can be removed quickly from the network registers. The message can be embedded directly into a computation using a *ldio* instruction or transferred into memory using DMA.

Synchronization in Sparcles uses two dataflow-like structures. The L structure is used for implementing spin-locks. The J structure forces a computation to block and wait for the data (*mutex locks*). Three types of operations are defined on J and L structures:

- *locking read*, which reads and deletes data making it unavailable to other processors (for example, acquiring a lock)
- *non-locking read*, which reads the data but does not delete it (to support multiple readers)
- *unlocking write*, which writes the data and sets a flag to indicate its availability.

A failure of locking read on an L structure causes the processor to spin; such an operation on a J structure blocks the process.

4. Software Implemented DSM Systems

In this section we describe systems that require little or no hardware support for maintaining coherence and synchronization among computations. A software layer is added to traditional operating systems to convert remote memory accesses into request messages. In fact, the earliest distributed shared memory was a software implementation that extended traditional virtual memory systems.

In general, the software layer must provide sufficient functionality to make programming easier on distributed memory systems. Some of the functionalities and issues that must be addressed by software DSM are now summarized:

- *Large address space.* A user should view the memory locations in all memory units as a single address space. Software must maintain "directories" on each node in order to distinguish between local and remote memory accesses. Efficiency of mapping an address to a physical location often leads to hierarchical and static mapping of addresses. Overheads incurred in maintaining data coherence favor coarser granularity of sharing at the risk of increasing false sharing.
- *Memory consistency:* In order to support sequential consistency, software must maintain directories about shared copies (copy set),

and send updates (or invalidations) to all remote nodes. It may be necessary to wait for acknowledgements before permitting actual updates to data. If release consistency is supported, then software must track synchronization variables, associate shared data with synchronization variables, and update memory on release operations.

- *Synchronization primitives:* The software should build on hardware provided atomic instructions such as test-and-set and fetch-and-add. These operations must be location-transparent. Issues related to the placement of synchronization variables, elimination of contention for locks, and co-location of data with a lock are critical to the performance of software-based DSM.

The systems described in this section can be classified as page-based, variable-based, and object-based.

- *Page-based* distributed shared memory systems are easier to design because they can be viewed as extensions to traditional virtual memory systems. An access to a datum that is not currently in local memory results in a page fault. Page-based DSMs utilize traps caused by page-faults to send requests to the remote nodes containing the data (instead of searching local hard drive for the missing data, as done in conventional virtual memory systems). The DSM software extends traditional page-tables to track the location of shared address space as well to maintain coherence of shared data. The granularity of sharing in such systems is necessarily a page, leading to false sharing and reduced concurrency.

- In *variable-based* systems, the granularity of sharing is a variable as defined by a programming language. Normally sharing may be limited only to large data structures such as arrays. A key attribute of these systems is that they represents the distributed shared memory in terms of language-based data objects rather than system-based objects such as pages and words. However, the finer granularity may cause excessive overhead.

- In *object-based* systems, sharing is at object level. Object-oriented programming is drastically different from the algorithmic model since each object defines both the data and the operations on the data. All accesses to the data necessarily imply a call to a method (or operation) defined by the object. Conceptually, such a model voids coherence related issues because an object is responsible for all (update) operations on its internal data. However, in practice, replication of objects for improving concurrency presents interesting coherence-related challenges.

4.1 IVY

One of the earliest implementations of DSM was the IVY system, which was termed *shared virtual memory* rather than distributed shared memory. The system extended conventional virtual memories to permit access to memory located at a remote node. IVY is a page-based system with 1 K pages. The software layer of IVY consists of five modules, as shown in Fig. 13.

The memory mapping module implements the mapping between local and remote memories and serves the role of a directory for maintaining coherence of pages. Each user address space consists of a private memory and a shared virtual memory. The memory coherence in IVY is based on invalidations. Processes initially receive pages in read-only mode. Any attempt to write to a page will result in a trap, leading to the invalidation of other copies of the page. For each processing node, the memory mapping module serves as the page manager (or directory controller) for the shared pages allocated on that node. IVY also experimented with distributed page managers where the management responsibilities of pages are dynamically determined as pages change ownership (owner is the process which writes to the page). IVY supports sequential consistency.

The remote operation module is responsible for remote request/reply operations needed for the implementation of shared virtual memory. IVY

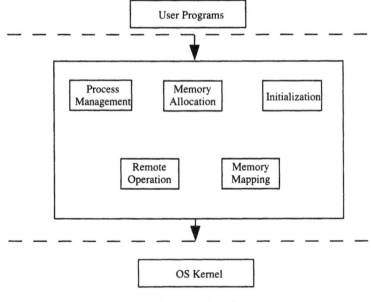

FIG. 13. An IVY module.

supported broadcasting and multicasting to simplify the search for a page, invalidations, and location of page managers (in the dynamically distributed algorithm). Request messages might automatically be forwarded to other nodes while searching for a page or a page manager.

The memory allocation module relies on "first fit" to allocate memory for a process in the shared virtual memory. Process Management module is responsible for the management of processes (or threads) and their migration.

The prototype was implemented on the Appollo Domain, an integrated system of workstations and servers connected by a 2 Mbit/s baseband token-ring network. IVY ran on a modified version of the Aegis operating system. This prototype demonstrated the feasibility of building software-only DSMs, relying on an existing system; however, the system experienced excessive overheads. More recent implementations (e.g., SHRIMP [43]) utilize specialized hardware for achieving higher performance and support relaxed memory consistency models (e.g., scope consistency), thus combining hardware and software solutions for the support of DSM.

4.2   Mirage

Mirage [44] is also a page-based system with modifications to the Unix System V kernel (within the UCLA's LOCUS distributed system [45, 46]) to process remote memory references. Unlike IVY, processes in Mirage share segments. Segments contain pages that are mapped to shared virtual address space. A process at a site can create a segment and define its shared properties. Processes at other sites may then map the shared segment into their virtual address space. Each segment is assigned a *library site* that keeps the directory information for the pages of the segment.

A bit in the user page table indicates if the page is shared or not. An auxiliary page table is consulted for shared pages. Each site maintains an auxiliary page entry for each shared page and links it to the library site for that page. Only the auxiliary page table information at the library site is guaranteed to be up-to-date. The library site using the auxiliary page tables and invalidation protocol maintains coherence.

In addition to the library site, each shared page is associated with a *clock site*. It is assumed that the clock site contains the most up-to-date copy of the page. The clock site is authorized to write to the page; other sites must send their updates to the clock site. If a page has no writers, then one of the sites is chosen arbitrarily as the clock site. After a chosen time window, a new clock site is assigned for shared pages by the library site. In general, in a distributed system, multiple writers to a page force page migration from writer to writer, causing "thrashing." Multiple writers will also imply excessive invalidations of copies held by other writers, leading to excessive network traffic. The use of a clock-site eliminates these performance problems involving multiple writers. However, the clock sites and the duration of the clock window should be chosen carefully to achieve optimal performance for a given application.

4.3 Millipede

Millipede [47] is a page-based software DSM for network of workstations running Microsoft NT operating systems interconnected by a Myrinet switch. However, Millipede reduces false sharing caused by 4 Kbyte pages of NT using a concept known as *Millipages* [48] and multiple views (multiviews) of a shared address space. Thus Millipede differs from Munin type systems that use variable-based shared memory since such shared variable granularity can cause excessive overheads in managing the coherence. When different processes are accessing different variables (or different portions of a shared page), there is no true sharing among the processes, even if the variables are located on the same shared page. By making the processes use different virtual addresses to access the page containing the shared variables, Millipede eliminates false sharing. Even though the variables reside on the same page, the application views them as residing on different (virtual) mini-pages. The Multiview allows the application to manage each memory element through dedicated view or a *vpage* associated with this element. The size of a mini-page can be as large as an OS page or as small as a single variable or a word (see Fig. 14).

No access, read only, and read–write protection is permitted with each mini-page:

- *no access* indicates non-present mini-page
- *read only* protection is set for read copies
- *read–write* is set for read copies and a writable copy.

This information is used for implementing coherence of shared variables. Mini-pages can be created either statically by the application or dynamically when allocated. Millipede creates two types of threads for running an application:

- *server threads*, which are used for management of the shared memory
- *application threads*, which execute the computation.

A single view known as the *privileged view* is used by all server threads (at least one per site)—this view presents the physical memory mapping. Server

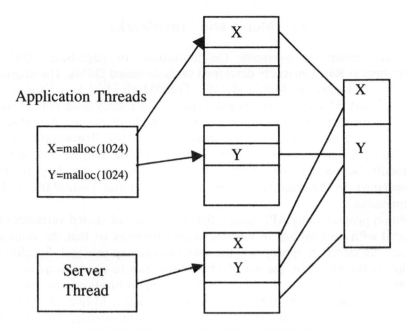

FIG. 14. Millipages and multiviews of Millipede.

threads use privileged view to process read and write requests by application threads to shared memory. Server threads can also perform updates to shared pages overwriting protection on the pages. Multiple views of a shared data object are created by using `MapViewOfFile` after the object is created using a `CreateFileMapping` library call. When a page contains n independent objects that can be shared, then Millipede permits $n + 1$ views: one for the privileged view and n application views.

Server threads use *mini-page tables* (MPT) for resolving addresses to remote data. A request for a remote data is sent to an appropriate server thread (or manager) at the remote node. Millipede supports application level multithreading using application threads. Thread and data migration is supported to achieve greater locality of data as threads migrate. Software libraries are used for supporting synchronization and locks.

The current implementation of Millipede supports only sequential consistency (with multiple readers and a single writer) as well as multiple writers to different millipages to minimize false sharing. However, other consistency protocols (e.g., release consistency or scope consistency) can be supported by first constructing necessary procedures defining the actions required for the protocols and then installing the DLLs into the Millipede environment.

4.4   Munin and TreadMarks

In an attempt to overcome the limitations of page-based DSMs, researchers at Rice University developed variable-based DSMs. The original system was known as Munin [49, 50]. TreadMarks [51] is a version of Munin updated by adding additional memory consistency models and other performance improvement measures. Another difference is that Munin employs a centralized directory manager whereas TreadMarks uses distributed directory managers. Both systems employ multiple consistency protocols (sequential consistency, release consistency and lazy release consistency). In this discussion we consider Munin and TreadMarks to be synonymous.

Munin programming APIs permit the declaration of shared variables (or objects) with annotations to describe access patterns so that the runtime system can select an appropriate memory consistency protocol. Synchronization is supported by the use of library routines to create, acquire, and release locks and wait at a barrier. Since all synchronizations are visible to the system (indicated by the use of library routines), Munin can support relaxed memory protocols (particularly release consistency; TreadMarks supports lazy release). Shared objects are annotated using the following:

- *Read-only:* These variables cause no coherence-related problems, and replicated copies can be kept on individual nodes.

- *Migratory:* At any given time only one process has (write or ownership) access to the variable. However, the ownership migrates from process to process. Replicated copies of such variables are not permitted.

- *Write-shared:* In an attempt to eliminate false sharing, large data structures (such as large arrays) can be written simultaneously by several processes, provided the updates are directed to different elements of the data structure. Updates to write-shared variables do not cause invalidates of other copies, but the updates are merged and the updated objects are sent to all processes.

- *Producer–consumer:* This annotation indicates that only one process updates the variable but several processes can read the updates. An update-based coherence protocol is better suited for such variables than invalidation-based protocols.

- *Reduction:* This annotation indicates that a single process manages all updates to a variable. Reduction is different from the producer–consumer type since a reduction variable does not have consumers.

- *Result:* This is similar to write-shared in that multiple processes can update the data structure simultaneously. Unlike write-shared, the merged updates are not sent back to all processes.
- *Conventional:* This annotation is used for variables requiring sequential consistency or for those variables for which the user could not determine accesses patterns. Invalidation-based protocols are used to maintain coherence of conventional variables.

Munin and TreadMarks support multiple protocols for maintaining data coherence and support both sequential consistency and release consistency of memory.

Table II shows how the access annotations are translated into coherence protocols. Munin and TreadMarks support both invalidation (I) and update-based coherence protocols. Data variables may or may not be replicated (R). Updates to a variable may or may not be delayed (D). Variables may have a fixed owner (FO) that is responsible for all updates to the variable. Some variable may have multiple owners (M) permitting write-shared annotation described above. S indicates that the shared object has a stable access pattern; that is, the same threads access the object in the same way during the entire program execution. Update protocol is used for such objects. FI indicates whether the updates should be "flushed" to the owner only (used for result variables), and finally, W indicates if a page is writable (or read-only).

The data object directory serves the purpose of the directory for shared data. Each entry tracks the size and address of shared object, the protocol used (Table II), the shared status of the object (valid, modified, shared), copy-set, and a pointer to the synchronization object (if any) associated with this object (for implementing release consistency). The data object directory also includes information about the home-node and probably the owner who may have the most up-to-date copy of the object. The implementation

TABLE II

MUNIN MAPPING OF SHARING ANNOTATIONS TO COHERENCE PROTOCOLS

Sharing annotations	I	R	D	FO	M	S	FI	W
Read-only	N	Y	—	—	—	—	—	N
Migratory	Y	N	—	N	N	—	N	Y
Write-shared	N	Y	Y	N	Y	N	N	Y
Producer–consumer	N	Y	Y	N	Y	Y	N	Y
Reduction	N	Y	N	Y	N	—	N	Y
Result	N	Y	Y	Y	Y	—	Y	Y
Conventional	Y	Y	N	N	N	—	N	Y

of release consistency model requires tracking of synchronization accesses. The object directory is used to track synchronization variables and implement release consistency. Each synchronization variable has one owner who manages acquires and releases on that lock. Likewise a single node is responsible for managing barrier variables; all join messages are sent to the owner and the owner sends release messages to all waiting processes. Queue-based locks are used in Munin to eliminate problems associated with spin locks as discussed in Section 2.

The performance of an application on Munin and TreadMarks depends on a correct choice of coherence protocols for each shared object. Researchers have investigated the use of profiling information and compiler support in the determination of sharing access patterns for variables, instead of relying on user annotations [52].

4.5   Brazos

Brazos [53, 54] is the latest software DSM system designed by the Rice researchers and was intended to be executed on NT operating systems. Like Munin and TreadMarks, Brazos uses a variable-based approach on top of page-based DMS implementations. Multiple consistency protocols are also supported; moreover, Brazos facilitates dynamic changes to the protocol used based on annotations or changes in sharing patterns. In addition, it supports the scope consistency model fully in software with no requirements for additional hardware or language support. The compiler determines the association of synchronization objects with data. Scopes are characterized as global or local scopes and shared data is guaranteed to be coherent only when global scope is exited. Brazos uses multicasting to reduce consistency related communication and thus reducing the overall communication cost for global synchronization. At each (global) barrier, the barrier manager receives notification from all processes along with an indication of invalid pages. The updates to pages are merged (as done in Munin and Treadmarks) and multicast to all processes synchronizing on the barrier.

Brazos supports both locks and barriers for synchronization. Synchronization objects can be shared among threads of multiple processes. Brazos supports two types of barriers: local for synchronization of threads within a process and global for synchronization of threads across processes. It also supports queue locks using NT-supported primitives for mutex variables, critical sections, and semaphores. Both eager and lazy release consistencies are supported to achieve better performance in the presence of false sharing resulting from large-grained critical sections. The eager release is achieved by having the manager distribute a list of newly updated pages provided by threads joining at a barrier (instead of merging all page updates before providing copies of the updated pages to all threads).

The process generates a large number of invalidations (greater than a threshold value). The use of the NT operating system instead of Unix required the designers to rethink the implementations used in Munin and TreadMarks. At the same time, they also benefited from the thread support provided by the NT kernel, including support for multiple types of synchronization objects.

4.6   CRL: C-Region Library

This software-only DSM [55] was designed for CM-5 and MIT's Alewife. CRL libraries can be used with standard C programs to make them run on a network of workstations or DMSs. The program must specify shared memory as C-Regions—a region is a contiguous portion of memory. Thus CRL can be considered as variable size page-based system. Regions can be created using `rgn_create(size)`, which returns a unique region number (or identification). This number is used to address data in the region. The region can be deleted using `rgn_delete`. Other processes sharing a region must first map the region into their virtual address space using `rgn_map(number)`. This binding of the region to a process's virtual address space can be deleted by using `rgn_unmap`. The use of shared region leads to the definition of a larger virtual address space than can be supported by an individual node. Hence it is necessary to map and unmap regions to make room for other regions. It should be noted that when a region is remapped it might be bound to a different virtual address space. Thus use of pointers may cause problems if the pointer points to data in other regions. Pointers do not cause any problems, however, if they point only to data within the same region. Example 7 is a simple example that uses regions.

Example 7   C-region library code.

```
double dotprod (rid_t x, double *y, int n)
{
    int I;
    double *z;
    double rslt;

    /* map 1st vector and initiate read */
    z = (double *) rgn_map(x);
    rgn_start_read(z);
    /* initiate read operation on 2nd vector */
    /* assumed that y is aready mapped */
    rgn_start_read(y);
```

```
/* compute result */
rslt = 0;
for (I = 0; I < n; I++)
    rslt = rstl + z[i]*y[i];
/* terminate read and unmap x */

rgn_end_read(y);
rgn_end_write(z);
rgn_unmap(z);

retrun rslt;
}
```

The functions `rgn_start_read` and `rgn_start_write` indicate to the runtime system the type of operation being performed on the region. This information is used for maintaining coherence of regions (using an invalidation protocol). Directory information is maintained for each region and directories are distributed among the nodes in the system. When a new region is created, its directory entry is assigned to a node chosen in a round robin fashion. Sharing among processes changes dynamically since new regions can be created (or deleted) and regions may be mapped (or unmapped) by processes.

As noted, CRL uses fixed-home for regions and invalidation of regions for maintaining coherence. It also uses unique version number with each region to overcome problems presented by "out of order" message delivery (as in CM-5), since it is necessary to construct the correct order in which updates to a region are made.

CRL implements entry consistency since access to a region is controlled using `rgn_read` and `rgn_write` (which can be viewed as acquiring a lock to the region) and `rgn_end_read` and `rgn_end_write` (which can be viewed as releasing a lock to the region). CRL permits caching of both mapped and unmapped regions. This can lead to a case where a processor may have a cached copy of a region that was subsequently unmapped and remapped. Mapping overhead can be minimized if the same virtual address binding is possible when a region is remapped. This is achieved using a table known as *unmapped region cache* (URC). The region can then be copied from URC to main cache without any binding overhead. It is possible that the copy of the region in URC is stale (invalidated by some other processor), making it useless.

The performance of applications using CRL depends heavily on the choice of sizes for C-Regions. Large regions limit concurrency since only one process can be writing to the region. Small regions can cause overheads in creation, mapping, and unmapping.

4.7   ORCA

Orca [56] is a portable, object-based distributed shared memory system designed and implemented at the Vrije University in Amsterdam. The programming language (Orca) and the runtime system (Panda) were implemented on a networked distributed operating system called Amoeba [57]. Orca differs from previously described software DSMs in several ways:

- In Orca, shared data structures are encapsulated in shared objects—an object is an abstract data type and encapsulated data can only be accessed by the operations defined with the object. Orca supports object-based models without inheritance.
- Orca is a language-based system and uses language construct such as fork a process and pass a shared object to the newly created processes. In addition, unlike other systems that use library extensions to define shared memory and require user annotations on sharing access patterns to achieve a higher performance, the sharing patterns can be deduced by the compiler.
- Orca integrates synchronization and data accesses. The object-model of Orca implies that all operations on an object are atomic. This atomicity is relied on to implement mutual exclusion to shared data. Additional synchronization is achieved using guards with operations.
- Orca supports sequential consistency model. More accurately, it supports entry consistency since all operations to any object are totally ordered.

The object model of Orca presents interesting challenges to the management of replicated objects. Consider what happens when different processes make multiple updates to the same object. In order to implement *update-based coherence protocols* on replicated objects, all update operations (or invoking of an operation on the object) must be executed at each site. The runtime system (Panda) supports totally ordered group communication and multitasking. The totally ordered group communication guarantees that all group members (i.e., processes) receive all messages in the same total order. When a write operation is invoked on a shared object, the operation is broadcast to all members of the shared group so that all shared copies of the object become consistent by invoking the operation.

Invalidation-based protocols require the system to differentiate between operations that modify the internal data of an object and those that do not. Any operation that modifies the object causes the invalidation (or deletion) of the entire object from all other sites, with subsequent supply of the object to requesting sites.

Both invalidation-based and update-based protocols can lead to excessive overheads when dealing with large objects and frequent update operations. An optimization strategy requires the knowledge of the frequency of read operations and write operations to an object. Replication of objects should be permitted only when the read/write ratio is high. If the read/write ratio is low, it is better to keep a single centralized copy of the object. The placement of the single copy will affect the performance since incorrect placement can lead to excessive update operations from the remote location. The Orca system tracks readers and writers of objects to determine if an object should be replicated and where non-replicated objects must be placed. Quantitative performance comparison of TreadMarks and CRL with Orca were reported in [1]. The comparisons showed that programs written for TreadMarks send far more messages than Orca, because the Orca system makes dynamic decisions regarding replication and placement of objects based on read/write ratios of shared data. Orca programs run faster than those written using CRL primarily because the object model of Orca provides for a more natural selection of the size of the shared data. In CRL the performance is affected by the size of a C-region and the regions have no natural link to a programming entity.

5. Summary and Conclusions

In this chapter we have surveyed DSM systems which are intended to combine the ease of programming of the shared-memory model with the scalability of the distributed-memory system. We have explored the design space for such systems and included case studies. We have included descriptions of both hardware- and software-supported DSM systems. We have not included any detailed performance evaluation of the systems, for several reasons. It is very difficult to design experiments that compare all systems fairly. The implementation prototypes of some of the systems were based on older technology and older software designs, making them appear to perform poorly. Although there is a wealth of published information on the performance of specific systems, researchers have not addressed a comprehensive comparative analysis of these systems. Interested readers are encouraged to consult the publications cited in this chapter for performance data.

Although distributed systems and DSM systems have been investigated for nearly 15 years, it is still unclear if the shared-memory model will dominate in all implementations. In almost all cases, DSM systems cannot outperform applications hand tuned to run on distributed-memory (or message-passing) systems. The advent of easy to use message-passing software (e.g., PVM and MPI) may draw some programmers away from DSM systems. Although shared-memory programming is considered simpler than its message-passing counterpart, synchronization and mutual exclusion among processes in a shared memory can be extremely difficult without the aid of sophisticated tools that can detect data races, incorrect and/or unwanted use of locks, loss of signals, and livelocks.

At the same time, as small-scale SMP systems replace today's high-end workstations, the shared-memory multithreaded programming model may become the norm for most programmers. Clustering such workstations in order to achieve high-performance computing systems may justify the use of DSM technology. In the meantime, we believe that both shared-memory (or distributed shared memory) and message-passing paradigms will continue to attract users.

REFERENCES

[1] Bal, H. *et al.* (1998). Performance evaluation of the Orca shared object system. *ACM Transactions on Computer Systems*, February, **16**(1), 1–40.

[2] Flynn, M. J. (1966). Very high-speed computing systems. *Proceedings of IEEE*, **54**(12), 1901–1909.

[3] Wulf, W. and Bell, C. G. (1972). C.mmp—a multi-mini-processor. *Proceedings of the AFIPS Fall Joint Computing Conference*, **41**(Part 2), 765–777.

[4] Swan, R. J., Fuller, S. H. and Siewiorek, D. P. (1997). Cm—a modular, multi-microprocessor. *Proceedings of the AFIPS National Computer Conference*, **46**, 637–644.

[5] Open MP (1997). *OpenMP Fortran Application Program Interface*, Version 1.0. October.

[6] Archibald, J. and Baer, J.-L. (1986). Cache Coherence protocols: evaluation using a multiprocessor simulation model *ACM Transactions on Computer Systems*, **4**(4), 273–298.

[7] Thacker, C. P., Stewart, L. C. and Satterthwaite, E. H. (1988). Firefly: a multiprocessor workstation. *IEEE Transactions on Computers*, **37**(8), 909–920.

[8] Lenoski, D., Laudon, J., Gharachorloo, K. *et al.* (1990). The directory-based cache coherence protocol for the DASH multiprocessor, *Proceedings of the 17th International Symposium on Computer Architecture*, Los Alamitos, CA, pp. 148–159.

[9] Lenoski, D., Laudon, J., Gharachorloo, K. *et al.* (1992). The Stanford DASH multiprocessor. *Proceedings of the International Symposium on Computer Architecture*, pp. 148–159.

[10] Veidenbaum, A. V. (1986). A compiler-assisted cache coherence solution for multiprocessors. *Proceedings of the International Conference on Parallel Processing*, pp. 1029–1036.

[11] Cheong, H. and Veidenbaum, A. V. (1988). Cache coherence scheme with fast selective invalidation. *Proceedings of the 15th Annual International Symposium on Computer Architecture (ISCA'88)*, June.

[12] Cheong, H. and Veidenbaum, A. V. (1989). A version control approach to cache coherence. *Proceedings of the ACM International Conference on Supercomputing*, New York, pp. 322–330.

[13] Lamport, L. (1979). How to make a multiprocessor computer that correctly executes multiprocess programs. *IEEE Transactions on Computers*, **28**(9), 241–248.

[14] Adve, S. V. and Hill, M. (1990). Weak ordering: a new definition. *Proceedings of the 17th International Symposium on Computer Architecture*, Los Alamitos, CA, pp. 2–14.

[15] Gharachorloo, K., Gupta, A. and Hennessy, J. (1991). Performance study of consistency model performance evaluation of memory consistency models for shared memory multiprocessors. *Proceedings of the 4th Symposium on Architectural Support for Programming Languages and Operating Systems (ASPLOS-IV)*, April, pp. 245–259.

[16] Keleher, P., Cox, A. L. and Zwaenepoel, W. (1992). Lazy release consistency for software distributed shared memory. *Proceedings of the 19th Symposium on Computer Architecture*, May, pp. 13–21.

[17] Bershad, B. N., Zekauskas, M. J. and Sawdon, W. A. (1993). The Midway distributed shared memory system. *Proceedings of the COMPCON*, pp. 528–537.

[18] Iftode, L., Singh, J. P. and Li, K. (1996). Scope consistency: a bridge between release consistency and entry consistency. *Proceedings of the 8th Symposium on Parallel Algorithms and Architectures*, pp. 277–287.

[19] Adve, S. V., Pai, V. S. and Ranganathan, P. (1999). Recent advances in memory consistency models for hardware shared-memory systems. *Proceedings of the IEEE*, March, **87**(3), 445–455.

[20] Hecht, D., Kavi, K. M., Gaede, R. and Katsinis, C. (1999). Implementation of recovery blocks on cache-coherent distributed shared memory systems. *Proceedings of the 1999 International Symposium on Parallel Architectures, Algorithms and Networks (I-SPAN '99)*, Fremantle, Western Australia, June.

[21] Anderson, T. E. (1990). The Performance of spin lock alternatives for shared-memory multiprocessors. *IEEE Transactions on Parallel and Distributed Systems*, **1**(1), 6–16.

[22] Graunke, G. and Thakkar, S. (1990). Synchronization algorithms for shared-memory multiprocessors. *Computer*, **23**(6), 60–69.

[23] Hensgen, D., Finkel, R. and Manber, U. (1988). Two algorithms for barrier synchronization. *International Journal on Parallel Programming*, **17**(1), 1–17.

[24] Lubachevsky, B. (1989). Synchronization barrier and related tools for shared memory parallel programming. *Proceedings of the 1989 International Conference on Parallel Processing*, August, II, 175–179.

[25] Mellor-Crummey, J. M. and Scott, M. L. (1991). Algorithms for scalable synchronization on shared-memory multiprocessors. *ACM Transactions on Computer Systems*, **9**(1), 21–65.

[26] Kuskin, J., Ofelt, Heinrich, D. M. *et al.* (1994). The Stanford FLASH multiprocessor. *Proceedings of the 21st International Symposium on Computer Architecture*, Chicago, IL, April, pp. 302–313.

[27] IEEE (1996). *ANSI/IEEE Standard 1596.3–1996: Scalable Coherent Interface*. IEEE, New York.

[28] James, D. V. (1994). The scalable coherent interface: scaling to high-performance systems. *Proceedings of the COMPCON '94: Digest of Papers*, pp. 64–71.

[29] Convex (1994). *CONVEX Exemplar Architecture*. CONVEX Press, Richardson, TX.

[30] Laudon, J. and Lenoski, D. (1997). The SGI Origin: a ccNUMA highly scalable server. *Proceedings of the 24th International Symposium on Computer Architecture*, June, pp. 241–251.

[31] Joe, T. and Hennessy, J. (1994). Evaluating the memory overhead required for COMA architectures. *Proceedings of the 21st International Symposium on Computer Architecture*, April, pp. 82–93.

[32] Frank, S., Burkhardt, H. III and Rothnie, J. (1993). The KSR1: bridging the gap between shared memory and MPPs. *Proceedings of the COMPCON '93*.

[33] Windheiser, Boyd, D. E. L., Hao, E. *et al.* (1993). KSR1 multiprocessor: analysis of latency hiding techniques in a sparse solver. *Proceedings of the 7th International Parallel Processing Symposium*, April, 454–461,

[34] KSR (1994). *KSR/Series Principles of Operations*, revision 7.0. Kendall Square Research
[35] Hagersten, E., Landin, A. and Haridi, S. (1992). DDM—a cache-only memory architecture. *Computer*, **25**(9), 44–54.
[36] Could Computer Systems (1984). *SCI-Clone/32 Distributed Processing System* (brochure).
[37] Oracle Corporation (1994). *Oracle Parallel Server in the Digital Environment*. Oracle Corporation White Paper, Part A19242, June.
[38] Fillo, M. and Gillett, R. B. (1997). Architecture and implementation of MEMORY CHANNEL 2. *Digital Technical Journal*, **9**(1), 27–41.
[39] Agarwal, A. *et al.* (1999). The MIT Alewife machine. *Proceedings of the IEEE*, March, **87**(3), 430–444.
[40] Agarwal, A., Kubiatowicz, Kranz, J. D. *et al.* (1993). Sparcle: an evolutionary processor design for large-scale multiprocessors. *IEEE Micro*, June, **13**(3), 48–61.
[41] Chaiken, D., Fields, Kurihara, C. K. and Agarwal, A. (1990). Directory-based cache-coherence in large-scale multiprocessors. *Computer*, **23**(6), 49–58.
[42] Kubiatowicz, J., Chaiken, D. and Agarwal, A. (1994). The Alewife CMMU: addressing the multiprocessor communications gap. *Extended Abstract for Hot Chips '94*, August.
[43] Dubncki, C., Bilas, A., Chen, Y. *et al.* (1998). Shrimp update: Myrinet communication. *IEEE Micro*, January/February, **18**(1).
[44] Fleisch, B. D. and Popek, G. J. (1993). Mirage: A coherent distributed shared memory design. *Proceedings of the 14th ACM Symposium on Operating System Principles*, December. pp. 211–223.
[45] Popek, G. *et al.* (1981). LOCUS: a network transparent, high reliability distributed system *Proceedings of the 8th Symposium on OS principles*, December, pp. 169–177.
[46] Walker, B. *et al.* (1983). The LOCUS distributed operating system. *Proceedings of the 9th Symposium on OS Principles*, December.
[47] Friedman, R., Goldin, M., Itzkovitz, A. and Schuster, A. (1997). Millipede: easy parallel programming in available distributed environments. *Software: Practice and Experience*, **27**(8), 929–965.
[48] Itzkovitz, A. and Schuster, A. (1999). MultiView and Millipage—fine-grain sharing in page based DSMs. *Proceedings of the 3rd Symposium on Operating Systems Design and Implementation (OSDI '99)*, New Orleans, LA, February.
[49] Bennett, J. K., Carter, J. B. and Zwaenepoel, W. (1990). Munin: distributed shared memory based on type-specific memory coherence. *Proceedings of the 2nd ACM SIGPLAN Symposium on Principles and Practice of Parallel Programming (PpoPP)*, March. pp. 168–176.
[50] Carter, J. B., Bennett, J. K. and Zwaenepoel, W. (1991). Implementation and performance of Munin. *Proceedings of the 13th ACM Symposium on Operating Systems Principles*, October. pp. 152–164.
[51] Amza, C. *et al.* (1996). TreadMarks: shared memory computing on networks of workstations. *Computer*, February, **29**(2), 18–28.
[52] Dwarkadas, S. *et al.* (1996). Combining compile-time and run-time support for efficient distributed shared memory. *Proceedings of the IEEE*, March, **87**(3), 476–486.
[53] Speight, E. and Bennett, J. K. (1997). Brazos: a third generation DSM system. *Proceedings of the 1997 USENIX Windows/NT Workshop*, August.
[54] Speight, E. and Bennett, J. K. (1998). Using multicast and multithreading to reduce communication in software DSM systems. *Proceedings of the 4th Symposium on High Performance Architecture (HPCA-4)*, February, pp. 312–323.
[55] Johnson, K. *et al.* (1995). CRL: high-performance all software distributed shared memory. *Proceedings of the 15th ACM Symposium on OS Principles*, December, pp. 213–228.

[56] Bal, H., Kaashoek, M. and Tanenbaum, A. (1992). Orca: a language for parallel programming of distributed systems. *IEEE Transactions on Software Engineering*, March, **18**(3), 190–205.
[57] Tanenbaum, A. *et al.* (1990). Experiences with the Amoeba distributed operating systems. *Communications of the ACM*, December, **33**(12), 46–63.

Resource-Aware Meta-Computing

JEFFREY K. HOLLINGSWORTH, PETER J. KELEHER AND
KYUNG D. RYU

Department of Computer Science
University of Maryland
College Park
Maryland 20742
USA
{hollings,keleher,kdryu}@cs.umd.edu

Abstract

Meta-computing is an increasingly popular and useful method of obtaining resources to solve large computational problems. However, meta-computer environments pose a number of unique challenges, many of which have yet to be addressed effectively. Among these are dynamicism in both applications and environments, and heterogeneity at several different levels. This chapter discusses current approaches to these problems, and uses them in the Active Harmony system as a running example. Harmony supports an interface that allows applications to export tuning alternatives to the higher-level system. By exposing different parameters that can be changed at runtime, applications can be automatically adapted to changes in their execution environment caused by other programs, the addition or deletion of nodes, or changes in the availability of resources like communication links. Applications expose not only options, but also expected resource utilization with each option and the effect that the option will have on the application's performance. We discuss how this flexibility can be used to tune the overall performance of a collection of applications in a system.

ADVANCES IN COMPUTERS, VOL. 53
ISBN 0-12-012153-0

109

1. Introduction

Meta-computing, the simultaneous and coordinated use of semi-autonomous computing resources in physically separate locations, is increasingly being used to solve large-scale scientific problems. By using a collection of specialized computational and data resources located at different facilities around the world, work can be done more efficiently than if only local resources were used. However, the infrastructure needed to efficiently support this type of global-scale computation is not yet available.

Private workstations connected by a network have long been recognized for use with computation-intensive applications. Since workstations are unused a large fraction of the time, idle cycles can be harnessed to run scientific computations or simulation programs as a single process or a parallel job. The usefulness of this approach depends on how much time the machines are available, and how well those available resources can be harnessed.

Mutka and Livny [1] found that on the average, machines were idle 75% of the time. Similarly, Krueger and Chawla [2] demonstrated that for 199 diskless Sun workstations on average the nodes were idle 91% of the time and only 50% of those idle cycles were made available for background jobs. The other half of the idle cycles could not be harnessed since they belonged either to intervals when the workstation owners were using their machines or during a waiting period to ensure that users were away. More recently, by analyzing machine usage traces from three academic institutions Acharya *et al.* [3] also observed that 60–80% of the workstations in a pool are available.

Both meta-computer environments and the applications that run on them can be characterized by distribution, heterogeneity, and changing resource requirements and capacities. These attributes make static approaches to resource allocation unsuitable. Systems need to dynamically adapt to changing resource capacities and application requirements in order to achieve high performance in such environments. The canonical way to run applications in current meta-computing environments is to pass the application's name, parameters, and number of required nodes to the system, and to hope for the best. The execution environment (hardware and system software) is expected to run the program efficiently with little or no information from the application about the application's needs or expectations. This model of application and system interaction is simple, and allows many applications to run well.

However, this model does not accommodate the full generality of application–system interactions required by current applications. In particular, an application may wish to alter its resource requests on the basis of knowledge of available resources. For example, a multimedia application might alter its resolution or frame rate on the basis of available bandwidth. Second, computational resources are not always static and fixed for the life of an application. For example, an application might be running on a system that batch schedules jobs on to idle workstations. To address the needs for these types of applications, the interface between applications and the execution environment needs to change. In this chapter, we present our approach to enhancing the application–system interface.

Most previous approaches to adapting applications to dynamic environments have required applications to be solely responsible for reconfiguration to make better use of existing resources. Although the actual means that applications use to reconfigure themselves are certainly application-specific, we argue that the decisions about when and how such reconfigurations occur are more properly made in a centralized resource manager.

Moving policy into a central manager serves two purposes.

- First, it accumulates detailed performance and resource information into a single place. Better information often allows better decisions to be made. Alternatively, this information could be provided directly to each application. Problems with this approach include duplicated effort and possible contention from the conflicting goals of different applications.
- More importantly, however, a centralized manager equipped with both comprehensive information on the system's current state, and knobs to permit runtime reconfiguration of running applications, can adapt any and all applications in order to improve resource utilization.

For example, consider a parallel application whose speedup improves rapidly up to six nodes, but improves only marginally after that. A resource allocator might give this application eight nodes in the absence of any other applications since the last two nodes were not being used for any other purpose. However, when a new job enters the system, it could probably make more efficient use of those two nodes. If decisions about application reconfiguration are made by the applications, no reconfiguration will occur. However, a centralized decision-maker could infer that reconfiguring the first application to only six nodes will improve overall efficiency and throughput, and could make this happen.

We target long-lived and persistent applications. Examples of long-lived applications include scientific code and data-mining applications. Persistent applications include file servers, information servers, and database management systems. We target these types of applications because they persist long enough for the global environment to change, and hence have higher potential for improvement. Our emphasis on long-lived applications allows us to use relatively expensive operations such as object migration and application reconfiguration since these operations can be amortized across the relatively long life of the application.

The focus of this chapter is on the interface between applications and the system. Specifically, we ask the following questions:

- Can we build an API that is expressive enough to define real-world alternatives?
- Can a system use this information to improve the behavior of applications during execution?
- How can we make accurate predictions of parallel and distributed applications?

We use the *Active Harmony* system as a running example of a resource manager that can make the tradeoffs discussed above. However, our intent is to foster a more general dialogue about the role of sophisticated resource managers, heterogeneous clusters, and tradeoffs between autonomy and efficiency. Other projects such as AppLeS, Condor, Globus, and Legion provide similar functionality with somewhat different abstractions. Section 5 describes these systems in more detail.

The remainder of this chapter is organized as follows. Section 2 presents an overview of Harmony and describes how it facilitates cooperation between applications and system software. Section 3 describes several subsystems that extend Harmony by performing sophisticated application adaptation. Section 4 describes how information about the execution environment can be gathered for use at runtime. Section 5 describes additional work related to dynamic resource management. Finally, Section 6 summarizes the issues raised in this chapter.

2. Harmony Structure

Harmony applications are linked with a Harmony communication library. Each library communicates with the centralized Harmony scheduler process, which runs on one node in the system. The overall system is shown in Fig. 1, and the major components are described below.

The *adaptation controller* is the heart of the scheduler. The controller gathers relevant information about the applications and the environment, projects the effects of proposed changes (such as migrating an object) on the system, and weighs competing costs and expected benefits of making various changes.

Active Harmony provides mechanisms for applications to export tuning options, together with information about the resource requirements of each option, to the adaptation controller. The adaptation controller then chooses among the exported options on the basis of more complete information than is available to individual objects. A key advantage of this technique is that the system can tune not just individual objects, but also entire collections of objects. Possible tuning criteria include network latency and bandwidth, memory utilization, and processor time. Since changing implementations or data layout could require significant time, Harmony's interface includes a frictional cost function that can be used by the tuning system to evaluate whether a tuning option is worth the effort required.

The scheduler uses a *metric interface* to provide a unified way to gather data about the performance of applications and their execution environment. Data about system conditions and application resource requirements flow into the metric interface, and on to both the adaptation controller and individual applications.

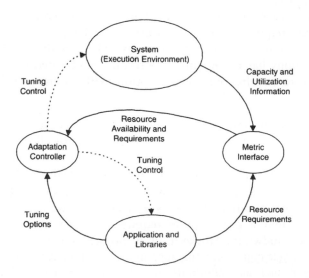

FIG. 1. Major components of Active Harmony.

The library stubs communicate with applications through a *tuning interface*, which provides a method for applications to export tuning options to the system. Each tuning option defines the expected consumption of one or more system resources. The options are intended to be "knobs" that the system can use to adjust applications to changes in the environment. The main concern in designing the tuning interface is to ensure that it is expressive enough to describe the effects of all application tuning options.

2.1 Application to System API

This section describes the interface between applications and the Harmony adaptation controller (hereafter referred to as "Harmony"). Applications use the API to specify tuning options to Harmony. Harmony differs from previous systems such as Matchmaker [4] and the Globus RSI [5] in that it uses simple performance models to guide allocation decisions. These models require more application information than previous systems. Whereas previous systems might accept requests for "a machine and a network," Harmony requires each resource usage to be specifically quantified. This is necessary because Harmony uses performance prediction to optimize an overall objective function, usually system throughput. Estimates of resource usage are employed to build simple performance models that can then predict the interaction of distinct jobs. Performance models give Harmony the ability to make judgements of the relative merits of distinct choices.

Harmony's decision-making algorithm can also consider allocation decisions that require running applications to be reconfigured. Hence, applications that are written to the Harmony API periodically check to see whether Harmony has reconfigured the resources allocated to them.

We therefore require our tuning option API to have the following capabilities:

- First, it must be able to express mutually exclusive choices on multiple axes. These options can be thought of as a way of allowing Harmony to locate an individual application in n-dimensional space, such that the choice corresponding to each dimension is orthogonal.

- Second, the interface must provide a means to specify the resource requirements of different options. For example, we need to be able to represent that a given option requires X cycles and Y amount of network bandwidth. However, it is problematic to express the "X cycles". Cycle counts are only meaningful with reference to a particular processor, such as "20 minutes of CPU time on a UltraSparc 5". To circumvent this problem, we specify CPU requirements with reference to an abstract machine, currently a 400 MHz Pentium II. Nodes then express their capacity as a scaling factor compared to the reference machine. Similar relative units of performance have been included in systems such as PVM [6].

- Third, the tuning options must be able to express relationships between entities. For example, we need to be able to express "I need 2 machines for 20 minutes, and a 10 Mbps link between them." Note that the link can be expressed relative to the machines, rather than in absolute terms. The system must therefore be able to understand the topology of the system resources, such as network connections between machines, software services, etc.

- Fourth, the interface must be able to represent the granularity at which the modification can be performed. For example, an iterative data-parallel HPF Fortran application might be able to change the number of processors that it exploits at runtime. However, this adaptation can probably only be performed at the completion of an outer loop iteration.

- Fifth, we need to express the frictional cost of switching from one option to another. For example, once the above data-parallel HPF application notices the change request from Harmony, it still needs to reconfigure itself to run with the new option. If two options differ in the number of processors being used, the application will likely need to change the data layout, change the index structures, and move data among nodes to effect the reconfiguration. This frictional cost is certainly not negligible, and must be considered when making re-allocation decisions.

- Finally, each option must specify some way in which the response time of a given application choice can be calculated by the system. This specification may be either explicit or left to the system. In the latter case, Harmony uses a simple model of computation and communication to combine absolute resource requirements into a projected finishing time for an application. An explicit specification might include either an expression or a function that projects response time on the basis of the amount of resources actually allocated to the application.

2.1.1 The Harmony RSL

The Harmony resource description language (RSL) provides a uniform set of abstractions and syntax that can be used to express both resource availability and resource requirements. The RSL consists of a set of interface routines, a default resource hierarchy, and a set of predefined tags that specifies quantities used by Harmony. The RSL is implemented on top of the TCL scripting language [7]. Applications specify requirements by sending TCL scripts to Harmony, which executes them and sends back resource allocation descriptions. An example of one such script is shown in Example 1.

Example 1 Harmonized applications: (a) simple parallel application; (b) bag-of-tasks application.

```
harmonyBundle Simple - {
  {-        {node "worker"
                  {hostname  "*"}
                  {os        "linux"}
                  {seconds   "300"}
                  {memory    32}}
           {variable worker "node" 4}}
           {communication    "2+2*4"}
  }}
```

(a) simple parallel application

```
harmonyBundle bag howMany {
    {default    {node      "worker"
      {hostname  "*"}
      {os        "linux"}
      {seconds   "200/workerNodes"}
      {memory    {32}}}
    {variable worker "workerNodes" 1 2 4 8}
    {communication    "2+2*workerNodes*workerNodes"}
    {performance {[interp workerNodes {1 1e5} {4 3e4} {8 2e4}]}
  }}
```

(b) bag-of-tasks application

Several things make TCL ideal for our purposes:

● it is simple to incorporate into existing applications, and easily extended

● TCL lists are a natural way to represent Harmony's resource requirements

● TCL provides support for arbitrary expression and function evaluation.

The last property is useful in specifying parametric values, such as defining communication requirements as a function of the number of processors. More to the point, much of the matching and policy description is currently implemented directly in TCL. Performance is acceptable because recent versions of TCL incorporate on-the-fly byte compilation, and updates in Harmony are on the order of seconds not microseconds.

The following summarizes the main features of the RSL:

- *Bundles*: Applications specify bundles to Harmony. Each bundle consists of mutually exclusive options for tuning the application's behavior. For example, different options might specify configurations with different numbers of processors, or algorithm options such as table-driven lookup vs. sequential search.

- *Resource requirements*: Option definitions describe requested high-level resources, such as nodes or communication links. High-level resources are qualified by a number of tags, each of which specifies some characteristic or requirement that the resource must be able to meet. For example, tags are used to specify how much memory and how many CPU cycles are required to execute a process on a given node.

- *Performance prediction*: Harmony evaluates different option choices on the basis of an overall objective function. By default, this is system throughput. Response times of individual applications are computed as simple combinations of CPU and network requirements, suitably scaled to reflect resource contention. Applications with more complicated performance characteristics, provide simple performance prediction models in the form of TCL scripts.

- *Naming*: Harmony uses option definitions to build namespaces so that the actual resources allocated to any option can be named both from within the option definition, and from without. A flexible and expressive naming scheme is crucial to allowing applications to specify resource requirements and performance as a function of other resources. More detail on the naming scheme is presented below.

Table I lists the primary tags used to describe available resources and application requirements. The "harmony-Bundle" function is the interface for specifying requirements. The "harmonyNode" function is used to publish resource availability.

2.1.2 Naming

Harmony contains a hierarchical namespace to allow the adaptation controller and the application to share information about the current instantiated application options and about the assigned resources. This

TABLE I

PRIMARY TAGS IN HARMONY RSL

Tag	Purpose
harmonyBundle	Application bundle
node	Characteristics of desired node (e.g., CPU speed, memory, OS, etc.)
link	Specifies required bandwidth between two nodes
communication	Alternate form of bandwidth specification. Gives total communication requirements of application, usually parameterized by the resources allocated by Harmony (i.e., a function of the number of nodes)
performance	Override Harmony's default prediction function for that application.
granularity	Rate at which the application can change between options
variable	Allows a particular resource (usually a node specification) to be instantiated by Harmony a variable number of times
harmonyNode	Resource availability
speed	Speed of node relative to reference node (400 MHz Pentium II)

namespace allows applications to describe their option bundles to the Harmony system, and also allows Harmony to change options.

The root of the namespace contains application instances of the currently active applications in the system. Application instances are two-part names, consisting of an application name and a system-chosen instance id. The next level in the namespace consists of the option bundles supported by the application. Below an option bundle are the resource requirements for that option, currently just nodes and links. In addition, nodes contain sub-resources such as memory, CPU, I/O, etc. Links currently contain only bandwidth estimates. An example of a fully qualified name would be

```
appliction.instance.bundle.option.resourcename.tagname
```

For example, if the client in Example 2 was assigned instance ID 66 by Harmony, the tag describing the memory resources allocated to the client of the data-shipping option would be

```
DBclient.66.where.DS.client.memory.
```

2.1.3 Simple parallel application

We next show the expressiveness of Harmony's interface. Our first example is shown in Example 1a. "Simple" is a generic parallel application that runs on four processors. There are two high-level resource requests. The first specifies the required characteristics of a worker node. Each node requires 300 seconds of computation on the reference machine and 32 Mbytes of memory. The "variable" tag specifies that this node definition should be used to match four distinct nodes, all meeting the same requirements. The "communication" tag is used to specify communication requirements for the entire application. Since specific endpoints are not given, the system assumes that communication is general and that all nodes must be fully connected.

2.1.4 Variable parallelism

Our second application, "Bag", is a parallel application that implements an application of the "bag-of-tasks" paradigm. The application is iterative, with computation being divided into a set of possibly differently-sized tasks. Each worker process repeatedly requests and obtains tasks from the server, performs the associated computations, returns the results to the server, and requests additional tasks. This method of work distribution allows the application to exploit varying amounts of parallelism, and to perform relatively crude load-balancing on arbitrarily shaped tasks.

Bag's interface with Harmony is shown in Example 2b. There are three additional features in this example.

- First, bag uses the "variable" tag to specify that the application can exploit one, two, four, or eight worker processes. Assuming that the total amount of computation performed by all processors is always the same, the total number of cycles in the system should be constant across different numbers of workers. Hence, we parameterize "seconds" on the "workerNodes" variable defined in the "variable" tag.

- Second, we use the "communication" tag to specify the overall communication requirements as a function of the number of processors assigned. The bandwidth specified by the communication tag defines that bandwidth grows as the square of the number of worker processes. Hence, "Bag" is an example of a broad domain of applications in which communication requirements grow much faster than computation.

- Third, we use the "performance" tag to tell Harmony to use an application-specific prediction model rather than its default model. This tag expects a list of data-points that specify the expected running time of the application when using a specific number of nodes. Rather than requiring the user to specify all of the points explicitly, Harmony will interpolate using a piecewise linear curve on the basis of the supplied values.

Other ways of modeling costs could also be useful. For example, a somewhat more accurate model of communication costs is CPU occupancy on either end (for protocol processing, copying), plus wire time [8]. If this occupancy is significant, cycles on all worker processes would need to be parameterized on the basis of the amount of communication.

2.1.5   Client–server database

Our third example is that of Tornadito, a hybrid relational database [9]. The database consists of clients and servers, with the distinction being that queries are submitted at clients and the data resides at servers. Queries can execute at either place. In fact, this is the main choice the application bundle exports to Harmony. We assume a single, always available server and one or more clients. The interface to Harmony is handled entirely by the clients. Each client that has queries to execute contacts Harmony with a choice bundle. The bundle consists of two options:

● *query-shipping*, in which queries are executed at the server
● *data-shipping*, where queries are executed at the client.

Each option specifies resource usage on behalf of both the client and the remote server. Although there is no explicit link between clients, Harmony is able to combine server resource usage on behalf of multiple independent clients in order to predict total resource consumption by the server.

Example 2 shows one possible bundle specification. The DBclient application specifies a bundle named "where," with two options: QS (query-shipping), and DS (data-shipping). In either case, cycles and memory are consumed at both the client and the server, and bandwidth is consumed on a link between the two. The distinction is that "QS" consumes more resources at the server, and "DS" consumes more at the client. All other things being equal, the query-shipping approach is faster, but consumes more resources at the server. Each option specifies two node resources, and a network link between the two. All numeric arguments are total requirements for the life of the job. Both assume that the server is at "harmony.cs.umd.edu". Clients and servers can locate each other given a machine name.

Example 2 Client–server database.

```
harmonyBundle Dbclient:1 where {
 {QS {node server
             {hostname harmony.cs.umd.edu}
             {seconds      9}
             {memory       20}}
       {node client
             {hostname      *}
             {os         linux}
             {seconds       1}
             {memory       42"}}
       {link client server 2}}
 {DS {node server
             {hostname harmony.cs.umd.edu }
             {seconds      1}
             {memory       20}}
       {node client
             {hostname      *}
             {os         linux}
             {memory      >=17}
             {seconds       9}}
       {link client server
             {44+(client.memory>24?24:
             client.memory)-17}}
    }}
```

Additionally, the nodes are qualified by "seconds", meaning the total expected seconds of computation on our reference machine, and "memory," which specifies the minimum amount of memory needed. Both options specify the nodes equivalently. The names "server" and "client" are used within the option namespace to identify which node is being referred to. For example, the link option specifies the total communication requirements between "server" and "client", without needing to know at application startup exactly which nodes are being instantiated to these names.

In addition to basic functionality, the example illustrates two relatively sophisticated aspects of Harmony's resource management.

- First, resource usage is higher at the server with query-shipping than data-shipping. This allows the system to infer that server load grows more quickly with the number of clients with query-shipping than with data-shipping. At some number of clients, the server machine will become overloaded, resulting in data-shipping providing better overall performance. The specification does not require the same option to be chosen for all clients, so the system could use data-shipping for some clients and query-shipping for others.

● Second, the memory tag ">= 32" tells Harmony that 32 MB is the minimal amount of memory the application requires, but that additional memory can be profitably used as well. The specification for bandwidth in the data-shipping case is then parameterized as a function of "client.memory." This allows the application to tell Harmony that the amount of required bandwidth is dependent on the amount of memory allocated on the client machine. Harmony can then decide to allocate additional memory resources at the client in order to reduce bandwidth requirements. This tradeoff is a good one if memory is available, because additional memory usage does not increase the application's response time, whereas additional network communication does.

2.2   Policies

A key piece of Harmony is the policies used by the automatic adaptation system to assign resources to applications. This section describes how Harmony matches application resource requirements to the available resources. We then describe how we compose the performance information from individual nodes into a global picture of resource utilization. Finally, we describe the overall objective function that Harmony optimizes. The current policies, although simple, allow us to gain experience with the system.

2.2.1   Matching resource needs

Resources are assigned to new applications under Harmony on the basis of the requirements described in the corresponding RSL. When Harmony starts execution, we get an initial estimate of the capabilities of each node and links in the system. For nodes, this estimate includes information about the available memory, and the normalized computing capacity of the node. For links, we note the bandwidth and latency attributes. As nodes and links are matched, we decrease the available resources on the basis of the application's RSL entries.

We start by finding nodes that meet the minimum resource requirements required by the application. When considering nodes, we also verify that the network links between nodes of the application meet the requirements specified in the RSL. Our current approach uses a simple first-fit allocation strategy. In the future, we plan to extend the matching to use more sophisticated policies that try to avoid fragmentation. However, for now our goal is to demonstrate the ability of our system to optimize application performance on the basis of the options, so any initial match of resource requirements is acceptable.

2.2.2   Explicit (response time) models

Harmony's decisions are guided by an overarching objective function. Our objective function currently minimizes the average completion time of the jobs currently in the system. Hence, the system must be able to predict the lifetime of applications. Harmony has a very simple default performance model that combines resource usage with a simple contention model. However, this simplistic model is inadequate to describe the performance of many parallel applications because of complex interactions between constituent processes. For example, we might use the critical path notion to take inter-process dependencies into account [10]. Other application models could model piecewise linear curves. Figure 2 shows an example of Harmony's configuration choices in the presence of our client-server database and an application with variable parallelism. The parallel application's speedup curve is described in an application-specific perform-ance model.[1]

In the future we plan to investigate other objective functions. The requirement for an objective function is that it be a single variable that represents the overall behavior of the system we are trying to optimize (across multiple applications). It really is a measure of goodness for each application scaled into a common currency.

2.2.3   Setting application options

The ability to select among possible application options is an integral part of the Harmony system. In order to make this possible, we need to evaluate the likely performance of different options and select the one that maximizes our objective function. However, the space of possible option combinations in any moderately large system will be so large that we will not be able to evaluate all combinations. Instead, we need a set of heuristics that select an application option to change and then evaluate the overall system objective function.

Currently, we optimize one bundle at a time when adding new applications to the system. Bundles are evaluated in the same lexical order as they were defined. This is a simple form of greedy optimization that will

---

[1] This performance model matches a simple bag of tasks parallel application and a client–server database we have modified to support Harmony.

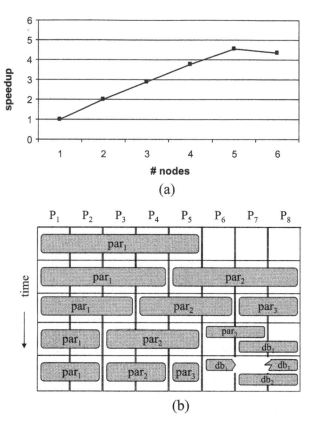

FIG. 2. Online reconfiguration: (a) the performance of a parallel application; (b) the eight-processor configurations chosen by Harmony as new jobs arrive. Note the configuration of five nodes (rather than six) in the first time frame, and the subsequent configurations that optimize for average efficiency by choosing relatively equal partitions for multiple instances of the parallel application, rather some large and some small.

not necessarily produce a globally optimal value, but it is simple and easy to implement. After defining the initial options for a new application, we re-evaluate the options for existing applications. To minimize the search space, we simply iterate through the list of active applications and within each application through the list of options. For each option, we evaluate the objective function for the different values of the option. During application execution, we continue this process on a periodic basis to adapt the system to allow for changes out of Harmony's control (such as network traffic due to other applications).

2.2.4 Search-space heuristics

To be effective, the system needs to find good configurations for each incoming application. Application configuration consists of two parts:

- "Harmonized" applications export mutually exclusive algorithmic alternatives for the system to choose among.
- A given application and tuning alternative can usually be mapped to multiple configurations of nodes in the system.

Hence, the search space of possible configurations is clearly too large for exhaustive search, especially since "looking" at each individual configuration alternative requires evaluating the performance model against that configuration. Thus, heuristics are needed to constrain the search space of configurations for a given application and among applications.

Heuristics are evaluated on the basis of cost and efficiency. A heuristic that performs anything like an exhaustive search clearly has too high a runtime cost to be useful. On the other hand, a cheap heuristic that leads to poor processor efficiencies and response times is of little use. As a starting point, simple variations on first-fit and best-fit heuristics show promising behavior whether or not currently running applications can be reconfigured. Another part of this strategy is to try satisfy a resource request with "local" machines before considering all connected remote machines. Although sophisticated approaches such as hill-climbing or simulated annealing have a number of advantages, our expectation is that simple heuristics will perform nearly as well and at a much lower cost than more complicated approaches.

2.2.5 Performance prediction subsystem

To effectively compare candidate configurations, we need accurate, lightweight models for the expected behavior of applications in any possible configuration. Accurate models allow the system to make good decisions about scheduling jobs on constrained resources. Consider a system with eight nodes and three incoming jobs: a two-node job, an eight-node job, followed by another two-node job. A simple first-come first-served (FCFS) system will delay each job until the others have finished. However, running the two smaller jobs at the same time might be a better approach. The reason that we can not say this with any assurance is that systems have historically not had a priori knowledge of expected running times. If the second two-node job runs much longer than the first, jumping it in front of the larger job will delay the larger job unfairly. *Backfilling* [11] schedulers use knowledge of running times to determine whether or not re-ordering will delay jobs that arrived first. However, such systems depend on accurate knowledge of the running times. Underestimating the times still delays the larger application unfairly. Overestimating times reduces the opportunity for re-ordering.

In addition to simple job duration, we want to be able to handle the more complex resource needs of supporting multiple applications in a system. For example, we need to manage the amount of memory and networking bandwidth used by applications. Furthermore, we want to be able to handle a reasonably large set of performance metrics, in addition to the more "traditional" ones, such as response time and throughput (this will become clearer as we discuss the applications below).

Even if accurate information on running time for a single configuration is available, a global system needs to be able to evaluate running times in a variety of configurations, on possibly heterogeneous hosts, and possibly in the presence of contention for a variety of resources. End-users clearly can not provide all of this information.

Thus, analytical models will allow us to develop expressive and accurate predictions of application behavior. We are currently adapting previous work on using simplified analytical models to represent complex systems (e.g., as in [12–15]).

2.2.5.1 *Model Generation*   We are using simple analytical models to predict performance at runtime. Efficient resource management depends on good resource usage predictions. Furthermore, better resource management decisions can be made dynamically, at runtime, when more information is available about the currently running applications and their resource demands. Such decisions must be made relatively quickly, and simple analytical models are well suited for these types of problems.

The constructed analytical models must have appropriate knobs that can be turned in order to make a resource allocation decision. The system can then automatically derive models from information provided by the applications. To construct the models automatically, knowledge of resources and the workload to be executed on these resources is required. Clearly, the adaptation control has information about available system resources; thus, what is needed is a proper workload characterization. In order to simplify matters for the application designers, the system needs to perform workload characterization from a variety of information sources. Specifically, the information given in the RSL description can be used as a source of resource demands of each application. More sophisticated models will be constructed on the basis of more detailed descriptions of application, which would require the use of an appropriate specification language. One possible way to represent the models is via an existing modeling language such as the Unified Modeling Language (UML) [16].

UML provides a standard means of describing software oriented designs and promises to be widely used in the software industry. It contains several types of diagrams which allow different properties of a system design to be expressed. Such diagrams (and the associated information) are useful in the generation of performance models. For instance, *use case* diagrams are useful in characterizing the system workload; *implementation* diagrams are useful in characterizing the mapping of software components onto hardware resources and in defining contention for these resources.

To facilitate automatic generation of analytical models, we are building a library of model components for each of the resources available in our system, which can be used in automatic construction of appropriate analytical models at runtime.

2.2.5.2 Multi-resolution models

More accurate analytical models generally produce better predictions, but also tend to increase the time needed to make resource management decisions. Thus, there is a tradeoff between the "goodness" of the resource management decision and the amount of time and resources required to make it. The optimum accuracy of the model, with respect to its cost and resulting benefits, will to a large extent depend on the application(s) being modeled. Thus, for better results, such decisions should also be made at runtime. To facilitate this, we plan to construct "multi-resolution" models and choose the appropriate resolution, on the basis of predicted benefits and costs, at runtime.

For instance, consider a system that manages a shared pool of resources where more resources are allocated to an application as the need for them arises (i.e., as the workload of that application crosses a predefined set of thresholds). In order to make such a system stable, one should include a hysteresis, i.e., the set of thresholds for adding resources should be distinct from the set of thresholds for removing resources. In this case, an analytical model that accurately represents both the hysteresis behavior and the non-instantaneous resource addition behavior can be quite costly to solve (details can be found in Golubchik and Liu [12]). However, a model that "ignores" this complex behavior is quite simple (actually, a simple birth–death stochastic process). The more accurate model will tend to give better performance predictions, but would also require quite a bit more time to solve. Thus, depending on the amount of time and resources available to the adaptation controller, it would choose one or the other model in making a decision about allocating more resources to an application.

2.2.5.3 System state

For many applications, it is important to model the behavior of multiple invocations, rather than just one. For example, consider a client–server database. There may be little incentive to run a single query on a client because we would need to migrate too much data. However, if multiple queries are considered, we might invest the time to migrate data to a client to allow a workload of queries to run faster.

Therefore the system must maintain state information (e.g., which data is being cached by a database client) and the performance models must incorporate that state can be passed from one invocation to the next (or between applications). We plan to incorporate state information into the workload characterization process by mapping workflow onto system resources (as described above). Options to represent state in the system include simple finite state automata.

2.2.5.4 *Runtime parameter measurement*   The accuracy of the performance prediction models can be further improved by increasing the accuracy of the parameters used by these models, which to a large extent reflect the current state of the system, in terms of resource and workload characteristics. To aid in increasing the accuracy of this information, we use runtime performance measurements, such as [10, 17].

2.3   Mechanisms

Most of the mechanisms needed by meta-computer schedulers are identical to those needed by local schedulers. One difference is that meta-computing on non-dedicated resources, such as idle machines, must be prevented from impacting the owners of those machines. This section briefly describes a set of techniques that allow remote jobs to co-exist with local jobs without the performance of the local jobs being affected. We describe how to realize fined-grained cycle stealing (the *linger-longer* approach), and the requirements that this approach imposes on local schedulers. The key feature of fine-grained cycle stealing is to exploit brief periods of idle processor cycles while users are either thinking or waiting for I/O events. We refer to the processes run by the workstation owner as *host processes*, and those associated with fine-grained cycle stealing as *guest processes*.

In order to make fine-grained cycle-stealing work, we must limit the resources used by guest processes and ensure that host processes have priority over them. Guest processes must have close to zero impact on host processes in order for the system to be palatable to users. To achieve that goal requires a scheduling policy that gives absolute priority to host processes over guest processes, even to the point of starving guest processes. This also implies the need to manage the virtual memory via a priority scheme. The basic idea is to tag all pages as either guest or host pages, and to give priority on page replacement to the host pages. The complete mechanism is presented in section 2.3.3.

Previous systems automatically migrate guest processes from non-idle machines in order to ensure that guest processes do not interfere with host processes. The key idea of our fine-grained cycle stealing approach is that migration of a guest process off of a node is *optional*. Guest processes can often co-exist with host processes without significantly impacting the performance of the latter, or starving the former.

A key question in evaluating the overhead of priority-based preemption is the time required to switch from the guest process to the host process. There are three significant sources of delay in saving and restoring the context of a process:

- the time required to save registers
- the time required (via caches misses) to reload the process's cache state
- the time to reload the working set of virtual pages into physical page frames.

We defer discussion of the latter overhead until section 2.3.3. On current microprocessors, the time to restore cache state dominates the register restore time. In a previous paper [18], we showed that if the *effective context-switch time* is 100 μs or less, the overhead of this extra context-switch is less than 2%. With host CPU loads of less than 25%, host process slowdown remains under 5% even for effective context switch times of up to 500 μs.

In addition, our simulations of sequential processes showed that a linger-based policy would improve average process completion time by 47% compared with previous approaches. On the basis of job throughput, the linger-longer policy provides a 50% improvement over previous policies. Likewise our *linger-forever* policy (i.e., disabling optional migrations) permits a 60% improvement in throughput. For all workloads considered in the study, the delay, measured as the average increase in completion time of a CPU request, for host (local) processes was less than 0.5%.

2.3.1 Linux kernel extensions

This section introduces the modifications to the local Linux scheduler necessary to support the linger-longer scheduling policy. These extensions are designed to ensure that guest processes cannot impede the performance of host processes. We first describe the general nature of our kernel modifications, and then describe how we modified the scheduler and virtual memory system of Linux to meet our needs.

One possible concern with our approach is the need for kernel modifications. In general, it is much harder to gain acceptance for software that requires kernel modifications. However, for the type of system we are building, such modifications are both necessary and reasonable. Guest processes must be able to stay running, yet impose only an unnoticeable impact on host processes. There is no practical way to achieve this without kernel modifications. Additionally, we feel that kernel modifications are a reasonable burden for two reasons:

- First, we are using the Linux operating system as an initial implementation platform, and many software packages for Linux already require kernel patches to work.
- Second, the relatively modest kernel changes required could be implemented on stock kernels using the kernInst technology [19], which allows fairly complex customizations of a UNIX kernel at runtime via dynamic binary rewriting. All of the changes we have made could be implemented using this technique.

Current UNIX systems support CPU priority via a per-process parameter called the *nice* value. Via nice, different priorities can be assigned to different processes. These priority levels are intended to reflect the relative importance of different tasks, but they do not necessarily implement a strict priority scheme that always schedules the highest priority process. The nice value of a process is just a single component that is used to compute the dynamic priority during execution. As a result, sometimes a lower *static priority* process gets scheduled over higher static priority processes to prevent starvation, and to ensure progress of the lower priority processes. However, we need a stricter concept of priority in CPU scheduling between our two classes of processes. Guest processes should not be scheduled (and can even starve) when any host process is ready no matter what its runtime priority is. Meanwhile, the scheduling between the processes in the same class should be maintained as it is under current scheduling implementation.

Although many UNIX kernels provide strict priorities in order to support real-time deadlines, these real-time priorities are *higher* than traditional UNIX processes. For linger-longer we require just the opposite, a lower priority than normal.

Current general-purpose UNIX systems provide no support for prioritizing access to other resources such as memory, communication, and I/O. Priorities are, to some degree, implied by the corresponding CPU scheduling priorities. For example, physical pages used by a lower-priority process will often be lost to higher-priority processes. Traditional pages replacement policies, such as least recently used (LRU), are more likely to page out the lower-priority process's pages, because it runs less frequently. However, this might not be true with a higher-priority process that is not computationally intensive, and a lower-priority process that is. We therefore need an additional mechanism to control the memory allocation between local and guest processes. Like CPU scheduling, this modification should not affect the memory allocation (or page replacement) between processes in the same class.

We chose Linux as our target operating system for several reasons.

- It is one of the most widely used UNIX operating systems.
- The source code is open and widely available.
- Since many active Linux users build their own customized kernels, our mechanisms could easily be patched into existing installations by end users. This is important because most PCs are deployed on people's desks, and cycle-stealing approaches are probably more applicable to desktop environments than to server environments.

2.3.2 Starvation-level CPU scheduling

The Linux scheduler chooses a process to run by selecting the ready process with the highest runtime priority, where the runtime priority can be thought of as the number of 10 ms time slices held by the process. The runtime priority is initialized from a static priority derived from the nice level of the process. Static priorities range from -19 to $+19$, with $+19$ being the highest.[2] New processes are given $20 + p$ slices, where p is the static priority level. The process chosen to run has its store of slices decremented by 1. Hence, all runnable processes tend to decrease in priority until no runnable processes have any remaining slices. At this point, all processes are reset to their initial runtime priorities. Blocked processes receive an additional credit of half of their remaining slices. For example, a blocked process having 10 time slices left will have 20 slices from an initial priority of zero, plus 5 slices as a credit from the previous round. This feature is designed to ensure that compute-bound processes do not receive undue processor priority compared to I/O bound processes.

This scheduling policy implies that processes with the lowest priority (nice $-$ 19) will be assigned a single slice during each round, whereas normal processes consume 20 slices. When running two CPU-bound processes, where one has normal priority and the other is *niced* to the minimum priority, -19, the latter will still be scheduled 5% of the time. Although this degree of processor contention might or might not be visible to a user,

---

[2] Nice priorities inside the kernel have the opposite sign of the nice values seen by user processes.

running the process could still cause contention for other resources, such as memory.

We implemented a new *guest priority* in order to prevent guest processes from running when runnable host processes are present. The change essentially establishes guest processes as a different class, such that guest processes are not chosen if any runnable host processes exist. This is true even if the host processes have lower runtime priorities than the guest process.

We also verified that the scheduler reschedules processes any time a host process unblocks while a guest process is running. This is the default behavior on Linux, but not on many BSD-derived operating systems. One potential problem of our strict priority policy is that it could cause *priority inversion*. Priority inversion occurs when a higher priority process is not able to run because of a lower-priority process holding a shared resource. This is not possible in our application domain because guest and host processes do not share locks, or any other non-revocable resources.

2.3.3 Prioritized page replacement

Another way in which guest processes could adversely affect host processes is by tying up physical memory. Having pages resident in memory can be as important to a process's performance as getting time quanta on processors. Our approach to prioritizing access to physical memory tries to ensure that the presence of a guest process on a node will not increase the page fault rate of the host processes.

Unfortunately, memory is more difficult to deal with than the CPU. The cost of reclaiming the processor from a running process in order to run a new process consists only of saving processor state and restoring cache state. The cost of reclaiming page frames from a running process is negligible for clean pages, but quite large for modified pages because they need to be flushed to disk before being reclaimed. The simple solution to this problem is to permanently reserve physical memory for the host processes. The drawback is that many guest processes are quite large. Simulations and graphics rendering applications can often fill all available memory. Hence, not allowing guest processes to use the majority of physical memory would prevent a large class of applications from taking advantage of idle cycles.

We therefore decided not to impose any hard restrictions on the number of physical pages that can be used by a guest process. Instead, we implemented a policy that establishes low and high thresholds for the number of physical pages used by guest processes. Essentially, the page replacement policy prefers to evict a page from a host process if the total number of physical pages held by the guest process is less than the low threshold. The replacement policy defaults to the standard clock-based pseudo-LRU policy up until the upper threshold. Above the high threshold, the policy prefers to evict a guest page. The effect of this policy is to encourage guest processes to steal pages from host processes until the lower threshold is reached, to encourage host processes to steal from guest processes above the high threshold, and to allow them to compete evenly in the region between the two thresholds. However, the host priority will lead to the number of pages held by the guest processes being closer to the lower threshold, because the host processes will run more frequently.

In more detail, the default Linux replacement policy is an LRU-like policy on the basis of the "clock" algorithm used in BSD UNIX. The Linux algorithm uses a one-bit flag and an age counter for each page. Each access to a page sets its flag. Periodically, the virtual memory system scans the list of pages and records which ones have the use bit set, clears the bit, and increments the age by 3 for the accessed pages. Pages that are not touched during the period of a single sweep have their age decremented by 1. Only pages whose age value is less than a system-wide constant are candidates for replacement.

We modified the Linux kernel to support this prioritized page replacement. Two new global kernel variables were added for the memory thresholds, and are configurable at runtime via system calls. The kernel keeps track of resident memory size for guest processes and host processes. Periodically, the virtual memory system triggers the page-out mechanism. When it scans in-memory pages for replacement, it checks the resident memory size of guest processes against the memory thresholds. If they are below the lower thresholds, the host process's pages are scanned first for page-out. Resident sizes of guest processes larger than the upper threshold cause the guest process's pages to be scanned first. Between the two thresholds, older pages are paged out first regardless of which process is using them.

Correct selection of the two parameters is critical to meeting the goal of exploiting fine-grained idle intervals without significantly impacting the performance of host processes. Too high of value for the low threshold will cause undue delay for host processes, and too low a value will cause the guest process to thrash constantly. However, if minimum intrusiveness by the guest process is paramount, the low memory threshold can be set to zero to guarantee the use of the entire physical memory by foreground process.

In a previous paper [20] we evaluated the effect of linger-longer on parallel applications on our test cluster. We used the Musbus interactive UNIX benchmark suite [21] to simulate the behavior of actual interactive users. Musbus simulates an interactive user conducting a series of compile–edit cycles. The benchmark creates processes to simulate interactive editing (including appropriate pauses between keystrokes), UNIX command line utilities, and compiler invocations. We varied the size of the program being edited and compiled by the "user" in order to change the mean CPU utilization of the simulated local user. In all cases, the file being manipulated was at least as large as the original file supplied with the benchmark.

The guest applications are Water and FFT from the Splash-2 benchmark suite [22], and SOR, a simple red–black successive over-relaxation application [23]. Water is a molecular dynamics code, and FFT implements a three-dimensional fast Fourier transform. All three applications were run on top of CVM [24], Harmony's user-level distributed shared-memory (DSM) layer. DSMs are software systems that provide the abstraction of shared memory to threads of a parallel application running on networks of workstations. These three applications are intended to be representative of three common classes of distributed applications. Water has relatively fine-grained communication and synchronization, FFT is quite communication-intensive, and SOR is mostly compute-bound.

In the first set of experiments, we ran one process of a four-process CVM application as a guest process on each of four nodes. We varied the mean CPU utilization of the host processes from 7% to 25% by changing the size of the program being compiled during the compilation phase of the benchmark. The results of these tests are shown in Fig. 3. Figure 3a shows the slowdown experienced by the parallel applications. The solid lines show the slowdown using our linger-longer policy, and the dashed lines show the slowdown when the guest processes are run with the default (i.e., equal priority). As expected, running the guest processes at starvation level priority generally slows them down more than if they were run at equal priority with the host processes. However, when the Musbus utilization is less than 15% the slowdown for all applications is lower with lingering than with the default priority. For comparison, running SOR, Water, and FFT on three nodes instead of four slows them down by 26%, 25%, and 30%, respectively. Thus for the most common levels of CPU utilization, running on one non-idle node and three idle would improve the application's performance compared to running on just three idle nodes. Our previous study [18] showed that node utilization of less than 10% occurs over 75% of the time even when users are actively using their workstations.

Figure 3b shows the slowdown experienced by the host Musbus processes. Again, we show the behavior when the guest processes are run using our linger-longer policy and the default equal priority. When the guest processes were run with moderate CPU utilization (i.e., over 10%), all three guest processes started to introduce a measurable delay in the host processes when equal priority was used. For Water and SOR, the delay exceeds 10% when the Musbus utilization reaches 13%. At the highest level of Musbus CPU utilization, the delay using the default priority exceeds 10% for all

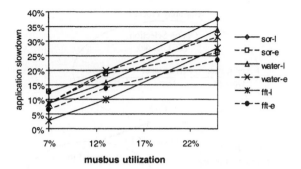

(a) slowdown of parallel application
(guest process)

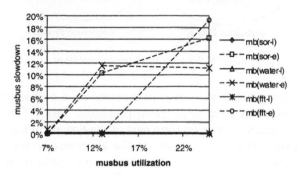

(b) slowdown of host Musbus process

FIG. 3. Impact of running one process of four-process CVM applications as a guest process: (a) slowdown of parallel application (guest process); (b) slowdown of host Musbus process.

three applications and 15% for two of the three applications. However, for all three parallel guest applications, the delay seen when running with linger-longer was not measurable. This experiment demonstrates that our new CPU priority and memory page replacement policy can limit the local workload slowdown when using fine-grained idle cycles.

2.4 Prototype

We have developed a prototype of the Harmony interface to show that applications can export options and respond to reconfiguration decisions made by system. The architecture of the prototype is shown in Fig. 4. There are two major parts, a Harmony process and a client library linked into applications.

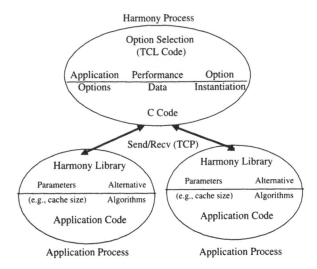

FIG. 4. Architecture of Harmony prototype.

The Harmony process is a server that listens on a well-known port and waits for connections from application processes. Inside Harmony is the resource management and adaptation part of the system. When a Harmony-aware application starts, it connects to the Harmony server and supplies the bundles that it supports. A Harmony-aware application must share information with the Harmony process. The interface is summarized in Table II. First, the application calls functions to initialize the Harmony runtime library, and define its option bundles. Second, the application uses special Harmony variables to make runtime decisions about how the computation should be performed. For example, if an application exports an option to change its buffer size, it needs to periodically read the Harmony variable that indicates the current buffer size (as determined by Harmony controller), and then update its own state to this size. Applications access the "Harmony" variables by using the pointer to a Harmony variable returned by the `harmony_add_variable()` function.

New values for Harmony variables are buffered in the until a `flushPendingVars()` call is made. This call sends all pending changes to the application processes. Inside the application, a I/O event handler function is called when the Harmony process sends variable updates. The updates are then applied to the Harmony variables. The application process must periodically check the values of these variables and take appropriate action.

Our system uses a polling interface to detect changes in variables at the application. Many long-running applications have a natural phase where it is

TABLE II

HARMONY API USED BY APPLICATION PROGRAMS

`harmony_startup(<unique id>, <use interrupts>)`
A program registers with the Harmony server using this call

`harmony_bundle_setup("<bundle definition>")`
An application informs Harmony of one of its bundles this way. The bundle definition looks like the examples given in section 2.1.1

`void *harmony_add_variable("variable name", <default value>, <variable type>)`
An application declares a variable that to communicate information between Harmony and the application. Harmony variables include bundle values, and resource information (such as the nodes that the application has been assigned to use). The return value is the pointer to the variable

`harmony_wait_for_update()`
The application process blocks until the Harmony system updates its options and variables

`harmony_end()`
The application is about to terminate and Harmony should re-evaluate the application's resources

---

both easier and more efficient to change their behavior rather than requiring them to react immediately to Harmony requests. For example, database applications usually need to complete the current query before reconfiguring the system from a query shipping to a data-shipping configuration. Likewise, scientific applications generally have a time-step or other major loop that represents a natural point to re-configure the application.

The Harmony process is an event driven system that waits for application and performance events. When an event happens, it triggers the automatic application adaptation system, and each of the option bundles for each application gets re-evaluated to see it should be changed (see section 2.2 for a complete description of the way the evaluation is done). When option bundles are changed, the appropriate variables are updated in each application.

2.5   An Example Application

To explore the ability of the Harmony server to adapt an application, we modified a hybrid client–server database to allow Harmony to reconfigure where queries are processed: on client nodes or on server nodes. The database system used was Tornadito, a relational database engine built on top of the SHORE (Scalable Heterogeneous Object REpository) storage manager [25, 26]. All experiments were run on nodes of an IBM SP-2, and used the 320 Mbps high performance switch to communicate between clients and the server. Each client ran the same workload, a set of similar, but randomly perturbed join queries over two instances of the Wisconsin benchmark relations [27], each of which contains 100 000 208-byte tuples. In each query, tuples from both relations are selected on an indexed attribute (10% selectivity) and then joined on a unique attribute. Although this is a fairly simple model of database activity, such query sets often arise in large databases that have multiple end users (bank branches, ATMs), and in query refinement.

The Harmony interface exported by this program is the set of option bundles shown in Example 2. For our initial experiments, the controller was configured with a simple rule for changing configurations on the basis of the number of active clients. We then ran the system and added clients about every 3 minutes. The results of this experiment are shown in Fig. 5. In this graph, the *x*-axis shows time and the *y*-axis shows the mean response time of the benchmark query. Each curve represents the response time of one of the three clients. During the first 200 seconds, only one client is active and the system is processing the queries on the server. During the next 200 seconds, two clients are active, and the response time for both clients is approximately double the initial response time with one active client.

At 400 seconds, the third client starts, and the response time of all clients increases to approximately 20 seconds. During this interval one of the clients has a response time that is noticeably better than the other two (client #1 for the first 100 seconds, and then client #2). This is likely due to cooperative caching effects on the server since all clients are accessing the same relations.

The addition of the third client also eventually triggers the Harmony system to send a reconfiguration event to the clients to have them start processing the queries locally rather than on the server. This results in the response time of all three clients being reduced, and in fact the performance

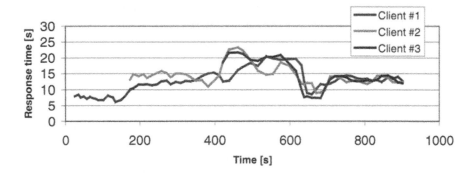

FIG. 5. Client–server database application: Harmony chooses query-shipping with one or two clients, but switches all clients to data-shipping when the third client starts.

is approximately the same as when two clients were executing their queries on the server. This demonstration shows that by adapting an application to its environment, we can improve its performance.

3. Transparent System-Directed Application Adaptation

Harmony has several means of adapting applications to their environments. Environments, consisting of local schedulers, can be controlled directly. Application execution can be steered explicitly through the RSL interface. This section describes a method transparently steering application execution, i.e., a method of dramatically reconfiguring running applications that have not been explicitly "harmonized."

Harmony provides an automatically reconfigurable shared memory abstraction (DSM) to parallel applications running on networks of workstations. DSM applications are multi-threaded, and assumed to have many more threads than the number of nodes used by any one application. Overall performance depends on parallelism, load balance, latency tolerance, and communication minimization. In this section, we focus on communication minimization through active correlation tracking [28], a mechanism for tracking data sharing between threads, and its implementation in CVM [29]. Consistency between data located on different processors is maintained by using virtual memory techniques to trap accesses to shared data and a protocol to ensure timely propagation of these updates to other processors. Information on the type and degree of data sharing is useful to such systems because the majority of network communication is caused by the underlying consistency system. When a pair of threads located on distinct machines (nodes) both access data on the same shared page, network communication can only be avoided by moving at least one of the threads so that they are located on the same node.

In order to minimize communication, therefore, the system needs to identify the thread pairs that will cause the most communication if not located on the same node. The information should be complete, in that we need information on all threads in the system, and it must be accurate, in that small errors in the relative ordering of thread pairs might cause large differences in communication.

Ideally, sharing behavior would be measured in terms of access rates. However, a naive implementation would add overhead to all writes, not just those that occur when the tracking mechanism is turned on. Function cloning could be used to create tracking and non-tracking versions, but every function that might possibly access shared data would have to be cloned. Current systems [30, 31], therefore, merely track the set of pages that each thread accesses. Changes in sharing patterns are usually accommodated through the use of an aging mechanism.

In any case, word-level access densities are not the proper abstraction for a page-based system. We therefore track data sharing between threads by correlating the threads' accesses to shared memory. Two threads that frequently access the same shared pages can be presumed to share data. We define *thread correlation* as the number of pages shared in common between a pair of threads. We define the *cut cost* to be the aggregate total of thread correlations for thread pairs that must communicate across node boundaries. Cut costs can then be used to compare candidate mappings of threads to nodes in the system. Once the best mapping has been identified, the runtime system can migrate all threads to their new homes in one round of communication.

3.1.1 Thread correlations and cut costs

The cut cost of a given mapping of threads to nodes is the pairwise sum of all thread correlations, i.e., a sum with n^2 terms, where n is the number of threads. This sum represents a count of the pages shared by threads on distinct machines.

We hypothesized that cut costs are good indicators of data traffic for running applications. We tested this hypothesis experimentally by measuring the correlation between cut costs and remote misses of a series of randomly generated thread configurations. A remote miss occurs any time a process accesses an invalid shared page. Pages are invalid either because the page has never been accessed locally, or because another process is modifying the page.[3]

In either case, the fault is handled by retrieving a current copy of the page from another node. For purposes of this experiment, we assume that all remote sites are equally expensive to access; thereby ensuring that the number of remote faults accurately represents the cost of data traffic.

In all but one case, we had correlation coefficients are at least 0.72. Aside from a single extraneous miss caused by CVM's garbage collection mechanism, one application's correlation coefficient would be 1.0.

3.1.2 Correlation maps

Thread correlations are used to create *correlation maps*. These are grids that summarize correlations between all pairs of threads. We can represent

---

[3] This is a gross simplification, but captures the essence.

maps graphically as two-dimensional squares where the darkness of each point represents the degree of sharing between the two threads that correspond to the x,y coordinates of that point. Correlation maps are useful for visualizing sharing behavior. For example, Fig. 6a shows a correlation map for a parallel FFT with 32 threads. Note the prevalence of dark areas near the diagonals, which imply the presence of nearest-neighbor communication patterns. However, the sharing is concentrated in discrete blocks of threads, rather than being continuous.

This correlation map represents a version of FFT with 32 threads distributed equally across four nodes. The points inside the dark squares represent those thread pairs that are located on the same nodes, and hence do not figure into cut costs or require network communication. There are four squares, since there are four nodes, or regions where sharing is free. Since all of the dark regions are inside the "free zones" that represent nodes, we can infer that communication requirements will be relatively minimal.

Now consider instead Fig. 6b. This picture represents a configuration of four threads running on each of eight nodes. The correlation map is the same, but the smaller "free zones" encompass only half of the dark areas. Hence, we can infer that this configuration has more communication than the four-node version. Together with information on the ratio of communication to computation in the application, a runtime system could potentially make a rough guess at whether the eight-node configuration would have any performance advantage over the four-node version.

Finally, consider Fig. 6c. This is the same application, with unchanged sharing patterns. However, we have randomly permuted the assignment of threads to nodes. Doing so results in a configuration with a much higher cut cost, which is not addressed effectively by either the four-node or eight-node configurations. Similar situations would arise with applications in which sharing patterns change slowly over time.

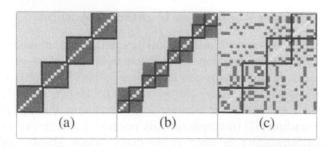

FIG. 6. 32-thread FFT, $2^6 \times 2^6 \times 2^6$: (a) on four nodes, squares indicate thread sharing that does not cause network communication; (b) on eight nodes, as above; (c) randomized thread assignments for four nodes.

3.1.3   Correlation-tracking mechanisms

Previous systems obtained page-level access information by tracking existing remote faults. Remote faults occur when local threads attempt to access invalid shared pages, and are satisfied by fetching the latest version of the shared page from the last node that modified it. The underlying DSM can overload this process to inexpensively track the causes of remote faults, slowly building up a pattern of the pages accessed by each thread.

The problem is that this approach only captures information about the first local thread that accesses a page, and captures no information about sharing between local threads. Even after multiple (10 or more) rounds of thread migrations, passive tracking only comes close to obtaining complete information for one of the applications that we tested, and this application is by far the least complex of our applications.

The solution used by Harmony is to use *active correlation tracking*. Multiple rounds of threads migrations can be avoided by obtaining additional information about correlations between local threads before any thread migration takes place. We obtain this information through an active correlation tracking phase, which iteratively obtains access information for each local thread. The reader is referred to [28] for details. In summary, however, the active approach consists of a discrete phase where page faults are forced to occur at the first access to each page by each local thread. This information is collected at the next global synchronization operation, giving the synchronization owner complete information about page accesses by all threads in the system. This information is complete, and collected without multiple rounds of migrations. Assuming static sharing behavior, the cost of the extra local page faults can be amortized across the entire execution of the application.

3.1.4   Using correlation maps to direct migration

Thread correlations are primarily useful as a means of evaluating cut costs (and, indirectly, communication requirements) of candidate mappings of threads to nodes. Such comparisons are only meaningful if applications can be configured to match arbitrary thread mappings. Hence, reconfigurations require thread migrations. We assume a DSM system that supports per-node multithreading [32] (multiple threads per node) and thread migration. Per-node multithreading is only problematic when DSMs only allow dynamically allocated data to be shared, like CVM. The problem is that it exposes an asymmetry in the threads' view of data. Threads on a single node share the same copy of statically allocated global data, but each node has distinct copies. This problem is usually handled by restricting threads from accessing any of these variables. Instead, threads can access only stack and globally shared data.

Given the above, thread migration can be accomplished through little more than copying thread stacks from one machine to another. Care must be taken to preserve the stack's address before and after a copy so that pointer values do not become orphaned. Additionally, thread migration in systems that support relaxed consistency models must ensure that the thread's view of shared data at the destination is not missing any updates that were visible at the source.

3.1.5 Identifying good thread assignments

The combination of finding the optimal mapping of threads to nodes is a form of the *multi-way cut* problem, the general form of which is NP-hard (meaning that it is at least as hard as any problem in NP, and possibly harder).

Although good approximation schemes have been found for the general form of the communication minimization problem [33], our problem is complicated by the fact that we must also address load balancing and parallelism. For the purposes of this chapter, we restrict the problem to merely identifying the best mapping of threads to nodes, given a constant and equal number of threads on each node. We investigated several ways of identifying good mappings. We used integer programming software to

TABLE III

EIGHT-NODE PERFORMANCE BY HEURISTIC

Applications	Assignment	Time (s)	Remote misses	Total Mbytes	Cut cost
Barnes	Min-cost	43.0	120 730	218.1	125 518
	Random	46.5	124 030	254.2	129 729
FFT7	Min-cost	37.3	22 002	172.2	8960
	Random	68.9	86 850	685.9	14 912
LU1 k	Min-cost	7.3	11 689	121.3	31 696
	Random	97.1	231 117	1136.2	58 576
Ocean	Min-cost	21.2	123 950	446.3	26 662
	Random	28.9	171 886	605.5	29 037
Spatial	Min-cost	240.1	125 929	551.8	273 920
	Random	273.7	249 389	870.8	289 280
SOR	Min-cost	3.6	881	5.4	28
	Random	5.9	8103	47.7	252
Water	Min-cost	19.3	20 956	49.0	21 451
	Random	21.1	33 188	72.0	23 635

identify optimal mappings. We developed several heuristics on the basis of cluster analysis [34], and showed that two heuristics identified thread mappings with cut costs that were within 1% of optimal for all of our applications. We refer to these heuristics collectively as *min-cost*.

Table III shows communication requirements, counts of remote misses, and overall performance for each application with both min-cost and a random assignment of threads to nodes.

4. Resource Information and Metrics

In order to make intelligent decisions about resource allocation and adaptation, data about the application and its behavior are required. Previously, two major types of information were available:

- First, static performance prediction has been used to try to predict the behavior on an application when it executes on a given collection of hardware.
- Second, runtime-profiling tools have been used to record information about application execution to allow programmers to revise their code between executions to improve its performance.

In this section, we review the first two types of information. We then present a new type of data we call *predictive metrics* that are a combination of performance prediction and runtime observation that allow adaptive systems to use data about their current execution to forecast the impact of possible runtime configuration changes.

4.1   Prediction Models

An important component of the Harmony approach to adaptive systems is to include performance prediction to allow the system to evaluate tuning alternatives. Although there has been considerable work in the area of performance prediction, much of the work has concentrated on abstract system performance prediction rather than predicting the performance of a specific application. However, there has been some recent work to allow accurate prediction of application performance.

The POEMS project [35] is developing an integrated end-to-end performance prediction environment for parallel computation. They are combining analytical modeling with discrete simulation to allow different levels of fidelity in their predictions on the basis of user need. The *Performance Recommender* allows an application programmer to select parameters for a specific problem instance by drawing on a database of information derived from previous program executions and inferred via modeling. The POEMS project differs from Harmony in that POEMS considers static information such as number of nodes, whereas the Harmony system also includes runtime information such as system load.

Schopf and Berman [36] have combined stochastic modeling of applications with runtime observations to create time varying predictions of the execution time of applications. Their approach represents the predicted application performance as a *structural model* that represents application behavior as component models and component interactions. Values for component models (such as the bandwidth used or functional unit operation counts) are modulated by runtime observations of available resources to provide accurate predictions of the completion time of a component operation for a system with multiple users. Component interactions capture the attributes of the parallel application such as synchronization points and data decomposition.

4.2   Runtime Performance Metrics

To effectively adapt an application, raw performance data needs to be distilled down into useful information. Historically, performance metrics have been used to provide programmers with data to allow them to improve the performance of their application. In a system that automatically adapts, the role of performance metrics is to provide similar insights not to the programmer, but to the tuning infrastructure. In this section, we review different performance metrics, and in the next section we describe how one of them has been adapted to support automatic application tuning.

4.2.1   Parallel Performance Metrics

Simply extending sequential metrics to parallel programs is not sufficient because, in a parallel program, improving the procedure that consumes the largest amount of time may not improve the program's execution time. Inter-process dependencies in a parallel program influence which procedures are important to a program's execution time. Different parallel metrics measure and report these interactions differently. A common way to represent the execution of a parallel program is in terms of a graph of the application's execution history that incorporates both these inter-process dependencies as well was the sequential (intra-process) time. We refer to this graph as a *program activity graph* (PAG). Nodes in the graph represent significant events in the program's execution (e.g., message sends and receives, procedure calls, and returns). Arcs represent the ordering of events within a process or the synchronization dependencies between processes. Each arc is labeled with the amount of process and elapsed time between events.

One of the first metrics specifically designed for parallel programs was *critical path analysis* [37, 38]. The goal of this metric is to identify the procedures in a parallel program that are responsible for its execution time. The *critical path* of a parallel program is the longest CPU time weighted path through the PAG. Non-productive CPU time, such as spinning on a lock, is assigned a weight of zero. The critical path profile is a list of the procedures or other program components along the critical path and the time each procedure contributed to the length of the path. The time assigned to these procedures determines the execution time of the program. Unless one of these procedures is improved, the execution time of application will not improve.

Although critical path provides more accurate information than CPU time profiles such as gprof, it does not consider the effect of secondary and tertiary paths in limiting the improvement possible by fixing a component on the critical path. An extension to critical path called *logical zeroing* [39] addresses this problem. This metric calculates the new critical path length when all of the instances of a target procedure are set to zero. The difference between the original and new critical paths is a prediction of the potential improvement achieved by tuning the selected procedure.

Critical path provides detailed information about how to improve a parallel program, but building the PAG and calculating the metric requires significant space and time. On-line critical path analysis [40] permits computing the critical path profile value or logical zeroing value of a selected procedure during program execution. This is done by "piggy-backing" instrumentation data onto the application messages or locks.

4.2.2 *Automating Performance Diagnosis*

Different performance metrics provide useful information for different types of bottlenecks. However, since different metrics are required for different types of bottlenecks the user is left to select the one to use. To provide better guidance to the user, rather than providing an abundance of statistics, several tools have been developed that treat the problem of finding a performance bottleneck as a search problem.

AtExpert [41] from Cray Research uses a set of rules to help users improve FORTRAN programs written with the Cray auto-tasking library. The auto-tasking library provides automatic parallelism for FORTRAN programs; however, there are a number of directives that can that greatly affect performance. AtExpert measures a program that has been auto-tasked and attempts to suggest directives that would improve the performance of the program. Since, the tool works on a very specific programming model, FORTRAN programs on small scale shared-memory multiprocessors, it is able to provide precise prescriptive advise to the user.

Cray also produced the MPP Apprentice for their T3D platforms [42, 43]. This tool differs from ATExpert in that it handles a larger variety of parallel programming semantics (not limited to helping with auto-tasking). As a result, it is more generally applicable, but provides a less definitive suggestions on how to fix your program. MPP Apprentice uses the compiler to automatically insert instrumentation into an application. This instrumentation is in the form of counters and timers, so is (relatively) compact and finite size. The compiler produces a *compiler information file* (CIF), as a guide to map the counter/timer information back to the source code of the application program. After the program completes, a *runtime information file* (RIF) is produced, containing the values of the counters and timers. MPP Apprentice includes a rich set of performance visualizations that correlate this information with the application source code. These tools allow the programmer to navigate quickly through the performance data.

Predicate profiling [44] permits comparing different algorithms for the same problem as well as the scalability of a particular algorithm. It defines a common currency, time, and then calibrate all losses in terms of how many cycles it consumed. Losses due to load imbalance, starvation, synchronization, and the memory hierarchy are reported. Results are displayed in a bar chart showing how the available cycles were spent (both to useful work and various sources of loss). Information is presented for the entire application, which provides descriptive information about the type of bottleneck. However, they do not include suggestions about how to fix the problem or information about which procedure contain the bottleneck.

Another approach is to provide a search system that is independent of the programming model and machine architecture. Paradyn's Performance Consultant [45] uses a hierarchical three-axis search model (the "why," "where," and "when" of a performance bottleneck). The "why" axis represents hypotheses about potential bottlenecks in a parallel program (i.e., message passing, computation, I/O). The "where" axis defines a collection of resource hierarchies (CPU, interconnect, disk) that could cause bottleneck. The "when" axis isolates the bottleneck to a specific phase of the program's execution. A unique feature of the Performance Consultant is that it searches for bottlenecks while the program is executing. This requires an adaptive style of instrumentation, but it can greatly reduce the volume of performance data that needs to be collected. Only the performance data required to test the current hypothesis for the currently selected resources need be collected.

4.3 Adaptation Metrics

In order to make informed choices about adapting an application, Harmony needs metrics to predict the performance implications of any changes. To meet this need, we have developed a metric called *load balancing factor* (LBF) to predict the impact of changing where computation is performed. This metric can be used by the system to evaluate potential application reconfigurations before committing to potentially poor choices.

We have developed two variants of LBF, one for process level migration, and one for fine-grained procedure level migration. *Process LBF* predicts the impact of changing the assignment of processes to processors in a distributed execution environment. Our goal is to compute the potential improvement in execution time if we change the placement. Our technique can also be used to predict the performance gain possible if new nodes are added. Also, we are able to predict how the application would behave if the performance characteristics of the communication system were to change.

To assess the potential improvement, we predict the execution time of a program with a virtual placement, during an execution on a different one. Our approach is to instrument application processes to forward data about inter-process events to a central monitoring station that simulates the execution of these events under the target configuration.

The details of the algorithm for process LBF are described in [46]. Early experience with process LBF is encouraging. Table IV shows a summary of the measured and predicted performance for a TSP application, and four of the NAS benchmark programs [47]. For each application, we show the measured running time for one or two configurations and the predicted running time when the number of nodes is used. For all cases, we are able to predict the running time to within 6% of the measured time.

Whereas process LBF is designed for course-grained migration, *procedure-level LBF* is designed to measure the impact of fine-grained movement of work. The goal of this metric is to compute the potential improvement in execution time if we move a selected procedure, from the client to the server or vice versa.

The algorithm used to compute procedure is on the basis of the *critical path* (CP) of a parallel computation (the longest process time weighted path through the graph formed by the inter-process communication in the program). The idea of procedure LBF is to compute the new CP of the program if the selected procedure was moved from one process to another.[4]

---

[4] Our metric does not evaluate how to move the procedure. However, this movement is possible if the application uses Harmony's shared data programming model.

TABLE IV

MEASURED AND PREDICTED TIME FOR LBF

Application target	Measured time	Predicted time	Error	%	Prediction	Error	%
TSP			4/1			4/1	
4/4	85.6	85.5	0.1	(0.1%)	85.9	−0.3	(−0.4%)
4/1	199.2	197.1	2.1	(1.1%)	198.9	0.3	(0.2%)
EP—class A			16/16			16/8	
16/16	258.2	255.6	2.6	(1.0%)	260.7	−2.5	(−1.0%)
FT—class A			16/16			16/16	
16/16	140.9	139.2	1.7	(1.2%)	140.0	0.9	(0.6%)
IS—class A			16/16			16/8	
16/16	271.2	253.3	17.9	(6.6%)	254.7	16.5	(6.0%)
MG—class A			16/16			16/8	
16/16	172.8	166.0	6.8	(4.0%)	168.5	4.3	(2.5%)

For each application, we show 1–2 target configurations. The second column shows the measured time running on this target configuration. The rest of the table shows the execution times predicted by LBF when run under two different actual configurations.

In each process, we keep track of the original CP and the new CP due to moving the selected procedure. We compute procedure LBF at each message exchange. At a send event, we subtract the accumulated time of the selected procedure from the CP of the sending process, and send the accumulated procedure time along with the application message. At a receive event, we add the passed procedure time to the CP value of the receiving process *before* the receive event. The value of the procedure LBF metric is the total effective CP value at the end of the program's execution. Procedure LBF only approximates the execution time with migration since we ignore many subtle issues such as global data references by the "moved" procedure. Figure 7 shows the computation of procedure LBF for a single message send. Our intent with this metric is to supply initial feedback to the programmer about the potential of a tuning alternative. A more refined prediction that incorporates shared data analysis could be run after our metric but before proceeding to a full implementation.

We created a *synthetic parallel application* (SPA) that demonstrates a workload where a single server becomes the bottleneck responding to requests from three clients. In the server, two classes of requests are processed: *servBusy1* and *servBusy2*. *ServBusy1* is the service requested by the first client and *servBusy2* is the service requested by the other two clients.

The results of computing procedure LBF for the synthetic parallel application are shown in Table V. To validate these results, we created two

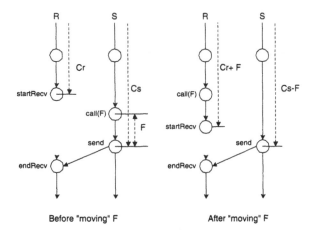

FIG. 7. Computing procedure LBF: The PAG before and after moving the procedure F. The time for the procedure F is moved from the sending process (which is on the application's critical path) to the receiving one (which is not).

modified versions of the synthetic parallel application (one with each of *servBusy1* and *servBusy2* moved from the server the clients) and measured the resulting execution time.[5] The results of the modified programs are shown in the third column of Table V. In both cases the error is small, indicating that our metric has provided good guidance to the application programmer.

For comparison to an alternative tuning option, we also show the value for the *critical path zeroing* metric (Table VI) [40]. Critical path zeroing is a metric that predicts the improvement possible due to optimally tuning the selected procedure (i.e., reducing its execution time to zero) by computing the length of the critical path resulting from setting the time of the selected procedure to zero. We compare LBF with critical path zeroing because it is

TABLE V

PROCEDURE LBF ACCURACY

Procedure	Procedure LBF	Measured time	Difference
ServBusy1	25.3	25.4	0.1 (0.4%)
ServBusy2	23.0	23.1	0.1 (0.6%)

[5] Since Harmony's shared data programming model is not yet fully implemented, we made these changes by hand.

TABLE VI

PROCEDURE LBF vs. CP ZEROING

Procedure	LBF	Improvement	CP Zeroing	Improvement
ServBusy1	25.3	17.8%	25.4	17.4%
ServBusy2	23.1	25.1%	16.1	47.5%

natural to consider improving the performance of a procedure itself as well as changing its execution place (processor) as tuning strategies.

The length of the new CP due to the movement of *servBusy1* is 25.4 and the length due to *servBusy2* is 16.1 while the length of the original CP is 30.7. With the critical path zeroing metric, we achieve almost the same benefit as tuning the procedure *servBusy1* by simply moving it from the server to the client. Likewise, we achieve over one-half the benefit of tuning the *servBusy2* procedure by moving it to the client side.

4.4 Other Sources of Information

In addition to gathering data directly from applications, it is important to incorporate performance data into the system from other sources such as the operating system or the network.

4.4.1 Operating System Instrumentation Techniques

Operating systems are another important source of data for adaptable systems. It is possible to instrument an operating system, but generally it is better if the basic instrumentation is already built into it. For example, most operating systems keep track of statistics about the virtual memory system, file system, and file cache. However, since this data is intended for use by the operating system or for system administration tools these counters are difficult to gather. To support application-oriented instrumentation systems, it is important that operating-system level counters be exposed via APIs that permit efficient access from user processes. An example of such a facility is the reading performance counters from the UNIX kernel memory via the/dev/kmem psuedo-device. Harmony (and other resource-aware meta-computing environments) run on top of commodity operating, and thus making this type of data available in current operating systems is critical.

4.4.2   *Active network monitoring*

There are two major ways to measure a network: passive monitoring and active monitoring. *Passive network monitoring* inserts measurement systems or instruments network components to observe and record the information about the traffic that passes through the network. *Active monitoring* involves injecting new traffic into the network, or changing the transmission of existing traffic. Active monitoring can gather additional information not available via passive monitoring; however, because it alters the traffic on the network it is more intrusive.

A basic type of passive monitoring for local area networks takes advantage of the fact many local area networks use broadcasts at the physical media level. For example, the *packet filter* [48] puts an Ethernet adapter into promiscuous mode and then observes all traffic on that segment. Since gathering all traffic on a network can result in an enormous amount of data, the packet filter provides a simple predicate language to filter traffic on the basis of packet content. With switched Ethernet, it is no longer possible to implement a packet filter at an arbitrary compute node. However, many switches provide a monitoring port that can be configured to receive all, or a filtered subset, of the traffic passing through the switch.

In addition, the RMON protocol [49] provides a way for hubs and switches to record and report statistics about the traffic passing through them. The RMON protocol defines a set of SNMP variables that can be extracted and displayed by any SNMP compliant monitoring station. RMON permits gathering statistics about packet counts, a matrix of traffic by sending and receiving host, and statistics about selected TCP and UDP ports.

A basic type of active monitoring is to use *internet control message protocol* (ICMP) echo packets, often called *ping* packets, to measure the network performance between two hosts. By sending an echo packet and noting the time it leaves the host and the time when it returns, it is possible to compute the average round-trip delay between hosts. By attaching a sequence number to each echo packet, estimates of network losses may be made by counting the number of lost packets. In addition, since the size of ICMP echo packets can be varied it is possible to use them to estimate the available bandwidth between hosts.

A second type of active monitoring is to exploit the time-to-live field in IP packets to discover the route taken between two hosts. This technique is used by the *traceroute* utility. All IP packets have a time-to-live field which limits the number of hops that a packet can travel. This field was originally intended to prevent packets from looping through the network when a routing error caused a cycle in the path between two hosts. At each hop in the network, the time-to-live field is decremented by 1. When the count reaches zero, the packet is dropped and an ICMP message containing the identity of the host where the packet was dropped is sent back to the originating host. By setting the time-to-live field to 1, a host can discover the first hop in routing a packet to a destination. By repeatedly incrementing the time-to-live field, a sender can discover the entire route to the desired destination. Since IP networks route traffic on a per-packet basis, it is possible that the routes taken by these probe packets may be different. However, over short periods of time, packets bound for the same destination tend to travel the same path. Like echo packets, trace-route packets can be used to gather information about the time packets take to reach their target. By comparing the return times of adjacent nodes it is possible to identify the bottleneck link between the source and destination.

Another way to estimate the delays in the network is on the basis of sending *packet pairs*, two back-to-back packets [50, 51]. The key idea of this approach is that by measuring the difference in the arrival times of the two packets it is possible to estimate the queuing delay of the bottleneck switch between the sender and receiver.

Network Weather Service [52, 53] provides dynamic resource forecasts in meta-computing environments. The service gathers the time-varying load data from a distributed set of sensors. The load data includes CPU availability and network performance (bandwidth between two nodes). Numerical models are then used to predict and forecast the load conditions for a given time frame. Their prediction models embody various stochastic techniques such as mean-based methods, median-based methods and autoregressive models. Since different estimation techniques yield the best forecasts at different times, the Network Weather Service dynamically chooses one prediction model on the basis of the error between all predictors and sampled data.

4.4.3 Hardware counters

Some performance information only can be provided efficiently with hardware support. This information includes high resolution timers, memory system performance, and internal details of processor use (such as floating point unit utilization or FLOP counts). Fortunately, many modern processors provide high-resolution performance data via special registers or memory-mapped locations.

A crucial hardware feature for instrumentation is an accurate clock. To be useful to measure fine-grained events, a clock should provide sufficient resolution so that it does not roll over during an application's execution. For example, at current processor clock rates, a 32-bit counter will roll in less than 10 seconds. Most recent micro-processors include high resolution clocks [54–57]: 64-bit clocks should be considered a basic requirement.

However, high resolution alone is not sufficient; for a clock to be useful, it must be accessible with low latency to permit measuring fine-grained events. Clock operations need to be supported by user-level instructions that execute with similar performance to register-to-register instructions. The Intel Pentium family provides a clock that meets this requirement, but SPARC v9 does not.

As more and more features are integrated on to a single chip, it is increasingly important that instrumentation be incorporated into the chips since many useful types of information are no longer visible to an external instrumentation system. Modern processors, such as the Sun UltraSPARC, Intel Pentium Pro, and IBM Power2 provide a rich collection of performance data. For example, the Pentium Pro provides access to its performance data through the *model specific registers* (MSRs). These registers include counts of memory read/writes, L1 cache misses, branches, pipeline flushes, instructions executed, pipeline stalls, misaligned memory accesses, bus locked cycles, and interrupts. The UltraSPARC, Power2, and MIPS R10000 provide similar sets of counters.

In addition to processors it is increasingly important that other system components provide instrumentation at the hardware level. For example, network interfaces and I/O systems are increasing using high speeds and higher levels of integration. One system that provided detailed system instrumentation was the IBM RP3 [58], which included a passive hardware monitor, with instrumentation built into almost every subsystem of the computer. Each device recognized its own events and passed the information through I/O pins to a *performance monitor chip* (PMC) which counts the events. The PMC also sampled memory references to provide statistics about memory usage. The capabilities were limited, however, owing to constraints on space and cost imposed on the designs.

5. Related work

Although we have tried to present much of the work in resourceware computing throughout this chapter, in this section we summarize some of the key enabling technology, and present a few projects that have looked at various aspects of the problem.

5.1 Meta-Computing and Adaptive Applications

Globus [59] and Legion [60] are major projects to build an infrastructure for meta-computing. They are trying to address various requirements to seamlessly aggregate heterogeneous computing resources. The required services include global naming, resource location and allocation, authorization, and communications. Prospero Resource Manager (PRM) [61] also provides a uniform resource access to the nodes in different administration domains so that users do not have to manage them manually. By contrast, our work concentrates on the specific problem of developing interfaces and policies to allow applications to react to their computing environment.

From the application's view, it is advantageous for the application to adjust itself to changing resource status since the application knows more than the underlying resource manager how to obtain good performance from different resources. Based on this concept, the AppLeS [62] project developed *application-centric scheduling*. AppLes allows applications to be informed of the variations in resources and presented with candidate lists of resources to use. In this system, applications are informed of resource changes and provided with a list of available resource sets. Then, each application allocates the resources based upon a customized scheduling to maximize its own performance. This is different from most other systems, which strive to enhance system-wide throughput or resource usage. The Network Weather Service [52] is used to forecast the network performance and available CPU percentage to AppLeS agents so that the applications can adapt by appropriate scheduling. Harmony differs from AppLes in that we try to optimize resource allocation between applications, whereas AppLes lets each application adapt itself independently. In addition, by providing a structured interface for applications to disclose their specific preferences, Harmony will encourage programmers to think about their needs in terms of options and their characteristics rather than as selecting from specific resource alternatives described by the system.

Dome [63] is another parallel programming model which supports application-level adaptation using load balancing and checkpointing. The load balancing for the different CPU and network performance is transparent, but the programmers are responsible for writing suitable checkpointing codes using provided interfaces.

The Odyssey [64] project also focuses on online adaptation. Odyssey gives resources, such as network bandwidth, to applications on a best-effort basis. Applications can register system callbacks to notify them when resource allocations stray outside of minimum and maximum thresholds. When the application is informed that the resource availability goes outside the requested bounds, it changes the fidelity and tries to register a revised window of tolerance. For example, when the available network bandwidth decreases, the video application can decrease the fidelity level by skipping frames, and thus displaying fewer frames per second.

EMOP [65] provides mechanisms and services (including object migration facilities) that allow applications to define their own load-balancing and communication services. Its programming model is on the basis of CORBA and uses an *object request broker* (ORB) for communications between application components. EMOP supports multiple, possibly user defined, communication protocols. Its automatic protocol selection adaptively chooses the most suitable protocol at runtime. However, the decision is made on the basis only of a predefined order. The first available protocol will be selected from an ordered list of preferred protocols. Therefore, EMOP cannot consider changing available bandwidth in choosing communication protocol. The load-balancing mechanisms are on the basis of *proxy server duality*. When the load increases, the server object acts as a proxy, and forwards the requests to other server objects. When the load decreases, it switches back to server mode, and processes the requests.

5.2 Computational Steering

Computational steering [66–69] provides a way for users to alter the behavior of an application under execution. Harmony's approach is similar in that applications provide hooks to allow their execution to be changed. Many computational steering systems are designed to allow the application semantics to be altered, for example adding a particle to a simulation, as part of a problem-solving environment, rather than for performance tuning. Also, most computational steering systems are manual in that a user is expected to make the changes to the program.

One exception to this is Autopilot [66], which allows applications to be adapted in an automated way. Sensors extract quantitative and qualitative performance data from executing applications, and provide requisite data for decision-making. Autopilot uses a fuzzy logic to automate the decision-making process. Their actuators execute the decision by changing parameter values of applications or resource management policies of underlying system. Harmony differs from Autopilot in that it tries to coordinate the use of resources by multiple applications.

5.3 Idle-Cycle Harvesting and Process Migration

Many research prototypes and practical systems have been developed to harvest those idle cycles. Condor [70] is built on the principle of distributing batch jobs around a cluster of computers. It identifies idle workstations and schedules background jobs on them. The primary rule Condor attempts to follow is that workstation owners should be able to access their machine immediately when they want it. To do this, as soon as the machine's owner returns, the background job is suspended and eventually migrated to another idle machine. This low perturbation led to successful deployment of the Condor system. For fault tolerance, Condor checkpoints jobs periodically for restoration and resumption. It also provides machine owners with the mechanisms to individually describe in what condition their machine can be considered idle and used. IBM modified Condor to produce a commercial version, Load Leveler [71]. It supports not only private desktop machines but also IBM's highly parallel machines.

Sprite [72] is another system providing process migration to use only idle machines and respecting the ownership of workstations. A migrated process is evicted when the owner reclaims their machine. The major difference from Condor is that job migration is implemented at the operating system level. The advantage is the migration overhead is much lower—a few hundred milliseconds, whereas user level evictions typically occur in a few seconds. However, the fully custom operating system kernel hinders the wide deployment and extension to the heterogeneous environment.

DQS [73] is an early non-commercial cluster computing system. Like Condor, it supports most of the existing operating systems. Different job queues are provided on the basis of architecture and group. DQS ensures the local autonomy of a private machine by suspending currently running background jobs when keyboard or mouse activities are detected. However, their emphasis is placed on distributing the jobs to different shared machine clusters in a balanced manner. Jobs can be suspended and resumed, but migration is not supported. DQS 3.0 [74], the latest version, is widely used by companies such as Boeing and Apple Computer.

Load Sharing Facility (LSF) [75] was developed to automatically queue and distribute jobs across a heterogeneous network of UNIX computers. This system was intended for much larger groups of workstation clusters consisting of thousands of machines. The basic assumption on each participating machine is that a host is by default sharable, which is opposite to the policy of Condor-like systems. Local autonomy is not respected, and hence few mechanisms are provided to protect machine owners. LSF focuses on two major goals:

● to place jobs on nodes that meet the application's requirement
● to balance the load across machine clusters to achieve better turn-around time of jobs and system utilization in the entirety.

Since job migration is not supported, the process should finish on the node it started. It also lacks the checkpointing mechanism, so remote jobs are vulnerable to node failure.

The Butler system [76] also gives users access to idle workstations. This system requires the Andrew system [77] for shared file access. The basic concept of this system is to provide transparent remote execution on idle nodes. Lack of support for job migration in Butler can lead to loss of work by remote jobs when the machine owner returns. The system will just warn the remote user, then kill the process so as not to disturb the machine owner.

There is one approach, which supports local autonomy of individual machines in a different way. The Stealth system [2] runs remote processes with lower priority to preserve the performance of local work. Thus, when the owner reclaims their machine, the remote job does not leave the node, rather keeps running with low priority. They prioritized several major resources including CPU, memory, and the file buffer cache on the MACH operating system so as not to interfere with local processes. This is similar to our fine-grain cycle stealing approach. However, lack of support for job migration can lead to extreme delay or even starvation of background jobs. Also, this system is not intended for parallel jobs.

There have been studies of specific issues involved in using idle cycles. Theimer and Lantz [78] investigated into how to find idle machines more efficiently. They found that a centralized architecture can be scaled better and can be more easily monitored, while a decentralized architecture is easier to implement. Bhatt *et al.* [79] investigated finding an optimal work size to run remotely assuming that the partial result will be lost when idle machines are reclaimed. In their cycle stealing model, too small chunks of remote work will suffer from high network overhead and too large chunks can waste cycles by losing larger partial work. While checkpointing can avoid this problem, a study showed that it should be carefully designed. Basney and Livny [80] used data from the Condor system to show that their initial matchmaking and checkpointing design could cause a bursty utilization of network bandwidth, and thus interfere with interactive processes and even unrelated remote job migrations. They suggested a better design that gives priority to applications with low network requirements. Also, this approach limits the bandwidth consumed by job placement and checkpointing for a given time period.

Immediate migration does not always satisfy machine owners since it takes a noticeable time to recover the previous state of machine such as CPU cache, I/O cache buffers and memory pages. Arpaci *et al.* [81] limited this perturbation by restricting the number of times when returning users notice disruptions on their machine to a fixed limit per day. Petrou *et al.* [82] present a more complex solution to increase the available time of idle machines. Their system predicts when a user will return on the basis of the past history and actively restores the memory-resident state in anticipation of a user returning.

General load balancing and process migration mechanisms have been studied extensively. MOSIX [83] provides load-balancing and preemptive migration for traditional UNIX processes. DEMO/MP [84], Accent [85], Locus [86], and V [87] all provide manual or semi-automated migration of processes.

5.4 Parallel Job Scheduling

Non-interactive computation-intensive applications are often found in the form of parallel programs. Since a collection of idle machines connected by a high speed network can be viewed as a virtual parallel machine, parallel computing in this environment is a natural match. However, this is far more complicated than running multiple independent sequential jobs on idle machines. Furthermore, multiple parallel jobs should be able to be served at the same time for two reasons. First, a very large pool of workstations can be wasted if only single parallel job can run at once. Second, the response time of each parallel job should be acceptable as well as the system throughput. In general, scheduling of multiple parallel programs is classified to two styles: time sharing and space sharing [88].

In *time shared scheduling*, different parallel jobs share the nodes and take turns for execution. However, global coordination across the processors are essential since independent process switching on each node will lead to large inefficiencies. In *gang scheduling*, context switches between different parallel jobs occurs simultaneously at all the processors in a synchronized manner. Thus, constituent processes(or threads) can interact at a fine granularity.

There have been extensive studies to efficiently implement gang scheduling. Ousterhout [89] suggested and evaluated a few algorithms for co-scheduling. He verified that avoiding fragmentation of slots for processes on processors are critical for system throughput. A number of variants of co-scheduling were also explored. Sbalvarro *et al.* [90] presented demand-based co-scheduling. This dynamic scheduling algorithm co-schedules the processes exchanging messages. The implicit co-scheduling work by Dessau *et al.* [91] shows that co-scheduling can be achieved implicitly by independent decisions of local schedules on the basis of the communication pattern. This study focuses more on how to immediately schedule the corresponding process and keep the communicating processes on the processors without blocking.

Space sharing partitions the nodes and executes a number of applications side by side. This has the advantage of reducing the operating system overhead on context switching [92]. However, an important constraint is that activities on one partition should not interfere with the others. Therefore, processor partitioning in a classic parallel machine needs to be aware of the interconnection architecture between processing units. The simplest way of space sharing is fixed partitioning. Fixed partitions are set by the system administrators. Certain partitions can be dedicated to a certain group of users or different job classes [93, 94]. Many commercial systems split the system into two partitions: one for interactive jobs and the other for batch jobs. This is because the responsiveness of interactive jobs should not be compromised by a heavy load of batch jobs. In spite of its simplicity, this system will suffer from internal fragmentation. Variable partitioning can change the partition size on jobs' requests. None the less, external fragmentation remains an issue because free processors left might not be enough for any queued jobs. Another issue is the scheduling decision: which job in the queue should be scheduled first. Obviously, FCFS will introduce more external fragmentation. "Shortest job first" can give better average response time, but starve long jobs. In addition, it is not easy to know the lifetime of submitted jobs in advance. Other policies such as "smaller job first" and the opposite, "longer job first" were explored and turned out to be not much better than simple FCFS scheduling. Backfilling [11] is another scheduling algorithm to reduce external fragmentation while still offering fairness to queued jobs with respect to their arrival time.

The flexibility of applications can give the scheduler more opportunity for global optimization. Many parallel programs can be written so that they can run on different number of processors. However, this does not necessarily mean that they can adapt the partition size at runtime. For these parallel jobs, the scheduler can decide the number of processors to be allocated. Fairness plays a more important role here since the decision is made mostly by the scheduler with little application involvement. Various on-line algorithms were suggested. Equipartition [95] allocates the same number of processors to all queued jobs. However, since "non-malleable" jobs cannot change the level of parallelism at runtime, all running jobs will not have the same number of processors as jobs come and go. Equipartition works as it is intended when treating "moldable" jobs that can adapt the partition size at runtime. However, too frequent reconfiguration should be avoided to limit overhead. For dynamic partitioning with moldable parallel jobs, two different schemes have been proposed: the *two-level scheduler* [96] designed at University of Washington and the *process control scheduler* [92] designed at Stanford University. An interesting study on running runtime reconfigurable parallel jobs was that by Zahorjan *et al.* [97]. They measured the job efficiency of different processor allocations and found the best configurations yielding maximum speedup at runtime. This self-tuning is on the basis of the fact that the speedup stops increasing after a certain size of the partition owing to a heavy communication overhead. Studies showed that the memory constraint should be considered since it can put a lower bound on the partition size [98] and below this lower bound, using virtual memory unacceptably degrades the parallel job performance owing to heavy paging [99].

The scheduling policies surveyed above were originally developed for dedicated parallel systems. Thus, they cannot be directly applied to the network of workstation environment where interactive jobs require a quick response time. In most such systems, local interactive processes are not controllable and should be protected from aggressive background jobs. Parallel jobs are much more difficult to run on idle machines than sequential jobs because the suspension of one constituent process can block the whole parallel job resulting in poor system usage.

There have been many studies on running parallel jobs on non-dedicated workstation pools. Pruyne and Livny [100] interfaced the Condor system and PVM [6] through CARMI (Condor Application Resource Management Interface) to support parallel programming. Their Work Distributor helped the parallel job adapt as the resources came and went. The MIST [101] project also extended PVM to use only idle machines. The distinction between the two systems is that CARMI requires a master–workers style of programming and the inclusion and exclusion of machines is handled by creation and deletion of new worker processes, whereas MIST migrates running PVM processes. Piranha [102] works similarly, but it is restricted to programs using Linda [103] tuple-space based communication, whereas CARMI and MIST can serve in a general message-passing environment. Cilk-NOW [104] also supports this adaptive parallelism for parallel programs written in Cilk. When a given workstation is not being used by its owner, the workstation automatically joins in and helps with the execution of a Cilk program. When the owner returns to work, the machine automatically retreats from the Cilk program.

The NOW project [105] investigated various aspects of running parallel jobs on a network of workstations. They developed the River system [106] which supports I/O intensive parallel applications, such as external sort, running on dynamically changing resources. Their load balancing scheme, using distributed queue and data replication, removes the drastic performance degradation of a I/O intensive parallel application due to the reduced I/O bandwidth on some nodes. Another study [81] in the NOW project investigated, through simulation, running parallel jobs and interactive sequential jobs of local users. This showed that a non-dedicated NOW cluster of 60 machines can sustain a 32-node parallel workload. Acharya *et al.* [3] also studied running adaptive parallel jobs on a non-dedicated workstation. Their experiments confirmed NOW's 2 : 1 rule in running parallel jobs. They also showed that the parallel job throughput depends on the flexibility of adaptive parallel jobs. Restricting the possible number of constituent processes to a certain number, such as a power of 2, would yield a poor performance since not all of the available nodes are used.

5.5 Local Scheduling Support by Operating Systems

The concept of "time-sharing" a machine has been widely adopted and served for a long time to provide a good response time to each process and better system utilization. For the same class of jobs, the system strives to ensure "fairness" in allocating the CPU time to existing processes. Most current UNIX systems [107, 108] use dynamic priority adjustment to achieve fair scheduling. For example, if a process releases the CPU before its time-quanta expires, it is rewarded by a temporary priority boost for the future. On the other hand, it is sometimes necessary to treat some types of processes differently or unfairly. A typical example is the case of running CPU-intensive jobs in background with interactive jobs. UNIX systems provide users with different user-level priorities so that processes that are more important can execute more frequently by using a higher priority. However, the definition of "priority" varies, depending on implementation. In addition, the priority is enforced only to CPU scheduling and thus can be compromised by competition for other resources such as memory and disk I/O.

Some systems provide special local resource scheduling for different classes of jobs. Host processes that belong to the machine owner should run as if there were no other activities. Guest processes, which are either initially intended as background jobs or moved from other machines to balance the load, can use only the time and resources which are not used by host processes. The Stealth Distributed Scheduler [2] supports this by a local scheduler that protects the performance of owner's processes. They prioritized not only CPU scheduling but also memory management and file accesses. Stealth was implemented on a network of Sun 3/50 and IBM RT workstations using a customized version of Mach 2.5.

Verghese *et al.* [109] investigated dynamic sharing of multi-user multi-processor systems. Their primary scheme is to isolate the performance of the processes belonging to the same logical entity, such as a user. Logical smaller machines named *software performance units* (SPU) were suggested to achieve two performance goals:

- *Isolation*: If the allocated resources meet the requirement of an SPU, its performance should not be degraded by the load placed to the systems by others,
- *Sharing*: If the allocated resources are less than the requirement, the SPU should be able to improve its performance utilizing idle resources.

Like Stealth, only idle time of the CPU and unused memory can be loaned to non-host SPUs and will be revoked immediately when the host SPU needs them. Their system was implemented in the Silicon Graphics IRIX operating system. Their approach requires changes to similar parts of the operating system, but their primary goal was to increase fairness to all applications, whereas our goal is to create an inherently unfair priority level for guest processes. Having logical smaller machines in this study is similar to the classic virtual machine concept developed by IBM [110]. However, the concept of virtual machines on a physical machine was developed mainly to provide an illusion of having multiple machines and running different operating systems on a single machine. The system efficiency can be limited owing to internal fragmentation resulted from lack of support for dynamic resource sharing between virtual machines.

In the current version of IRIX operating system [111], the Miser feature provides deterministic scheduling of batch jobs. Miser manages a set of resources, including logical CPUs and physical memory, that Miser batch jobs can reserve and use in preference to interactive jobs. This strategy is almost the opposite of our approach, which promotes interactive jobs.

6. Conclusions

Tying together multiple administration domains and systems is the most cost-effective method of meeting today's high-end computational demands. However, this approach poses a number of difficult challenges, most notably that of dealing with dynamic and heterogeneous environments. We feel the best way to address the issue of dynamic environments is to use a rich interface between applications and the system and to allow the system fine-grained control over application resource use. Much of our work has focused on building an API that is expressive enough to define real-world alternatives, and the scheduling infrastructure that can use this information to improve application performance. The remaining missing piece is that of deriving simple, accurate performance models. A great deal of work has been done in performance models in other domains. It remains to be seen whether this work can be directly applied to meta-computing.

ACKNOWLEDGEMENTS

We thank the other members of the Harmony Project (Bryan Buck, Hyeonsang Eom, Dejan Perkovic, Kritchalach Thitikamol) for their contributions to the project. We also thank Dr. Leana Golubchik for her insights about performance modeling and prediction. We gratefully acknowledge the sponsors of the project: NSF (awards ASC-9703212, CCR-9624803 and ACI-9711364), and DOE (Grant DE-FG02–93ER25176).

REFERENCES

[1] Mutka, M. W. and Livny, M. (1991). The available capacity of a privately owned workstation environment. *Performance Evaluation*, **12**, 269–284.

[2] Krueger, P. and Chawla, R. (1991). The Stealth distributed scheduler. *International Conference on Distributed Computing Systems (ICDCS)*, Arlington, TX, May, pp. 336–343.

[3] Acharya, A., Edjlali, G. and Saltz, J. (1997). The utility of exploiting idle workstations for parallel computation. *SIGMETRICS'97*, Seattle, WA, May, pp. 225–236.

[4] Raman, R., Livny, M. and Solomon, M. (1998). Matchmaking: distributed resource management for high throughput computing. *7th International Symposium on High-Performance Distributed Computing*, Chicago, IL, July, pp. 28–31.

[5] Czajkowski, K., Foster, I. Kesselman, C. *et al.* (1998). A resource management architecture for metacomputing systems. *IPPS/SPDP '98 Workshop on Job Scheduling Strategies for Parallel Processing*.

[6] Geist, A., Beguelin, A., Dongarra, J. *et al.* (1994). *PVM: Parallel Virtual Machine*. MIT Press, Cambridge, MA.

[7] Osterhout, J. K. (1990). Tcl: an embeddable command language. *USENIX Winter Conference*, January, pp. 133–146.

[8] Culler, D. E., Karp, R. M., Patterson, D. A. *et al.* (1993). LogP: towards a realistic model of parallel computation. *Fourth ACM SIGPLAN Symposium on Principles and Practice of Parallel Programming*, May, pp. 262–273.

[9] Padua-Perez, N. (1997). Performance analysis of relational operator execution in *N*-client 1-server DBMS architectures. Masters thesis, Computer Science department, University of Maryland.

[10] Hollingsworth, J. K. (1998). Critical path profiling of message passing and shared-memory programs. *IEEE Transactions on Parallel and Distributed Computing*, **9**(10), 1029–1040.

[11] Feitelson, D. G. and Weil, A. M. A. (1998). Utilization and predictability in scheduling the IBM SP2 with backfilling *2nd International Parallel Processing Symposium*, Orlando, Florida, April, pp. 542–546.

[12] Golubchik, L. and Lui, J. C. S. (1997). Bounding of performance measures for a threshold-based queueing system with hysteresis. *Proceedings of ACM SIGMETRICS Conference*, Seattle, WA.

[13] Lui, J. C. S. and Golubchik, L. (1999). Stochastic complement analysis of multi-server threshold queues with hysteresis. *Performance Evaluation Journal*, **35**, 19–48.

[14] Leung, M. Y.-Y., Lui, J. C.-S. and Golubchik, L. (1997). Buffer and I/O resource pre-allocation for implementing batching and buffering techniques for video-on-demand systems. *Proceedings of the International Conference on Data Engineering (ICDE '97)*, Birmingham, UK.

[15] Golubchik, L., Lui, d. S. e., Silva, J. C. S. E. and Gail, H. R. (1998). Evaluation of tradeoffs in resource management techniques for multimedia storage servers. Technical report CS-TR # 3904, University of Maryland, May.

[16] Pooley, R. and Stevens, P. (1998). *Component Based Software Engineering with UML*. Addison-Wesley, Reading, MA.

[17] Miller, B. P., Callaghan, M. D., Cargille, J. M. *et al.* (1995). The Paradyn parallel performance measurement tools. *IEEE Computer*, **28**(11), 37–46.

[18] Ryu, K. D. and Hollingsworth, J. K. (1998). Linger longer: fine-grain cycle stealing for networks of workstations. *SC'98*, Orlando, November. ACM Press.

[19] Tamches, A. and Miller, B. P. (1999). Fine-grained dynamic instrumentation of commodity operating system kernels. *3rd Symposium on Operating Systems Design and Implementation (OSDI)*, New Orleans, February.

[20] Ryu, K. D., Hollingsworth, J. K. and Keleher, P. J. (1999). Mechanisms and policies for supporting fine-grained cycle stealing. *ICS*, Rhodes, Greece, June, pp. 93–100.

[21] McDonell, K. J. (1987). Taking performance evaluation out of the "stone age." *Summer USENIX Conference*, Phoenix, AZ, June, pp. 8–12.

[22] Woo, S. C., Ohara, M., Torrie, *et al.* (1995). The SPLASH-2 Programs: characterization and methodological considerations. *Proceedings of the 22nd Annual International Symposium on Computer Architecture*, pp. 24–37.

[23] Amza, C., Cox, A., Dwarkadas, S. *et al.* (1996). TreadMarks: shared memory computing on networks of workstations. *IEEE Computer*, February, **29**(2), 18–28.

[24] Keleher, P. (1996). The relative importance of concurrent writers and weak consistency models. *ICDCS*, Hong Kong, May, pp. 91–98.

[25] Carey, M. *et al.* (1994). Shoring up persistent applications. *ACM SIGMOD*. Minneapolis, MN, 24–27 May.

[26] Zaharioudakis, M. and Carey, M. (1997). Highly concurrent cache consistency for indices in client–server database systems. *ACM SIGMOD*, Tucson, AZ, 13–15 May, pp. 50–61.

[27] Gray, J. (1993). *The Benchmark Handbook for Database and Transaction Processing Systems*, 2nd edn. Morgan Kaufmann, San Mateo, CA.

[28] Thitikamol, K. and Keleher, P. J. (1999). Active correlation tracking. *19th International Conference on Distributed Computing Systems*, June, 324–331.

[29] Keleher, P. (1996). The relative importance of concurrent writers and weak consistency models. *Proceedings of the 16th International Conference on Distributed Computing Systems*, May.

[30] Itzkovitz, A., Schuster, A., and Wolfovich, L. (1996). Thread migration and its applications in distributed shared memory systems. LPCR # 9603, Technion IIT, July.

[31] Sudo, Y., Suzuki, S., and Shibayama, S. (1997). Distributed-thread scheduling methods for reducing page-thrashing. *Proceedings of the 6th IEEE International Symposium on High Performance Distributed Computing*.

[32] Thitikamol, K. and Keleher, P. (1997). Multi-threading and remote latency in software DSMs. *17th International Conference on Distributed Computing Systems*, May.

[33] Dahlhaus, E., Johnson, D. S., Papdimitriou, C. H. *et al.* (1994). The complexity of multiterminal cuts. *SIAM Journal on Computing*, **23**, 864–894.

[34] Jarvis, R. A. and Patrick, E. A. (1973). Clustering using a similarity based on shared near neighbors. *IEEE Transactions on Computers*, **22**(11).

[35] Deelman, E. *et al.* (1998). Poems: end-to-end performance design of large parallel adaptive computational systems. *WOSP: International Workshop on Software and Performance*. Santa Fe, NM, October, pp. 18–30.

[36] Schopf, J. M. and Berman, F. (1998). Performance prediction in production environments. *IPPS/SPDP*. Orlando, FL, April. IEEE Computer Society, pp. 647–53.

[37] Yang, C.-Q. and Miller, B. P. (1988). Critical path analysis for the execution of parallel and distributed programs. *8th International Conference on Distributed Computing Systems*. San Jose, CA, June, pp. 366–375.

[38] Yang, C.-Q. and Miller, B. P. (1989). Performance measurement of parallel and distributed programs: A structured and automatic approach *IEEE Transactions on Software Engineering*, **12**, 1615–1629.

[39] Hollingsworth, J. K., Irvin, R. B. and Miller, B. P. (1991). The integration of application and system based metrics in a parallel program performance tool. *ACM SIGPLAN Symposium on Principals and Practice of Parallel Programming*, Williamsburg, VA, 21–24 April, pp. 189–200.

[40] Hollingsworth, J. K., (1996). An online computation of critical path profiling. *SPDT'96: SIGMETRICS Symposium on Parallel and Distributed Tools.* Philadelphia, PA, 22–23 May, pp. 11–20.

[41] Kohn, J. and Williams, W. (1993). ATExpert. *Journal of Parallel and Distributed Computing,* **18**(2), 205–222.

[42] Williams, W., Hoel, T. and Pase, D. (1994). The MPP Apprentice performance tool: delivering the performance of the Cray T3D. In *Programming Environments for Massively Parallel Distributed Systems.* North-Holland, Amsterdam.

[43] Pase, D. and Williams, W. (1996). A performance tool for the Cray T3D. In *Debugging and Performance Tuning of Parallel Computing Systems,* ed. M. L. Simmons *et al.,* IEEE Computer Society Press, New York, pp. 207–230.

[44] Crovella, M. E. and LeBlanc, T. J. (1993). Performance debugging using parallel performance predicates. *ACM/ONR Workshop on Parallel and Distributed Debugging,* San Diego, CA, 17–18 May, pp. 140–150.

[45] Hollingsworth, J. K. and Miller, B. P. (1993). Dynamic control of performance monitoring on large scale parallel systems. *7th ACM International Conference on Supercomputing,* Tokyo July, pp. 185–194.

[46] Eom, H. and Hollingsworth, J. K. (1998). LBF: a performance metric for program reorganization. *International Conference on Distributed Computing Systems,* May, 222–229.

[47] Bailey, D. H., Barszcz E., Barton, J. T. and Browning, D. S. (1991). The NAS parallel benchmarks. *International Journal of Supercomputer Applications,* **5**(3), 63–73.

[48] Mogul, J. C., Rashid, R. F., and Accetta, M. J. (1987). The Packet filter: an efficient mechanism for user-level network code. *11th SYMPOSIUM ON OPERATING SYSTEMS PRINCIPLES,* Austin, TX, November, pp. 39–51.

[49] Waldbusser, S. (1995). Remote network monitoring management information base, *RFC* (Request for Comments) *1757,* February IETF (Internet Engineering Task Force).

[50] Keshav, S. (1991). A control-theoretic approach to flow control. *Proceedings of SIGCOMM'91.* Zurich, Switzerland, September, pp. 3–15.

[51] Carter, R. L. and Crovella, M. E. (1996). Measuring bottleneck link speed in packet-switched networks. *Proceedings of Performance '96.* Lausanne, Switzerland, October, vol. 27–28, pp. 297–318.

[52] Wolski, R. (1997). Forecasting network performance to support dynamic scheduling using the Network Weather Service. *High Performance Distributed Computing (HPDC),* Portland, Oregon, August. IEEE Press, pp. 316–325.

[53] Wolski, R. (1997). Dynamic Forecasting Network Performance Using the Network Weather Service. TR-CS96–494, May, UCSD.

[54] Mathisen, T. (1994). Pentium secrets. *Byte,* **19**(7), 191–192.

[55] DEC (1994). *DECchip 21064 and DECchip21064A Alpha AXP Microprocessors— Hardware Reference Manual* EC-Q9ZUA-TE, June. DEC.

[56] Zagha, M., Larson, B., Turner, S. and Itzkowitz, M. (1996). Performance analysis using the MIPS R10000 performance counters. *Supercomputing,* Pittsburg, PA, November.

[57] SPARC (1994). *The Sparc Architecture Manual, Version 9.* SPARC International.

[58] Brantley, W. C., McAuliffe, K. P. and Ngo, T. A. (1989). RP3 Performance monitoring hardware. In *Instrumentation for Future Parallel Computer Systems,* ed. M. Simmons, R. Koskela, and I. Bucker, Addison-Wesley, Reading, MA, pp. 35–47.

[59] Foster, I. and Kesselman, C. (1997). Globus: a metacomputing infrastructure toolkit. *International Journal of Supercomputer Applications,* **11**(2), 115–128.

[60] Lewis, M. J. and Grimshaw, A. (1996). The core legion object model. *Proceedings of the 5th International Symposium on High Performance Distributed Computing.* Los Alamitos, CA, pp. 551–561.

61] Neuman, B. C. and Rao, S. (1993). Resource management for distributed parallel systems. *2nd Symposium on High Performance Distributed Computing*, July, pp. 316–323.

62] Berman, F. and Wolski, R. (1996). Scheduling from the perspective of the application. *15th Symposium on High Performance Distributed Computing*, Syracuse, NY, 6–9 Aug.

63] Arabe, J., Beguelin, A., Lowekamp, B. *et al.* (1995). Dome: Parallel programming in a heterogeneous multi-user environment. CMU-CS-95-137, March, Carnegie Mellon University.

64] Noble, B. D., Satyanarayanan, M., Narayanan, D. *et al.* (1997). Agile application-aware adaptation for mobility. *Proceedings of the 16th ACM Symposium on Operating Systems Principles*, Saint-Malo, France, 5–8 Oct.

65] Diwan, S. and Gannon, D. (1998). Adaptive utilization of communication and computational resources in high performance distribution systems: the EMOP approach. *7th International Symposium on High Performance Distributed Computing*, Chicago, IL, 28–31 July, pp. 2–9.

[66] Ribler, R. L., Vetter, J. S., Simitci, H. and Reed, D. A. (1998). Autopilot: adaptive control of distributed applications. *High Performance Distributed Computing*, Chicago, IL, July, pp. 172–179.

[67] Gu, W., Eisenhauer, Kraemer, G. E. *et al.* (1995). Falcon: on-line monitoring and steering of large-scale parallel programs. *Frontiers '95*, McLean, VA, 6–9 February, IEEE Press, pp. 422–429.

[68] Geist, A. G., Kohl, J. A., and Papadopoulos, P. M. (1997). CUMULVS: Providing fault tolerance, visualization, and steering of parallel applications. *International Journal of Supercomputer Applications and High Performance Computing*, **11**(3), 224–235.

[69] Parker, S. G. and Johnson, C. R. (1995). SCIRun: a scientific programming environment for computational steering. *Supercomputing*, San Diego,. November, vol. II, pp. 1419–1439.

[70] Litzkow, M., Livny, M. and Mutka, M. (1988). Condor—a hunter of idle workstations. *International Conference on Distributed Computing Systems*, June, pp. 104–111.

[71] IBM (1996). *IBM LoadLeveler: General Information*, September. IBM, Kingston, NY.

[72] Douglis, F. and Ousterhout, J. (1991). Transparent process migration: design alternatives and the sprite implementation. *Software—Practice and Experience*, **21**(8), 757–785.

[73] Green, T. and Snyder, J. (1993). DQS, a distributed queueing system. March. Florida State University.

[74] Duke, D., Green, T. and Pasko, J. (1996). Research toward a heterogeneous networked computing cluster: the distributed queueing system version 3.0. May. Florida State University,

[75] Zhou, S., Zheng, X., Wang, J. and Delisle, P. (1993). Utopia: a load sharing facility for large, heterogeneous distributed computer systems. *Software—Practice and Experience*, **23**(12), 1305–1336.

[76] Dannenberg, R. B. and Hibbard, P. G. (1985). A Butler process for resource sharing on spice machines. *ACM Transactions on Office Information Systems*, July **3**(3), 234–52.

[77] Morris, J. H., Satyanarayanan, M., Conner, M. *et al.* (1986). Andrew: a distributed personal computing environment. *Communications of the ACM*, **29**(3), 184–201.

[78] Theimer, M. M. and Lantz, K. A. (1988). Finding idle machines in a workstation-based distributed system. *8th International Conference on Distributed Computing Systems*, San Jose, CA, June, pp. 13–17.

[79] Bhatt, S. N., Chung, F. R., Leighton, K. F. T. and Rosenberg, A. L. (1997). On optimal strategies for cycle-stealing in networks of workstations. *IEEE Transactions on Computers*, **46**(5), 545–557.

[80] Basney, J. and Livny, M. (1999). Improving Goodput by co-scheduling CPU and network capacity. *International Journal of High Performance Computing Applications*, fall, **13**(3).

[81] Arpaci, R. H., Dusseau, A. C., Vahdat, A. M. *et al.* (1995). The interaction of parallel and sequential workloads on a network of workstations. *SIGMETRICS*, Ottawa, May, pp. 267–278.

[82] Petrou, D., Ghormley, D. P. and Anderson, T. E. (1996). *Predictive state restoration in desktop workstation clusters*, CSD-96–921, 5 November, University of California.

[83] Barak, A., Laden, O. and Yarom, Y. (1995). The NOW Mosix and its preemptive process migration scheme. *Bulletin of the IEEE Technical Committee on Operating Systems and Application Environments*, **7**(2), 5–11.

[84] Powell, M. L. and Miller, B. P. (1983). Process migration in DEMOS/MP. *Symposium on Operating Systems Principles*, pp. 110–119.

[85] Zayas, E. R. (1987). Attacking the process migration bottleneck. *Symposium on Operating Systems Principles*, pp. 13–24.

[86] Thiel, G. (1991). Locus operating system, a transparent system. *Computer Communications*, **14**(6), 336–346.

[87] Theimer, M. M., Lantz, K. A. and Cheriton, D. R. (1985). Premptable remote execution facilities for the V-system. *Symposium on Operating Systems Principles*, December, pp. 2–12.

[88] Feitelson, D. G. and Rudolph, L. (1995). Parallel job scheduling: issues and approaches. In *Job Scheduling Strategies for Parallel Processing*, Lecture Notes in Computer Science 949, Springer-Verlag, New York.

[89] Ousterhaut, J. K. (1982). Scheduling techniques for concurrent systems. *3rd International Conference on Distributed Computing Systems*, October, pp. 22–30.

[90] Sobalvarro, P. and Weihl, W. (1995). Demand-based coscheduling of parallel jobs on multiprogrammed multiprocessors. In *Job Scheduling Strategies for Parallel Processing*, Lecture Notes in Computer Science 949, Springer-Verlag, New York.

[91] Dusseau, A. C., Arpaci, R. H. and Culler, D. E. (1996). Effective distributed scheduling of parallel workloads. *SIGMETRICS*, Philadelphia, PA, May, pp. 25–36.

[92] Tucker, A. and Gupta, A. (1989). Process control and scheduling issues for multi-programmed shared memory multiprocessors. *12th Symposium on Operating Systems Principles*, December, pp. 159–166.

[93] Messina, P. (1993). The Concurrent Supercomputing Consortium: year 1. *IEEE Parallel and Distributed Technology*, **1**(1), 9–16.

[94] Naik, V. K., Setia, S. K. and Squillante, M. S. (1993). Scheduling of large scientific applications on the distributed shared memory multiprocessor systems. *6th SIAM Conference Parallel Processing for Scientific Computing*, August, vol. 2, pp. 174–178.

[95] Setia, S. and Tripathi, S. (1991). An analysis of several processor partitioning policies for parallel computers. CS-TR-2684, May, Department of Computer Science, University of Maryland.

[96] Zahorjan, J. and McCann, C. (1990). Processor scheduling in shared memory multiprocessors. *ACM SIGMETRICS*, May, pp. 214–255.

[97] Nguyen, T. D., Vaswani, R., and Zahorjan, J. (1996). Maximizing speedup through self-tuning of processor allocation. *Proceedings of IPPS'96*.

[98] McCann, C. and Zahorjan, J. (1995). Scheduling memory constrained jobs on distributed memory parallel computers. *ACM SIGMETRICS*, Ottawa, Ontario, Canada, pp. 208–219.

[99] Setia, S. (1995). The interaction between memory allocation and adaptive partitioning in message-passing multicomputers In *Job Scheduling Strategies for Parallel Processing*, Lecture Notes in Computer Science 949, Springer-Verlag, New York.

[100] Pruyne, J. and Livny, M. (1996). Interfacing Condor and PVM to harness the cycles of workstation clusters. *Future Generation Computer Systems*, **12**(1), 67–85.

[101] Casas, J. D., Clark, L., Galbiati, P. S. *et al.* (1995). MIST: PVM with transparent migration and checkpointing. *Annual PVM Users' Group Meeting*, Pittsburgh, PA, 7–9 May.

[102] Carriero, N., Freeman, E., Gelernter, D. and Kaminsky, D. (1995). Adaptive parallelism and Piranha. *IEEE Computer*, **28**(1), 40–59.

[103] Gelernter, D., Carriero, N. Chandran, S. and Chang, S. (1985). Parallel programming in Linda. *International Conference on Parallel Processing*, March, pp. 255–263.

[104] Blumofe, R. D. and Lisiecki, P. A. (1997). Adaptive and reliable parallel computing on networks of workstations. *USENIX Annual Technical Conference*, Anaheim, CA, 6–10 January, USENIX Association, Berkeley, CA, pp. 133–47.

[105] Anderson, T. E., Culler, D. E. and Patterson, D. A. (1995). A case for NOW (networks of workstations). *IEEE Micro*, **15**(1), 54–64.

[106] Arpaci-Dusseau, R. H., Anderson, E., Treuhaft, N. *et al.* (1999). Cluster I/O with River: making the fast case common. *IOPADS '99*, Atlanta, Georgia, May.

[107] Leffler, S., McKusick, M., Karels, M. and Quarterman, J. (1988). *4.3 BSD UNIX Operating System*. Addison-Wesley, Reading, MA.

[108] Goodheart, B. and Cox, J. (1993). *The Magic Garden Explained: The Internals of UNIX System V Release 4*. Prentice-Hall, Englewood Cliffs, NJ.

[109] Verghese, B., Gupta, A. and Rosenblum, M. (1998). Performance isolation: sharing and isolation in shared-memory multiprocessors. *ASPLOS*, San Jose, CA, October, pp. 181–192.

[110] Meyer, R. A. and Seawright, L. H. (1970). A Virtual Machine time-sharing system. *IBM Systems Journal*, **9**(3), 199–218.

[111] SiliconGraphics (1998). IRIX 6.5 Technical Brief. *www.sgi.com/software/irix6.5/techbrief.pdf*.

Knowledge Management

WILLIAM W. AGRESTI

Software Engineering and Economic Analysis Center
Mitretek Systems, Inc.
7525 Colshire Drive, McLean, VA 22102 USA

Abstract

Knowledge management (KM) is the practice of transforming the intellectual assets of an organization into business value. This chapter takes a comprehensive look at KM, structured around five key questions that organizations face: what knowledge should be managed, where is it, how does it get where it is needed, what is the role of innovation, and what is the influence of organizational culture. Addressing these questions leads naturally to the consideration of intellectual capital, communities of practice, learning, knowledge sharing, knowledge packaging, and the life cycle of knowledge in organizations. The architecture and technology components of KM systems are described as they provide capabilities for publishing, profiling, content structuring, content delivery through push and pull mechanisms, collaboration, interface and portal design, and data mining. The discussion of KM systems includes references to representative tools and technologies such as case-based reasoning and XML. The strategic and tactical design of an organizational KM program is described, including program elements, success criteria, and the role of the Chief Knowledge Officer. Many examples and references are provided. Also discussed are issues surrounding KM and observations on its future.

ADVANCES IN COMPUTERS, VOL. 53
ISBN 0-12-012153-0

171

1. Introduction

Successful companies of the 21st century will be those who do the best jobs of capturing, storing, and leveraging what their employees know [1].

When we take two everyday words, knowledge and management, and put them together, they spark an energetic reaction across the business and technology landscape. Long-established companies re-write their mission statements, vendors re-target their products, consultants launch lucrative new practice areas, and people with bright ideas create high-technology start-ups. Knowledge management (KM) addresses the most fundamental information problem as we begin a new century—how to get the right information, at the appropriate level of granularity, to the right people at the right time for decisions and actions.

The objective of this chapter is for readers to learn what KM is; how it involves people, work practices, and technology; and what it means for the success of organizations. With KM changing so rapidly, a concern is that any characterization of it will be driven by the suite of practices and tools existing when the description was written. For that reason, this chapter will stress the emerging foundational aspects of KM. The only additional expansion of the topic is to consider KM in the context of organizations. Other than stressing fundamentals and an organizational context, the goal is to paint a comprehensive picture of KM and to provide extensive references so readers can pursue specific aspects in more detail.

This first section defines knowledge management, the motivation for it, and its relationship to other improvement strategies.

1.1 Definition

Knowledge management is the practice of transforming the intellectual assets of an organization into business value [2].

The payoff in terms of business value must not imply that KM is for the private sector alone. Government agencies and other public sector organizations are attuned to the absolute necessity to understand their customers, their competitors, and their value in business terms. KM applies to any organization.

Without "intellectual" in the definition, it appears nearly to define management in general. This observation foreshadows criticisms (discussed in section 6.2) that claim either that KM is just part of management, or that all management is KM. Certainly, effective managers are addressing KM objectives if they make best use of the intellectual assets (people) in their organizations.

However, whenever we have "*resource* management"—for example, property management, time management, or financial management—we are actively focusing on that resource and paying special attention to the way it is managed. With regard to space management, suppose a company has 250 000 square feet of office space. It costs money. How will the company best manage that space to advance the business goals?

What is similar with KM is the active attention to a specific resource. KM strikes a nerve with business because it raises the question whether executives are effectively managing this resource to meet organizational objectives.

What is different with KM is that knowledge is not just another resource. It is "the" resource. More than just another competence, like manufacturing or marketing, knowledge is a meta-competence [3]. It enables a company to do manufacturing and marketing and everything else.

With space management, the company knew it had 250 000 square feet of space. How much knowledge does it have? What are the corresponding units of measure? Or is it misguided to talk about knowledge management, because knowledge is not an object that can be controlled and manipulated [3]. And unlike space, when someone in the organization gives away knowledge, she still has it.

Although the quantity of knowledge is not obvious, a company can count its employees. A big part of KM is managing people, because they certainly have knowledge. However, KM is more than managing people. It raises more focused questions:

- Is there an effective way to characterize the knowledge of the entire organization?
- How does knowledge get into the company's products and services?
- Do the employees have sufficient depth and breadth of the right kind of knowledge to keep the company competitive?

As a relatively new term, KM has many definitions; for example, see [4]. Nor is KM not the only name for this area, although is the most widely used: *intellectual capital management* or *knowledge networking* are perhaps the most popular alternatives. Other definitions of KM often provide more detail about the creation, storing, and use of knowledge. These activities are important and will be discussed in this chapter. However, whenever definitions start listing component activities, some will be left out. KM is a broad concept, so we prefer the definition above to convey that breadth.

Figure 1 is a different look at our component words, knowledge and management. It is an example of *visualization*, an important technology for supporting KM. The Theseus Institute in France created the figure using the UMAP tool from TriVium. The figure shows the result of applying the tool to the Internet with the keywords "knowledge" and "management." UMAP visualizes using a tree metaphor, with trunks and branches showing the clusters of content radiating from the position of the user, marked by "X." C. Despres and D. Chauvel of Theseus have annotated the structure with their interpretation of the themes of the tree segments. We can see the many aspects of knowledge, such as behavioral and business themes, and the relative amount of material on each aspect. With the wealth of content on the Internet, tools like UMAP help us summarize material and express semantic relationships [6].

1.2 Examples

A few examples will expand on the definition of KM and illustrate its scope. They will show the interactions of people, work practices, and technology indicative of KM. The examples raise key points that will be discussed more thoroughly later in the chapter.

Example 1 Ford Motor Company had a strong success with Taurus, the top-selling car in the US in 1992–95. When Ford was preparing for a new vehicle design cycle, it was anxious to re-create the Taurus design

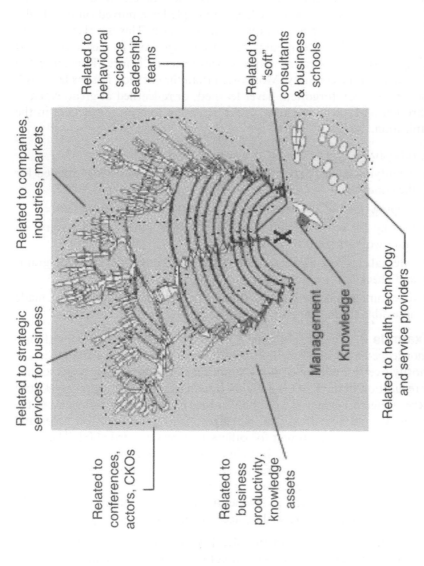

FIG. 1. Visualization of "knowledge" and "management" (© Theseus Institute. Reprinted by permission. Also published in [5]).

experience, and, it hoped, Taurus-like success in the marketplace. When it went looking to find who in the company knew the Taurus design experience, it came up empty [4].

The Ford example has been repeated countless times. Hard-won lessons and experiences are lost. Knowledgeable people have moved on or left the company. The process was not captured in any form. This is a classic case of "losing the recipe." The company cannot leverage from its past success and is likely to stumble over the same impediments as before. Repeating the earlier success is no certainty. More often than the cliched "lessons learned," we see lessons lost, forgotten, never learned, or re-learned at great expense.

Through KM, there would be active attention to critical practices in the organization:

- recognizing vehicle design as a core competence [7]
- identifying people and teams who have the key knowledge needed for the competence
- keeping track of the people involved in the successful experience
- looking for opportunities to creatively staff vehicle design teams so more workers learn the practices
- externalizing key aspects of the practice, through workflow diagrams and checklists
- determining precisely how this critical knowledge will be made accessible to the company in the future.

Example 2   The US Atlantic Command has transformed itself into a knowledge-based organization (KBO). As the largest command, it has authority over 1.2 million of the 1.5 million active duty military personnel. The realization of the KBO is a highly interactive intranet that enables staff to access reference materials, obtain distance learning, keep informed of the latest events and directives, send messages securely, and publish notes and reports directly to the intranet for others to access as needed [8]. The KBO runs itself. Staff can use capabilities in the intranet to form into workgroups with shared space for collaboration, threaded discussions, and document creation and review. Outcomes of electronic meetings can be posted immediately to the intranet. Everyone in the organization is running on the same information, which is visible, accessible, and current [9].

This example shows a comprehensive KM strategy rather than a focus on a particular problem. KM becomes a vehicle for cultural change, removing stovepipes and integrating the organization. The organization-wide intranet provides a unifying framework. Internet technology provides for sharing and accessing knowledge, with collaboration, e-mail, and search and retrieval tools. Everyone in the command sees the organization through the KBO home page, a portal for accessing knowledge resources.

Example 3   Wal-Mart is well known for its effectiveness in analyzing its data and using it to competitive advantage. Its data mining has advanced to the point of providing the rationale for changing the physical layout of stores at different times during the day. A customer shopping in the afternoon may find product displays that are different than in the morning. Transaction data shows the time of day when items are purchased at the stores. The data mining uncovers trends reflecting the changing demographics of customers and their needs during the day: information that is used to redesign store layouts.

Data mining can provide a competitive advantage to companies by discovering patterns in their masses of data. It is a vehicle for transforming data into meaningful information. It is especially effective when the data mining algorithms work across previously distinct databases. Data warehouses and smaller data marts provide an enterprise-level source for data mining, with data on advertising and promotion, in-store transactions, competitive intelligence, marketing trends, and regional demographics.

Example 4   An employee drafts an e-mail message to Ann and Bob, and hits the send button. A dialogue box opens, "It looks like Carl would be interested in this too, shall I send it to him too?" When people purchase by mail order, the company can learn about individual preferences, life style, and timing of purchases over the year. A company that knows Jim buys white button-down shirts every fall can "push" personalized offers to him at that time every year. Also possible is the company mining its data to reveal that other people who bought these shirts also purchased particular styles of ties and slacks. This "collaborative filtering" can lead to another message to Jim, with an offer on ties and slacks. The company believes it has increased the chances of a successful sale, because of its analysis. Push technology and collaborative filtering predate the world wide web.

The example shows collaborative filtering with a twist. It operates in the dynamic environment of electronic mail in an organizational intranet, so people's interests are being continually updated by the messages and documents they generate and receive. An automated agent is working behind the scenes to perform semantic analysis on e-mail, documents, and anything else it can access. The agent is generating and refining interest profiles of people. The message to send the e-mail to Carl may be prompted by having seen messages with similar content that were sent to Ann, Bob, and Carl. Perhaps the employee sending the message doesn't know Carl, but the system has identified him as someone in the organization who may share the employee's interests.

The targeted delivery of content to people who are interested in that content—and to no one else—is a goal of KM. However, any implementation must be done with great care. The system's suggestion to send the e-mail to Carl may be seen as helpful and constructive or as intrusive and time-wasting, depending on the human–computer interface design and the working styles and preferences of the employees.

Example 5   When soldiers from the US Army's 25th Infantry Division began house-to-house searches in Haiti for the first time in 1994, they had "seen" these situations before. Training simulations enabled them to practice searches in multimedia environments, re-living what the 10th Mountain Division had found in Somalia in the previous year. The experiences in Somalia were synthesized as 25 vignettes. The 25th Infantry re-encountered 24 of them in Haiti [10].

This example brings out two points:

- formal education and training have a role in KM, and should not be ignored
- multimedia can greatly enhance learning.

The troops in the example are learning how to do something that involves physical activity. More senses are involved than when a person reads a document. The learning environment tries to match the actual circumstances as much as possible, with training exercises and simulations. Exploiting the same advances used in computer games can greatly enhance the training effect through integrated sight and sound with movement through virtual spaces. The troops are reusing knowledge about physical experiences, and multimedia is needed to attempt to capture that knowledge.

The intention is that these five diverse examples will suggest the breadth of KM. They are instances of organizations taking steps to actively manage their knowledge, who has it and who needs to know it, so they can they operate more effectively and efficiently in the future.

As a provocative term, KM has been stamped on all manner of products, services, and solution strategies. Stories that would have been characterized as testimonials about process redesign or quality improvement are now KM successes. More to the point, is there something done anywhere that is not KM? After all, knowledge and information and intelligence are involved everywhere.

To explore the boundaries of KM, consider a product described as a *knowledge management scanner*, which uses optical character recognition

(OCR) to extract text from business cards [11]. Labeling a scanner as KM may appear to be stretching the point, much like using pretentious job titles in place of simple and clear ones. However, it is clearly in the spirit of KM to get critical information content into a system where it can be organized with other content and accessed not only by the individual who has the physical business card.

Accepting the scanner as a KM product raises the question whether KM subsumes all imaging applications and, while we are at it, all of information management. Vendors of document management products are now marketing KM solutions. Again, the management of documents containing information needed by an organization, providing enterprise-wide search and access, is certainly a component of KM.

For our purposes, it is not essential that we draw hard boundary lines around KM, or spend unwarranted effort mediating borderline cases. We are open to activities, practices, and products that advance the KM objective of transforming intellectual assets into business value.

1.3 Motivation

Organizations pursue KM for two primary reasons: improving the organization in general or solving a specific problem.

Organizational improvement KM is a comprehensive approach at the enterprise, line-of-business, or critical function level. Results of an IBM survey of 431 CEOs in the US and Europe show the motivation for enterprise-wide KM. Over 87% agree with the following statements [12]:

- Knowledge is critical to our competitive advantage.
- We are struggling to make personal knowledge explicit and sharable.
- It would be possible for us to leverage knowledge to a greater degree.

An organizational KM program that is responsive to the survey results would identify the critical knowledge the organization needs, and get it captured and easily accessible so it can be shared with decision-makers throughout the enterprise.

When organizational improvement is pursued at levels below the enterprise level, it is primarily because the success criteria (see section 5.5) are strongest at those intermediate levels, especially the essential senior executive sponsorship. Another reason is that the success of the entire enterprise may depend critically on one function, so fixing that function has a significant impact on the enterprise. We saw this in our example of Ford starting its KM program not for the entire enterprise but for the critical function of new vehicle development.

We are using the broad category of organizational improvement KM to include a variety of motivations related to maximizing the benefits of institutional knowledge:

- installing an infrastructure that enables workers to communicate and share documents and data
- improving the support for collaborative work teams
- mitigating worker shortage by getting the most from the current workers.
- demonstrating returns on investments in intellectual capital
- establishing a culture where knowledge sharing is valued
- enhancing the knowledge of individual workers
- stimulating innovation in the organization.

We can expand on any of these points to find a strong argument for KM. For example, the shortage of IT workers dictates that every organization must fully use the talents of the workers it has. Of the 3.5 million knowledge worker jobs in the US, 10% are unfilled [13]. The excitement of winning a large systems development job is often muted by the challenging reality of needing to hire or find outsourcing support to meet the new staffing needs.

A related motivation for KM is to compensate for lack of training among workers in general. Echo, Inc., a maker of outdoor power equipment, was motivated by no longer being able to hire staff with the same level of training as in the past. The company reacted by launching a program to capture problem-solving techniques used on the job, for re-use across the company [14].

Knowledge has outdistanced other organizational assets as a means to gain a competitive edge. Where quality had been a discriminator, it is now more often a required attribute just to be considered a player in a market. Where exclusive access to distribution channels may have provided a competitive advantage to a firm, the Internet has furnished a worldwide distribution channel so the smallest enterprise can reach individuals in their homes and businesses at virtually no cost. Through high-yielding global manufacturing capabilities, products can be readily duplicated and brought to market rapidly.

Knowledge stands alone as an asset with the potential not to be copied so as to eliminate a company's competitive advantage. Chapparal Steel's key to continuing success lies in its niche as a low-cost producer of specialty steels. Its knowledge of how to accomplish that low-cost production—embedded in its culture and practices—is the core of its distinction [15].

The global nature of competition puts a further premium on knowledge to provide the competitive edge. Being the best provider of products or services in a market defined any narrower than the entire world should bring no measure of comfort. Consider the change in Mercedes, which for decades built cars in Germany for export to the US. Now it builds cars in the US. What is being exported is not the cars but the knowledge—embedded in culture, designs, and work practices—of how to build Mercedes vehicles. The knowledge transactions are not limited to complex products. A firm from the Netherlands won a contract for facilities maintenance at New York's JFK Airport. What is coming from the Netherlands is not an army of maintenance workers, but rather exported knowledge in the forms of work practices and management practices [16].

When we claim KM is allied with business strategy, the discussion holds equally well for public sector organizations. A key trend of the last decade of the 20th century is holding public sector organizations and workers accountable to performance standards indicative of the best of the private sector. Mayor Goldsmith of Indianapolis is credited with the "Yellow Pages" test: if there are five companies offering the same service as the city government, that service will be outsourced. The Information Technology Management Reform Act (ITMRA) in the US reinforces this message of high performance expectations and measurable improvement for the US Government. KM is possibly even more challenging in the public sector, which must deal with public law, access to data through the Freedom of Information Act, a mission of service to all citizens, generally lower pay scales, no stock options, and limited bonuses or other incentives to attract and retain the best knowledge workers.

Underlying the motivation for KM to improve organizations is the singular role of knowledge as the discriminating characteristic of a successful organization. "KM isn't about helping us to know more. It's about helping us to understand." [17] Organizations launch KM programs because they want to understand the knowledge that makes them competitive and to provide for its sustainment and enhancement.

A second broad class of motivations for pursuing KM is problem solving, a targeted approach to address a problem or pursue an opportunity that has knowledge at its core. Two examples of problems that motivate a focused KM solution are *information overload* and *cycle time*.

With the wealth of information on the Internet, search engines can return millions of hits on queries. Workers need human or automated help to identify a manageable number of information sources that best match the query. Even within the context of a single organization, workers can be overwhelmed with responses from internal sources unless steps are taken through improving the search services or restructuring the content.

The internet is justifiably praised for providing much greater direct access to factual information. The trend of *disintermediation*, or Penzias' law, is that intermediaries between a person and the needed information or service will be eliminated by the market, unless real value is provided. Paradoxically, the overload of information and lack of time to digest it is frustrating people so they sometimes place increased reliance on less factual sources such as "tips" or the subjective experience of others.

There is a corresponding business trend for intermediaries to provide a value-added service, often related to providing structure to the vast information on the web. Strong recent examples include intermediaries, like the Health Information Technology Institute (HITI), which are sorting out and evaluating the extensive, often confusing, and sometimes conflicting information on the internet about treatments and therapies for medical conditions.

Companies are pressured to compress the cycle time of critical processes, to bring products and services to market more quickly. The critical paths through these processes often have delays caused by work teams waiting for necessary information to become available. KM initiatives at pharmaceutical companies are dramatically reducing the time required to get new drugs through approval by the Food and Drug Administration by redesigning the processes around the knowledge flows.

Whether the motivation is organizational improvement or problem solving, KM is not a fad. Surveys, interviews, and companies' internal investment decisions are in agreement on this point. If it were, why would top companies want to be the best at it? For example, the goal at IBM is to turn it into the world's premier knowledge management company.

In a survey of over 500 professionals, 37% see KM as "a major new strategic imperative for staying competitive" and another 43% regard KM as "a new way to add value to information inside and outside the organization" [18]. An *Information Week* survey found similar results: over 94% of the 200 IT managers surveyed consider KM strategic to their business [19].

With business success tied to knowledge, there is abundant motivation for organizations to pay explicit attention to the management of this key resource.

1.4   Relationship to Other Practices

A look at the origins of KM begins to show the relationships to other disciplines and activities. KM grew out of the increasing realization that knowledge is at the core of an organization's ability to compete. One of the earliest accounts of KM followed from the strategic planning of Roger Nelson, the Managing Partner of Ernst & Young's US consulting practice. In 1993, Nelson identified five meta-processes as the keys to success: sales, service, delivery, people, and knowledge [20]. What is striking is the prominence and visibility given to knowledge; it is no longer a supporting player. Tom Davenport and Larry Prusak were principals with E&Y, and were instrumental in developing KM in a follow-on strategic planning workshop sponsored by the firm [21].

Prusak sees the origins of KM in the ideas and trends in information management consulting, business strategy, human capital, and economics [21]. Perhaps most influential is the resource-based theory of the firm, which says ideas run the world. A firm is defined and bounded by its cognitive and decision-making culture.

From the examples it is clear that KM touches on many other management practices and information technologies. On occasion, KM is not only related, but equated with other subjects, as in

- *Isn't knowledge management just like business intelligence?* No, KM has been applied to manage information about customers, markets, and competitors because that is an application every organization has in common. KM applies to applications other than business intelligence.
- *Isn't KM really just data mining?* Data mining is very influential technique of its own, and a contributor to KM. Data mining is the use of sophisticated algorithms for detecting patterns and discovering new relationships in large databases, especially over data warehouses that combine data from different functional areas of an organization. The patterns can be exploited to provide new or improved products or services, cut costs, or increase revenues. But KM involves more than data mining because it looks at all opportunities to take advantage of the intellectual assets in an organization.

There are other cases where KM is claimed to be "just like" something else. Rather than treating each one, we will examine clusters of practices and technologies in Fig. 2, and discuss their relationships to KM.

1.4.1 The People Cluster

People are the heart of knowledge management. There is a wealth of experience relevant to KM about how people learn, how people feel about sharing what they know, how people interact in groups when they perform tasks, and the personal preferences and styles of people. KM can draw on selective portions of established behavioral sciences like psychology and sociology. There are specialty areas within those disciplines that focus on knowledge, knowledge acquisition, learning, organizational behavior, and social interaction.

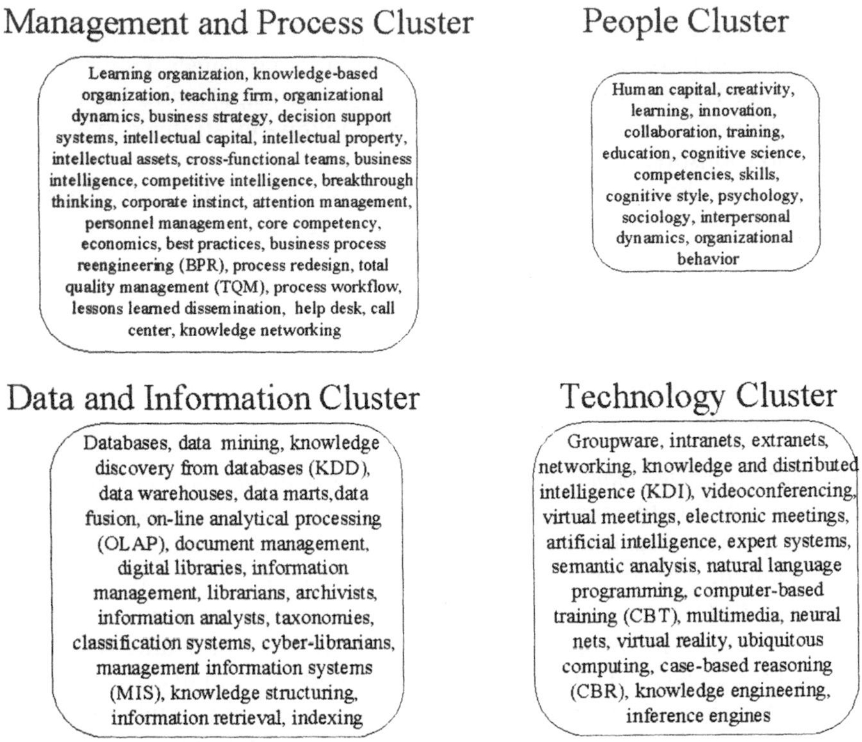

Management and Process Cluster

Learning organization, knowledge-based organization, teaching firm, organizational dynamics, business strategy, decision support systems, intellectual capital, intellectual property, intellectual assets, cross-functional teams, business intelligence, competitive intelligence, breakthrough thinking, corporate instinct, attention management, personnel management, core competency, economics, best practices, business process reengineering (BPR), process redesign, total quality management (TQM), process workflow, lessons learned dissemination, help desk, call center, knowledge networking

People Cluster

Human capital, creativity, learning, innovation, collaboration, training, education, cognitive science, competencies, skills, cognitive style, psychology, sociology, interpersonal dynamics, organizational behavior

Data and Information Cluster

Databases, data mining, knowledge discovery from databases (KDD), data warehouses, data marts, data fusion, on-line analytical processing (OLAP), document management, digital libraries, information management, librarians, archivists, information analysts, taxonomies, classification systems, cyber-librarians, management information systems (MIS), knowledge structuring, information retrieval, indexing

Technology Cluster

Groupware, intranets, extranets, networking, knowledge and distributed intelligence (KDI), videoconferencing, virtual meetings, electronic meetings, artificial intelligence, expert systems, semantic analysis, natural language programming, computer-based training (CBT), multimedia, neural nets, virtual reality, ubiquitous computing, case-based reasoning (CBR), knowledge engineering, inference engines

FIG. 2. Relationship of KM to other practices and technologies.

Education is a profession with its own associated body of knowledge and practices. When we say education is part of KM, it is not to diminish education but to recognize it as offering one route towards increasing the knowledge of people. Formal and informal education and training can be explicit elements of KM strategies.

Disciplines in this cluster have the greatest potential to impact the elusive but very influential "culture" element of KM. Organizations need to understand their culture and the messages it sends to workers about sharing or hoarding knowledge and about behaviors that are rewarded. Designers of KM programs should take advantage of available research and experiences on these subjects, which are briefly discussed in section 3.5.

1.4.2 The Management Cluster

Economists were among the earliest to explicitly consider the relationship of knowledge to their discipline. An assumption of a perfect market, which is more prominently discussed now because of buying and auctioning on the internet, is that every event becomes known instantaneously to all members of a community. People know automatically all that is relevant for their decisions. In a 1936 paper, Freidrich Hayek examined the implications for equilibrium analysis when that assumption is relaxed. How does the knowledge that people actually possess affect economic analysis? His question immediately focused attention on a core issue for KM: How do people acquire knowledge, including knowledge from experience? [22]

Hayek continued to pose questions and stimulate discussion of the links between knowledge and economics. In 1945, he recognized the critical issue of knowledge being distributed among people: "The economic problem of society is thus not merely a problem of how to allocate 'given' resources ... it is rather a problem of how to secure the best use of resources known to any of the members of society, ... it is a problem of the utilization of knowledge which is not given to anyone in its totality" [23].

With the obvious linkage between learning and knowledge, the viewpoint of the learning organization [24] is clearly related to KM. A learning organization has an ingrained culture of learning from people's experiences so they can be incorporated into a continuous cycle of improvement of products and services. A related concept is the teaching firm [25], which holds that teaching can be a model for knowledge sharing in an organization.

Help desks and call centers are examples of knowledge-intensive functions providing information on demand to a community. Those services can be greatly enhanced by automated support to enhance the service and reduce the cost. Tools can rapidly access a wide range of knowledge, including the caller's context, others who have encountered similar problems or who have similar environments, solutions to problems, and answers to questions.

KM is informally associated with total quality management (TQM) and business process reengineering (BPR) because KM has an image as following TQM and BPR as the latest management fad. The similar structure of the terms, KM and TQM, helps to reinforce a notion that KM is a fleeting notion. A concept or management approach may no longer be as popular, but, if it has substance, the value-adding aspects of it can be embedded into the culture and work practices of organizations. TQM followed this route, as characteristics such as building quality into processes became ingrained in quality organizations. Like TQM, KM has enduring principles: leveraging intellectual assets for competitive advantage. By implication, it may be the case that KM will not endure as a title, but its essential features will be woven into the fabric of the firm.

The strongest linkage between KM and TQM on substantive matters is the quality improvement that comes from capturing knowledge at all points in the product life cycle and getting that knowledge to people who can improve the product. Quality organizations want to understand how their products and services are being used, and want to capture and capitalize on information about failures and suggested improvements. The flow of information and knowledge is critical to effective quality management. In defect causal analysis, information on a defect detected anywhere in an internal process or in the field will be propagated to the source of the defect insertion so the corresponding practice can be corrected. Sun Microsystems uses its corporate intranet SunWeb to share information about "train wrecks," like discrepancies in orders, late deliveries, and dead-on-arrival products [26].

KM is similar to BPR in its attention to processes, with KM stressing the flow of knowledge necessary in work practices. Like BPR, KM has had a suite of early success stories that heighten enthusiasm. Ongoing improvement projects are being rechristened KM initiatives, even when the connection may be tenuous. But the evolution of BPR is not one that new management approaches would seek to emulate. One survey found 66 of 99 completed reengineering initiatives produced results judged as mediocre, marginal, or failed. In the opinion of those active in the genesis of BPR, it failed because it forgot about people. Reengineering "has become a word that stands for restructuring, layoffs, and too-often failed change programs" [27]. A 1994 report showed that 73% of surveyed companies said they were using BPR to eliminate jobs [27]. Where BPR was motivated by "a performance gap," now there is "an opportunity gap," to revitalize organizations to revenue growth through KM [28].

As a first-level filter for people dreaming up the newest management approach, Davenport, who started both BPR and KM, offers some advice. Ask yourself, "Would I like this management approach applied to me and my job? If yes, do it to yourself first; you'll set a great example" [27].

Several other items in the management and process cluster, such as best practices and lessons learned dissemination, are activities that can advance a KM program. Core competence is a very influential management concept of clearly identifying and nurturing those competencies that distinguish an organization and will keep it competitive over an extended timeframe. Attention management, another in the "resource" management style, argues that the really scarce resource is the attention which people are able to give, based on overwhelming competition for that attention, given the accessibility of so much through the internet [29].

1.4.3 The Data and Information Cluster

As we have seen with data mining, KM is strongly related to a wide range of practices and technologies involving data and information. The content for a KM system resides on databases, accessible over networks. Enterprise-wide document management systems provide sophisticated search algorithms, flexible document indexing, and back-up capabilities.

Librarians and information analysts have long been practising KM by providing access to information resources and finding answers from recorded material based on queries.

Advances in information search and retrieval, for example, context-sensitive search to increase relevance, are being introduced into search engines to help users of KM systems to find the right answers.

1.4.4 The Technology Cluster

Intranets and extranets provide a delivery mechanism and framework for KM capabilities like collaboration, document sharing and review, threaded discussions, and search and retrieval. KM has provided a market for semantic analysis tools that analyze a corpus of documents and enable context-sensitive search.

Artificial intelligence (AI) research has long been involved with subjects at the heart of KM: knowledge, knowledge capture, knowledge structuring, human and machine cognition, semantic networks, semantic analysis, learning, natural language processing, and inferencing mechanisms. Expert systems first introduced the notion of a knowledge base to a wide audience. The idea of automated reasoning from a body of stored knowledge has been around in AI research since the 1950s. Knowledge engineering, which predates KM and evolved independently from it, involves developing expert systems and automated support for decision making. A long-running effort, CYC, is attempting to equip a system with everyday knowledge [30], thus exploring a key area of KM, the influence of informal background knowledge. Advances in AI have provided the foundations of tool support to KM, such as help desk technology featuring case-based reasoning.

Knowledge and Distributed Intelligence (KDI) is a National Science Foundation (NSF) initiative that seeks ideas exploring the potential for Internet-like structures in which the nodes are not raw data, but rather structured intelligence [31]. Digital libraries are huge electronic repositories with sophisticated search, access, and delivery capabilities on multimedia content [32].

Figure 2 and the discussion in this section suggest that KM shares similarities with other management approaches and is intimately and intricately related to a wide array of ideas, practices, disciplines, and technology.

2.   Knowledge

"Philosophers disagree about what knowledge is, about how you get it, and even about whether there is any to be gotten." [33]

To address KM, we first need to reach a level of understanding on what it is we are attempting to manage. The quote above implies that the task will not be straightforward. Dictionary definitions describe knowledge as "all that has been perceived or grasped by the mind; the body of facts, principles accumulated by mankind" [34]. This definition succeeds in offering a first hint of two aspects of knowledge, roughly subjective and objective. This duality will persist through more detailed treatments of knowledge and will influence the style and emphasis of KM programs.

With an orientation to KM, Davenport and Prusak [4] describe knowledge as "a fluid mix of framed experience, values, contextual information, and expert insights that provides a framework for evaluating and incorporating new experiences and information."

In this section, we explore what knowledge means, the various kinds of knowledge, and its relationship to data and information.

2.1   The Meaning of Knowledge

Knowledge has been a subject of contemplation by philosophers for centuries. To Plato, knowledge was justified true belief. Over time, it became associated with more than one meaning. These multiple meanings will directly relate to issues we will face in KM. Three interpretations of what is means for a subject S to know an object X are:

- *acquaintance:* S is familiar with X
- *competence:* S is able to X
- *veracity*: S recognizes X as true information.

Knowing, in the sense of being familiar with, is fairly straightforward. It is perhaps easiest to understand when the object is another person, as in, "I know Karen." If instead, the statement were, "I know New York City," the inference by a reader or listener would be that the speaker knows a great deal if information about New York City, more than simple facts. The speaker has a strong familiarity, knowing the neighborhoods, sights, restaurants, and other information about the life of the city.

Competence is most clearly being expressed when "know" is followed immediately by "how," as in "I know how to cook"; "I know how to play the piano"; and "I know how to ride a bicycle." For KM, this kind of knowing raises the question whether the knowledge to be managed includes certain skills. An example of a skill-based competency, which requires the application of specialized knowledge in a task, is installing a local area network. Less obvious, but still in the realm of competence-oriented knowledge, is "I know about being a program chair for a scientific conference." A person expressing confidence having this knowledge knows many things, undoubtedly learned from observation of others in that position, participation as a program committee member, and personal experience performing the role herself.

Veracity is the notion of knowledge nearest to justified true belief. Our template for veracity, S recognizes X as true information, seems to confuse matters by describing a kind of knowledge in terms of information. The sense expressed here is that if one were exposed to data or purported information, he must have knowledge to recognize whether the input constitutes information (i.e., is meaningful and true) or not.

If someone is talking about chemistry and tells you, "When you combine sulfur trioxide with water, you get sulfuric acid," you may or may not have the basis of knowledge to recognize the veracity of that statement. We are beginning to see why "justified" and "belief" appear in Plato's definition. A third key concept is acceptance. If the statement were read in a chemistry book or spoken by a chemistry professor who is known to you, you might accept it as a true fact, even if you lack the knowledge on your own to recognize it as such.

Not all expressions of knowledge fit neatly into only one of the three categories. If racing car legend Richard Petty says, "I know cars," that statement draws from all three meanings of knowledge. He is certainly expressing familiarity with cars. The starkness of that statement implies someone who has a range of competencies and factual knowledge about cars: he has driven them, raced them, fixed them, torn them apart and rebuilt them, and so on. Because of our knowledge of Richard Petty, we are willing to accept that the statement is true information and that he has familiarity and competence.

A consequence of the extensive use of computers is to call into question what it means for a person to know something. Before the widespread use of instrumentation and computers in the workplace, workers had a sense of ground truth. They knew because they had direct physical contact that furnished a full range of sensory experience. Now many workers operate at a level removed from reality. They know because they see a display showing information about the physical condition, but it is a transformed sense of knowing. In the domain of manufacturing, a few people in a windowed control room look out over a vast factory space of machines and materials with no other people in sight.

This notion of mediated knowledge is explored by Zuboff, who observed operations at a pulp and paper mill. A worker, who is inside a central control room looking at a display about mill operations, comments:

> "With computerization I am further away from my job than I have ever been before. I used to listen to the sound the boiler makes and know just how it was running. I could look at the fire in the furnace and tell by its color how it was burning .... Now I only have numbers to go by. I am scared of that boiler, and I feel that I should be closer to it in order to control it." [35, pp. 200–201]

At this point, the numbers still resonate with the events and activities being measured because this worker has had the first-hand experience. What will happen if the next generation of workers has not had that direct experience, when the only realities are the numbers, when "... the action context is paved over by the data highway?" [35, p. 204] Will it be knowledge of a less satisfactory kind?

We wanted to achieve a basic sense of the meanings of knowledge, to contribute to our coverage of KM. Our expectations for absolute clarity are perhaps too high.

> Philosophy remains the residual pot of unsolved problems. To date, theories of knowledge have remained in the pot [33].

The richness and subtlety of knowledge and its meanings are the subjects of an extensive literature. Recommended next steps are *Belief, Justification, and Knowledge* [36] and *Contemporary Theories of Knowledge* [37].

The consideration of various kinds of knowledge will bring us closer to the roles of knowledge as they affect KM.

2.2   Kinds of Knowledge

If knowledge has more than one meaning, then it follows that there are attempts to partition knowledge into classes. Many of the observations about different kinds of knowledge mention one kind that is objective, rational, and associated with facts and formal learning and a second kind that is subjective, intuitive, and learned by experience. Table I presents pairs of contrasting characteristics denoting these two kinds of knowledge.

One of the earliest discussions of the duality of knowledge is by Hayek. He viewed scientific knowledge as concentrated in specific individual experts. His second kind was unorganized knowledge but absolutely

TABLE I

THE DUALITY OF KNOWLEDGE

Explicit knowledge	Tacit knowledge
Cognition/thinking/of the mind	Experience/doing/of the body
Objective	Subjective
Theoretical	Practical
Digital	Analog
Rational	Intuitive [39]
Scientific	Unorganized [23]
Focal	Background [48]
Given through formal education	Earned through experience
Specific	General [38]
Body of facts and principles	All that has been perceived or grasped [34]
Expressible in words	Hard to articulate
Easy to transmit and share	Embedded in individual experience
Expressed/declared	Implied/understood
Lends itself to automation	Resists automation
Text	Multimedia/virtual reality
Intellectual property	People
Yang	Yin [39]

essential to society. This "knowledge of particular circumstances of time and place" was distributed among all the people and routinely used by all to live and work [23].

Jensen and Mechling [38] continue this theme, describing knowledge as being either specific or general. They call attention to the implications of these two kinds of knowledge in three aspects that are important for the consideration of KM in organizations:

● distribution of both kinds of knowledge across the organization

● implications of these kinds of knowledge for decision making that takes place

● relative cost to transfer or transmit knowledge of each kind to get it to the point of decision.

This dual nature of knowledge can be viewed from the perspective of different cultures. With the success of science, Denning observes that rational knowledge is highly valued in western culture. In the east, the Upanishads recognize a higher knowledge and a lower knowledge, but sciences are part of the lower knowledge. It is not that knowledge is divided into two kinds, but rather it has a complementary nature: the rational and the intuitive, the mind and body, the yin and yang [39].

In KM, we most often use the terms explicit and tacit to represent the duality of knowledge. *Explicit knowledge* corresponds to the information that is captured in media and, thus, is easier to reuse across an organization. *Tacit knowledge* is constantly changing and highly personal, embedded in the individual experiences of the workers [40]. Organizations can best tap a worker's tacit knowledge by getting her on the team or consulting her personally.

Although many of the observations about kinds of knowledge have focused on its dual nature, it has been decomposed further. Fleck identifies six kinds of knowledge, and, relevant to KM, ties each kind to the form of embodiment which carries the information associated with it. For each of the six kinds, Table II shows an example, the primary mode of learning, and the form in which that kind of knowledge is embodied [41].

Tacit knowledge is one of the six kinds of in Table II, but explicit knowledge is not. Explicit knowledge most closely matches the table entry

TABLE II

KINDS OF KNOWLEDGE (ADAPTED FROM [41])

Kind of knowledge	Examples	Primary mode of learning	Embodied in ...
Formal knowledge	Physics, law	Formal education	Codified theories
Instrumentalities	Using a telescope or camera	Demonstration and practice	Tool use
Informal knowledge	Rules of thumb in gardening, fishing, cooking	Interaction within a specific milieu such as a laboratory or office	Verbal interaction
Contingent knowledge	What a taxicab driver needs to know about locality to get a license; the way claims are processed in a insurance firm, and the things that can go wrong	On-the-spot learning	The specific context
Tacit knowledge	Research idea that will be groundbreaking	Perception, experience	People
Meta-knowledge	How to handle an offensive comment; how to treat co-workers	Socialization	Organization or society

for formal knowledge. Instrumentalities are a kind of knowledge we saw in section 2.1 as aligned with the competence meaning of knowledge. *Contingent knowledge* captures Hayek's notion of the knowledge of time and place.

Quinn proposes a five-level knowledge hierarchy that moves us closer to the roles that knowledge fulfills in KM [42]. The "professional intellect of an organization" is captured in these five kinds of knowledge, presented in Table III in order of increasing importance to the organization [43].

A key contribution of Quinn is to rank order the kinds of knowledge, The increase in value appears logarithmic as we move up from one level to the next. It is necessary, but not sufficient, to have people with basic factual knowledge (level 1) of an area. Organizations need people who can apply that knowledge (level 2). Even more highly valued are people who have achieved true understanding (level 3) so they can see patterns and relationships that are not obvious. These first three levels are embodied (in Fleck's sense) in the people, systems, and practices of the organization. Quinn says level 4 knowledge is embodied in the culture of the organization—does it encourage and reward new ideas? Organizations with impressive credentials in the first three areas can be overrun by organizations that have nurtured the fourth. People with level 4 knowledge keep organizations out in front of the competition.

The finer granularity in the Fleck and Quinn knowledge categories is helpful when organizations look at their competencies in terms of the extent to which each kind of knowledge is present. These classifications of

TABLE III

QUINN'S PROFESSIONAL INTELLECT OF THE ORGANIZATION [42, 43]

Rank order	People with ...	Can ...
1. (Lowest)	Cognitive knowledge	Know disciplines because of education and experience
2.	Advanced skills	Apply what they know to solve problems and to address business needs
3.	Systems understanding	See relationships and interactions among disciplines
4.	Self-motivated creativity	Generate new ideas and approaches, are adaptive to changing conditions
5. (Highest)	Synthesis and trained intuition	Perceive how and why, possess instinctive feel for subtle issues and opportunities

knowledge can contribute to characterizing intellectual capital (section 3.1.2) and measuring knowledge (section 5.4).

To manage knowledge means that you first know what it is you are managing. It is no easy task to know what you know. In addition to breaking down knowledge into different kinds, another dimension is the awareness of knowledge. Awareness is important in KM, because we may be asking people what they know as a way to understand the collective knowledge in an organization. The answers may not be complete. People may be cooperating and responding truthfully, but will not say certain things because they are unconscious about even knowing them.

Figure 3 plots the two dimensions of knowledge and awareness, identifying four quadrants of interest. To probe the awareness of knowledge, we give examples for each quadrant. In two quadrants, an organization is aware of what it knows and what it doesn't:

- *Conscious knowledge*: We know how to develop systems to access legacy databases from web browser front-ends. We have done it many times.

- *Conscious lack of knowledge*: We recognize that we don't know how to develop systems with hard real-time requirements. Our staff members have not worked on those systems.

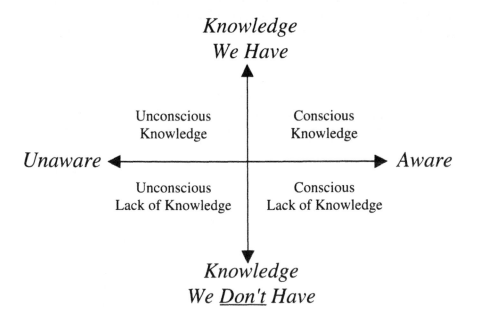

FIG. 3. Quadrants of knowledge and awareness.

When an organization lacks awareness of knowledge, there are two cases:

- *Unconscious knowledge*: One of your employees is an active volunteer in a social service agency. Your company is trying to get business from that agency. Your employee's knowledge of the agency's operations and executive staff would be very helpful in approaching the agency for work, but your organization is unaware of the valuable knowledge it has. We speculate that companies have probably failed, while unaware that the knowledge of its employees or data in its databases held the answers that would have saved it.

- *Unconscious lack of knowledge*: The examples here take the form of not knowing something, and, worse, not being aware that it was important or valuable for you to know it. For example, next week a start-up company will bring to market a product that will make a line of your business obsolete—and you didn't know that was a subject area you needed to track. A petroleum pipeline company starts laying fiber optic cable. The company is exploiting its asset, the right-of-way it has. A telecommunications company may not think to look to a petroleum company as competition. It is insufficient for companies to know who their competitors are now; companies must know who their competitors will be in the future.

2.3 Data, Information, and Knowledge

Data, information, and knowledge are frequently confused with one another, and sometimes used interchangeably. They are not interchangeable, and the relationships among them are not always simple. We saw the first glimpse of this in section 2.1, in which we saw that a person needs to have knowledge to recognize something as information.

It is common to show the three concepts in a strict hierarchy of value, with data on the bottom and knowledge at the top. Sometimes the hierarchy doesn't stop with knowledge. What is higher in value than knowledge? There are several contenders:

- *wisdom*, as in possessing the wisdom to judge when certain knowledge is relevant or not to a situation
- *understanding*, as in people may have all the knowledge in the world, but without understanding, they have nothing
- *decision*, stressing the purpose of knowledge is to contribute to decision-making
- *action*, because knowledge must be put to use to make a difference.

The hierarchy has been criticized as being too limited because it doesn't reveal where many concepts—such as instinct, intuition, perception, judgement, intelligence, and hunches—fit in with data, information, and knowledge.

At the bottom of the hierarchy, the distinction between data and information is based on information having meaning. Information is

- "data endowed with relevance and purpose" [44]
- "data passed through a human's mind and found meaningful" [45]
- "data that makes a difference" [4].

Information has been studied and analyzed from multiple viewpoints. Shannon pioneered the concept of information theory, and the information content of messages [46]. The association of information with a message is useful for our purposes because it causes attention to be focused on the receiver of the message. A discriminator between data and information is to determine whether the item had any effect. If it is information, it must inform a receiver.

Although we subscribe to the notion that information is an improvement over data, as in "we need less data and more information," the latter still does not take us very far up the value chain. An organization can be awash in both data and information and lack understanding of its business and its competitive environment.

> Information seems more like dirt than money; it's everywhere you look, accumulates into piles, and can be difficult to turn into something useful. [29].

As we move from information to knowledge, we are adding context, experience, interpretation, and reflection [4]. These sound like elements that only people can contribute, and, indeed, the distinction between information and knowledge is the role of people. We share the view that "knowledge is what knowers know" [21].

The hierarchy is useful in properly depicting the relative value of data, information, and knowledge. However, it must not be interpreted to imply that all knowledge evolves neatly from a lockstep transformation of data into information and information into knowledge [17]. This transformation does occur with data mining, in which meaningful patterns are deduced from masses of data. But knowledge comes from doing things as well as from synthesizing masses of information.

To help clarify the distinctions among data, information, and knowledge, we examine four cases in which more than one concept is present:

- *There is information associated with knowledge.* People can generate information based on their knowledge. They can convey messages that are meaningful to other people as a way to share some of what they know.

- *It takes knowledge to recognize true information.* We encountered this case in section 2.1. A related circumstance is that people can possess information and still not have knowledge. Consider an example in which you are at an airport, and see a monitor that says Flight 644 will arrive at 5:10. Someone asks you when Flight 644 will arrive. You possess information, but you lack knowledge, because you are ignorant of the reliability of the source of information. You lack justified true belief.

- *Converting data into information requires knowledge* [44]. Two people are intently watching a stock ticker. One person is seeing the ticker for the first time and does not know how to interpret the symbols and the numbers. The second person has knowledge of what the symbols and numbers mean. For the second person, the ticker has meaning; it is information to her. She sees quantities of shares of stock being traded at specified prices.

- *Taking action based on information requires more than knowledge.* Consider the same situation as in the previous case, except both people have knowledge of how to read the ticker. One person jumps from her seat and calls her broker to execute a trade. The other person stays seated wondering what he has missed. The first person had knowledge about a certain industry and market. The trading information carried additional meaning for her. She had a particular focus and frame of reference for interpreting the information as an indication of a trend, prompting her to take action.

Figure 4 shows the differences between what is known, what is communicated as information, and what is stored as data. In the figure, a person shares information about her knowledge by using a word processing application to write a report and publish it to the corporate intranet for others to use. Knowledge is personal. She has it. An automaton can be very impressive, but it doesn't have knowledge. It can possess a rich store of rules and cases, highly context-sensitive and flexible. When combined with its inferencing mechanisms, it can exhibit remarkably sophisticated behavior, including the development and execution of strategies and plans. Notable examples include Big Blue, the IBM chess-playing system that defeated the world champion. But for purposes of describing knowledge and KM in this chapter, we consider knowledge as something that people have and automata do not.

In the figure, our knowledgeable worker is generating information (messages that can be meaningful) related to her knowledge. The resulting

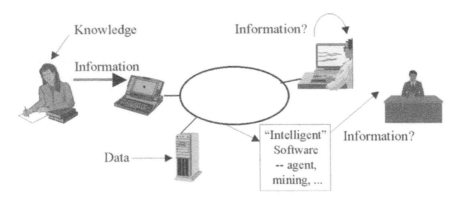

FIG. 4. Data, information, and knowledge.

artifact, the electronic version of the report, is data. Again, we acknowledge that documented reports like this are called information or knowledge elsewhere. When the information represents hard-won lessons learned from experience, it is tempting to say that knowledge is stored. But we hold that all explicitly recorded material is data. Some data is potentially more valuable to people than others.

The data (report) resides on a server, shown in Fig. 4. It has the potential to be information if it accessed and read by a person or automaton that finds meaning in the data. Storage media "carry" information associated with the knowledge [41]. Figure 4 shows a person reading the report. Now, consistent with a message being received, there is information gleaned from the data. The information is contributing to the knowledge of the person who is reading it. If the data were never read, it never would be information. If the data carried no meaning for the person (e.g., it were in a foreign language), it would not be information. Also shown is an "intelligent" software application operating on the data. It may recognize patterns in the data as information, that if read by a human may increase his knowledge.

We acknowledge that the uses of data, information, and knowledge in Figure 4 are not universally shared. Later sections will casually refer to knowledge capture and knowledge bases, but we believe Fig. 4 expresses the true roles of data, information, and knowledge. Knowledge transfer occurs when information about a person's knowledge is communicated. Databases are termed knowledge bases to reflect that the content (data) is information (if someone reads it) about precious knowledge, obtained at high cost or unique experience.

Next we examine what knowledge means in the context of organizations.

3. Knowledge and Organizations

Knowledge is the genome of a company. If you could write down all the knowledge, you could clone the company [47].

Knowledge is the centerpiece of the modern organization. The industrial era, "physical laborers processing physical resources to create tangible products," has moved into the knowledge era, "knowledge workers converting knowledge into intangible structures." [48, p. 27] The transition point may be marked as 1991, the year when "money spent on equipment to gather and process information first exceeded the money expended on equipment to gather and process physical resources." [49]

Peter Drucker described the coming knowledge-based organization in 1988. It will be filled with specialists, more like a symphony orchestra than a manufacturing company. As a "bassoonist aspires to move from second bassoon to first bassoon, and possibly from a second-rank orchestra to a first-rank one," specialists will aspire to advance within their specialty, rather than into management [44].

The specialists, or knowledge workers, "respond to events (issues, opportunities, or problems) within their domain by assembling relevant information, collaborating with others who share responsibility for or provide expert knowledge to the domain, and taking an action or making a decision" [50]. Knowledge work is ad hoc, demand driven, and creative.

Laboratories of research and development (R&D) scientists provided an early model of an organization of knowledge workers. Outside of R&D, advancement was primarily through the management chain until the 1950s. General Electric was one of the first US companies to establish a separate career path for individual professional contributors. The presence of a dual career path brought recognition to the individual contributor, but did not alter the basic hierarchical, command-and-control industrial model.

In the transition from primarily physical labor, it is not necessarily that knowledge workers are different people, but rather, "hourly workers are doing knowledge work" [51]. At Corning Glass in 1972, "2/3 of the employees chiefly used their hands and worked with things; today, 2/3 chiefly use their minds and work with concepts, data, and information" [51, p. 43].

Effectively managing knowledge workers presented a challenge to managers accustomed to a command-and-control model. In the industrial age, the worker worked with resources owned by the company, and so had to link up with those resources again to be productive. A knowledge worker does not rely on the physical resources of the employer and so is more portable [51]. Unlike the industrial model, critical knowledge on which the company depends for survival is chiefly in the knowledge workers, not in the managers. Managers cannot order about knowledge workers "like the ditch diggers or assembly-line bolt turners of yore." [52, p. 47]

In successful knowledge-based organizations, everyone takes responsibility for information, asking periodically "who in this organization depends on me for what information? And on whom, in turn, do I depend?" [44]

This section examines the critical role of knowledge in organizations by addressing five key questions:

- *What knowledge should be managed?* Not all knowledge is equally valuable, not all documents merit retention
- *Where is the critical knowledge?* Who has it in the organization, how much needed knowledge is outside the firm
- *What is the role of innovation?* Some organizations' survival depend on a steady stream of innovations
- *How does knowledge get where it is needed?* How is knowledge created, organized, and applied to benefit customers
- *What is the culture?* If knowledge sharing is not happening, the culture may be the reason.

3.1 What Knowledge Should Be Managed?

It is easy to claim that all of an organization's knowledge should be managed. Certainly anecdotes throughout this chapter illustrate that we do not always know the specific knowledge that will turn out to be valuable. But a stronger thread is that an organization must also recognize that not all of its knowledge is equally influential in its success. To the extent that managing knowledge requires an investment of time and money, organizations may conserve their discretionary investment dollars by focusing their attention on the knowledge worth managing. The prudent organization will want to understand, as specifically as possible, the knowledge that is key to its success.

Although determining what knowledge to manage is the first question in KM, it follows from a series of more basic questions every organization needs to ask itself:

- What business are you in?
- Who are your customers and competitors?
- Why do customers buy from you now? Why will they in 10 years?
- What are the distinctive competencies that will keep you competitive in 10 years?

Your answer to the last question on competencies will lead naturally to the KM question of what knowledge should be managed. By a competency we mean "a logical grouping of productive resources (human, technical, and intellectual) that represent leading-edge and differentiated thinking that is valued in the marketplace" [45]. The knowledge that enables your distinctive and core competencies must be made visible, so it can be nurtured and cultivated. It is the wellspring [15] that sustains your business.

In our Ford Motor Company example, the critical knowledge supported new vehicle development practices. At Cigna Corporation, an insurance company, knowledge is critical if it informs the fundamental decision to underwrite or not. They discovered key information was being collected but stuffed into drawers. Their KM program made it visible and accessible. Now, if a nursing home in California wants insurance, underwriters can associate the location of the nursing home to the nearest earthquake fault line and other risk factors. More important, when new information comes in, it updates the knowledge base [51].

The core knowledge is not always obvious from the company's products and services. At Kao Corporation, it is surface science, technologies for coating the surface of materials. It may not be obvious to someone seeing a list of Kao products—detergents, cosmetics, and floppy disks—that they result from a focused pursuit and manifestation of the core competence [53].

The core competence at AccessHealth, a call-in medical center, is the set of patterns it establishes over time between patients' symptoms and successful courses of action. The company built a knowledge repository that can index from a callers' symptoms to search possible conditions, and finally recommend what the caller should do next: pursue home remedies, visit a doctor, or go immediately to an emergency room. The technology investment is in the critical software to map from various combinations of symptoms to recommended courses of action. AccessHealth makes money on the reuse of that knowledge. The first 300 patterns that the company developed are used on average, over 8000 times each per year [54].

Another approach to identify the critical knowledge is to manage over a wide range of practices, but establish thresholds, as does EDS, for declaring something to be worth keeping. Ernst & Young has knowledge editors continually pruning the thousands of documents submitted to its knowledge bases, so that it can eliminate the clutter and allow the gems to shine through.

Organizations should determine what kinds of information will be most needed in the future, such as:

- lessons learned, helpful hints, "gotcha's" from current projects
- templates or checklists that can be reused easily

- procedures and processes for doing work
- expertise areas of the workers
- customer information
- reference information like estimating relationships and industry benchmark data
- proposal or other highly reused information like "boilerplate" text on corporate capabilities, recurring contract clauses.

Determining the knowledge to be managed is tied to the business strategy of the organization and becomes the basis of its intellectual capital.

3.3.1 Business Strategy

Knowledge is the linchpin in the creation of new industries and the survival of current ones. Schumpeter says new industries arise from a process of creative destruction, as innovators create new technology that is superior and causes existing firms that are based on the inferior technology to be replaced. In this way, knowledge-based corporate strategy "strikes not at the margins of the profits and outputs of the existing firms but at their foundations and their very lives." [55, p. 439] "Competitive pressures are so brutal, no outsider could ever begin to understand" [56]. Skandia Financial Services is planning to offer "competence insurance," appealing to an organization's reliance on the availability of critical knowledge resources [57].

The essential role of knowledge to business strategy is not limited to private companies. The US Army is transforming itself into an organization "that leverages its intellectual capital to better organize, train, equip, and maintain a strategic land combat Army force" [58]. The Army envisions its future as a "knowledge-centric" force [59].

The knowledge driving the business strategy may not be obvious. The Virgin Group is a presence in a range of markets, including music retailing, airlines, soft drinks, and insurance. Behind this seeming lack of focus is a corporate strategy tried to the needs of an age group, roughly teenagers through young adults. The company manages its critical knowledge of this age group, and, through lateral thinking, conceives of products and services for its target customers [60].

With knowledge so prized as the distinctive asset of a knowledge-based organization, it would seem to follow that companies should aggressively pursue legal avenues, such as patents and trademarks, to erect barriers to competition. Kodak and IBM in the US have pursued this strategy. However, knowledge-based firms are also successful when they pursue concurrently both competition and cooperation.

An example of sharing knowledge to build a market is Sun Microsystems' licensing of RISC technology to competitors. Sun started its RISC design effort in 1983, leading to its Scalable Processor Architecture (SPARC) microprocessor in 1985. Sun's license agreements allowed Fujitsu, Texas Instruments, and other competitors to implement their own designs for SPARC. In contrast, MIPS kept control of the chip design, delivering only masks to its licensees. With SPARC market share at 63%, compared to 16% for MIPS, "Sun's strategy of freely licensing its intellectual property thus appears to have been the more successful" [55, p. 447].

Companies are using knowledge-sharing alliances to achieve their strategic objectives. A survey by Booz, Allen revealed that the number of alliances has increased 25% per year since 1985. Over 20 000 alliances in the US during 1988–92 accounted for 16% of the revenues of the top US corporations. Half of the alliances were between competitors [55].

Standards are a mechanism for establishing a body of knowledge that can enhance interoperability among products and enable further knowledge creation and applications through the use of a common vocabulary. Government organizations, industry consortia, and professional societies such as the IEEE have been effective in developing standards. Part of a company's business strategy is to establish a position on proposed standards that may influence its products or services. The resulting strategy may call for the company to become active in standards development, working to reach consensus on knowledge that can be very influential in the industry.

Another way that knowledge affects business strategy is in the potential for knowledge-based products and services to generate a bandwagon effect, in which positive feedback can accelerate technologies or companies to market dominance or failure [55]. We witnessed this phenomenon in the 1980s in the decision to purchase a VHS format or Betamax format video recorder, where we were influenced by the extent to which other people have adopted the product or complementary products. We continue to see this effect with users who invest time in achieving a degree of mastery in the use of a knowledge-based product, like a software application. They are more likely to stay with that product rather than switch to a new one [61].

3.1.2 Intellectual Capital

With intellectual capital (IC), we get serious about accounting for knowledge and intellectual assets in an organization [62]. John Kenneth Galbraith coined the term intellectual capital in 1969 to account for the difference between the market value and the book value of a company. This difference is most visible when a company is being acquired. In the volatile world of internet-related companies, we have seen millions of dollars spent to acquire companies that are short on tangible assets of "bricks and mortar" and production capital. What is being bought is the potential for creating new value, and this concept is precisely what Galbraith meant by IC.

Not as visible as acquisitions, but equally striking, are the drastic differences between the market value and book value for today's companies. Using traditional accounting methods, 95% of the 1999 market value of Microsoft cannot be accounted for. Perhaps more surprising is the result of the same calculation for a company known to have extensive physical assets: for the international petroleum firm BP, the figure is 93% [63]. Overall, the median market-to-book value ratio of US public corporations increased from 0.82 in 1973 to 1.692 in 1992 [64]. Because of the magnitude difference between market value and book value and the importance of knowledge to companies and their survival, IC needs more thorough analysis, accounting, and management. "Intellectual capital is at least as important as financial in providing an accurate picture of an enterprise's true worth" [65].

These hidden IC assets have never been entirely unknown. In qualitative terms, Caterpillar has intellectual assets such as a well-known brand (Cat), a dealership network, and the knowledge of its workers [60]. The motivation for understanding intellectual capital is simply to account for these substantial hidden assets and give them visibility so they can be managed. Sveiby attributes the failure of the international advertising firm Saatchi and Saatchi to the loss of intangible assets [48]. "The business imperative is to manage intellectual capital or die!" [60]

Skandia Financial Services has been at the forefront of attempts to account for its intellectual capital, as emphasized by its issue of an IC supplement to its 1994 annual report. The basis for Skandia's IC accounting is to break it down into human capital and structural capital. Human capital is obviously the employees, and the competencies, talents, and loyalties they bring to their positions. The challenge with managing human capital is the connection with the company: "our assets have legs; they walk home every day" [65].

Structural capital is the IC that the company still has when the employees go home at night. The most obvious element of structural capital is intellectual property owned by the company through legal mechanisms such as patents, trademarks, brands, and copyrights. Less obvious is structural capital in the form of prices, practices, and procedures that may be documented or not, but are embedded in the company's way of doing business.

Other elements of structural capital are the knowledge of customers, relationships with them, delivery channels, and relationships with partners and suppliers. For individual elements of structural capital, we may have quantitative evidence of its value. Achieving a sale with a new customer is estimated to be 20 times more expensive than achieving the same sale with an existing customer. The approach at Skandia was to break down IC into elements that could be described in sufficient detail to suggest metrics or indicators of the value to the firm.

As indicators of its internal structural capital, Skandia uses gross insurance premiums per employee, administrative expenses as a percentage of gross insurance premiums, and information technology (IT) employees as a percentage of all employees. Indicators like these relate to the efficiency of the internal operations. Other metrics quantify the growth and renewal of IC, and its stability. For example, measures of human capital are counts of knowledge workers in various categories, the levels of education and experience, and the amount invested in the training and education of workers. Canadian Imperial Bank of Commerce (CIBC) measures human capital in the context of 48 model competencies [49].

Measures of external structural capital include counts of customers, the length of customer relationships, customer satisfaction scores, the percentage of income from new revenue streams, and the timeliness of complaint resolution [48]. Key to all these measures is not to focus excessively on the totals, but rather on the trends—are they moving in the right direction over time?

Is more intellectual capital always better? In an empirical study of 128 UK manufacturing firms, the most significant result was that asset complementarity is more crucial than particular assets. An organization can score high in knowledge assets, yet fail because it lacks sufficient strength in complementary assets. Companies were more successful when they had greater alignment between their functional assets (production costs, customer service, and distribution networks) and their knowledge assets (manufacturing know-how, skill in research and design, and understanding of the market) [66]. So although organizations will want to see the IC metric trends moving in the right direction, it is more important that the IC metrics make sense in the context of a broader range of measures, such as the balanced scorecard [67].

Other attempts to account for IC have been influenced by the Skandia "Business Navigator." CIBC also assesses IC as three components: individual skills needed to meet customers' needs (human capital), organizational capabilities demanded by the market (structural capital), and the strength of its franchise (customer capital) [49]. Similar to Skandia, Celemi has developed an "Intangible Assets Monitor." [48]

One of the threads in second-generation IC measurement is to integrate over the set of individual metrics to form a single IC bottom line. The IC-index of Roos is a weighted composition of four separate indices for relationship capital, human capital, infrastructure capital, and innovation capital [60]. Once again, instead of focusing intently on the meaning of the aggregate number itself, track how it changes over time.

An overarching goal with IC is to transform human capital into structural capital. This is a recurring theme in KM. We will see a variation of it when we discuss transforming tacit knowledge into explicit knowledge in section 3.4.2. In IC terms, human capital is the source of innovation and competence, but it is not an asset the company can own. Structural capital, on the other hand, can be owned; it belongs to shareholders.

An example of transforming human capital into structural capital is our investment at Mitretek Systems to develop an institutional practice in the assessment of large software designs. There was recurring work, but the effectiveness of its execution depended strongly on the individuals assigned. Pooling the experiences of the practitioners, we developed a tool-supported practice that is partially independent of the individuals. We captured the essence of the practice in procedural steps, guidance information, and software tools. Workers with less direct experience are able to execute the work better because the structural capital gives them leverage to build on the embedded experience of previous workers. This design assessment instrument is now structural capital of the company. Through this transformation, we have new IC that can be managed. As with other structural capital, it required human capital to create it.

Although the focus here is on hidden assets, companies should also manage more formal intellectual property. To manage its portfolio of patents, Dow Chemical introduced a management process so it would ensure attention to its intellectual assets: [49]

- "Define the role of knowledge and innovation in your business
- Assess your competitor's strategies and knowledge assets
- Classify your portfolio to show patents being used
- Determine the value of your assets, the cost to maintain them, and the investment needed to maximize their value
- Based on the evaluation, decide whether to keep them, sell them, or abandon them
- Identify gaps that must be filled to defend against competitors
- Assemble your new portfolio, and start the process over."

When an organization understands the knowledge it should be managing, it must identify where that knowledge resides.

3.2 Where is the Critical Knowledge?

There are several aspects to understanding where critical knowledge is, so it can be managed. The key knowledge may be in your own organization, or outside it, for example with suppliers or customers. It may be knowledge your organization should have but does not. For the knowledge in your organization, it may be with individuals or instilled into the work practices. Information about the knowledge, in the sense of section 2.3, may be explicit in tools, guidance documents, or products. We will first examine the distribution of key knowledge between your organization and your partners.

A valuable aid to determining where key knowledge resides is to build a knowledge supply chain, which starts with the customer and the product or service it gets from your organization. Where did the knowledge in that end product or service come from? By tracing back from the customer into your organization, you identify the knowledge contributed at each stage. When you are done, you will have identified the sources of the knowledge, and understand your reliance, if any, on external partners for critical knowledge. It is important to understand the extent to which you have control over sources of knowledge critical to your business.

IBM used strategic knowledge links to help transform it from a mainframe hardware supplier to a computer and telecommunications provider of networks for transmitting voice, data, and images. More than a dozen alliances forged by IBM USA provided needed knowledge in molecular simulation software, image processing, insurance transactions processing, and signal converters for fiber optic communications [68].

The use of nearly synonymous terms, knowledge link and learning alliance, calls attention to whether any learning is involved. A company may set up a *knowledge link* with the intention of remaining dependent on an outside entity for the needed knowledge. In contrast, a *learning alliance* is intended to transfer knowledge so the company will be left with an in-house capability when the alliance concludes. Organizations must be clear which relationship they are pursuing. If the objective is to set up a learning alliance, include activities and time in the budget for employees to work along with the partner entity so knowledge is transferred.

Certain partnerships fall somewhere in between—a degree of learning takes place, but the organization continues the alliance. The reasons vary, and may include establishing a higher level internal competency is not in alignment with the core business, the partner relationship is more cost-effective or provides more flexibility, or the knowledge is scarce.

There are additional reasons why knowledge transfer may not occur across the boundaries of the alliance. In international alliances, a lack of intercultural skills, including language competence, may inhibit learning. It may not be career enhancing for personnel to participate in the alliance, so the people whose participation would most benefit the organization are not involved [69].

When organizations are tightly defined and staffed around core competencies, it increases the likelihood that external partners will be needed. The pattern of relationships is called a *shamrock organization*, in which essential executives and knowledge workers in core competencies are supplemented by contracting to an array of leaf organizations [70]. The shamrock can succeed through the tight integration of the partner/providers. As an example of cluster around a dominant firm, Nintendo manages a network of 30 principal hardware subcontractors and 150 software developers [55]. The core management retains the flexibility to hold leaf organizations to high levels of accountability and to select the best organizations to meet its needs. At the same time, vulnerabilities exist when capable and reliable knowledge partners are scarce. When Motorola had 3000 job openings at its Chicago plant, it found that only 1 applicant in 10 met its requirements of seventh grade mathematics and ninth grade reading. "We worried about the other nine, because they went to work for our suppliers. That's a quality problem for us." [71]

Company alliances are only a part of the knowledge web. Partnerships with government institutes and universities, including spin-offs and incubation centers for small start-ups, establish linkages between sources of innovative ideas and the development of products and services to meet real needs.

Critical knowledge for your organization may be in universities. Your ability to sustain success may be driven by your ability to attract and retain knowledge workers with particular skills. If you require people with specialized knowledge typically associated with graduate or professional education, you may face difficult employment markets. Of particular concern are the high salaries offered by industry to attract students immediately after bachelor's degrees, or sometimes, before their degree is complete. A consequence is fewer students entering fulltime graduate school, which decreases the capacity of universities to conduct research because they lack the graduate research assistants. Companies hoping to hire students with graduate degrees find fewer students to hire. This critical situation has been the subject of task forces and conferences to find strategies to correct it [72].

> Without providers of scientific and technical knowledge such as universities and research institutes, most new industries, particularly knowledge-intensive industries, would fail to develop [55, p. 440].

3.2.1 Organizational Structure

Drucker [44] traces the fundamental changes in organizational structure since the beginning of the modern business enterprise. Until that time, management implied ownership. The first evolutionary change pulled apart these roles in the restructuring of US railroads and steel industries, and we began to see managers who were not owners. The second change was to the command-and-control organization that has continued to evolve from the first instances at DuPont and General Motors through to the late 20th century.

The transition from the industrial model occurred when data began to be used for information rather than control. Companies discovered layers of middle managers, busy relaying data up and down the line, who were no longer needed. Corporate leaders found the information they needed in the knowledgeable workers at the operational front lines of the company. So, the third evolutionary change is flattening the hierarchical divisions and departments into an information-based organization of knowledge specialists [44]. When there have been only three major evolutionary changes, and knowledge has been the decisive factor in one of them, then clearly knowledge has been very influential in organizational structure.

Exemplifying the third change, BP is a flat, lean organization with $70 billion in revenues. No one stands between the general managers of the 90 business units and the 9 operating executives who oversee the business with the CEO. The headquarters staff of the company and its business units was reduced from 4000 in 1989 to 350 in 1997 [73].

Hayek foresaw the inflexibility of the industrial model and the influential role of knowledge:

> We cannot expect that this problem [of rapid adaptation to changes] will be solved by first communicating all this knowledge to a central board which, after integrating all knowledge, issues its orders. [22]

This rapid adaptation necessarily must rely on some form of decentralization of decision-making. In a flexible and agile organization, knowledge must be distributed so that the decision-making authority and the capacity to act are collocated [74].

Knowledge-based organizations have inverted the hierarchical structure to be successful, tailoring their structure to the way "professional intellect creates value" [43, p. 195]. In bureaucracies, higher levels possessed greater information. In a knowledge-based organization, knowledge will be primarily at the bottom. Knowledge workers will be the keepers of the organization's most detailed knowledge of the customers' needs and interests [44].

> If knowledge workers are any good at all, they soon learn more about what they are doing on a specific project than their boss. Knowledge work

inherently has a large component of self-direction and teamwork and is hampered by remote control from distant bosses. [52, p. 47]

Recalling our discussion of different kinds of knowledge and competencies, we may moderate the claim that all knowledge is at the bottom of the organization. As Sveiby observes, managers and professionals have different competencies—managers use organizational competence, professionals use professional competence. There is a place even in knowledge-based organizations for "finders, grinders, and minders," [48]—those with competencies, respectively, to get business, execute the tasking, and manage its execution.

A knowledge-based company should be organized around "the source of knowledge, where the knowledge is modified for customer use, and the direction of the flow of this knowledge from point to point" [42]. In a *starburst origination*, the critical knowledge is concentrated in a group of experts who define products, which are distributed to others, who deliver them to customers. The core knowledge flows from the center to the outer nodes of the organization. Even in a starburst organization, such as a financial services firm, true KM recognizes the benefit of the information feeding back from the point of value where the company's representatives work with customers.

Medical practices have characteristics of model knowledge-based organizations. There is high autonomy in the work of physicians in a hospital. The sources of knowledge are the nodes of the organization, coincident with the place knowledge is modified for customer use. As a patient's case requires specialized knowledge of other experts, they are consulted, setting up a knowledge-web organizational structure [42].

The KM strategy and program (see section 5) must resonate with the organizational structure. The core business of NovaCare is with the 5000 occupational, physical, and speech therapists who minister to individual patients at 2090 locations in 40 states. They have a database with relevant company rules, customer information, and regional resources information. They exercise high levels of autonomy in patient care, with a database of best practices, built up from tracking their own therapeutic-care practices in 10 minute blocks of time. The executives of the organization are committed to serving the therapists by removing administrative roadblocks and time wasters, like billing, scheduling, and marketing. This inverted pyramid works because the individual experts/practitioners are the keepers of the corporate knowledge; they can operate independently and individually [43].

Consulting firms share similarities with medical practices in the location of expertise with the practitioners who work with customers. The web structure shows the linking of domain knowledge, market knowledge, functional knowledge, and other specialties into teams that are formed dynamically to meet customer needs and business opportunities. Ideally the entire resources of the firm are brought to bear as needed, with the potential knowledge links activated to instantiate the right team for the assignment.

Although the organizational structure shows formal relationships, it does not capture the social networks. Stephenson believes, "Real working knowledge lies in the relationships between employees" [75]. She looks at the ways work gets accomplished in organizations. Her mapping of the actual social networks can reveal shortcomings in communication among individuals and teams that need to have stronger interactions [76].

3.2.2 Communities of Practice

In this section, we examine two key aspects concerning where knowledge resides: what is the appropriate level of granularity of the unit with the knowledge, and is the knowledge in tacit or explicit forms. Much of the discussion relates the locus of knowledge and expertise with various groups of workers, especially communities and teams. To provide a basis for this discussion, we use Curley's definitions [77]:

- *community*: a self-organizing structure held in place by relationships of trust
- *team*: a small group of identifiable individuals committed to a common, clear, measurable, and short-term goal that requires interdependent effort.

A community of practice (COP) is the collection of people and work groups performing the same or similar work activities. The scope of a COP may be an organization, for example, a COP consisting of all the people who perform cost–benefit analyses or all the work teams who conduct software process audits. A COP may be organized through a professional society, such as people who are directors of college computer centers.

A COP, in addition to an individual worker, is a unit with which we associate knowledge and competence in an organization. An organization will want to understand its COPs to assess the depth and breadth of its knowledge and its capacity to deliver products and services. Organizations want confidence that critical knowledge can be counted on to provide competitive advantage. To provide that confidence, the knowledge must be instilled in the routine practices of the organization [78], rather than tied to individuals.[1] When an organization has attained this degree of embedding

---

[1] Although they are more stable, even groups of practitioners are vulnerable. When Booz Allen perceived it was behind in KM, it hired 15 staff from McKinsey [79].

its ways of doing business into the company culture, it can be very open about its operations. Chapparal Steel has such confidence in its culture and work practices that it gives plant tours without hesitation. It has reached the stage in which it "... can show competitors everything and give away nothing" [79]

Knowledge is in the COPs because that is where the learning takes place. People are learning when they work. They can be nurtured in their professional growth through assignments in COPs. Curley [77] calls this "time to talent," the time needed to take novices and make them experts. Managers' staffing decisions play a crucial role in the professional growth of individuals and the robustness of COPs. In this sense, skilled knowledge managers predate KM. They have been practising KM without being aware of it when they artfully staff their teams so there is a blend of expert knowledge, while providing career-enhancing challenges at the same time.

Knowledge managers are conscious of the potential impact of losing workers with critical knowledge. As a mitigating step, companies develop rotational assignments through COPs and teams to provide cross training. The job rotation, learning-by-doing, can reduce the need for formal training and enhance the ability of work groups to solve problems and generate new ideas because of the diversity of viewpoints. From the knowledge workers' perspective, these crossover experiences can naturally expand the depth and breadth of their knowledge, while providing opportunities to grow their leadership and organizational skills. Individuals can increase their versatility, visibility, and contribution to the firm.

Closely related to a COP is a community of expertise (COE), a collection of individuals who have in common a high level of knowledge in a particular subject area. One simple strategy to identify expertise in individuals, a starting point for COEs, is to follow a practice akin to "six degrees of separation." Begin by asking people about the individuals they call when they have a question about database technology. Then go to the people mentioned, and ask them. You will soon reach the point where you are only hearing names you have heard before. This will be a first cut at the COE on database technology in your organization. Then move on to a new topic.

Clearly, this works best with smaller organizations, although, if the objective is to identify the top handful of people in a subject area, it can work in large corporations as well. In the process, you will reveal the informal networks present in the organization. If you also ask, "how did you learn about the people you are naming, and why do you consider them to be knowledgeable about the subject", you will also learn more about people who share knowledge and about ways people gain visibility for their expertise.

The COEs for large companies are virtual groups that literally span the world. The technology groups at Computer Sciences Corporation (CSC) most often work electronically, but then convene somewhere in the world for face-to-face interaction. At these sessions, they may develop the corporate position on new software architectures, while, important for KM culture, they build personal relationships that will sustain their community over the electronic interchanges in the coming months.

IBM has competency networks, showing the core team and extended team for each core competency of the corporation [45]. Each network is responsible for creating, evaluating, and structuring the IC that gets added to the database, and then sharing it with the rest of the company.

A knowledge audit is a more formal way of identifying COEs. The audit typically is conducted by using a data collection instrument, for example, a questionnaire. To enhance participation, it should be brief, no more than 5–6 questions. With an interactive intranet in an organization (see section 4), conducting an audit can be relatively easy.

A knowledge audit raises questions about how to interpret the results. People vary considerably in their own perception of what they know, what they do, and how well they do it. To help with consistent terminology, and to suggest the appropriate level of detail that is intended, it is desirable to show a few examples, or have lists of options from which to choose. Again, when implemented electronically, features such as pull-down lists can be very helpful. The most difficult aspect of a knowledge audit is its maintenance. It gets out-of-date as soon as it is completed. People gain new experiences, change work assignments, and begin to lose currency in areas in which they no longer work.

This situation is reminiscent of the corporate resume initiatives in which employees are told to get their resumes into a central system, but there is no procedure for updating the resumes or, sometimes, even accessing the system. The importance of knowledge and the nature of the work practices in certain organizations, such as consulting firms, have caused them to maintain up-to-date resumes accessible across the firm. A technique at Ernst & Young, introduced when the individual resume initiative was flagging, was to have supervisors be responsible for the accuracy and currency of expertise characterization for the people they supervise. But for many other companies, resume systems have not worked. From a KM viewpoint, they are not always essential. There are other approaches to identify individual expertise, such as using tools that will mine your documents and e-mail to identify themes in your explicit products, and associate those themes with the authors. The advantages lie in the automation and the currency of the information. Accuracy is improved when a human edits the raw results.

More important than a resume system is knowing the COPs and COEs and how to reach them.

A variation on a knowledge audit is a knowledge map. Where an audit is a snapshot of the knowledge in COPs at a point in time, a knowledge map should be continually evolving and current. A knowledge map allows users to navigate, stressing the relationships among the "islands of knowledge" [49]. A map uses a graphic showing the connections among the areas of expertise, whereas the audit typically results in a directory of expertise. Both the knowledge audit and the knowledge map can assist with exposing gaps; that is, areas in which the organization believed it had (more) strength. With the visibility provided by the audit or map, the organization can take corrective action without having the weakness uncovered during work with a customer.

When knowledge maps are implemented as hierarchical directories, they resemble the familiar structure of the Yahoo or Open Directory home pages. A user clicks through pages to find more detailed content in a subject. Xerox Palo Alto Research Center (PARC) advanced the use of a hyperbolic tree to give a fisheye view that helps a user maintain perspective with large hierarchies [80]. Figure 5 shows the evolution of the PARC research in a commercial product from a Xerox company, Inxight Software, Inc. Figure 5a shows knowledge about the San Francisco Museum of Modern Art organized by Inxight's Site Lens. When the user is interested in public programs, and moves that named object to the center, the structure moves as shown in Fig. 5b. Note that all the structure and contents are still there. The direct manipulation by the user can make selected information very prominent, while other content recedes into the background. The user can click on any node to obtain detailed information. In addition to mapping the content of a web site, a knowledge map similar to Figure 5 can be used to represent the interrelated knowledge of COPs in an organization.

The organization benefits when a COP captures its work practices explicitly. This transformation from tacit to explicit makes the work practices more consistent and repeatable. Good Samaritan Regional Medical Center, a 650-bed teaching hospital in Phoenix, developed a computer alert system that pulled together information from a patient's medical records, lab results, and prescriptions. It took about 400 person hours to develop its systems, using the Discern Expert tool from Cerner Corp. An alert may signal something that was forgotten, such as routine medication that should have been prescribed but wasn't. The professional staff, not a separate team of programmers, was able to use the tool to capture its own rules for prescribing medication under different conditions. In a 6-month study involving 1116 alerts, it was almost evenly split when the

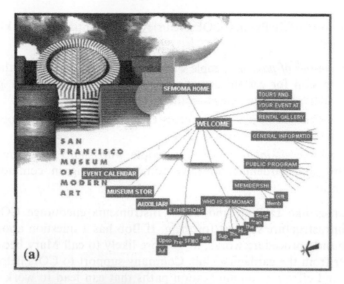

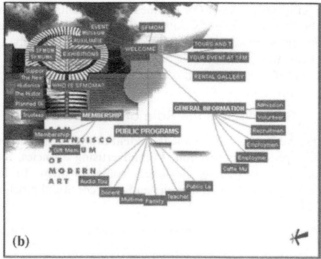

FIG. 5. (a) Knowledge map. San Francisco Museum of Modern Art. (b) Using Site Lens—shifting the focus to specific content. (Both figures © Inxight Software, Inc. Reprinted by permission).

doctor agreed with the recommendation produced by the system or overruled it. The point is that the work practices of the professional staff have been enhanced by the complementary use of tacit and explicit knowledge [81].

In addition to COPs and COEs, Curley [77] identifies other kinds of communities:

- *communities of passion:* people who share a high degree of enthusiasm and passion for certain activities, such as trading online or playing particular adventure games on the internet
- *communities of purpose:* task forces that come together in a period of time to do a job and then disband
- *communities of interest (COIs):* people who share an interest in a hobby, like gardening, or have some something in common, like parenting.

Companies like DuPont and Texas Instruments encourage COIs and provide infrastructure support for them. If Bob has a question about how the purchasing procedure works, he is more likely to call Mary because he knows her from the gardening club. Company support to COIs helps build informal and effective communication paths that can lead to work getting done more efficiently. An EDS business unit wants to know about employees' hobbies and interests outside of work. When it learned that a new business prospect was an avid motorcyclist, it quickly identified employees who were members of the same club and could build a relationship that led to new business.

3.3   What is the Role of Innovation?

Every organization must determine the extent to which its competitiveness and survival depend on innovation. For advertising agencies, innovation and creativity are the reasons customers come to them. In fast-paced technology markets, companies may depend on a continual pipeline of new products.

> When our new cellular telephone comes out, we can get $3000 for it. After 6 months, our competitors have reverse-engineered their clones. Now we have to sell ours for $1500. At the end of another 6 months—or a total of 12 months—we feel lucky if we can give the phones away for the service contract. This means that we have to re-capture all of our investment in the first 18 months, including the R&D, production, sales, profit, plus enough to fund the R&D for the next wave of telephones [82].

Innovation sounds as though every organization should want a high level of it, but your success may not be based on innovation. The Gartner Group characterizes organizations as being one of three types with respect to new technology, ranging from early adopters on the leading edge, to risk-averse organizations who want technology that is mature. A similar classification is possible regarding the role of innovation in achieving the goals of the organization. For particular organizations, success either—

- depends on a steady stream of new products or services, or
- requires innovation in applications and implementations, with only infrequent innovations at the level of new products or services, or
- does not require innovation

Other attributes may be more important than innovation:

You don't want a creative surgeon, you don't want an accountant to create a whole new accounting system for you. You want people who can deliver a particular skill in a timely fashion, at the state of the art, every single time. [42]

Although you may not want a creative surgeon, people are routinely advised when searching for the best care, to look for teaching hospitals, where there are leading-edge practitioners.

Innovation may be important to your survival, but you may cultivate it through outsourcing or partnerships. Although it may seem odd to outsource innovation, there are companies, such as IdeaFisher Systems and Inventive Logic, which specialize in working with you to generate ideas. Also your company may choose partners, such as universities and other outside consultants, specifically as a source of new ideas. In our highly interconnected world, your partners for innovation may be anywhere in the world. For Hewlett-Packard, in California, one of its longest sustained research partnerships with a university is with one in Israel for research on data compression. Organizations will be drawn to the expertise, wherever it may be.

Innovation and the discovery of knowledge have occurred in a myriad of settings over the years. During the nineteenth century, invention "was seen as the product of genius, wayward, uncontrollable, often amateurish; or if not genius, then of accident and sudden inspiration" [83]. The world of communications provides examples such as Guglielmo Marconi and Alexander Graham Bell.

When innovation is seen as highly individual activity, marked by brilliant insight and creative thinking, it may follow that any kind of group activity or organization would have a detrimental effect. The creative impulses will be dulled by necessary adherence to administrative regulations and hierarchical reporting structures. Of course, it need not be this way. Companies like 3M, and research centers like Xerox PARC, IBM Watson Research Center, and Bell Laboratories, are famous for generating new ideas and inventions.

Extensive research and fieldwork by Kanter [84] confirm that organizations can actually foster innovation. Key elements to stimulate innovation include close contact with users who are sources of needs, cross-fertilization of ideas, high connectivity among workers and functional areas, broadly scoped jobs, coalition building, open communication, cross-cutting teams, continuity of personnel, and flexibility to adapt to changing conditions.

One way organizations can help stimulate innovation is to take into account cognitive differences when creating teams. Especially important are the ways people approach, perceive, and assimilate data. To begin to understand the cognitive styles of their workers, organizations may use a diagnostic instrument, such as the Hermann Brain Dominance Instrument (HBDI) [85] or the Myers–Briggs Type Indicator [86]. HBDI helps reveal a person's preferences for right-brained or left-brained thinking. MBTI uses a series of questions to assess where individuals lie on a range of attribute pairs: extroversion vs. introversion, sensing vs. intuition, thinking vs. feeling, and judging vs. perceiving. A team constituted with consideration of cognitive styles may benefit from multiple approaches to problems and a wider range of alternative solutions to explore.

Beyond carefully staffing teams based on cognitive styles, organizations also take more overt steps to stimulate creativity and innovation. Companies bring people with diverse talents together in "creative chaos" [53] or "creative abrasion." [15] These practices are related to the principle of requisite variety in cybernetics, which would call for team members to possess sufficiently diverse talents and skills to meet the challenges posed by the environment [87]. Matsushita used this strategy when it wanted to develop an automatic breadmaking machine. Instead of assigning the development to a single division, the company intentionally wanted to stir up innovation. It formed a team with people from three divisions (computer-control, induction heaters, and rotating motors) and charged the team with the development task. Familiar approaches, acceptable in the cultures of the individual divisions, were challenged in the cross-division team setting. The successful outcome also provided a lesson that too much chaos can be disruptive. Matsushita learned that the team needed to establish some common language so there was clarity on the meaning of key processes involved in electrical equipment. The company used a 3-day retreat for this purpose, and considered the common language, or "overlapping knowledge," to be essential to successful team innovation [53].

A metaphor for innovation has been the *breakthrough*—punching through the boundaries of existing knowledge or technology. Recent examples of innovation, for example in optoelectronics, suggest that innovation may be perceived in the future more as the fusion of different types of technology [55]. The implications for KM are to place increasing value on KM systems (see section 4) that can integrate information across lines of business, technologies, domains of practices, and internal and external sources.

A recent historical analysis of innovation in computing shows both the critical role of individuals and the positive influence of a nurturing climate for creativity. Ted Codd's idea of a new way to organize data led to new industry standard, commercial products, and a multibillion-dollar market in relational databases. Innovation in computing has been fostered by the free movement of researchers between institutions, by flexible and diverse approaches to investigation, and by synergistic relationships among universities, industry, and government [88].

Xerox PARC is widely known for pioneering the graphical user interface, object-oriented programming, and other innovations. It chides itself for "fumbling the future," [89], that is, failing to capitalize on its brilliant research advances for the benefit of Xerox. Seeking to capitalize on its innovations, PARC is now studying "local innovation," on the front lines where Xerox employees work. In the interaction between the company and customers, "innovation is everywhere; the problem is learning from it." [89, p. 156]

Xerox uses an "unfinished document" video as a way to communicate the possibilities of new technology. Researchers knowledgeable in a new technology not only talk about the potential, but also show how the technology may be used. The objective is to stimulate the executives who are watching, by conveying imaginative probes into the future use of the technology—and, by so doing, stimulate even more futuristic excursions. In this sense, new technologies are not so much developed in a laboratory, but "co-produced" with people outside the lab—the employees, executives, and customers who will become engaged in the process of enriching the concept and enhancing its eventual impact [89].

DARPA also uses professionally-produced videos to portray visions of technology-enhanced military operations in the future. By showing a future desirable end state, the video calls attention to specific instances in which innovation needs to occur:

● What are the technology problems that must be solved to get to this point?
● What prevents us from transforming information and knowledge to achieve the battlefield situational awareness shown in the video?

The use of multimedia, virtual reality, and other information technologies can enhance this practice of "collaborative imagining." A distinctive feature of the "envisioning laboratory" at PARC is giving customers access to the tools. They can quickly explore the consequences of evolving new technology in their own environments and business settings. The outcome of a customer's exploration is captured by the tool so it can contribute to the evolution of the technology [89].

An organization innovating with its customers is an instance of a more general case of transorganizational innovation. With individual firms increasingly defined along core competencies, it may require a cluster of firms to achieve the kind of diversity of experiences and perspectives needed for innovation. Effective multifirm learning and collaboration is essential to this networked innovation [90].

A closing recommendation, considering that innovation rests with people, is that "if you want an innovative organization, you need to hire, work with, and promote people who make you uncomfortable." [91]

3.4   How Does Knowledge Get Where It Is Needed?

We have seen how the flow of knowledge influences organizational structure, in starburst, knowledge web, and inverted pyramid organizations. There is much more to discover about how an organization gets knowledge, transforms it, shares it, and applies it to advance the needs of the organization.

In this section, we examine the life cycle of knowledge in an organization and the packaging of knowledge in products and services.

3.4.1   The Knowledge Life Cycle

The notion of a life cycle for knowledge draws attention to emergence of knowledge, operations on it during its lifetime, and the reality of a time when particular knowledge is no longer useful. We will lay out the knowledge life cycle, then discuss the stages and the transformations between them.

The stages in the knowledge life cycle, as shown in Figure 6, are originate, capture, transform, access, and apply. The cycle begins with the emergence of knowledge in the organization; information about it is captured in explicit forms; the explicit knowledge is structured and classified; and the tacit and explicit knowledge are accessed and applied.

3.4.1.1   Originate   In the originate stage, we include bringing in people who have knowledge and acquiring information and data that can contribute to the knowledge of the employees.

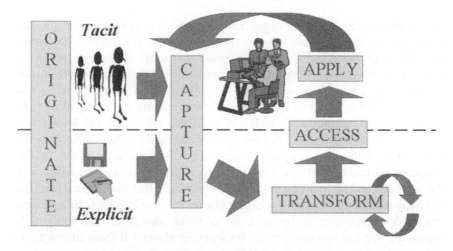

Consider a company that has a job requiring the development of a Visual Basic (VB) front-end for a system. The company does not have the needed expertise. There are several options, assuming the company is committed to completing the job assignment. The company can:

- send current employees to learn what is needed
- hire someone with the needed expertise
- bring in a consultant or a temporary worker to work alongside its employees
- contract with an outside firm.

Whether these are realistic options depends on factors such as consultant availability, local employment conditions, and the ability of current employees to learn new technology.

The choice of options should be guided by the more fundamental issues associated with our first question, what knowledge should be managed.

- How does VB development relate to the core competencies and knowledge of the company?
- Is this a competence the company wants to grow?
- How volatile is the knowledge?
- Is the company willing and able to make the financial commitment to establish and sustain a competence in this area?

The decision can affect the intellectual capital of the company. If the decision is to hire a new employee, that person will contribute to the knowledge and the IC of the organization. If the task is contracted out, the contribution will not persist beyond the scope of the assignment. However, even the impression of discrete options, a variation on the rent/buy decision, is deceiving. From a KM perspective, there is a continuous spectrum of alternatives according to their effects on organizational knowledge. If the decision is to get someone outside the company to do the work, there can be vastly different persistent effects on the knowledge base of the organization. In one case, we may hire a consultant who does the work away from the company setting, and delivers a product to the company (assuming that the VB front-end can be partitioned in this way and later integrated with the rest of the system). After this experience, the company would still not have a capability in VB development. In a second case, a VB developer is brought in to work alongside the company's employees. We can imagine employees learning about VB from interactions with the temporary employee, while he is learning about the company culture and its development environment. In both cases there is a transaction, but in the second case, there is more knowledge transfer to the company.

The emergence of knowledge in an organization is associated with bringing in new people who have knowledge and the learning that occurs as people do their jobs, work together, and participate in formal programs of education, training, idea generation, and brainstorming.

As Figure 6 suggests, we also include cases of acquiring information, such as a company buying a report that analyzes an industry or market. The information may be very valuable and contribute to decision-making. We also include acquiring data, such as a database with data on software development projects: their characteristics, sizes, effort expended in various development activities, defects found, and so on. Again, the database may be very useful and contribute to the knowledge of people who use it.

3.4.1.2 Capture

The straightforward part of the capture stage in Fig. 6 is to keep track of the newly acquired explicit resources, such as new reports or databases, so they can be combined with previously captured data and made visible to the organization to help it do its work. Because they are already in explicit forms, they can be integrated with other data with only technical issues to resolve.

The more challenging aspect of this stage is to capture knowledge, because we have consistently held that knowledge is in people and the way they work together. This subject is at the heart of KM: how much and what kinds of knowledge can be captured?

When we refer to capture, we mean to record information about the knowledge in a form that can be stored and accessed for use by an organization. To appreciate why knowledge capture is so important, we need only look at the extraordinary effect on the human experience when information about people's thoughts and lives has been recorded in some way. The act of capturing information in an explicit form allows it to reach across space and time. No metric can register what it has meant to people around the world for writings of early civilizations to have been captured—drawings on cave walls, inscriptions in the pyramids of Egypt and Mexico, the Bible and other religious works, or the dialogues of Plato [39]. We revere the invention of movable type for its incalculable impact on the transference of ideas. Where the human experience has not been captured, we are left to wonder at the experience of Greek theater or the dancing of Nijinsky. By the act of recording, we permit uncountable others to ponder the meaning of the recorded material and interpret it for their own circumstances.

Capturing what we know into explicit forms, and then bringing it to bear in our lives and work, is fundamental to the human experience. Alfred Whitehead said,

> Civilization advances by extending the number of important operations which we can perform without thinking about them. We make constant use of formulas, symbols, and rules whose meaning we do not understand and through the use of which we avail ourselves of the assistance of knowledge which individually we do not possess. [23]

When Larry Prusak was asked to write about what it was like growing up in New York City, he wrote a few pages. How do those few pages compare with what he knows about it? It is not even appropriate to say it is some percentage or another. The explicit part is the visible tip connected to a great mass of tacit knowledge that is beneath the surface. No matter how well intentioned the person, what is written is information about something that is qualitatively richer than information. Reading *The Art of Hitting* by Ted Williams, may help an aspiring baseball player, but only to a limited degree. Knowledge is embodied in people [21].

The act of capturing tacit knowledge into explicit forms is *externalization*. When an employee writes a white paper on lessons learned managing a complex system development project, the organization now has two resources to draw from, the person and the white paper. Both are valuable. No matter how thorough, the white paper, like *The Art of Hitting*, is no match for the person. "There is no way I can write something to make you understand the subject the way I do." [92]. But the white paper can be transmitted instantaneously around the world over the company's network, and every manager who wants it, can benefit from one person's experiences, even after that person has left the company. The multiplier effect of explicit resources can make them extremely valuable.

Depending on the nature of the work activities, coordinated multimedia—text, graphics, audio, and video—can be brought to bear for knowledge capture. Training simulators will even include additional sensory experience in the form of haptic interfaces to convey the feeling of pressure and resistance based on movements.

A new manager, preparing for the next project, may find a wide range of explicit resources from which to obtain guidance. These resources may include lessons learned white papers, postmortems from previous projects, old project plans, profiles of technical staff members who are candidates for the project team, customer requirements documents, data from past projects, and videotaped interviews with customer managers. The human act of assimilating this explicit information is *internalization*. This internalized information will contribute to the tacit knowledge of the new manager.

Externalization, and internalization create knowledge for an organization. With externalization, a new artifact containing information is created. With internalization, the tacit knowledge of the worker is enhanced.

Nonaka and Takeuchi [53] identify two complementary processes that, together with externalization and internalization, create a continuous spiral of knowledge creation. *Combination* is a process of organizing explicit resources into structures that lend themselves to internalization by people. Suppose our new manger went searching for documents and reports to help her, and found dozens of project plans and "lessons learned" documents. An act of combination would be to synthesize the relevant documents into a single guide for new managers, removing outdated or redundant information, and structuring it as a new manager would like to see it.

Through *socialization*, senior managers would talk to new managers about what they have experienced. They would answer questions and tell stories to give new managers a feel for what they will soon face. Tacit knowledge shared this way can never be externalized in a way that matches the real thing. The nearest approximation would be a video of the interaction, to be replayed for other new managers. Even a professionally produced video is likely to come up short, because the act of recording will adversely influence the free flow of ideas and questions, or the nuance of the personal contact will not be conveyed satisfactorily.

Now the knowledge spiral of Nonaka and Takeuchi [53] is in place, with knowledge creation in all four activities:

- *Externalization (tacit to explicit):* People capture information about their knowledge into explicit forms.
- *Combination (explicit to explicit):* Multiple sources of explicit knowledge are combined and structured into more useful forms.

- *Internalization (explicit to tacit):* People internalize information from explicit forms to enhance their tacit knowledge.

- *Socialization (tacit to tacit):* People talk to each other and work with each other, sharing their knowledge and experience.

The processes in the knowledge spiral provide an excellent organizing framework for much of the technology associated with KM, which will be discussed in section 4. The technology can be viewed as supporting one or more of these processes:

- *externalization:* personal publishing tools such as personal digital assistants (PDAs), word processors, presentation support tools, spreadsheet tools; audio and video recorders; interactive tools so workers can publish to an enterprise-wide intranet

- *combination:* on-line editing tools for people to synthesize and repackage related materials; software tools for creating taxonomies and indexing content; tools for data mining; software agents that look across internal and external sources to pull together related topical material

- *internalization:* software tools to present content to people, including web browsers, relevance ranking technology, push technology, collaborative filtering, interest profiles, semantic retrieval, visualization, natural language processing

- *socialization:* e-mail, threaded discussions, chat rooms, instant messaging, dynamic workgroup creation, groupware, electronic meetings, process workflow

3.4.1.3 Transform
This stage includes any actions that contribute to making explicit or tacit knowledge easier for people to access and easier to internalize after they have accessed it. There are many transforming actions:

- organizing content into structures
- classifying content by its attributes
- providing indexes of the content
- synthesizing content into new forms
- creating templates or model objects
- visualizing the content
- assuring the quality of content
- providing access controls

- mining the content for patterns and relationships

- removing obsolete content.

Organizing activities do not change the stored resources, but rather place them into categories or bins to simplify the collection and provide easier access. The structure may be a list or directory or semantic map, and it may have a hierarchical structure. Good examples of directory structures are the familiar portals on the internet. Information can also be structured in time, with a series of menus to show the hierarchical relationships.

Content can be classified according to many dimensions, such as document type (e.g., proposals, project plans, or system architectures), project type, industry type, and customer. In a similar way, people often prefer to gain access to other people, rather than documents. Organizations can classify the stored information about people, for example, according to their areas of expertise or roles in projects—those who have been database administrators, lead architects, project managers, or configuration managers. Section 4.2 describes content structuring activities.

Certain actions change the original resources into new forms. The project manager's guidebook was an example of synthesizing many explicit resources to develop a more usable form of information. These transforming actions include building models or templates. Instead of managers looking through reports showing planned and actual expenditures on past projects, a structuring action is to build a software tool that provides an estimation model developed by analyzing the data. This kind of structuring action requires effort, but can be very cost effective.

Visualizations of stored information can characterize a wealth of data in a concise way. Figures 1 and 5, along with more examples in section 4, show how contemporary visualization tools can summarize a mass of content into its prevailing themes.

Quality-related transforming actions include removing restricted information of any kind, such as customer-sensitive data or information, before others reuse it. It is extremely important, for obvious reasons, to examine stored data to ensure it is correct and accurate.

Data mining can be performed to uncover patterns and relationships that people find meaningful, surprising, and valuable. Data mining alone does not create knowledge, but it can expose patterns people recognize as meaningful information, thus increasing their knowledge.

We include the transforming action of retiring knowledge to emphasize the need for current information and to recognize that people leave organizations. One company gives cash "knowledge bounties" of up to $5000 at exit interviews, based on the information shared by the departing employee [93].

The profile of work in an organization changes over time. The organization needs to ensure that a competence, and its associated knowledge, is no longer listed if it is not a current capability. Information about outdated knowledge must be removed from the content stores. Updating of knowledge is a continuing process. Especially in technical areas, knowledge becomes obsolete relatively quickly, with knowledge half-life perhaps being the best way to express it.

3.4.1.4 Access Access is the essential activity of obtaining the knowledge a worker needs when it is needed. Access is enabled in most organizations through intranets connecting workers with repositories of documents, tools, and directories of people and their expertise. Figure 7 shows a typical presentation interface on a corporate intranet. The user can see a directory of content by subject area and also has a search capability in the upper part of the screen.

The key to the effectiveness of access methods, as with any content retrieval delivery process, is to understand what the people who are doing the accessing really want. Research has shown that people do not always

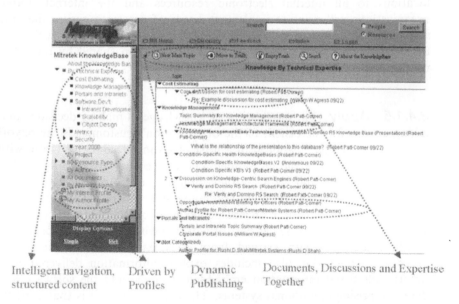

Intelligent navigation, structured content | Driven by Profiles | Dynamic Publishing | Documents, Discussions and Expertise Together

FIG. 7. Accessing content with a corporate intranet (© 1999 Mitretek Systems, Inc. All rights reserved).

know what they want. They may be trying to contact a person because they believe the person has the answer they seek, when their original need was for an answer to a question. They would have been more successful if they had submitted that question to a fuzzy search engine (see section 4.3.1) operating on a repository of already answered questions. Or, they might have fared better if their KM infrastructure provided full-text search across documents, e-mail, and expertise profiles of people. The outcome from the search would have indicated whether the returned item was a document, an e-mail message, or a pointer to a person with the needed expertise.

Accessing knowledge is not limited to search and retrieval, that is, pull technologies. As section 4.3.2 will discuss, workers can use push technology, alert mechanisms, and filters to gain access to needed information. Individuals can set up profiles so that relevant and needed information is automatically sent to them when the information first hits the information repository. Figure 7 shows the person's profile is readily accessible on the screen so it can be updated. Workers who need access to individuals can use groupware technology to meet with them in a virtual space over a network, and can use threaded discussions and chat facilities to get the contact they want with other workers.

With the advances in internet technology, most organizations have, or are working towards, networked access from employees' desktops or mobile locations to all internal electronic resources and the internet. Often organizations will want to implement levels of access to ensure that the sensitivity of information is preserved. Collaboration groups will want to establish their own work areas, with information shared by them but no one else.

3.4.1.5 Apply The application of knowledge in making decisions and taking actions for the benefit of the organization's customers is the payoff for KM. Knowledge is applied in a host of settings leading to its use with customers. People use and re-use their knowledge when they work together in internal teams and with partner organizations. Ideally, the use of knowledge reflects the collective and integrated experiences of the entire enterprise, brought to bear on the problem or question of the customer. Tacit knowledge being used as part of working with customers incorporates the best that has been learned from socialization and internalization processes. Application also includes explicit information delivered in a report, rule-based information embedded in tools, and the software and data comprising operational systems. The common thread is that workers have been able to access the most relevant knowledge, so they can apply it in a way that represents the best work of the organization.

3.4.2 Packaging Knowledge

We have already seen how people can record information about their knowledge into explicit forms, such as software tools, databases, and technical reports. We focus in this section on embedding knowledge in products and services. This subject draws on the distinction between information and knowledge (see section 2.3), so we consider a few examples of knowledge-intensive work and the resulting products.

In the first example, an organization is retained to perform a technical analysis to solve a problem. The organization delivers a final technical report, presenting the analysis and the solution. The organization is not delivering knowledge; it is delivering information. It has knowledgeable people, who presumably enhanced their knowledge by doing the work.

As a second example, consider an organization whose business is providing information. For example, Avenue Technologies sells research and profiles on 30 000 companies. Organizations that perform competitive analyses of markets will often charge thousands of dollars for the reports presenting their results. They also are delivering information. The price of the report may be high, reflecting the extent of analysis that went into the product. But the high price does not mean there is knowledge in the report.

In this section we examine how knowledge gets into products and services. One way is to make knowledge into a product, like the market analysis report, even when your organization is not primarily in the business of selling information. In the course of doing its traditional business, an organization realizes that it can also make money by organizing some of its knowledge into a package for sale. A second way is to enhance an existing product or service by adding information-rich features. To exaggerate, it is as though the product or service comes with a person who is knowledgeable about it.

Examples will clarify the two kinds of knowledge packaging. For a company that is turning knowledge into a product, consider Bay State Shippers [94]. They decided to package some of what they know about the shipping business into a product that other shippers could use. With this REZ1 product, shippers can reserve rail containers, track shipments, and do billing and forecasting operations. The distinguishing characteristic is that Bay State was not in the information business. It turned knowledge it had into a product.

Air Products, which sells liquid gases, turned its knowledge about how to store and handle hazardous substances into a service [48]. The form of "selling knowledge" can translate into providing a specified number of days of consulting support to organizations that buy the product. Once the consulting relationship is established, it can grow into a more substantial revenue stream. Lotus gets 20% of its revenues from selling knowledge, not software, and they expect it to grow to 40% by 2001 [94].

Copying machines illustrate the second kind of knowledge packaging. We start with a copier lacking any information features. When it stops working, it gives no indication of the problem, leaving everything to the user. Enhancing the product with a built-in user manual is adding information from a knowledgeable person. Flip cards on the machine itself guide the user through recovering from common problems such as jammed paper. Still more embedded knowledge is in a machine able to identify the kind of problem and its location. Lights and displays tell the user what is wrong and where to look.

Advancing along the spectrum of knowledge embedding, consider high-end Xerox copiers containing 30 microprocessors on a LAN. The product has built-in logic to continually monitor itself, collect information, and use it to improve performance and quality. Xerox's "remote interactive communication" feature is an expert system that predicts when the next breakdown will occur, and automatically calls a branch office to communicate its predicted breakdown time and the accompanying reasoning. On the receiving end at the branch office is another computer that conducts further analysis and schedules a technician to attend to the copier before the predicted failure [89]. This example is more in the spirit of true knowledge embedding because it has the capability for flexible behavior and can initiate action in response to sensory input.

Tom Stewart describes what may be the ultimate scenario for packaged knowledge, a Thanksgiving in the future, in which intelligent turkeys with embedded chips will signal when they need basting and shut off the oven when they are done. Users will be able to program the signal, for example, a gobble sound [94].

Help desk and call center operations are prime candidates for embedding knowledge to improve performance and effectiveness. At Hewlett-Packard, questions coming in from dealers by phone were growing at 40% annually. The company put frequently asked questions (FAQ) on a dialup database, HP Network News, later converted to Lotus Notes. By continually editing the data to remove useless information and by highlighting lists of the top 10 encountered problems and FAQs, the company was able to stem the need for staff increases to cope with the increased calls [95]. This example highlights the role of technology to make it feasible to scale up to higher volume operations. A variation on the same theme is an organization saving money because the embedded knowledge in its computer systems enables it to use lower paid workers. Referring to a computer system that controls a paper and pulp mill, Zuboff notes, "Most Cedar Bluff managers agreed that the computer system made it possible to do a better job running the plant with an inexperienced work force than otherwise would have been possible. ... " [35, p. 204]

Through tools for managing the relevant knowledge, helpdesk operators can be more effective. Several current tools enable operators to look up users' configurations when they call and to search to see if the same or a similar call was answered before. Capturing data from helpdesk calls can enable operators to detect hot spots, schedule preventive maintenance, and recommend training.

Of course, the ability to search for similar problems and their solutions can be pushed down to users. At Valero Energy, employees can search a knowledge base for answers that others have used to solve problems, instead of calling the helpdesk [96]. Raymond James Financials' helpdesk support web site provides access to 3000 packaged and custom how-to scripts that guide users so they can fix problems themselves. Although the company, with 6000 employees, has grown 20% per year, the self-service approach is credited with keeping costs steady, with a 15-person staff. The biggest challenge was getting users to depend on technology and not on people. Key to success was ensuring the site was easy to use and current. They also used incentives like scavenger hunts, with prizes for people who found the right information in the knowledge base [96].

Organizations use knowledge embedding to differentiate their products and services from competitors. The differentiation may be very simple addition of needed information, such as an airline reservation web site that will tell the customer the assigned gate at the airport for the selected flight. The purpose in providing more information with its service is to distinguish itself in what may be seen as a commodity service.

An example of more extensive knowledge embedding is AMP Inc., which designs and manufactures electronic devices. AMP developed a knowledge-rich service, AMP Connect, providing digital engineering data using a multilingual internet catalog so its 24 000 customers can search by text or picture for information on the company's 67 000 parts. If potential customers are choosing suppliers, the added benefit of AMP Connect may make the difference in deciding on their company. As with help desk tools, AMP Connect frees up the expensive time of technical staff. The company also avoids the $7 million annual cost of publishing and distributing the product catalogs [26].

To demonstrate the range of industries instilling knowledge to differentiate and supplement their products, we note that Lincoln Re, the reinsurance part of Lincoln National Corp., developed LincUP, so its self-insured customers can calculate their exposure to risk. In the same spirit as AMP's Internet catalog and self-service help desks, LincUP allows customers to use their location, work force demographics, and occupational categories online against Lincoln Re's actuarial data [94].

We have seen in these examples that, as knowledge is embedded in products and services, it can differentiate them, generate savings in company operations, and provide more value to users.

3.5   What is the Culture?

Organizational culture is the most critical determinant of KM success and the most difficult to define. It is the extent to which people trust each other, feel positively about the goals of the organization and the leadership, and are willing to go beyond the bounds of their job definitions to help each other be successful. Developing a knowledge culture was cited as the number one obstacle to successful KM, named by 54% of respondents in a survey of 431 executives [97]. Signaling the key role of culture, Arthur Andersen hired 30 anthropologists for their skills at understanding the culture of work. "If I don't trust my co-workers, I can have all the collaborative technology the world, but collaboration is not going to happen." [98]

The leadership of the organization sets the tone through its messages and behavior about what is valued in the organization. If knowledge sharing is important, workers will know it. If an employee who is known to be generous and unusually helpful to those in need of her knowledge is not rewarded for that behavior, then no amount of talking about the importance of knowledge sharing will counter the prevailing culture. If the organization has determined that innovation is crucial to success, the culture needs to stimulate it.

Organizations need to appreciate that knowledge workers may feel possessive about their knowledge. It is the basis for their livelihood—why should they give it away? It is left to the organization to create an atmosphere where the knowledge workers will be encouraged following their first, perhaps tentative, ventures into knowledge sharing. When the reaction is the free flow of knowledge from other workers, there is positive feedback, and the organization benefits from the liberating spirit of generating new ideas and sharing experiences. Knowledge sharing should be encouraged, because the knowledge of the organization increases.

An executive in a Danish company noted how often he saw people talking in the hallways. The reaction might have been to send a memo admonishing people to get in their offices and "back to work." His reaction was to redesign the building to have wider hallways and informal meeting spaces so people could find it easier to talk [21]. These informal conversations can provide valuable knowledge sharing. "The stories tech-reps tell each other—around the coffee pot, in the lunchroom ... are crucial to continuous learning." [89, p. 166]

Recalling that the purpose of KM is understanding, an indicator of understanding is that there are stories being told. Story telling, used at organizations such as the World Bank [99], involves a narrative unfolding of events and relationships, all in a context and over time. It has been shown to be very effective in communicating tradition and culture within an organization. Weinberger [17] observed that, at a company he worked for, and which had failed, no one was able to tell the story of the company, a circumstance that he equates to no one really understanding what went wrong.

Bipin Junnarkar encouraged employees to take pictures when they attended business conferences. He found employees more interested in taking pictures than in taking notes. Back in the office, they shared the pictures, much like family vacation photos. The idea was to recreate context as a means of recalling the interactions and events, to stimulate discussion [99].

Even when the conversations are not about business, the act of sharing helps establish the culture. In the Japanese practice of *cho rei*, people take a few minutes in the morning to say whatever they want. Americans who initially saw it as a waste of time realized they were learning from it. Cho rei gave them insight into people and their values—"where they were coming from"—that was not easy to understand through work alone. This personal context setting helped people work together [100].

Socialization has played a role in discovery and innovation over the years. The coteries and clubs of the nineteenth century were described as sources of lively new ideas: "the object of the proposed Society was to be at the same time friendly and scientific. The members were to exchange views with each other on topics relating to literature, arts, and science; each contributing his quota of entertainment and instruction" [83, p. 82]. In a "knowledge-friendly" culture [101], the flow of conversation can move freely among topics that are work-related and those that are not.

In exploring the role of culture, we devote particular attention to two critical aspects: the sharing of knowledge and its relationship to learning.

3.5.1 Learning

When we talk about the knowledge people have, it is because they have learned through experience, observation, apprenticeship, and formal education and training. Learning and knowledge are intimately intertwined. Among management strategies, the concept of a learning organization [24] predates KM as a management strategy. A learning organization is one "skilled at creating, acquiring, and transferring knowledge and at modifying its behavior to reflect new knowledge and insights" [102, p. 51]. In a learning organization, "you cannot *not* learn, because learning is so insinuated into the fabric of life" [24].

New ideas are a necessary, but not sufficient, condition for a learning organization. Garvin [102] identifies five building blocks:

- systematic problem solving
- experimentation with new approaches
- learning from its own experience and past history
- learning from the experiences and best practices of others
- transforming knowledge quickly and efficiently throughout the organization.

The overall similarity to KM is obvious; the chief difference is one of emphasis. A learning organization focuses on continual feedback from what has been learned, so it can apply the revised lessons to solve problems and improve practices. KM stresses a comprehensive look at knowledge and information in all its tacit and explicit forms, to advance the aims of the organization. Both approaches seek organizational improvement.

A view that integrates the two strategies is to interpose "knowing" as one stage in an endless cycle of "doing" the business of the organization, which causes "learning," which contributes to "knowing," which enables "doing," and so on.

An organization can use a learning history (LH) as a structured mechanism for capturing experiences. Developed at MIT's Center for Organizational Learning, the LH is a written description of an organization's recent event, program, or project. The LH, which can run from 20 to 100 pages, is structured into two columns. On the right-hand column, people who participated in or were affected by the experience record their observations on what took place. Alongside this narrative, in the left-hand column, is analysis and comment from outside learning historians. Ideally the outside experts find themes, weave the observations together and otherwise identify issues. The LH is the basis for discussion and improvement of practices [103].

Informal learning refers to any learning that happens directly in the process of doing work. Consider the informal learning that can occur from an employee being supervised. The employee may learn performance expectations, ways of integrating feedback, a leadership style of the supervisor, boundaries of acceptable behavior, and levels of risk tolerance. Organizations can take steps to facilitate informal learning by providing a social environment conducive to giving and receiving constructive feedback and sharing ideas. Also helpful are an organizational policy and culture that encourage frequent interactions between supervisor and subordinate [25].

We believe informal learning is valuable, and the Education Development Center [25] corroborated its value in a disciplined evaluation with the following results:

- The economic benefit of informal learning to firms is statistically significant.
- Informal learning can be influenced by the organization and its management.
- Many skills acquired informally cannot be acquired formally.
- Approximately 70% of the way employees learn their jobs is through informal learning.

Learning must not be left to happen through chance assignments or encounters. McKinsey & Company is similar to many firms that assign staff so each position is a learning experience. The company uses a very structured process of staffing five-person teams. New consultants prepare the assignment report, which requires them to spend a great deal of time searching the company database of assignment reports, using the global computer network, and reading the 300-page book, *Perspectives on McKinsey*, written by longtime McKinsey leader, Marvin Bower. Through these initial assignments, new staff members learn in their areas of professional competence by working with more senior colleagues. They learn informally the company's practices, include building on previous engagements and accessing corporate databases. In subsequent assignments, staff members take on roles of increasing scope and leadership in the team, continuing to learn as they go [48].

Learning takes place in more than the mind. The familiar learning experiences of childhood, such as riding a bicycle and tying shoelaces, are early instances that continue to challenge us to write down how we do it. This is quintessentially tacit learning, with the knowledge embodied in our entire physical and emotional being.

The same notion of shared physical and emotional experience is used to dramatic effect with team-building exercises. Action exercises and more extensive Outward Bound adventures can leave indelible marks on the participants. In one case, all someone had to do was say, "Remember the raft," and it brought back a flood of feelings and physical memories of the team being successful accomplishing a challenging task together. The confidence from that shared success, against great odds, carried over to their business challenges [100].

There are many paths to becoming a learning organization. Some companies stress formal training and education, and certainly teaching is a form of knowledge sharing. One strategy maintains that a culture and leadership style based on teaching will reduce the lead-time between teaching and learning [26]. Motorola is an example of a "teaching firm," with its Motorola University providing extensive education and training courses with a goal of improving team performance. Software engineers receive nearly 2 months of training per year [71].

The Corporate University Xchange (CUX) claims more than 1600 companies run corporate universities, including Bain Virtual University (for the consulting firm Bain & Co.), Conoco, and Cox Communications. They take advantage of the internet, real-time videoconferencing, and other technology to deliver course material, often to a worldwide student body of employees [104].

Another implementation strategy is to charge employees with the responsibility for learning, and provide them with resources and supportive culture to be successful. One company took this approach, abolishing the formal training it had been using. It found it was spending $30 million a year on training, with only "one penny out of a hundred hitting the mark." Now it is up to employees to get the knowledge they need to do their current jobs, to improve their performance on their current jobs, or prepare for new ones. Employees are provided software learning resources, such as computer-based training, and they can still take courses if they want to do so. They have a learning culture that offers another option: they can make arrangements to work alongside colleagues to learn new skills [49].

The challenge for KM is that an organization takes advantage of everything it learns: "It's up to you to make a lot of mistakes. And it's up to you that no mistake is repeated, anywhere in the world."[2]

3.5.2 Knowledge Sharing

Knowledge sharing is not new. Direct knowledge sharing between people has occurred throughout history, "from palavers under the baobab, village square debates, and town meetings, to conclaves, professional consultations, meetings, workshops, and conferences." [39]

Knowledge can be shared directly or indirectly. Direct knowledge sharing is from the source of knowledge, a person, to other people. An instance of direct knowledge sharing with potentially dramatic effect is a CEO's sharing of a personal vision for a company with all the employees. Even with the extensive use of computers, direct knowledge sharing remains very influential, with more than half of all knowledge worker communication being person-to-person [105].

Indirect knowledge sharing uses explicit information as an intermediary. Information about the knowledge is captured into explicit forms, and

[2] Anonymous quote to software engineers at Motorola on what is expected of them for continuous learning in their organizations, quoted in [71].

accessed by other people who learn from it. A metaphor is that the knowledgeable person is "teaching" an unknown reader by capturing information about the knowledge. It is important to be very clear and logical because there is no immediate feedback to sense if the eventual reader is getting the message and no opportunity to answer questions in real time. Also, information cannot be returned once it is released [94].

In an organization, interactive knowledge sharing takes place from one individual to another and in group work activity. IBM believes the team or group environment is the "sweet spot" for sharing both tacit and explicit knowledge [45]. "Original ideas emanate from autonomous individuals, diffuse within the team, and then become organizational ideas" [53, p. 76].

Indirect knowledge sharing is essential if the opportunities for person-to-person interaction are limited or there is a need to leverage the knowledge to a wide audience. In section 1.2, we mentioned the US Army's extensive use of multimedia simulation to share experiences from house-to-house searches through its Center for Army Lessons Learned. Booz Allen's Knowledge OnLine intranet enables the firm to leverage its 12 innovation teams so they can share expertise across the 90 offices worldwide [79].

When it comes time to select people to capture the knowledge for later sharing, it is best to directly engage people who have knowledge of the activity, rather than resorting to higher level managers or designated procedure writers. An electronics firm faced with creating International Standards Organization (ISO) documentation asked the employees to write down the procedures they used. During the cross-training that followed, the employees regarded the drafted procedures highly because they knew that people who actually worked on the machines wrote those parts of the document [25].

The GM-UAW Quality Network provides for knowledge sharing and communication between managers and automobile workers. This network also illustrates the replacement of a hierarchical management structure with a flat organization of 85 self-empowered work teams. The defect rate of 2 parts per million on precision hydraulic valve lifters is far better than its international competitors' or international quality standards. Here the knowledge sharing leads to tangible outcomes, the development and continuous refinement of a new production approach, and intangible benefits of building trust [26].

The US Department of Labor wanted to achieve greater leverage from the funds it dedicated to improving the information processing in the states' unemployment insurance operations. It established the Information Technology Support Center (ITSC) through the State of Maryland, to serve as a central resource for all the states in their improvement efforts. The ITSC achieves high leverage from the good ideas and best practices discovered in the states. It shares knowledge through prototypes, specification templates, planning tools, workshops, traditional and distance training, reports, data models, and especially, its web site. Now the good idea one state had about how to structure an appeals process or what to include in a proposal for imaging automation can be leveraged for all to benefit.

Xerox's Eureka project is aimed at sharing experiences of service technicians for on-line access worldwide. Technicians write tips on fixing equipment and solving problems encountered in the field. A peer review panel validates tips, which are then added to the on-line repository. Xerox consulted industrial psychologists to develop an incentive plan for sharing experiences. Financial incentives did not work as well as giving name recognition to the contributors, so the names of the technician and the review panelists appear with the tip itself in the knowledge base. Eureka was first introduced in France, where 30% of the technicians generated validated tips; 85% of them accessed tips; and there are 5000 accesses per month to the tip database. Results show a 5% cost savings in parts and labor [106].

When there are such demonstrated economic benefits from knowledge sharing, some people lament those who seem to get it for free. The knowledge shared by early users of a company's products provides an extremely valuable benefit to the company. By one estimate, a large software producer got the equivalent of roughly $1 billion of benefit from the testing and debugging performed at beta test sites [107]. In the beta-testing scenario, the knowledge was valuable, yet no money was charged for it. What is the "market" for knowledge? Under what circumstances will people pay for knowledge or expect to get it for free? Do the forces of supply and demand work for knowledge? Davenport and Prusak [4] make the case for knowledge being shaped and buffeted by market dynamics, with knowledge buyers and sellers, in an analogous way to goods and services.

What are you buying when you purchase a business intelligence report on particular industry? When you hire a consultant? We expect a consultant to be retained for her knowledge rather than specific information she possesses. This view is consistent with knowledge involving a deeper, more reflective quality than information (see section 2.3). When someone pays an informant or a spy, a monetary value is being placed on the information that is provided. Companies pay for data on consumers' purchasing practices or analyses of markets or competitors. The data can be information to an individual who can see the patterns in the data and what those patterns imply. That information can lead to decisions and actions, so a business case can be made to pay for the information.

Knowledge is given away in an organizational setting because of reciprocity, repute, and altruism [4]. Sharing knowledge may place the giver in a better position to request knowledge in the future (*reciprocity*).

She may be held in higher esteem within the organization by sharing knowledge (*repute*). Some people genuinely want to help others who need their help and their knowledge because they know it will contribute to the common good of the organization (*altruism*).

Motivated by reciprocity, a knowledge giver may be willing to share because of direct reward, such as money or frequent flier miles, or indirect reward, because knowledge sharing "counts" in performance evaluations, which translate into higher salaries or bonuses. One company executive has a simple approach: "If you promote the people who do the best job of sharing, you don't need any other incentives". [108]

Sometimes elements of all three incentives are present when knowledge is shared. At Ernst & Young, consultants are evaluated for salary increments and bonuses in part on their contributions to the corporate knowledge base. By contributing, a partner is adding to the common good (*altruism*), enhancing a reputation for sharing (*repute*), and, to the extent the contribution helps complete a task in less time, increasing the profits of the firm, which are returned to the partners (*reciprocity*).

Knowledge grows when it is shared. "He who receives an idea from me, receives instruction himself without lessening mine; as he who lights his taper at mine receives light without darkening me". [109] The act of sharing can deepen the understanding on the part of the knowledge giver, providing another slant on reciprocity. Anyone who has taught knows that, by teaching a concept, the teacher can learn too. The process of explaining a principle deepens the understanding of the teacher, perhaps by prompting her to think about a relationship for the first time. Some organizations try to formalize the "win" for the expert providing the knowledge. When the questioner has learned something from the expert, the questioner is responsible for codifying that knowledge and sending it back to the expert. This action captures the knowledge and also provides a service to the learner to organize what he has learned, and have it validated by the expert that the correct messages were received. In this model the expert gets something back, and it is her responsibility to submit it to the organization's knowledge base. The benefit to the expert is credit for submitting the knowledge [99].

Incentives for knowledge sharing touch on all aspects of the motivations of reciprocity, repute, and altruism. Microsoft has given out polo shirts in addition to financial awards [110]. To encourage use of knowledge bases, the nearly 2000 internal educators at Hewlett-Packard gave out free airline frequent flier miles. By early 1996, more than two-thirds of the target community had read at least one posting, and more than one-third had submitted a posting or comment themselves. But, even with free miles and e-mail and voice mail reminders, the knowledge sharing effort would have failed "without an evangelist." [95]

Rewards for contributing to the knowledge base are built into the performance system at many consulting firms, such as Ernst & Young and PriceWaterhouse Coopers. Texas Instruments presents knowledge-sharing employees the "Not Invented Here But I Did It Anyway" prize [110]. The incentives at Booz Allen address both reciprocity and repute. The prominent display of the author's name along with the contribution becomes a way to showcase one's accomplishments. Also, one-third of a consultant's evaluation is "contributions that cause the firm to gain client business." [79]

With knowledge transfer being so important, the attention to incentives is understandable. "The best kind of knowledge transfer is informal, but the best way to get knowledge to be transferred is ... to reward them for transferring it" [111]. But incentives can backfire. After one company started giving away televisions and trips, infighting developed among analysts. They started taking more work home to get ahead, and teamwork suffered [112].

If incentives are used, they must be introduced with a clear idea of the messages they are sending and the behaviors they are reinforcing. Any incentive program must be aligned with organization goals and fit naturally with the culture.

4. KM Systems

They expect to solve the problem by installing the software. It's never worked in applications software, and it's not going to work in KM [113].

A KM system is the automated part of an organizational knowledge management program. It may involve an array of interrelated custom applications, databases, and commercial products on a network infrastructure. The purpose of the KM system is to provide maximum effective automated contribution to the objectives of the KM program.

The principal delivery mechanisms for KM systems are intranets and extranets. They provide users the connectivity to other people and to servers containing explicit resources that can be accessed and shared. With the increasingly focused expertise of individual organizations (see section 3.1), extranets are becoming more widely used as the KM platform, because they transparently link business partners, suppliers, and customers. As a cautionary note, the multi-organization span of extranets places increased attention on security and the definition of access privileges.

It does not require a sophisticated KM system to get dramatic results. Buckman Laboratories used CompuServe to provide a forum for question answering and discussion groups organized around industries. Buckman is a specialty chemical maker that provides customized solutions to customers in 90 countries. Because it relies extensively on the individual expertise of its front-line workers, its KM strategy was to share their solutions across the company. Before its KM program, only 16% of Buckman's employees were out selling. Now the figure is 40%, and the company credits KM for making it more successful [51].

This section examines the architecture and administration of KM systems, and the underlying technology elements that provide its capabilities.

4.1 KM Conceptual Architecture

Figure 8 shows the KM architecture used at Mitretek Systems [114]. As a conceptual architecture, it captures the basic elements and relationships for an organizational KM system, and serves as the reference point for implementation.

The content stores at the bottom of Fig. 8 are the data and information resources at the heart of the organization. The content can include documents, e-mail, transaction data, financial data, project data, and information about employees, customers, and markets. At this conceptual level, it is easy to show that content from diverse systems and applications should be resources for a KM system. Actually making an implementation

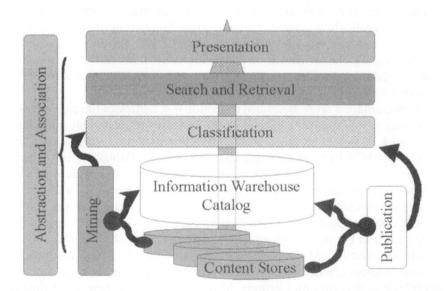

FIG. 8. KM conceptual architecture [114] (© 1999 Mitretek Systems, Inc. All rights reserved).

appear to move seamlessly across all this content can be challenging. The approach shown in Fig. 8 is to use an *information warehouse catalog*, which knows what is in the content stores.

A catalog has three components:

- *catalog entries* identifying the resources in the content stores
- *reference data* about the content, especially relationships showing the logical organization of the content and the ways it will be accessed
- a *programming interface* to create, delete, and manage entries and reference data.

A catalog allows for maximum flexibility in managing diverse content stores. Multiple attributes can be defined for entries and relationships. For example, the catalog can associate a person to a document, a document to a document, a person and a document to a project, and so on. In addition to supporting retrieval for the work of the organization, the catalog generally needs to support managerial (report generation and query) and archival (back-up and recovery) functions as well.

The classification element in Fig. 8 provides the principal axes for structuring the resources for retrieval. Classification axes must be designed to clearly track business practices and expected access patterns. Section 4.2 discusses the structuring and classification of content.

The search and retrieval layer provides capabilities to access content, aided by classification schemes and a catalog. The notion of searching and retrieving here conveys the pulling of content, but we also include the increasingly significant action of delivering content when the person has not searched for it. Both push and pull technologies are discussed in section 4.3.

The presentation layer, described in section 4.4, addresses the challenge of packaging capabilities for a variety of users so they can get what they want from the KM system. A key feature of the interface is to make it easy for people to publish items to the organizational intranet. Publishing is a vehicle for the externalization of tacit knowledge. It is not the sole province of individual contributors. The results of electronic meetings and taped presentations can also be directly published as a means to get timely information accessible to a broad community.

As shown in Fig. 8, publishing and mining interact with the central layers in the architecture. Mining, discussed in section 4.6, is the analysis of content to uncover nuggets of meaning—patterns and relationships that can contribute to decisions and actions. Mining can generate new and valuable content that must be added to the content stores and cataloged in the information warehouse catalog.

The abstraction and association activities in Fig. 8 imply the continual learning that must occur in any KM system. KM architects will want to improve the system so it anticipates changing business needs and knowledge requirements. As new technology becomes available, it must be considered for its potential to improve KM operations. KM designers should be examining content stores for new abstractions and associations that can improve access. The eXtensible Markup Language (XML) (see section 4.3.3) is a leading example of promising technology that will affect the information warehouse catalog, content structuring, and retrieval.

The conceptual architecture in Fig. 8 can be a reference point leading to a wide variety of implementations. The implementation decisions should be guided by the state of the supporting infrastructure, the nature of the work practices, and the capabilities and maturity of the commercial products that will be components of the system. Vendors' products do not always neatly match the layers in Fig. 8. Implementation approaches may merge certain layers and split others.

This section continues by taking key architectural elements from Fig. 8 and describing their role in KM systems.

4.2   Content Structuring

We use "content" intentionally so as not to limit the kinds of materials that may be knowledge resources for an organization. Content may be in file systems, structured relational or object-oriented databases, data stores in special purpose applications, enterprise document management systems, or in enterprise resource planning (ERP) systems that support financial, personnel, and other functional areas of the organization. Figure 7 showed that even a threaded discussion is treated as any other content, and can be retrieved as a unit.

The appropriate content to include is driven in part by the same considerations we discussed in section 3.1—content corresponding to the critical knowledge of the organization. In building its KM system, Arthur D. Little used a task force to identify the knowledge content and to characterize its importance to individuals, groups, and corporate objectives [115]. The critical knowledge will vary by the user communities served by the KM system. Senior executives typically want ready access to information about customers, competitors, and markets. They also want distilled information about the operation of the organization, to support their decision-making. Often the decision-making and planning information comes from enterprise systems tracking revenues and costs.

Technical contributors want access to information, from both internal and external sources, that will contribute to their project work. Relevant content may be in technical documents, threaded discussions, and e-mail. Project leaders need access to the same information, plus limited financial information related to their projects.

Sometimes the knowledge that sets an organization apart from its competitors is knowledge that is outside its doors. Users may want notification of events of interest, news, product announcements, and security alerts from software product vendors. In the mid-1980s, Zurich-American Insurance Group started a quality program focused on its customers. Through extensive analysis, research, and training of its front line and support staff, the company is able to offer customers data on how they compare to industry benchmarks. Their knowledge of their customers is a competitive advantage [26].

One organizational approach to identifying the content to be structured is to look for information that is needed by several user communities. Obvious content here is reference material such as policies, procedures, forms, and information for new employees. Look first to populate the KM system with content to support COPs engaged in cross-cutting activities, such as writing proposals or project plans, that span the organization. Other content of wide interest is dated material such as events and news about people: who is joining or leaving the organization, being promoted or reassigned. Corporate "yellow pages" also fall in this category. Users throughout an organization want to query a KM system to find out who in the organization knows about a subject. The subject may be a technical topic, an organizational topic (e.g., purchasing), a customer, or a line of business. In addition to corporate yellow pages, Stewart [94] says the basic content should include lessons learned and competitor intelligence.

The content selected for inclusion needs to fit with the organizational strategy for KM. Booz Allen's KOL system includes whom to call for help, detailed resumes, frameworks for solving problems, best practices, case studies, trends, and glossaries. But in developing KOL, the firm also learned something about what not to include. Providing access to a lot of leading edge technical material worked against its KM strategy to get consultants to collaborate and contact the experts [79].

Content should be structured according to how it will be used. If users logically associate the organization's work products with the customer for the work, then it may make sense to use customer as one axis on which to identify content. Searching for content by specific customer name will be faster if the search can be conducted over the customer field alone rather than a full text search over all the content. Other candidates for classification axes include author, project, application domain, and technical area. Individual categories may be hierarchical, such as the technical area of database technology unfolding into more detailed categories like relational and object-oriented.

Patt-Corner [114] identifies six parameters to guide the classification of resources:

- *theme:* What am I about?
- *security:* Who can see me?
- *ownership:* Who do I belong to?
- *valuation:* How am I valuable?
- *association:* How do I relate to other knowledge?
- *management:* How am I maintained?

For a given parameter, resources should be classified is ways that are useful to people doing the work. For example, the valuation parameter can include issues such as [114]:

- *utility:* Is this meaningful information in its present form, or is it raw data that would need to be combined or interpreted to have value?
- *currency:* To what extent is this representative of current operations?

The same parameters used to classify content should be used when workers publish new content to the KM system [114]. Often a simple contribution interface will be pre-filled with information the system knows, such as the name and organization of the person. For the few remaining fields, the system should provide pop-up boxes showing the predetermined values from which users can select.

Representative parameters and their values will vary depending on the organization. For document content, parameters could be

- *finality:* draft, preliminary version, final form
- *visibility:* owner, named work group, department, division, organization, customer, partners, unrestricted external visibility
- *type:* proposal, statement of work, specification, design, test plan, technical report, user's manual, product description, strategic plan
- *form:* text, spreadsheet, audio, video, graphic.

A *taxonomy*, providing a comprehensive classification of a category, may be used to classify content. Subject matter experts or software tools can define the taxonomy. When a software tool is employed, it is extracting structure from a corpus of unstructured content. SemioMap is a product that develops a hierarchical taxonomy of information from repositories of text. An interesting feature is to allow people to establish the top-level categories of the taxonomy, for example, to align them with lines of business or core competencies. Then SemioMap automatically fills out the lower levels of the taxonomy. In this way, the tool may develop useful organizing relationships based solely on the content, yet within a top-level structure that is guaranteed to relate to the business.

4.3 Content Delivery

There are a variety of strategies, techniques, and tools for delivering desired content to people who need it. This section might easily have been titled "search and retrieval," but that is only one approach. The real issue is content delivery at the personal level: show me only what matters to me and only when I need to know it. So in addition to looking for desired material and pulling it in, a person may have content pushed to her because her supervisor wants her to see it or because a software agent has found something that matches the interest profile she entered. Her interest profile may be operating against various channels of content coming from internal and external sources.

The delivered content can be overwhelming, but summarization and visualization can make it approachable and understandable. At the level of an individual document, content summarization addresses people's interest in knowing what the document is about. There is emerging technology aimed at effectively summarizing documents automatically. To do this requires software that uncovers the meaning in documents, their semantics rather than their syntax. An example system is KNOW-IT, from TextWise LLC, which evolved from DARPA funding. KNOW-IT automatically extracts concepts and their relationships to build a knowledge base from raw text.

Visualization tools can present a graphic depiction of a body of content. The ThemeScape product from Cartia, Inc., uses a map metaphor for its visualizations. Figure 9 shows ThemeScape used to visualize a week's worth of technology news, 535 documents in all. The mountains, valleys, and islands in the graphic express relationships that are difficult to represent through text. Seeing Fig. 9, we get an overall sense of the themes in the content, suggested by the height of the mountains. A user still has access to the individual documents, which are marked by dots. Moving the cursor over a topographical region reveals the names of documents related to each theme. Clicking on a dot will display the corresponding document. A user can also search over the content and mark key documents with flags for future reference.

An excellent use for visualization is to summarize the themes for a new person who is assigned to a project and needs to get up-to-date quickly. The frequent occurrence in the era of hard-copy documents was to place a stack of them in front of the new arrivals so they can learn the background and get oriented. An electronic equivalent may be to point them to a folder

FIG. 9. Visualization of 535 technical articles using Cartia ThemeScape. (© Cartia, Inc., Reprinted by permission).

containing many documents. But this would still not be much help. The new worker would still need to open each document to learn about its content. A major step forward is to point a visualization tool at a directory to get the high-level themes of the project and provide a framework for more detailed examination of the content.

Content delivery is affected by content structuring. As we noted in section 4.2, structure should be introduced to facilitate the way content will be used. In our organization, the project and the customer are key attributes that characterize plans, technical reports, and prototypes. When we organize content, these terms are part of the metadata to describe the content. By doing so, we make it easier for users to access material, both by pull and push technology:

- We can search for content by fielded search on the metadata, where the customer field is "Company X," rather than full-text search of the content itself.

- We can enter a profile or subscription expressing interest in any new items, for which the project field in the metadata description is "Project Y"

We discuss content delivery from these two basic approaches: search and pull, and profile and push. The two are related in the sense that, for push technology to work, there must be mechanisms, such as search engines and software agents, operating in the background to find relevant content based

on the expressed interest profiles. In effect the interest profile becomes a
query term to drive the push technology. A very promising emerging
technology, the eXtensible Markup Language (XML), is discussed in
section 4.3.3, because it offers great potential to improve content delivery.

4.3.1 Search and Pull

Searching may be performed over structured or unstructured content,
based on trying to match a query or search term. When dealing with a
database or a document management system, the structured organization of
the content provides an aid. The user may search based on fields in the
metadata description or relations in the data.

> Often what people want from a search query is not the material itself; they
> want to use the material to figure out who they should call to talk about the
> problem they have right now [116].

Searching over unstructured content is increasingly important with the
wealth of information available on the Internet. Web search technology is a
widely used means of finding relevant material. Early Internet search tools
were Archie (1990), for searching FTP servers, and Veronica (1992) and
Jughead (1993) for gopher servers. Search engines for the world wide web
typically include programs called crawlers or spiders that access web sites,
and follow links to other sites, continually building up an index of text and
uniform resource locators (URLs) found along the way. A user of the search
engine enters a search term: a word, a string of words enclosed in quotation
marks, or words connected by Boolean operators such as "and" and "or."
Search engine software operates on its index, returning names and URLs of
web pages that match the search term.

In its response, the search engine will list the sites in ranked order, trying
to reflect the semantic closeness of the site to the search term. A familiar
ranking approach is to list the sites according to the number of times the
query term appears in the web page. Search engines operating on documents
in an enterprise document management system may give greater weight
when terms appear earlier in the document, or in titles, section headings, or
larger font. The approach of the Google search engine from Stanford
University is taken from the academic world, where the number of citations
of a publication is a proxy for the importance of that publication. So Google
ranks a site by how many other web pages link to that site. Where Google is
based on static information, the presence of hyperlinks on a web page, the
Direct Hit search engine looks at dynamic data. It ranks the relevance of
web pages using a proprietary algorithm that monitors the web pages users
access, the time they spend, and the hyperlinks they take.

The Clever search algorithm iteratively converges on a rank for a web page based on scoring web pages two ways, as hubs or authorities. A highly valued *hub* is a web page that points to the best authoritative web pages for a subject. A web page ranks high as an *authority* if the best hubs point to it. The algorithm starts with a base set of web pages, and assigns them scores both as hubs and authorities. The highest scoring authority pages are used to identify the best hubs. An analysis of these top-ranked hub sites points to a new set of authorities. The process is repeated until the rankings begin to stabilize. A side effect is to establish clusters of web pages along major sub-areas of a subject. When someone searches for a subject, the authority scores are used to respond with the relevant web pages in priority order [117].

A tactical problem is that spamming can skew the results of searches. To gain high relevance rankings, commercial web sites may repeat words ("auto loans auto loans auto loans") in metatags, which are HTML tags that do not affect the appearance of the page but provide keywords and other information about the contents of the page. Search services are countering by not scanning metatags or by reducing the relevance ranking of sites that use keywords unrelated to the content of the page [118].

A fundamental problem is that the most relevant document to meet a particular need may scarcely include the query term, perhaps because it is using a synonym or has quickly moved from a general concept to more specific ones. Search engines supplemented by semantic networks can take a query for "heart attack" and relate it to "cardiac arrest" and search on both strings [119].

The KM perspective is to question the extent to which keyword searching captures the way people think about what information they need. More often, people want concept search—all the information relevant to a concept in their minds and not always easy to capture in a few words connected by Boolean operators. Search engines have been enhanced by allowing users to pose a question in natural language as they would with another person. One of the most widely used examples is the AskJeeves search service, which uses natural language processing to parse the text in the query. The intention is to more nearly identify the concept being searched by taking advantage of the grammar and syntax of the entire query expression. Another feature of AskJeeves, also used by other search services, is to use multiple search engines (AskJeeves uses five), so the user gets the benefit of the searching, indexing, and ranking strategies of several engines with a single query.

Natural language queries are an improvement over keywords, but we are still far removed from concept search. A closer approximation is to point to a paragraph or entire document and ask the search service to find other documents "like this one." Sophisticated search algorithms can make use of the additional information to provide context by comparing it to semantic networks that place weighted values on relationships between words. The search algorithm will find words that reinforce each other to create themes. Consider a user who wants data on automobile sales. Entering "auto" and "sales," or even "auto sales," as keyword search terms on most search engines will generate high-relevance responses about automobiles for sale and special sales announced by automobile dealers. Consider the difference if the query were based on a paragraph about the numbers of automobiles sold during the year, and the trends in those numbers. An intelligent search for similar documents would pick up on the theme and attach more relevance to documents that truly match the intent of the user.

A directory, such as Yahoo, provides structure to content, so a user can navigate through the hierarchical directory structure to find web pages of interest. The search capability accompanying a directory service allows a user first to navigate into the general topic of interest (e.g., automobiles) and restrict the search space to pages associated with that topic. When directory search services operate without a web crawler, human editors produce descriptive text for each web page. When a query term is entered, the search software scans these descriptions to find matches. The strength, over web crawlers, is the editor can write the descriptions in ways that will help to bring the most relevant pages to the top of the rankings. We used a web crawler based search engine with the query term, "Bristol Connecticut." We clearly want to go to comprehensive home pages about the city, but those responses were not among the top 15 rankings in the list. A weakness, when a web crawler is not used, is the directories do not always find changes in web pages. NEC's Research Institute estimated that more than 5% of the search results of one search service were dead links [118]. To counter this problem, search services like Netscape are using hybrid approaches, incorporating automated crawlers and directories.

Although we have contrasted searching over structured and unstructured sources, users typically don't care where the answer comes from. Certain search capabilities will accept a query term and produce a ranked list of responses integrated from multiple sources such as structured databases, files systems, web sites, resume repositories, and e-mail. Figure 10 shows the outcome of a search using PC DOCS/Fulcrum across multiple content sources. The middle of the figure shows the responses ranked by relevance, indicated by the length of the cross-hatched bar.

To improve search performance, companies are exploring a range of options, technical and otherwise. Fast Search & Transfer is implementing faster indexing algorithms and architectures that will scale with the increase in web pages. Northern Light reduces the search space through context-sensitivity. If a user indicates an interest in certain application domains or

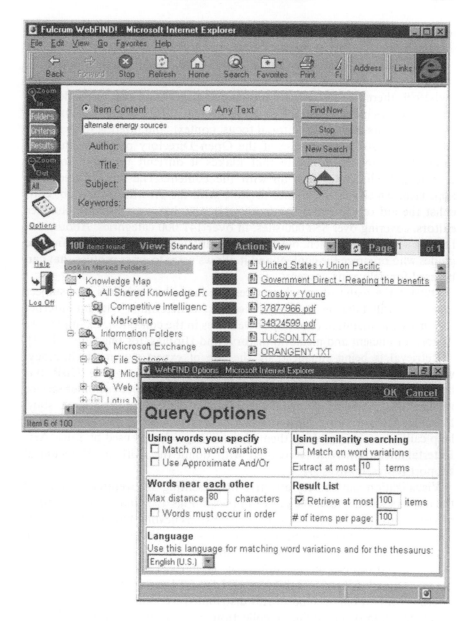

FIG. 10. Outcome of search with PCDOCS/Fulcrum. (© Hummingbird/PCDOCS/ Fulcrum, Reprinted by permission).

regions, the search engine can take advantage of that information to deliver more relevant matches [118].

A variation on limiting the range of resources being searched is for the search service to exercise control over the web pages that are indexed. By mid-1999, there were over 350 million web pages, and one of the leading search services indexed only 140 million of them. [118] LookSmart currently uses 200 editors to provide editorial focus, context, and filtering to its search technology [120]. The premise of the Open Directory project is that the Internet is growing at a rate that makes it difficult for any group of commercial editors to keep up with the content. The Open Directory's approach, which has the chance to scale with the growth of the web, is to enlist the aid of the entire community. It now has over 14 000 volunteer editors, covering over 850 000 sites, in over 141 000 categories. About.com follows a similar approach, but significant differences are that it certifies the guides who organize the content and it allows users to enter profiles that can be used for delivering content.

Outside the realm of search services are individual scholars in a subject area who will take on the role of editor to determine relevant internet resources and maintain currency of web sites in the collection. Examples are Argos, for ancient and medieval history, and Hippias, for philosophy [121].

Retrieval is being enhanced by the use of expert systems technology, where knowledge can be captured by rules. *Case-based reasoning* (CBR) has been especially valuable for helpdesk, call center, and other customer service applications, allowing companies to handle calls without a large staff. Inference Corporation's CBR product generates a series of questions that help callers resolve problems themselves. The product is used by LucasArts Entertainment, where it is credited with doing the work of 33 technical support representatives [122].

Visualization can be very effective in presenting an overarching view of the responses to a query. We saw examples in Figs 1, 5, and 9. An advantage of visualization is the expression of relationships beyond binary ones. People can see fuzzy relationships between concepts, as in the topographic view in Fig. 9 showing semantic closeness, breadth, and depth.

Search and retrieval in the context of the internet has been the challenge of the Digital Libraries Initiative (DLI). DLI researchers envision an internet with "a billion repositories distributed over the world, where each small community maintains a collection of their own knowledge" [32]. Accessing this knowledge will require enhanced semantic and concept-based searches that will facilitate knowledge networking—making it easy for outsiders to search the specialized terminology of an individual repository. Advances in indexing would make the searches effective not only across text, video, voice, and image sources, but across languages and cultures. The vision is to transform the Internet into the Interspace, where users easily access and analyze information from heterogeneous repositories [32].

DLI and the US National Science Foundation initiative on Knowledge and Distributed Intelligence [31] raise the prospect of greatly improved technology in the future to access and integrate information from disparate worldwide sources. It may not be obvious that advances like these will affect KM in an organization, in which there is more control. However, most of the knowledge in any particular field is generated outside of a single organization. For knowledge workers to stay abreast of developments in their fields, they need better tools for conducting concept-based analysis of external resources.

4.3.2 Profile and Push

Another fundamental approach to delivering content is to selectively send content to individuals, based on understanding their interests. Users may complete profiles describing the kinds of information they want and how they want the information to be sent to them.

A factor affecting the ability of systems to push information is the extent to which people are willing to submit interest profiles or engage in on-line transactions that reveal data about them. While there is general acknowledgment that people are concerned about personal privacy on the web, a study by AT&T Labs provided data on the subject. Among people who say they are reluctant to supply personal data, 58% would do so if the site had a privacy policy and a recognizable approval seal. Among people who were willing to supply personal data, 78% do so in return for a customized service [123].

When relevant information is found, there is a range of alternatives for sending the information to the user, in addition to a notification when the user signs on. As an example, BackWeb Technologies' products offer these options, all configurable based on user preferences:

- *Flash:* A small box automatically appears on your desktop, announcing the new content. The flash box can be configured based on time settings and to operate with certain applications.

- *Ticker:* a scrolling line of text, configured to bring a specified content channel, such as stock trades or news headlines, to your screen. The ticker can be configured to use the title bar of the active window to conserve desktop space. The user can click on a scrolling item to obtain a summary of the content in a pop-up box.

- *Screensaver:* Configured to bring any channel to your desktop as a screensaver.

Collaborative filtering allows a software tool to tailor its communications to you on the basis of what other people have done. It may suggest a new item for you to purchase, not because you asked for it, but because other people with similar purchasing histories or interest profiles bought the item. One of the most familiar examples of collaborative filtering is its use by Amazon.com, in connection with selling books over the internet.

Apple Data Detectors are intelligent agents that extract structured information from unstructured documents [124]. Someone reading a message will invoke the agent to detect whatever structures it can. Apple Data Detectors can detect highly formatted text, such as URLs, and less-structured content, such as names and addresses or the dates and times for meetings. For each detected structure, the agent generates a pop-up menu with likely actions for that structure:

- *URLs:* open them or add them to a bookmark list
- *names and addresses:* add them to an address book
- *meeting dates and times:* enter them in an appointment book.

4.3.3 XML

There is a high level of enthusiasm about the eXtensible Markup Language (XML) as the new "language of business" [125]. The World Wide Web Consortium (W3C) endorsed it in 1997 as a future standard for data interchange. Each element of content can be tagged in XML for relevant information, such as source of the data or the business unit that owns the data. In this sense, we have the potential to get the benefits of structure and organization—for example, searching for material associated with a specific business unit—with unstructured content.

> For knowledge management, XML promises to be nothing short of revolutionary, providing an infrastructure for KM functionality to finally become enmeshed in the fabric of company operations. [125].

Among mark-up languages, XML owes more to the more flexible Standard Generalized Mark-up Language (SGML) than to the widely used HyperText Markup Language (HTML). Whereas HTML tags prescribe the formatting and displaying of the content, XML is not restricted. The potential is for users to operate from XML-based browsers to find specific information without extensive searching against repositories and programming into database systems.

A DLI project illustrates the more flexible tagging of content. The project developed a retrieval system called DELIVER (Desktop Link to Virtual Engineering Resources) [126]. It was implemented as a testbed at the

University of Illinois at Urbana-Champaign for researching federated search over heterogeneous sources. DELIVER operates on a document collection of 66 000 articles from five professional societies in physics, engineering, and computer science. The articles are captured in full text, SGML format, with bit-mapped images.

This structural tagging can align indexing and searching with the way people read documents. A study of engineers found that, when they encounter an article for the first time, they tend to use parts of it in a consistent way [126]. First they read the title and abstract. Next, they skim section headings and look at lists and illustrations. Content tagged in XML can deliver content by unfolding greater detail in a way that is natural for users.

The generality of the attribute-tagging concept is suggested by ongoing XML efforts for 3D and voice. The Web 3D consortium is developing a 3D specification so that, in the future, clicking on a component in an engineering document will bring you a 3-dimensional schematic of the component. A Voice eXtensible Markup Language (VXML) is aimed at enabling users to easily create interactive voice applications, for example, to access e-mail and calendar information from a voice response system [125].

Early XML applications encourage the optimism about its potential to manage content across applications and trading partners. The US General Services Administration uses it to provide a unified catalog of products, so users do not need to access multiple individual electronic catalogs. Conexant and Agile Software have used XML in their businesses to standardize supply chain information among vendors, manufacturers, and customers. The XML documents can describe product data and bills of materials, so that all parties work with consistent information regardless of the individual companies or application systems used [125].

> XML can do for data what Java has done for programs, which is to make the data both platform-independent and vendor independent [127].

4.4   User Interface

Intranets have evolved into corporate portals that provide a tailorable window for viewing information flowing from within the organization, from external partners, and from the entire internet. The scope of internal information includes the relatively static policies, procedures, phone books, and forms as well as dynamic information about ongoing operations, like transaction flows and performance levels. Emphasizing the channeling of information from a wide range of sources into one place, IBM refers to its interface as a *knowledge cockpit* [45].

Getting the presentation interface right for an intranet means understanding all the stakeholders and their needs. To the extent possible, systems
should allow users the flexibility to accommodate their varying styles and
preferences. But the overall framework needs to be consistent, so that people
are not jolted by a different appearance every time they access the system.
There will certainly be a visible presence for an ability to search for content
by attributes, by example, and by name. Many users also want to browse
through a more detailed directory of all content. Systems need to provide
site maps and navigation aids so users can know where they are and easily
access what they want. Visualizations, like tree structures and topographic
maps, can be especially useful in showing many relationships in a concise
way. We saw with Inxight's hyperbolic tree (Fig. 5) that the structure can
remain with the content, obviating the need for a separate site map.

KM tools allow organizations to move beyond intranets to develop
portals into a wide range of content. Figure 11 shows an example of
personalization using the Plumtree portal product, which uses XML to
provide flexibility. Users can contour their presentation interface so that it

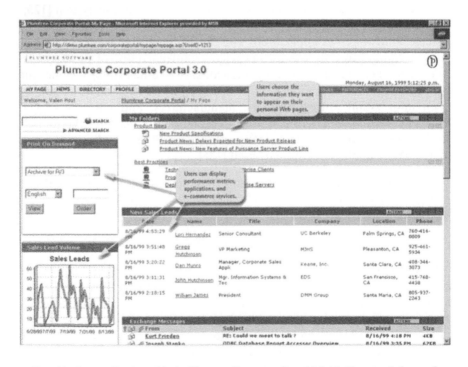

FIG. 11. Personalization with the Plumtree Corporate Portal 3.0 (© Plumtree Software, Inc.,
www.plumtree.com Reprinted by permission).

has the content and layout that makes them more productive. In the figure, the user has organized folders representing information from both internal and external sources. Security features make it feasible to use the product with external partners. On the left side, windows keep an active e-commerce tool and a performance graph on the desktop. Software agents are working in the background to search internal content stores and external web pages, so they can refresh the interface with current information. The bottom window shows the day's appointment book.

The metaphor of asking a human, encouraged by AskJeeves, is further explored by the Big Science Company, whose web site presents the user with the image of a person, Andrette, who responds to users' questions. Her facial expressions change depending on the response she provides: happy for a question she can answer, a puzzled look for a question outside her domain, and so on. This interface perhaps can provide an element of personality to a search process or help service.

4.5 Collaboration

The importance of collaboration to KM should be clear from the extensive treatment of knowledge sharing and communities of practice in section 3. Bill Gates observes, "To recruit and retain smart people, you need to make it easy for them to collaborate with other smart people" [110]. Collaboration is a principal way that knowledge gets created, transferred, and applied. Valuable collaboration capabilities are already available without any KM system. The communications infrastructure of many organizations includes e-mail along with audio and video teleconferencing. Quite common also is the ability of users to specify access privileges for files and folders on servers so a work group can maintain a common repository. An essential element of a KM system is to provide additional capabilities to make it easy for people to collaborate. Automated support for collaboration takes many forms:

- *Threaded discussions*, in which an individual can post a question to the KM system, and others can respond. The record of the original question and associated responses can build over time. Key to KM is treating the entire threaded discussion as another unit of content that can be managed and accessed in response to search queries.

- *Chat*, for synchronous communication in which participants are online at the same time, and able to type their comments one after another as if they were chatting in a face-to-face experience.

- *Online meeting*, where, instead of typing discussion comments as with chat, each person's screen can show the image of the other person, with audio. Supporting capabilities include the ability to designate one person to possess special privileges to moderate the discussion. More important is the ability for meeting participants to have a shared space. This space can be a document, so that people can circle text while the audio track makes a point about that part of the document. An open whiteboard can be made accessible, so if one person draws a diagram, all parties can see it on their screens. People can give up control of their screens so another person can actively manipulate an electronic artifact.

- *Instant messaging*, or *on-demand linking*, in which a user can see, for example, who is reviewing a document and establish an immediate connection if the other person allows it.

- *Virtual workspace*, which carries the metaphor of a physical place to an electronic collaboration. By examining the project workroom region of their screen, participants in the project can see other team members who are in the room and eligible to join discussions. Team members can make electronic artifacts available to the team by dragging and dropping them into the room. The metaphor is that everything about the project is contained in that virtual space.

- *Electronic meeting rooms*, guided by an expert facilitator can be powerful environments for knowledge sharing and knowledge creation. Meeting room software enables all participants to brainstorm ideas and propose solutions in parallel, generating a lot of material in a short amount of time. Software also allows participants to rank ideas and vote for them, thereby producing ordered lists that carry the message from the meeting about the leading ideas. Everything gets captured, unlike a conversation, in which a good idea may be put forward, but never recognized at the time for its merit, and is ultimately lost to the organization. A much-touted benefit of electronic meeting rooms is the lack of attribution. Participants are able to express what is really on their minds. More important is the ability of an electronic meeting room to allow people to get their ideas out to others, where they may not be as successful in person due to interpersonal dynamics.

"I've worked with you guys for 20 years, and this is the first time I've ever heard you. When you're talking, I'm always trying to figure out what I'm going to say in response. Here, I get to see all the comments without the emotion, so I'm overwhelmed."[3]

---

[3] Anonymous manager quoted by Doug Stover of Hewlett-Packard, based on his experiences conducting groupware sessions, from [100].

Highly effective collaboration capabilities are increasingly important because of the growth of telecommuting, mobile and independent knowledge workers, and international operations. Each method of collaboration has its strengths and weaknesses. For example, same-time collaboration methods, like on-demand linking and chat, can create an effective immediate collaboration, but also can be difficult to accomplish because of the mobility—and sometimes multiple time zones—of knowledge workers.

Organizations should select groupware and other collaboration-support tools that offer the capabilities for the collaborative styles they use. The role of innovation (see section 3.3) will help determine the importance of selecting tools to support brainstorming and idea generation. In some organizations, the most critical collaboration is in communities of practice that are active over many years because they represent core practices. Other organizations are known for the rapid creation of teams who work in very close collaboration full-time for a short period of time and then disband.

With the increasing use of teams and task forces, one of the current trends in groupware products is to provide more support for them through "instant groupware." The working assumption is that the team members are separated by distance and are thrown together to solve a problem. They need to establish a workspace immediately to collaborate and share materials, often across scattered time zones.

When a mix of collaborative styles are used, organizations should look to products featuring an array of capabilities, so that the various collaborative groups can select the ones that meet their needs.

4.6   Mining

There are many words preceding "mining," such as data mining, information mining, knowledge mining, skills mining, or talent mining. The term may vary but the concept is the same: applying sophisticated algorithms to a mass of data to uncover relationships and patterns that can contribute to improved decision-making and organizational success. Much of the mining is perhaps more properly prospecting, since the existence of nuggets is not at all assured.

Consistent with our practice of using data to refer to all electronic content (see section 2.3), we do not distinguish among data mining, information mining, and knowledge mining. In each case we are analyzing electronic content. If meaningful patterns are discovered, then there is information. Skills mining or talent mining involves analyzing content to determine who possesses certain skills or who may be knowledgeable about a subject. The content may be resumes, but it also could be documents, whose authors might be presumed to have the skills.

Data about individual buying profiles have always been valuable. An off-line lead can fetch up to $300 from a financial services firm [123]. With electronic commerce, the quantity of data available for mining is staggering. NetCreations has a database of over 2 million people who participate ("opt-in") by having their interest profiles listed. Presented with a topical interest, the company will sell the matching e-mail addresses for 20–25 cents apiece [123, 128].

The success of data mining in yielding information is due to the effectiveness of the analysis routines and the extent to which the content facilitates the mining. Data mining methods include statistical methods, concept learning, collaborative filtering, association rules, neural networks, genetic algorithms, and other means of evolutionary computation.

Keys to success in data mining are knowing the business, knowing the data, and formulating the right question. An example involving all three factors is a data mining project to predict the attrition of users of a specific product. It turned out that part of the attrition was desirable because the product was being fraudulently used by some users. Understanding the business and the data helped determine that the well-formed question involved dealing with seven different types of attrition [129].

Data mining can be very effective in finding relationships from disparate data sources. For this reason, data mining is often discussed along with data warehousing, to emphasize the potential for surprising results when multiple and diverse data sources are mined. Data mining has been effective in determining the most successful product mixes and sales promotions for Kraft, a producer of a variety of food products. The data mining uncovered relationships across two different data sources: marketing and demographic data from the producer, and point-of-sale data from the supermarkets [130].

Data mining, or knowledge discovery in databases, is a significant field of study and application, discussed in greater detail in [131].

> Data mining will become much more important and companies will throw away nothing about their customers because it will be so valuable. If you're not doing this, you're out of business [132].

4.7 System Administration

A KM system needs an ongoing systems administration function. The content needs to be managed to assure quality, security, access control, backup, recovery, and compliance with legal and accounting practices and standards. KM professional staff will need a development environment to assure that applications, interfaces, and changes are robust before they are released for use across the organization.

The design of the KM system can reduce the level of effort required for administration. The successful Knowledge Today system at the US Atlantic Command is largely self-managed. A user can publish to the intranet and can set up a work group to collaborate and share documents without needing to send requests to a central administrative function [8]. Similarly, authority to create home pages is driven down in BP's organization, so anyone can create a home page [73].

Administrative costs can be further reduced by taking advantage of organization-wide systems administration for user login, helpdesk, product upgrade, remote access, networking, and other support functions.

Ideally, the KM systems administration function is free to focus on KM-specific activities. It is important to create a set of indicators that give visibility into the evolving system. Monitoring the size of the KM content stores and the number and activity of collaborative workgroups will provide advance warning when additional capacity is required. KM administrators may need to watch for opportunities to combine groups or archive the work of inactive groups.

With the assistance of subject matter experts and management, the KM staff should take the lead in several aspects of managing content:

- achieving consensus on organization-wide taxonomies
- retiring obsolete or extraneous content
- restructuring content as the organization evolves, to support new competencies and lines of business.

KM systems can be overwhelmed with information. A useful KM indicator is to monitor the growth of content in subject areas, to signal the transforming action of packaging content, as we discussed in section 3.4, with the synthesis of project management information into a guidebook. If the organization relies on search technology to retrieve relevant material, the KM staff should ensure, through its understanding of the search engine, that this guidebook will be the highest relevance hit on any reasonable searches. The newly developed guidebook should be advertised on the KM system, through push technology based on user interests (see section 4.3.2), so workers are aware of the latest developments.

Packaged knowledge may be tailored to specific audiences. For a CEO, the package may focus on trends in recent projects in a subject area, while, for a technical staff member, it may summarize the results of cost estimations for large software projects that feature integration of commercial off the shelf (COTS) components. If possible, the package should be market-tested with a sample of its intended audience [133].

Ernst & Young calls its packaged reports "power packs," whose preparation is triggered by the volume of content in the area and its criticality. A power pack is limited to 50 Mbytes so consultants can carry it on laptops. To enhance usability, all power packs follow the same format, with the material divided into eight categories: people, sales and marketing, leading practices, articles and research, learning resources, regulations and standards, service delivery, and software [134].

In addition to preparing power packs of synthesized knowledge, KM staff also may need to unpack documents, as Ernst & Young does, to create reusable chunks, like interview guides and work schedules, that are best suited to reuse. The knowledge objects populate a repository that is staffed by 250 people in Ernst & Young's Center for Business Knowledge [54]. Disaggregating artifacts must be performed with care so as not to lose the context that gives meaning to the extracted information.

An indication of the administrative effort to maintain a KM system is provided by Booz Allen. Its KOL system had 1.5 Gbytes of content in 1997, fed by approximately 100 documents per month. Documents are text-only, appropriate for worldwide consultants who may be connecting on low speed modems. The 1997 budget for technology upgrades and support for KOL was $250 000. The cost of content management was $750 000, which does not include the cost to prepare documents. To place these numbers in perspective, Booz Allen in 1997 was a $1.4 billion company with 8500 employees [79].

5. KM Programs

Technology without people will never work, but people without technology can not scale [135].

This section aims to pull together the material on knowledge sharing and collaboration in organizations, along with the automated support of a KM system, to focus on the task of defining a KM program. We will consider KM strategy, ways to structure the program, how to get started, measures and indicators of progress, success criteria, and the role of a Chief Knowledge Officer (CKO) or similar KM leader.

5.1 KM Strategy

Business strategy drives KM strategy. Hansen *et al.* [54] describes two overarching KM strategies of codification and personalization, based on the business and work practices of the organization.

A *codification* strategy is appropriate for companies whose products and services have high similarity. These organizations are positioned to take advantage of the reuse of artifacts generated as part of the business. Consulting firms such as Andersen Consulting and Ernst & Young pursue this strategy. The KM approach would stress capturing documents, plans, proposals, and other objects produced during assignments and providing access to them so can be adapted for use with other jobs. There is extensive investment in infrastructure for repositories, content structuring, indexing, and search capabilities, so people can be linked to documents. Skandia worked on packaging its cumulative experiences into administrative modules that could be reused easily. As a result, the time required to set up operations in a new country was reduced from 7 years to 7 months [130].

In contrast, a business strategy founded on providing solutions to unique problems leads to a very different KM approach. The *personalization* strategy of consulting firms like McKinsey and Boston Consulting Group is based on the individual expertise of senior consultants who establish close personal relationships with client executives and provide custom contributions rich in tacit knowledge. Companies with a personalization business strategy would invest in KM to achieve people-to-people linkages. Consultants encountering a problem want to easily tap the personal knowledge of others in the company who have encountered similar problems. The KM system would emphasize being able to search on problem types and industry types to identify the most appropriate consultants who can help. Collaboration tools, video conferencing, and instant team collaboration support would be key KM tools [54].

Arthur Andersen pursued a dual strategy, characterized as divergent and convergent paths. The *divergent path*, AA Online, provides an organizational forum where anyone can post a question or document, without any editing. The emphasis is on openness: sharing ideas, following threaded discussions, and posting questions and announcements. Global Best Practices (GBP) represents the *convergent path* at Arthur Andersen. Its focus is to help consultants sell work and execute on the engagements. GBP is managed so it constitutes the best practices of the firm in each practice area, as well as presentations that can be customized [134].

Unless an organization understands its business strategy and the kinds of knowledge (tacit or explicit) and work practices critical to its success, it risks pursuing a KM strategy that is not appropriate for it [54].

5.2 Structuring a KM Program

Guided by an overall KM strategy, an organization has a variety of elements from which to choose in structuring an initiative for KM. We have already seen in section 1.3 how KM programs may be motivated by a broad organizational improvement goal or a more specific objective, such as reducing cycle time or improving collaboration. Also we noted that the program might be directed at the entire enterprise or a more narrow focus, such as a functional area or line-of-business unit.

Ideally, KM will address needs in all parts of the organization. Stowe Boyd has a useful three-tier pyramid to depict different perspectives on KM.

- The top strategy tier is the executive perspective, which is the success of the company and the contribution of knowledge towards that success.
- The mid-level business tier is the world of the line-of-business manager—deliver value to customers, reduce costs, and create a climate for knowledge sharing and innovation.
- The bottom foundation of the pyramid is the technology manager, who focuses on how best to employ information technology to support the business layer [136].

In structuring a KM program, Arthur D. Little believes the most critical aspect is to pursue KM from a multidimensional perspective, in the four domains of content, culture, process, and infrastructure. To be successful at KM, it is more important to do a credible job at all four, than to excel at three and fail at one [115].

KM projects tend to be composed of one or more of the following activities [130]:

- capturing and reusing structured knowledge
- capturing and sharing lessons learned
- identifying sources and networks of expertise
- structuring and mapping knowledge needed to enhance performance
- synthesizing and sharing knowledge from external sources
- embedding knowledge in products and processes
- measuring and managing the economic value of knowledge.

Surveys are revealing that companies' actual KM activities are different from what they believe they should be doing. An IBM survey showed that most KM initiatives are in intranets, groupware, data warehouses, and decision-support tools. What company executives say they should be doing is mapping sources of internal expertise, establishing new knowledge roles, and creating networks of knowledge workers [12].

Figure 12 shows the leading areas for applying KM, based on Delphi Group survey research of over 300 organizations [137]. The principal

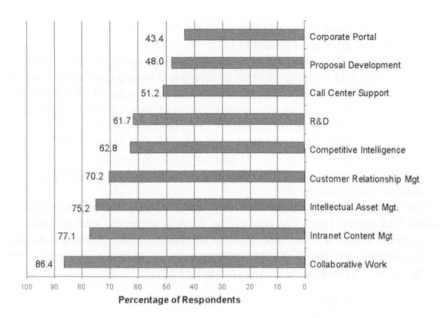

FIG. 12. Current and planned KM applications: survey of 300 organizations, March 1999. (Source: The Delphi Group, Inc. [137]).

application areas, collaborative work and intranet content management, are basically in agreement with the IBM survey.

Some organizational KM programs are directed at a single project type from the list in Fig. 12. Both Eli Lilly [138] and Hoffman-LaRoche used a KM approach to reduce the time-to-market for new drugs, in a market where a single day's delay can mean $1 million in lost revenue [130]. Hoffman-LaRoche organized knowledge from R&D, legal, and other functional areas. Then it created a knowledge map of the new drug application process to show what knowledge had to be developed and packaged, to reduce delays in answering questions from the FDA.

Platinum's KM initiative is also quite focused. The goal is to give its global sales force a single source of current information. Platinum's web knowledge portal was one of the earliest to use XML-based indexing. Platinum calculates a return of $6 million on its investment of $750 000. Much of the return was in costs avoided to print and mail sales information. Revenue per salesperson has jumped by 4%, but, as is often the case, it is difficult to attribute the increase solely to the KM initiative. More direct measurement shows 2 hours per week saved per salesperson in searching for information. Another indicator of success is Platinum's continuing program to develop six more web portals around COPs, in business development, consulting, and education groups [139].

We discussed in section 3.3 that the role of innovation influences an organization's KM strategy. A team at Hewlett-Packard developed a novel electronic oscilloscope and associated interface, and wanted to inform the rest of the company. They considered the predictable path of writing a product description along with answers to frequently asked questions, and publishing it within the company, but concluded that the knowledge they wanted to convey was too rich to communicate in writing. Instead, they visited other divisions and transferred the knowledge through meetings and conference presentations [54].

The successful World Bank KM program has elements of more than a single KM project type. The goal of the Bank is to be the leading place to turn for information about development worldwide, incorporating not only Bank projects, but those of other development organizations as well. The Bank's KM initiative provides the following [39]:

- support to COPs
- access to an on-line knowledge base
- helpdesks and advisory services
- directory of expertise
- key sectoral statistics
- transactions and engagement information
- dialogue space for professional conversations
- access and outreach to external clients, partners, and stakeholders.

It is important to structure the KM program to advance its strategic objectives, with an appropriate mix of codification, personalization, content delivery mechanisms, and collaboration tools to meet the needs of the organization.

5.3 Getting Started

The KM project must be phased and staged over time, and with consideration of available budget. Each stage needs to deliver visible and real benefits to a specific community in the organization. Most critical is the selection of the first stage of the KM program. It should have the following qualities [140]:

- *visible:* this is the time to call on the high level sponsors to communicate the KM objective to the organization

- *valuable:* providing early visible returns, a real benefit to a community of practice, preferably a COP that cuts orthogonally across the enterprise, like business development
- *doable:* scoped so it will be successful; but begin working the high risk elements in the background
- *leveraged:* building from the experiences of people in the organization to others who can benefit from them
- *scalable:* don't postpone the tough issues; tackle a project that, when successful, can scale more broadly, for example, to other COPs
- *instrumented:* so the KM team learns as it tries this first activity, with quantitative and qualitative feedback, including interviews and surveys of people affected by the change.

5.4 Measures and Indicators

Our discussion of intellectual capital in section 3.1.2 provided an early look at the use of quantitative indicators. In this section, we examine the use of measures and indicators for understanding the degree of success in KM initiatives. Two dimensions of indicators are the degree of objectivity and the scope of measurement. Indicators for KM range from objectively defined quantitative measures to very subjective qualitative indicators. The scope of the indicators corresponds to the scope of the KM initiative, ranging from organization-wide indicators to those more narrowly defined around a problem or activity.

KM requires investment and expects returns. The value proposition for KM must include a timeline of clearly defined expected outcomes based on the investment.

> [KM] doesn't run on air; it takes money. If you think you can do this without funding it and ask people to do it in their spare time, it won't happen [141].

> Unless KM falls under someone's job description, it won't get done [97].

Often the investment part of the equation is strikingly clear in dollar terms, although the returns resist quantification.

> How much does it cost an organization to forget what key employees know, to be unable to answer customer questions quickly or not at all, or to make poor decisions based on faulty knowledge? [141].

In an era of "internet time," an organization may need to make a significant investment to keep track of the information relevant to its business and to package it for use. We mentioned Ernst & Young's staff of

250 serving this role. BP Amoco spent $12.5 million to install KM technologies and $20 million more over the years on coaching employees and codifying best practices. They claim the sharing and applying of best practices worldwide have justified the investment [99]. The World Bank KM program is funded at 4% of its administrative budget, but they are able to pull together relevant knowledge from development projects worldwide in minutes to support their organizational mission [39].

At the level of the organization or line-of-business, using a familiar quantitative measure such as return on investment (ROI) allows KM investments to be evaluated along with other proposals for improving the business. There are clear cases of ROI used in KM, although one report claims, "We have found no convincing case where the ROI for KM has been done in a rigorous, methodical way" [143]. We do not know the specific cases that led to this observation, but we have seen many reports from reputable organizations describing their KM returns in quantitative measures, as increased revenue, increased profit, or costs avoided.

MITRE, a not-for-profit organization, reports returns of $54.91 million in reduced operating costs and improved productivity on an investment of $7.19 million in its corporate information infrastructure [144]. Dow Chemical classified its 29 000 patents, deciding which ones offered strategic advantage and revenue opportunities, and which should be abandoned to reduce tax burden. This KM effort, focused on intellectual property, saved $4 million in the first year alone and is expected to generate more than $100 million in licensing revenues [130]. Through knowledge sharing on energy use, Chevron saved $150 million annually in power and fuel expenses. By leveraging internal knowledge and best practices, Texas Instruments avoided the cost of building a $500 million wafer fabrication plant [14]. Booz Allen claims an ROI of 1400% on its KM system, with 62% of its consultants accessing the system each month [79].

Motorola looks to KM to help it reach its goal of fewer than 3.4 defects per million opportunities for error. This goal inspires innovative approaches to continuous learning and sharing of knowledge. On its investment in knowledge sharing and training at Motorola University, the company calculates a return of $3.1 billion between 1987 and 1992, or a return of $29 for every $1 invested [71].

Although quantitative measures are generally preferable, some organizations use qualitative indicators either exclusively or to supplement ROI measures. Eli Lilly & Co. uses subjective indicators to rate the success of its KM projects. They are scored from 1 to 10 on each of 5 areas: technology, profit, context, people, and content [138]. Arthur Andersen's KM Assessment tool lists the 24 practices that it uses in KM. The firm rates itself on two 1–5 scales—the extent to which the practice is established, and importance of the practice to the firm [134].

Whether the measures are quantitative or qualitative, a guiding principle is to look for trends in changes in the indicators. Even if there are no standards for KM measurement, as there are in managerial accounting, organizations should care about measures that make sense for them alone. They want to assess the returns and progress on KM investments for their benefit to their operations and their competitiveness. Most critical is to thoughtfully define the measurement instrument so it is measuring something of value, directly related to work practices. By applying the measurement instrument consistently, the most valuable knowledge will arise from tracking the indicators over time. Because the indicators will have been defined to be meaningful and relevant, the trends will show how the organization is progressing in its returns on KM.

5.5 Success Criteria

The experiences of early KM adopters are providing a rich source of knowledge on the key criteria that need to be present for a successful program. Success criteria must be aligned to the objectives of the KM program, which, as we have seen, may be broadly addressing organizational improvement or more narrowly focused. Critical success factors fall into three areas: leadership, project characteristics, and organizational context.

Organizations may find success with narrowly scoped KM efforts simply because smaller communities of practice are self-motivated. There are islands of knowledge across an organization. For example, a department may decide to collect all its documents, reports, and reference material and post them to a local server. The department technical staff members are growing weary of repeatedly answering the same questions and continually e-mailing reports to new staff to serve as examples of good practice. They don't need to draft a business case; they can readily see the benefit.

When we move beyond self-motivated communities of practice, larger KM programs require formal vision and structure. Top management involvement and commitment are essential, where the top corresponds to the planned scope of the KM initiative, at the level of the enterprise or a business unit. Surveys confirm that one of the major reasons for failure of KM programs is that top management didn't signal its importance to the rest of the organization [12]. As with other improvement practices (see section 1.4), employees must perceive genuine commitment to the goals of the KM initiative through the actions, more so than the words, of the organizational leadership.

Business users, not information systems staff, should drive the KM projects. KM initiatives risk failure unless they are tied to line-of-business practices [28]. Organizations must present a business case for the KM investment and manage it as with other projects. Experience suggests that the returns on KM may take longer than with practices more pointed to specific operational practices.

Project characteristics can predispose a KM project to success or failure. For a substantial KM initiative to provide knowledge sharing, document access, and project team collaboration, the KM team needs people with specific skills. The program cannot be expected to succeed if its design and execution is assigned to whomever in the organization is currently not otherwise busy. KM team members need to understand the sociological and technological issues associated with knowledge capture, document management, and corporate networked infrastructures. The team needs to maintain a window on emerging technology in specific KM areas such as search and retrieval, "push" tools, semantic analysis, skills profiling, collaboration, and data mining.

Key success criteria in the organizational context are a technological infrastructure and a "knowledge friendly" culture [101]. A major reason for failures of KM programs is a culture of knowledge hoarding [12]. To the extent the organization is not knowledge friendly, KM requires change in behavior and organizational values. The path to success will be more challenging, because change is difficult for people. In a survey of 200 IT managers by Information Week Research, two-thirds said behavior modification required of employees is the biggest obstacle to implementing KM [145].

Also crucial to success is to build KM on a firm technological foundation. Basic infrastructure includes appropriate-bandwidth network connectivity among employees, distributed storage across the network, e-mail, internet access, and web browsers. Individual knowledge workers are expected to have basic applications for knowledge capture, which typically include word processing, spreadsheet, graphic presentations, and may include industry-specific and organization-specific capabilities such as advanced graphics, design tools, or multimedia.

Although the principal success criteria lie in the realms of leadership, team characteristics, technological foundation, and organizational context, there are a host of tactical steps to help ensure success. For KM to bring benefits, it needs to be used. We have mentioned incentives such as frequent flier miles used to encourage knowledge sharing. It maybe as simple as gradually liberating people from familiar paper-based reference material, to get them started using the corporate intranet that is the hub of KM. At Mitretek, years ago we began migrating essential information (required forms, phone book, policies, company newsletters), so the only place to find it was on the corporate intranet. Once people are there, they will have overcome one obstacle and will be in the intranet on which they will start finding technical knowledge content. Organizations sponsor scavenger hunts to encourage employees to move beyond the static reference information and start exploring areas of the intranet that have useful items for them. Another simple tactic is to post information that people want to know. People in organizations are typically keenly interested in the latest rumors. One large organization used its infrastructure to maintain a newsgroup on the latest rumors about reorganization, so everyone could access the latest "information."

Not so obvious as a key tactic to make KM a success is to provide for sustainment. This crucial follow-up process at Sun Microsystems includes the KM leaders interviewing a vice president and her senior staff every 6–7 weeks to learn about the most current issues and problems they are facing. Through these interviews, the KM program keeps oriented to the top and most timely business objectives [99].

There are clear messages from early adopters about the characteristics of KM programs that have been successes and failures. Organizations have an opportunity to learn and benefit from these experiences to ensure success in their own KM programs.

5.6 The Chief Knowledge Officer

KM and the growing awareness of the key role of knowledge in organizations have given rise to new roles and titles. None is more visible and provocative than that of Chief Knowledge Officer (CKO), the executive charged with leveraging the intellectual assets in the organization. The title has been in place sufficiently long that there is even a CKO Emeritus at Booz Allen. But the prominence of CKOs should not imply that this is the only route to success or that the idea of a CKO is universally praised. In this section, we examine the CKO and other organizational roles aimed at making KM a success in organizations.

The responsibilities of the CKO include setting the priorities for KM in the organization and working with the CEO and senior managers to build the sponsorship for the program. Regardless of the specific thrust of the program, CKOs will be leading the organization in highly visible initiatives, such as managing intellectual property, obtaining customer satisfaction information, or capturing global best practices. The greatest challenge is to change an organization into a knowledge-sharing environment [146].

Much of our understanding of CKOs comes from three sources:

- a study of 52 CKOs by Bob Guns, partner at Probe Consulting [146]
- a study of 20 CKOs in North America and Europe by Earl and Scott [147]

- a series of interviews with 25 companies about the role of CKOs, by the Delphi Group [148].

Many of the CKOs in the Probe Consulting study were brought into this new and ill-defined role because they were thought to possess the skills to succeed, acquired through a broad base of experience rotating through functional areas with the organization. Both the Probe Consulting and the Earl and Scott studies show strong agreement on desirable traits of successful CKOs. They must be adept at influencing by persuasion and energizing others. Successful CKOs tend to be enthusiastic, bordering on evangelists or promoters, and comfortable operating as entrepreneurs within the organization. They must be skillful as agents of change, excellent communicators, and able to withstand pressure and tolerate ambiguity.

The interpersonal skills are put to a test as many CKOs become involved in changing performance measurement and executive appraisal systems. CKOs will be working closely with information systems directors and human resources directors to get programs implemented across the organization. They will be cultivating allies and KM partners in the administrative and business units.

CKOs typically will create advisory councils or other linkages to business units and stakeholders. Ernst & Young has a Knowledge Council, operating at a high level in the organization to ensure consistency across business units. The Council gives advice on major KM decisions involving architecture and technology. Within each business unit, a Knowledge Advisory Committee, consisting of 10–12 senior partners, ensures that KM aligns with business [130]. KPMG plans include a Shared Knowledge Center, a Director of Knowledge, and a web council [149]. Arthur D. Little has a similar structure, in which the Global Director of KM, at the corporate level, works with Knowledge Coordinators associated with each practice. Within a practice there is a Knowledge Advocate (the champion for KM) and the Knowledge Steward(s) having operational responsibility for KM [115].

We see in the case above that the executive KM title need not be CKO. In addition to Director of KM, other titles include Chief Learning Officer (CLO) or Director of Knowledge. Of course, with different titles, the responsibilities of the position may vary somewhat from that of the CKO.

In some organizations, the same person is both CKO and Chief Information Officer (CIO). However, based on what we are learning about the range of talents needed for a successful CKO, the CIO may be "good at running a substantial function but short on nurturing and leading a transitory team" [147]. Also, CIOs have their own array of challenges. PriceWaterhouseCoopers current CKO is also CIO, in what must be a demanding position with over 150 000 consultants worldwide.

If organizations wonder whether having a CKO is essential for successful KM, Earl and Scott conclude the CKO role is neither necessary nor sufficient. The results of interviews by the Delphi Group offer a substantial reason why CKOs may not be right for all organizations. Investing someone as the chief officer of knowledge runs counter to the sense of creating a knowledge sharing culture, a "hierarchical title applied to what is naturally a diffuse process" [148]. A CKO, and KM leadership in general, may be a temporary role to get KM to critical mass in the company, after which it is no longer needed. The knowledge sharing infrastructure and practices will have become embedded in the culture. Declare success and move on.

6. The World of KM

Knowledge forms the basis for value in almost all business transactions. That will not change in our lifetime [150].

The KM milieu is replete with conferences, journals, magazines, industry newspapers, and gurus. There are discussions of KM standards in the Association of Imaging and Information Management (AIIM) and the Knowledge Management Consortium (KMC). An internet search on KM will bring readers quickly to web repositories that will point to all aspects of the KM community. An excellent synopsis of KM books appears in Silverstone [151].

In this section, we briefly characterize KM products and services, issues and controversies, and perspectives on the future of KM.

6.1 Products and Services

Part of the world of KM is the array of products that enable it. Ovum predicts the worldwide market for KM software will reach $1.6 billion by 2002 [152]. The market for KM-related products is rapidly changing. In 1998 over $100 million in venture capital went to start-up companies in KM. In this chapter, it is not appropriate to present profiles of specific products, because any such snapshot will soon be out of date. Previous sections have included examples and screen shots from representative KM products.

We want to offer a broad characterization of the KM market to stress the primary themes that may be expected to have some stability over time. There is no comprehensive KM product offering a complete spectrum of capabilities, so organizations are left to structure their own KM system by configuring existing commercial products into a composite system that meets their needs.

The KM market consists of two kinds of suppliers: vendors who have a strong installed base in a principal KM capability, such as databases and collaboration, and vendors who target specific niche areas of KM with products that provide one or a very few capabilities, such as in visualization and data mining. By December 1998, Lotus/Domino had an installed base of over 26 million seats, compared to an estimated 16 million seats for Microsoft Outlook/Exchange [153]. Products in many specialty areas like process workflow are being re-christened "knowledge management" products to present themselves as candidates for KM system solutions.

The major vendors in databases, collaboration technology, desktop and local area network applications, and enterprise document management are all strong forces in KM. A comprehensive KM vendor would be capable in all four areas. As of March 1999, the KM vendors with more than $25 million in annual revenue were [154]:

- IBM/Lotus
- Microsoft
- Dataware
- Documentum
- Excalibur
- Infoseek
- INSO
- PCDOCS/Fulcrum
- Verity
- Opentext.

Vendors generally are trying to expand the scope of their offerings to encompass additional capabilities through product extensions and acquisitions. For example, Microsoft acquired FireFly, a start-up with innovative collaborative filtering technology. An orthogonal trend in KM, as with other applications, is the expanding role of the Internet and the offering of capabilities through the web via application service providers (ASPs).

An organization seeking to build a comprehensive KM system on top of a distributed network infrastructure will very likely be choosing one or more of the major vendors and adding selectively to bring in specialized software tools, for example, for skills profiling or data visualization.

A wide range of consulting firms and product vendors will perform KM readiness assessments, conduct knowledge audits, and design KM systems for organizations. Consulting firms especially are known for projecting their internal experiences to outside engagements. In some instances, firms will develop supporting tools or create brands to distinguish their services. For example, Enterprise IQ, from KPMG LLP, is a proprietary assessment tool for benchmarking an organization's KM capabilities, focusing on people, process, strategy, and technology. The benchmark of industry trends is based on the firm's experiences building 50 knowledge-based systems. The Delphi Group has KM2, a methodology for conducting a KM audit.

There are many diverse specialty service firms addressing KM-related subjects. Companies specializing in brainstorming can be brought in to an organization to generate out-of-the-box ideas. Organizational dynamics consultants will help firms improve their internal communication and culture. Certain research firms, such as Teltech Resource Network Corporation, have established themselves as single points of contact for external knowledge by maintaining networks of experts who are on call when their expertise is needed.

For timely information on KM providers, searching the internet will bring you to comprehensive KM sites that maintain directories of products and services.

6.2 Issues and Controversies

KM is not without its share of controversy. The view that "all management is knowledge management" [3] exemplifies one persistent observation—that managers of all kinds routinely do KM as part of their jobs. They don't bring in a specialist every time they need one. Managers conduct meetings without calling in facilitators and counsel employees without calling in industrial psychologists. What is different with KM? Organizations simply need effective managers, not necessarily knowledge managers. "The quality of knowledge always matters less than the quality of management" [155].

A second area of controversy surrounds the development and promulgation of best practices. It may sound impossible to quarrel with best practices, but there can be a downside. "Best" practice can get confused with codifying a single standard and dogmatic corporate approach to every problem. At its worst, individuals set themselves up as gatekeepers of a technology or practice area, always on the lookout to discourage anyone who may unseat them. The unthinking reuse of what has been blessed and codified as the standard practice can stifle innovation and promote a "culture of compliance" [155]. Employees should seek to understand the customers' needs, rather than bending the standard practice to fit every situation.

Even when the motives are not so insidious, organizations also falter when they create a burdensome process for employees to get a practice anointed a best practice. Employees can become cynical and poison the KM culture. Organizations should be encouraging workers to make the "best" practices better.

It is not difficult to see how an admonition to "avoid best practices at your peril" can originate. Consider hospitals and managed care firms that, in the spirit of KM, develop databases containing standard therapies for diseases or other medical conditions. Does a physician risk a lawsuit if she tries something that is not the standard practice?

For some people, KM has an ominous tone, appearing as a step on an inevitable progression to thought management [156]. Related to this observation is the extent to which KM is perceived and pursued as a computer-based, systems-analytic corporate initiative or a people-oriented, knowledge-sharing, culture-building movement. Is it KM when a CEO uses commercially available software tools to get reports on how many employees read his latest on-line memo, and for how long the memo was on their screens? Or is it KM when a CEO orders the redesign of the offices to create more informal seating areas so employees can share experiences?

6.3   Future of KM

In 1998 KM was at the very top of the Gartner Group hype curve of inflated expectations. If it follows course, it will diminish in visibility over the next few years. The key question is whether its underlying principles will endure. In section 1.4, we questioned whether KM would evolve more similarly to TQM or BPR, or chart a new path. There is strong sentiment that KM is striking at the essence of competitiveness in the 21st century. "There are sufficient strategic reasons to suggest that KM as a concept and practice will survive" [146].

Prusak thought that by 1999 the term KM would have died [21]. "Intellectual capital" may have more staying power [6]. IBM's knowledge initiative is called IC management [45]. Whatever the name, the themes of KM—understanding what knowledge you have in your organization, what knowledge you need to be competitive and thrive, how to design structures and practices that take best advantage of knowledge so it can be brought to bear on your core business—will only grow in relevance.

Although technology makes it scalable, KM is ultimately about people and what they know. We prefer to see it evolving in the spirit of calm computing [157]. Facing a torrent of dazzling new technology, KM will take advantage of it, but always as a supporting player. Enduring KM will remind us that it is okay to talk about simple things, like people sharing knowledge and doing better work because of it.

ACKNOWLEDGEMENTS

I am grateful to Marv Zelkowitz for his review and his recommendations throughout this exercise. I thank Mary Brick for providing much needed graphic talent. I benefited from the knowledge-friendly and technology-savvy culture at Mitretek Systems and the sharing of insights by the KM team. My deep appreciation for all the helpful comments and stimulating discussions goes to Linda K. Stone, for her leadership, vision, and inspiration; Bob Lewis, Robert Patt-Corner, Clem McGowan, Mary Harlow, Jim Ackermann, Don Plebuch, Steve McCabe, Archna Bhandari, Jeffrey Michaels, Bonnie Long, and Paul Gonzalez. For the family-friendly culture with Risa, Aimee, and Karen, thank you for understanding.

REFERENCES

[1] Platt, L. E. (1996). Chairman, president, and CEO of Hewlett-Packard, quoted in Bowles, J. and Hammond, J. Competing on knowledge. *Fortune* magazine, supplement.

[2] Definition adapted from Ivers, J. (1998). Bringing out brilliance. *Enterprise Solutions*, November/December, 25–27.

[3] Jordan, J. (1998). Competing through knowledge: an introduction. *Technology Analysis and Strategic Management* 9(4), 379–381.

[4] Davenport, T. H. and Prusak, L. (1998). *Working Knowledge.* Harvard Business School Press, Boston, MA.

[5] Despres, C. and Chauvel, D. (1999). Knowledge Management. *Journal of Knowledge Management*, 3(2), 110–119.

[6] Despres, C. and Chauvel, D. (1998). *Notes on Knowledge Management.* Theseus Institute, April.

[7] Prahalad, C. K. and Hamel, G. (1990). The core competence of the corporation. *Harvard Business Review*, May–June, 79–91.

[8] Lewis, B. (1999). Guidelines for building a knowledge-based organization. In Knowledge management—for my organization? *ACM Professional Development Seminar*, Washington, DC ACM Chapter, April, ed. W. Agresti, B, Lewis, C. McGowan, and R. Patt-Corner.

[9] Finegan, J. (1997). Joining forces. *CIO Web Business*, Section 2, 1 December.

[10] Hiemstra, M. A. (1999). How the U. S. Army learns and shares knowledge. *Proceedings of the Leveraging Knowledge Conference*, Giga Information Group, Orlando, FL, March.

[11] Enterprise Solutions (1998). Lotus talks about knowledge management. *Enterprise Solutions*, November/December, 19–22.

[12] IBM (1998). Knowledge management: lost in search of a map. Downloaded from IBM Global Services UK web site, *www-5.ibm.com/services/uk/news/biresult.htm*, 20 December.

[13] ITAA (1999). Help wanted 1998. Executive summary. Downloaded from Information Technology Association of America web site, *www.itaa.org/workforce/studies/hw98.htm*, 8 April.

[14] Dataware Technologies (1998). *Seven Steps to Implementing Knowledge Management in Your Organization.* Dataware Technologies, Inc., Cambridge, MA.

[15] Leonard, D. (1998). *Wellsprings of Knowledge.* Harvard Business School Press, Boston, MA.

[16] Schlier, F. (1998). The information- and technology-enabled enterprise of 2004. *Gartner Group Symposium/ITxpo 98*, Lake Buena Vista, FL, 12–16 October.

[17] Weinberger, D. (1999). Narrative knowledge. Downloaded from *http://idm.internet.com/opinion/narrknow.shtml*, 2 April.

[18] Delphi Group (1998). Knowledge management is not management fad. Downloaded from *www.delphigroup.com/pressreleases/1998-PR/043011998KMSurvey.html*, Delphi Group, Boston, MA, 20 December.

[19] Information Week (1999). Stay in touch with information. *Information Week*, 5 April, 116.

[20] Davenport, T. H. (1997). Knowledge management at Ernst & Young 1997. Downloaded from University of Texas web site, *www.bus.utexas.edu/kman/e_y.htm*, 15 December.

[21] Prusak, L. (1999). Knowledge management's future. *Proceedings of the Leveraging Knowledge Conference*, Giga Information Group, Orlando, FL, March.

[22] Hayek, F. A. (1937). Economics and knowledge. *Economica*, **IV** (new series), 33–54.

[23] Hayek, F. A. (1945). The use of knowledge in society. *American Economic Review*, **35**(4). Also in *Knowledge Management and Organizational Design*, ed. P. S. Myers, Butterworth-Heinemann, Boston, MA.

[24] Senge, P. (1990). *The Fifth Discipline*. Doubleday/Currency, New York.

[25] EDC (1998). The teaching firm, phase II. Education Development Center, Inc., Sewickley, PA. Downloaded from *www.edc.org/CWD/oview.htm*, 23 March.

[26] Bowles, J. and Hammond, J. (1996). Competing on knowledge. *Fortune* magazine, supplement.

[27] Davenport, T. H. (1995). The fad that forgot people. *Fast Company*, **1**, 70ff.

[28] Moore, C. (1999). A roadmap for leveraging knowledge. *Proceedings of the Leveraging Knowledge Conference*, Giga Information Group, Orlando, FL, March.

[29] Davenport, T. H. (1998). We've got to pay attention! *CIO*, Section 1, 1 November.

[30] Lenat, D. B. (1995). CYC: A large-scale investment in knowledge infrastructure. *Communications of the ACM*, **38**(11), 32–38.

[31] NSF (1997). KDI: knowledge and distributed intelligence. Downloaded from the National Science Foundation web site, *www.nsf.gov/od/lpa/news/publicat/nsf9860/start.htm*, 18 September.

[32] Schatz, B. and Chen, H. (1999). Digital libraries: technological advances and social impacts. *Computer*, **32**(2), 45–50.

[33] Lehrer, K. (1990). *Theory of Knowledge*. Westview Press, Boulder, CO.

[34] Guralnik, D. (ed.) (1984). *Webster's New World Dictionary*. Simon and Schuster, New York.

[35] Zuboff, S. (1996). The abstraction of industrial work. In *Knowledge Management and Organizational Design*, ed. P. S. Myers, Butterworth-Heinemann, Boston, MA.

[36] Audi, R. (1988). *Belief, Justification, and Knowledge*. Wadsworth, Belmont, CA.

[37] Pollack, J. L. (1986). *Contemporary Theories of Knowledge*. Rowman and Littlefield, Totosa, NJ.

[38] Jensen, M. C. and Mechling, W. H. (1996). Specific and general knowledge, and organizational structure. In *Knowledge Management and Organizational Design*, ed. P. S. Myers, Butterworth-Heinemann, Boston, MA.

[39] Denning, S. (1998). What is knowledge management? World Bank KM Board, World Bank, Washington, DC.

[40] Polonyi, M. (1966). *The Tacit Dimension*. Routledge & Kegan Paul, London.

[41] Fleck, J. (1997). Contingent knowledge and technology development. *Technology Analysis and Strategic Management*, **9**(4), 383–397.

[42] Quinn, J. B., and Gary, L. (1997). Organizing around intellect: an interview with James Brian Quinn. In *Creating a System to Manage Knowledge*, Harvard Business School Publishing, Boston, MA, pp. 1–6.

[43] Quinn, J. B., Anderson, P. and Finkelstein, S. (1996). Managing professional intellect. In *Harvard Business Review on Knowledge Management*. (1998). Harvard Business School Press, Boston, MA.

[44] Drucker, P. F. (1988). The coming of the new organization. In *Harvard Business Review on Knowledge Management*. (1998). Harvard Business School Press, Boston, MA.

[45] Huang, K.-T. (1998). Capitalizing on intellectual assets. *IBM Systems Journal*, **37**(4). Downloaded from the IBM web site, *www.almaden.ibm.com/journal/sj/374/huang.html*, 14 May.

[46] Shannon, C. and Weaver, W. (1949). *The Mathematical Theory of Communication*. University of Illinois Press, Urbana, IL.

[47] Kanevsky, V., quoted in Stewart, T. A. (1994). Your company's most valuable asset: intellectual capital. *Fortune*, 3 October, 68–74.

[48] Sveiby, K. E. (1997). *The New Organizational Wealth*. Berrett-Koehler, San Francisco.

[49] Stewart, T. A. (1994). Your company's most valuable asset: intellectual capital. *Fortune*, 3 October, 68–74.

[50] Harris, K. (1999). So, you're a knowledge worker: what do you do all day? Research Note, Gartner Group, 24 March. Downloaded from *gartner.gartnerweb.com/public/static/ note/nc00077668.html*, 5 April.

[51] Stewart, T. A. (1995). Getting real about brainpower. *Fortune*, 27 November.

[52] Pinchot, G. and Pinchot, E. (1996). The rise and fall of bureaucracy. In *Knowledge Management and Organizational Design*, ed. P. S. Myers, Butterworth-Heinemann, Boston, MA.

[53] Nonaka, I. and Takeuchi, H. (1995). *The Knowledge-Creating Company*. Oxford University Press, Oxford.

[54] Hansen, M. T., Nohria, N. and Tierney, T. (1999). What's your strategy for managing knowledge? *Harvard Business Review*, March–April, 106–116.

[55] Chen, S. (1997). A new paradigm for knowledge-based competition: building an industry through knowledge sharing. *Technology Analysis and Strategic Management*, 9(4), 437–452.

[56] Miraglia, J., Senior Vice President of Motorola, quoted in Aring, M. K. (1994). Motorola Corporation: a case study of a teaching firm. Education Development Center, Inc., Newton, MA, February.

[57] Skandia (1999). Competence insurance. Downloaded from the Skandia web site, *www.skandia.se/group/future/competence/main.competence.htm*, 11 August.

[58] General Dennis J. Reimer, US Army, quoted in Army knowledge online, 20 November. Downloaded from the US Army web site, *www.army.mil.ako*, 13 June 1999.

[59] US Army (1998). Army knowledge online, 20 November. Downloaded from the US Army web site, *www.army.mil.ako*, 13 June 1999.

[60] Roos, J., Roos, G., Edvinsson, L. and Dragonetti, N. C. (1998). *Intellectual Capital*. New York University Press, New York.

[61] Fudenberg, D. and Tirole, J. (1983). Learning-by-doing and market performance. *Bell Journal of Economics*, **14**, 522–530.

[62] Stewart, T. A. (1998). *Intellectual Capital: The New Wealth of Organizations*. Doubleday/Currency, New York.

[63] McGowan, C. (1999). KM issues, community, and references. In Knowledge management—for my organization? *ACM Professional Development Seminar*, Washington, DC ACM Chapter, April, ed. W. Agresti, B. Lewis, C. McGowan, and R. Patt-Corner.

[64] Edvinnson, L. and Malone, M. S. (1997). *Intellectual Capital*. Harper Collins, New York.

[65] Edvinsson, L., Director of Intellectual Capital at Skandia AFS, quoted in Sveiby, K. E. (1997). *The New Organizational Wealth*. Berrett-Koehler, San Francisco.

[66] Taylor, P. and Lowe, J. (1997). Are functional assets or knowledge assets the basis of new product development performance? *Technology Analysis and Strategic Management*, 9(4), 473–488.

[67] Kaplan, R. S. and Norton, D. P. (1996). *The Balanced Scorecard : Translating Strategy into Action*. Harvard Business School Press, Boston, MA.

[68] Baldaracco, J. (1996). Knowledge links. In *Knowledge Management and Organizational Design*, ed. P. S. Myers, Butterworth-Heinemann, Boston, MA.

[69] Pucik, V. (1996). Strategic alliances, organizational learning, and competitive advantage: the HRM agenda. In *Knowledge Management and Organizational Design*, ed. P. S. Myers, Butterworth-Heinemann, Boston, MA.

[70] Handy, C. (1996). The numbers. In *Knowledge Management and Organizational Design*, ed. P. S. Myers, Butterworth-Heinemann, Boston, MA.

[71] Aring, M. K. (1994). Motorola Corporation: a case study of a teaching firm. Education Development Center, Inc., Newton, MA, February.

[72] Freeman, P., and Aspray, W. (1999). The supply of information technology workers in the United States. Computing Research Association, Washington, DC.

[73] Prokesch, S. E. (1997). Unleashing the power of learning: an interview with British Petroleum's John Browne. In *Creating a System to Manage Knowledge*, Harvard Business School Publishing, Boston, MA, pp. 7–24.

[74] Bahrami, H. (1996). The emerging flexible organization: perspectives from Silicon Valley. In *Knowledge Management and Organizational Design*, ed. P. S. Myers, Butterworth-Heinemann, Boston, MA.

[75] Stephenson, K., quoted in Hildebrand, C. (1998). Mapping the invisible workplace. *CIO Enterprise*, Section 2, 15 July, 18–20.

[76] Hildebrand, C. (1998). Mapping the invisible workplace. *CIO Enterprise*, Section 2, 15 July, 18–20.

[77] Curley, K. (1999). Communities of practice: why are they the "hot" interest in KM? *Proceedings of the Leveraging Knowledge Conference*, Giga Information Group, Orlando, FL, March.

[78] Myers, P. S. (ed.) (1996). *Knowledge Management and Organizational Design*. Butterworth-Heinemann, Boston, MA.

[79] Tristram, C. (1998). Intranet profile: common knowledge. *CIO Web Business*, Section 2, 1 September, 54–59.

[80] Lamping, J., Rao, R. and Pirolli, P. (1995). A focus+context technique based on hyperbolic geometry for visualizing large hierarchies. *Proceedings of CHI'95*.

[81] Gotschall, M. G. (1999). Good samaritan implements decision support system. *Knowledge Inc.*, 4(1), 1ff.

[82] Miraglia, J., Senior Vice President of Motorola, quoted in Aring, M. K. (1994). Motorola Corporation: a case study of a teaching firm. Education Development Center, Inc., Newton, MA, February.

[83] Burns, T. and Stalker, G. M. (1996). The organization of innovation. In *Knowledge Management and Organisational Design*, ed. P. S. Myers, Butterworth-Heinemann, Boston, MA.

[84] Kanter, R. M. (1996). When a thousand flowers bloom: structural, collective, and social conditions for innovation in organizations. In *Knowledge Management and Organisational Design*, ed. P. S. Myers, Butterworth-Heinemann, Boston, MA.

[85] Hermann, N. (1999). Hermann Brain Dominance Instrument. The Ned Hermann Group, Lake Lure, NC. Downloaded from the HBDI web site at *www.hbdi.com*, 18 September.

[86] Briggs Myers, I., McCaulley, M. H., Quenk, N. L., and Hammer, A. L. (1998). *MBTI Manual*. Consulting Psychologists Press.

[87] Ashby, W. R. (1956). *Introduction to Cybernetics*. Chapman & Hall, London.

[88] NRC (1999). *Funding a Revolution*. Computer Science and Telecommunications Board, National Research Council. National Academy Press, Washington.

[89] Brown, J. S. (1991). Research that reinvents the corporation. In *Harvard Business Review on Knowledge Management*. (1998). Harvard Business School Press, Boston, MA.

[90] Millar, J., Demaid, A. and Quintas, P. (1997). Trans-organizational innovation: a framework for research. *Technology Analysis and Strategic Management*, 9(4), 399–418.

[91] Leonard, D. and Straus, S. (1997). Putting your company's whole brain to work. In *Harvard Business Review on Knowledge Management*. (1998). Harvard Business School Press, Boston, MA.

[92] Torsilieri, J., principal at Booz Allen, quoted in Tristram, C. (1998). Intranet profile: common knowledge. *CIO Web Business*, Section 2, 1 September, 54–59.

[93] Glasser, P. (1999). The knowledge factor. *CIO*, 15 December 1998/1 January 1999, 108–118.

[94] Stewart, T. A. (1998). Packaging what you know. *Fortune*, 9 November.

[95] Davenport, T. H. (1996). Knowledge Management at Hewlett-Packard, early 1996. Downloaded from University of Texas web site, *www.bus.utexas.edu/kman/hpcase.htm*, 15 December 1998.

[96] Stackpole, B. (1999). Cooking up self-service support. *PC Week*, 22 February, 91–94.

[97] Webb, D. (1998). Corporate culture blocks better use of knowledge. *Computing Canada*, **24**(32), 27.

[98] Smith, S., managing principal of global knowledge management consulting services, IBM, quoted in Corporate culture counts. *Information Week*, 15 March, 113.

[99] Wah, L. (1999). Making knowledge stick. *Management Review*, **88**(5), 24–25.

[100] Durrance, B. (1998). Some explicit thoughts on tacit learning. *Training and Development*, December, 24–29.

[101] Davenport, T. H., De Long, D. W., Beers, M. C. (1999). Working paper: building successful knowledge management projects. Downloaded from Ernst & Young web site, *www.businessinnovation.ey.com/mko/html/kproje.html*, 25 September.

[102] Garvin, D. A. (1993). Building a learning organization. In *Harvard Business Review on Knowledge Management*. (1998). Harvard Business School Press, Boston, MA.

[103] Kleiner, A. and Roth, G. (1997). How to make experience your company's best teacher. In *Harvard Business Review on Knowledge Management*. (1998). Harvard Business School Press, Boston, MA.

[104] Stuart, A. (1999). Continuing ed. *CIO Web Business*, Section 2, 1 September, 31–42.

[105] Bair, J. (1998). Knowledge management innovation. *Proceedings of the Gartner Group Symposium*, Lake Buena Vista, FL, 12–16 October.

[106] Ruddy, T. M. (1999). Eureka: new techniques for the exchange of knowledge and solutions. *Proceedings of the Leveraging Knowledge Conference*, Giga Information Group, Orlando, FL, March.

[107] Manasco, B. (1999). Knowledge strategies generate lasting value. *Knowledge Inc.*, 4(1), 1 ff.

[108] Buckman, R., CEO of Buckman Laboratories, quoted in Stewart, T. A. (1995). Getting real about brainpower. *Fortune*, 27 November.

[109] Jefferson, T., quoted in NRC (1999). *Funding a Revolution*. Computer Science and Telecommunications Board, National Research Council. National Academy Press, Washington.

[110] Gates, W. H. (1999). *Business @ the Speed of Thought*. Warner Books, New York.

[111] Davenport, T. O. principal in Towers, Perrin, global human resources consultants, quoted in Wah, L. (1999). Making knowledge stick. *Management Review*, **88**(5), 24–25.

[112] Gilhooly, K. (1999). Can you avoid culture shock when moving to a solution-centered support model? *Service News*, April, 31 ff.

[113] Sivan, M., leader of KM consulting practice in the Toronto office of Ernst & Young, quoted in Webb, D. (1998). Corporate culture blocks better use of knowledge. *Computing Canada*, **24**(32), 27.

[114] Patt-Corner, R. (1999). Knowledge management architectural framework. In Knowledge management—for my organization? *ACM Professional Development Seminar*, Washington, DC ACM Chapter, April, ed. W. Agresti, B. Lewis, C. McGowan, and R. Patt-Corner.

[115] Chait, L. P. (1999). Creating a successful knowledge management system. *Journal of Business Strategy*, 19 March. Downloaded from Dialog File 781: UMI Newsstand.

[116] Mahon, A., senior manager of strategic marketing, Lotus Development Corporation, quoted in Hapgood, F. (1998). Tools for teamwork. CIO Web Business, Section 2, November 1, (1998). 68–74.

[117] Clever Project (1999). Hypersearching the web. *Scientific American*, June. Downloaded from *www.sciam.com/1999/0699issue/0699raghavan.html*, 2 July.

[118] Greenberg, I. and Garber, L. (1999). Searching for new search technologies. *Computer*, **32**(8), 4–11.

[119] Bair, J. (1998). Dimensions of KM technology selection. Research Note, Gartner Group, 13 October.

[120] Tomassi, P. (1999). Adding human intellect to search technology. *4th Search Engine Conference*, Boston, MA, 19–20 April.

[121] Williams, M. (1999). New engines that zoom right to the site. *Washington Technology*, 15 March, 22.

[122] Paquette, P. (1999). Knowledge management: creed for the new millennium. *High Tech Careers*, September/October, 14.

[123] Cukier, K. N. (1999). Is there a privacy time bomb? *Red Herring*, September, 91–98.

[124] Nardi, B. A., Miller, J. R. and Wright, D. J. (1998). Collaborative, programmable intelligent agents. *Communications of the ACM*, **41**(3), 96–104.

[125] Lawton, G. (1999). Unifying knowledge with XML. *Knowledge Management*, **2**(8), 39–45.

[126] Schatz, B., Mischo, W., Cole, T. *et al.* (1999). Federated search of scientific literature. *Computer*, **32**(2), 51–59.

[127] Bosak, J. (1999). Media-independent publishing: four myths about XML. *Computer*, **31**(10), 120–122.

[128] NetCreations (1999). Web site of NetCreations, Inc., *www.netcreations.com*.

[129] Makulowich, J. (1999). Government data mining systems defy definition. *Washington Technology*, 22 February, 21–22.

[130] DeLong, D., Davenport, T. and Beers, M. (1997). What is a knowledge management project? Research Note, University of Texas, 17 February.

[131] Fayyad, U. M., Piatetsky-Shapiro, G., Smyth, P. and Uthurusamy, R. (1996). (eds) *Advances in Knowledge Discovery and Data Mining*. MIT Press, Cambridge, MA.

[132] Penzias, A., Nobel Laureate, in an interview with *Computerworld* in January 1999, quoted in: Nobel laureate calls data mining a must. Information Discovery, Inc., Marketing Communications Special Release, 8 February.

[133] Myers, P. S. and Swanborg, R. W. (1998). Packaging knowledge. *CIO Enterprise*, Section 2, 15 April, 26–28.

[134] Garvin, D. A. (1997). A note on knowledge management. In *Creating a System to Manage Knowledge*, Harvard Business School Publishing, Boston, MA, pp. 55–74.

[135] Stewart, T. A. quoted in Curley, K. (1999). Communities of practice: why are they the "hot" interest in KM? *Proceedings of the Leveraging Knowledge Conference*, Giga Information Group, Orlando, FL, March.

[136] Boyd, S. (1997). Knowledge management: three perspectives. *Business Process Strategies*, *Modus Operandi*, Reston, VA, October.

[137] Delphi Group (1999). Delphi Group research identifies leading business applications of knowledge management. Downloaded from *www.delphigroup.com/pressreleases/1999-PR/03291999KMBusApps.html*, Delphi Group, Boston, MA, 2 April.

[138] Fusaro, R. (1998). Rating intangibles no easy task. *Computerworld*, 8 November, 8.

[139] Davis, R. and Riggs, B. (1999). Get smart. *Information Week*, 5 April, 40–50.

140] Agresti, W., Lewis, B., McGowan, C. and Patt-Corner, R. (1999). Knowledge management—for my organization? *ACM Professional Development Seminar*, Washington, DC ACM Chapter, April.

[141] Denning, S., World Bank Program Director of KM, quoted in Wah, L. (1999). Making knowledge stick. *Management Review*, **88**(5), 24–25.

[142] Manasco, Britton, Editor and Publisher, Knowledge, Inc., quoted in *Seven Steps to Implementing Knowledge Management in Your Organization*. (1998). Dataware Technologies, Inc., Cambridge, MA.

[143] Skyrme, David, author of the Business Intelligence Report *Measuring the Value of Knowledge*, quoted in Vowler, J. (1998). How do you know when the price is right in measuring knowledge? *Computer Weekly*, 17 September, 56.

[144] Field, T. (1999). Common knowledge. *CIO*, 1 February, 50–52.

[145] Information Week (1999). Corporate culture counts. *Information Week*, 15 March, 113.

[146] Duffy, D. (1998). Knowledge champions. *CIO Enterprise*, Section 2, 15 November, 66–71.

[147] Earl, M. J. and Scott, I. A. (1999). What is a chief knowledge officer? *Sloan Management Review*, **40**(2), 29–38.

[148] Delphi Group (1998). A summary of Delphi's knowledge leadership study. Downloaded from *www.delphigroup.com/pubs/best-prac-in-know-lead-summ.htm*, Delphi Group, Boston, MA, 17 December.

[149] Alavi, M. (1997). KPMG Peat Marwick US: one giant brain. In *Creating a System to Manage Knowledge*, Harvard Business School Publishing, Boston, MA, pp. 75–95.

[150] Koulopoulos, T. M. (1988). President of the Delphi Group, quoted in: Knowledge management is not management fad. Downloaded from *www.delphigroup.com/press-releases/1998-PR/04301998KMSurvey.html*, Delphi Group, Boston, MA, 20 December.

[151] Silverstone, S. (1999). A knowledge manager's bookshelf. *Knowledge Management*, **2**(8), 55–64.

[152] ComputerWire (1998). Knowledge management vendors poised for battle. *Computergram International*, 2 October.

[153] Enterprise Solutions (1998). Interview with Jeff Papows. *Enterprise Solutions*, November/December, 9–12.

[154] Harris, K. (1999). Knowledge management: a field of start-ups. Research Note, Gartner Group, March 16.

[155] Schrage, M. (1999). When best practices meet the intranet, innovation takes a holiday. *Fortune*, **139**(16), 29 March, 198.

[156] Schrage, M. (1998). Why no one wants knowledge management. *Computerworld*, 7 December.

[157] MSNBC (1998). Mark Weiser: in his own words. Interview with MSNBC's Bob Sullivan, 4 December. Downloaded from *msnbc.com/news/220559.asp*, 27 May 1999.

A Methodology for Evaluating Predictive Metrics

JARRETT ROSENBERG

Sun Microsystems
901 San Antonio Road
Palo Alto, CA 94303
USA
Jarrett.Rosenberg@acm.org

Abstract

A central question in software metrics is how well one or more metrics predict some measure of interest, such as defect density or developer effort. Numerous proposals for new metrics have been made over the past decades, some with attempts at empirical evaluation.

Unfortunately, many evaluations of metrics are crude at best, and often completely invalid. This chapter describes a conventional approach to the evaluation of predictive ability of one or more metrics, using well-established statistical methods. Such topics as the importance of examining data prior to analysis, avoidance of model violations such as collinearity, and the proper use of univariate and multivariate techniques are discussed and illustrated, as well as common mistakes such as the use of automated procedures like stepwise regression. More advanced statistical techniques such as logistic regression and signal detection theory are briefly discussed.

1. Introduction

For over 30 years, software engineers have been interested in the ability to accurately measure characteristics of software and its production, which could lead to improvements in both. In that time, a large number of metrics have been proposed, some with attempts at empirical validation of their effectiveness. Unfortunately, many if not most of these laudable efforts at empirical validation have foundered on a lack of knowledge about the appropriate methods to use.

For example, a central goal in software metrics is the prediction of software characteristics based on other metrics of the software or its production process. This prediction problem is a quintessentially statistical one, but the lack of statistical training in the typical crowded engineering curriculum leaves most engineers uncertain of how to proceed. The result has been many well-intentioned but poorly executed empirical studies. This chapter addresses this problem by providing a simple methodology for the predictive evaluation of metrics, one that reflects what most statisticians would recommend in general terms. Not all of these steps are necessarily required, and often more will be needed, but they are a suitable framework for addressing the problem. Many statistical niceties are omitted in order to make the general approach clear, and a real example is used to illustrate the method. The dataset used in this chapter comes from an excellent study by MacDonell, Shepperd, and Sallis [1]. Since their dataset consisted of only 70 multivariate observations, they thoughtfully published it along with their analysis.[1] MacDonell et al. described their sample as follows:

> The systems comprising the sample were built over a period of 5 years by groups of senior students in the Department of Information Science at the University of Otago. Every system was built to satisfy the real requirements of an external client, normally a small business or a department in a larger organisation. ... A wide variety of systems was constructed over the period. A few examples should help to provide an indication of their general nature. The set included: client management systems for two dental surgeries, a law firm

---

[1] The reader may find it instructive to compare their analysis with the one given here; it is similar in basic approach, although different in detail.

and an accountant; stock/inventory management systems for five utility firms and four retail stores; membership record systems for two leisure clubs, exhibit management systems for two museums; a freight scheduling system for a transport firm; and three school course and student administration systems. ... The systems were all of small to medium size. ... One of the positive features of the sample is the degree of commonality of several process attributes across the set. All but a few of the systems were built by groups of four developers; the same development methodology was employed in every case; all systems were implemented using the same tool, the Cognos 4GL Powerhouse; and the systems were all of the same generic class-transaction-oriented data processing and retrieval systems. (pp. 100–101)

From the requirements and design documentation and the implemented code, the authors obtained the following measures:

- *Entities:* The number of entities depicted in the entity–relationship (E–R) diagram
- *Relationships:* The number of relationships depicted in the E–R diagram
- *Attributes:* The number of attributes associated with the E–R diagram
- *MenuFunctions:* The number of menus depicted in the functional decomposition chart
- *DataScreens:* The number of data entry/edit screens depicted in the functional decomposition chart
- *Reports:* The number of reports depicted in the functional decomposition chart
- *NonMenuFunctions:* The number of non-menu functions depicted in the functional decomposition chart
- *TotalFunctions:* The total number of functions depicted in the functional decomposition chart
- *SourceSize:* The total number of source statements in the implemented project.

Note that one of the measures, *NonMenuFunctions*, is the sum of two others, *DataScreens* and *Reports*, and another, *TotalFunctions*, is the sum of *MenuFunctions* and *NonMenuFunctions*. Because of these relationships, these measures will necessarily be highly correlated with each other, and some of them will have to be eliminated from the analysis. Our goal with these data is to predict the final size of a project (in source statements), given the information we can obtain from the project's requirements, as depicted in its entity–relationship diagram and functional decomposition chart. That is, we will want to derive some functional relationship

$$Y = b_0 + b_1 X_1 + b_2 X_2 + \cdots + b_n X_n + error$$

where Y is the code size of the project and the X_is are one or more of the requirements-based measures. We want this model to fit as accurately as possible, minimizing the error term. Our job then is to estimate the b_is. The reader may wish to refer to the Appendix for a brief review of the the basic concepts of the linear regression model.[2]

2. Preparing the Data for Analysis

The first step, which is surprisingly easy to neglect, is simply to *look* at the data; visual inspection can quickly spot points of interest and potential problems. Using several different graphical methods can also be quite helpful.[3] A striking demonstration of this fact was provided by Anscombe [2] and can be seen in Fig. 1. All four datasets produce exactly the same regression line, even though they are quite different in structure. Without graphing the data, it is impossible to tell from the regression results alone which case we are dealing with.

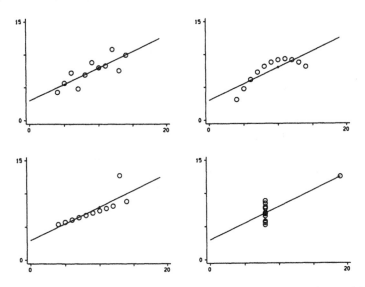

FIG. 1. Four different data sets fit equally well by the same regression model.

[2] This is phrased in terms of a linear model because such a simple model is preferable if possible. If a linear model can't be found, we may decide to try more complicated ones.

[3] The analyses and graphics in this chapter were done with the statistical package Stata (*www.stata.com*).

Let us start with the dependent (to-be-predicted) variable, *SourceSize*. Since there are only 70 data points, it is useful to just plot the points directly, as shown in Fig. 2.

Right away we can spot a potential problem: the range of sizes for the 1995 projects is much less than that for the preceding 4 years. There are many possible reasons for this which it would be interesting to investigate, but the immediate problem is that the 1995 projects may be of a different type than those in the other years, thus confusing the analysis. At the very least, the difference makes it difficult to validate the sample by fitting a model to the first 4 years and then predicting the last year.[4] Figure 3 shows the histogram of the distribution of program sizes, both overall, and by year. This way of looking at the data reveals a second problem: the distribution of sizes is somewhat skewed. The graphs include a plot of a normal distribution with the same mean and standard deviation as the data, and the curve and histogram are clearly different.[5] Skewness seriously affects many commonly used statistics such as the mean and variance, as well as statistical tests based

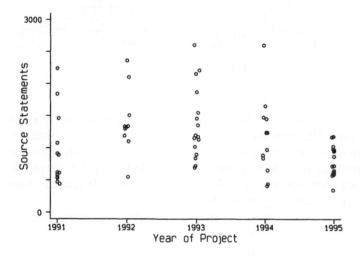

FIG. 2. Size of projects by year.

[4] Are these differences between the different years' project sizes real, or just due to sampling variation? A one-way analysis of variance of the mean size of each year's projects indicates that they are not all the same. Given the small sample size (and the skewness in the data, see below), it might be better to use the non-parametric analogue of the ANOVA, namely the Kruskal–Wallis test. It too indicates that the groups are different.

[5] There are several tests available to determine whether or not a sample is likely to be from a normally distributed population; all of the them agree that it is unlikely here.

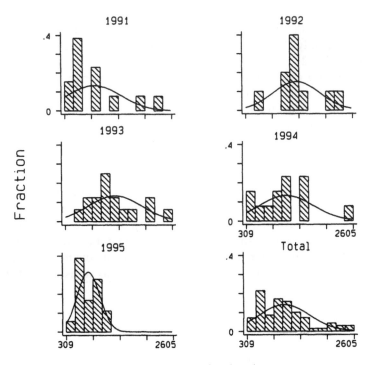

FIG. 3. Distribution of project sizes.

on them, and so it is preferable to work with data with a more symmetrical distribution. The simplest way to achieve this is with some invertible transformation: we do our statistical tests on the transformed data and then transform back into the original scale as needed. Figure 4 shows the results of various transforms of the *SourceSize* values; as frequently happens, a logarithmic transform gives the best result.

Let us now look at the independent (predictor) variables; Figure 5 shows that they, too, are somewhat skewed, and that is confirmed by tests of departure from normality. It turns out that log transforms correct the problems (although a square-root transform turns out to be better for the number of *Reports*), and so we will be performing our analyses on the transformed variables. As can be seen in Fig. 6, the number of menus in the functional decomposition chart is a very unusual variable: no project has less than 4 (suggesting that less than 4 is a practical impossibility), roughly half the projects have exactly 4, and the remaining half have a few more than 4, but 2 have a total of 14. This suggests that we have a mixture of 2 or more kinds of projects in terms of number of menu functions. The correct procedure is to try to understand and model this variability directly, but to keep this chapter short

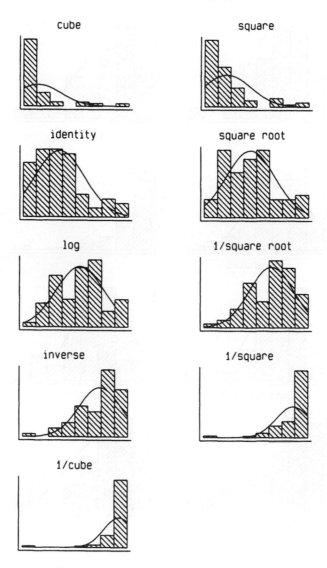

FIG. 4. Various transformations of source size.

we will simply drop this problematic variable from the analysis for now. We will come back to it later.

At this point we have to decide what to do about the definitionally related function measures: *DataScreens*, *Reports*, *MenuFunctions*, *NonMenuFunctions*, and *TotalFunctions*. In the absence of any information as to whether menu, data, or report functions are more important, and given that the

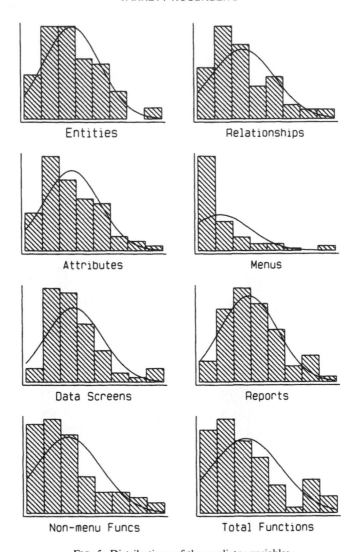

FIG. 5. Distributions of the predictor variables.

MenuFunctions variable itself is problematic, the best thing to do is simply drop the component measures and just use the *TotalFunctions* measure. Were the *MenuFunctions* variable not problematic, an alternative would be to drop *TotalFunctions* and *NonMenuFunctions* and use the three component measures instead. For demonstrative purposes, however, we keep *DataScreens* and *Reports* as well as *TotalFunctions*, to see the effects of collinearity.

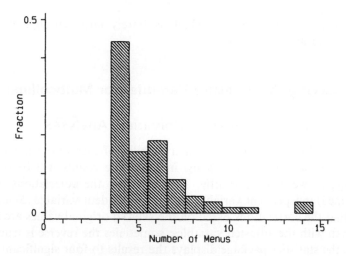

FIG. 6. Distribution of number of menus.

3. Creating the Fitting and Validation Samples

Given that we want not only to fit a model to the current data, but also to construct a model that can be used to predict the size of future projects, we need to divide our sample into two parts: one for developing a model that fits the data as well as possible, and one for validating that model by seeing how well it fits new data. There are two possibilities: the first is that, since we have some historical data and want to predict the size of future projects, we could use the data from the first 3–4 years and then see how well it predicts what happened in the next year or two. This strategy won't work here, however, since we have seen that the most recent year's data are somewhat different from those that went before, so it will be harder for a model developed from the former to fit the latter well. The second method, which is the more commonly used anyway, is to randomly split the sample into two parts. There is a tradeoff here, however: the larger the development part, the more accurate the model; the larger the validation part, the more accurate the assessment of its predictive value. A good compromise is a 50–50 split. This can easily by done by assigning each observation a random number, ordering the observations by that number, and then choosing every other one. An alternative that may be better for such a small sample is to randomly choose half of the projects from each year; this *stratified sampling* method guarantees that each sample will have exactly the right proportions of projects from each year. Whichever way we construct our two samples, note that our model-building sample is now just 35 observations, however, which is barely large enough given the number of variables involved.

4. Checking the Predictor Variables for Multicollinearity

4.1   The Pitfall of Univariate Analyses

Let us start by looking at the predictive ability of each of our independent variables (*Entities* to *TotalFunctions*) in turn. The results will be seriously misleading, as we will see shortly. Table I shows the correlations of each (transformed) independent variable with the dependent variable, *SourceSize*.

Note that the correlations based on the skewed original values are mostly higher than with the adjusted variables; sometimes the reverse is true. Note also that the statistics package displays the results to four significant digits, not because our estimate is actually that accurate, but so that we can use the results in other calculations with as little rounding error as possible. From these results we might conclude that each of the variables has a large effect on the size of a project, but the results of our multivariate analysis will show that that conclusion is seriously misleading. This reason for this is the phenomenon called *multicollinearity*.

4.2   Checking for Multicollinearity

It is has been established that children's handwriting skill is strongly correlated with their shoe size, and that the decline in the birthrate in Germany is strongly correlated with the decline in the number of storks there. The correlation is due, of course, to an additional variable (age and industrialization, respectively) that is correlated with the other two and produces the

TABLE I

CORRELATIONS OF INDEPENDENT VARIABLES WITH PROJECT SIZE ($N = 35$).

	ln *SourceSize*	Untransformed
ln *Entities*	0.5199	0.5792
ln Relationships	0.5197	0.5643
ln Attributes	0.7521	0.7098
ln TotalFunctions	0.7431	0.7807
ln DataScreens	0.6767	0.7212
sqrt Reports	0.6109	0.6742

all with $p < 0.01$.

association. It is therefore critical in performing a correlation or regression analysis with multiple independent variables that all the relevant independent variables be included, *and that they not be correlated with each other.* Otherwise, at best the model estimates will be very imprecise, and at worst, the wrong model may be fit. Figure 7 depicts the collinearity graphically.

Let us look, then, at the independent variables in our study. Table II shows the correlations among the (log-transformed) independent variables. All the correlations have $p < 0.01$ except for those marked by an asterisk.[6] Figure 8 shows them graphically in a scatterplot matrix.

It's clear that some pairs of variables are highly correlated with each other. *TotalFunctions* correlates moderately with everything, and *Entities* and *Relationships* are very highly correlated. This suggests that the variables in these clusters may reflect some underlying factor that they all are measuring. This makes sense: we would expect that the number of entities and the

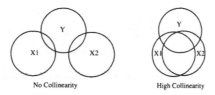

No Collinearity   High Collinearity

FIG. 7. Collinearity between two predictor variables X_1 and X_2.

TABLE II

CORRELATIONS OF (TRANSFORMED) INDEPENDENT VARIABLES ($N = 35$)

	TotalFuncs	Entities	Relationships	DataScreens	Attributes	Reports
TotalFunctions	—					
Entities	0.61	—				
Relationships	0.59	0.97	—			
DataScreens	0.88	0.66	0.65	—		
Attributes	0.71	0.63	0.62	0.68	—	
Reports	0.79	0.25	0.22	0.50	0.53	—

[6] Note that by calculating a large correlation matrix, we run the risk that some may meet our criterion for statistical significance purely by chance. For example, if our criterion were the usual one of 0.05, then we would expect a spuriously significant result about one time in 20. A correlation matrix of all the independent variables contains 28 correlation coefficients, so we would expect one of them to be falsely significant at the 0.05 level. This phenomenon is called the *experiment-wise error rate.*

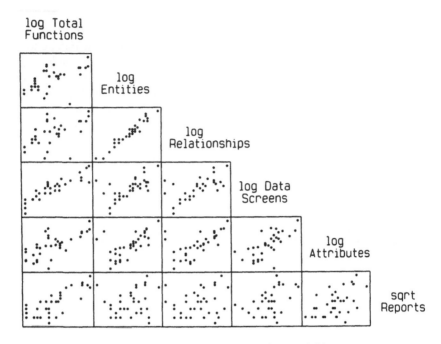

FIG. 8. Scatter plots of the predictor variables.

number of relationships in the E–R diagram would grow together as the size of the diagram increases, so either one of them could be taken as a measure of its size. It may also be that the number of functions is a good indicator of the size of a project, and thus generally related to other measures of it.

It would be nice if there were some more direct way of uncovering the presence of these underlying factors, especially without computing dozens of correlation coefficients and incurring the high risk of a falsely significant result which that entails. There is such a method, called *exploratory factor analysis*. There are many variations depending on the situation, but the basic model is this: the covariation among the variables is examined to extract some number of "dimensions" or "factors" with respect to which the observations can be located.[7] Table III shows the results of a factor analysis of our independent variables.

[7] The technique of principal components analysis works in a similar way; the chief difference is that it uses the raw variances rather than first standardizing them as done in factor analysis. This may be an issue when the independent variables are measured on scales with widely varying magnitudes, as use of the unstandardized variances may then cause more weight to be given to variables simply because they have larger values and hence larger variances. Factor analysis avoids this problem.

TABLE III

FACTOR ANALYSIS OF INDEPENDENT VARIABLES ($N = 35$)

(a) Factors and eigenvalues

Principal factor analysis

Factor	Eigenvalue	Proportion	Cumulative
1	4.012	0.774	0.774
2	1.022	0.197	0.971
3	0.227	0.044	1.015
4	0.002	0.000	1.065

(b) Factor loadings for each variable

	Factor loadings				
Variable	F1	F2	F3	F4	Uniqueness
ln TotalFunctions	0.922	0.345	−0.076	−0.024	0.025
ln Entities	0.846	−0.483	0.120	−0.006	0.037
ln Relationships	0.835	−0.506	0.105	−0.008	0.036
ln DataScreens	0.879	0.086	−0.356	0.004	0.093
ln Attributes	0.767	0.054	0.041	0.039	0.406
sqrt Reports	0.624	0.635	0.260	−0.001	0.139

Table IIIa shows how many factors appear to be present. The eigenvalue here can be viewed as a measure of the prominence of the factor; factors with eigenvalues less than 1 can be ignored. The second column lists the amount of total covariance among the variables that can be accounted for the factor, and the third columns lists the cumulative variance of all the factors so far. It can be seen that Factor 1 accounts for roughly 75% of the variability, and Factor 2 for roughly 20%. The other factors account for a much smaller amount, and thus can be ignored. Even Factor 2 is only a third the size of Factor 1.

Table IIIb shows the *factor loadings* of each variable on the underlying factors; these can be thought of as how strongly each variable correlates with or reflects the underlying factor. Almost all of the variables have high loadings on Factor 1, with *TotalFunctions* being the highest, so this may be some "size" factor underlying its overall high correlation with the other variables.

The highest loading on Factor 2 comes from the number of reports. It may represent the "data requirements" of the project, but it is hard to tell.

The "uniqueness" values in the last column represent the amount of variance in the variable's values that is *unexplained* by any of the factors. As can be seen, almost all of the variance can be accounted for by these two underlying factors, with the exception of the number of attributes in the E–R diagram; this seems to represent something different.

It is usual to do a "factor rotation" in a factor analysis, whereby the axes of the factor space are rotated to create a more interpretable picture (much as one rotates a camera to frame the subject more appropriately; nothing substantive is changed). In this case, the results are clear enough that the rotations do not improve things, and so are omitted here.

What do we conclude from all this? That a number of our measures are in fact measuring the same thing. This will produce seriously misleading results if we do not address the problem. For example, even though each of the variables has a high correlation with *SourceSize*, a multivariate regression at this point will produce a surprise: only the number of E–R diagram attributes will have a significant independent effect!

The problem is the redundancy, or *multicollinearity*, among the independent variables; jointly they have an effect, but individually they don't, since most of their variance is shared and not unique. Having identified these redundant independent measures, what are we to do? There are several possibilities:

- *Drop them:* This will prevent problems with multicollinearity, but we may drop the wrong ones and underestimate their effect, while overestimating that of the remaining ones.
- *Leave them in:* Ignore the per-variable effects and just look at the omnibus *F*-test for the regression of all the variables jointly. This is somewhat unsatisfying, however, since we would like to know the effect of each individual variable.
- *Combine them:* Either by some simple arithmetic method (e.g., adding them), or by using factor scores from a factor analysis.

We will use this last approach.

The reason for spending the time doing the factor analysis is thus twofold: it gives us insight into the independent variables, and it allows us to simplify and correctly perform the subsequent analyses when required.

5. Multivariate Analyses

5.1 Multivariate Rather Than Multiple Univariate Analyses

The purpose of a multivariate analysis is to simultaneously examine the effect of several variables on another one.[8] This simultaneously

---

[8] A generalization called *canonical correlation* handles multiple dependent variables as well.

allows for

- determining the joint effect of variables and their interactions
- adjusting for related variables
- avoiding the high experiment-wise error rate involved in doing many sequential univariate analyses.

Let's pretend that we don't know about the multicollinearity problems and just do a multiple regression, as in Example 1.[9]

Example 1

```
Number of obs =       35      Raw R-squared = 0.6635
F( 6,    28) =     9.20      Adj R-squared = 0.5914
Prob > F      = 0.0000      Root MSE      = .32642
```

ln SourceSize	Coeff.	Std. Err.	[95% CI]		t	P>|t|
ln TotalFunctions	.177	.737	-1.333 --	1.687	0.240	0.812
ln Entities	-.258	.571	-1.428 --	.911	-0.452	0.654
ln Relationships	.220	.450	- .701 --	1.141	0.489	0.628
ln DataScreens	.196	.411	- .646 --	1.038	0.477	0.637
ln Attributes	.536	.208	.111 --	.961	2.584	0.015
sqrt Reports	.145	.201	- .267 --	.557	0.719	0.478
Constant	3.436	1.155	1.069 --	5.803	2.974	0.006

Our model with six variables does a significantly better job of predicting size than just using the mean ($p < 0.0001$); in fact, it accounts for 59% of the variance. And yet it appears that only the number of attributes in the E–R diagram is a predictor of size. This is the result of having correlated independent variables: there is so much shared variance among them that none of them has a significant unique effect.

Now let us try using the results of the factor analysis. We create *factor scores* for each factor, which are weighted functions of the independent variables based on their factor loadings, and do the regression again using them and the *Attributes* variable, which was not well accounted-for by the two factors (Example 2).

---

[9] In this analysis and all the other multivariate ones in this chapter we examine only main effects of variables and not interaction terms. There are two reasons for this: first, interaction terms greatly complicate the analysis (see [3]); second, interaction effects are typically much smaller than those of main effects, and thus frequently have less practical significance.

Example 2

```
Number of obs =      35      Raw R-squared = 0.6564
F( 3,    31) =  19.74      Adj R-squared = 0.6231
Prob > F     = 0.0000      Root MSE      = .31349
```

Ln SourceSize	Coeff.	Std. Err.	[95% CI]		t	P>|t|
Factor 1	.209	.086	.034 --	.384	2.441	0.021
Factor 2	.093	.056	-.021 --	.206	1.666	0.106
Ln Attributes	.522	.203	.108 --	.937	2.571	0.015
Constant	4.747	.828	3.059 --	6.435	5.736	0.000

The fit is just as good, but now we see that the variance is explained by the first factor ("size") and the number of E–R diagram attributes. The result of just using those two is shown in Example 3.

Example 3

```
Number of obs =      35      Raw R-squared = 0.6256
F( 2,    32) =  26.73      Adj R-squared = 0.6022
Prob > F     = 0.0000      Root MSE      = .32206
```

Ln SourceSize	Coeff.	Std. Err.	[95% CI]		t	P>|t|
Factor 1	.199	.088	.012 --	.378	2.264	0.031
Ln Attributes	.553	.208	.130 --	.977	2.662	0.012
Constant	4.622	.847	2.897 --	6.347	5.458	0.000

5.2 Evaluating Model Fit

A high adjusted R^2 is not enough; we have to examine the results more closely.

The first step is to examine the residuals (the discrepancies between the predicted Y values and the actual observations) in order to make sure that they are as random as our linear regression model assumes. When we plot the residuals against the predicted values, as shown in Fig. 9, we look for any sort of apparent pattern: such a pattern may indicate the presence of an unaccounted-for variable, or that one of the assumptions of the linear regression model has been violated.

A second step is to see if any of the individual observations is exerting too much of an influence on the overall fit of the model. This is typical with outliers. The problem doesn't seem to occur in these data, fortunately.

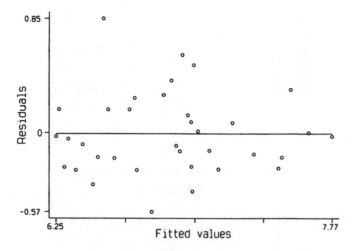

FIG. 9. Plot of residual prediction error.

A further step is to examine the fit of each variable, adjusting for the others. Such plots are called *adjusted variable plots*, or sometimes *partial leverage plots*. They are shown here in Fig. 10.

5.3   Validating the Model

After fully evaluating the fit of the model on our "training" sample, we must then validate the model by seeing how well it can predict the observations in our validation sample. In this case, our model equation accounts for 56% of the variance in the validation sample, very close to the fit in the original sample.

There are many other ways of assessing the predictive accuracy available from the forecasting literature (e.g., [4]) such as mean absolute deviation (MAD), or mean absolute percent error (MAPE), which have different properties; it is up to the researcher to decide which one fits best with the goals of the research.

Whatever measure of fit we choose, we must again closely examine the fit; Fig. 11 shows the residuals in the validation sample; overall it looks fine, but the lowermost point invites investigation.

5.4   Refining the Model

Having evaluated our model's fit and validated it against a new dataset, we are now ready to look for possible refinements to it. One of the

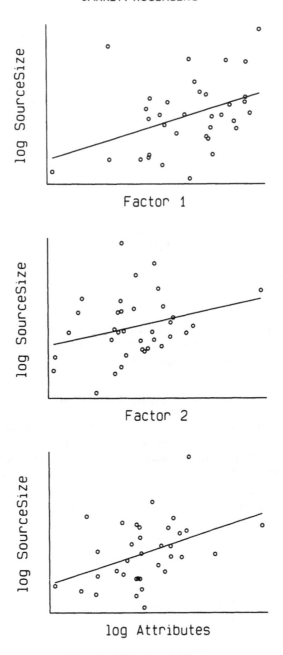

FIG. 10. Adjusted variable plots.

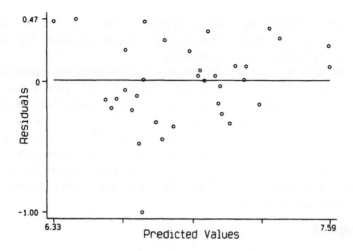

FIG. 11. Residual prediction error in validation sample.

differences between science and engineering is that the latter strives to be *useful*. Although factor analysis is a valuable research tool, it clearly is unreasonable to expect to tell someone outside the laboratory to run a factor analysis to predict the size of a source module. Our challenge then is to see if we can find a simpler model that works almost as well as the "true" model our analysis has revealed. An obvious candidate in this case would be one that uses the variables directly instead of by way of factor scores. For example, we can use the variable with the highest loading on Factor 1 (*TotalFunctions*) for our estimation (Example 4).

Example 4

```
Number of obs =      35     Raw R-squared = 0.6549
F( 2,    32) = 30.36     Adj R-squared = 0.6333
Prob > F     = 0.0000     Root MSE      = .3092
```

Ln SourceSize		Coeff.	Std. Err.	[95% CI]		t	P>|t|
Ln TotalFunctions		.617	.215	.180 --	1.055	2.877	0.007
Ln Attributes		.553	.179	.188 --	.917	3.085	0.004
Constant		2.695	.540	1.595 --	3.796	4.988	0.000

The fit is as good, and it is much easier to take the logs of the original variables than to do a factor analysis, so this model is probably preferable, even though it gives the misleading impression that *TotalFunctions* is more relevant than, say, *Entities* or *Relationships*. Figure 12 shows that the two models make almost identical predictions.

If we are lucky, we might be able to get a good fit using the untransformed observations, but that doesn't work very well here: the overall fit is as good, suggesting that the transformed and untransformed variables would make equally accurate predictions, but the number of functions is given a higher weight than it really deserves, and the number of attributes is actually judged to be insignificant. So although the overall predictive results might be the same, our model of the factors involved would be seriously misleading. This is the result of the skewness and outliers present in the original observations (Example 5).

Example 5

```
Number of obs =      35      Raw R-squared = 0.6468
F( 2,   32) = 29.30      Adj R-squared = 0.6247
Prob > F    = 0.0000      Root MSE      = 344.28
```

SourceSize		Coeff.	Std. Err.	[95% CI]		t	P>|t|
TotalFunctions		34.603	9.613	15.021 --	54.185	3.599	0.001
Attributes		6.121	3.329	-0.660 --	12.902	1.839	0.075
Constant		-133.743	170.427	-480.891 --	213.406	-0.785	0.438

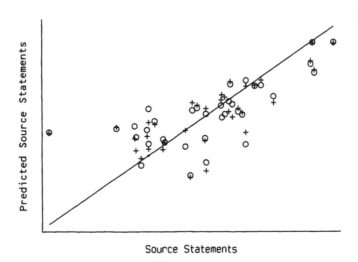

FIG. 12. Predicted vs. actual source statements for the two models.

After examining various refinements of the model, we may conclude that we can best express our predictions in the following equation:

$$\ln SourceSize = 2.7 + 0.62 \; (\ln TotalFunctions) + 0.55(\ln Attributes)$$

5.5 The Pitfall of Automated Procedures

A common mistake in doing multivariate analyses is to use some type of automated procedure to find the best-fitting model. The most common example is stepwise regression, which can take a variety of forms (forward, backward, hierarchical) and use a variety of criteria to guide its search.[10]

Although it was statisticians themselves who developed these methods of exploratory data analysis, most statisticians today discourage their use because it has become clear that there are a number of serious problems with them. Their main problem is that although they sometimes work, they often do not, and there is little indication to the user as to when they have failed (see, for example, the discussion in [5]).

The basic problem with automated procedures is that regression methods (for estimating coefficients and their confidence intervals, for testing whether a result is due to chance or not, etc.) are based on the assumption that the method is applied once, not over and over. Violating this basic assumption means that the reported results are misleading, since they are calculated relative to the *final* set of variables in the model, rather than the *initial* candidate set (and thus, for example, the adjusted R^2 value is a serious overestimate, not being adjusted fully, see [6] and [7]). Furthermore, the *p*-values and Type I error estimates are ones for a single regression calculation, not the multiple ones that were done. Just as when there is a risk of spurious correlations when computing a large matrix of correlations, there is the risk of a spurious model fit in a repetitive automated procedure. Additionally, automated procedures are especially vulnerable to the problem of multicollinearity since there is no human judgement involved, and so the resulting model can easily be one that a human analyst would have rejected as implausible based on knowledge of the domain. Different algorithms may also produce different results from the same dataset.

---

[10] One must distinguish automated procedures such as stepwise regression from various iterative fitting methods such as classification (e.g., CART) or machine learning/neural net techniques. The latter use iterative methods to solve an optimization problem in fitting a model to data, with a single final test of the significance of the fit; stepwise regression merely automates the tedious process of doing one regression test after another, with its attendant increase in the experiment-wise error rate.

In short, although automated procedures can sometimes be useful, their results are frequently misleading and can sometimes be seriously wrong, all without any warning to the user. They should be used only as a last resort. If they are used, they should be used in a hierarchical manner: variables or sets of variables should be entered based on their degree of permanence. Some variables reflect attributes which are essentially unchangeable (e.g., the age or sex of a person), whereas others reflect attributes that could easily have taken on a different value (e.g., location of residence). Since the unchangeable factors will always be present, they are in some sense logically prior and should be included first in the model, since they are the presumed source of any variance that they share with other independent variables.

6. Categorical Dependent Variables

The above procedure has assumed that the dependent variable is a continuous scale; what do we do if it is not? The most common case is the one in which the dependent variable is binary—some characteristic is either present or absent. However, the reduction of the dependent variable to a dichotomy creates a special situation: we are no longer able to state the "degree" to which the outcome is present; it must be either completely present or completely absent. Such a situation is called a *diagnostic* or *signal detection* problem.

There are several related techniques for such situations; *discriminant analysis* was the earliest one to be developed and is thus the most widely known, but statisticians currently prefer *logistic regression*, which transforms the dichotomous dependent variable in a way that allows it to be analyzed within the well-developed framework of ordinary linear regression. Consequently, most diagnostic studies (e.g., in medicine) use logistic regression as a starting point.

6.1 Logistic Regression

To illustrate logistic regression, let us revisit the problematic variable *MenuFunctions*. Suppose that we would like to predict whether or not a project will have more than the minimum number of 4 menu functions, using the other variables (apart from *SourceSize*) as possible predictors. We can create a new variable, *ExtraMenus*, which has the value 0 if the project has 4 menu functions, and the value 1 if it has more. (This loses information, of course, but that may not be important depending on the researcher's goals.)

Note that the mean of a dichotomous variable Y coded as 0/1 is simply the proportion of observations whose value is 1. Thus it can be thought of as the probability p that $Y = 1$. (The probability that $Y = 0$ is then $1 - p$.) Our goal then is to predict this probability that $Y = 1$ for each project with a linear model like the ones we have constructed so far.

The problem with the usual linear model in this case ($p = a + bX$) is that p must take on values between 0 and 1, but there is no constraint on the right-hand side of this equation to ensure that. One could try $p = e^{a+bX}$, but that will only guarantee that p is positive. The solution is the *logit* or *logistic* transformation $p = e^{a+bX}/(1 + e^{a+bX})$ which ranges from 0 to 1 as X ranges from $-\infty$ to $+\infty$. To get back to a simple linear form, note that $p/(1 - p) = e^{a+bX}$ and so taking logs of both sides gives us $\ln p/(1 - p) = a + bX$.

Since $p/(1 - p)$ is the *odds ratio* of p and its complement, the logistic model is sometimes called the *log odds* model. In particular, in logistic regression the regression coefficients are log odds ratios, rather than raw probabilities, although we can easily obtain the latter by the inverse transformation $p = 1/(1 + e^{-L})$, where L is the log odds ratio. The odds ratios are actually more desirable in many cases. Example 6 shows the result of a logistic regression of *ExtraMenus* on the variables *TotalFunctions* and *Attributes*.

Example 6

```
-------------------------------------------------------------
            | Odds   Std.
ExtraMenus  | Ratio  Err.        [95% CI]        z      P>|z|
------------+------------------------------------------------
TotalFuncs  | 1.375  0.113   1.170 -- 1.614    3.878   0.000
Attributes  | 0.977  0.017   0.950 -- 1.018   -0.926   0.355
-------------------------------------------------------------
Area under ROC curve = 0.880
```

Here we see that *TotalFunctions* significantly predicts the presence of extra menus, whereas *Attributes* does not (note that since we are dealing with odds ratios here, the confidence interval for a significant odds ratio must not include 1). The interpretation of the odds ratio for *TotalFunctions* is that every one-unit increase in *TotalFunctions* increases the odds of there being extra menus by 38%.

6.2   Predictive Accuracy and Signal Detection Theory

The fact that there are only two outcomes to predict shifts the emphasis in predictive accuracy and model goodness of fit from numerical accuracy (called *model calibration*) to discriminative accuracy (*model discrimination*). This is because the actual values predicted by the model are less important than their correlation with the two outcomes. Since R^2 in the case of logistic regression typically has a maximum value less than 1, depending on the prevalence of the "1" outcome, it is rarely reported (though see [8] for a discussion of its usefulness). Various "pseudo-R^2" statistics are sometimes used, but the most common measure of fit in logistic regression is one of discriminative accuracy: the area under the ROC curve. To see why, let us examine the concept of predictive accuracy in a diagnostic or detection framework. The situation is depicted in Fig. 13.

The items being assessed fall into one of two categories: positive or negative depending on whether $Y = 1$ or $Y = 0$ (in our example, whether or not the application has extra menus). The cases in these two categories have different values of the predictor variables (Fig. 13 depicts only one predictor, X, for simplicity; in our example, it is the total number of functions); but the distributions of these X values overlap (hence the discrimination problem). As the value of X increases, so does the probability that a case with that X value belongs to the positive category; at some point (the decision criterion), we will decide to call cases with larger X values positive, and those with smaller ones negative. Shifting the criterion downwards increases sensitivity, since more positive cases will correctly be predicted, but at a cost of more false positive predictions. Conversely, moving the criterion upwards decreases sensitivity but increases specificity, since it decreases the number of false positives and

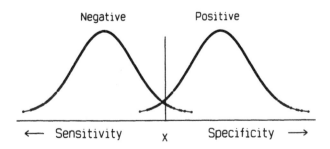

FIG. 13. Schematic representation of the diagnostic task.

increases the number of true negatives, but at a cost of more false negatives ("misses"). Given that the two distributions overlap, the placement of the criterion specifies one out of many possible 2 × 2 tables (Example 7).

Example 7

```
                    --- Actual Observation ---

Prediction      |  ExtraMenus=1   ExtraMenus=0      Total
----------------+----------------------------------+-------
ExtraMenus=1    |    true pos       false pos    |
ExtraMenus=0    |    false neg      true neg     |
----------------+----------------------------------+-------
Total           |                                 |
```

There are thus four outcomes:

- correct prediction of the presence of extra menus (a *hit* or *true positive*)
- correct prediction of the absence of extra menus (a *correct rejection* or *true negative*)
- incorrect prediction of extra menus when there are none (a *false alarm* or *false positive*)
- incorrect prediction of no extra menus where there are some (a *miss* or *false negative*).

From this we can define a few critical concepts:

- *sensitivity:* The probability of signalling the presence of the characteristic when it is in fact present: *truepos*/(*truepos* + *falseneg*)
- *specificity:* The probability of not signalling the presence of the characteristic when it is in fact not present: *trueneg*/(*trueneg* + *falsepos*)
- *false positive rate:* 1 − specificity
- *false negative rate:* 1 − sensitivity
- *positive predictive value:* The probability of a correct positive prediction: *truepos*/(*truepos* + *falsepos*)
- *negative predictive value:* The probability of a correct negative prediction: *trueneg*/(*trueneg* + *falseneg*)
- *accuracy:* The probability of a correct prediction: (*truepos* + *trueneg*)/ *Total*.

The table for our logistic regression is shown in Example 8.

Example 8

```
                      --- Actual Observation ---

Prediction      |  ExtraMenus=1  ExtraMenus=0      Total
----------------+------------------------------+-------
ExtraMenus=1    |       30             6        |   36
ExtraMenus=0    |        9            25        |   34
----------------+------------------------------+-------
Total           |       39            31        |   70


Classified pos if predicted Pr(ExtraMenus) >= 0.5
-------------------------------------------------------
Sensitivity                                  76.92%
Specificity                                  80.65%
Positive predictive value                    83.33%
Negative predictive value                    73.53%
-------------------------------------------------------
False pos rate for classified pos            16.67%
False neg rate for classified neg            26.47%
-------------------------------------------------------
Correctly classified                         78.57%
-------------------------------------------------------
```

From the preceding discussion, however, we know that any 2×2 diagnostic table is based not only on the evidence, but also on some implicit or explicit criterion about when to declare the evidence sufficient to make a positive prediction. The setting of the criterion is based on the relative costs of making false positive and false negative errors; reducing the likelihood of one results in increasing the likelihood of the other. *A change in the decision criterion changes the accuracy, even if the data stay the same.* As a result, such 2×2 tables and their associated accuracy values are only part of the story. For example, here are the same data, but using a decision criterion of 0.6 rather than 0.5; this small change in the criterion leaves the overall accuracy unchanged, but alters everything else (Example 9).

Example 9

```
                      --- Actual Observation ---

Prediction      |  ExtraMenus=1  ExtraMenus=0      Total
----------------+------------------------------+-------
ExtraMenus=1    |       28             4        |   32
ExtraMenus=0    |       11            27        |   38
----------------+------------------------------+-------
Total           |       39            31        |   70
```

```
Classified pos if predicted Pr(ExtraMenus) >= 0.6
------------------------------------------------
Sensitivity                                71.79%
Specificity                                87.10%
Positive predictive value                  87.50%
Negative predictive value                  71.05%
------------------------------------------------
False pos rate for classified pos          12.50%
False neg rate for classified neg          28.95%
------------------------------------------------
Correctly classified                       78.57%
------------------------------------------------
```

Consequently, what we would like to have is some diagram of the sensitivity/specificity tradeoff for our model, and some measure of accuracy that encompasses the range of possible criterion values. This is the receiver operating characteristic (ROC) curve, shown in Fig. 14. The diagonal line represents 50% accuracy or chance performance. The ROC curve draws away from the diagonal and towards the 100% accuracy of the upper-left corner and its adjacent sides. The area under the ROC curve (between the curve and the diagonal) thus ranges from 0.5 to 1.0 and is thus analogous to R^2. In our example, the area is a respectable 0.88. The points along the curve represent the various pairs of sensitivity/specificity values possible with the

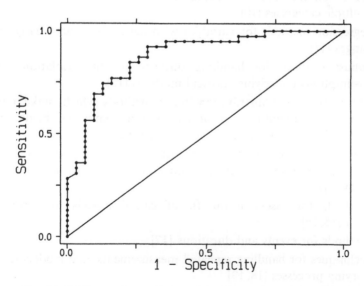

FIG. 14. ROC curve for prediction of extra menus by total functions.

model. The relative accuracy of predictive models can be graphically compared by plotting their ROC curves on the same graph.

It is to address these issues that *signal detection theory* was developed, providing a useful framework for modeling the various aspects of any sort of diagnostic procedure, including such things as the optimum placement of the decision criterion given differing costs for false positive and false negative errors. The concept of the ROC curve has been one of its most important contributions (our logistic regression model can thus be viewed as a sort of "receiver" trying to detect the "signal" of the positive cases amid the "noise" of the negative cases). It is beyond the scope of this chapter to discuss signal detection theory further, but it is essential that researchers pursuing the question of predicting dichotomous variables be familiar with it. A good introduction is [9].

7. More Advanced Methods

This chapter has used only a small set of very basic statistical tools, since for many situations they are all that is needed. However, there are many additional statistical techniques available to researchers to deal with a wide variety of situations. For example:

- regression methods for ordinal data, or for categorical data with multiple categories [10]
- regression methods for variables with naturally or artificially limited ranges [11]
- robust methods for handling outliers or other violations of the assumptions underlying classical methods [12]
- non-parametric ("distribution-free") methods which make minimal assumptions about the type of distribution from which the data come, and which do not require large sample sizes [13]
- computationally intensive techniques which work with very small samples, or sample statistics whose sampling distributions are unknown [14]
- methods for assessing the fit of causal models to correlational data [15, 16]
- methods for events and durations [17]
- techniques for handling repeated measurements, and models for time-varying processes [18, 19]
- techniques for compensating for missing observations [20].

However, these techniques require extensive training to use effectively. Rather than try them yourself, you are better off asking your friendly local statistician for assistance.

8. Summary

This simultaneously involved and sketchy presentation has attempted to convey a fairly simple yet effective model of how to properly conduct an empirical evaluation of a predictive metric. The tools themselves are rather simple, yet their flexibility requires an extensive acquaintance with their advantages and disadvantages. The basic steps in the method are easy to follow:

1. Look at the data first
2. Exclude or adapt problem variables
3. Be skeptical of univariate analyses
4. Check for correlations among the independent variables
5. Split the data into model-building and model-validation halves
6. Construct a model and fit it with multivariate methods
7. Examine the model fit
8. Validate the model against the validation sample
9. Examine the model fit
10. Refine the model

A conscientious application of this method increases the likelihood of a correct and insightful analysis.

9. Appendix: The Linear Regression Model

In evaluating a predictive metric, what we are looking for is some correlation (positive or negative) between the predictor and predicted measures. We could just calculate a correlation coefficient, which would tell us in standardized terms the strength of the relationship, but we are interested in actual numerical predictions as well (e.g., calculating the size of an application based on, say, the number of attributes in the E−R diagram of the system specification), so we will build a linear regression model. We could use non-linear regression, of course, but we should look at simpler models first to see if they do the job.

   The idea of bivariate linear regression is that we have a set of observation pairs $\langle x_i, y_i \rangle$, and would like to be able to predict the Y values as accurately as possible. That is, we are looking for a high degree of covariation between the two variables. Figure 15 diagrammatically depicts the variances of two variables, X and Y, and the concept of covariance, a mathematical linkage between the values of the X and Y variables. The covariance is sometimes referred to as the *shared variance* of the two variables.

We know a priori that, in the absence of any other information, the mean of the Y values, Y, is our best guess for any particular y_i, but we are hoping that knowing the value of an observation's X measure will allow us to make a more accurate prediction. The total of the (squared) differences between the Y values and their mean Y is called the *total sum of squares* (TSS) of Y. If we were to predict the values of the y_i from just Y alone, then the TSS of Y could be viewed as the total inaccuracy of such a (simplistic) prediction. The "$y_i = Y$" model is the simplest plausible model (it ignores the X data altogether), and serves as the comparison point for any other model we care to construct using additional information such as the X values.

In bivariate linear regression, such models have a linear form: $y_i = a + bx_i + \varepsilon_i$ where ε is an *error term* that embodies the inaccuracy in our model's predictions from a variety of reasons (measurement error, sampling variation, factors other than X). We cannot produce estimates for the slope and intercept parameters in this model without making some assumptions about the error terms, and a plausible (and very useful) one is that they independently come from the same normal distribution, which has a mean of zero.[11]

We will say that our model works if its predictions are better than those obtained from the "$y_i = Y$" model. This is equivalent to saying that our model estimates that b is not equal to zero (a being equal to Y in this model). The statistical procedures in linear regression produce *estimates* of the model parameters, and also measures of how precise those estimates are (the *standard errors* of the estimates, from which the so-called "confidence

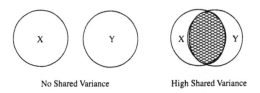

No Shared Variance   High Shared Variance

FIG. 15. Shared variance between two variables.

---

[11] The statistical jargon for this is that they are "independently and identically normally distributed with mean zero and variance σ^2". The drawback of this is that if the error terms are not so distributed, then most statistical procedures silently produce incorrect results.

intervals" for the estimates are constructed). The standard errors are critical, since an estimate with a very wide confidence interval is not very useful.

9.1   Assessing Model Goodness of Fit

Our predicted values of the y_is are each some distance from the actual observed values. The total of the (squared) differences between the predicted values of the y_is and their mean is the *model sum of squares* (MSS). The total of the (squared) differences between the observed and predicted values of the y_is is the *residual sum of squares* (RSS) and is the total inaccuracy of our model. The ratio of the MSS to the TSS is thus a good measure of how well our model fits the observations, compared to the "null" model of just using Y. This measure is called R^2, because in the bivariate case it turns out to be the square of the correlation coefficient r. It is also called the *coefficient of determination* and the amount of *explained variance* of the model. In terms of Fig. 15, a high degree of overlap gives a large R^2.

Another measure of goodness of fit is *root mean square error*, which is simply the square root of the average squared differences between observed and predicted values. This "average" error gives us another perspective on a model's fit, albeit unstandardized, since it is not a percentage of total error.

9.2   An Example

To make this concrete, let us look at an example: *Entities* and *SourceSize*. The two have a correlation of 0.58. A regression of *SourceSize* on *Entities* gives us the results shown in Example 10, typical of regression reports from most statistical packages.

Example 10

Source	Sum of Sqrs	df	Mean Sqr			
				Number of obs =		35
				F(1, 33) =		16.66
Model	3601792.82	1	3601792.82	Prob > F	=	0.0003
Residual	7135825.35	33	216237.132	R-squared	=	0.3354
				Adj R-squared =		0.3153
Total	10737618.2	34	315812.299	Root MSE	=	465.01

SourceSize	Coeff.	Std. Err.	[95% CI]		t	P>|t|
Entities	64.589	15.824	32.388 --	96.778	4.081	0.000
Constant	337.674	200.930	-71.120 --	746.47	1.681	0.102

The small table at the upper left gives the MSS and RSS, and the mean sums-of-squares on which the overall test of the regression model is based. On the right, the number of observations is given, then the value of the F-statistic which assesses whether or not the entire regression model is different from the $y_i = Y$ null model. The probability of getting such an F value if the null model is true is then printed; in this case the probability is 0.0003, and we are justified in concluding that the null model is not accounting for our results—our alternate model is. The raw and adjusted R^2 ("explained variance") indicates how well the model fits: in this case, the number of entities in the E–R diagram accounts for roughly 30% of the variation in the source size of the project.

Another measure of goodness-of-fit, the root mean square error, is printed next. Then come the actual estimates for the parameters in the model:

$$SourceSize = a + b \times Entities$$

The estimate for b is 65, with a standard error of 16, giving a 95% confidence interval for its actual value of 32 to 97. The t-statistic tests whether or not this parameter is different from zero; the probability is given next (the "0.000" means "less than 0.001"). Here there is a clear indication that the number of entities has an effect. The last line gives an estimate for the constant a in the equation; it is not significantly different from zero (note that the confidence interval for it includes zero), meaning that we could probably drop it from the model, and use simply the number of entities if we wished.

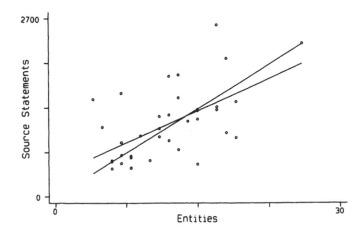

FIG. 16. Linear models for source size with zero and non-zero intercepts.

If we were to do so, we would get the result shown in Example 11. This model fits somewhat better, since the standard error of the slope parameter is only half as large. Note that by omitting the constant term a from our new model, our null model is now that $a = 0$, rather than $a = Y$ as before; since that is a less plausible null model, it's not surprising that our R^2 is much higher here. But note that the Root MSE is actually slightly larger; the model fit is really about the same. This illustrates the pitfall of using just one measure of goodness of fit. Figure 16 shows the data and the two regression lines; it's clear that the two models are very similar.

Example 11

```
Source    | Sum of Sqrs  df    Mean Sqr     Number of obs =       35
----------+---------------------------       F( 1,    34) = 196.44
Model     | 44755715.5    1    44755715.5   Prob > F      = 0.0000
Residual  | 7746539.51   34    227839.397   R-squared     = 0.8525
----------+---------------------------       Adj R-squared = 0.8481
Total     | 52502255.0   35    1500064.43   Root MSE      = 477.33
-------------------------------------------------------------------

                          Std.
SourceSize      Coeff.    Err.        [95% CI]            t      P>|t|
------------+------------------------------------------------------------
Entities    |   89.057    6.354   76.144 -- 101.970   14.016   0.000
-------------------------------------------------------------------
```

From this analysis we conclude that the model

$$SourceSize = 89 \times Entities$$

is perhaps preferable to

$$SourceSize = 338 + 65 \times Entities$$

with either model accounting for about a third of the variance in the number of source statements. Good introductory references for linear regression are [21] and [22]. More comprehensive discussions can be found in [23–26]. A brief but especially informative work is [27].

ACKNOWLEDGEMENTS

The author thanks Steve MacDonnell, Martin Shepperd, and Peter Sallis for generously providing their data and graciously commenting on this chapter. Thanks also to Barbara Kitchenham, Shari Lawrence Pfleeger, Khaled El-Emam, and several anonymous reviewers for their comments and suggestions.

References

[1] MacDonell, S., Shepperd, M. and Sallis, P. (1997). Metrics for database systems: an empirical study. *Proceedings of the 4th International Software Metrics Symposium*, Albuquerque, NM, pp. 99–107.

[2] Anscombe, F. (1973). Graphs in statistical analysis. *American Statistician*, **27**(1), 17–21.

[3] Aiken, L. and West, S. (1991). *Multiple Regression: Testing and Interpreting Interactions*. Sage, Thousand Oaks, CA.

[4] Makridakis, S., Wheelwright, S. and Hyndman, R. (1998). *Forecasting: Methods and Applications*, 3rd edn. Wiley, New York.

[5] Judd, C. and McClelland, G. (1989). *Data Analysis: A Model Comparison Approach*. Harcourt Brace Jovanovich, San Diego, CA.

[6] Copas, J. B. (1983). Regression, prediction and shrinkage (with discussion). *Journal of the Royal Statistical Society* B, **45**, 311–354.

[7] Derksen, S. and Keselman, H. (1992). Backward, forward and stepwise automated subset selection algorithms: frequency of obtaining authentic and noise variables. *British Journal of Mathematical and Statistical Psychology*, **45**, 265–282.

[8] Ash, A. and Shwartz, M. (1999). R^2: a useful measure of model performance when predicting a dichotomous outcome. *Statistics in Medicine*, **18**, 375–384.

[9] Swets, J. (1996). *Signal Detection Theory and ROC Analysis in Psychology and Diagnostics*. Erlbaum, Hillsdale, NJ.

[10] Hosmer, D. and Lemeshow, S. (1989). *Applied Logistic Regression*. Wiley, New York.

[11] Long, J. (1997). *Regression Models for Categorical and Limited Dependent Variables*. Sage, Thousand Oaks, CA.

[12] Birkes, D. and Dodge, Y. (1993). *Alternative Methods of Regression*. Wiley, New York.

[13] Sprent, P. (1993). *Applied Non-Parametric Statistical Methods*, 2nd edn. Chapman & Hall, New York.

[14] Good, P. (1994). *Permutation Tests*. Springer-Verlag, New York.

[15] Retherford, R. and Choe, M. (1993). *Statistical Models for Causal Analysis*. Wiley, New York.

[16] Kline, R. (1998). *Principles and Practice of Structural Equation Modeling*. Guilford, New York.

[17] Blossfeld, H.-P., Hamerle, A. and Mayer, K. (1989). *Event History Analysis: Statistical Theory and Application*. Erlbaum, Hillsdale, NJ.

[18] Diggle, P., Liang, K. and Zeger, S. (1994). *Analysis of Longitudinal Data*. Oxford University Press, Oxford.

[19] Bowerman, B. and O'Connell, R. (1993). *Forecasting and Time Series: An Applied Approach*. Wadsworth, New York.

[20] Little, R. and Rubin, D. (1987). *Statistical Analysis with Missing Data*. Wiley, New York.

[21] Hamilton, L. (1990). *Modern Data Analysis*. Duxbury, Belmont, CA.

[22] Hamilton, L. (1992). *Regression with Graphics*. Duxbury, Belmont, CA.

[23] Draper, N. and Smith, H. (1998). *Applied Regression Analysis*, 2nd edn. Wiley, New York.

[24] Freund, R. and Wilson, W. (1998). *Regression Analysis*. Academic Press, New York.

[25] Rawlings, J., Pantula, S. and Dickey, D. (1998). *Applied Regression Analysis*, 2nd edn. Springer-Verlag, New York.

[26] Ryan, T. (1996). *Modern Regression Methods*. Wiley, New York.

[27] Kennedy, P. (1998). *A Guide to Econometrics*, 4th edn. MIT Press, Cambridge, MA.

An Empirical Review of Software Process Assessments

KHALED EL EMAM

National Research Council, Canada
Institute for Information Technology
Ottawa, Ontario
Canada K1A OR6
Khaled.El-Emam@iit.nrc.ca

DENNIS R. GOLDENSON

Software Engineering Institute
Carnegie Mellon University
Pittsburgh, PA 15213-3890
USA
dg@sei.cmu.edu

Abstract

In the recent past there has been a rapid increase in the use of process assessments in the software industry. Such assessments play an important role in initiating and tracking process improvements. In addition, there has been a proliferation of best practice models that are the basis for the assessments. The purpose of this chapter is to review the empirical evidence that exists to date on the efficacy of process assessments, with a specific focus on the CMM for software and the emerging ISO/IEC 15504 international standard. The available evidence is quite extensive, and supports the claims that assessments can be an effective tool for process improvement. We also highlight gaps in the literature where further work needs to be done.

ADVANCES IN COMPUTERS, VOL. 53
ISBN 0-12-012153-0

319

1. Introduction

Over the last decade and a half there has been a rapid growth of interest by the software industry in Software Process Improvement (SPI). An industry to support SPI efforts has also been burgeoning. SPI can, and has, played an important role in achieving improvements in product quality and the ability to meet budget and schedule targets [1, 2].

Two general paradigms to SPI have emerged, as described by Card [3]. The first is the *analytic paradigm*. This is characterized as relying on "quantitative evidence to determine where improvements are needed and whether an improvement initiative has been successful." The second, what Card calls the *benchmarking paradigm*,[1] "depends on identifying an

---

[1] This may also be called "experiential," since the term "benchmarking" is often used to describe the collection of quantitative data that can be used to describe the "state of the art" among similar organizations in the software industry.

'excellent' organization in a field and documenting its practices and tools."
The analytic paradigm is exemplified by the work at the Software
Engineering Laboratory [4]. The benchmarking paradigm is exemplified
by the Capability Maturity Model (CMM) for software [5] and the emerging
ISO/IEC 15504 international standard [6].[2] Benchmarking assumes that if a
less-proficient organization adopts the practices of the excellent organization, it will also become excellent. Our focus in this chapter is on the
benchmarking paradigm.

An essential ingredient of SPI following the benchmarking paradigm is a
best practice model,[3] e.g., the CMM for software [5]. Such a model codifies
what are believed to be best software engineering practices. By comparing
their own processes to those stipulated in the best practice model, software
organizations can identify where improvements in their processes should be
made. The above process of comparison is known as a *software process
assessment* (SPA).[4]

A key feature of contemporary best practice models is that they group
their software engineering practices into a series of "stages" that an
organization (or a process) should go through on its improvement path. By
knowing which stage you are at, you can then identify the actions necessary
to progress to the next higher stage. An SPA can be used to identify the
current stage of an organization or process.

The objective of this chapter is to review the empirical evidence on the use
of SPAs. The importance of such a review is perhaps best exemplified
through a historical interlude. Hence, we first trace the path of Nolan's stage
hypothesis. This is arguably the first "stage" model, which initially appeared
in print in 1973.

---

[2] Following the benchmarking paradigm involves using structured frameworks of best
practice as identified by expert working groups and corroborated by external review. Although
such frameworks rely heavily on experience, they have in fact been based at least partially from
the beginning on empirical analytic evidence as well.

[3] The model that is used as the basis for an assessment has been referred to differently over the
years. For example, ISO/IEC 15504 refers to it as an "assessment model." The SW-CMM is
referred to as a "reference model" by the SEI, which means something very different in the
context of ISO/IEC 15504. To avoid confusion we shall use the term "best practice model" in
this chapter.

[4] Here we use the term SPA in the general sense, not in the sense of an earlier SEI assessment
method (which was also called an SPA). The successor to the SPA is the CBA IPI [8]. The term
"assessment" is often reserved only for methods that are meant to be used by organizations for
their own self-improvement. The term "evaluation" is then used to refer to methods meant to be
used by others for acquisition or source selection. However, "assessment" also is commonly
used to cover both kinds of methods interchangeably. We use the term in its broader sense
throughout this chapter.

1.1   The Stage Hypothesis

One of the earliest stage models was Nolan's stage hypothesis [7]. Nolan observed the rise in the information systems (IS) budget of three firms, and interpreted this rise as following an S-shaped curve. From the points of inflection on these curves, he derived four stages that an IS organization goes through during its evolution: *initiation, contagion, control,* and *integration.* For example, the integration stage is characterized by the establishment of controls to allow the exploitation of computing without cost overruns. Planning is well established, Users are knowledgeable and capable in their uses of computing. Operations are rationalized, and economic analyses (e.g., cost/benefits analysis) are performed to justify and prioritize development work. And systems analysts are appropriately decentralized to user departments to encourage improved systems development. The stage hypothesis came to be regarded as a well-grounded empirical theory of IS organizational evolution [9], and became well entrenched in the management information systems (MIS) discipline through its appearance in textbooks (e.g., [10–13]).

Subsequent to the initial descriptive hypothesis, Nolan and his colleagues further refined it into a prescriptive model [14, 15], with guidelines to aid the management of the IS function. Other work expanded the initial four-stage model into a six-stage model [9, 16]: *initiation, contagion, control, integration, data administration,* and *maturity.*

The importance and influence of Nolan's model also attracted a good amount of empirical evaluation. Researchers empirically evaluated the basic premises of the model as well as the accuracy of its predictions [17–20]. One review and interpretation of the empirical evidence concluded that

> most of the testable hypotheses have not been confirmed ... the overall weight of the accumulated evidence to date in the evolution of IS research, is nonsupportive of the stage hypothesis .... The general conclusion of all of the studies summarized here is that empirical support for the stage hypothesis is unconvincing .... The empirical studies surveyed here indicate that the various maturity criteria do not reliably move together, or even always in the same direction, this refuting one of the requirements for claiming the existence of a stage theory [21].

Some other authors have questioned the logical structure of the model, identifying a number of problems in its formulation [22].

Despite this evidence, the stage hypothesis was seen as a useful tool for the MIS discipline in that it promoted "a more organized approach to research on the subject", and it has value for its "conceptual contribution in the stage idea" [23]. Recently, some authors have argued that the observations embodied in Nolan's model were in fact essentially accurate, but that the model needed further refinement [24].

1.2   The Second Wave

Independent of Nolan's stage model, another stage model was developed in the mid-1980s. Humphrey [25] initially described the software process maturity framework, which consists of five stages: *initial, repeatable, defined, managed,* and *optimizing* (Fig. 1). The framework was based on earlier experiences at IBM [26]. It is both a descriptive and a guidance framework. It is descriptive of the "actual historical phases of evolutionary improvement of real software organizations" [25]. However, these software organizations can be considered best-in-class since the framework provides "a set of immediate priorities, once an organization's state in this framework is known." By addressing the identified priority items, you would then follow the path of the best-in-class organizations and gain the consequent performance improvements.

The software process maturity framework was not driven by academic research. Rather, it was meant to address a practical need:

the increasing importance of software in DoD procurements and the need of all the [US DoD] services to more effectively evaluate the ability of their software contractors to competently perform on software engineering contract [28].

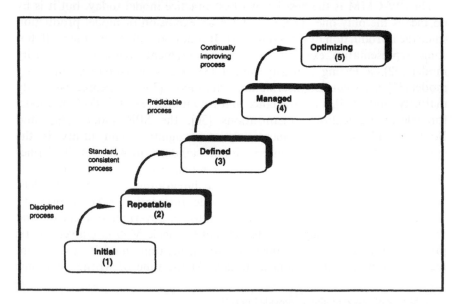

FIG. 1. The stages of software process maturity according to the Humphrey framework (from [27] © 1999 IEEE, reproduced with permission).

Software procurement problems were not unique to the DoD. Drouin [29] describes similar problems encountered by the UK Ministry of Defence. Other large commercial procurers faced special difficulties, including the procurement of mission-critical software before it is actually complete and that is expected to evolve to meet new requirements and continue to operate correctly for a number of decades [30]. In such cases, it is necessary to look at the capability of the supplier to deliver and maintain the product.

Humphrey and Sweet [28] operationalized the process maturity framework into a basic capability evaluation method that used a questionnaire to identify the "stage" at which an organization resided. The "stage" is known as the maturity level of the organization, taking on values from 1 (least mature) to 5 (most mature). The maturity level provides a simple quantification of the capability of a particular supplier, and can be used as input into the procurement process.

Early on, it was also realized that process assessments can be beneficial for SPI [25, 31]. Process assessments were typically conducted to initiate and monitor improvement progress as part of larger SPI efforts. Hence, both capability evaluation of suppliers and process improvement became the two primary purposes for performing SPAs.

Humphrey's maturity framework evolved into the Capability Maturity Model for Software (SW-CMM) [5].[5]

The SW-CMM is the best-known best practice model today, but it is by no means the only one. There has been an explosion of model production since the introduction of the SW-CMM. It is not possible to list them all, but some representative examples are the requirement engineering maturity model [32], a testing maturity model [33, 34], a measurement maturity model [35], a systems engineering maturity model [36], the people capability maturity model [37], a maintenance maturity model [38], the Trillium model for telecommunications organizations [30], the SPR model [39], and Bootstrap [40–42]. Also, increasing in recognition and utility is the emerging ISO/IEC 15504 international standard [6, 44], which defines requirements for models as well as an exemplar best practice model.

There have been some recent efforts at integrating the various models, most notably the Capability Maturity Model Integration (CMMI) project.[6] The CMMI project is a joint effort of industry, government agencies, and the Software Engineering Institute (SEI) at Carnegie Mellon University. Its product suite includes a framework for generating models, assessment methods, and related training materials. At the time of writing, a public

---

[5] A history of this evolution is provided in [43].

[6] Further information about the CMMI project may be found at *www.sei.cmu.edu/cmm/cmmi/*.

review is currently under way of a model that integrates concepts from both software and systems engineering. A program of test and evaluation is about to commence in coordination with the international SPICE trials.

An important question that needs to be answered at the outset is, how prevalent are assessments that use these models? Herbsleb *et al.* [45] note that there are probably "thousands" of assessments that have been performed using the SW-CMM, and the resources expended on CMM-based improvement are in the "billions of dollars." A study by El Emam and Garro [92] estimated that between September 1996 and June 1998, approximately 1250 assessments using the emerging ISO/IEC 15504 standard were performed.[7] On the basis of the above numbers, it is reasonable to conclude that there are indeed many "thousands" of assessments being performed worldwide, and that these assessments represent a considerable investment of software engineering resources.[8]

1.3 Empirical Evaluation

So far we have established that SPAs are used for process improvement and procurement, and that they enjoy considerable usage worldwide by the software engineering community. But what empirical evidence exists to support and justify their use? Given the experiences with Nolan's stage hypothesis, are we repeating the same pattern again? Shouldn't we exercise prudence in empirically evaluating a technology first before deploying it so widely?

Some of the comments that have appeared, and continue to appear, in the literature would make one think that the practical use of SPAs proceeds in an empirical vacuum. For instance, in the context of SW-CMM based assessments, Hersh [46] stated "despite our own firm belief in process improvement and our intuitive expectation that substantial returns will result from moving up the SEI [CMM] scale—we still can't prove it." Fenton [47] noted that evaluating the validity of the SEI's process maturity scheme is a key contemporary research issue. Jones, commenting on the SW-CMM effort at the SEI, stated that [48] "Solid empirical information is lacking on the quality and productivity levels associated with the SEI five

---

[7] A point estimate of 1264 with a 90% confidence interval between 916 and 1895 was calculated using a capture–recapture model.

[8] There are dissenting opinions: For example, Gray and Smith [49] stated (in 1998) that SPAs are not yet widely employed in the software industry, although they do not present any evidence to support that argument. The authors make some claims about the general inefficacy of SPAs. However, none of these claims is supported by evidence either. This is surprising given that the main thrust of the article was the lack of empirical evidence supporting the use of SPAs.

levels of maturity." Gray and Smith [49] present severe criticism of SPAs, mainly due to a presumptive lack of empirical evidence. For example, they state

> The whole CMM style approach is based on untested assertions and opinions, ... there is a lack of evidence to support the notions of repeatability and reproducibility of software process assessments .... Currently software process assessment schemes are being applied and resultant process improvement plans being drawn up and acted upon without answers to the questions of repeatability and reproducibility being in place ... the validity of the SEI's maturity model remains unproven .... If anyone states that existing process assessment schemes or the attempted world standard [ISO/IEC 15504] are based on a full understanding and sound theoretical underpinnings, let it go in one ear and out the other.

The above criticisms are undoubtedly rather severe. It is fair to say that at the outset when best practice models and SPAs were first introduced to the software engineering community, there was indeed little empirical evidence supporting their use. For example, in relation to SPAs, Pfleeger makes the point that

> many development organizations grab new, promising technologies well before there is clear evidence of proven benefit. For instance, the US Software Engineering Institute's Capability Maturity Model was embraced by many companies well before the SEI and others began empirical investigations of the nature and magnitude of its process improvement effects [50].

Jones argues that

> the SEI Capability Maturity Model was deployed without any kind of serious evaluation or testing of the concept .... The SEI assertions about quality and productivity were initially made without any kind of study or empirical evidence [48].

However, since their initial development and deployment, a considerable amount of empirical evaluative studies have in fact been performed. Especially when compared to other widely used software engineering technologies such as object-oriented techniques, the SPA field is remarkably rich in empirical evidence.

That empirical results lag the actual adoption of technology is not a problem unique to software engineering. In the allied discipline of MIS, this particular problem has been well recognized. Specifically, Benbasat and Zmud [51] state that rapid technological change

> results in our chasing after practice rather than leading practice, and [this] typically leads to reporting results from (rigorous) studies involving new technologies years after the technology's acceptance (and, occasionally,

rejection) by practice .... Needless to say, pronouncements in the future about today's technological and associated business challenges are just not going to be considered relevant by most practitioners.

Herbsleb [52] provides a further elaboration:

If, for example, we are trying out a new technology that we believe has enormous potential, it may be a serious error for managers to wait until conclusive results are available. Management is the art of placing good bets, and as soon as a manger is convinced that the likelihood of significant benefits outweighs the risks and justifies the cost, managers should act.

Most of the empirical evidence did indeed come after wide initial adoption. When one considers the classical technology adoption stages [53], it becomes clear that empirical evidence serves the needs of early majority adopters who follow rather than lead, and who are willing to try new things only when they are demonstrated to be effective by others [50]. Innovators and early adopters need no such assurances. However, without the existence of innovators and early adopters, it is doubtful that realistic empirical evaluation studies can be performed at all.

Empirical evaluation serves two objectives:

● It can validate or refute claims made by developers about the costs and benefits of their technologies. In practice, usually one finds that some of the claims are confirmed under certain conditions, and are unsupportable under other conditions.

● Perhaps more importantly, empirical evaluation can identify opportunities for enhancing the technology in the spirit of continuous improvement.

In this chapter we attempt to provide some answers to the concerns just voiced. We review the empirical evidence on SPAs to date, attempt to draw conclusions from existing studies, and distill what we have learned thus far. To be clear, those studies are not the last word on SPAs. More remains to be done to confirm and refine their conclusions, so we also attempt to identify promising areas for additional work.

1.4 Scope and Caveats

We limit our scope in this review largely to SPAs that are performed for the purpose of SPI rather than capability evaluation. Although there are important differences between the two usages, much of the work on SPAs can be reasonably generalized to both SPI and capability evaluation, and a limited scope makes the review more focused.

In this review we focus mainly on the SW-CMM and ISO/IEC 15504, but we do provide some coverage of ISO 9000 because of its prevalence [54]. We are collectively most familiar with them, and a considerable amount of detailed information is publicly available about them. They have been used extensively worldwide, and a considerable number of empirical studies have evaluated them and their use.

At the outset we have to make clear two further caveats about this review.

- First, we only consider published works that we judge to be reasonably methodologically sound. Frequently it is heard at conferences or in meetings that company X has performed an empirical study that demonstrated Y, but the detailed results are not in the public record. Without access to a fully documented report, one cannot make an informed judgement about the weight of the evidence. A poorly done study lacks credence even if it supports a commonly held view. For the same reason, we deliberately have excluded studies that we judged to be based on questionable data or analytic methods.

- Second, there does exist a feedback loop whereby any weaknesses in best practice models and assessment methods that were identified in empirical studies were addressed in subsequent versions. The most recent versions of these models and methods in use today may actually be better than the available evidence suggests.[9]

2. Summary of Review Findings

SPAs are ubiquitous in today's software engineering industry. Encouraged by an increasing number of success stories, many organizations have begun to rely heavily on SPAs since their introduction in the mid-1980s. Some commentators continue to bemoan the adoption of a technology that has not been empirically evaluated. This criticism may have been acceptable a few years ago, it is no longer defensible: An increasing number of empirical studies now exist. Of course, they do not demonstrate that SPAs are the solution to all of our problems. However, the studies do highlight many strengths, as well as identify opportunities for continuing improvement.

In this chapter we provide a detailed review of the empirical evidence about the efficacy of SPAs. What follows here is an overall summary of that

---

[9] We assume that if empirical studies identify a strength in the various models and methods, the feature(s) in question will be retained. Therefore, we can safely claim that models and methods in use today are not likely to be worse than the evidence suggests.

review. The summary provides a comprehensive picture of the empirically based state of knowledge about SPAs, and also identifies promising areas for further exploration:

- At the time of writing, evidence exists that organizations perform assessments for the following reasons (see Section 4.3):
  - Sponsors expect a SPA to generate buy-in and create a climate for change within the organization.
  - Sponsors believe that process improvement based on the results of assessments will lead to bottom-line improvements in their projects and organizations.
  - Sponsors perceive SPAs as a valuable, objective measurement procedure.
  - Sponsors expect that a SPA will lead to the introduction of best practices within their organizations.
- The concept of "stages" found in best practice models is perceived to be useful by organizations performing SPAs. Further work needs to be performed, however, to clarify whether this is indeed the natural order in which historically successful software organizations improve (see Section 5.1).
- Approximately one third of respondents on SPI surveys report marked changes in their organizations as a consequence of their assessments. Organizations appear to have (unrealistically) high expectations from assessment-based SPI, and these need to be better managed. Despite the above, sponsors of assessments and assessment participants remain enthusiastic about the value of SPAs (see Section 5.2).
- Assessments increase "buy-in" for SPI for the participants in the assessments and the organizations' technical staffs. This is particularly encouraging since these are the individuals who are most likely to be initially skeptical about SPI, and to resist change from "yet another" management initiative (see Section 5.3).
- The most important factors that affect the success of SPI initiatives are (see Section 5.4):
  - management commitment and support of SPI (e.g., management monitoring of the initiative, or making resources available)
  - involvement of technical staff in the SPI effort
  - ensuring that staff understand the current software processes and their relationship to other business activities
  - clear SPI goals that are understood by the staff
  - tailoring the improvement initiatives
  - respected SPI staff (change agents and opinion leaders).

- In the chapter, we provide some general guidelines that may be useful in better managing expectations about the cost of SPI (see Section 5.5).

- The groupings of processes and practices within best practice models tend to be based largely on expert judgements made by model builders. Further empirical work needs to be performed in corroborating such judgements (see Section 6).

- A growing number of studies have empirically demonstrated the reliability of SPA results. Our ability to provide such evidence provides confidence in those results, and is particularly important given the high stakes of conducting process assessments (see Section 7). Studies of inter-rater agreement in ISO/IEC 15504-based assessments indicate that most ratings by independent teams are sufficiently reliable (at least 75%):
  - There exists evidence that more reliable assessments may prove to be less costly. When assessors agree in their initial rating judgements, the consolidation phase appears to require less consensus-building. Hence the consolidation progresses faster, resulting in an overall reduction in cost.
  - Early evidence suggests that the reliability of SPAs deteriorates with inexperienced assessors
  - Some systematic bias has been witnessed when assessment teams did not include both internal and external assessors. Mixed teams appear to be less prone to such unreliability.
  - The nature of the assessment method also appears to have a demonstrable impact on inter-rater agreement. One study found that rating judgements about lower capability levels were more reliable when they were deferred until later in the assessment when all of the evidence was collected and considered together.

- Further systematic empirical investigation is necessary, but a survey based study of assessment experts suggests a number of factors that may affect the reliability of assessments (see Section 7):
  - clarity of the best practice model, and knowledge of it by the assessment team
  - the extent to which the assessment process is defined and documented
  - amount of data that is collected during the assessment
  - commitment to the assessment by both its sponsor and others in the assessed organization
  - assessment team composition and stability

- By now there is ample evidence from a number of case studies that higher process capability is associated with improved performance.

More methodologically defensible studies of predictive validity also suggest that higher process capability tends to result in better performance. Similar results exist both at the project and organizational levels. (see Section 8)

- Further studies need to be performed to determine the rate of returns as an organization improves its processes according to current best practice models.

As we said at the outset, a considerable amount of empirical evidence already exists about the conduct and impact of software process assessments. However much more remains to be done, especially if we are to promote a more cumulative accumulation of knowledge:

- It is important that researchers use standardized instruments in their studies. For example, studies of predictive validity ought to reuse measures of process capability that were used in previous studies to allow comparability of the results. Without this, there will always be uncertainty as to what the body of knowledge really indicates.

- One of the vexing problems in correlational and observational studies of SPAs is the lack of appropriate sampling frames. This means that samples that are used for study most often are convenience samples. While this is driven by the constraints of a particular study, we encourage more effort to be placed on improved sampling. This will give us far greater confidence in the generalizability of our results.

3. Background

3.1 The Context of Assessments

The context of process assessment is depicted in Fig. 2. This shows that process assessment provides a means of characterizing the current process capabilities of an organization. An analysis of the assessment results identifies the process strengths and weaknesses. For SPI, this would lead to an improvement initiative, which identifies changes to the processes in order to improve their capabilities. For capability determination, the assessment results identify whether the assessed processes meet some target capability. If the processes do not scale up to the target capability, then this may initiate an improvement effort.

The performance of an assessment requires three different types of inputs:

- First is an *assessment definition*, which includes the identification of the assessment sponsor, the purpose and scope of the assessment, any

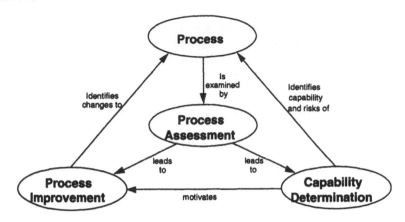

FIG. 2. The context of process assessment (from [44]).

relevant constraints, and identifying the assessment responsibilities (e.g., who will be on the assessment team, and who will be interviewed).

- It is also necessary to have an *assessment method* that describes the activities that need to be performed during an assessment.[10]
- Finally, an underlying *best practice model* is required. This model consists of the definitions of the processes that will be assessed, the assessment criteria, and a scheme to produce quantitative ratings at the end of the assessment.

Since our focus is SPI, process assessment's positioning within an overall SPI cycle can be seen in the IDEAL model [55] shown in Fig. 3.[11] It consists of five phases: Initiating (the improvement program); Diagnosing (the current state of practice); Establishing (the plans for the improvement program); Acting (on the plans and recommended improvements); and Leveraging (the lessons learned and the business results of the improvement effort)

- The *initiating* phase establishes the business reasons for undertaking a software process improvement effort. It identifies high-level concerns in the organization that can be the stimulus for addressing various aspects of quality improvement. Communication of these concerns and business perspectives is needed during the Initiating phase in order to

---

[10] The distinction between assessment definition and method is made in ISO/IEC 15504. Definition in that sense is part of "method" in CMM-based appraisals.

[11] The description of IDEAL here is based on that given in [27].

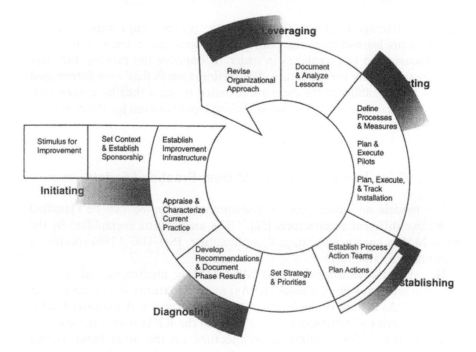

FIG. 3. The SEI's IDEAL model for SPI (source [27] © 1999 IEEE, reproduced with permission).

gain visible executive buy-in and sponsorship at this very early part of the improvement effort.

- The *diagnosing* phase is used to build a common understanding of the current processes of the organization, especially the strengths and weaknesses of those current processes. It will also help identify priorities for improving your software processes. This diagnosis is based on an SPA.

- The *establishing* phase finalizes the strategy and supporting plans for the software process improvement program. It sets the direction and guidance for the next 3–5 years, including strategic and tactical plans for software process improvement.

- The *acting* phase takes action to effect changes in organizational systems that result in improvements in these systems. These improvements are made in an orderly manner and in ways that will cause them to be sustained over time. Techniques used to support and institutionalize change include defining software processes and measurements, pilot testing, and installing new processes and measurements throughout the organization.

- The *leveraging* phase completes the process improvement cycle. Lessons learned from the pilot projects and improvement efforts are documented and analyzed in order to improve the process improvement program for the future. The business needs that were determined at the beginning of the cycle are revisited to see if they have been met. Sponsorship for the program is revisited and renewed for the next cycle of software process improvement.

3.2   The Architecture of Best Practice Models

The models on which process assessments are based can be classified under two different architectures [56].[12] The architecture exemplified by the SW-CMM is known as a "staged" architecture. ISO/IEC 15504 specifies a "continuous" architecture.

The staged architecture of the SW-CMM is unidimensional since it defines a set of *key process areas* (KPAs) at each maturity level (except level 1). The KPAs at each of the levels are shown in Table I. A maturity level is defined in terms of satisfaction of the goals of the KPAs within those levels. The ISO/IEC 15504 continuous architecture, on the other hand, is two dimensional as shown in Fig. 4. One dimension consists of the processes that are actually assessed. As seen in the figure, they are grouped into five categories on the Process dimension. The second dimension consists of the capability scale that is used to evaluate process capability (the Capability dimension). The same capability scale is used across all processes (see Table II for further elaboration.)

The initial versions of ISO/IEC 15504 embodied the concept of a process instance. A *process instance* is defined as a singular instantiation of a process that is uniquely identifiable and about which information can be gathered in a repeatable manner [6]. It is typical, but not necessary, that a process instance corresponds to a project. For example, if we were assessing the design process, then there would be one instance of the design process for each project within the organizational scope of the assessment. In this continuous architecture, a rating is made for each process instance. The ratings for each of the process instances are then aggregated to produce a rating for the design process of the organization. In the most recent version of ISO/IEC 15504 [44] it is no longer required to rate at the process instance, but rather one can produce a single rating for the process at the organizational level directly without explicit aggregation. The latter

---

[12] Current work in the CMMI project aims to harmonize the two architectures. CMMI models can have both staged and continuous representations.

TABLE I

KEY PROCESS AREAS IN THE SW-CMM (FROM [27])

Level	Focus	Key process areas
5 Optimizing	Continual process improvement	Defect prevention Technology change management Process change management
4 Managed	Product and process quality	Quantitative process management Software quality management
3 Defined	Engineering processes and organizational support	Organization process focus Organization process definition Training program Integrated software management Software product engineering Intergroup coordination Peer reviews
2 Repeatable	Project management processes	Requirements management Software project planning Software project tracking and oversight Software subcontract management Software quality assurance Software configuration management
1 Initial	Competent people and heroics	

approach is more congruent with the rating scheme in the SW-CMM where the satisfaction of the KPA goals is rated at the organizational level [57].

The rating scheme used in SW-CMM based assessments also allows the aggregation of ratings across the KPAs to produce a single maturity level for the entire organization (within the scope of the assessment). For ISO/IEC 15504, the capability level rating is per process rather than for the whole of the organization.

Perhaps the biggest difference between the two architectures is that in a staged architecture the processes are ordered, while in a continuous architecture it is the capabilities that are ordered. For example, ISO/IEC 15504 does not require that a particular process must be defined at a level different than any other process, and any process can vary independently in its capability.[13] On the other hand, the SW-CMM groups its KPAs into maturity levels, each of which represents increasing organizational capability.

---

[13] This distinction is not definitive, since the two dimensions in ISO/IEC 15504 are not completely orthogonal. There are strong links between some of the processes and capabilities.

TABLE II

THE LEVELS OF ISO/IEC 15504 DEFINED, AND THEIR ASSOCIATED ATTRIBUTES (FROM [44]).[a]

Level	Title	Notes
0	Incomplete process	There is general failure to attain the purpose of the process. There are no easily identifiable work products or outputs of the process
1	Performed process	The purpose of the process is generally achieved. The achievement may not be rigorously planned and tracked. Individuals within the organization recognize that an action should be performed, and there is general agreement that this action is performed as and when required. There are identifiable work products for the process, and these testify to the achievement of the purpose
1.1		Process performance attribute
2	Managed process	The process delivers work products of acceptable quality within defined timescales. Performance according to specified procedures is planned and tracked. Work products conform to specified standards and requirements. The primary distinction from the Performed level is that the performance of the process is planned and managed and progressing towards a defined process
2.1		Performance management attribute
2.2		Work product management attribute
3	Established process	The process is performed and managed using a defined process based on good software engineering principles. Individual implementations of the process use approved, tailored versions of standard, documented processes. The resources necessary to establish the process definition are also in place. The primary distinction from the Managed level is that the process of the Established level is planned and managed using a standard process
3.1		Process definition attribute
3.2		Process resource attribute
4	Predictable process	The defined process is performed consistently in practice within defined control limits, to achieve its goals. Detailed measures of performance are collected and analyzed. This leads to a quantitative understanding of process capability and an improved ability to predict performance. Performance is objectively managed. The quality of work products is quantitatively known. The primary distinction from the Established level is that the defined process is quantitatively understood and controlled
4.1		Process measurement attribute
4.2		Process control attribute
5	Optimizing process	Performance of the process is optimized to meet current and future business needs, and the process achieves repeatability in meeting its defined business goals. Quantitative process effectiveness and efficiency goals (targets) for performance are established, based on the business goals of the organization. Continuous process monitoring against these goals is enabled by obtaining quantitative feedback and

TABLE II

CONTINUED

Level	Title	Notes
		improvement is achieved by analysis of the results. Optimizing a process involves piloting innovative ideas and technologies and changing non-effective processes to meet defined goals or objectives. The primary distinction from the Predictable level is that the defined process and the standard process undergo continuous refinement and improvement, based on a quantitative understanding of the impact of changes to these processes
5.1		Process change attribute
5.2		Continuous improvement attribute

[a] This is the capability scale that was in effect during the studies that are reported in this chapter, although it has undergone some revisions since then.

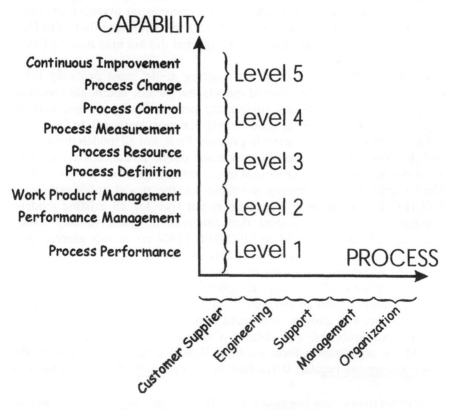

FIG. 4. The architecture of ISO/IEC 15504.

In the remainder of this chapter we shall refer to the measurement of *process capability* to denote measurements using either of the architectures. This greatly simplifies the presentation since it reduces the amount of repetitive qualification that would otherwise be necessary. Moreover, one can in principle convert an ISO/IEC 15504 process capability profile into an overall organizational maturity rating through an appropriate aggregation. Hence we will refer to the finer-grained measures here.

4. Software Process Assessment: Models and Methods

4.1   Coverage of Best Practice Models

Of course, best practice models do not necessarily cover all of the processes that are important for a particular organization. For example, in an early analysis of assessment data from 59 sites representing different business sectors (e.g., DoD contractor and commercial organizations) and different project sizes (from less than 9 peak staff to more than 100) [58], more than half of the sites reported findings that did not map into the KPAs of the software CMM.[14]

The lack of full coverage in any existing model most probably helps explain the current proliferation of models that include additional processes beyond the core of software engineering per se. One can argue that an organization should use the models that are most pertinent to its needs. However, that is far from simple in practice. First, not all models are equally well developed. For instance, by now much public guidance is available to assist in assessments and subsequent improvements based on the SW-CMM. Similar guidance is becoming available for the model specifications in ISO/IEC 15504. However, the same is not true for all existing models. Furthermore, it is not evident that the reliability and validity results obtained with the SW-CMM and ISO/IEC 15504 are readily generalizable to all competing models (see later in this chapter).

It also is far from obvious that the results of assessments based on different models are directly comparable. For example, what if an organization performs an assessment using one model and obtains a rating of x, and performs another assessment using a different model that focuses on different processes, and obtains a rating of $x - 1$? Which processes should the organization focus on first? Would it be those covered in the latter assessment because it resulted in a lower rating? One has no way

---

[14] Note that revisions have been made to the CMM since that study, partly as a consequence of these findings.

of knowing a priori, since the measurement scales most probably are not comparable.

ISO/IEC 15504 may be helpful in this regard since it provides an overall framework that is intended to be applicable to many different models. The ISO/IEC 15504 documents define a set of requirements and the claim is that all ratings using best practice models that meet the requirements are comparable. However, this remains an empirical question. Similarly, the current CMMI effort aims to obtain consistent results for the same organizational and model scope of an assessment, regardless of the model representation that is used (staged or continuous).

4.2 Assessment Methods

An assessment method constitutes the activities that must be performed in order to conduct an assessment. Many methods are used in practice, most of them tailored to the needs of the assessed organizations. Examples of methods that have been described in the literature are [57, 59]. Perhaps one of the best known methods is the SEI's CBA IPI, which is described in brief in [8], and with much greater detail in [57].

Some assessments that are performed with small organizations may last only a single day, whereas assessments in larger, high maturity organizations can take over 2 weeks of interviews, document reviews, and consolidation of findings.[15] A typical week-long assessment would be organized as shown in Fig. 5.

The CMM Appraisal Framework (CAF) documents a set of requirements for assessment methods based on the SW-CMM [105]. The ISO/IEC 15504 documents contain another set of requirements (largely based on the CAF) [44]. Both sets of requirements are based on considerable expert knowledge and review. To our knowledge, however, there have been no systematic empirical investigations in this area.

Aggregate data were collected as part of the SPICE trials on the distribution of effort among the activities of a typical assessment. Assessors were asked to estimate the effort (in person-hours) spent on each of the following during the assessment:

- preparing the assessment input
- briefing the sponsor and/or organizational staff about the methodology to be used

[15] In an analysis of feedback data from CBA IPI assessments [68], about one third of lead assessors report spending 3 days on pre-onsite activities; another third report spending 4–8 days. Almost 40% report devoting 5 days to on-site activities of the assessment; over an additional half of the lead assessors said that they spend 6 or more days on on-site activities.

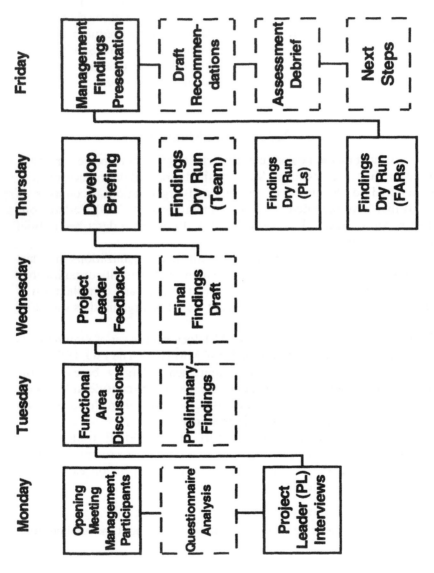

FIG. 5. Organization of a typical week-long assessment (from [62] © 1999 IEEE, reproduced with permission).

- collecting evidence (e.g., reviewing documentation, interviewing organizational staff/management)
- producing and verifying ratings
- preparing the assessment results
- presenting the results to management.

The results are shown in Fig. 6. Evidence collection is typically the most effort-consuming phase of an ISO/IEC 15504 assessment, followed by the production of the ratings. The initial phases of defining the assessment input and the initial briefing consume a non-negligible amount of effort as well.

4.3 Why do Organizations Perform Assessments?

It has been stated that SPAs for process improvement are performed for two reasons [8]:

- to support, enable, and encourage an organization's commitment to software process improvement
- to provide an accurate picture of the strengths and weaknesses of an organization's software processes.

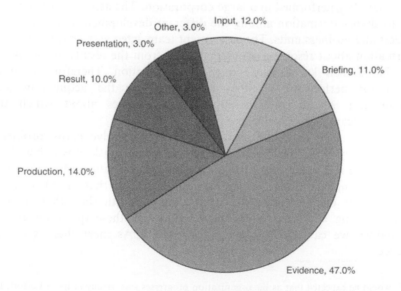

FIG. 6. Distribution of effort during assessments conducted in the SPICE trials.

The former implies creating a climate for change within the organization.[16] In fact, it has been stated that [61] "the bottom line is that many [Process Improvement Program] activities succeed or fail based on the level of buy-in from the people involved." The latter implies obtaining a quantitative rating (or ratings) as a consequence of the assessment. Such ratings characterize the capability of the organization's processes.

Different authors will assign different weights to each of these two reasons for doing process assessments. For example, Dymond [62] asserts that the essence of an SPA is to "Agree on Process Issues." An assessment should generate consensus from management and the work force on the important process problems in the organization, and a commitment to address them. It is essentially a social ritual from that perspective. A prominent accident of assessments, according to Dymond, is the quantitative rating that is usually produced at the end.

Another posited reason for performing assessments is key customer or market pressure. This has been articulated in the case of the SW-CMM and DoD contractors [63] for the former. Also, some large procurers of software systems are including SPAs as an important ingredient in their supplier selection process [30, 64], prompting suppliers to possess and demonstrate necessary process capabilities. For market pressure, a good example is ISO 9001, which often is required to do business in European Union nations [65, 66].

Herbsleb and Grinter [67] describe a further benefit of SPAs based on a case study they performed in a large corporation: The assessment team was able to share information among the different development groups, across projects and business units. The assessment team acted as a central point for information about resolving problems raised from the results of the SPAs, and shared their knowledge across the corporation. Therefore, another reason for performing a SPA is to facilitate the acquisition and dissemination of information about best practices about which the assessment team is knowledgeable.

As can be seen from the above, an SPA may solve many problems simultaneously. The first question that one needs to ask is whether these problems are really important for the assessed organizations. For example, is it really important for the assessed organizations that an SPA create a climate for change? How does this compare with the other reasons for performing an assessment? Once we answer these questions in the affirmative, we can then evaluate how well SPAs meet these goals in practice.

---

[16] It would be expected that as the organization progresses successfully in its SPI effort, the effort required for creating a climate for change will be reduced.

An analysis performed by the SEI based on CBA IPI feedback data collected from assessment sponsors showed that over half of the sponsors stated that the primary goals of their assessments were either to monitor the progress of their existing software process improvement programs or to initiate new programs [68]. Furthermore, over a third of the sponsors said that validating an organization's maturity level was a primary goal of their assessment.

In an attempt to further provide some empirically grounded answers to the above questions, below we present a study of assessment sponsors that was performed during the SPICE trials.[17]

In this study, assessment sponsors were asked about the reasons for performing the assessments in their organizations. The sponsors completed a questionnaire immediately after their assessments. Data are available from 70 assessments. All of the sponsors supported their respective organizations in performing at least one assessment using the emerging ISO/IEC 15504 standard. The questions are summarized in Table III.[18]

The range plot in Fig. 7 shows the mean for each one of the reasons and the 95% confidence interval. This means that if we were to repeat this study a large number of times, and each time calculate the confidence interval, this interval will contain the population mean 95% of the time. To test a hypothesis of "indifference" (i.e., that the respondent did not think that the reason was neither important nor not important for conducting an assessment), then we can use the tails of the confidence interval. Indifference

---

[17] An overview of the SPICE trials is provided in the appendix, section 9.1.

[18] In our data set, some organizations were assessed more than once during the SPICE trials. For some of these assessments, there were missing values on some of the 12 responses in Table III. To deal with the missing values, we used the multiple imputation approach of Rubin [69]. Imputation techniques use auxiliary models to estimate the missing values. In multiple imputation, these estimates are performed more than once, and then the analyses of the multiple data sets are combined.

There are two general approaches that one can take for imputation for this study:

Assume that the reasons for conducting an assessment may vary for the same organization across different assessments. In this case, the unit of analysis is the assessment and the imputation approach allows for different response patterns for the same organization across different assessments.

Assume that the reasons for conducting an assessment are constant for the same organization across multiple assessments. In this case the unit of analysis would be the organization, and the imputation approach would provide only one set of values for each organization.

Inspection of our data set indicates that the first assumption is more realistic. There were sponsors who expressed different reasons for conducting an assessment across multiple assessments of the same organization. This may have been due to a different sponsor of the assessment. As another example, an organization may have conducted an initial assessment under customer pressure, but then the second assessment was driven by the organization itself after realizing the benefits of assessments and wanting to track their SPI efforts.

TABLE III

THE REASONS WHY AN ASSESSMENT WAS PERFORMED

No.	Reason	Variable name
1	Gain market advantage	ADVANTAGE
2	Customer demand to improve process capability	DEMAND
3	Improve efficiency	EFFICIENCY
4	Improve customer service	CUSTOMER
5	Improve reliability of products	PRODREL
6	Improve reliability of services in supporting products	SERVREL
7	Competitive/marketing pressure to demonstrate process capability	COMPETITIVE
8	Generate management support and buy-in for software process improvement	MANAGEMENT
9	Generate technical staff support and buy-in for software process improvement	TECHSTAFF
10	Establish best practices to guide organizational process improvement	BESTPRACT
11	Establish project baseline and/or track projects' process improvement	TRACKPROJ
12	Establish project baseline and/or track organization's process improvement	TRACKORG

The wording of the question was "To what extent did the following represent important reasons for performing a software process assessment?". The response categories were: "don't know", "very important", "important", "somewhat important", "not very important", "not at all important".

The "Don't Know" responses were treated as missing data. We therefore have a 5-point scale of importance (instead of the original 6). There are two obvious alternatives for identifying the importance for each one of the above 12 reasons. The first is to dichotomize the 5-point scale into "important" and "not important" categories. This was discounted, however, because we had difficulty deciding which category the response "somewhat important" should be in. This can be somewhat alleviated by dichotomizing around the median, for example. However, because the distributions that we obtained on these 12 questions tended to have sizeable clusters around the middle, the choice of the breakpoint as >median or <median would have had dramatic impact on the resulting dichotomous distribution. The second alternative, and the one that we opted for, was to use the mean.

can be defined as a response of "Somewhat Important", which has a value of 3. If the tails cross the value of 3, then there is evidence, at a two-tailed α level of 0.1, that the mean response for that question is not different from 3. Only the SERVREL and ADVANTAGE variables demonstrate indifference.

Note first the reasons that were perceived *not* to be important. Clearly competitive/marketing pressure to demonstrate process capability (COMPETITIVE) was not a reason for performing assessments. This may be a reflection of the fact that those organizations that participated in the SPICE trials are innovators and early adopters, and therefore their priorities may be different from the general population of organizations.

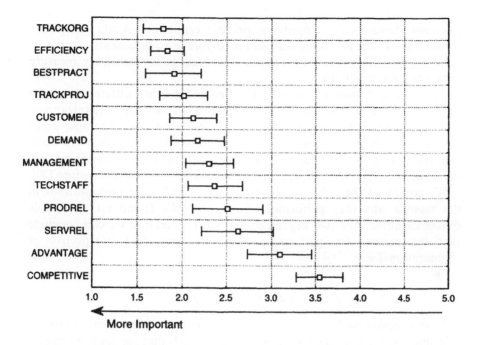

FIG. 7. Mean of importance scores with 95% confidence interval. Low scores indicate higher importance, and the higher scores indicate less importance.

The sponsors also exhibited indifference on gaining market advantage and improving the reliability of services in supporting products as reasons for performing an assessment.

The most important reasons these sponsors chose for conducting their process assessments were to establish process capability baselines and/or track progress with project and organizational process improvement, to improve efficiency, and customer service, and to identify best practices for process improvement. The importance that the sponsors assigned to establishing capability baselines clearly indicates that they tended to recognize that assessments are in fact an important measurement procedure. Improving efficiency and customer service indicates that these sponsors believed that SPI based on the assessment would in fact provide tangible benefits to their projects. The identification of best practices is consistent with the conclusions of Herbsleb and Grinter [67], but also likely indicates that the sponsors expected the good practices embodied in the models would be transferred to their organizations.

In the middle range were the need to generate support and buy-in for process improvement among the technical staff and management, and customer demands for improving process capability. Again, these are consistent with the two basic reasons for performing assessments, namely to build support for process improvement as well as to accurately measure organizational capability.

An interesting issue to consider is whether there are differences in the reasons for performing assessments between small and large organizations. We dichotomize IT staff size into small and large organizations, small organizations being those with no more than 50 IT staff. This is the same definition of small organizations that has been used in a European project that is providing process improvement guidance for small organizations [70].

We computed the differences between small and large organizations in the reasons why they performed assessments. We found no discernible difference among the two organizational sizes. Therefore we can conclude that the reasons for performing SPAs are consistent irrespective of organizational size.

4.4 Summary

In this section we have provided an overview of process assessments for SPI, and have summarized the models and methods that are used to conduct them. Based on the results of a recent survey, we also described the reasons sponsors support process assessments in their organizations. These results provide a concrete set of criteria for evaluating SPAs to see if they meet their expectations. Specifically:

- Sponsors expect a SPA to generate buy-in and create a climate for change within the organization.
- Sponsors believe that process improvement based on the results of assessments will lead to bottom-line improvements in their projects and organizations.
- Sponsors perceive SPAs as a measurement procedure.
- Sponsors expect that a SPA will lead to the introduction of best practices within their organizations.

In the remainder of this chapter we review existing empirical evidence about how well SPAs in fact meet those criteria.

5. Software Process Improvement

In this section we review the studies performed on assessment-based SPI, how and why it succeeds.

5.1   The Order of Process Improvement

One of the basic tenets of all models on which process assessments are based is that the implementation of process improvements should follow a specific path, and this is the path stipulated in the best practice model. The existence of a path serves an important purpose, as articulated by Paulk:

> The advantage of the maturity levels is that they provide clear priorities, which provide guidance for selecting those few improvement activities that will be most helpful if implemented immediately. This is important because most software organizations can only focus on a few process improvement activities at a time [43].

Indeed, surveys of sponsors and assessors consistently find that they believe that feature to be a useful one, since it provides concrete guidance about the next process improvement steps that one should follow. In addition, the improvement steps are small and manageable. For example, 93% of the sponsors of ISO/IEC 15504 assessments who took part in the SPICE trials agreed or strongly agreed with the statement that "the assessment provided valuable direction about the priorities for process improvement in the organization" [71]. In a survey of individuals whose organizations were assessed using the SW-CMM it was reported that over 80% believe that the "CMM provides valuable direction about the order in which process improvement should be made" [72].

However, an obvious question that one may ask is, what is the basis for such an ordering of practices? The logic of this sequencing is that this is the natural evolutionary order in which, historically, software organizations improve [25], and that practices early in the sequence are prerequisite foundations to ensure the stability and optimality of practices implemented later in the sequence [5].

The little evidence that does exist is not pertinent for contemporary models, but nevertheless fails to support the argument that earlier models embody the natural evolution of software engineering practices. In particular, one study investigated whether the maturity path suggested by Humphrey and Sweet's process maturity framework [28] follows a natural evolutionary progression [73].[19] Their analysis was based on the

[19] Another unpublished study examined the ordering of capabilities in ISO/IEC 15504. However, this was done with organizations that were participating in the SPICE trials, and therefore they were a priori predisposed to follow the stipulated path. Furthermore, the assessors may be predisposed in a manner that is consistent with the ordering of attributes in the capability dimension. As expected, the results provided a strong indication that organizations follow the ISO/IEC 15504-stipulated order of achieving capability. Ideally, such studies should be done with organizations that are not already familiar with, or already using, a particular model to guide their improvement efforts.

basic idea that questions representing maturity levels already passed by organizations would be endorsed (i.e., answered yes) whereas items representing maturity levels not reached would fail. Their results did not support the original maturity path and led the authors to suggest that the original model seemed "arbitrary" in its ordering of practices and is "unsupported." The first five levels of the alternative maturity model that they empirically derived are shown in Table IV. Of course, further studies are necessary to confirm this alternative model, but at least it enjoys some empirical support thus far.

It should be noted that the ordering shown in Table IV does not come solely from organizations or projects that were successful, so it is not known whether this empirically derived ordering actually represents a path to success or to failure. Therefore, in reality we, as a community, still do not have systematic evidence as to the natural ordering of practices as followed by successful organizations and projects.

There are three implications of this:

- First, as of now, we still cannot make strong claims that best-practice models capture the true evolution of the implementation of software engineering practices in organizations.

- Second, that the current ordering of practices (or capability) in best practice models may still represent a logical ordering. This means that it is logical that some practices occur after others. It is also plausible that another ordering would be just as good and lead you to the same end state.

- Third, it is prudent to take the prescribed path in an best practice model as a suggestion rather than as gospel. If an alternative path or a modified path also makes business sense for a particular organization or project, then there is no compelling reason not to adopt it. In fact, in a report of SPI based on the CMM [74] it is noted that "Business demands often necessitate improvements in an order which is counter to the CMM." In that particular case, the organization initiated some process improvements that were not necessarily congruent with their next level of maturity, but driven by their business objectives.

5.2 SPI Experiences

There does exist evidence that SPI efforts succeed and bring benefits. However, not all organizations that attempt SPI based on an assessment are successful. Below we review the results of two studies on the success of assessment-based SPI initiatives.

TABLE IV

EMPIRICALLY DERIVED MATURITY MODEL (FIRST FIVE LEVELS ONLY)

Level	Function	HS[a]
1	*Reviews and change control*	
	Is a mechanism used for controlling changes to the code? (Who can make changes and under which circumstances?)	L2
	Are internal software design reviews conducted?	L3
	Are software code reviews conducted?	L3
	Is a mechanism used for controlling changes to the software requirements?	L2
2	*Standard process and project management*	
	Is a mechanism used for controlling changes to the software design?	L3
	Does the software organization use a standardized and documented software development process on each project?	L3
	Do software development first line managers sign off on their schedules and cost estimates?	L2
	Is a formal procedure used in the management review of each software development prior to making contractual commitments?	L2
	Is a formal procedure used to produce software development schedules?	L2
	Are formal procedures applied to estimating software development cost?	L2
	Is a mechanism used for managing and supporting the introduction of new technologies?	L4
3	*Review management and configuration control*	
	Are the action items resulting from code reviews tracked to closure?	L3
	Are the actions items resulting from design reviews tracked to closure?	L3
	Are the review data gathered during design reviews analyzed?	L4
	Is there a software configuration control function for each project that involves software development?	L2
	Are code review standards applied?	L4
	Is a formal procedure used to make estimates of software size?	L2
	Is a mechanism used for periodically assessing the software engineering process and implementing indicated improvements?	L4
4	*Software process improvement*	
	Are analyses of errors conducted to determine their process related causes?	L4
	Is a mechanism used for ensuring compliance to software engineering standards?	L3
5	*Management of review and test coverage*	
	Are design and code review coverages measured and recorded?	L4
	Is test coverage measured and recorded for each phase of functional testing?	L4

[a] The values in this column refer to the levels in the original Humphrey and Sweet framework [28]. This table is based on the results in [73].

5.2.1 The CMM Study

In an SEI survey [72], a sample of representatives from 61 assessments (in different organizations) were contacted. These assessments were conduced at least 1 year prior to the survey. Three respondents per organization were sought:

- the project level software manager most knowledgeable about the assessment
- the most knowledgeable and well-respected senior developer or similar technical person available
- an organizational level SEPG manager, or someone with equivalent responsibilities, if such a person existed.

In total, responses from 138 individuals representing 56 of the 61 organizations were returned. This gives an average of about 2.5 responses per organization. The pooled observations from all three roles were used for the analysis, giving a total of 138 observations.

Over two-thirds of the respondents reported that their organization's SPI efforts were largely determined by the findings and recommendations that were raised in the assessment. However, when asked "How successfully have the findings and recommendations [from the assessment] been addressed?", 70% of the respondents said "moderate", "limited", or "little if any." Over one-fourth said that the recommendations resulting from their assessments proved to be too ambitious to accomplish in a reasonable period of time, 26% acknowledged that "nothing much has changed" since the assessment, 49% said that there "has been a lot of disillusionment over the lack of improvement", 42% said that process improvement has been overcome by events and crises and that other things have taken priority, 72% report that process "improvement has often suffered due to time and resource limitations", 77% say that process improvement has taken longer than expected, and 68% reported that it has cost more than they expected.

The above summary of the results indicate a number of things:

- SPI is difficult, with many organizations not being able to address the assessment recommendations and to demonstrate tangible changes to their processes as a consequence of the assessments.
- One potential reason can be seen from the responses, that there is not sufficient commitment of resources and energy within the organizations to make SPI happen.
- Also, it is clear that the expectations of organizations need to be managed better, in terms of the cost and time to make SPI happen.

However, 84% of the disagreed or strongly disagreed with assertions that software processes had become more rigid and bureaucratic or that it had become harder to find creative solutions to difficult technical solutions, and only 4% said that the assessments had been counter-productive and that the progress of SPI had actually worsened since their assessments.

5.2.2 The SPICE Trials Study

We summarize the results of a follow-up study of organizations that participated in an ISO/IEC 15504 assessment [75]. In this particular study, sponsors of assessments in the SPICE trials were administered a questionnaire approximately 1 year after the assessment to determine their perceptions on the extent to which the assessment influenced their SPI efforts. This study was performed in the context of the SPICE trials (an overview of the trials is provided in the appendix, section 9.1).

For the description of sponsors' perceptions, we used percentages of respondents who are supportive (as opposed to critical) of their experiences with assessment-based SPI. For example, assume that a question asked the respondents to express their extent of agreement to the statement "the assessment was well worth the money and effort we spent; it had a major positive effect on the organization", and that it had the following four response categories: "Strongly Agree", "Agree", "Disagree", and "Strongly Disagree." As shown in Table V, the "Strongly Agree" and "Agree" responses would be considered supportive of assessment-based SPI, and the "Disagree" and "Strongly Disagree" responses would be considered to be critical of assessment-based SPI.

We received a total of 18 responses to our questionnaire. However, some of the assessments were done too recently for any accurate information about the progress of SPI to be collected. Therefore, we excluded all observations that were conducted less than 30 weeks before the response time. This left us with data from 14 valid assessments and subsequent SPI efforts. The variation of elapsed time since the assessment is given in Fig. 8. This indicates that the organizations from which we have data have

TABLE V

SCHEME FOR DEFINING SUPPORTIVE AND CRITICAL RESPONSES

Supportive responses	Critical responses
Strongly agree	Disagree
Agree	Strongly disagree

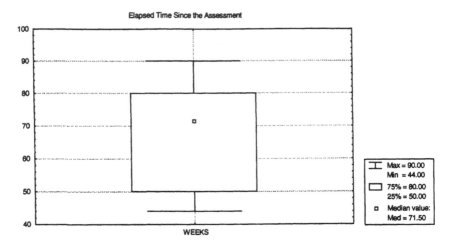

FIG. 8. Distribution of elapsed time since the assessment.

conducted their assessments from 44–90 weeks before responding to the questionnaire. This provides sufficient time for SPI efforts to have started and for some progress to have been made.

Our results on the perceptions about assessment based SPI are summarized in Table VI. Counter to what has sometimes been heard, all of the sponsors do not believe that software processes have become more bureaucratic due to their SPI efforts (see question 1). Neither do they believe that other important issues facing the organization have been neglected (see question 2). Almost all of the sponsors (93%) do not agree with the statement that things have deteriorated (see question 3). Almost three-quarters of the respondents (77%) disagree with the statement that there has been disillusionment due to a lack of improvement (see question 4).

However, a sizable group of respondents (54%) believe that SPI is costing more than they have anticipated (see question 5). Approximately three-fifths do not believe that the assessment has had a major impact on the organization (see question 6). This may be due to there not being sufficient time since the assessment for SPI to have taken root, or due to the organization's not being able to act on the recommendations and findings from the assessment. To deal with this issue we can consider the recommendation that it can be very important to make some "quick wins" to ensure that the assessment is seen to have had an impact and to maintain momentum.

This is further reinforced by the finding that only 28% disagree with the statement that nothing much has changed since the assessment (see question 7). It is interesting to note that 79% believe that SPI was overcome by events

TABLE VI

PERCENTAGES OF SUPPORTIVE AND CRITICAL RESPONSES ON THE ASSESSMENT-BASED SPI

No.	Question	Number supportive	%
1	Software processes have become more rigid and bureaucratic; it is harder to find creative solutions to technical problems	14/14	100
2	Because of the assessment, we have neglected other important issues facing the organization	14/14	100
3	The assessment was counter-productive; things have gotten worst	13/14	93
4	There has been a lot of disillusionment over the lack of improvement	10/13	77
5	Process improvement is costing more than we expected	6/13	46
6	The assessment was well worth the money and effort we spent; it had a major positive effect on the organization	5/14	36
7	Nothing much has changed since the assessment	4/14	28
8	Process improvement was overcome by events and crises; other things took priority	3/14	21
9	Process improvement is taking longer than expected	2/13	15
10	Process improvement has often suffered due to time and resource limitations	1/14	7
11	Process change has been easier than we expected	0/14	0

and crises (see question 8), indicating potentially that the organizations were not ready for long-term SPI initiatives (i.e., there were other more important things to attend to). Some further reasons are forthcoming from the following responses: 85% believe that SPI is taking longer than expected (see question 9), and not surprisingly 93% believe that SPI suffered due to time and resource limitations (see question 10). None of the respondents believe that SPI has been easier than expected (see question 11).

Two general problems emerge from the above descriptive statistics:

- First, that expectations of organizational sponsors may not have been managed optimally, given that many believe that SPI costs more than expected, and is taking longer than expected.

- Second, in many cases insufficient resources were made available for SPI, and insufficient priority was given to SPI. This can lead us to the conclusion that an SPI effort must be treated as a project in its own right with a plan, resources and commitment. However, these problems do not seem to have dampened the enthusiasm within the organizations for assessments and assessment based SPI.

5.2.3 Summary

The results of the two studies above demonstrate a remarkable consistency:

- Approximately two-thirds of respondents on SPI surveys do not report marked changes in their organizations as a consequence of their assessments: 70% of the SW-CMM survey respondents state that they had "moderate", "limited", or "little if any". When asked about how successful they were in addressing the recommendations from the assessment, 64% of the SPICE trials survey respondents "disagree" or "strongly" disagree with the statement that the assessment had a major positive effect on the organization.[20]
- Organizations seem to have (unrealistically) high expectations from assessment-based SPI, and these need to be managed better.
- Despite the above, sponsors of assessments and assessment participants still remain enthusiastic about SPAs.

It is therefore important to consider the actual costs of SPI to provide more realistic expectations (see section 5.5), and identify the critical success factors to make SPI happen to ensure that more organizations succeed in their assessment based SPI efforts (see section 5.4).

5.3 Creating Buy-in

One of the major objectives of an assessment is to create "buy-in" for SPI within the organization. As part of the SPICE trials survey described above (section 5.2.2), the respondents were requested to give their perceptions about the extent of buy-in for SPI for before the assessment and since the assessment. This was done for four different roles in the organization: participants in the assessment, the organization's technical staff, the organization's management, and the assessment sponsor. A Wilcoxon matched pairs test was used to compare the "before" and "since the assessment" responses [76]. Hypothesis testing was all one-tailed since we expect the effect to be directional: an assessment increases buy-in.

The results are summarized in Table VII. It can be seen that participants in the assessment and the organization's technical staff increased their buy-in since the assessment. However, the organization's management and sponsor were not perceived to have increased their buy-in. This is evidenced

---

[20] However, it should be noted that the SPICE trials study was a relatively small scale survey, and therefore its results are only tentative.

TABLE VII

THE ABILITY OF THE ASSESSMENT TO CREATE "BUY-IN" FOR
VARIOUS ROLES IN THE ORGANIZATION

Role	p-value
Participants in the assessment	**0.00**
Organization's technical staff	**0.00**
Organization's management	0.18
Assessment sponsor	0.12

A Wilcoxon matched pairs test was used to compare the "before" and
"since the assessment" responses [76]. Hypothesis testing was all one-
tailed since we expect the effect to be directional: an assessment increases
buy-in. Statistically significant results are in **bold** in the p-value column.

by the results in the previous analysis, whereby the insufficient resources and
priority were given to the SPI initiatives.

In summary, then, the assessments did not manage to significantly
increase the buy-in of the organization's management nor sponsor. This
may explain the low priority and low resources given to the SPI effort in
many of the assessments, but may also be due to the management and
sponsor already having "bought-in" before the assessment, and hence their
support of the assessment already existed (and therefore the assessment did
not lead to significant changes in that). More encouraging is that the
assessment increased buy-in among the participants in the assessment and
the technical staff.

The results from the SEI survey (see section 5.2.1) show that there
were increases in buy-in among all four roles. What is clear though is that
support for SPI increased most markedly among the people who actually
participated in the assessments.

5.4   Factors Affecting Improvement Success

In the CMM study (section 5.2.1), respondents were asked about the
extent of success their organizations have had in addressing the findings and
recommendations that were raised as a result of the assessment. A series of
questions were also asked about factors that may have an impact on SPI
Success. These questions can be categorized as Organizational Factors or
Barriers. Subsequently, bivariate associations between each of these factors
and SPI Success were investigated.[21] Only the results of statistical testing of

---

[21] A bivariate association looks at the relationship between only two variables.

this association were presented. A chi-square test was used for these purposes.[22] The "Organizational Factors" and "Barriers" that were found to be statistically significant are summarized in Table VIII.

Another study was performed as a follow up to organizations that performed assessments using ISO/IEC 15504 [75] (see section 5.2.2). This found that the more an organization's SPI effort is determined by the findings of an assessment, the greater the extent to which the assessment findings are successfully addressed during the SPI effort. Therefore, it is important to ensure that the SPI effort is determined by the assessment findings.

To increase the possibility that the assessment's findings determine the SPI effort of the organization, the following factors were found to be important:

- senior management monitoring of SPI
- compensated SPI responsibilities

TABLE VIII

ORGANIZATIONAL FACTORS AND BARRIERS THAT
WERE FOUND TO BE RELATED TO SPI SUCCESS [72]

Organizational factors
Senior management monitoring of SPI
Compensated SPI responsibilities
SPI goals well understood
Technical staff involved in SPI
SPI people well respected
Staff time/resources dedicated to process improvement

Barriers
Discouragement about SPI prospects
SPI gets in the way of "real" work
"Turf guarding" inhibits SPI
Existence of organizational politics
Assessment recommendations too ambitious
Need guidance about how to improve
Need more mentoring and assistance

---

[22] A chi-square test, as applied in the SEI study, is a statistical test that is used to find out whether there is an association between two variables when both variables are on a categorical scale. In the bivariate analysis that was performed, one variable was either an Organizational Factor or a Barrier, and the second was SPI Success. They are categorical in the sense that they were responses to a question with a fixed number of response options (categories).

- ensuring that SPI goals are well understood
- technical staff involvement in SPI
- staff and time resources should be made available for SPI
- SPI people well respected

Stelzer and Mellis [77] provide a comprehensive review of the literature with the objective of identifying the factors affecting the success of organizational change in the context of SPI. They came up with 10 factors that were perceived to be important, and these are summarized in Table IX. They then carefully reviewed 56 published case reports of SPI using ISO 9000 and the SW-CMM to produce a ranking of the 10 factors. The ranks are based on the percentage of case reports that mention a particular factor as important. The rankings are summarized in Table X.

As can be seen across the three studies, there is considerable consistency in the factors that have been found to be important in ensuring the success of an SPI initiative. We can distill the following factors that are the most critical:

- management commitment and support of SPI (as a demonstration of commitment this would include management monitoring of the initiative and making resources available)
- involvement of technical staff in the SPI effort
- ensuring that staff understand the current software processes and their relationship to other business activities
- clear SPI goals that are understood by the staff
- tailoring the improvement initiatives
- respected SPI staff (change agents and opinion leaders).

5.5 The Cost of Software Process Improvement

The most common and interpretable measures of the costs of SPI are in terms of dollars and/or effort. A recent study sponsored by the US Air Force [78] found that government organizations tend to characterize investments in process improvement in terms of costs, whereas industry tend to characterize it in terms of effort expended on SPI activities. In some cases, cost measures such as calendar months have also been used. The studies that we summarize below show the costs of SPI using different approaches. The amount of detail that we can present is directly a function of the amount of publicly available information.

TABLE IX

FACTORS AFFECTING THE SUCCESS OF ORGANIZATIONAL CHANGE IN SPI (FROM [77])

Success factor of organizational change	Explanation
Change agents and opinion leaders	Change agents initiate and support the improvement projects at the corporate level, opinion leaders at a local level.
Encouraging communication and collaboration	Degree to which communication efforts precede and accompany the improvement program (communication) and degree to which staff members from different teams and departments cooperate (collaboration)
Management commitment and support	Degree to which management at all organizational levels sponsor the change
Managing the improvement project	Degree to which a process improvement initiative is effectively planned and controlled
Providing enhanced understanding	Degree to which knowledge of current software processes and interrelated business activities is acquired and transferred throughout the organization
Setting relevant and realistic objectives	Degree to which the improvement efforts attempt to contribute to the success of the organization (relevant) and degree to which the objectives may be achieved in the foreseeable future (realistic)
Stabilizing changed processes	Degree to which software processes are continually supported, maintained, and improved at a local level
Staff involvement	Degree to which staff members participate in the improvement activities
Tailoring improvement initiatives	Degree to which improvement efforts are adapted to the specific strengths and weaknesses of different teams and departments
Unfreezing the organization	Degree to which the "inner resistance" of an organizational system to change is overcome

5.5.1 Costs of Improvement Based on the CMM

A number of companies have publicized the cost details of their process improvement efforts based on the CMM. Some of these are summarized in Table XI. Another study conducted at the SEI determined the amount of time it takes organizations to increase their maturity levels on the CMM for the first three levels [83]. The distribution of assessments that used the original SPA method and the replacement CBA IPI method in the data set is

TABLE X

RANKING OF SUCCESS FACTORS (FROM [77])

Success factor	ISO cases ($n = 25$)		CMM cases ($n = 31$)		All cases ($n = 56$)	
	%	Rank	%	Rank	%	Rank
Management commitment and support	84	1	97	1	91	1
Staff involvement	84	1	84	8	84	2
Providing enhanced understanding	72	3	87	6	80	3
Tailoring improvement initiatives	68	4	90	3	80	3
Managing the improvement project	56	6	94	2	77	5
Change agents and opinion leaders	52	7	90	3	73	6
Stabilizing changed processes	52	7	90	3	73	6
Encouraging communication and collaboration	64	5	74	9	70	8
Setting relevant and realistic objectives	44	9	87	6	68	9
Unfreezing the organization	24	10	52	10	39	10

not clear however, and whether any differences in method would have had any effect on the time it takes to move up one maturity level.

Two groups of organizations were identified: those that moved from level 1 to level 2, and those that moved from level 2 to level 3. On average, it takes organizations 30 months to move from level 1 to level 2. Those organizations, however, varied quite dramatically in the amount of time it takes to move up one maturity level. A more outlier-resistant measure would be the median. In this case, the median was 25 months. Organizations that moved from level 2 to level 3 took on average 25 months (the median was also 25 months).

It is plausible that the size of the organization would have an impact on the number of months it takes to move from one maturity level to another; however, the variation in the size of the organizational units that were assessed was not given in the report. Therefore, these results should be taken as general guidelines to check an organization's own estimates of the time it takes to move up the maturity ladder.

Another study of US companies found results that are consistent with those mentioned above [78]. It was found that organizations at level 2 spend 12–36 months at level 1 with an average of 21 months, and organizations at level 3 had spent 22–24 months at level 1 with an average of 23 months. Organizations at level 3 spent 12–20 months at level 2 with an average of 17.5 months. This is corroborated with data from the improvement efforts at AlliedSignal [74] where advancement from level 1 to 2 and from level 2 to level 3 took 12–14 months across different sites.

TABLE XI

ORGANIZATIONAL EXPERIENCES ILLUSTRATING THE COSTS OF SPI

Ref.	Organization and SPI Program	Costs
[79]	SPI effort at the Software Engineering Division of Hughes Aircraft. The division had 500 professional employees at the time	The assessment itself cost US$45 000 Cost of a 2-year SPI program was US$400 000 Implementation of the action plan to move from ML1 to ML2 was 18 calendar months
[80]	SPI effort led by the Schlumberger Laboratory for Computer Science	Large engineering centers (120–180 engineers) have 1–5 fulltime staff on SPI Smaller centers (50–120 engineers) have up to 3 fulltime staff on SPI
[78] [81]	Data was collected from 33 companies using questionnaires and/or interviews	The authors present examples of data on the costs of activities related to SPI. For example, some organizations increased from 7% to 8% of total effort on data collection, and increase up to 2% of project costs on fixing design defects
[74]	Corporate-wide SPI effort at AlliedSignal Aerospace starting in 1992	Using data on SEPG investment measured in full-time equivalent headcount for eight sites, the maximum was 4%
[82]	SPI initiative started in 1988 at Software Systems Laboratory in Raytheon, employing 400 software engineers. Results reported after 5 years. Organization has progressed from level 1 to level 3 during that period	US$1 million invested every year

5.5.2 Costs of Registration to ISO 9001

A multiple regression model has recently been constructed to estimate the effort it would take an organization to meet the requirements of ISO 9001 [84]. Data was collected from 28 software organizations that were registered to ISO 9001 in Canada and the USA. There are two inputs to the model:

- the size of the organization in number of employees
- the degree of noncompliance to ISO 9001 clauses.

Both sets of data were collected by questionnaire and a sample of responses were verified with the respondents to increase confidence in the reliability of the responses. The model to predict effort in man-months is:

$$\text{Ln (effort)} = -2.793 + 0.692 \times \text{Ln } (x_1) + 0.74 \times \text{Ln } (x_2)$$

where x_1 is the number of employees within the scope of registration, and x_2 is the degree of compliance of the organization to the ISO 9001 clauses prior to the improvement effort.

The model was validated using data collected from five organizations that were not included in the model development sample. A brief comparison of the model prediction versus the actual effort is given in Table XII.

5.5.3 Other Models

Jones [39] presents the stages of Software Productivity Research (SPR) Inc.'s improvement model as follows:

- stage 0:   software process assessment and baseline
- stage 1:   focus on management technologies
- stage 2:   focus on software processes and methodologies
- stage 3:   focus on new tools and approaches
- stage 4:   focus on infrastructure and specialization
- stage 5:   focus on reusability
- stage 6:   focus on industry leadership.

From the data that SPR has collected, the costs per capita (in US $) for small and large organizations to progress through the stages are presented in Table XIII, and the time it takes to make these progressions are summarized in Table XIV.

TABLE XII

COMPARISON OF ACTUAL VERSUS PREDICTED EFFORT FOR ISO 9001 REGISTRATION

No.	Size	Non-compliance (%)	Predicted	Actual	Residual
1	175	35%	30.3	31.2	0.9
2	108	15%	11.6	13	1.4
3	170	30%	26.5	27	0.5
4	45	100%	25.8	36	10.2
5	100	70%	34.4	37	2.6

TABLE XIII

COSTS PER CAPITA ($) TO PROGRESS THROUGH SPR'S STAGE MODEL (FROM [39])

	Stage	Company size[a]			
		Small	Medium	Large	Giant
0	Assessment/baseline	100	125	150	200
1	Management	1500	5000	5000	8000
2	Methods/process	1500	2500	3000	3500
3	New tools	5000	7500	15000	25000
4	Infrastructure	1000	1500	3500	5000
5	Reusability	500	3000	6000	7500
6	Industry leadership	15000	2500	3000	4000
	Approximate total	11100	22120	35650	48200

The costs include training, consulting fees, capital equipment, software licenses, and improvements in office conditions.
[a] Small < 10 staff, medium 101–1000 staff, large 1001–1000 staff, giant > 10 000 staff.

TABLE XIV

CALENDAR MONTHS IT TAKES TO PROGRESS THROUGH THE STAGES OF THE SPR MODEL (FROM [39])

Stage		Company size			
		Small	Medium	Large	Giant
0	Assessment/baseline	2	2	3	4
1	Management	3	6	9	12
2	Methods/process	4	6	9	15
3	New Tools	4	6	9	12
4	Infrastructure	3	4	6	9
5	Reusability	4	6	12	12
6	Leadership	6	8	9	12
Total		26	38	57	76

[a] Small, < 10 staff, medium 101–1000 staff, large 1001–1000 staff, giant > 10 000 staff.

5.6 Summary

The following are the main points from the review of the literature on SPI:

- There is no evidence supporting or refuting that the ordering of processes or process capabilities in contemporary best practice models really reflects the natural evolution of successful software organizations.

However, this does not necessarily diminish the utility of the "stage" concept of best practice models: assessed organizations find the stages concept to be very useful for prioritizing their improvement efforts.

- Approximately one-third of respondents on SPI surveys report marked changes in their organizations as a consequence of their assessments.

- Organizations seem to have (unrealistically) high expectations from assessment-based SPI, and these need to be managed better.

- Despite the above, sponsors of assessments and assessment participants still remain enthusiastic about SPAs.

- Assessments increase "buy-in" for SPI for the participants in the assessments and the organization's technical staff. This is certainly encouraging as these are the individuals who are most likely to be skeptical about SPI and resist change to yet another management initiative.

- The most important factors that affect the success of SPI initiatives are (there are other factors that are important, but the ones below seem to be the most important):
  - management commitment and support of SPI (as a demonstration of commitment this would include management monitoring of the initiative and making resources available)
  - involvement of technical staff in the SPI effort
  - ensuring that staff understand the current software processes and their relationship to other business activities
  - clear SPI goals that are understood by the staff
  - tailoring the improvement initiatives
  - respected SPI staff (change agents and opinion leaders).

- We have provided some general guidelines on the costs of SPI that may be useful in managing the expectations of organizations better.

6. The Dimensions of Process Capability

In section 4.3 we saw that the measurement property of software process capability measures represents an important criterion for evaluating SPAs. The embedded assumption in contemporary best practice models is that process capability is a unidimensional construct. This can be seen in the unidimensional nature of the SW-CMM and the capability scale of ISO/IEC 15504. In this section we review studies that test this assumption.

Studies that investigate dimensionality have been exploratory in nature. For this, principal components analysis (PCA) has been used as the investigative technique [85]. PCA identifies groups in a set of variables.

One of the first such studies was performed by Curtis [86]. He collected data from a large number of individuals in three organizations about their software engineering practices following the SW-CMM. Questions on satisfying the goals of the KPAs were posed. A PCA was performed on each organization's data individually, and then the overall results were collectively interpreted. His results are shown in Table XV.

One immediate conclusion is that process capability, as defined in the SW-CMM, is a multidimensional construct. Also, it is clear that the goals of

TABLE XV

RESULTS OF THE CURTIS PCA [86]

	Goal[a]	
Planfulness		
Project planning	G1	Software estimates are documented for each use in planning and tracking the software project
Project planning	G2	Software project activities and commitments are planned and documented
Project tracking	G1	Actual results and performance are tracked against the software plans
Project tracking	G2	Corrective actions are taken and managed to closure when actual results and performance deviate significantly from the software plans
Integrated software management	G2	The project is planned and managed according to the project's defined software process
Coordinated commitments		
Project planning	G3	Affected groups and individuals agree to their commitments related to the software project
Project tracking	G3	Changes to software commitments are agreed to by the affected groups and individuals
Intergroup coordination	G1	The customer's requirements are agreed to by all affected groups
Intergroup coordination	G2	The commitments between the engineering groups are agreed to by the affected groups
Intergroup coordination	G3	The engineering groups identify, track, and resolve intergroup issues
Subcontractor management		
Subcontractor management	G1	The prime contractor selects qualified software subcontractors
Subcontractor management	G2	The prime contractor and the software subcontractor agree to their commitments to each other
Subcontractor management	G3	The prime contractor and the software subcontractor maintain ongoing communications
Quality assurance		
Software quality assurance	G1	Software quality assurance activities are planned

TABLE XV

CONTINUED

	Goal[a]	
Software quality assurance	G2	Adherence of software products and activities to the applicable standards, procedures, and requirements is verified objectively
Software quality assurance	G3	Affected groups and individuals are informed of software quality assurance activities and results
Software quality assurance	G4	Noncompliance issues that cannot be resolved within the software project are addressed by senior management
Configuration management		
Configuration Management	G1	Software configuration management activities are planned
Configuration management	G2	Selected software work products are identified, controlled, and available
Configuration management	G3	Changes to identified software work products are controlled
Configuration management	G4	Affected groups and individuals are informed of the status and content of software baselines
Process definition		
Organization process focus	G1	Software process development and improvement activities are coordinated across the organization
Organization process focus	G2	The strengths and weaknesses of the software processes used are identified relative to a process standard
Organization process focus	G3	Organization-level process development and improvement activities are planned
Organization process definition	G1	A standard software process for the organization is developed and maintained
Organization process definition	G2	Information related to the use of the organization's standard software process by the software projects is collected, reviewed, and made available
Integrated software management	G1	The project's defined software process is a tailored version of the organization's standard software process
Training		
Training program	G1	Training activities are planned
Training program	G2	Training for developing the skills and knowledge needed to perform software management and technical roles is provided
Training program	G3	Individuals in the software engineering group and software-related groups receive the training necessary to perform their roles

[a] Entries in this column are references to the goals of the associated KPA.

individual KPAs do not load on the same component. For example, the "planfulness" dimension is covered by goals from three separate KPAs, the "Coordinated Commitments" dimension is covered by goals from two different KPAs, and the "Process Definition" dimension by goals from three different KPAs. Although, there is also some consistency. The "Subcontractor Management", "Quality Assurance", and "Configuration Management" dimensions are composed of goals from the same KPA.

Clark, in his PhD thesis [87], provided the correlation matrix for 13 SW-CMM KPAs for data collected from 50 organizations. This can be used to perform a PCA, which we did. The results are shown in Table XVI.

It is clear that the dimensionality of SW-CMM process capability is different between these two studies. For example, Clark's data indicate that the Intergroup Coordination and Software Project Tracking are different dimensions, whereas Curtis's results shows that they are strongly related at the goal level. Apart from the Subcontractor Management KPA and the anomaly above, one would say that the KPAs studied by Curtis load on the same dimension in Clark's data. For example, from Clark's data, configuration management, quality assurance, and training are all in the same dimension, whereas they represent three different dimensions in Curtis's results.

There are a number of ways of explaining these results, unfortunately none of them substantive. First, Curtis collected data from individuals from

TABLE XVI

FACTOR STRUCTURE FOR THE FIRST 13 KPAS (FROM [87])

	PC 1	PC 2	PC 3
Requirements management	0.224205	**0.793343**	0.167607
Software project planning	**0.661053**	0.349884	0.443339
Software project tracking and oversight	**0.705950**	0.420637	0.414642
Software subcontract management	0.056427	−0.056777	**−0.917932**
Software quality assurance	**0.696583**	0.460522	0.175482
Software configuration management	**0.521998**	0.493161	−0.049939
Organization process focus	**0.910695**	0.153472	−0.070893
Organization process definition	**0.924298**	0.047921	−0.013578
Training program	**0.605227**	0.337231	0.216687
Integrated software management	**0.841650**	0.148948	−0.058104
Software product engineering	0.122982	**0.747144**	0.012944
Intergroup coordination	0.230563	**0.719089**	0.072065
Peer reviews	**0.900477**	0.213542	0.027097
Expl.Var	50.384027	20.669933	10.334092
Prp.Totl	0.414156	0.205379	0.102622

the same organization. Therefore, all the respondents within a PCA were responding about the same practices (i.e., the unit of observation was the individual rather than the organization). This type of design is useful for reliability studies, but ideally the unit of observation should be the organization or the project. Such was the case in Clark's thesis [87], and therefore one is tempted to conclude that Clark's results are more likely to be stable. In addition, the two studies did use different measurement approaches. Curtis asked questions on the satisfaction of KPA goals. Clark asked about the frequency of implementation of the KPAs.

Another study by El Emam investigated the dimensionality of the ISO/IEC 15504 capability scale [88]. He found that to be two dimensional, with the attributes in the first three levels of the capability scale representing one dimension, and the attributes in levels 4 and 5 representing the second dimension.

It is clear from the above studies that process capability is not a unidimensional construct. Beyond that it is quite difficult to draw strong conclusions about the dimensionality of the SW-CMM practices. For ISO/IEC 15504 two dimensions have been identified. If indeed further research confirms and identifies the dimensions of process capability, then it may be plausible to define different measures of capability with higher reliability and validity rather than attempt to have single universal measures.

7. The Reliability of Process Capability Measures[23]

Reliability is an enduring concern for software process assessments. The investment of time, money, and personal effort needed for assessments and successful software process improvement is quite nontrivial, and decisions based on assessment results are often far-reaching. Organizations and acquirers of software systems must be confident that the assessment results are well-founded and repeatable.

Reliability is defined as the extent to which the same measurement procedure will yield the same results on repeated trials and is concerned with random measurement error [97]. This means that if one were to repeat the measurement under similar or compatible conditions the same outcomes would emerge.

There has been a concern with the reliability of assessments. For example, Card discusses the reliability of software capability evaluations in an earlier article [98], where he commented on the inconsistencies of the results

---

[23] This section is based partially on material from [89–91, 94, 95].

obtained from assessments of the same organization by different teams. At the same time, another report noted that comparisons of SCE outcomes being cited as evidence of their lack of reliability were frequently based on SCEs performed on different subsets of the organization (or at least had different interviewees), and therefore one would not expect identical results [99]. Mention is also made of reliability in a contract award situation where emphasis is placed on having one team assess different contractors to ensure consistency [64]. Bollinger and McGowan [93] criticize the extent to which the scoring scheme used in the SEI's software capability evaluations contributes towards reduced reliability (see also [118] for a response). The interim profile method of the SEI [96] includes specific indicators to evaluate reliability. Furthermore, a deep concern with reliability is reflected in the empirical trials of the prospective SPICE standard whereby the evaluation of the reliability of SPICE-conformant assessments is an important focus of study [89].

One important implication of the extent of unreliability is that the rating obtained from an assessment is only one of the many possible ratings that would be obtained had the organization been repeatedly assessed. This means that, for a given level of confidence that one is willing to tolerate, an assessment rating has a specific probability of falling within a range of ratings. The size of this range increases as reliability decreases. This is illustrated in Fig. 9.

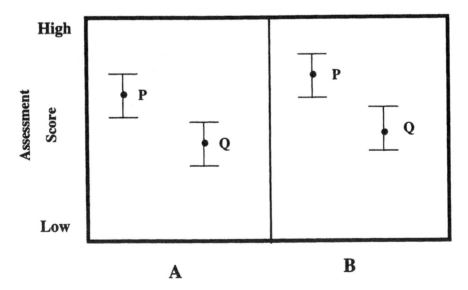

FIG. 9. Example hypothetical assessment ratings with confidence intervals.

Assume Fig. 9 shows the profiles of two organizations, A and B, and that P and Q are two different processes being assessed. Due to random measurement error, the ratings obtained for each process are only one of the many possible ratings that would be obtained had the organization been repeatedly assessed. The ratings obtained for organization B are in general higher than those of organization A, but this may be an artifact of chance. Without consideration of random measurement error, organization A may be unfairly penalized in a contract award situation. Turning to a self-improvement scenario, assume that Fig. 9 shows the profiles of one organization at two points in time, A and B. At time A, it may seem that the rating for process Q is much lower than for process P. Thus, the organization would be tempted to pour resources on improvements in process Q. However, without consideration of random measurement error, one cannot have high confidence about the extent to which the difference between P and Q ratings is an artifact of chance. Furthermore, at time B, it may seem that the organization has improved. However, without consideration of random measurement error, one cannot have high confidence about the extent to which the difference between A and B ratings (for processes P and Q) are artifacts of chance.

The above examples highlight the importance of evaluating the extent of reliability of software process assessments. A recent study also found evidence that more reliable assessments are indeed less costly [101]. The reason for that is when assessments are reliable (i.e., the assessors agree in their initial ratings), the consolidation phase progresses faster with less consensus building, hence resulting in an overall reduction in cost.[24]

7.1 Reliability Theory and Methods

Two theoretical frameworks for ascertaining the extent of reliability are presented below: the classical test theory framework, and the generalizability theory framework. Associated with each theoretical framework are a number of empirical research methods that can be applied.

7.1.1 Classical Test Theory Framework

Classical test theory states that an observed rating consists of two additive components, a true rating and an error: $X = T + E$. Thus, X would be the rating obtained in an assessment, T is the mean of the theoretical distribution of X ratings that would be found in repeated assessments of

---

[24] Note that this effect was identified for certain types of processes rather than for all processes that were studied.

the same organization,[25] and E is the error component. The reliability of measurement is defined as the ratio of true variance to observed variance.

There are four methods for estimating reliability under this framework. All of the four methods attempt to determine the proportion of variance in a measurement scale that is systematic. The different methods can be classified by the number of different assessment procedures necessary and the number of different assessment occasions necessary to make the estimate, as summarized in Table XVII. These methods are briefly described below:

TABLE XVII

A CLASSIFICATION OF CLASSICAL RELIABILITY ESTIMATION METHODS

		Number of assessment procedures required	
		1	2
Number of assessment occasions required	1	Split-halves Internal consistency	Alternative forms (immediate)
	2	Test–retest	Alternative forms (delayed)

7.1.1.1 Test–Retest Method
This is the simplest method for estimating reliability. In an assessment one would have to assess each organization's capability at two points in time using the same assessment procedure (i.e., the same instrument, the same assessors, and the same assessment method). Reliability would be estimated by the correlation between the ratings obtained on the two assessments. Test–retest reliability suffers from three disadvantages:

- First is the expense of conducting assessments at more than point in time. Given that the cost of assessments is an enduring concern [103, 104], the costs of repeated assessments for the purpose of estimating reliability would generally be unacceptable.
- Second, it is not obvious that a low reliability coefficient obtained using test–retest really indicates low reliability. For example, a likely

[25] In practice the true score can never be really known since it is generally not possible to obtain a large number of repeated assessments of the same organization. If one is willing to make some assumptions (e.g., an assumption of linearity), however, point estimates of true scores can be computed from observed scores [102].

explanation for a low coefficient is that the organization's software process capability has changed between the two assessment occasions. For instance, the initial assessment and results may (should) sensitize the organization to specific weaknesses and prompt them to initiate an improvement effort that influences the results of the subsequent assessment.

- Finally, carry-over effects between assessments may lead to an over-estimate of reliability. For instance, the reliability coefficient can be artificially inflated due to memory effects. Examples of memory effects are the assessees knowing the "right" answers that they have learned from the previous assessments, and assessors remembering responses from previous assessments and, deliberately or otherwise, repeating them in an attempt to maintain consistency of results.

7.1.1.2 Alternative Forms Method

Instead of using the same assessment procedure on two occasions, the alternative forms method stipulates that two alternative assessment procedures be used. This can be achieved, for example, by using two different assessment instruments or having two alternative, but equally qualified, assessment teams. This method can be characterized either as immediate (where the two assessments are concurrent in time), or delayed (where the two assessments are separated in time). The correlation coefficient (or some other measure of association) is then used as an estimate of reliability of either of the alternative forms.

7.1.1.3 Split-Halves Method

With the split-halves method, the total number of items in an assessment instrument are divided into two halves and the half-instruments are correlated to get an estimate of reliability. The halves can be considered as approximations to alternative forms. A correction must be applied to the correlation coefficient though, since that coefficient gives the reliability of each half only. One such correction is known as the *Spearman–Brown prophecy formula* [106]. A difficulty with the split-halves method is that the reliability estimate depends on the way the instrument is divided into halves. For example, for a 10 question instrument there are 126 possible different splits, and hence 126 different split-halves reliability estimates. The most common procedure is to take even numbered items on an instrument as one part and odd numbered ones as the second part.

7.1.4.4 Internal Consistency Methods

With methods falling under this heading, one examines the covariance among all the items in an assessment instrument. By far the most commonly used internal consistency estimate is the Cronbach alpha coefficient [100].

7.1.4.5 Selection Among Methods
Since there exists more than one classical method for estimating reliability, a relevant question is "which method(s) should be used?" One way to answer this is to consider what the research community perceives to be the most important reliability evaluation techniques. If we take the field of management information systems (MIS) as a reference discipline (in the sense that MIS researchers are also concerned with software processes, their measurement, and their improvement), then some general statements can be made about the perceived relative importance of the different methods.

In MIS, researchers developing instruments for measuring software processes and their outcomes tend to report the Cronbach alpha coefficient most frequently [107]. Furthermore, some researchers consider the Cronbach alpha coefficient to be the most important [108].

Examples of instruments with reported Cronbach alpha coefficients are those for measuring user information satisfaction [109, 110], user involvement [111, 112], and perceived ease of use and usefulness of software [113]. Moreover, recently, reliability estimates using other methods have also been reported, for example, test–retest reliability for a user information satisfaction instrument [114], and for a user involvement instrument [115].

In software engineering, the few studies that consider reliability report the Cronbach alpha coefficient. For example, the reliability estimate for a requirements engineering success instrument [116], for an organizational maturity instrument [117], and for level 2 and 3 of the SEI maturity questionnaire [118].

7.1.2 Generalizability Theory Framework

The different classical methods for estimating reliability presented above vary in the factors that they subsume under error variance. Some common sources of random measurement are presented in Table XVIII [89]. This means that the use of different classical methods will yield different estimates of reliability.

Generalizability theory [119], however, allows one to explicitly consider multiple sources of error simultaneously and estimate their relative contributions. In the context of process assessments, the theory would be concerned with the accuracy of generalizing from an organization's obtained rating on an assessment to the average rating that the organization would have received under all possible conditions of assessment (e.g., using different instruments,

TABLE XVIII

DEFINITION OF SOME SOURCES OF ERROR IN PROCESS ASSESSMENTS

Source of error	Description
Different occasions	Assessment ratings may differ across time. Instability of assessment ratings may be due to temporary circumstances and/or actual process changes
Different assessors	Assessment ratings may differ across assessors (or assessment teams). Lack of repeatability of assessment ratings may be due to the subjectivity in the evaluations and judgement of particular assessors (i.e., do different assessors make the same judgements about an organization's processes?)
Different instrument contents	Assessment ratings may differ across instruments. Lack of equivalence of instruments may be due to the questions in different instruments not being constructed according to the same content specifications (i.e., do different instruments have questions that cover the same content domain?)
Within-instrument contents	Responses to different questions or subsets of questions within the same instrument may differ among themselves. One reason for these differences is that questions or subsets of questions may not have been constructed to the same or to consistent content specifications. Regardless of their content, questions may be formulated poorly, may be difficult to understand, may not be interpreted consistently, etc.

different assessment teams, different team sizes). This average rating is referred to as the *universe rating*. All possible conditions of assessment are referred to as the *universe of assessments*. A set of measurement conditions is called a *facet*. Facets relevant to assessments include the assessment instrument used, the assessment team, and assessment team size.

Generalizability theory uses the factorial analysis of variance (ANOVA) [120] to partition an organization's assessment rating into an effect for the universe rating, an effect for each facet or source of error, an effect for each of their combinations, and other "random" error. This can be contrasted to simple ANOVA, which is more analogous to the classical test theory framework. With simple ANOVA the variance is partitioned into "between" and "within." The former is thought of as systematic variance or signal, the latter as random error or noise. In the classical test theory framework one similarly partitions the total variance into true rating and error rating.

Suppose, for the purpose of illustration, one facet is considered, namely assessment instrument. Further, suppose that in an evaluation study two instruments are used and N organizations are assessed using each of the two instruments. In this case, one intends to generalize from the two instruments to all possible instruments. The results of this study would be analyzed as a two-way ANOVA with one observation per cell (e.g., see [120]). The above example could be extended to have multiple facets (i.e., account for multiple sources of error such as instruments and assessors).

7.1.3 Applications

The studies that have been performed thus far on the reliability of assessments only utilize classical methods. Specifically, the evaluation of internal consistency using the Cronbach alpha coefficient and the alternative forms (immediate) methods. For the latter the alternative form is a different assessor or assessment team. This is commonly called an interrater agreement study where instead of using the correlation coefficient, other approaches are used to quantify reliability.

7.2 Internal Consistency

A basic concept for comprehending the reliability of measurement is that of a *construct*. A construct refers to a meaningful conceptual object. A construct is neither directly measurable nor observable. However, the quantity or value of a construct is presumed to cause a set of observations to take on a certain value. An observation can be considered as a question in a maturity questionnaire (this is also referred to as an *item*). Thus, the construct can be indirectly measured by considering the values of those items.

For example, organizational maturity is a construct. Thus, the value of an item measuring "the extent to which projects follow a written organizational policy for managing system requirements allocated to software" is presumed to be caused by the true value of organizational maturity. Also, the value of an item measuring "the extent to which projects follow a written organizational policy for planning software projects" is presumed to be caused by the true value of organizational maturity. Such a relationship is depicted in the path diagram in Fig. 10. Since organizational maturity is not directly measurable, the above two items are intended to estimate the actual magnitude or true rating of organizational maturity.

The type of scale used in the most common assessment instruments is a summative one. This means that the individual ratings for each item are summed up to produce an overall rating. One property of the covariance matrix for a summative scale that is important for the following formulation

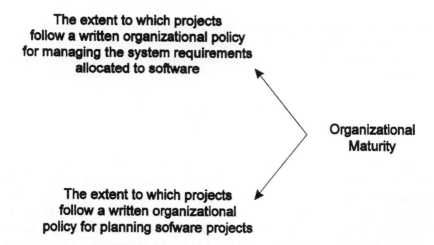

FIG. 10. The organizational maturity construct and example items for its measurement.

is that the sum of all the elements in the matrix give exactly the variance of the scale as a whole.

One can think of the variability in a set of item ratings as being due to one of two things:

- actual variation across the organizations in maturity (i.e., true variation in the construct being measured); this can be considered as the signal component of the variance
- error, which can be considered as the noise component of the variance.

Computing the Cronbach alpha coefficient involves partitioning the total variance into signal and noise. The proportion of total variation that is signal equals Cronbach alpha.

The signal component of variance is considered to be attributable to a common source, presumably the true rating of the construct underlying the items. When maturity varies across the different organizations, ratings on all the items will vary with it because it is a cause of these ratings. The error terms are the source of unique variation that each item possesses. Whereas all items share variability due to maturity, no two items are considered to share any variation from the same error source.

Unique variation is the sum of the elements in the diagonal of the covariance matrix $\sum \sigma_i^2$ (where $i = 1, \ldots, N$ items). Common variation is the difference between total variation and unique variation, $\sigma_y^2 - \sum \sigma_i^2$ where the first term is the variation of the whole scale. Therefore, the proportion of common variance can be expressed as $(\sigma_y^2 - \sum \sigma_i^2)/\sigma_y^2$. To express this in relative terms, the number of elements in the matrix must be considered. The total number of elements is N^2, and the total number of elements that are communal is $N^2 - N$. Thus the corrected equation for coefficient alpha becomes:

$$\alpha = \frac{N}{(N - 1)} \left[1 - \sum \sigma_i^2 / \sigma_y^2 \right]$$

The Cronbach alpha coefficient varies between 0 and 1. If there is no true rating but only error in the items, then the variance of the sum will be the same as the sum of variances of the individual items. Therefore, the coefficient alpha will be equal to zero (i.e., the proportion of true ratings in the scale is 0%). If all items are perfectly reliable and measure the same thing, then coefficient alpha is equal to 1 (i.e., the proportion of true rating in the scale is 100%).

What a satisfactory level of internal consistency is depends on how a measure is being used. In the early stages of the research on assessment instruments, reliabilities of 0.7 or higher are considered sufficient. For basic research, a value of 0.8 is acceptable. However, in applied settings where important decisions are made with respect to assessment ratings, a reliability of 0.9 is considered a minimum [106].

To illustrate the calculation of Cronbach's alpha through an example, let's assume that we have an instrument with five items. Also, let the variances of each of these items be 4.32, 3.86, 2.62, 2.55, and 2.46. The sum of the variances, $\sum \sigma_i^2$, is 15.81. For this 5-item instrument, the variance of the sum of the 5 items, $\sum \sigma_y^2$, is say 53.95. Then the Cronbach alpha coefficient would be $1.25(1 - (15.81/53.95)) = 0.88$. The values for the sample variances can be computed as

$$\left(\sum (x_j - x)^2 \right) / N_{\text{OBS}} - 1,$$

where the x_j's are the actual values for each observation j ($j = 1, \dots, N_{\text{OBS}}$), and $\bar{x}$ is the mean of all observations, and N_{OBS} is the total number of observations.

Cronbach's alpha is a generalization of a coefficient introduced by Kuder and Richardson to estimate the reliability of scales composed of dichotomously scored items. Dichotomous items are scored 1 or 0 depending on whether the respondent does or does not endorse the particular characteristic under investigation. To determine the reliability of scales composed of dichotomously scored items, the Kuder–Richardson formula (denoted by KR20) is [121]:

$$KR20 = \frac{N}{(N-1)} \left[1 - \sum p_i q_i / \sigma_y^2 \right]$$

where N is the number of dichotomous items; p_i is the proportion responding positively to the ith item; $q_i = 1 - p_i$; and σ_y^2 is the variance of the total composite. Since KR20 is simply a special case of alpha, it has the same interpretation as alpha.

A series of studies investigated the internal consistency of the CMM maturity questionnaire (the questionnaire described in [28]) [95, 118], the initial version of the ISO/IEC 15504 capability dimension [95], and the second version of the ISO/IEC 15504 capability dimension [88].

Before presenting the results, it is worth noting that the Cronbach alpha coefficient depends on the number of items in an instrument. Therefore, to compare different instruments, or present their internal consistency in a comparable manner, the coefficient is adjusted to an instrument of the same size.

Table XIX shows the internal consistency results for the first set of studies [95, 118]. The coefficients are presented for two instruments, an 85-item instrument (to be compatible with the maturity questionnaire size), and a 26-item instrument (to be compatible with the ISO/IEC 15504 version 1 capability dimension). In general, it can be seen that these instruments have a remarkably high internal consistency.

However, as we saw earlier on, the above capability measures are not all unidimensional. The Cronbach alpha coefficient assumes unidimensionality. Therefore, it is not obvious how to interpret the results in Table XIX. As noted earlier, a subsequent study [88] found that the ISO/IEC 15504 capability dimension actually consisted of two separate dimensions: "Process Implementation" and "Quantitative Process Management." The

TABLE XIX

COMPARISONS OF EARLY INTERNAL CONSISTENCY RESULTS

	1987 MQ[a] Dataset 1	1987 MQ[a] Dataset 2	Estimates based on [118]	SPICE v1[b] Dataset 1	SPICE v1[b] Dataset 2
85 item instrument	0.94	0.94	0.92	0.98	0.99
26 item instrument	0.84	0.84	0.78	0.94	0.97

[a] 1987 maturity questionnaire.
[b] SPICE v1 Capability Dimension.

internal consistency for these are shown in Table XX. Here, the results demonstrate a high internal consistency for each dimension individually.

7.3   Interrater Agreement

A number of interrater agreement studies have been performed on software process assessments [94, 122, 123, 124]. All of these were performed in the context of the SPICE trials.

For conducting interrater agreement studies, the assessment team is divided into two or more groups. Ideally all groups should be equally competent in making attribute ratings. In practice, assessors in each group need only meet minimal competence requirements (described in [44]) since this is more congruent with the manner in which the ISO/IEC 15504 documents would be applied.

Both groups would participate in the preparation of the assessment. During evidence collection, each group would be provided with the same information (e.g., all would be present in the same interviews and provided with the same documentation to inspect),[26] and then they would perform their ratings independently. It is these independent ratings that are used in interrater agreement studies.

Subsequent to the independent ratings, the groups would meet to reach a consensus in their findings and ratings, and produce a consolidated rating which is the final outcome of an assessment. This is the consolidation phase. Subsequently the assessment team may discuss the findings and ratings with the initial interviewees (debriefing), which may lead to refinement of the findings and ratings. Then they present the final results to the organization. Consolidation, debriefing, and reporting are activities that are not necessary for evaluating interrater agreement, but they must be performed so that the organization that sponsored the assessment gets value out of it. Given the expense of an assessment, few, if any, organizations will sponsor

---

[26] Under this requirement, one group may obtain information that was elicited by the other group, which they would have not asked for. The alternative to this requirement is that the different groups interview the same people at different times to make sure that they only obtain the information that they ask for. However, this requirement raises the risk that the interviewees "learn" the right answers to give based on the first interview, or that they volunteer information that was asked by the first group but not the second. Furthermore, from a practical perspective, interviewing the same people more than once to ask the same questions would substantially increase the cost of assessments, and thus the cost of conducting a study. It is for this reason that these studies are referred to as "interrater" agreement since, strictly speaking, they consider the reliability of ratings, rather than the reliability of whole assessments. The study of "interassessment" agreement would involve accounting for variations in the information that is collected by two (or more) different groups during an assessment.

TABLE XX

CRONBACH ALPHA COEFFICIENTS FOR DIFFERENT NUMBERS OF
ATTRIBUTES

Attributes up to level 3	Attributes in levels 4 and 5
5 attributes	4 attributes
$n = 312$	$n = 232$
0.89	0.90

assessments that produce no output. General guidelines for conducting interrater agreement studies are given in Table XXII.

Since all of the interrater agreement studies that have been conducted thus far were in the context of the SPICE Trials, we briefly review the general rating scheme of ISO/IEC 15504 to aid in understanding the methods used [6]. The rating scheme consists of a 4-point achievement scale for each attribute. A summary of the definition for each of these response categories is given in Table XXI.

Data from an interrater agreement study of an ISO/IEC 15504 assessment can be represented in a table such as Table XXIII. Here we have two groups that have independently made a number of ratings on the 4-point scale described above. The table would include the proportion of ratings that fall in each one of the cells. In this table P_{ij} is the proportion of ratings classified in cell (i, j), P_{i+} is the total proportion for row i, and P_{+j} is the total proportion for column j:

$$P_{i+} = \sum_{j=1}^{4} P_{ij}$$

$$P_{+j} = \sum_{i=1}^{4} P_{ij}$$

TABLE XXI

THE FOUR-POINT ATTRIBUTE RATING SCALE

Rating	Designation	Description
Not achieved	N	No evidence of achievement of the defined attribute
Partially achieved	P	Some achievement of the defined attribute
Largely achieved	L	Significant achievement of the defined attribute
Fully achieved	F	Full achievement of the defined attribute

TABLE XXII

GUIDELINES FOR CONDUCTING INTERRATER AGREEMENT STUDIES

For each process, divide the assessment team into $k \geqslant$ two groups with at least one person per group

The groups should be selected so that they both meet the minimal assessor competence requirements with respect to training, background, and experience

The groups should use the same evidence (e.g., attend the same interviews, inspect the same documents, etc.), assessment method, and tools

Each group examining any physical artifacts should leave them as close as possible (organized/marked/sorted) to the state that the assessees delivered them

If evidence is judged to be insufficient, gather more evidence and the groups should inspect the new evidence before making ratings

The groups independently rate the same process instances

After the independent ratings, the groups then meet to reach consensus and harmonize their ratings for the final ratings profile

There should be no discussion among the groups about rating judgement prior to the independent ratings[a]

[a] This requirement needs special attention when the assessment method stipulates having multiple consolidation activities throughout an assessment (e.g., at the end of each day in an assessment). Observations that are discussed during such sessions can be judged as organizational strengths or weaknesses, and therefore the ratings of the different groups would no longer be independent. This can be addressed if consolidation is performed independently by the different groups. Then, before the presentation of findings to the organization, overall consolidation of ratings and findings by the different groups is performed.

TABLE XXIII

4×4 TABLE FOR REPRESENTING PROPORTIONS FROM AN ISO/IEC 15504 INTERRATER AGREEMENT STUDY WITH TWO GROUPS

Group 2	Group 1				
	F	L	P	N	
F	P_{11}	P_{12}	P_{13}	P_{14}	P_{1+}
L	P_{21}	P_{22}	P_{23}	P_{24}	P_{2+}
P	P_{31}	P_{32}	P_{33}	P_{34}	P_{3+}
N	P_{41}	P_{42}	P_{43}	P_{44}	P_{4+}
	P_{+1}	P_{+2}	P_{+3}	P_{+4}	

The most straightforward approach to evaluating agreement is to consider the proportion of ratings upon which the two groups agree:

$$P_{\text{o}} = \sum_{i=1}^{4} P_{ii}$$

However, this value includes agreement that could have occurred by chance. For example, if the two groups employed completely different criteria for assigning their ratings to the same practices (i.e., if the row variable was independent from the column variable), then a considerable amount of observed agreement would still be expected by chance.

Hartmann [125] notes that percentage (or proportion) agreement tends to produce higher values than other measures of agreement, and discourages its use since the tradition in science is to be conservative rather than liberal. A more detailed analysis of the behavioral literature where proportion agreement was used concluded that large fractions of these observations would be deemed unreliable if corrections for chance were considered [126]. Therefore, in general, the use of percentage or proportion agreement is not recommended as an evaluative measure.

There are different ways for evaluating extent of agreement that is expected by chance. We will consider two alternatives here. The first assumes that chance agreement is due to each of the groups rating randomly at equal rates for each of the categories of the four-point scales. In such a case chance agreement would be:

$$P_{\text{e}} = \frac{1}{k} \tag{1}$$

where in our case k would be 4.

An alternative definition of chance agreement considers that the groups' proclivity to distribute their ratings in a certain way is a source of disagreement:

$$P_{\text{e}} = \sum_{i=1}^{4} P_{i+} P_{+i} \tag{2}$$

The above marginal proportions are maximum likelihood estimates of the population proportions under a multinomial sampling model. If each of the assessors makes ratings at random according to the marginal proportions, then the above is chance agreement (derived using the multiplication rule of probability and assuming independence between the two groups).

A general form for agreement coefficients is [127]:

$$Agreement = \frac{P_{\text{o}} - P_{\text{e}}}{1 - P_{\text{e}}}$$

The observed agreement that is in excess of chance agreement is given by $P_o - P_e$. The maximum possible excess over chance agreement is $1 - P_e$. Therefore, this type of agreement coefficient is the ratio of observed excess over chance agreement to the maximum possible excess over chance agreement.

When there is complete agreement between the two groups, P_o will take the value 1. In this case, the agreement coefficient is 1. If observed agreement is greater than chance, then the agreement coefficient is greater than 0. If observed agreement is less than would be expected by chance, then the agreement coefficient is less than 0.

An agreement coefficient[27] that considers chance agreement as in equation (1) is Bennett et al.'s S coefficient [128]. An agreement coefficient that considers chance agreement as in equation (2) is Cohen's kappa (κ) [129].

A priori it would seem more reasonable to assume that each group has a proclivity to distribute their ratings in a certain way rather than assume that both groups distribute their ratings in exactly the same way. This therefore suggests that Cohen's kappa is a more appropriate coefficient. Furthermore, as Cohen notes, it is also desirable to take account of disagreement in marginal distributions in an agreement coefficient [129].[28]

Cohen's kappa is therefore defined as:[29]

$$\kappa = \frac{P_o - P_e}{1 - P_e}$$

where the definition of P_e is as in equation (2).

---

[27] It should be noted that "agreement" is different from "association." For the ratings from two teams to agree, the ratings must fall in the same achievement category. For the ratings from two teams to be associated, it is only necessary to be able to predict the achievement category of one team from the achievement category of the other team. Thus, strong agreement requires strong association, but strong association can exist without strong agreement. For instance, the ratings can be strongly associated and also show strong disagreement.

[28] A further problem with the S coefficient is that it is dependent on the number of categories in a rating scheme [130]. For example, the chance agreement for a 2-category rating scheme is 0.5, whereas chance agreement for a 4-category rating scheme is 0.25. Therefore, by definition, the S coefficient rewards rating schemes with larger numbers of categories. Although this is not a major problem when the number of categories is fixed, as is the case with ISO/IEC 15504-based assessments, it provides another reason for not using this coefficient in general.

[29] There is also a weighted version of the Kappa coefficient [131]. The weighting schemes that have been suggested are based on mathematical convenience. However, thus far no weighting scheme has been developed that has a substantive meaning in the context of software process assessments.

The minimum value of kappa depends upon the marginal proportions. However, since we are interested in evaluating agreement, the lower limit of kappa is not of interest.

7.3.1 Example Kappa Calculation

Here we illustrate the computation of the kappa coefficient through an example. Consider Table XXIV, which contains the proportions calculated from a hypothetical assessment.

For this particular table we have:

$$P_o = 0.051 + 0.128 + 0.154 + 0.051 = 0.384$$

$$P_e = (0.256 \times 0.051) + (0.384 \times 0.282)$$

$$+ (0.307 \times 0.461) + (0.051 \times 0.205) = 0.273$$

$$\kappa = (0.384 - 0.273)/(1 - 0.273) = 0.153$$

7.3.2 Interrater Agreement Results

A recent study that summarized the results from the interrater agreement studies that have been performed produced the benchmark shown in Table XXV [91]. This indicates the quartile values for the kappa coefficient from actual studies. Therefore, 25% of the assessed ISO/IEC 15504 process instances had kappa values below or equal to 0.44, and 25% had values greater than 0.78.

It is clear that variation in interrater agreement exists, and the factors that may be causing such variation are discussed below. In order to determine whether these values are indicative in general of a reasonable amount of

TABLE XXIV

4×4 TABLE CONTAINING PROPORTIONS FROM A HYPOTHETICAL ASSESSMENT

	Group 1				
Group 2	F	L	P	N	
F	0.051	0.128	0.077	0	0.256
L	0	0.128	0.230	0.026	0.384
P	0	0.026	0.154	0.128	0.307
N	0	0	0	0.051	0.051
	0.051	0.282	0.461	0.205	

TABLE XXV

ISO/IEC 15504 SOFTWARE PROCESS ASSESSMENT KAPPA BENCHMARK

Kappa statistic	Strength of agreement	Percentile interpretation	
≤ 0.44	Poor	(bottom 25%)	
≤ 0.44–0.62	Moderate		(bottom 50%)
0.62–0.78	Substantial		(top 50%)
> 0.78	Excellent	(top 25%)	

reliability or not, it is informative to compare this benchmark with one used in medicine to evaluate the reliability of doctors' diagnoses. The benchmark provided by Fleiss [132] is shown in Table XXVI. We can see that what is characterized as poor diagnosis reliability falls in the lowest quartile on the assessment benchmark. Therefore, at least by these standards, the majority of process assessments have a respectable level of interrater agreement.

7.4 Factors Affecting Reliability

A survey was conducted to prioritize the factors that have an impact on the reliability of process assessments [94]. The data collection was conducted during a meeting of the SPICE project that took place in Mexico in October 1996. These meetings are of sizeable number of experienced assessors with substantial experience in various assessment methods and models, such as the CMM, CBA IPI, Trillium, Bootstrap, and other proprietary models and methods. During the meeting, the authors generated a list of factors that may potentially have an impact on the reliability of assessments. The authors relied largely on their experiences and the prior comments of other assessors. This is justifiable given that no comprehensive study of the factors influencing reliability had been conducted.

This list was reviewed by two other experienced assessors to ensure completeness of coverage. The list is given in Table XXVII. The refined list

TABLE XXVI

THE FLEISS KAPPA BENCHMARK

Kappa statistic	Strength of agreement
< 0.40	Poor
0.40–0.75	Intermediate to good
> 0.75	Excellent

TABLE XXVII

RANKING OF FACTORS AFFECTING THE RELIABILITY OF ASSESSMENTS

ID	Factor	Number	%
A	Lead assessor's experience/competence in conducting assessments	24/26	92
B	Lead assessor's knowledge of ISO/IEC 15504 documents	22/25	88
C	Clarity of the semantics of the process definition in the ISO/IEC 15504 documentation	22/26	84.6
D	The extent to which the assessment process is defined and documented	20/26	77
E	Team members' knowledge of ISO/IEC 15504 documents	16/25	64
F	Amount of collected data objective evidence and/or interviews	16/26	61.5
G	Assessees' commitment	13/25	52
H	Assessment team stability	13/25	52
I	Rating just after collecting the evidence, and validation at the end of the assessment	12/25	48
J	Assessment team composition unidisciplinary vs. multidisciplinary competencies	11/25	44
K	Sponsor commitment	11/25	44
L	Team building curve	10/25	40
M	Competence of the interviewed assessees	10/25	40
N	Number of assessed projects in the organizational unit	9/25	36
O	Assessment duration	9/25	36
P	Lead assessor's experience/competence in conducting audits	8/25	32
Q	Assessment team size number of assessors including lead assessor	8/25	32
R	Rating only at the end of the assessment	8/25	32
S	Language used during the assessment	8/25	32
T	Time allocation between artifact reviews and interviews	8/25	32
U	Management of the assessment logistics, e.g., availability of facilities	6/25	24
V	The capability of the organizational unit's processes	5/25	20
W	Whether the assessors are external or internal	3/26	11.5

was turned into a rating form. The rating form was piloted with four assessors to ensure that it was understandable and to identify ambiguities. Based on this feedback, a new form was developed and was distributed to all attendees at the closing session of the meeting. In total, approximately 50 individuals attended the project meeting, and we believe a slightly smaller number attended the closing session. A total of 26 valid responses were received back and were used for analysis.

The form consisted of an unordered list of factors that are believed to have an impact on the reliability of assessments. The respondent was requested to rate each factor on a 5-point scale, where 1 means that the factor has "very high influence" on the reliability of assessments, and 5 means that it has "very low influence." The objective was to prioritize these factors. The responses on the 5-point scale were dichotomized into high influence (scores 1 and 2) and low influence (scores 3–5). For each factor, the percentage of respondents who rated a factor as high influence was calculated. this percentage is used for ranking. The results are shown in Table XXVII. We use the letters A to W in the discussions to indicate items in the table.

7.4.1 Assessor Competence

Given that assessment are a subjective measurement procedure, it is expected that assessor competence will have an impact on the reliability of assessments. We consider mainly the competence of the lead assessor since s/he is the key person on the assessment team. The types of competencies covered here include knowledge of the ISO/IEC 15504 documents (B), experience and competence in conducting assessments (A), and audits (P). Indeed, a subsequent study demonstrated that assessors lacking experience can give results that are quite different from experienced assessors [133]. Also, knowledge of the ISO/IEC 15504 documents (E) was perceived to be important since the team members will be collecting, organizing, and interpreting information during an assessment; they must know ISO/IEC 15504 well to collect the right information, organize it efficiently, and interpret it properly.

7.4.2 External vs. Internal Assessors

Previous research has identified potential systematic biases of internal or external assessors [122] (i.e., one assessor would systematically rate higher or lower than the other). For example, an internal assessor may favor the organization in his/her ratings or may have other information not available to the external assessor which may influence the ratings. Similarly, an external assessor may not know the organization's business well and therefore may systematically underrate the implementation of its practices. This issue is covered in item (W).

7.4.3 Team Size

Practice and recommendation on team size have tended to be confusing. In some assessment methods it is stipulated that teams range in size from 5 to 9 [62]. In the first version of the ISO/IEC 15504 documents the recommendation has been team sizes of at least two assessors. From a practical point of view it has been suggested that a single assessor would find it difficult to collect and record information at the same time, and therefore more than one person is recommended. Item (Q) covers this issue from the perspective of its impact on reliability.

7.4.4 Backgrounds of Assessors

It has been noted by some assessors that multidisciplinary assessment teams (i.e., not consisting of only software engineering staff, but also those with backgrounds in, for example, human resources management and marketing) are better able to collect the right evidence (i.e., ask the right questions and request the appropriate documents) and better able to interpret it for certain processes. This would likely increase the reliability of assessments. This issue is covered in item (J).

7.4.5 Number of Assessed Projects

During an assessment, a sample of projects is selected for assessment. It is usually not feasible to assess all of the projects within the scope of the organization. It is assumed, through this selection process, that the selected projects are representative of the whole organization. Clearly, the more projects that are assessed, the more representative and hence repeatable the ratings that are made. This is covered in item (N). Of course, this item applies only when one is giving ratings to whole organizations, and has less influence when the unit of analysis is a process instance.

7.4.6 Assessment Duration

Long assessment may lead to fatigue of the assessors and assessees, may reduce their motivation, and hence reduce the reliability of ratings. Short assessments may not collect sufficient information to make reliable ratings. This is covered in item (O).

7.4.7 Team Building Curve

In team-based assessments, it is expected that the assessor judgements would converge as the assessment progresses. This would be due to a better appreciation of the other team members' experiences, backgrounds, and due to the consensus building activities that usually take place during an assessment. This is covered in item (L).

7.4.8   Clarity of Documents

Ambiguities and inconsistencies in the definition of practices or in the scales used to make ratings would potentially lead to different interpretations of what practices mean and how to rate them. This would in turn reduce reliability. This issue is covered in item (C).

7.4.9   Definition of the Assessment Process

Having a clearly defined assessment process potentially ensures that the process is repeatable, which in turn has an impact on the repeatability of ratings. This is covered in item (D).

7.4.10   Amount of Data Collected

The more time spent on data collection (item F), the more data will be collected. The more data that is collected, the more likely that the assessment team will have a more objective basis to make their ratings. Furthermore, the extent to which time is allocated to different methods for data collection may have an impact on the amount of data collected (item T).

7.4.11   Capability of Organization and its Processes

It is hypothesized that higher capability processes are easier to rate because of the existence of more objective evidence and process stability to make consistent judgements. This is covered in item (U).

7.4.12   Assessment Method

A feature of the assessment method is when the ratings are actually made. One approach is to collect data about a process and then make the ratings right afterwards (item I). Another approach is to collect data on all of the processes within the scope of the assessment, and then rate them all afterwards (item R). The latter allows the assessors to build an overall picture of the implementation of software engineering practices in the organization, and also to get a better understanding of the organization's business and objectives (especially for external assessors) before making ratings. This could potentially increase the reliability of assessments.

One study investigated the impact of the method on the agreement among independent assessors in their ratings [94]. The results indicate that for low capability levels, there is a difference in reliability between rating processes early in assessment versus late in an assessment. For higher capability processes, it does not make a difference whether ratings are done early or late in an assessment.

7.4.13   Sponsor and Assessee Commitment

A lack of commitment by members of the assessed organization can lead to insufficient or inappropriate resources being made available for the assessment. This may compromise the assessment team's ability to make repeatable ratings. This issue is covered in items (K) and (G).

7.4.14   Assessment Team Stability

If the assessment team changes during an assessment, the disruption can break the consensus building cycle. Furthermore, knowledge about the organization that has been gained by an assessor that leaves would have to be regained by a new assessor. This is covered in item (H).

7.4.15   Logistics Management

Inappropriate management of the logistics may distract the assessors and waste time. This could potentially lead to insufficient evidence being collected and hence to lower reliability. This issue is covered in item (V).

7.4.16   Assessee Competence

Assessees provide the necessary information during an assessment. If the assessees are not competent then they may provide inconsistent information to the assessors, which may consequently lead to inconsistent interpretations of the process' capability. This issue is covered in item (M).

7.4.17   Assessment Language

Assessments are now being conducted all around the world. In fact, in the first phase of the SPICE trials certain documents were translated to a language other than English. The issue of the impact of language on the reliability of assessments is covered in (S).

7.4.18 Discussion

The results clearly indicate that assessment team competence and the clarity of the documents are perceived to be the two most important factors that have an impact on the reliability of assessments.

Equally interesting are the factors that were rated to be of least priority. This does not mean that they are not important, only that they are less important than the other factors. These factors were whether the assessors were internal vs. external, the capability of assessed processes, and the assessment logistics.

7.5 Summary

In summary, this is what we have learned thus far about the reliability of process assessments:

- The reliability of SPAs is important to give confidence in the decisions based on assessment results, but also a recent study found evidence that more reliable assessments are less costly. The reason for that is when assessments are reliable (i.e., the assessors agree in their initial ratings), the consolidation phase progresses faster with less consensus building, hence resulting in an overall reduction in cost.
- A number of studies have evaluated the internal consistency of assessment instruments. However, most of these assumed unidimensionality, which, as noted above, was found subsequently not to be the case. One study evaluated the internal consistency of the ISO/IEC 15504 capability scale dimensions and found it to be sufficiently high for practical usage.
- Studies of interrater agreement in ISO/IEC 15504-based assessments indicate that most ratings by independent teams are sufficiently reliable (in at least 75% of studied ratings).
- Current evidence demonstrates that the reliability of SPAs deteriorates with inexperienced assessors (the sole study compared inexperienced with experienced assessor ratings during a training course).
- In reliability studies with both internal and external assessors on an assessment team, systematic bias was witnessed in some cases. Assessment methods should be designed to alleviate this possibility.
- It has been suggested by assessment experts in a survey that the following are the most important factors that affect the reliability

of assessments:
- clarity of the best practice model, and knowledge of it by the assessment team
- the extent to which the assessment process is defined and documented
- amount of data that is collected during the assessment
- assessee and sponsor commitment to the assessment
- assessment team composition and stability.

However, many of these factors require further systematic empirical investigation.

- It was found that the assessment method has an impact on the reliability of assessments (interrater agreement). A feature of the assessment method is when the ratings are actually made. One type of method stipulates that the assessment team collect data about a process and then make the ratings right afterwards. Another method would be to collect data on all of the processes within the scope of the assessment, and then rate them all afterwards. The latter allows the assessors to build an overall picture of the implementation of software engineering practices in the organization, and also to get a better understanding of the organization's business and objectives (especially for external assessors) before making ratings. One study found that for low capability levels, there is a difference in reliability between rating processes early in assessment versus late in an assessment. For higher capability processes, it does not make a difference whether ratings are done early or late in an assessment, but for low capability processes late ratings are more reliable.

8. The Validity of Process Capability Measures

8.1 Types of Validity

The validity of measurement is defined as the extent to which a measurement procedure is measuring what it is purporting to measure [134]. During the process of validating a measurement procedure one attempts to collect evidence to support the types of inferences that are to be drawn from measurement scores [135]. In the context of SPAs, concern with validity is epitomized by the question "are assessment ratings really measuring best software process practices?"

A basic premise of SPAs is that the resultant quantitative ratings are associated with the performance of the project and/or organization that is assessed. This premise consists of two parts:[30]

- that the practices defined in the best practice model are indeed good practices and their implementation will therefore result in improved performance
- that the quantitative assessment rating is a true reflection of the extent to which these practices are implemented in the organization or project; and therefore projects or organizations with higher assessment ratings are likely to perform better.

Validity is related to reliability in the sense that reliability is a necessary but insufficient condition for validity. The differences between reliability and validity are illustrated below by way of two examples.

For instance, assume one seeks to measure intelligence by having children throw stones as far as they could. The distance the stones are thrown on one occasion might correlate highly with how far they are thrown on another occasion. Thus, being repeatable, the stone-throwing measurement procedure would be highly reliable. However, the distance that stones are thrown would not be considered by most informed observers to be a valid measure of intelligence.

As another example, consider a car's fuel gauge that systematically shows 5 liters higher than the actual level of fuel in the gas tank. If repeated readings of fuel level are taken under the same conditions, the gauge will yield consistent (and hence reliable) measurements. However, the gauge does not give a valid measure of fuel level in the gas tank.

We consider here two types of validity that we believe are most important for SPAs: content and predictive validity.

8.1.1 Content Validity

Content validity is defined as the representativeness or sampling adequacy of the content of a measuring instrument [134]. Ensuring content validity depends largely on expert judgement.

---

[30] The fact that the premise behind the use of quantitative scores from SPAs consists of two parts means that if no empirical evidence is found to support the basic premise, then we would not know which part is at fault. For example, if we find that there is no relationship between the assessment score and performance it may be because:

- the practices are really not good practices, but the measurement procedure is accurately measuring their implementation, or
- the practices are really good practices, but the measurement procedure is not accurately measuring their implementation.

From a practical standpoint it does not matter which of the above two conclusions one draws since the practices and measurement procedure are always packaged and used together.

In the context of SPAs, expert judgement would ensure that assessments are at least perceived to measure best software engineering practice. This centers largely on the content of the models.

At least for the best practice models that we are intimately associated with, the models have been extensively reviewed by experts in industry and academe, and their feedback has been accounted for in the revision of these models. This exercise, coupled with the feedback obtained from actual field applications of the models, ensures to a certain degree that the models adequately cover the content domain.

To further ensure content validity, it is necessary that all assessment instruments include questions that adequately sample from the content domain. However, this requirement is easily met since most assessment instruments are derived directly from the best practice models.

8.1.2 Predictive Validity

A predictive validity study typically tests for a relationship between process capability and performance. This relationship is expected to be dependent upon some context factors (i.e., the relationship functional form or direction may be different for different contexts, or may exist only for some contexts).

The hypothesized model can be tested for different units of analysis [90]. The three units of analysis are the life cycle process (e.g., the design process), the project (which could be a composite of the capability of multiple life cycle processes of a single project, such as design and coding), or the organization (which could be a composite of the capability of the same or multiple processes across different projects). All of the three variables in the model can be measured at any one of these units of analysis.

The literature refers to measures at different units of analysis using different terminology. To remain consistent, we will use the term "process capability", and preface it with the unit of analysis where applicable. For example, one can make a distinction between measuring process capability, as in ISO/IEC 15504, and measuring organizational maturity, as in the SW-CMM [56]. Organizational maturity can be considered as a measure of organizational process capability.

8.2   Predictive Validity Hypotheses[31]

The basic hypotheses related to predictive validity can be explained with reference to Fig. 11 (see [27]). The first improvement that is expected when

---

[31] Material in this section is based partially on [136, 139].

process capability increases is in predictability. The difference between targeted results and actual results is expected to decrease. The second expected improvement is in control. The variation in actual results around target results gets narrower. The third expected improvement is in effectiveness. The actual

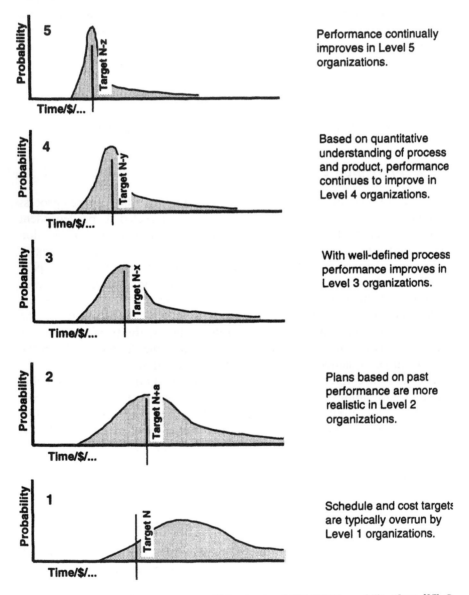

FIG. 11. Hypothesized improvements at higher levels of SW-CMM capability (from [27] © 1999 IEEE, reproduced with permission).

targeted results improve as process capability increases. The hypotheses can be stated with respect to project performance or organizational performance.

The predictive validity studies that have been performed focused on the first and third issues. Demonstrating a reduction in variation has, to our knowledge, not been studied.

8.3   Validation Approaches

Two classes of empirical studies have been conducted and reported thus far: case studies and correlational studies [90]. Case studies describe the experiences of a single organization (or a small number of selected organizations) and the benefits it gained from increasing its process capability. Case studies are most useful for showing that there are organizations that have benefited from increased process capability. Examples of these are reported in [79, 80, 82, 137, 138, 140–143] (see also [1] for a recent review). However, in this context, case studies have a methodological disadvantage that makes it difficult to generalize the results from a single case study or even a small number of case studies. Case studies tend to suffer from a selection bias because:

- Organizations that have not shown any process improvement or have even regressed will be highly unlikely to publicize their results, so case studies tend to show mainly success stories (e.g., all the references to case studies above are success stories), and

- The majority of organizations do not collect objective process and product data (e.g., on defect levels, or even keep accurate effort records). Only organizations that have made improvements and reached a reasonable level of maturity will have the actual objective data to demonstrate improvements (in productivity, quality, or return on investment). Therefore failures and non-movers are less likely to be considered as viable case studies due to the lack of data.

With correlational studies, one collects data from a larger number of organizations or projects and investigates relationships between process capability and performance statistically. Correlational studies are useful for showing whether a general association exists between increased capability and performance, and under what conditions.

Correlational approaches to evaluating the predictive validity of a process capability measure can be classified by the manner in which the variables are measured. Table XXVIII shows a classification of approaches. The columns indicate the manner in which the criterion is measured. The rows indicate the manner in which the process capability is measured. The criterion can be

TABLE XXVIII

DIFFERENT CORRELATIONAL APPROACHES FOR EVALUATING PREDICTIVE VALIDITY

	Measuring the criterion		
Measuring capability	Questionnaire	Measurement program	
Questionnaire	Q1	Q2	(low cost)
Assessment	Q3	Q4	(high cost)
	(across organizations)	(within one organization)	

measured using a questionnaire whereby data on the perceptions of experts are collected. It can also be measured through a measurement program. For example, if our criterion is defect density of delivered software products, then this could be measured through an established measurement program that collects data from defects found in the field. Process capability can also be measured through a questionnaire whereby data on the perceptions of experts on the capability of their processes are collected. Alternatively, actual assessments can be performed, which are a more rigorous form of measurement.[32]

A difficulty with studies that attempt to use criterion data collected through a measurement program is that the majority of organizations do not collect objective process and product data (e.g., on defect levels, or even keep accurate effort records). Primarily organizations that have made improvements and reached a reasonable level of process capability will have the actual objective data to demonstrate improvements (in productivity, quality, or return on investment). This assertion is supported by the results in [78] where, in general, it was found that organizations at lower SW-CMM maturity levels are less likely to collect quality data (such as the number of development defects). Also, the same authors found that organizations tend to collect more data as their CMM maturity levels rise. It was also reported in another survey [144] that for 300 measurement programs started since 1980, less than 75 were considered successful in 1990, indicating a high mortality rate for measurement programs. This high mortality rate indicates that it may be difficult right now to find many organizations that have implemented measurement programs.

This means that organizations or projects with low process capability would have to be excluded from a correlational study. Such an exclusion would reduce the variation in the performance measure, and thus reduce

---

[32] "More rigorous" is intended to imply greater reliability and construct validity.

(artificially) the validity coefficients. Therefore, correlational studies that utilize objective performance measures are inherently in greater danger of not finding significant results.

Furthermore, when criterion data are collected through a measurement program, it is necessary to have the criterion measured in the same way across all observations. This usually dictates that the study is done within a single organization where such measurement consistency can be enforced, hence reducing the generalizability of the results.

Conducting a study where capability is measured through an assessment as opposed to a questionnaire implies greater costs. This usually translates into smaller sample sizes and hence reduced statistical power. Therefore, the selection of a quadrant in Table XXVIII is a tradeoff among cost, measurement rigor, and generalizability.

Many previous studies that evaluated the relationship between process capability (or organizational maturity) and the performance of projects tended to be in quadrant Q1: For example, [72, 87, 145]. These studies have the advantage that they can be conducted across multiple projects and across multiple organizations, and hence can produce more generalizable conclusions.

A more recent study evaluated the relationship between questionnaire responses on implementation of the SW-CMM KPA's and defect density [146], and this would be placed in quadrant Q2. However, this study was conducted across multiple projects within a single organization, reducing its generalizability compared with studies conducted across multiple organizations.

The ISO/IEC 15504 studies in [136, 139] can be placed in quadrant Q3 since the authors use process capability measures from actual assessments, and questionnaires for evaluating project performance. This retains the advantage of studies in quadrant Q1 since it is conducted across multiple projects in multiple organizations, but utilizes a more rigorous measure of process capability. Similarly, the study of Jones can be considered to be in this quadrant [39, 147].[33]

---

[33] Since it is difficult to find low maturity organizations with objective data on effort and defect levels, and since there are few high maturity organizations, Jones' data relies on the reconstruction of, at least, effort data from memory, as noted in [148]: "The SPR approach is to ask the project team to reconstruct the missing elements from memory." The rationale for that is stated as "the alternative is to have null data for many important topics, and that would be far worse." The general approach is to show staff a set of standard activities, and then ask them questions such as which ones they used and whether they put in any unpaid overtime during the performance of these activities. For defect levels, the general approach is to do a matching between companies that do not measure their defects with similar companies that do measure, and then extrapolate for those that don't measure. It should be noted that SPR does have a large data base of project and organizational data, which makes this kind of matching defensible. However, since at least some of the criterion measures are not collected from measurement programs, we place this study in the same category as those that utilize questionnaires.

Studies in quadrant Q4 are likely to have the same limitations as studies in Q2: being conducted across multiple projects within the same organization. For instance, the study of McGarry *et al.* was conducted within a single company [149], and the AFIT study was conducted with contractors of the Air Force [150, 151].

Therefore, the different types of studies that can be conducted in practice have different advantages and disadvantages, and predictive validity studies have been conducted in the past that populate all four quadrants. It is reasonable then to encourage studies in all four quadrants. Consistency in the results across correlational studies that use the four approaches would increase the weight of evidence supporting the predictive validity hypothesis.

8.4 Main Effects

There have been a few correlational studies in the past that evaluated the predictive validity of various process capability measures. For example, Goldenson and Herbsleb [72] evaluated the relationship between SW-CMM capability ratings and organizational performance measures. They surveyed individuals whose organizations have been assessed against the SW-CMM. The authors evaluated the benefits of higher process capability using subjective measures of performance. Organizations with higher capability tend to perform better on the following dimensions (respondents chose either the "excellent" or "good" response categories when asked to characterize their organization's performance on these dimensions): ability to meet schedule, product quality, staff productivity, customer satisfaction, and staff morale. The relationship with the ability to meet budget commitments was not found to be statistically significant.

A more recent study considered the relationship between the implementation of the SW-CMM KPA's and delivered defects (after correcting for size and personnel capability) [146]. They found evidence that increasing process capability is associated with fewer delivered defects. Another correlational study investigated the benefits of moving up the maturity levels of the SW-CMM [150, 151] (also see the reanalysis of the data from this study in the appendix, section 10). They obtained data from historic US Air Force contracts. Two measures were considered:

- *cost performance index* which evaluates deviations in actual vs. planned project cost
- *schedule performance index* which evaluates the extent to which schedule has been over/under-run.

Generally, the results show that higher maturity projects approach on-target cost, and on-target schedule. McGarry *et al.* [149] investigated the relationship between assessment ratings using an adaptation of the SW-CMM process capability measures and project performance for 15 projects within a single organization. They did not find strong evidence of predictive validity, although they were all in the expected direction. Clark [87] investigated the relationship between satisfaction of SW-CMM goals and software project effort, after correcting for other factors such as size and personnel experience. His results indicate that the more KPAs are implemented, the less effort is consumed on projects. Jones presents the results of an analysis on the benefits of moving up the 7-level maturity scale of Software Productivity Research (SPR) Inc.'s proprietary model [39, 147]. This data were collected from SPR's clients. His results indicate that as organizations move from level 0 to level 6 on the model they witness (compound totals): 350% increase in productivity, 90% reduction in defects, 70% reduction in schedules.

Deephouse *et al.* evaluated the relationship between individual processes and project performance [145]. As would be expected, they found that evidence of predictive validity depends on the particular performance measure that is considered. One study by El Emam and Madhavji [117] evaluated the relationship between four dimensions of organizational process capability and the success of the requirements engineering process. Evidence of predictive validity was found for only one dimension.

The results from recent studies that evaluate the predictive validity of the process capability measures in ISO/IEC 15504 [136, 139] are shown in Table XXIX. In general, these indicate that process capability for some processes is related to performance, but mainly only for large organizations. The evidence for small organizations is rather weak.

Many software organizations are being assessed in terms of the clauses of ISO 9001. A number of surveys have been conducted that evaluate the benefits of ISO 9001 registration in industry in general and in software organizations in particular. Some of the results of these surveys have been presented in [170]. Below we summarize some of the relevant findings:

- One survey conducted in 1993 had 292 responses with almost 80% of the responding organizations being registered to ISO 9001. The findings included:
  - 74% felt that the benefits of registration outweighed the costs
  - 54% received favorable feedback from their customers after registration.
- A survey of companies in the UK had 340 responses from companies that were registered. It was found that 75% of the respondents felt that registration to ISO 9001 improved their product and/or service.

TABLE XXIX

SUMMARY OF THE FINDINGS FROM THE PREDICTIVE VALIDITY STUDY

Small organizations	
Ability to meet budget commitments	
Ability to meet schedule commitments	Develop software design
Ability to achieve customer satisfaction	
Ability to satisfy specified requirements	
Staff productivity	
Staff morale/job satisfaction	
Large organizations	
Ability to meet budget commitments	Develop software design
Implement software design	
Ability to meet schedule commitments	Develop software design
Ability to achieve customer satisfaction	Develop software design
Ability to satisfy specified requirements	Develop software design
Staff productivity	Develop software requirements
	Integrate and test software
Staff morale/job satisfaction	Develop software design

In the first column are the performance measures that were collected for each project. In the second column are the development processes whose capability was evaluated. The results are presented separately for small (≤ 50 IT staff) and large organizations (> 50 IT staff).

- A survey of companies that were registered in the USA and Canada with 620 responses found that:
  - the most important internal benefits to the organization included: better documentation (32.4%), greater quality awareness (25.6%), a positive cultural change (15%), and increased operational efficiency/productivity (9%)
  - the most important external benefits to the organization included: higher perceived quality (33.5%), improved customer satisfaction (26.6%), gaining a competitive edge (21.5%), and reduced customer quality audits (8.5%).
- A survey of 45 software organizations in Europe and North America that have become ISO 9001 registered found that:
  - 26% reported maximum benefit from increased efficiency
  - 23% reported maximum benefit from increased product reliability
  - 22% reported maximum benefit from improved marketing activity
  - 14% reported maximum benefit from cost savings
  - 6% reported maximum benefit from increases exports.

Thus, with respect to registration to ISO 9001, the few studies that have been conducted are consistent in their findings of benefits to registration.

However, many of these studies were not specific to software organizations. Therefore, more research specifically with software organizations would help the community better understand the effects of registration.

8.5   Moderating Effects

A recent article noted that existing evidence suggests that the extent to which a project's or organization's performance improves due to the implementation of good software engineering practices (i.e., increasing process capability) is dependent on the context [152]. This highlights the need to consider the project and/or organizational context in predictive validity studies. However, it has also been noted that the overall evidence remains equivocal as to which context factors should be considered in predictive validity studies [152].

One of the important moderating variables that has been mentioned repeatedly in the literature is organizational size. Previous studies provide inconsistent results about the effect of organizational size. For example, there have been some concerns that the implementation of some of the practices in the CMM, such as a separate quality assurance function and formal documentation of policies and procedures, would be too costly for small organizations [153]. Therefore, the implementation of certain processes or process management practices may not be as cost-effective for small organizations as for large ones. However, a moderated analysis of the relationship between organizational capability and requirements engineering process success [152] (using the data set originally used in [117]) found that organizational size does not affect predictive validity. This result is consistent with that found in [72] for organization size and [145] for project size, but is at odds with the findings from [136, 139, 153].

To further confuse the issue, an earlier investigation [154] studied the relationship between the extent to which software development processes are standardized and MIS success.[34] It was found that standardization of life cycle processes was associated with MIS success in smaller organizations but not in large ones. This is in contrast to the findings cited above. Therefore, it is not clear if and how organization size moderates the benefits of process and the implementation of process management practices.

8.6   Diminishing Rates of Return

Some studies suggest that there may be diminishing returns with greater process capability. For example, the functional form of the relationship

---

[34] Process standardization is a recurring theme in process capability measures.

between the SW-CMM based maturity measure and field defects as reported in [146] is shown in Fig. 12. As can be seen there, the number of defects decreases as process capability increases. However, the rate of the decrease diminishes and further improvements in process capability produce only marginal improvements in field defects.[35]

A similar interpretation can be made based on the results of Clark's analysis [87]. In that study, the process measure was coded so that smaller values mean higher capability. Larger values mean smaller capability. The functional form of the relationship in that study is shown in Fig. 13. As process capability increases, person-months spent on the projects decrease. That is, there tends to be greater productivity. Similar to the previous study, however, the rate of decrease goes down as process capability increases.[36]

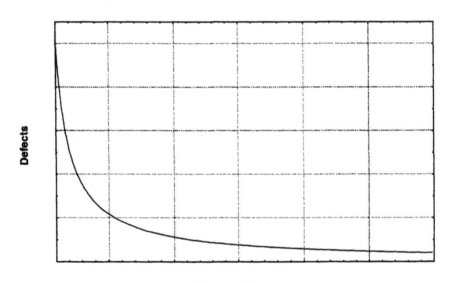

Process Measure

FIG. 12. Functional form of the relationship between the process measure and number of defects found (from [146]). We do not show the values on the axes since they would be meaningless without describing in detail how process capability was measured. This is not necessary here, since we are only interested in showing the functional form of the relationship.

---

[35] The authors controlled for the size of the product in their analysis, so the graph can be interpreted as applicable regardless of product size.

[36] Also similar to the other study, the model adjusted statistically for the effect of size and other covariates.

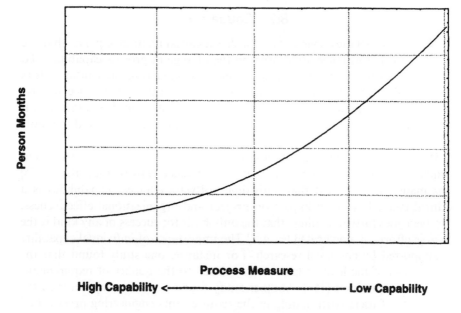

FIG. 13. Functional form of the relationship between the process measure and person-months (from [87]). We do not show the values on the axes since they would be meaningless without describing in detail how process capability was measured. This is not necessary here, since we are only interested in showing the functional form of the relationship.

These results do suggest that there may be diminishing returns at higher levels of process capability, at least with respect to product defects and development effort. However, the results should not be overinterpreted. There are no software projects that take zero time to complete, and the proportion of software products in the world that originally shipped with zero defects is likely rather small. Such ceiling/floor effects, associated with the measures of effort and quality may appear in the form of asymptotic limits in the relationships studied.

Depending on an organization's quality goals, there is still room for improvement until one reaches zero defects. Continuing attention to process capability may be necessary to maintain such patterns over time, particularly if the remaining defects may differ in severity. Moreover, at higher levels of capability, organizations may choose to focus on other aspects of process and product improvement. The point where the rate of return is "not worth the additional effort" remains an empirical question.

8.7   Causality

None of the studies reviewed establishes a causal relationship, i.e., that the changes in performance are caused by the change in process capability. To establish causation one must at least rule out other possible causal factors that could have led to the performance changes (also, experience reports documenting benefits of SPI would have to rule out natural progress, i.e., if the organization did not make any changes, would it have achieved the same benefits?).

It is clear that implementation of processes or process management practices are not the only factors that will influence performance. Bach [155] has made the argument that individual software engineer capabilities is a critical factor having an impact on project and organizational effectiveness. He even goes further, stating "that the only basis for success of any kind is the 'heroic efforts of a dedicated team.'" The importance of individual capability is supported by empirical research. For instance, one study found that the capabilities of the lead architect were related to the quality of requirements engineering products [156]. Another study found a relationship between the capability of users participating in the requirements engineering process and its success [157]. Other field studies of requirements and design processes also emphasized the importance of individual capabilities [158, 159].

The implementation of automated tools has been advocated as a factor that has an impact on effectiveness. This assertion is supported by empirical research. For instance, one study of the implementation of an Information Engineering toolset achieved increases in productivity and decreases in post-release failures [160].

The best that can be attained with studies that focus only on process factors is strong evidence that process capability is associated with performance or that organizations could benefit from SPI activities. In order to improve our understanding of the influences of other factors on performance more sophisticated empirical studies would have to be conducted. These would include building multivariate models that take the influence of non-process factors into account and investigate the interactions between process and non-process factors. Good current examples of these are the studies in [87, 146].

8.8   Summary

In summary, we can make the following general statements:

- There is ample evidence through case studies that higher process capability is associated with improved performance. These demonstrate that it is plausible to improve performance as capability is improved.

- The results of more methodologically defensible predictive validity studies of capability measures tend to demonstrate an association between increased process capability and increased performance. Performance was measured both at the project and organizational levels. No evidence exists to our knowledge that demonstrates a reduction in variability in performance as process capability increases.

- Current studies indicate potential diminishing rates of return to increased process capability. It is not yet clear whether this means that there exists a maximal gain from SPI based on contemporary best practice models or whether the effect observed in the studies is a statistical artifact. This is a topic that should be further investigated in future studies.

- Few predictive validity studies attempt to control confounding variables. This should be an area deserving of more methodological attention in future studies.

9   Appendix

9.1   An Overview of the SPICE Trials

There has been a general concern among some researchers that existing software engineering standards lack an empirical basis demonstrating that they indeed represent "good" practices. For instance, it has been noted that [161] "standards have codified approaches whose effectiveness has not been rigorously and scientifically demonstrated. Rather, we have too often relied on anecdote, 'gut feeling', the opinions of experts, or even flawed research", and [162] "many corporate, national and international standards are based on conventional wisdom [as opposed to empirical evidence]." Similar arguments are made in [163–165].

Unique among software engineering standardization efforts, the developers of ISO/IEC 15504 deliberately initiated an international effort to empirically evaluate ISO/IEC 15504. This effort is known as the SPICE trials [60, 166, 168].

The SPICE trials have been divided into three broad phases to coincide with the stages that the ISO/IEC 15504 document was expected to go through on its path to international standardization. The analyses presented in this chapter come from phase 2 of the SPICE trials.

During the trials, organizations contribute their assessment ratings data to an international trials database located in Australia, and also fill up a series of questionnaires after each assessment. The questionnaires collect information about the organization and about the assessment. There is a network of SPICE trials co-ordinators around the world who interact directly with the assessors and the organizations conducting the assessments. This interaction involves ensuring that assessors are qualified, making questionnaires available, answering queries about the questionnaires, and following up to ensure the timely collection of data. A total of 70 assessments had been conducted within the context of the trials (phase 2). The distribution of assessments by region is given in Fig. 14.[37] In total 691 process instances were assessed. Since more than one assessment may have occurred in a particular organization (e.g., multiple assessments each one looking at a different set of processes), a total of 44 organizations were assessed. Their distribution by region is given in Fig. 15.

Given that an assessor can participate in more than one assessment, the number of assessors is smaller than the total number of assessments. In total, 40 different lead assessors took part. The variation in the number of years of software engineering experience and assessment experience of the assessors is shown in Fig. 16. The median experience in software engineering is 12 years, with a maximum of 30 years experience. The median experience in assessments is 3 years, indicating a non-trivial background in assessments.

The median number of assessments performed in the past by the assessors is six, and the median number of 15504-based assessments is two. This indicates that, in general, assessors had a good amount of experience with software process assessments.

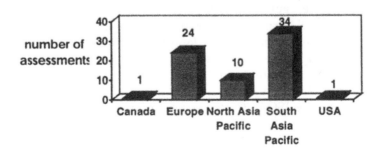

FIG. 14. Distribution of assessments by region.

---

[37] Within the SPICE trials, assessments are coordinated within each of the five regions shown in the figures above.

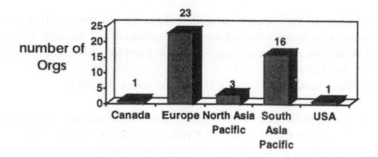

FIG. 15. Distribution of assessed organizations by region.

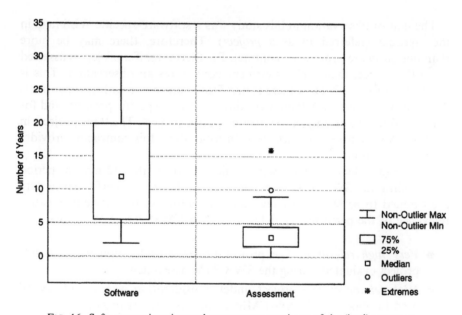

FIG. 16. Software engineering and assessment experience of the (lead) assessors.

9.2   A Reanalysis of the AFIT Study Data

The authors provide a detailed report of a predictive validity study of the SW-CMM maturity rating [150, 151, 169] using historic Air Force contracts data. Specifically, they looked at the relationship between SW-CMM maturity ratings and the ability to meet budget and schedule targets. The advantage of the data set that they use is that all contractors have to report project cost and schedule data in a consistent format, ensuring comparability of data across projects. The Air Force product centers from which data were collected were the Aeronautical Systems Center at Wright-Patterson Air Force base, and the Electronic Systems Center at Hanscom Air Force Base.

The authors used the following criteria to select projects:

- software specific cost and schedule data were tracked according to Cost/Schedule Control System Criteria (C/SCSC) guidelines
- the contractors were rated against the SW-CMM
- the relevance of the cost and schedule data to the SW-CMM rating could be established.

The unit of observation in this study was a software-specific WBS item in the contract (referred to as a *project*). Therefore, there may be more than one software project per contract. Furthermore, if a project is assessed more than once, then each assessment constitutes an observation. This is illustrated in Fig. 17. Here there is one DoD contractor with two contracts A and B. For contract A there were three software specific projects, and for contract B there was only one software-specific project. The three projects in contract A were assessed twice each. In total, then, this contractor provides seven observations.[38]

Cost and schedule data were collected over the 12-month period surrounding the SW-CMM assessment date. Hence, the performance data are claimed to be temporally relevant. The authors also define associative relevance of the performance data to the SW-CMM rating as follows:

- *Very high relevance*: The project under consideration was the sole project evaluated during the SW-CMM assessment.
- *High relevance:* The project under consideration was one of several used in obtaining the SW-CMM rating for the organization.
- *Medium relevance:* The project under consideration was not used to establish the SW-CMM rating, but the organization or personnel who participated in the project were also responsible for projects evaluated in the SW-CMM assessment.
- *Low relevance:* Neither the project nor the personnel responsible for the project under consideration were used to obtain the organization's SW-CMM rating; the rating for the contractor as a whole is considered to apply to the organization responsible for the project under consideration.

---

[38] Strictly speaking, under this scheme, the observations for the three projects in contract A are not independent, hence violating one of the assumptions of statistical tests.

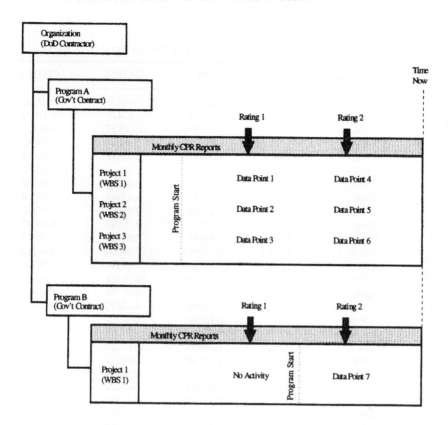

FIG. 17. Relationship between rating period, project, and contract.

For the purposes of our analyses, we only considered the very high relevance and high relevance projects. Furthermore, we excluded all assessments that were performed using the SCE method. The reason is that the focus of this paper is process improvement, and the SCE is essentially an audit rather than assessment. It is known that an assessment for the purposes of capability evaluation and for process improvement can yield different results for the same organization [103]. Finally, we also ignored all observations which the authors themselves deemed of dubious quality. We end up with data on 25 software projects, and these are included in Table XXX. The authors did not perform an analysis with this particular subset, which is the subset most relevant for this review. Also note that none of the projects rated had a maturity rating greater than 3.

The performance criteria were intended to measure ability to meet budget and schedule targets. These are defined as follows.

TABLE XXX

SUBSET OF THE AFIT DATA USED FOR THE ANALYSIS PRESENTED IN THIS PAPER

	CMM rating	SPI	CPI	SPIDEV	CPIDEV
1	3.000	0.954	1.03526	0.04626	0.03526
2	3.000	1.024	1.11050	0.02420	0.11050
3	3.000	1.007	1.06107	0.00725	0.06107
4	3.000	0.934	1.04982	0.06646	0.04982
5	1.000	1.056	0.84981	0.05599	0.15019
6	3.000	1.026	1.12719	0.02618	0.12719
7	3.000	0.987	0.98222	0.01318	0.01778
8	2.000	0.966	0.38626	0.03404	0.61374
9	1.000	1.868	0.20188	0.86762	0.79812
10	2.000	1.077	0.34957	0.07744	0.65043
11	2.000	1.047	0.83683	0.04736	0.16317
12	3.000	1.000	0.96737	0.00000	0.03263
13	3.000	1.172	0.79640	0.17241	0.20360
14	3.000	1.086	0.98556	0.08641	0.01444
15	3.000	1.092	0.95995	0.09190	0.04005
16	3.000	1.221	0.79240	0.22072	0.20760
17	2.000	0.973	0.86808	0.02737	0.13192
18	2.000	1.000	1.21799	0.00000	0.21799
19	2.000	0.908	1.45455	0.09220	0.45455
20	2.000	0.904	1.11139	0.09572	0.11139
21	2.000	0.915	1.75556	0.08494	0.75556
22	2.000	0.988	2.05063	0.01220	1.05063
23	2.000	0.919	0.77919	0.08144	0.22081
24	2.000	0.973	1.14790	0.02713	0.14790
25	1.000	0.551	0.23626	0.44935	0.76374

The projected rate of funds expenditure (the baseline) is expressed in the *budgeted cost of work scheduled* (BCWS). The *budgeted cost of work performed* (BCWP) represents the earned value of the work performed, and is an estimate of the work completed in dollars. The difference between the BCWS and BCWP is the schedule variance expressed in dollars, and captures the amount of work which was scheduled but not performed. The *actual cost of work performed* (ACWP) is the sum of funds actually expended in the accomplishment of the planned work tasks. Cost variance is the difference between what the project was expected to cost (BCWP) and what the project actually cost (ACWP).

Two indices were then defined. The *schedule performance index* (SPI) was defined as:

$$SPI = BCWP/BCWS \tag{3}$$

An SPI value less than 1 implies that for every dollar of work scheduled, less than one dollar has been earned—a schedule *overrun*. An SPI of more than 1 implies that for each dollar of work scheduled, more than one dollar of work has been earned—a schedule *underrun*. An SPI of 1 implies that the project was on-target. Similarly for cost we have the *cost performance index* (CPI):

$$CPI = BCWP/ACWP \qquad (4)$$

A CPI value less than 1 indicates a cost overrun, a value greater than 1 indicates a cost underrun, and a value of 1 indicates an on-target condition.

The hypothesis that the authors were testing was explicitly stated as

> Given that the goal of any project is to meet the target budget and schedule, an organization's success can be measured by evaluating the CPI and SPI of a particular project. The closer the CPI and SPI are to the value of 1.00, the more successful the project can be considered, at least in terms of cost and schedule. Thus, it is reasonable to expect that as an organization's process matures, its success or ability to consistently meet target budgets and schedules will increase [150].

In fact, this is the general SW-CMM hypothesis stated as "As maturity increases, the difference between targeted results and actual results decreases across projects."

The authors then proceed to test this hypothesis using the Kruskal–Wallis test [76]. This allows the authors to test the null hypothesis that there is no difference (in the medians) among projects in each of the groups, where each group is characterized by its maturity rating (there were three groups with maturity levels 1, 2, and 3). The alternative hypothesis is that there is a difference among the groups, which would be the case if the above hypothesis was true.

However, the actual hypothesis that one wants to investigate is not whether there is any difference among the groups, but that there is better improvement as one moves from level 1 to level 3. Therefore, the alternative hypothesis is an ordered one. A better statistical test to use is therefore the Jonckheere–Terpstra (JT) test [167], which is more powerful than the Kruskal–Wallis test for ordered alternatives.

The data for the SPI performance measure are shown in Fig. 18. It is seen that the median value for level 1 projects is slightly above 1 but has a large variance. It drops below 1 for level 2 projects, and goes back again above one for level 3. The JT test produces a J value of 1.446 which has a one-sided asymptotic p-value of 0.074. This indicates that indeed there is an ordered association between SPI and maturity levels at an alpha level of 0.1.

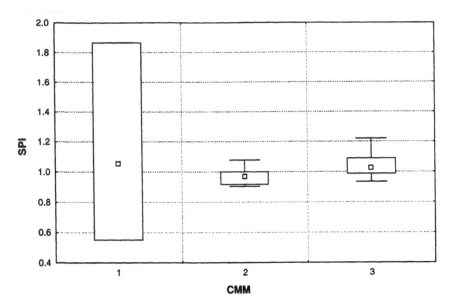

FIG. 18. SPI values for the three levels. The J is 1.446.

The data for CPI are shown in Fig. 19. As can be seen there is a dramatic shift from gross cost overruns for level 1 to almost meeting cost targets at levels 2 and 3. The JT test, however, produced a value of J of 0.9554, which has an asymptotic one-sided p-value of 0.1697, indicating lack of statistical significance at an alpha level of 0.1.

The above results would seem to indicate that there is a relationship between meeting schedule targets and SW-CMM maturity ratings, but not with meeting cost targets.

However, a careful examination of the hypothesis that is being stated indicates that we are actually testing the wrong hypothesis quantitatively. The hypothesis that was tested above was whether higher level projects tend to underrun their costs and schedules targets. Thus, if level 3 projects dramatically underrun costs and schedule targets then the results would be overwhelming good using the above approach. The hypothesis that we want to test is whether higher maturity is associated with meeting schedule and cost targets, not underrun them (i.e., SPI and CPI closer to 1, not greater than 1). It is known in the literature that both overrunning targets and underrunning targets is undesirable.

A proper test of the SW-CMM hypothesis as stated would therefore be to use the JT test with the following performance measures:

$$SPIDEV = |(BCWP - BCWS)/BCWS| \qquad (5)$$

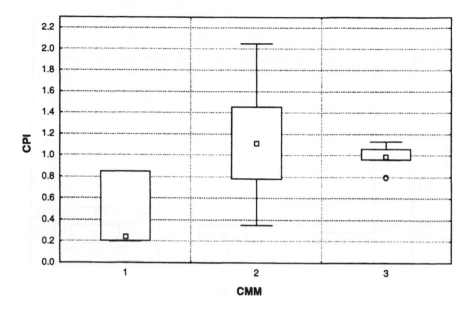

FIG. 19. CPI values for the three levels. The J is 0.9554.

and

$$CPIDEV = |(BCWP - ACWP)/ACWP| \qquad (6)$$

These deviation indices will increase as one deviates from target, over or under, and would provide the correct test of the hypothesis.

Figure 20 shows the data expressed in terms of SPIDEV. Here we see a clear decrease in deviation from target as maturity level increases. The J value of -1.291 has an asymptotic one-sided p-value of 0.0983, which is statistically significant at an alpha level of 0.1.

Similarly, the results for the CPIDEV variable are illustrated in Fig. 21. The J value of -3.744 is highly statistically significant with an asymptotic one-sided p-value of 0.0001.

Therefore, our reanalysis of the AFIT data made two methodological contributions. First, we used the JT test which is known to be more powerful for ordered alternatives than the K–W test used by the authors. Second, we argued that the original analysis was not testing the authors' own hypothesis nor the SW-CMM hypothesis, and therefore we modified the performance measures to actually measure deviations from targets and used that directly.

Our results indicate that there is an association between higher capability level ratings and the ability to meet schedule and cost targets.

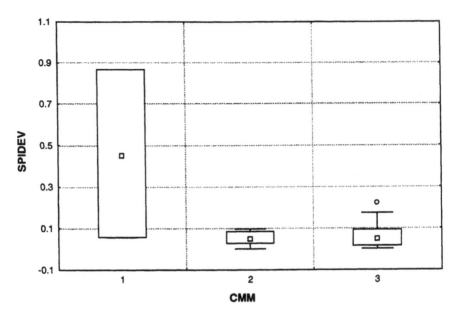

FIG. 20. SPIDEV values for the three levels. The J is -1.291.

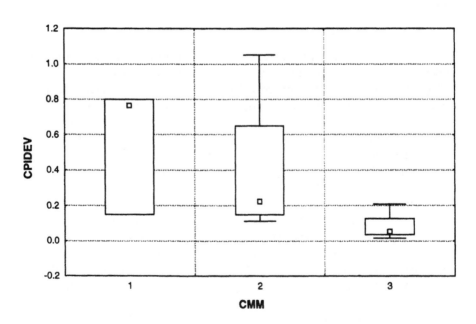

FIG. 21. CPIDEV values for the three levels. The J is -3.744.

ACKNOWLEDGEMENTS

We wish to thank Will Hayes and Shadia El Egazzar for providing us with thorough reviews of earlier versions of this chapter.

CMM and Capability Maturity Model are registered in the US Patent and Trademark Office. SM CMMI and IDEAL are service marks of Carnegie Mellon University. The Software Engineering Institute (SEI) is a federally funded research and development center sponsored by the US Department of Defense and operated by Carnegie Mellon University.

REFERENCES

[1] Krasner, H. (1999). The payoff for software process improvement: what it is and how to get it. In *Elements of Software Process Assessment and Improvement*, ed. K. El Emam and N. H. Madhavji, IEEE CS Press, New York.

[2] McGibbon, T. (1999). A business case for software process improvement revised: measuring return on investment from software engineering and management. DoD Data and Analysis Center for Software (DACS), Technical Report, September (available from *www.dacs.dtic.mil/techs/roispi2/roispi2.pdf*).

[3] Card, D. (1991). Understanding process improvement. *IEEE Software*, July, 102–103.

[4] Software Engineering Laboratory (1995). *Software Process Improvement Guidebook*. NASA/GSFC, Technical Report SEL-95-002.

[5] Software Engineering Institute (1995). *The Capability Maturity Model: Guidelines for Improving the Software Process*. Addison-Wesley, Reading, MA.

[6] El Emam, K., Drouin, J.-N. and Melo, W. (1998). *SPICE: Theory and Practice of Software Process Improvement and Capability Determination*. IEEE CS Press, New York.

[7] Nolan, R. (1973). Managing the computer resource: a stage hypothesis. *Communications of the ACM*, 16(7), 399–405.

[8] Dunaway, D. and Masters, S. (1996). CMM-based appraisal for internal process improvement (CBA IPI): method description. Technical Report CMU/SEI-96-TR-007, Software Engineering Institute.

[9] Nolan, R. (1979). Managing the crisis in data processing. *Harvard Business Review*, March/April, 115–126.

[10] Ahituv, N. and Neumann, S. (1982). *Principles of Information Systems for Management*. W. Brown,

[11] Alter, S. (1980). *Decision Support Systems: Current Practices and Continuing Challenges*. Addison-Wesley, Reading, MA.

[12] Ein-Dor, P. and Segev, E. (1978). *Managing Management Information Systems*. Lexington.

[13] Keen, P. and Scott Morton, M. (1978). *Decision Support Systems: An Organizational Perspective*. Addison-Wesley, Reading, MA.

[14] Gibson, C. and Nolan, R. (1974). Behavioral and organizational issues in the stages of managing the computer resource. In *Managing the Data Resource Function*, ed. R. Nolan. West Publishing Company.

[15] Gibson, C. and Nolan, R. (1974). Managing the four stages of EDP growth. *Harvard Business Review*, 76–88.

[16] Nolan, R. (1975). Thoughts about the fifth stage. *Database*, 7(2), 4–10.

[17] Benbasat, I., Dexter, A. and Mantha, R. (1980). Impact of organizational maturity on information system skill needs. *MIS Quarterly*, 4(1), 21–34.

[18] Lucas, H. and Sutton, J. (1977). The stage hypothesis and the S-curve: some contradictory evidence. *Communications of the ACM*, 20(4), 254–259.

[19] Goldstein, R. and McCririck, I. (1981). The stage hypothesis and data administration: some contradictory evidence. *Proceedings of the 2nd International Conference on Information Systems*, pp. 309–324.

[20] Drury, D. (1983). An empirical assessment of the stages of data processing growth. *MIS Quarterly*, **7**(2), 59–70.

[21] Benbasat, I., Dexter, A., Drury, D. and Goldstein, R. (1984). A critique of the stage hypothesis: theory and empirical evidence. *Communications of the ACM*, **27**(5), 476–485.

[22] King, J. and Kraemer, K. (1984). Evolution and organizational information systems: an assessment of Nolan's stage model. *Communications of the ACM*, **27**(5), 466–475.

[23] Huff, S., Munro, M. and Martin, B. (1988). Growth stages of end user computing. *Communications of the ACM*, **31**(5), 542–550.

[24] Gregoire, J.-F. and Lustman, F. (1993). The stage hypothesis revisited: an EDP professionals' point of view. *Information and Management*, **24**, 237–245.

[25] Humphrey, W. (1988). Characterizing the software process: a maturity framework. *IEEE Software*, March, 73–79.

[26] Radice, R., Harding, J., Munnis, P. and Phillips, R. (1985). A programming process study. *IBM Systems Journal*, **24**(2), 91–101.

[27] Paulk, M., Weber, C. and Chrissis, M.-B. (1999). The capability maturity model for software. In *Elements of Software Process Assessment and Improvement*, ed. K. El Emam and N. H. Madhavji, IEEE CS Press.

[28] Humphrey, W. and Sweet, W. (1987). A method for assessing the software engineering capability of contractors. Technical Report CMU/SEI-87-TR-23, Software Engineering Institute.

[29] Drouin, J.-N. (1998). Introduction to SPICE. In *SPICE: Theory and Practice of Software Process Improvement and Capability Determination*, ed. K. El Emam, J-N Drouin and W. Melo, IEEE CS Press.

[30] Coallier, F., Mayrand, J. and Lague, B. (1999). Risk management in software product procurement. In *Elements of Software Process Assessment and Improvement*, ed. K. El Emam and N. Madhavji, IEEE CS Press.

[31] Craigmyle, M. and Fletcher, I. (1993). Improving IT effectiveness through software process assessment. *Software Quality Journal*, **2**, 257–264.

[32] Sommerville, I. and Sawyer, P. (1997). *Requirements Engineering: A Good Practice Guide*. John Wiley, New York.

[33] Burnstein, I., Suwannasart, T. and Carlson, C. (1996). Developing a testing maturity model: Part I. *Crosstalk*, August, 21–24.

[34] Burnstein, I., Suwannasart, T. and C. Carlson (1996). Developing a testing maturity model: Part II. *Crosstalk*, September, 19–24.

[35] Budlong, F. and Peterson, J. (1995). *Software Metrics Capability Evaluation Guide*. Software Technology Support Center, Ogden Air Logistics Center, Hill Air Force Base.

[36] Software Engineering Institute (1994). *A Systems Engineering Capability Maturity Model, Version 1.0*. Handbook CMU/SEI-94-HB-04, Software Engineering Institute.

[37] Curtis, B., Hefley, W., Miller, S. and Konrad, M. (1999). The people capability maturity model for improving the software workforce. In *Elements of Software Process Assessment and Improvement*, ed. K. El Emam and N. Madhavji, IEEE CS Press.

[38] Drew, D. (1992). Tailoring the Software Engineering Institute's (SEI) Capability Maturity Model (CMM) to a software sustaining engineering organization. *Proceedings of the International Conference on Software Maintenance*, pp. 137–144.

[39] Jones, C. (1999). The economics of software process improvements. In *Elements of Software Process Assessment and Improvement*, ed. K. El Emam and N. H. Madhavji, IEEE CS Press.

[40] Bootstrap Project Team (1993). Bootstrap: Europe's Assessment Method. *IEEE Software*, May, pp. 93–95.

[41] Haase, V., Messnarz, R., Koch, *et al.* (1994). Bootstrap: fine-tuning process assessment. *IEEE Software*, July, pp. 25–35.

[42] Steinen, H. (1999). Software process assessment and improvement: 5 years of experiences with Bootstrap. In *Elements of Software Process Assessment and Improvement*, ed. K. El Emam and N. Madhavji, IEEE CS Press.

[43] Paulk, M. (1995). The evolution of the SEI's capability maturity model for software. *Software Process—Improvement and Practice*, Pilot Issue, 1–15.

[44] ISO/IEC TR 15504 (1998). *Information Technology—Software Process Assessment*. (parts 1–9; part 5 was published in 1999). Available from *www.seq.itt.nrc.ca/spice*.

[45] Herbsleb, J., Zubrow, D., Goldenson, D. *et al.* (1997). Software quality and the capability maturity model. *Communications of the ACM*, **40**(6), 30–40.

[46] Hersh, A. (1993). Where's the return on process improvement? *IEEE Software*, July, 12.

[47] Fenton, N. (1993). Objectives and context of measurement/experimentation. In *Experimental Software Engineering Issues: Critical Assessment and Future Directions*, ed. H. D. Rombach, V. Basili, and R. Selby, Springer-Verlag, Berlin.

[48] Jones, C. (1995). Gaps in SEI programs. *Software Development*, **3**(3), 41–48.

[49] Gray, E. and Smith, W. (1998). On the limitations of software process assessment and the recognition of a required re-orientation for global process improvement. *Software Quality Journal*, **7**, 21–34.

[50] Pfleeger, S.-L. (1999). Understanding and improving technology transfer in software engineering. *Journal of Systems and Software*, **47**, 111–124.

[51] Benbasat, I. and Zmud, R. (1999). Empirical research in information systems: the practice of relevance. *MIS Quarterly*, **23**(1), 3–16.

[52] Herbsleb, J. (1998). Hard problems and hard science: on the practical limits of experimentation. *IEEE TCSE Software Process Newsletter*, 11, 18–21. (available at *www.seq.iit.nrc.ca/spn*)

[53] Raghavan, S. and Chand, D. (1989). Diffusing software-engineering methods. *IEEE Software*, July, 81–90.

[54] Weissfelner, S. (1999). ISO 9001 for software organizations. *Elements of Software Process Assessment and Improvement*, ed. K. El Emam and N. Madhavji, IEEE CS Press.

[55] McFeeley, B. (1996). IDEAL: a user's guide for software process improvement. Technical Report CMU/SEI-96-HB-001, February, Software Engineering Institute.

[56] Paulk, M. and Konrad, M. (1994). Measuring process capability versus organizational process maturity. *Proceedings of the 4th International Conference on Software Quality*, October.

[57] Dunaway, D. (1996). *CMM-Based Appraisal for Internal Process Improvement (CBA IPI) Lead Assessor's Guide*. Handbook CMU/SEI-96-HB-003, Software Engineering Institute.

[58] Kitson, D. and Masters, S. (1993). An analysis of SEI software process assessment results: 1987–1991. *Proceedings of the International Conference on Software Engineering*, pp. 68–77.

[59] Simon, J.-M. (1998). Assessment using SPICE: a case study. In *SPICE: Theory and Practice of Software Process Improvement and Capability Determination*, ed. K. El Emam, J-N Drouin, and W. Melo, IEEE CS Press.

[60] Maclennan, F., Ostrolenk, G. and Tobin, M. (1998). Introduction to the SPICE Trials. In *SPICE: Theory and Practice of Software Process Improvement and Capability Determination*, ed. K. El Emam, J.-N. Drouin and W. Melo, IEEE CS Press.

[61] Klein, D. (1998). If you get straight A's, you must be intelligent—respecting the intent of the capability maturity model. *Crosstalk*, February, pp. 22–23.

[62] Dymond, K. (1999). Essence and accidents in SEI-style assessments or "maybe this time the voice of the engineer will be heard." In *Elements of Software Process Assessment and Improvement*, ed. K. El Emam and N. Madhavji, IEEE CS Press.

[63] Saiedian, H. and Kuzara, R. (1995). SEI capability maturity model's impact on contractors. *IEEE Computer*, January, 16–26.

[64] Rugg, D. (1993). Using a capability evaluation to select a contractor. *IEEE Software*, July, 36–45.

[65] Dadoun, G. (1992). ISO 9000: a requirement for doing business. *Proceedings of the CAS (Centre for Advanced Studies) Conference*, IBM Canada Ltd., pp. 433–437.

[66] Huebner, A. (1992). ISO 9000 implementation in software development of IBM Germany. Paper presented at SDC 1992, IBM, Application development Germany, 7 May.

[67] Herbsleb, J. and Grinter, R. (1998). Conceptual simplicity meets organizational complexity: case study of a corporate metrics program. *Proceedings of the 20th International Conference on Software Engineering*, pp. 271–280.

[68] Dunaway, D., Goldenson, D., Monarch, I. and White, D. (1998). How well is CBA IPI working? User feedback. *Proceedings of the 1998 Software Engineering Process Group Conference*.

[69] Rubin, D. (1987). *Multiple Imputation for Nonresponse in Surveys*. John Wiley, New York.

[70] SPIRE Project (1998). *The SPIRE Handbook: Better Faster Cheaper Software Development in Small Companies*. ESSI Project 23873, November.

[71] El Emam, K. and Goldenson, D. (1996). An empirical evaluation of the prospective international SPICE standard. *Software Process—Improvement and Practice*, **2**, 123–148.

[72] Goldenson, D. R. and Herbsleb, J. D. (1995). After the appraisal: a systematic survey of process improvement, its benefits, and factors that influence success. Technical Report, CMU/SEI-95-TR-009, Software Engineering Institute.

[73] Drehmer, D. and Dekleva, S. (1993). Measuring software engineering maturity: a Rasch calibration. *Proceedings of the International Conference on Information Systems*, pp. 191–202.

[74] Buchman, C. (1996). Software process improvement at AlliedSignal Aerospace. *Proceedings of the 29th Annual Hawaii International Conference on Systems Science, Vol. 1: Software Technology and Architecture*, pp. 673–680.

[75] El Emam, K., Smith, B., and Fusaro, P. (1999). Success factors and barriers for software process improvement: an empirical study. In *Better Software Practice for Business Benefit: Principles and Experiences*, ed. R. Messnarz and C. Tully, IEEE CS Press.

[76] Siegel, S. and Castellan, N. J. (1988). *Nonparametric Statistics for the Behavioral Sciences*. McGraw-Hill, New York.

[77] Stelzer, D. and Mellis, W. (1998). Success factors of organizational change in software process improvement. *Software Process—Improvement and Practice*. **4**(4), 227–250.

[78] Brodman, J. and Johnson, D. (1995). Return on investment (ROI) from software process improvement as measured by US industry. *Software Process: Improvement and Practice*, Pilot Issue, pp. 35–47.

[79] Humphrey, W., Snyder, T. and Willis, R. (1991). Software process improvement at Hughes Aircraft. *IEEE Software*, July, 11–23.

[80] Wohlwend, H. and Rosenbaum, S. (1993). Software improvements in an international company. *Proceedings of the International Conference on Software Engineering*, pp. 212–220.

[81] Brodman, J. and Johnson, D. (1996). Return on investment from software process improvement as measured by US industry. *Crosstalk*, **9**(4), 23–29.

[82] Dion, R. (1993). Process improvement and the corporate balance sheet. *IEEE Software*, **10**(4), 28–35.

[83] Hayes, W. and Zubrow, D. (1995). Moving on up: data and experience doing CMM-based process improvement. Technical Report CMU/SEI-95-TR-008, Software Engineering Institute.

[84] Rahhal, S. (1995). An effort estimation model for implementing ISO 9001 in software organizations. Master's thesis, School of Computer Science, McGill University, October.

[85] Kim, J. and Mueller, C. (1978). *Factor Analysis: Statistical Methods and Practical Issues.* Sage, Thousand Oaks, CA.

[86] Curtis, B. (1996). The factor structure of the CMM and other latent issues. Paper presented at the *Empirical Studies of Programmers: 6th Workshop*, Washington DC.

[87] Clark, B. (1997). The effects of software process maturity on software development effort. PhD thesis, University of Southern California, April.

[88] El Emam, K. (1998). The internal consistency of the ISO/IEC 15504 software process capability scale. *Proceedings of the 5th International Symposium on Software Metrics*, pp. 72–81, IEEE CS Press.

[89] El Emam, K. and Goldenson, D. R. (1995). SPICE: An empiricist's perspective. *Proceedings of the 2nd IEEE International Software Engineering Standards Symposium*, August, pp. 84–97.

[90] Goldenson, D., El Emam, K., Herbsleb, J. and Deephouse, C. (1999). Empirical studies of software process assessment methods. In *Elements of Software Process Assessment and Improvement*, ed. K. El Emam and N. H. Madhavji, IEEE CS Press.

[91] El Emam, K. (1999). Academic Publishers. Benchmarking kappa: interrater agreement in software process assessments. *Empirical Software Engineering: An International Journal*, **4**, 113–133.

[92] El Emam, K. and I. Garro: Estimating the extent of standards use: the case of ISO/IEC 15504. To appear in *Journal of Systems and Software* (2000).

[93] Bollinger, T. and McGowan. C. (1991). A critical look at software capability evaluations. *IEEE Software*, July, pp. 25–41.

[94] El Emam, K., Smith, B. and Fusaro, P. (1997). Modeling the reliability of SPICE based assessments. *Proceedings of the 3rd IEEE International Software Engineering Standards Symposium*, pp. 69–82.

[95] Fusaro, P., El Emam, K. and Smith, B. (1997). The internal consistencies of the 1987 SEI Maturity Questionnaire and the SPICE Capability Dimension. *Empirical Software Engineering: An International Journal*, **3**, 179–201.

[96] Whitney, R., Nawrocki, E., Hayes, W. and Siegel, J. (1994). Interim profile: development and trial of a method to rapidly measure software engineering maturity status. Technical Report, CMU/SEI-94-TR-4, Software Engineering Institute.

[97] Carmines, E. and Zeller, R. (1979). *Reliability and Validity Assessment*. Sage, Beverly Hills, CA.

[98] Card, D. (1992). Capability evaluations rated highly variable. *IEEE Software*, September, pp. 105–106.

[99] Springsteen, B., Brykczynski, B., Fife, D. *et al.* (1992). Policy assessment for the software process maturity model. Report IDA-D-1202, Institute for Defense Analysis.

[100] Cronbach, L. (1951). Coefficient alpha and the internal structure of tests. *Psychometrika*, **16**(3), 297–334.

[101] El Emam, K., Simon, J.-M., Rousseau, S. and Jacquet, E. (1998). Cost implications of interrater agreement for software process assessments. *Proceedings of the 5th International Symposium on Software Metrics*, pp. 38–51, IEEE CS Press.

[102] Lord, F. and Novick, M. (1968). *Statistical Theories of Mental Test Scores*. Addison-Wesley, Reading, MA.

[103] Besselman, J., Byrnes, P., Lin, C. *et al.* (1993). Software capability evaluations: experiences from the field. *SEI Technical Review*.

[104] Japan SC7 WG10 SPICE Committee (1994). *Report of Japanese trials process assessment by SPICE method*. A SPICE Project Report.

[105] Masters, S. and Bothwell, C. (1995). *CMM Appraisal Framework—Version 1.0*. Technical Report CMU/SEI-TR-95–001, Software Engineering Institute.

[106] Nunnally, J. and Bernstein, I. (1994). *Psychometric Theory*. McGraw Hill, New York.

[107] Subramanian, A. and Nilakanta, S. (1994). Measurement: a blueprint for theory building in MIS. *Information and Management*, **26**, 13–20.

[108] Sethi, V. and King, W. (1991). Construct measurement in information systems research: an illustration in strategic systems. *Decision Sciences*, **22**, 455–472.

[109] Ives, B., Olson, M. and Baroudi, J. (1983). The measurement of user information satisfaction. *Communications of the ACM*, **26**(10), 785–793.

[110] Tait, P. and Vessey, I. (1988). The effect of user involvement on system success: a contingency approach. *MIS Quarterly*, March, 91–108.

[111] Amoako-Gyampah, K. and White, K. (1993). User involvement and user satisfaction: an exploratory contingency model. *Information and Management*, **25**, 1–10.

[112] Baroudi, J., Olson, M. and Ives, B. (1986). An empirical study of the impact of user involvement on system usage and information satisfaction. *Communications of the ACM*, **29**(3), 232–238.

[113] Davis, F. (1989). Perceived usefulness, perceived ease of use, and user acceptance of information technology. *MIS Quarterly*, 319–340.

[114] Galletta, D. and Ledrer, A. (1989). Some cautions on the measurement of user information satisfaction. *Decision Sciences*, **20**, 419–438.

[115] Torkzadeh, G. and Doll, W. (1994). The test–retest reliability of user involvement instruments. *Information and Management*, **26**, 21–31.

[116] El Emam, K. and Madhavji, N. H. (1995). Measuring the success of requirements engineering processes. *Proceedings of the 2nd IEEE International Symposium on Requirements Engineering*, pp. 204–211.

[117] El Emam, K. and Madhavji, N. H. (1995). The reliability of measuring organizational maturity. *Software Process: Improvement and Practice*, **1**(1), 3–25.

[118] Humphrey, W. and Curtis, B. (1991). Comments on "a critical look." *IEEE Software*, July, 42–46.

[119] Cronbach, L., Gleser, G., Nanda, H., and Rajaratnam, N. (1972). *The Dependability of Behavioral Measurements: Theory of Generalizability of Scores and Profiles*. John Wiley. New York.

[120] Neter, J., Wasserman, W. and Kunter, M. (1990). *Applied Linear Statistical Models: Regression, Analysis of Variance, and Experimental Designs*. Irwin,.

[121] Allen, M. and Yen, W. (1979). *Introduction to Measurement Theory*. Brooks/Cole,.

[122] El Emam, K., Briand, L., and Smith, B. (1996). Assessor agreement in rating SPICE processes. *Software Process Improvement and Practice Journal*, **2**(4), 291–306.

[123] El Emam, K., Goldenson, D., Briand, L., and Marshall, P. (1996). Interrater agreement in SPICE-based assessments: some preliminary results. *Proceedings of the International Conference on the Software Process*, pp. 149–156.

[124] El Emam, K. and Marshall, P. (1998). Interrater agreement in assessment ratings. In *SPICE: Theory and Practice of Software Process Improvement and Capability Determination*, ed. K. El Emam, J-N Drouin, and W. Melo. IEEE CS Press, New York.

[125] Hartmann, D. (1977). Considerations in the choice of interobserver reliability estimates. *Journal of Applied Behavior Analysis*, **10**(1), 103–116.

[126] Suen, H. and Lee, P. (1985). The effects of the use of percentage agreement on behavioral observation reliabilities: a reassessment. *Journal of Psychopathology and Behavioral Assessment*, **7**(3), 221–234.

[127] Zwick, R. (1988). Another look at interrater agreement. *Psychological Bulletin*, **103**(3), 374–378.

[128] Bennett, E., Alpert, R. and Goldstein, A. (1954). Communications through limited response questioning. *Public Opinion Quarterly*, **18**, 303–308.

[129] Cohen, J. (1960). A coefficient of agreement for nominal scales. *Educational and Psychological Measurement*, **XX**(1), 37–46.

[130] Scott, W. (1955). Reliability of content analysis: the case of nominal scale Coding. *Public Opinion Quarterly*, **19**, 321–325.

[131] Cohen, J. (1968). Weighted kappa: nominal scale agreement with provision for scaled agreement or partial credit. *Psychological Bulletin*, **70**, 213–220.

[132] Fleiss, J. (1981). *Statistical Methods for Rates and Proportions*. John Wiley, New York.

[133] Khurana, M. and El Emam, K. (1998). Assessment experience and the reliability of assessments. *Software Process Newsletter*, IEEE Technical Council on Software Engineering, No. 13, Fall.

[134] Kerlinger, F. (1986). *Foundations of Behavioral Research*. Holt, Rinehart, and Winston, New York.

[135] Cronbach, L. (1971). Test validation. In *Educational Measurement*, ed. R. Thorndike. American Council on Education,.

[136] El Emam, K. and Birk, A. (2000). Validating the ISO/IEC 15504 measures of software development process capability. *Journal of Systems and Software*, **52**(2), 119–149.

[137] Herbsleb, J., Carleton, A., Rozum, J. *et al.* (1994). Benefits of CMM-based software process improvement: initial results. Technical Report CMU-SEI-94-TR-13, Software Engineering Institute.

[138] Dion, R. (1992). Elements of a process improvement program. *IEEE Software*, **9**(4), 83–85.

[139] El Emam, K. and Birk, A. (2000). Validating the ISO/IEC 15504 measures of software requirements analysis process capability. *IEEE Transactions on Software Engineering*. To appear.

[140] Benno, S. and Frailey, D. (1995). Software process improvement in DSEG: 1989–1995. *Texas Instruments Technical Journal*, **12**(2), 20–28.

[141] Lipke, W. and Butler, K. (1992). Software process improvement: a success story. *Crosstalk*, **5**(9), 29–39.

[142] Butler, K. (1995). The economic benefits of software process improvement. *Crosstalk*, **8**(7), 14–17.

[143] Lebsanft, L. (1996). Bootstrap: experiences with Europe's software process assessment and improvement method. *Software Process Newsletter*, IEEE Computer Society, No. 5, Winter, pp. 6–10 (available at *www-se.cs.mcgill.ca/process/spn.html*).

[144] Rubin, H. (1993). Software process maturity: measuring its impact on productivity and quality. *Proceedings of the International Conference on Software Engineering*, pp. 468–476.

[145] Deephouse, C., Goldenson, D., Kellner, M. and Mukhopadhyay, T. (1995). The effects of software processes on meeting targets and quality. *Proceedings of the Hawaiian International Conference on Systems Sciences*, January, vol. 4, pp. 710–719.

[146] Krishnan, M. and Kellner, M. (1999) Measuring process consistency: implications for reducing software defects. *IEEE Transactions on Software Engineering*, **25**(6), 800–815.

[147] Jones, C. (1996). The pragmatics of software process improvements. *Software Process Newsletter*, IEEE Computer Society TCSE, No. 5, Winter, pp. 1–4 (available at *www.seq.iit.nrc.ca/spn*).

[148] Jones, C. (1994). *Assessment and Control of Software Risks*. Prentice-Hall, Englewood Cliffs, NJ.

[149] McGarry, F., Burke, S. and Decker, B. (1998). Measuring the impacts individual process maturity attributes have on software projects. *Proceedings of the 5th International Software Metrics Symposium*, pp. 52–60.

[150] Flowe, R. and Thordahl, J. (1994). A correlational study of the SEI's capability maturity model and software development performance in DoD contracts. MSc thesis, Air Force Institute of Technology.

[151] Lawlis, P., Flowe, R. and Thordahl, J. (1996). A correlational study of the CMM and software development performance. *Software Process Newsletter*, IEEE TCSE, No. 7, Fall, pp. 1–5 (available at *www.seq.iit.nrc.ca/spn*).

[152] El Emam, K. and Briand, L. (1999). Costs and benefits of software process improvement. In *Better Software Practice for Business Benefit: Principles and Experience*, ed. R. Messnarz and C. Tully. IEEE CS Press, New York.

[153] Brodman, J. and Johnson, D. (1994). What small businesses and small organizations say about the CMM. *Proceedings of the 16th International Conference on Software Engineering*, pp. 331–340.

[154] Lee, J. and Kim, S. (1992). The relationship between procedural formalization in MIS development and MIS success. *Information and Management*, **22**, 89–111.

[155] Bach, J. (1995). Enough about process: what we need are heroes. *IEEE Software*, **12**(2), 96–98.

[156] El Emam, K. and Madhavji, N. H. (1994). A method for instrumenting software evolution processes and an example application. *Notes From The International Workshop on Software Evolution, Processes, and Measurements*, Technical Report 94–04 NT, Software Engineering Test Laboratory, Department of Computer Science, University of Idaho.

[157] El Emam, K. and Madhavji, N. H. (unpublished). The impact of user capability on requirements engineering success. Submitted for publication.

[158] Curtis, B., Krasner, H. and Iscoe, N. (1988). A field study of the software design process for large systems. *Communications of the ACM*, **31**(11), 1268–1286.

[159] El Emam, K. and Madhavji, N. H. (1995). A field study of requirements engineering practices in information systems development. *Proceedings of the 2nd IEEE International Symposium on Requirements Engineering*, pp. 68–80.

[160] Finlay, P. and Mitchell, A. (1994). Perceptions of the benefits from the introduction of CASE: an empirical study. *MIS Quarterly*, December, 353–370.

[161] Pfleeger, S.-L., Fenton, N. and Page, S. (1994). Evaluating software engineering standards. *IEEE Computer*, September, 71–79.

[162] Pfleeger, S.-L. (1994). The language of case studies and formal experiments. *Software Engineering Notes*, October, 16–20.

[163] Fenton, N., Littlewood, B. and Page, S. (1993). Evaluating software engineering standards and methods. In *Software Engineering: A European Perspective*, ed. R. Thayer and A. McGettrick. IEEE CS Press, New York.

[164] Fenton, N. and Page, S. (1993). Towards the evaluation of software engineering standards. *Proceedings of the Software Engineering Standards Symposium*, pp. 100–107.

[165] Fenton, N., Pfleeger. S.-L., Page, S. and Thornton, J. (1994). The SMARTIE standards evaluation methodology. Technical Report, Centre for Software Reliability, City University, UK.

[166] Goldenson, D. R. and El Emam, K. (1996). The international SPICE trials: project description and initial results. *Proceedings of the 8th Software Engineering Process Group Conference*, May.

[167] Hollander, M. and Wolfe, D. (1999). *Nonparametric Statistical Methods*. John Wiley, New York.

[168] Smith, B. and El Emam, K. (1996). Transitioning to phase 2 of the SPICE trials. *Proceedings of SPICE'96*, pp. 45–55.

[169] Lawlis, P., Flowe, R. and Thordahl, J. (1995). A correlational study of the CMM and software development performance. *Crosstalk*, September, pp. 21–25.

[170] Staff: "A survey of the surveys on the Benefits of ISO 9000". In Software Process, Quality & ISO 9000, 3(11): 1–5, November 1994.

State of the Art in Electronic Payment Systems

N. ASOKAN

Nokia Research Center
Helsinki
Finland
n.asokan@nokia.com

P. JANSON, M. STEINER, AND M. WAIDNER

IBM Research Division
Zurich Research Laboratory
Rüschlikon
Switzerland
{pj, sti, wmi}@zurich.ibm.com

Abstract

Electronic funds transfer over financial networks is reasonably secure, but securing payments over open networks like the Internet poses challenges of a new dimension. This paper lays out the security requirements for electronic payment systems, surveys the state of the art in electronic payment technologies and sketches emerging developments.

ADVANCES IN COMPUTERS, VOL. 53
ISBN 0-12-012153-0

425

1. Introduction

The exchange of goods conducted face-to-face between two parties dates from before the beginning of recorded history. As trade became more and more complicated, increasingly abstract representations of value were devised, progressing from barter through bank notes, payment orders, checks, credit cards, and now, to electronic payment systems.

Traditional means of payment suffer from various well-known security problems: Money can be counterfeited, signatures can be forged, and checks can be overdrawn. Electronic means of payment retain the same drawbacks. In addition, they entail some additional risks: Unlike paper, digital "documents" can be copied perfectly and arbitrarily often; digital signatures can be produced by anybody who knows the secret cryptographic signing key; a buyer's name can be associated with every payment, eliminating the anonymity of cash.

Thus without new security measures, widespread electronic commerce is not viable. On the other hand, properly designed electronic payment systems can actually provide better security than traditional means of payments, in addition to flexibility of use. This paper provides an overview of electronic payment systems, focusing on issues related to security.

A wide variety of payment systems have been proposed and/or implemented in the last few years. Our aim is not to cover all of these payment system. Instead, we focus on systems that satisfy one of the following criteria:

● historical importance (pioneering role)
● popularity and/or widespread current deployment
● novelty and/or potential for widespread future deployment.

The rest of the chapter is organized as follows. In section 2 we outline an informal model of electronic payment systems. In section 3 we identify desirable security requirements for electronic payments. In section 4 we survey the state of the art in the technological tools which can help meet the requirements identified earlier. In section 5 we present some example payment systems and discuss their properties. In the next two sections, we touch upon some advanced issues: In section 6 we motivate the need for a general framework within which multiple payment systems can be used and we also describe research efforts in building such frameworks, and in section 7 we refer to the problem of handling disputes, which will inevitably arise when electronic payment systems are deployed widely. In section 8 we describe the current state of standards activity. Finally, in section 9 we conclude with some observations about the current status and future possibilities regarding electronic payment systems. Section 10, the Appendix, provides a brief overview of some of the relevant basic concepts in security and cryptography.

2. Electronic Payment Models

Commerce always involves a *payer* and a *payee* who exchange money for goods or services. There is also at least one financial institution—which links "bits" to "money." In most existing payment systems, the latter role is divided into two parts: An *issuer* (used by the payer) and an *acquirer* (used by the payee). Electronic payment is implemented by a flow of money from the payer via the issuer and acquirer to the payee.

Figure 1 shows typical flows of money in the case of pre-paid, *cash-like* payment systems. In these systems, a certain amount of money is taken away from the payer before purchases are made. This amount of money can be used for payments later. Smartcard-based electronic purses, electronic cash, and bank checks (such as certified checks) fall into this category.

Figure 2 shows typical flows of money in the case of systems based on bank accounts, which include pay-now systems and pay-later systems. In pay-now payment systems, the payer's account is debited at the time of payment. Automated teller machine (ATM) cards fall into this category. In pay-later (credit) payment systems, the payee's bank account is credited the amount of sale before the payer's account is debited. Credit card systems fall into this category. From a protocol point of view, pay-now and pay-later systems belong to the same class: Because a payment is always done by sending a "form" from the payer to the payee (whether it be a check or a credit card slip or some other form), we call these systems *check-like*.

Both types of payment systems introduced above are *direct* payment systems: A payment requires a direct interaction between payer and payee. There are also *indirect* payment systems in which either the payer or the

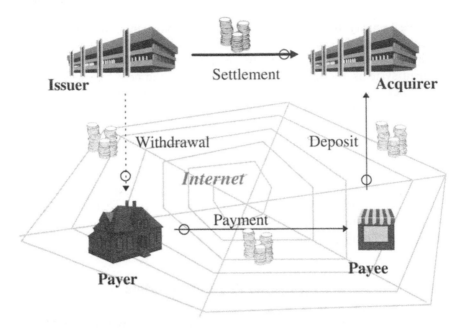

FIG. 1. Money flow in a cash-like payment system (circle in arrow indicates party initiating the flow).

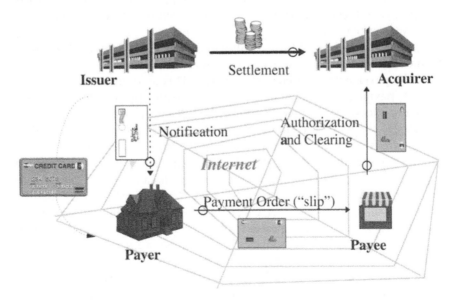

FIG. 2. Money flow in a check-like payment system (circle in arrow indicates party initiating the flow).

payee initiates payment without the other party involved being online. Electronic funds transfer is one example of an indirect payment system.

Although we can consider electronic funds transfer over financial networks reasonably secure, we face challenges of a new dimension in securing payments over open networks like the Internet. This paper surveys the state of the art in payment technologies and sketches emerging developments, focusing mainly on protocols suitable for use in open networks.

3. Security Requirements

The concrete security requirements of electronic payment systems vary, depending both on their features and on the trust assumptions placed on their operation. In general, however, electronic payment systems must exhibit integrity, authorization, confidentiality, availability, and reliability. The interests of the payer, payee, and bank contradict each other to some degree, so the trust which a system requires from the parties in each other should be as little as possible. This requirement is often referred to as *multiparty security*. One way of reducing trust is to make actions, in particular authorization, accountable. Digital signatures are a core ingredient to achieve *accountability*.

3.1 Integrity and Authorization

The integrity requirement at a global level is that the payment system should guarantee that no new monetary value is created by any player within the digital system. The integrity requirement from an individual player is that no money is taken from him without his explicit authorization. A user may also require that receipt of payments without his explicit authorization be disallowed in order to prevent, for example, unsolicited bribery. Payment can be authorized in three ways: via out-band authorization, using passwords, and using signatures. The latter two are based on sender authentication of authorization messages.

- *Out-band authorization:* In this approach, the verifying party (typically a bank) notifies the authorizing party (the payer) of a transaction. The latter is required to approve or deny the payment using a secure, out-band channel such as surface mail or the phone. This is the current approach used for credit card transactions for mail orders and phone orders: Anyone who knows a user's credit card data can initiate transactions. Legitimate users must carefully check their account statements and complain about any unauthorized transactions. If the user does not complain within a certain time, transactions are considered "approved" by default.

- *Password authorization:* In the password-based approach, every message from the authorizing party includes a cryptographic check value computed using a secret known only to the authorizing and verifying parties. This secret can be a personal identification number, a password, or any form of shared secret. See section 10.1.1 for more explanation on message authentication based on shared secrets.

- *Signature authorization:* In this type of transaction, the verifying party requires a digital signature of the authorizing party. Digital signatures also provide *nonrepudiation* of origin. See section 10.1.2 for more explanation on digital signatures.

3.2 Confidentiality

Some parties involved may wish confidentiality of transactions. Confidentiality in this context means the restriction of knowledge about various pieces of information related to a transaction: the identity of payer/payee, purchase content, amount, and so on. Typically, the confidentiality requirement dictates that this information be restricted only to the parties involved. Where *anonymity* is desired, the requirement may be to further limit this knowledge to certain subsets of the parties only, as described later.

3.3 Availability and Reliability

All parties require the ability to make or receive payments whenever necessary. Payment transactions must be *atomic*: They occur entirely or not at all, but they never hang in an unknown or inconsistent state. No payer would accept a loss of money (not a significant amount, in any case) due to a network or system crash.

Availability and reliability presume that the underlying networking services and all software and hardware components are sufficiently dependable. Recovery from crash failures requires that some form of stable storage be available to all parties as well as specific resynchronization protocols. These fault tolerance issues are not discussed here: Most payment systems do not address them explicitly and the standard mechanisms to increase availability and reliability [2] can be applied to most protocols in a rather straightforward manner.

4. Technology Overview

As we saw, electronic payment systems must enable an honest payer to convince the payee to accept a legitimate payment and at the same time prevent a dishonest payer from making unauthorized payments, all the while ensuring the privacy of honest participants. In this section, we describe some of the technologies that can be used to meet the security requirements.

4.1 Online versus Offline

Offline payments involve no contact with a third party during payment— the transaction involves only the payer and payee. The obvious problem with offline payments is that it is difficult to prevent payers from spending more money than they actually possess. In a purely digital world a dishonest payer can, after each payment, easily reset the local state of his system to a prior state. This is known as the *double spending* problem. Typically, double spending is prevented by the use of *tamper-resistant* hardware (see section 4.2). Another way to achieve protection against double spending is to use *preauthorization*: The payee is known to the payer in advance, and the payment is already authorized during withdrawal, as in the case of certified bank checks.

A weaker solution is to detect rather than prevent double spending. Double spending detection techniques guarantee that if a user spends more money than allowed, he can be identified and made accountable. Identification of double spenders can be achieved even if the user was (unconditionally) anonymous during "legal" transactions [3, 4]! Techniques for detection of double spending can serve as a second line of defense when they are used in conjunction with prevention based on tamper-resistant hardware.

Online payments involve an authorization server (usually as part of the issuer or acquirer) in each payment. Online systems obviously require more communication. In general, they are considered more secure than offline systems. Most proposed internet payment systems are online.

4.2 Trusted Hardware

As we saw, prevention of double spending requires tamper-resistant hardware at the payer end. The smartcard is an example. Tamper-resistant hardware may also be used at the payee end. An example is the security module of a point-of-sale (POS) terminal. This is mandatory in the case of shared-key systems and in cases where the payee forwards only the total volume of transactions (rather than every individual transaction) to the bank. In a certain sense, tamper-resistant hardware is a "pocket branch" of a bank and must be trusted by the issuer. However, such trust might not always be justified because smartcards are vulnerable to a number of attacks [5–9]. Therefore utmost care is necessary in designing protocols which rely on the tamper resistance of a device for their security.

Independent of the issuer's security considerations, it is in the payer's interest to have a secure device that can be trusted to protect his secret keys and to perform the necessary operations correctly. Initially, this could simply be a smartcard, but in the long run, it should become a smart device of a different form factor with secure access to a minimal keyboard and display. Such a device is usually referred to as an *electronic wallet*. Without such a secure device, payers' secrets and hence their money are vulnerable to anyone who can access their computers. This is obviously a problem in multiuser environments. It is also a problem even on single-user computers which can be accessed directly or indirectly by others. A virus, for example, installed on a computer could steal personal identification numbers (PINs) and passwords as they are entered. This is an instance of the more general *fake-terminal* attack (see section 10.2.1). Even when a smartcard is available to store keys, a virus program may directly ask the smartcard to make a payment to an attacker's account. Thus for true security, trusted input/output channels between the user and the smartcard must exist [10].

4.3 Micropayments

Micropayments are low-value payments (probably less than $1). In some scenarios, such as paying for each tick of a phone call, micropayments need to be made repeatedly and very quickly. Given these constraints, micropayment techniques must be both inexpensive and fast. Achieving both requires certain compromises, either by reducing the (multiparty) security or in making assumption on the usage of such systems. We return to micropayments in section 5.3.

4.4 Cryptography

Using no cryptography at all implies reliance on out-band security. For example, goods ordered electronically may not be delivered until a fax arrives from the payer confirming the order. The first proposals for internet payment systems were of this type. Later proposals rely on cryptography to provide reasonable security guarantees.

A wide variety of cryptographic techniques have been developed for user and message authentication, secret communication, and nonrepudiation.

They are essential tools in building secure payment systems over open networks that have little or no physical security. See section 10 for a quick introduction of basic concepts in cryptography and security.

4.4.1 Shared-Key Cryptography

Authentication based on shared-key cryptography requires that the prover (the payer) and a verifier (the issuer) both have a shared secret. The shared key may be, for example, a password or a PIN or a key in a shared-key cryptosystem. The most commonly used shared-key cryptosystem is the Data Encryption Standard (DES) and its stronger variant, triple DES [11]. However, the US National Institute of Standards Technology (NIST) is in the process of selecting a new standard for shared-key encryption (see *www.nist.gov/aes*). Once finalized, this Advanced Encryption Standard (AES) will become the most commonly used shared-key cryptosystem.

Because both sides have exactly the same secret information, shared-key cryptography does not provide nonrepudiation. If payer and issuer disagree about a payment, there is no way to decide if the payment was initiated by the payer or by an employee of the issuer. Authenticating a transfer order on the basis of shared keys is therefore not appropriate if the payer bears the risk of forged payments [12].

If authentication is to be done offline, each payer–payee pair needs a shared secret. In practice this means that a common master key is present at each payee end, to enable the payee to derive the payer's key. Tamper-resistant security modules are required to protect the master key.

4.4.2 Public-Key Digital Signatures

Authentication based on public-key cryptography requires that the prover has a secret signing key and a certificate for its corresponding public signature verification key. The certificate is issued by a well-known authority. Most systems now use RSA [13] signatures, but there are several alternatives.

Digital signatures can provide nonrepudiation—disputes between sender and receiver can be resolved. Digital signatures should be mandatory if the payer bears the risk of forged payments. A special form of signatures called blind signatures [4, 14] is used to construct payment systems that provide user anonymity (see section 4.5). A blind signature on some message is made in such a way that the signer does not know the exact content of the message.

4.5   Payer Anonymity

Payers prefer to keep their everyday payment activities private. Certainly they do not want outsiders not involved in their transactions to be able to observe and track their payments. Often, they prefer the payees (shops, publishers, and the like) and in some cases even banks to be incapable of observing and tracking their payments.

There are two levels of anonymity of a payer:

- *untraceability* simply means that an adversary cannot determine a payer's identity in a run of the payment protocol
- *unlinkability* means that, in addition, participation by the same player in two different payments cannot be linked.

Some payment systems provide untraceability and unlinkability of the payer. Both are considered useful for cash-like payments since cash is also untraceable and unlinkable. By encrypting the contents and addressing information in all message flows between payer and payee, any payment system can be made unlinkable by outsiders. Payer untraceability with respect to the payee can be achieved by using pseudonyms instead of real identities. Some electronic payment systems are designed to provide untraceability or even unlinkability with respect to the payee (*i*KP [15], for example, offers this as an option).

5.   Representative Payment Systems

Table I lists some examples of payment systems along with an indication of relevant properties. Pointers to more up-to-date information on these payment systems and others may be found at *www.semper.org/sirene/ outsideworld/ecommerce.html*.

A rather general security scheme that uses public-key signatures is Secure Socket Layer (SSL). SSL is a socket-layer communication interface that allows two parties to communicate securely over the internet. It is not a payment technology per se (and hence does not fit into Table I), but is often used as a means to secure payment messages. SSL does not support nonrepudiation.

Many of the complete payment systems were proposed and implemented during the 1990s, but the protocol ideas themselves are much older. The use of digital signatures for both online and offline payments, anonymous accounts with digitally signed transfer orders, and anonymous electronic cash were all introduced during the 1980s (see [23] for an early survey).

TABLE I

INFORMATION SOURCES FOR REPRESENTATIVE PAYMENT SYSTEMS

System[a]	Online/Offline	Anonymity	Cryptography	Trusted h/w
Check-like payment systems				
First Virtual [16]	Online	None	None	None
iKP [15]	Online	None	Public-Key	None
OpenMarket [17]	Online	None	Public-Key	None
echeck [18, 19][b]	Offline	None	Public-Key	Tamper resistant
SET [20]	Online	None	Public-Key	Proposed
Cash-like payment systems				
e-cash[c]	Online	Unlinkable	Blind Signatures	None
CAFÉ [21]	Offline	Unlinkable	Blind Signatures	Tamper resistant
Mondex[d]	Offline	None	Public-Key	Tamper resistant
CEPS	Offline	None	Public-Key	Tamper resistant
NetCash [22]	Online	Unlinkable	Shared-Key Only	None
Anonymous credit cards [23, 24]	Online	Unlinkable	Public-Key	None
Micropayments				
NetBill [25]	Online	None	Shared-Key	None
CAFÉ Ticks [26]	Offline	None	OWHF[e]	None
MilliCent [27]	Online	None	Shared-key + OWHF	None
μ-iKP [28]	Offline	None	Public-key + OWHF	None
IBM Micro Payments [29][f]	Offline	None	Public-key	None

[a] Proposed or existing standards are indicated in **bold type**.
[b] By FSTC (*www.echeck.org*).
[c] By Digicash.
[d] www.mondex.com/
[e] One-way hash function.
[f] Previously known as Minipay.

5.1 Check-Like Systems

First Virtual was an example of a payment system that did not use cryptography. A user had an account and received a password in exchange for a credit card number. However, the password was not protected as it traversed the Internet. Such a system is vulnerable to eavesdropping. First Virtual achieved some protection by asking the payer for an acknowledgment of each payment via e-mail, but the actual security of the system was based on the payer's ability to revoke each payment within a certain period. In other words, there was no definite authorization during payment. Until the end of this period, the payee assumed the entire risk.

The realization that cryptographic techniques are necessary to provide a reasonable level of security for Internet credit card payments led to several proposals. In particular *i*KP [15] set the theoretical foundations for such protocols in clearly specifying the involved security requirements and providing a systematic and modular approach to satisfy them. These efforts culminated in the proposed standard Secure Electronic Transactions (SET), described in Section 8.

A payment switch is an online payment system that implements both the pre-paid and pay-later models, as exemplified by the OpenMarket payment switch [17]. OpenMarket's architecture supports several authentication methods, depending on the payment method chosen. The methods range from simple, unprotected PIN-based authentication to challenge–response-based systems. In the latter case, it is possible to use a smartcard or other hand-held device for computing the response. User authentication is therefore based on shared-key cryptography. However, authorization is based on public-key cryptography: The OpenMarket payment switch digitally signs an authorization message, which is forwarded to the payee. The payment switch is completely trusted by users who use shared-key cryptography.

The Financial Services Technology Consortium (FSTC) Electronic Check project [18] uses a tamper-resistant PCMCIA card and implements a check-like payment model. A primary design principle in the FSTC electronic check mechanism appears to be to mirror the steps in paper check transactions as much as possible.

5.2 Cash-Like Systems

There are two main motivations for cash-like systems: Avoiding the need to have an account with a financial institution (e.g., as in pre-paid phone cards) and/or the possibility of untraceable, and possibly even unlinkable, transactions. So far, the only payment systems mentioned here that provide unconditional untraceability and unlinkability against payee and issuer are Digicash e-cash, an online system and Conditional Access For Europe (CAFE) [21], an offline system. Both are cash-like payment system based on blind signatures.

In an e-cash system, users can withdraw e-cash coins from a bank and use them to pay other users. Each e-cash coin has a serial number. To withdraw e-cash coins, a user prepares a "blank coin" that has a randomly generated serial number, blinds it, and sends it to the bank. If the user is authorized to withdraw the specified amount of e-cash, the bank signs the blind coin and returns it to the user. The user then unblinds it to extract the signed coin. The signed coin can now be used to pay any other e-cash user. When a payee deposits an e-cash coin, the bank records its serial number to prevent double spending. However, because the bank cannot see the serial number when it signs the coin, it cannot relate the deposited coin to the earlier withdrawal by the payer.

NetCash [22] and anonymous credit cards [23, 24] also provide untraceability and unlinkability. But they are based on the use of trusted intermediate systems that change electronic money of one representation into another representation, without revealing the relation. Neither e-cash nor CAFE assume the existence of such trusted third parties.

Most proposed payment systems based on electronic hardware are offline cash-like systems. All these systems can be used for Internet payments, but at the time of writing none actually are, except in small scale trials. The main technical obstacle is that they require a smartcard reader attached to the payer's computer. Inexpensive PCMCIA smartcard readers and standardized infrared interfaces on notebook computers will solve this connectivity problem.

CEPS is a proposed standard for smartcard-based cash-like systems. It evolved from systems already deployed such as Geldkarte (*www.zka.de*) or Proton (*www.protonworld.com*). Mondex is the only system that enables offline transferability: The payee can use the amount received to make a new payment himself, without having to go to the bank in between. However, this seems to be a politically unpopular feature as the risks are rather hard to control in such systems. CAFE is the only offline system that provides strong payer untraceability and unlinkability. CAFE also provides loss tolerance, which allows the payer to recover from coin losses (but at the expense of some anonymity in case of loss) [30]. CEPS, Mondex and CAFE are all capable of handling multiple different currencies simultaneously.

A class of payment systems known as "fair" cash-like payment systems support untraceability for the payer (like e-cash or CAFE) but allow a third party to trace selected payments under certain conditions [31–33]. The development of such systems is motivated by concerns related to law enforcement—e.g., that completely unlinkable payment systems can aid in money laundering, or in committing "perfect crimes" [34, 35]. The latter means that in untraceable payment systems it is possible to remotely blackmail users or the bank without leaving any traces. So far none of these systems has left the stage of theoretical designs.

5.3 Micropayments

Content servers on the internet will probably have to process such a large number of low-value transactions that it will be impractical to use computationally complex and expensive cryptographic protocols to secure them. One solution is to use flat-fee subscription services. Another more flexible approach is the use of micropayment systems. As mentioned in section 4.3, such micropayments achieve efficiency only based on some compromises.

Two very prominent examples of micropayment systems are MilliCent [27] and IBM Micro Payments [29] (previously known as "Minipay"). The former gains its speed by putting complete trust in the payment system provider, the latter achieves its efficiency relying on the assumption that in the case of small payments *a posteriori* fraud detection is sufficient. A number of proposals [26, 28, 36, 37] were especially designed for situations where a sequence of small payments need to be made to the same merchant. Such situations occur in pay-per-web-page services, or in streaming data services such as video-on-demand. These systems amortize the cost of an initial setup operation over extremely efficient subsequent payment operations, without any loss of multi-party security. They can even be used in paying for network connectivity from anonymous internet kiosks similar to the use of pre-paid cards in phone booths.

A noteworthy side effect of such scenarios of payment for streaming data services is that the risks of loss for both parties is very small: At most one payment or chunk of streaming data is outstanding, both of them can easily be made of negligible value by shortening the period of unit price. So we achieve highly efficient fair exchange [38] of payments for electronic goods.

All of these proposals use computationally secure one-way hash functions to implement micropayments. In this section, we describe μ-iKP [28], the micropayment proposal for iKP. Informally, a function $f(\ )$ is one-way if it is difficult to find the value x given the value $y = f(x)$. The value x is the *preimage* of y. Given such a one-way function, the payer will randomly choose a seed value X and recursively compute:

$$A_0(X) = X$$

$$A^{i+1}(X) = f(A^i(X))$$

The values $A_0, ..., A_{n-1}$, known as *coupons*, will enable the payer to make n micropayments of a fixed value v to the same payee: First, the payer forwards A_n and v to the payee in an authenticated manner. Authentication can be achieved by sending these values to the payee as the payload of a normal iKP payment. The payee ensures, possibly via its bank, that A_n does in fact correspond to a good preimage chain that can be used for subsequent micropayments. The micropayments are then carried out by revealing components of the chain $A_{n-1}, A_{n-2}, ..., A_0$ successively to the payee. To clear the payments, the payee presents the partial chain

$$A_i, ..., A_j \qquad (0 \leqslant i < j \leqslant n)$$

to its bank in return for a credit of value $v(j-i)$.

The overhead of the setup phase is justified only when it is followed by several repeated micropayments. However, nonrepeated (or rarely repeated) micropayments are also a likely scenario in the electronic marketplace: A user surfing the web may chance upon a single page that costs $0.01. Neither the micropayment setup overhead nor the cost of a normal payment is justified in this case.

μ-iKP solves this problem with a broker: An isolated micropayment from payer P to payee Q is carried out by P making one or more micropayments to broker B. Broker B then makes an equivalent micropayment to Q. In other words, a non-repeating financial relationship between P and Q is achieved by leveraging on existing relationships between B and P and between B and Q.

On the other hand, if the amount of the transaction is small, developers can assume a lower risk and so opt to reduce security (for example, by foregoing nonrepudiation). A notable example is NetBill, which is founded on the shared key technology Kerberos. It implements a check-like debit-payment model. The use of shared-key technology is justified by the performance required to process many micropayments in a short time.

6. Generic Payment Service

As we saw, a large number of electronic payment systems have been proposed in the past few years. The many different payment systems are incompatible with each other. Each individual party will have the ability to use only a subset of these payment systems. When a party wants to make a payment, he must first identify what payment systems he has in common with the payee, and then pick a suitable one among them for the payment.

For application developers this implies the need to understand the details of different systems, to adapt the code as soon as new payment systems are introduced, and also to provide a way of picking a suitable payment instrument for every transaction. Ideally, an application should be able to make use of any of the several common means of payment available to payer and payee. A unifying framework enabling business applications to use different payment systems in a transparent manner can greatly ease the task of business application developers by relieving them from having to

- make sure that the application knows how to use all the various different payment systems its users are likely to have available
- in case multiple payment instruments are available, provide a way of choosing one of them.

Several projects aiming at building such a framework have been reported in the literature [39–41]. One of the earliest and most complete of these efforts is the Generic Payment Service Framework developed as part of the European Commission project SEMPER [42–44]. An important aspect of this framework is a set of generic APIs which define common electronic payment services.

An important part of a common payment system framework is the negotiation of a mutually acceptable payment system and other related parameters between the parties. This implies a language to represent the necessary meta-information and a protocol for negotiation of parameters. There have been several efforts in this direction. Notable among them are Joint Electronic Payments Initiative by the World Wide Web Consortium, Open Trading Protocol (*www.otp.org*) by an industry consortium (and the related Internet Open Trading Protocol by the *trade* working group of the Internet Engineering Task Force), and Electronic Commerce Modeling Language (*www.ecml.org*), also by an industry consortium. None of these efforts has yet led to a widely accepted standard, but their very presence underlines the importance of the problem.

7. Handling Disputes

Support for handling disputes is a crucial aspect of any system providing accountability [45]. However, many payment systems limit themselves only to the generation and collection of evidence. It is assumed that such evidence can be used in some dispute resolution procedure external to the system. Such procedures are usually left unspecified.

A discussion of the issues can be found in [46]. This chapter also discusses how the SEMPER generic payment service framework could provide *dispute services* while retaining its generality: To the extent possible, users and applications must be allowed to initiate or respond to payment disputes in a payment-system-independent manner. In general, dispute claims can be expressed in terms of *statements* about a (possibly alleged) transaction. The terms of these statements correspond to the parameters used during the invocation of payment services themselves (such as the identities of the parties involved and the amount of transaction) and a finite set of other "environmental" terms (such as the time of transaction). [46] contains the grammar of a proposed language to express payment dispute claims.

8. Standards

Two proposals, Visa's Secure Transaction Technology (STT) and MasterCard's Secure Electronic Payment Protocol (SEPP) began as competing standards for credit-card-based online payment schemes. The SET (Secure Electronic Transactions) standard, designed by MasterCard, Visa, GTE, IBM, Microsoft, Netscape, SAIC, Terisa, and Verisign, has replaced these competing proposals. SET is likely to be widely adopted for credit card payments over the internet.

SET is a pragmatic approach that paves the way for easy, fast, secure transactions over the internet. It seeks to preserve the existing relationships between merchants and acquirers as well as between payers and their bank. SET concentrates on securely communicating credit card numbers between a payer and an acquirer gateway interfacing to the existing financial infrastructure.

In our classification, SET falls under the check-like model. The transaction is initiated with a handshake, with the merchant authenticating itself to the payer and fixing all payment data. The payer then uses a sophisticated encryption scheme to generate a payment slip. The goal of the encryption scheme is to protect sensitive payment information (such as the credit card number), limit encryption to selected fields (to ease export approval), cryptographically bind the order information to the payment message, and maximize user privacy. Next the payment slip is signed by the payer and is sent to the merchant. The merchant sends the slip to its acquirer gateway, to authorize and capture the payment. The acquirer checks all signatures and the slip, verifies the creditability of the payer, and sends either a positive or negative signed acknowledgment back to merchant and payer.

Currently, discussions on SET dominate the stage of internet payment systems, but there is a parallel demand for international standards of electronic cash-like payment schemes and schemes for micropayments. Europay, MasterCard, and Visa (known collectively as EMV), are working on standards for smartcard-based electronic payment systems. In 1999 Europay, Visa and others published the first version of the Common Electronic Purse Specifications (CEPS). First implementations of CEPS are expected for 2001. There are currently no efforts to standardize an unlinkable, offline payment system.

9. Status and Outlook

The most frequent form of payment supported by internet businesses today is to send the credit card number in an SSL encrypted channel from the payer's web browser to the merchant server. The reasons for this are twofold:

- being able to receive payments in this manner involves very minimal set-up effort by the merchant

- implementations of the other, more secure, electronic payment systems have been perceived as too complex.

However, SSL-based internet payments cannot provide nonrepudiation of origin. There has been at least one case where an internet pornography merchant claimed fraudulent payments on a massive scale by exploiting the fact that most internet credit card payments today do not provide nonrepudiation [47]. This case is also a striking example that even though the monetary damage to a single user is small ($39.90 in this case), the actual damage to their lives can be much greater.

The technology to provide high-grade security for internet payments already exists. It is now possible to achieve security for all parties, including the perfect unlinkability of the payer. The correct political and business conditions for the widespread deployment of highly secure payment systems are yet to arrive. No one system will prevail; several payment systems will coexist. Micropayments (less than $1), low-value payments ($1 to $100), and high-value payments have significantly different security and cost requirements.

High values will be transferred using non-anonymous, online payment systems based on public-key cryptography implementing a check-like payment model. The most promising candidates are SET and the FSTC Electronic Checks. SET has had a slower start than expected, but within the next 3–5 years, it could nevertheless become the predominant method for credit card purchases on the Internet. Initially it is implemented in software only, but will later be supported by smartcards. For some time, the currently preferred method of using SSL to encrypt payment details on their way from payer to payee will coexist with SET.

It is likely that FSTC Electronic Checks will be deployed within the US— there is currently a larger trial involving the US Department of the Treasury, the Defence Finance and Accounting System and the Federal Reserve Bank—but it is not clear if the FSTC design will, or indeed can, be used internationally.

Within the next few years, smartcard readers will become widely available on PCs and workstations. This will enable payments of small amounts using pre-paid, offline payment systems that provide a certain degree of unlinkability. Several smartcard-based electronic purse schemes are already deployed on a national basis, in particular in Europe, and within a few years most of us will carry smartcards that can be used to buy things offline and in shops, as well as over the internet. There are good chances that CEPS will become an accepted standard but so far most purses cannot be used for cross-border payments.

Several micropayment systems will be used with microservice providers, but it is not clear yet whether there will be a single winner in the end.

It is difficult to predict the future of privacy protecting payment systems. CAFE and Digicash's e-cash have demonstrated the technical feasibility of strongly untraceable payment systems, but neither has yet been successful on the market. The increasing awareness for privacy risks, in particular on the internet, might create the necessary demand for such systems.

Payment systems with and without tamper-resistant hardware at the payer's end will coexist for some time. Ultimately, payment systems based on smartcards and electronic wallets (having secure access to some display and keyboard, and communicating with the buyer's terminal via an infrared interface) will become prevalent for two reasons: They enable mobility of users and they clearly provide better security, allowing the payer to use untrusted terminals without endangering security.

A few almost equivalent payment systems with the same scope (in terms of the payment model and maximum amounts) will possibly coexist. The reasons are various cultural differences in the business and payment processes, national security considerations that might disqualify some solutions in some countries, and competition between payment system providers.

10. Appendix: Basic Concepts in Cryptography and Security

Cryptographic techniques are essential tools in securing payment protocols over open, insecure networks. Here we outline some relevant basic concepts. Additional information on cryptographic techniques can be found in excellent reference works on the subject [48, 49].

10.1 Message Authentication

To authenticate a message is to prove the identity of its originator to its recipient. Authentication can be achieved by using shared-key or public-key cryptography.

10.1.1 Shared-Key Cryptography

Because the prover and the verifier share a common secret, this is also called *symmetric authentication*. A message is authenticated by means of a cryptographic check value, which is a function of both the message itself and the shared secret. This check value is known as the *message authentication code* (MAC). The MAC function is such that it is infeasible to compute a valid MAC for a new message without knowing the shared secret. This means that we can detect any modification to a message by an attacker. HMAC [50] has become the standard way to construct MAC functions and is based on a suitable one-way hash function such as SHA-1 [51].

Shared secrets that are short—such as a six-digit personal identification number (PIN)—are inherently susceptible to various kinds of attacks. They cannot in themselves provide a high degree of security. They should only be used to control access to a physical token like a smartcard (or a wallet) that performs the message authentication using secure cryptographic mechanisms, such as digital signatures (see next section).

10.1.2 Public-Key Cryptography

Authentication using public-key cryptography is based on digital signatures. A digital signature system consists of a signature algorithm and a verification algorithm. In addition, each entity that needs to sign has a matching pair of keys. One, known as the *signature key*, is used for computing signatures and is kept secret. The other, known as the *verification key*, is used to verify signatures made with the corresponding signing key. The verification key is made public along with a certificate binding an entity's identity to its verification key. Certificates are signed by a well-known authority whose verification key is known *a priori* to all verifiers. To sign a message, the prover executes the signature algorithm with the message and his signing key as input. Thus, the signature can be generated only by the entity that knows the signing key. Given a digital signature and a certificate for its verification key, a verifier can authenticate the message by executing the matching signature verification algorithm. Any verifier who knows the corresponding public verification key can verify the authenticity of a signature; once a signature has been verified, the verifier can be sure that the signer cannot repudiate having signed the message. This property is known as nonrepudiation of origin. Authentication of messages using MACs does not provide nonrepudiation of origin for the message, whereas authentication using digital signatures does.

10.2 Attacks

Electronic payment protocols can be attacked at two levels: The protocol itself or the underlying cryptosystem.

10.2.1 Protocol-Level Attacks

Protocol attacks exploit weaknesses in the design and/or implementation of the high-level payment system. Even if the underlying cryptographic techniques are secure, their inappropriate use may open up vulnerabilities that an attacker can exploit.

- *Freshness and replay:* A protocol may be attacked by replaying some messages from a previous legitimate run. The standard countermeasure is to guarantee the freshness of messages in a protocol. Freshness means that the message provably belongs to the current context only (that is, the current payment transaction) and is not a replay of a previous message. A *nonce* is a random value chosen by the verifying party and sent to the authenticating party to be included in its reply. Because nonces are unpredictable and used in only one context, they ensure that a message cannot be reused in later transactions. Nonces do not require synchronization of clocks between the two parties. Consequently, they are very robust and popular in cryptographic protocol design. In general, nonces are an example of the challenge–response technique.

- *Fake-terminal:* Protocols that perform authentication in only one direction are susceptible to the fake-terminal attack. For example, when a customer uses an ATM, the bank and the machine check the authenticity of the customer using a PIN. The customer, however, cannot be sure whether the ATM is a genuine bank terminal or a fake one installed by an attacker for gathering PINs. Using a trusted personal device, such as a smartcard or electronic wallet, helps avoid this attack. See [52] for a more detailed discussion on the fake-terminal problem and potential solutions.

10.2.2 Cryptosystem Attacks

Cryptosystem attacks exploit weaknesses in the underlying cryptographic building blocks used in the payment system.

- *Brute force attack:* The straightforward cryptosystem attack is the brute force attack of trying every possible key. The space from which cryptographic keys are chosen is necessarily finite. If this space is not large enough, a brute force attack becomes practical. Four-digit PIN codes have a total of 10 000 permutations in the key space. If a value X is known to be the result of applying a deterministic transformation to the PIN, one can use this X to search the set of all possible PINs for the correct one. In some applications one can increase the protection against brute force attacks by randomization. Even if the key space is large, the probability distribution of keys is not necessarily uniform (especially for user-chosen PINs, which are likely to be related to the user's birthday, phone number, and so on). It might then be possible to mount dictionary attacks. Instead of trying every possible key as in the brute force attack, the attacker will only try the keys in "dictionary" of likely words, phrases, or other strings of characters.

● *Cryptanalysis:* More sophisticated attacks, called cryptanalysis, attempt to explore weaknesses in the cryptosystem itself. Most cryptosystems are not proven secure but rely on heuristics, experience, and careful review and are prone to errors. Even provably secure cryptosystems are based on the intractability of a given mathematical problem (such as the difficulty of finding graph isomorphism), which might be solvable one day.

ACKNOWLEDGEMENT

Part of the work of N. Asokan was carried out while the author was at the IBM Zurich Research Laboratory.

REFERENCES

[1] Asokan, N., Janson, P., Steiner, M. and Waidner, M. (1997). State of the art in electronic payment systems. *IEEE Computer,* **30**(9), 28–35. A Japanese translation of the article appeared in *Nikkei Computer (nc.nikkeibp.co.jp/jp/)* 30 March 1998, 195–201.
[2] Lee, P. A. and Anderson, T. (1990). *Fault Tolerance—Principles and Practice,* 2nd rev. edn., *Dependable Computing and Fault-Tolerant Systems* Vol. 3, Springer-Verlag, Wien.
[3] Chaum, D., Fiat, A. and Naor, M. (1990). Untraceable electronic cash. *Advances in Cryptology—CRYPTO '88,* Santa Barbara, California, 21–25 August 1988. Lecture Notes in Computer Science **403**, ed. S. Goldwasser, Springer-Verlag, Berlin, pp. 319–327.
[4] Brands, S. (1993). Untraceable off-line cash in wallet with observers. *Advances in Cryptology—CRYPTO '93.* Lecture Notes in Computer Science *773,* ed. Douglas R. Stinson, Springer-Verlag, Berlin, pp. 302–318.
[5] Anderson, R. and Kuhn, M. (1996). Tamper resistance—a cautionary note. *2nd USENIX Workshop on Electronic Commerce,* Oakland, California, pp. 1–11.
[6] Boneh, D., DeMillo, R. A. and Lipton, R. J. (1997). On the importance of checking cryptographic protocols for faults. *Eurocrypt '97.* Lecture Notes in Computer Science **1233**, Springer-Verlag, Berlin, pp. 37–51.
[7] Kocher, P., Jaffe, J. and Jun, B. (1999). Differential power analysis. *Advances in Cryptology—CRYPTO '99,* August. Lecture Notes in Computer Science **1666**, ed. M. Wiener, Springer-Verlag, Berlin, pp. 399–397.
[8] Chari, S., Jutla, C., Rao, J. R. and Rohatgi, P. (1999). A cautionary note regarding evaluation of AES candidates on smart-cards. *2nd Advanced Encryption Standard (AES) Candidate Conference,* Rome, Italy, March *(csrc.nist.gov/encryption/aes/round1/conf2/ aes2conf.htm).*

[9] Chari, S., Jutla, C., Rao, J. R. and Rohatgi, P. (1999). Towards sound approaches to counteract power-analysis attacks. *Advances in Cryptology—CRYPTO '99*, August. Lecture Notes in Computer Science **1666**, ed. M. Wiener, Springer-Verlag, Berlin, pp. 398–412.

[10] Pfitzmann, A., Pfitzmann, B., Schunter, M. and Waidner, M. (1997). Trusting mobile user devices and security modules. *IEEE Computer*, **30**(2), 61–68.

[11] National Institute of Standards Technology (1999). *Data Encryption Standard (DES)*. Federal Information Processing Standards Publication 46–3 (FIPS PUB 46–3), November.

[12] Anderson, R. (1994). Why cryptosystems fail. *Communications of the ACM*, **37**(11), 32–41.

[13] Rivest, R. Shamir, L. A. and Adleman, L. M. (1978). A method for obtaining digital signatures and public-key cryptosystems. *Journal of the ACM*, **21**(2), 120–126.

[14] Chaum, D. (1989). Privacy protected payments: Unconditional payer and/or payee untraceability. In *Smartcard 2000*, ed. D. Chaum and I. Schaumueller-Bichl, Elsevier North-Holland, Amsterdam, pp. 69–93.

[15] Bellare, M., Garay, J., Hauser, R. *et al.* (1999). Design, implementation and deployment of a secure account-based electronic payment system. *IEEE Journal on Selected Areas in Communications*, **18**(4), Apr. 2000.

[16] Borenstein, N. S. (1996). Perils and pitfalls of practical cybercommerce. *Communications of the ACM*, **39**(6), 36–44

[17] Gifford, D., Stewart, L., Payne, C. and Treese, G. (1995). Payment switches for open networks. *IEEE COMPCON '95*, San Francisco, March, IEEE.

[18] Anderson, M. M. (1998). The electronic check architecture. Technical Report Version 1.0.2, September, Financial Services Technology Consortium.

[19] Kravitz, J. (ed.) (1998). FSML—Financial service markup language. Technical Report Version 1.17.1, October, Financial Services Technology Consortium.

[20] Mastercard and Visa (1997). *SET Secure Electronic Transactions Protocol*, version 1.0 edition, May Book One: Business Specifications, Book Two: Technical Specification, Book Three: Formal Protocol Definition (*www.setco.org setspecifications:html*).

[21] Boly, J.-P., Bosselaers, A., Cramer, R. *et al.* (1994). The ESPRIT project CAFE—high security digital payment systems. *Proceedings of the 3rd European Symposium on Research in Computer Security (ESORICS)*, Brighton, UK, November. Lecture Notes in Computer Science **875**, ed. Dieter Gollmann, Springer-Verlag, Berlin.

[22] Medvinsky, G. and Neuman, B. C. (1993). NetCash: A design for practical electronic currency on the internet. *1st ACM Conference on Computer and Communications Security*, Fairfax, Virginia, November, ed. Victoria Ashby, ACM Press, pp. 102–106.

[23] Bürk, Holger and Pfitzmann, A. (1989). Digital payment systems enabling security and unobservability. *Computers and Security*, **8**(5), 399–416.

[24] Low, S., Maxemchuk, N. and Paul, S. (1994). Anonymous credit cards. *2nd ACM Conference on Computer and Communications Security*, Fairfax, Virginia, November, ed. Jacques Stern, ACM Press, pp. 108–117.

[25] Cox, B. J., Tygar, D. and Sirbu, M. (1995). NetBill security and transaction protocol. *1st USENIX Workshop on Electronic Commerce*, New York, July. USENIX.

[26] Pedersen, T. P. (1996). Electronic payments of small amounts. *Cambridge Workshop on Security Protocols*, April. Lecture Notes in Computer Science **1189** Springer-Verlag, Berlin, pp. 59–68.

[27] Glassman, S., Manasse, M., Abadi, M. *et al.* (1995). The MilliCent protocol for inexpensive electronic commerce. *4th International Conference on the World-Wide Web*, MIT, Boston, December.

[28] Hauser, R., Steiner, M. and Waidner, M. (1996). Micro-payments based on iKP. Research Report 2791 (No. 89269), February, IBM Research.

[29] Herzberg, A. and Yochai, H. (1997). Mini-pay: Charging per click on the web. *6th International Conference on the World-Wide Web*, Santa Clara, California, April.

[30] Pfitzmann, B. and Waidner, M. (1997). Strong loss tolerance of electronic coin systems. *ACM Transactions on Computer Systems*, **15**(2), 194–213.

[31] Jakobsson, M. and Yung, M. (1996). Revokable and versatile electronic money. *3rd ACM Conference on Computer and Communications Security*, New Delhi, India, March, ed. Clifford Neuman, ACM Press, pp. 76–87.

[32] Frankel, Y., Tsiounis, Y., and Yung, M. (1996). Indirect discourse proofs: achieving efficient fair off-line e-cash. *Asiacrypt '96*, Lecture Notes in Computer Science **1163**, Springer-Verlag, Berlin, pp. 286–300.

[33] Camenisch, J., Maurer, U. and Stadler, M. (1996). Digital payment systems with passive anonymity-revoking trustees. *4th European Symposium on Research in Computer Security (ESORICS '96)*, Rome, Lecture Notes in Computer Science **1146**, Springer-Verlag, Berlin, pp. 33–43.

[34] von Solms, S. and Naccache, D. (1992). On blind signatures and perfect crimes. *Computers and Security*, **11**(6), 581–583.

[35] Petersen, H. and Poupard, G. (1997). Efficient scalable fair cash with off-line extortion prevention. *1st International Conference on Information and Communications Security (ICICS)*, Lecture Notes in Computer Science **1334**, Springer-Verlag, Berlin, pp. 463–477.

[36] Rivest, R. L. and Shamir, A. (1996). PayWord and MicroMint: Two simple micropayment schemes. *Cambridge Workshop on Security Protocols*, April, Lecture Notes in Computer Science **1189**, Springer-Verlag, Berlin, pp. 69–88.

[37] Anderson, R., Manifavas, H. and Sutherland, C. (1996). NetCard—a practical electronic cash system. *Cambridge Workshop on Security Protocols*, April, Lecture Notes in Computer Science **1189**, Springer-Verlag, Berlin.

[38] Schunter, M. Fair exchange: A new paradigm for e-commerce. *SEMPER—Secure Electronic Marketplace for Europe*. Lecture Notes in Computer Science, ed. G. Lacoste, B. Pfitzmann, M. Steiner, and M. Waidner, Springer-Verlag, Berlin (to appear).

[39] Bahreman, A. (1996). Generic electronic payment services: Framework and functional specification. *2nd USENIX Workshop on Electronic Commerce*, Oakland, California, November, pp. 87–103.

[40] Ketchpel, S. P., Garcia-Molina, H., Paepcke, A. *et al.* (1996). U-PAI: A universal payment application interface. *2nd USENIX Workshop on Electronic Commerce*, Oakland, California, November, pp. 105–121.

[41] Sun Microsystems (1998). The Java Wallet (TM) architecture white paper, March. (*java.sun.com/products/commerce/docs/whitepapers/arch/architecture.ps*).

[42] Abad-Peiro, J. L., Asokan, N., Steiner, M. and Waidner, M. (1996). Designing a generic payment service. Research Report RZ 2891 (No. 90839), IBM Research, December. A later version is also available [43

[43] Abad-Peiro, J. L., Asokan, N., Steiner, M., and Waidner, M. (1998). Designing a generic payment service. *IBM Systems Journal*, **37**(1), 72–88.

[44] Asokan, N. and Steiner, M. The payment framework. *SEMPER—Secure Electronic Marketplace for Europe*. Lecture Notes in Computer Science, ed. G. Lacoste, B. Pfitzmann, M. Steiner, and M. Waidner, Springer-Verlag, Berlin, (to appear).

[45] Pfitzmann, B. and Waidner, M. (1996). Properties of payment systems—general definition sketch and classification. Research Report RZ 2823 (No. 90126), IBM Research, May.

[46] Asokan, N., Van Herreweghen, E. and Steiner, M. (1998). Towards a framework for handling disputes in payment systems. *3rd USENIX Workshop on Electronic Commerce*, Boston, MA, September, USENIX, pp. 187–202.

[47] Wallich, P. (1999). How to steal millions in chump change. *Scientific American*, **281**(2), 21. (More information on this fraud case at *www.labmed.umn.edu/john/ccfraud.html*.)

[48] Schneier, B. (1996). *Applied Cryptography: Protocols, Algorithms, and Source Code in C*. John Wiley, New York.

[49] Menezes, A. J., van Oorschot, P. C. and Vanstone, S. A. (1997). *Handbook of Applied Cryptography*. CRC Press, Boca Raton, FL.

[50] Bellare, M., Canetti, R. and Krawczyk, H. (1997). HMAC: Keyed-hashing for message authentication. Internet RFC 2104, February.

[51] NIST (1995). National Institute of Standards and Technology (Computer Systems Laboratory). *Secure hash standard*. Federal Information Processing Standards Publication FIPS PUB 180–1, April.

[52] Asokan, N., Debar, H., Steiner, M. and Waidner, M. (1999). Authenticating public terminals. *Computer Networks*, **31**(8), 861–870.

Defective Software: An Overview of Legal Remedies and Technical Measures Available to Consumers

COLLEEN KOTYK VOSSLER

Shaw Pittman
2300 N Street, N.W.
Washington, D.C.
20037, USA
colleen.Vossler@Shawpittman.com

JEFFREY VOAS

Reliable Software Technologies
21351 Ridgetop Circle, Suite 400
Dulles, VA 20166 USA
jmvoas@rstcorp.com

Abstract

The rapid growth of the computer industry has given rise to new legal and developmental challenges. Legal liability for software developers is unclear and nonuniform, and faulty software persists. Systems integrators and users are responsible for protecting their own interests when they contract for new software. However, a new uniform law, the Uniform Computer Information Transactions Act, is before US state legislatures; the law addresses agreements whose primary purpose is to require a party either to create, modify, license or transfer informational rights in computer information. If legislatures pass the Act, system integrators and users will have a new avenue for pursuing claims arising from computer information transactions. However, the law is the subject of much controversy because it is not neutral and is described as pro-vendor. This chapter outlines the legal remedies available to systems integrators when software fails and suggests defensive steps that system integrators and users can employ to minimize the risk of faulty software.

This chapter provides general information and represents the authors' views. It does not constitute legal advice and should not be used or taken as legal advice relating to any specific situation.

ADVANCES IN COMPUTERS, VOL. 53
ISBN 0-12-012153-0

451

1. Introduction

Legal liability for software developers is unclear and, as yet, nonuniform. When software malfunctions or has errors, it can cause various types of harm to the user. The harm can be economic or personal to property or to self. The degree to which software affects lives and livelihoods cannot be underestimated. As evidence, Cisco announced in June of 1999 that the top 20 companies in internet revenues have a combined market value of over $2.4 trillion dollars [1]. This shows how software, the backbone of the internet, is gradually gaining a higher degree of predominance in commerce and industry than it previously enjoyed. Such prominence only adds to the need that software work correctly.

Unfortunately, software fails. These failures are not limited to the software underlying the internet. Because of this, courts are beginning to wrestle with the concept of imposing liability on development organizations.

The key questions facing the industry are how courts will assign blame and determine whether a particular software package is defective. Whether software development organizations are liable, and to what extent, is a body of law that is in its infancy. This chapter aims to provide developers, system analysts, and systems integrators with a basic foundation of the types of liability they may incur. In addition, this chapter explores expectations for defect-free software, the basic concepts of tort and contract liability, the status of a proposed uniform law on computer information transactions, recommendations to developers for avoiding liability, and recommendations to users on how to avoid licensing problematic software.

2. Defect-Free Software: An Oxymoron?

The fundamental question underlying the issue of software liability is whether software must be free of defects before it is licensed to consumers. If software is legally allowed to have defects prior to release, the courts must then determine what defects are harmful to consumers and what defects are acceptable (either because they do not cause harm or cause minimum harm). To do so, the courts will need to define the term "defect."

Interestingly, software programs can have flaws that are not readily noticeable by developers or end-users. There are numerous reasons for this. One is that testing can fail to discover a fault in a program simply by not selecting a test case that exercises the fault. Here, the developer is unlikely to debug the software and hence the software will be released with an existing error. The reason that testing often fails to reveal the existence of defects is directly tied to the three events that must occur for software to fail as the result of a defect. Those are events are that:

- the bug must be executed
- the bug must infect the state of the program
- the infected state must propagate through the program and cause the output to be incorrect.

Even if those three events do occur, it is still possible that the testing tool or person observing the output of the program will fail to recognize that the output is incorrect and, in fact, may determine that the flawed output is actually correct output. Therefore, testing—even when it is rigorous and thorough—permits bugs to go undetected.

Another reason why end-users may not notice the effect of a code defect is that the end-users may not use the functionality of the software in which the defect is resident. For example, on a modern word-processing package, there are many options that the average user will not exploit. If the bulk of the defects for the word-processing system reside in the logic for these rarely used features, the defects can remain latent for long periods of time. In this type of situation, the software publisher likely will receive few complaints.

As a result, errors can exist in functioning systems that are still highly usable and robust. Although software errors can result in economic or personal disasters, they more often than not merely cause inconveniences to users. It is simply the "high profile" defects that make the nightly news— and those are far and few between.

Assessing the consequences of software failure is something with which the legal system is just beginning to grapple. To complicate matters, what may seem like a flaw or defect to a user may in fact be a performance limitation or the result of a design decision. Sorting out such issues is increasingly complex, given the types of highly integrated systems that are being designed today. These systems rely on multiple vendors to supply multiple components. Assigning blame for system failures from such systems is important to consumers, although difficult to accomplish.

Until the mid-1980s, most consumers used computers configured as standardized mini or mainframe systems. The industry then moved toward "distributed networks." These systems are comprised of hardware and software from different vendors. Distributed networks are often connected across long geographic distances, enabling system-level tasks to be performed with no predetermined sequence or combination of events. This is a vastly different computing paradigm than systems from the 1970s that performed tasks through a structured series of "time-ordered event sequences" [2]. The move toward distributed computation makes liability assessment a complex maze of hypotheses, assumptions, and variables that simply cannot be measured.

For example, suppose that one workstation gets handed an enormous task to perform that is independent of other tasks that the distributed network needs performed by that workstation. If the priority for the independent task is raised above the priority settings for the network-related tasks, the shift will reduce the workstation's ability to complete the network-related tasks in time. Any design assumptions about when the workstation will finish the network-related tasks may become invalid. Unless synchronization is properly implemented in this distributed system, the other workstations may continue with their tasks without waiting for the results from this workstation. A situation can arise that is virtually impossible to reproduce during testing, and therefore the incorrect coding of the synchronization will not get detected prior to software release. In essence, the slowdown of the workstation is a variable that cannot easily be measured and hence, assigning blame becomes very difficult to do.

In order for a developer to build software that is less likely to create a legal problem as a result of poor quality, there are a variety of well-known steps that the developer should employ during design and development. For example, the developer should use a standard process such as one of those promulgated by the International Standards Organization, the National Institute of Standards and Technology, the Institute of Electronics and Electrical Engineers, or the Software Engineering Institute. Whether the development organization adheres to any of these schemes rigorously is not important since none of these schemes claims to guarantee defect-free code. However, showing that the processes chosen were reasonable and in line with the state-of-the-art is the key and may be important in a legal battle.

Further, the developer should employ some combination of the well-known testing methods to assure that the software's actual behavior matches its desired behavior. Ample evidence exists which demonstrates the value added by the techniques (as well as their limitations), and therefore there is no reasonable defense for failing to employ them [3].

The most common test method that developers employ for satisfying themselves that particular software is ready for release is *operational, system-level* testing. This form of testing attempts to show that a system will behave reliably (with respect to the software's specifications) in a fixed environment. The fixed environment that developers usually test against is the one that represents the largest portion of their perceived user base. This form of testing can be thought of as the standard against which courts and the commercial public can assess the developer's liability. The developer can then assert that for the typical user, the software will function appropriately. Unfortunately, however, when the environment changes, this form of testing will need to be re-performed to reflect the nuances of the new environment. Further, if the developer's perception concerning how the typical user will use the product is incorrect, the testing will likely mislead the developer into believing that the software is ready for release when indeed it may not be.

Not all types of software need the same level of testing. For example, games software does not need the same level of assurance as safety-critical software. Business software such as banking systems needs high levels of assurance, but arguably not as high as safety-critical software. Therefore, the level of assurance must match the criticality of the application. One size does not fit all. The lack of a uniform standard may, however, prove costly to developers who may not employ the correct level of assurance.

Safety-critical software is unique because it requires a very special type of system-level testing: "exhaustive testing to assess every possible sequence, permutation, and combination of events" [2]. This, however, is not possible. In fact, except for non-trivial (simple) systems, it is widely accepted and theoretically valid that the relentless pursuit of perfection for correct software is not feasible. This reality requires a change in our thinking about software testing. Developers must strive to make software testing a more intelligent process, as opposed one of brute force. Removing all defects is an unattainable goal; developers should thus strategize and focus testing resources toward the most egregious errors when possible. Specialized testing and analysis techniques exist that attempt to accomplish this goal; however, they are not foolproof.

From a developer's standpoint, the key difficulty with operational, system-level testing is the developer's frequent lack of information concerning in which environments the software will be embedded. The developer can hypothesize about how the typical environment will look and can even generalize about how she believes the typical user will use the product. But without detailed, specialized information on a user-by-user basis, it will be rare for the operational, system-level testing that the developer conducts to match the accuracy of such testing when it is performed by the user at its own site.

Therefore, as this chapter discusses, it is prudent for users to do some level of in-house, specialized operational system-level testing before opting to incorporate a third-party product into their environment. If users do not conduct their own testing, the assurance afforded by the developer's testing is limited at best and highly questionable at worst. If users do not have the ability to do in-house testing, then those users should either request that the software publisher do it for them or contact a third-party independent laboratory or consultant to performing the testing.

It is fair to say that the main problem contributing to inferior "commercial grade" software quality stems from inferior testing, even when tools and numerous books on the subject exist:

> Automated testing tools capture the input of a human tester and generate test scripts to be run repeatedly. Errors are detected and testing resumes once the cause is determined and the fault repaired. However, each subsequent error is more difficult to detect and correct. Although automated testing tools are increasingly available, only about 75% of the code in the 60 leading products in the software industry has been tested. In the overall development community, only about 35% of the code in a typical application is tested. The top four development organizations, however, have been reported to be committed to quality development, detecting up to 95% of software defects before delivery to users [2].

The question then that begs to be answered concerns the 5% of defects that get released. What are the consequences? A competing imperative between the goals of users and developers exists. Users increasingly demand software that is rich in both features and quality, whereas developers want their software on the market as quickly as possible [4]. The question is, who loses in terms of the remaining defects—the user or the developer?

When discussing liability, two different types of software defects must be clarified, because each may have a different impact on liability. The two types of defects that exist in released software are patent defects and latent defects. A *patent defect* is one that is evident on its face. In this situation, the developer knows that the defect is in the software. A *latent defect* is one that manifests itself later. Under these circumstances, the developer is unaware of the defect when putting the software on the market. An issue arises over what defects—patent, latent, or both—for which the developer should be held accountable. Furthermore, if the developer discloses a patent defect, an issue arises as to whether the developer avoids liability based on the disclosure. To date, the law does not require disclosure of known defects, but as laws regarding software are promulgated at the state and national level, disclosure may become mandatory. Another sub-issue arises, however, if disclosure of known defects becomes mandatory—does the developer completely avoid liability, or does she limit her liability, if she discloses any known defects?[1]

The burden on developers to disclose any and all defects is a heavy one.

> The increasingly complex computing environment has made it more difficult to develop complex systems, correct in terms of the design specifications, with no defects. Even if it were possible, the development team would certainly be unable to foresee and accommodate all unanticipated circumstances which may arise during use [2].

The remainder of this chapter presents remedies that are available to affected users when developers release defective software. The discussion will also expand a developer's knowledge of the legal pitfalls inherent in producing software in today's marketplace.

3. Legal Remedies

As technology becomes increasingly intertwined with everyday life and its occurrences, the possibility of defects causing economic or physical harm rises as well. Software is being used to automate and run increasing numbers of systems every day, including medical systems, telecommunications networks, financial markets, and manufacturing and design systems, among others. The more software is intertwined with everyday life, the greater the chance of a defect causing economic or physical harm. There are many legal theories that a plaintiff might apply to a software defect that causes some type of harm. This chapter does not intend to cover all potential theories, but rather the most likely theories.[2] Those theories fall into two distinct legal categories: contract and tort theories of recovery.

A theory sounding in contract occurs when a good or service does not conform to the specifications of the contractual agreement between two or more parties. The underpinning for a contract theory of recovery is that a contract, express or implied, is the foundation of the transaction. A contract, in its most basic form, is an "agreement between two or more persons that creates an obligation to do or not to do a particular thing" [5 at 306, 322].[3]

---

[1] These questions remain to be resolved by the legal system.

[2] Furthermore, the authors do not claim to cover every aspect of the theories and approaches discussed. Rather, it is their intent to provide the reader with a broad-based understanding of the current and likely future legal landscape.

[3] Consideration is the "cause, motive, price, or impelling influence which induces a contracting party to enter into a contract." [5, at 306]. Legal consideration is consideration permitted or recognized by law.

The essentials of a contract are: competent parties, subject matter, legal consideration, mutuality of agreement, and mutuality of obligation" [5 at 306, 320].

In contrast, a tort theory of recovery is any other theory of recovery other than one sounding in contract.

> Recovery in tort is generally independent of the existence or nature of any associated contract or agreement. Instead, it is based on a finding that certain conduct was wrongful (and therefore tortious) as a matter of public policy and that the tortfeasor should be required to bear the cost of the injury [6, p. 203].

A tort is a "private or civil wrong or injury, including action for bad faith breach of contract, for which the court will provide a remedy in the form of an action for damages" [5, at 1489]. The wrong committed upon either person or property must be independent of contract. It can be "either (1) a direct invasion of some legal right of the individual; (2) the infraction of some public duty by which special damage accrues to the individual; or (3) the violation of some private obligation by which like damage accrues to the individual" [5, at 1489].

A plaintiff is more likely to succeed on a contract theory of recovery for information transactions, but tort remedies may be available. The following discussion highlights potential tort theories of recovery and explores contract recovery, in the form of a uniform act, in depth.

4. Tort Remedies

Negligence, fraud, and misrepresentation are three torts for which a software developer likely may be liable.[4] The application of tort law to information transactions is far from uniform; courts are wrestling with applying traditional common law concepts to ever-changing technologies. Such application is particularly difficult when a claim centers on a cutting-edge technology about which neither party knows the true potential.

4.1 Negligence

Negligence is a kind of conduct-conduct "which falls below the standard established by law for the protection of others against unreasonable risk of

---

[4] This discussion of tort remedies is not meant to be comprehensive; a plaintiff may find that other tort remedies are available. However, negligence, misrepresentation and strict liability are the three most likely causes of action that a plaintiff might bring. In addition, although plaintiffs have asserted professional malpractice as a cause of action, courts have rejected such a theory in the field of computer consulting. See [7], aff'd in part, remanded in part, [8].

harm" [9]. To prove negligence, a plaintiff must show:

- the existence of a legal duty of care owed to the injured party
- a breach of the duty of care
- actual and proximate cause of the injury by the breach of the duty of care
- damages.[5]

A legal duty of care is a duty or obligation to affirmatively act in a particular manner [12]. If a party has no duty to act in a particular manner, a negligence theory cannot succeed. If a duty exists, and the party breaches it by failing to conform to the standard of care, a cause of action may exist. The party asserting negligence must go further in its proof; a "reasonably close causal connection between the conduct and the resulting injury" is necessary [10, §30, at 165]. Finally, actual loss or damage must be the result of the breach of the duty of care. Without damages, the plaintiff's claim fails. Nominal damages or the threat of future harm are insufficient to establish actual damages. "Negligent conduct in itself is not such an interference with the interests of the world at large that there is any right to complain of it, or to be free from it, except in the case of some individual whose interests have suffered" [10, §30, at 165].

In addition to the ordinary standard of care imposed upon parties, a court may impose a professional standard of care.[6] Rather than measure the party's actions against what a reasonable person might do, the court will measure the actions against a higher standard that asks whether the party failed to act reasonably in light of superior knowledge and expertise in a particular area. Because computer and information transactions are highly specialized, courts may judge the conduct of developers and other professionals in the software industry against this higher standard. In

---

[5] "Reasonableness is one of the two major standards utilized in negligence to give content to the concept of duty. As a general matter, the conduct of the defendant is measured against the objective standard of the reasonable person. If such a mythical being, aware of the surrounding circumstances, would not have acted in the way the defendant did, the defendant's conduct is unreasonable, and the defendant has failed to exercise the duty of reasonable care" [10, at 164–165].

"The second major standard utilized in negligence to measure the scope of a defendant's duty is that of foreseeability. Since duty is expressed in terms of apparent risk, liability cannot be imposed unless the risk of injury is reasonably foreseeable. In addition, foreseeability defines the scope of duty by limiting the number of persons to whom the duty is owed. Negligence does not exist in a vacuum, ordinarily, a duty of care is not owed to the entire world. Reasonable care is due only to those whose injury is reasonably foreseeable" [11].

[6] The same elements for negligence apply regardless of the standard of care a court may apply.

Diversified Graphics, Ltd. v. Groves [13] the Eighth Circuit upheld a jury's finding that an accounting firm failed to exercise professional care when it assisted its client in the purchase and implementation of a turnkey data processing system.

The Court of Appeals stated that "[p]rofessional persons *and* those engaged in any work or trade requiring special skill must possess a minimum of special knowledge and ability as well as exercise reasonable care" [14].[7] Whether a professional has exercised the appropriate degree of skill and care is a question for the jury [13, at 296]. The jury found, and the appellate court agreed, that the defendants had not exercised the necessary degree of skill and care, in part because the defendants failed to meet their own internal standards that they expressly adopted [13, at 296–297].

Because Diversified Graphics, Ltd. lacked computer expertise, it relied on Ernst & Whinney to select and implement an in-house computer data processing system [13, at 294]. Ernst & Whinney promised Diversified that it would "locate a 'turnkey' system which would be fully operational without need of extensive employee training" [13, at 294]. The system that Diversified received was "difficult to operate and failed to adequately meet its needs" [13, at 294]. To procure a turnkey system, which is customized and fully operational, the party engaged in procuring the system must "carefully detail a business's needs" and "properly develop specifications for the computer system" [13, at 297]. During the selection process, potential vendors must be carefully investigated to discover any inadequacies in the system; once selected, proper implementation is imperative to ensure that the system truly is turnkey [13, at 297]. The Court of Appeals upheld the jury's findings that the data processing system that Ernst & Whinney selected and implemented required Diversified to "incur considerable expense necessary for modifications, employee training, and additional staffing and consultation" [13, at 297]. The system was not, in fact, turnkey.

The import of this decision and the court's application of a professional standard of care should give pause to developers, consultants, and others whose expertise is utilized in the development or selection of systems or programs. Such individuals may not only be held to the ordinary standard of care to which all individuals would be held. Instead, those individuals may find that a more stringent standard—the duty of professional care—is applicable. Regardless of which negligence standard a court applies, the

---

[7] "Reasonable care" is "[t]hat degree if care which a person of ordinary prudence would exercise in the same or similar circumstances …. That degree of care which ordinarily prudent and competent person engaged in the same line of business or endeavor should exercise under similar circumstances" [5, at 1265].

developer or consultant may be liable in tort if a party can demonstrate the four prongs of negligence.

4.2 Fraudulent Misrepresentation

To prove fraudulent misrepresentation (also known as *deceit*), a plaintiff must show [15]:

- a false representation of fact
- knowledge or belief that the representation is false
- intent to induce action or inaction in reliance on the representation
- justifiable reliance on the representation by the person to whom it is made
- damages resulting from reliance on the misrepresentation.

In the software context, a plaintiff's likely argument would be that the developer stated that the software would function in a certain way or meet the user's specifications. Another means of alleging fraud is for the plaintiff to claim that the developer knew of specific problems in the software and did not disclose those shortcomings.

In *RKB Enterps., Inc. v. Ernst & Young*, plaintiff **RKB** entered into a contract with defendant Ernst & Young to perform computer consulting services relating to RKB's procurement of a new data processing system [8]. RKB experienced cost increases and delays based on difficulties it encountered in adapting the computer program and system to its business [8].

> The court determined that it was error to dismiss plaintiff's allegation because "it relied upon the advice and the opinion of defendants and was thereby induced to enter into the contracts, that the inducements made by defendants were deliberately misleading and fraudulent, and that defendants knew plaintiff was relying upon their special knowledge and skill when they rendered their opinions [8, at 972–973].

Fraud claims are an excellent option for recovery for the average consumer. The public policy interest "protected by the law of deceit is an interest in formulating business judgements without being misled by others —in short, not being cheated." However, not all theorists agree with the application of fraud claims in this context:

> Fraud claims play a significant role in commercial litigation in the computer industry because they create litigation advantages for parties able to make a colorable allegation that fraud occurred in the transaction. Depending on the

circumstances and the nature of the dispute, these litigation advantages include creating factual issues that bring the case to a jury, the ability to circumvent some contract disclaimers and other barriers, and the ability to claim and potentially recover enhanced damages in a dispute with contract overtones that would not otherwise support such damage claims [16, 10–6].

Asserting this type of claim is not a sure success, however. One problem with asserting fraudulent misrepresentation or deceit is that, when a contract exists in a dispute, it is hard to distinguish the contract claim from the tort claim. The former deals in a failed promise and one party's failure to perform as a result, whereas the latter centers around a party's liability for disseminating false information or, alternatively, for failing to disclose information that is important or integral to the other party [16, 10–6]. When fraud is alleged in a case in which a contract exists, the courts must distinguish between what the contract covers and what is outside the four corners and independent of the contract. If the contract does not control a particular issue, the plaintiff may succeed in bringing a valid tort claim [17].

In *Ritchie Enterps. v. Honeywell Bull, Inc.*, the district court determined that a claim of negligent misrepresentation[8] was not viable because the integrated purchase contract specifically disclaimed all prior representations and warranties:

> The effect of confusing the concept of contractual duties, which are voluntarily bargained-for, with the concept of tort duties, which are largely imposed by law, would be to nullify a substantial part of what the parties expressly bargained for—limited liability .... The careless and unnecessary blanket confusion of tort and contract would undermine the carefully evolved utility of both [18].

The *Ritchie* court held that the negligent misrepresentation claim was invalid because the agreement between the parties "contains an integration clause stating that it represents the parties' entire agreement and 'supersedes' all prior oral and written proposals and communications" [18]. As a result, Ritchie's claim that Honeywell induced it to purchase a mainframe computer was dismissed.

---

[8] Three basic types of misrepresentation exist: fraudulent, negligent, and reckless. Negligent misrepresentation occurs when the party does not know its statement is false and very well may believe it is true, but a reasonably cautious person would discover the error or would not speak further before undertaking a further investigation. Reckless misrepresentation occurs when the party does not know the statement is false but there was substantial probability that the statement is false; alternatively, the party may not have an idea whether it is speaking truthfully. Regardless of the form of misrepresentation, courts still must distinguish the tort claim from the contract claim.

A misrepresentation claim will be difficult to establish when a contract regulates the deal that has occurred between two parties. Unless the party alleging misrepresentation can sufficiently demonstrate that the elements of misrepresentation can be met without relying on the contract, the claim will likely fail. The result is a difficult cause of action for a party to establish.

4.3   Strict Liability

Strict liability is another tort theory under which a plaintiff can bring a claim. To find a developer subject to strict liability, the courts must determine that the software is a product. Strict product liability is defined as:

> One who sells any product in a defective condition unreasonably dangerous to the user or consumer or to his property is subject to liability for physical harm thereby caused [even though] the seller has exercised all possible care in the preparation and sale of his product, and ... the user or consumer has not bought the product from or entered into any relationship with the seller [10, §95].

To date, strict liability has not been applied successfully to software in the United States. *Sparacino v. Andover Controls Corp.* [19] is indicative of the success rate (or lack thereof) for strict liability claims. Andover manufactured microprocessing equipment at the time of the incident; it sold an energy management system to another company, CMC, which in turn installed it in a high school. Sparacino, a chemistry teacher, prepared an experiment that produced chlorine gas in the laboratory; the experiment occurred in senior chemistry once a semester and Sparacino had performed it numerous times prior to that date [19, at 432]. However, the fan failed to operate and, when Sparacino opened the windows to provide ventilation to avoid inhalation of the noxious fumes, the air drew the noxious fumes toward him and he was forced to inhale them [19, at 433]. He suffered injury as a result.

The fan, part of the system that Andover manufactured and CMC installed, was scheduled to be inoperative until 6:30 a.m., 15 minutes later than the time at which Sparacino attempted to turn the fan on. No notices or other postings were on or near the fan [19, at 433]. Sparacino asserted that Andover was strictly liable because the energy management system was "inherently dangerous, defective, and unreasonably unsafe in design and manufacture" [19, at 433].

The court disagreed, stating that

[a] product is unreasonably dangerous where it fails to perform in the manner reasonably expected in light of its nature and intended function ... and where the defect in the product subjects those exposed to it to an unreasonable risk of harm [19, at 434].

The court held that the energy management system "did not fail to perform in the manner reasonably expected in light of its nature and intended function" because the system is user programmable, allowing the user to determine and write in its specifications [19, at 433, 435]. Further, the system was not inherently dangerous as assembled [19, at 435].

Because of the very high burden placed on the party alleging strict liability, it is a difficult standard to satisfy. It is not impossible, however, to succeed in proving the theory in information transactions, and courts are likely to award damages in the future to a party who can prove all the elements. If courts do begin to find developers strictly liable, developers will indeed need to reassess the way they currently do business because they could, regardless of the steps taken to prevent unintended or unforeseeable consequences, incur liability without fault.

5. Contract Remedies

When parties have contracted to perform certain duties, the question of a breach occurs when one or both parties fail to perform their respective duties. In certain situations, it may be relatively simple to determine whether a party has breached the contract based on its performance. However, certain conduct may not be specifically defined in the contract, and therefore, it may be difficult to determine whether a party has in fact breached.

Drafting a contract is an art. The contract should be specific enough to protect the party, and yet flexible enough to protect the party.[9] For example, defining acceptable performance is a key element of protection. Without such a definition, a software developer may find herself in the position of being accused of a breach of contract for non-performance. The resulting

---

[9] Often, issues that arise in litigation or other means of dispute resolution "can be controlled before the fact by careful bargaining and drafting. The frequency of reported litigation, however, documents that this often fails to achieve the desired clarity or outcome" [16, § 6.01 at 6–4]. As the law develops and gives parties direction regarding issues that arise, the legal precedent will drive the bargaining process, both in terms of economics and expectations.

mediation, arbitration, or litigation can be costly and lead to an unsatisfactory result. Contracts increasingly include a provision that states how the parties will resolve a conflict. These provisions will usually dictate a means of resolving a dispute.[10]

For many years, software and related technology issues have stymied courts, practitioners, parties, and academics because of the nature of the transaction and the resulting difficulty when attempting to apply existing law to the issues arising from software transactions.[11] The challenge is the subject matter because software is unlike the traditional transactional framework. One reason is the conditional nature of the transaction—information and rights are severable from the tangible aspect (e.g., a diskette). The value is in the intangibles, not the goods. Whether a technology-related transaction is one of goods or services arises frequently. Several laws exist that a court could apply to software; the Uniform Commercial Code (UCC) applies to a sale of goods, whereas common and statutory law applies to a services contract. Courts have applied both types of laws to software contracts. To remedy this tension, a uniform law has been crafted to regulate transactions where the

---

[10] For example, the following clause outlines a dispute resolution process to which the parties agree as a core element of the contract:

Binding Arbitration and Jury Trial Waiver. Any dispute with respect to this Agreement which is not resolved within ten (10) days after referral to the parties' senior executives, shall at any time thereafter at the initiation of either party, be submitted to arbitration which shall be the exclusive means for resolving any such disputes. Such arbitration shall be held in the City [determined by parties], and shall be conducted by an arbitration association mutually acceptable to both parties. However, in the event the parties do not agree within seven (7) days, then in such event the entity shall be the American Arbitration Association, in accordance with its arbitration rules and procedures then in effect or such other arbitrator or dispute resolution organization as the parties shall mutually agree. The arbitrators will be selected from a panel of retired judges and will have familiarity with dispute resolution in the information technology industry. Any costs associated with the arbitration shall be borne by the non-prevailing party. All decisions of the arbitrators shall be binding on both parties. Judgment upon the award rendered by the arbitrators may be entered in any court having jurisdiction. THE PARTIES HEREBY KNOWINGLY AND VOLUNTARILY AND IRREVOCABLY WAIVE THEIR RIGHT TO A TRIAL BY JURY and agree that if the foregoing binding arbitration provision is determined for any reason to be unenforceable or inapplicable to a particular dispute, then such dispute shall be decided solely by a judge, without the use of a jury, sitting in a court of competent jurisdiction. This binding arbitration and jury trial waiver provision shall survive termination of this Agreement.

[11] "[G]iven the complexity of technology and the often over enthusiastic expectations that parties bring to a deal, new technology and systems often fall short of expectations unless those expectations have been carefully defined and delimited in the bargaining and design phases of a transaction. When the delivered quality fails to meet expectations, the cost of the disparity between performance and expectation must be apportioned between the vendor and the buyer. This involves a determination of the rights of the parties under the applicable agreements" [16], § 6.01 at 6–4.

purpose is to convey rights in intangible property and information. If adopted by any of the states, it will be the standard against which state courts will judge technology transactions.

5.1 The Uniform Commercial Code

Under the UCC (§2–105), "goods" are defined as "things that are movable at the time of identification to the contract." Whether software is considered a good or a service is often dependent upon the nature of the software–whether it is mass-marketed or custom-made.[12] Courts face three possible approaches to classification: goods, services, or a goods/services combination. Under current law, if the court determines that the contract deals with goods, the UCC will apply [20–22]. For example, shrinkwrapped software, because it is mass-marketed, is often considered to be a good.

However, if the court classifies the transaction as one that is predominantly services, common or statutory law will apply. Courts are likely to determine that a custom-designed system is a service, particularly since it is not movable at the time of identification to the contract. It does not even exist when the parties are negotiating and finalizing the contract. The most difficult contract for a court to classify is one that sells software and provides maintenance or another type of service.[13]

In *Advent Sys., Ltd. v. Unisys Corp.* [23], the Third Circuit held that software is in fact a "good" within the meaning of the UCC as codified in Pennsylvania. In *Advent Systems*, the issue before the Court of Appeals was whether software was a good or intellectual property. The Official Commentary in the Pennsylvania Code states:

> The Act is drawn to provide flexibility so that, since it is intended to be a semi-permanent piece of legislation, it will provide its own machinery for expansion of commercial practices. It is intended to make it possible for the law embodied in this Act to be developed by the courts in light of unforeseen and new circumstances and practices [24].

The Court of Appeals cited other Pennsylvania cases recognizing goods as having a "very extensive meaning" under the UCC, and noted that the

---

[12] Hardware of any type would be considered goods because a monitor, CPU, or other component is "movable at the time of identification to the contract" [16, §6.02 at 6–4]. Two articles under the UCC can apply to such transactions: Article 2, which governs the sale of goods, or Article 2A, which governs the lease of goods.

[13] The test courts most frequently employ to determine whether the contract is goods- or services-based is the predominant purpose test. Under this test, the court will look at the entire contract and determine whether it is predominantly goods or predominantly services. Once it has made the determination, it applies the appropriate law to the whole contract.

contract's main objective was to transfer products and the compensation structure focused on goods [23, at 675–676]. As a result, the court applied Article 2 to the contract and its subject matter.[14]

Although Articles 2 and 2A of the UCC are well-crafted, many argue they neither adequately reflect or remedy the issues that software and other technology-related areas present. To remedy this tension, a uniform law has been crafted to regulate transactions where the purpose is to convey rights in intangible property and information.

5.2 Uniform Computer Information Transactions Act

On 7 April 1999, the National Conference of Commissioners on Uniform State Laws (NCCUSL) and the American Law Institute (ALI) announced that "computer information transactions w[ould] not be promulgated as Article 2B of the Uniform Commercial Code, but [NCCUSL] w[ould] promulgate the rules for adoption by states as the Uniform Computer Information Transactions Act" ("UCITA" or "the Act") [27]. The transformation from a uniform commercial code section to a uniform law was attributed to "[l]ack of uniformity and clarity of the legal rules governing these transactions engender uncertainty, unpredictability, and high transaction costs" [27]. These qualities would not "allow the sort of codification that is represented by the Uniform Commercial Code" [27].

The NCCUSL's shift has important ramifications. UCITA met serious opposition in the form of Article 2B; it was unlikely that the states would enact the law as a part of the commercial code. The law's metamorphosis into a uniform law was much more palatable; NCCUSL adopted UCITA on 29 July 1999.[15] The 50 states, the District of Columbia, Puerto Rico, and the US Virgin Islands had the opportunity to vote on the law, beginning in the fall of 1999.[16] NCCUSL "believes that UCITA can provide a framework in which sound business practices may further evolve in the marketplace bounded by standards of appropriate policy" [27]. The Act is based on five fundamental principles:

- Computer information transactions primarily involve licenses, not sales.
- Small companies play a large role in computer information transactions.

---

[14] Other courts have also applied Article 2 to software contracts [25, 26].

[15] Twenty-five state Attorneys General, the American Intellectual Property Law Association and many other groups opposed UCITA's passage. For a list of individual groups, see *www.badsoftware.com/oppose.htm*.

[16] At the time of writing, UCITA was before the California legislature.

- Computer information transactions implicate fundamental free speech issues.
- Parties to computer information transactions should be free to contract as they wish.
- The law must be technology-neutral [28].

Through these principles, UCITA purports to satisfy the need for "coherent and predictable legal rules to support the contracts that underlie" the information economy [29]. Legislative initiatives in many states attempt to clarify the legal rules that are applicable to electronic commerce, but the diversity "creates a potential nightmare for industries which are national and indeed international in scope" [29]. The Act's drafters intend the act to function as "an intermediate legal step that will bring greater uniformity and certainty to the law until the practice and the law in this area has developed sufficient maturity" [29]. By adopting a uniform law, opportunities for legal abuse, huge expenditures on legal research, and unfair surprises for developers and users are reduced because the parties will know what to expect [30]. It is crucial to remember, however, that the Act will function largely as a framework for parties whose contract does not specifically address particular issues.

The Act applies to computer information transactions, which the Act defines as "an agreement and the performance of that agreement to create, modify, transfer, or license computer information or informational rights in computer information" (UCITA §102(a)(12), Final Text).[17] The scope is carefully drawn; for a transaction to fall under the Act, "if a computer information is the primary subject matter, th[e] Act applies to the entire transaction ... [and if] the computer information is not the primary subject matter, th[e] Act applies only to the part of the transaction pertaining to the computer information." (UCITA §103(b)). The broad categories which are expressly excluded within the scope of the Act are: (UCITA §103 Note 3):

- service contracts
- casual exchanges of information
- contracts where computer information is not required or is insignificant
- employment contracts
- computers, televisions, VCRs, DVD players or similar goods

---

[17] "Computer information" is "information in electronic form that is obtained from or through the use of a computer, or that is in digital or similar form capable of being processed by a computer. The term includes a copy of information in that form and any documentation or packaging associated with the copy." (UCITA §102(11)).

- print books, magazines or newspapers
- motion pictures, sound recordings or musical works
- broadcast or cable programs.

The Act contains an opt-out provision; subject to certain restrictions, "if the subject matter of a transaction includes computer information ... the parties may agree that this [Act] including contract formation rules, governs the transaction in whole or in part or that other law governs the transaction and this [Act] does not apply" (UCITA §103(e)). If parties choose to opt out by agreement, several restrictions apply. Parties may not, in mass-market transactions, opt out of the applicability of good faith, fundamental public policy, or unconscionability (UCITA §103(e)(2)). Under UCITA, good faith is "honesty in fact and the observance of reasonable commercial standards of fair dealing" (UCITA §102(a)(34)).[18] This is a test that has both subjective and objective components. If a contract term violates fundamental public policy, a court has three options (UCITA §105(b)):

- refuse to enforce the contract
- enforce the remainder of the contract exclusive of the impermissible term
- limit that term to avoid any result contrary to public policy.

A court has the same three options—refuse entirely, enforce the remainder, or limit the term—if it finds that "in light of the general commercial background and the commercial needs of the particular trade or case, the terms involved are so one-sided as to be unconscionable under the circumstances existing at the time of the making of the contract" (UCITA §111, Note 2).

Although the opt-out provision may seem attractive to parties whose transactions fall within the scope of the Act, the provision is not as user- or vendee-friendly as it may seem. For example, the adoption of UCITA will implicitly ratify certain provisions in contracts. Because the Act aligns itself with standard protections found in vendor agreements, it is unlikely that a vendor will agree to opt out of the many protections that UCITA provides for such parties. As a result, the opt-out provision, although theoretically a sound concept, is just that; the reality of the commercial marketplace is likely to ignore the existence of the opt-out provision. Consumers are likely to receive reduced protections, other than those specifically stated above, based on this opt-out provision.

---

[18] There is no mirror-image called "bad faith" for which there is a compatible standard; rather, courts will determine whether a party demonstrated a lack of good faith.

5.2.1   Mass-Market Licenses

One area of the Act that aims to protect consumers is the provision that addresses and regulates mass-market licenses,[19] which are standard forms prepared for and used in mass-market transactions (UCITA §102(a)(45)). A mass-market transaction is a transaction under the Act that is:

> (A) a consumer transaction; or (B) any other transaction with an end-user licensee if: (i) the transaction is for information or informational rights directed to the general public as a whole including consumers, under substantially the same terms for the same information; (ii) the licensee acquires the information or rights in a retail transaction under terms and in a quantity consistent with an ordinary transaction in a retail market; and (iii) the transaction is not: (I) a contract for redistribution or for public performance or public display of a copyrighted work; (II) a transaction in which the information is customized or otherwise specially prepared by the licensor for the licensee other than minor customization using a capability of the information intended for that purpose; (III) a site license; or (IV) an access contract" (UCITA §102(a)(46)).

So what exactly does this mean? The Reporter's Notes give the definitions significantly more substance. The intended and fairly limited function of mass market indicates

> small dollar value, routine and anonymous transactions involving information that is directed to the general public in cases where the transaction occurs in a retail market available to and used by the general public

and includes all consumer transactions as well as certain transactions among business in the retail market (UCITA §102, Note 40). For example, a consumer who walks into a computer store and purchases pre-packaged software would receive the protections granted under this provision. By the same token, the company selling the shrink-wrapped software would be obligated to give those protections and otherwise act in conformity with this provision. Despite the opt-out provisions in the Act, an agreement that the Act will not apply does not free parties from the applicability of unconscionability, fundamental public policy, or good faith, as mentioned above.

Three features characterize a mass-market transaction:

- the context in which it occurs
- its terms
- the nature of the information involved.

[19] A mass-market transaction includes shrink-wrap licensing.

The context of the transaction occurs in the retail market involving information in a pre-packaged form with generally similar terms available to the general public (UCITA §102, Note 40). Most of the transactions involve fairly small quantities, lack negotiated terms, and deal with an end-user; "[t]he products are available to anyone who enters the retail location and can pay the stated price" (UCITA §102, Note 40).[20] The evolution of click-wrap licenses, in which a consumer can purchase and download software from the internet, falls within the purview of the Act. The notes in the definitional section state that on-line, consumer transactions are mass-market transactions; equating on-line and in-store transactions "gives commerce room to develop while preserving consumer interests" (UCITA §102, Note 40). However, several types of transactions do not fall under the requirements of this provision, including:

- specialty software for business or professional uses
- information aimed at specifically-targeted, limited audiences
- any commercial software distributed in non-retail transactions
- software for professional use.

Regarding the terms of the license, the Act attempts to protect the consumer in a mass-market transaction by regulating licenses that are presented both at the beginning of the transaction and afterwards. First, a licensee—the consumer—adopts the terms of the license *only* if he agrees to the license by manifesting assent at one of two times: either before or during his initial performance or during use of (or access to) that information (UCITA §102, Note 40).[21] The licensor must provide the licensee with the chance to review a mass-market license (or a copy of it) before the licensee becomes obligated to pay; if the licensee does not agree to the license by manifesting assent to the license after having the opportunity to review it, the licensee is entitled to a return. In addition, the licensee may demand reimbursement of reasonable expenses incurred in the return or destruction of the information and compensation for the restoration of an information processing system to the extent necessary to reverse changes caused by

---

[20] The Act focuses on the consumer end-user who, although not defined in the body of the Act, is an individual with the intent to use the information (or informational rights) for its own personal or business affairs.

[21] Similarly, §210(c) protects a licensor who does not have an opportunity to review a record (defined as "information that is inscribed on a tangible medium or that is stored in an electronic or other medium and is retrievable in perceivable form" (UCITA §102(a)(58))) prior to the time the licensor either delivers or becomes obligated to deliver the information. The licensor is entitled to a return if he has not agreed to the transaction.

installation of the information (UCITA §210(b)).[22] The licensor can state that it is opting out of the provisions of the Act (bearing in mind it may not opt out of the applicability of unconscionability, fundamental public policy, or good faith) on the packaging. The consumer must choose whether to accept the opt-out, in addition to any other terms and conditions stated on the packaging. If the consumer does not like the terms, it has no option other than to not buy the software.

The notes to the mass-market licenses provision indicate three limiting principles that govern mass-market licenses irrespective of the time a party has assented to the license.

- First, a "party cannot [manifest assent] unless it had an opportunity to review the record before the assent occurs" (UCITA §210, Note 2(a)). Therefore, the licensor must make the record available and must call the record to the party's attention to the extent that a reasonable person should have noticed the record (UCITA §210, Note 2(a)). For example, printing the terms of the transaction on the outside of a shrink-wrapped software package, rather than on a piece of paper inside of the shrink-wrapped box, might provide an adequate opportunity to review the record, assuming that the requisite notice element was satisfied.

- Second, if a term is bizarre, oppressive, and hidden in boilerplate language, a court should invalidate such a term because it is unconscionable. Unconscionability is a principle of that seeks to prevent both oppression and unfair surprise; it does not disturb allocation of risks because of one party's superior bargaining power. There is a greater likelihood in a mass-market transaction because one of the parties is necessarily a consumer; the licensor might use the elements of surprise or oppression to the detriment of the consumer. For example, a mass-market license cannot grant a license back to licensor of all trademarks and/or trade secrets of the licensee unless the parties had discussed such a reversion prior to the manifestation of assent (UCITA §210, Note 2(b)).

- Third, a conflict with the agreed terms is not permissible. If the parties expressly agree to particular terms and the agreement becomes part of their bargain, standard terms in a mass-market form cannot alter those agreed-upon terms (UCITA §210, Note 2(c)). The implication is that the licensor can not use standard terms to avoid its duty to provide

---

[22] Compensation is permitted only if the installation occurred before the licensee could review the license and altered the system or information but does not restore it upon removal after rejection of the license.

compatible software to the licensee when compatible software was a requirement in the transaction and the licensor has agreed to provide such software (UCITA §210, Note 2(c)).

It is important to remember that if a licensee manifests assent to a contract and has had the opportunity to review a mass-market license before the licensee pays, the non-negotiability of the terms does not invalidate the contract. Although a court will review the terms for unconscionability, the key under this provision of the Act is whether the licensor made the terms available to the licensee before the licensee manifested assent so as to prevent unfair surprise. A mass-market license by its very nature imposes non-negotiable terms. Therefore, the Act guarantees a consumer licensee that if she has not had the opportunity to review those non-negotiable terms before manifesting assent, she is not obligated to remain a party to the contract.

The Act specifically addresses pre-transaction disclosures when a licensor makes its computer information available to a licensee via the internet (UCITA §212). A licensor "affords an opportunity to review the terms of a standard form license" if it permits a licensee to download or copy the standard terms for archival or review purposes or makes the terms available to the licensee before the licensee either becomes obligated to pay or downloads the information (UCITA §212(1),(2). The licensor can make the terms available in one of two ways (UCITA §213):

- First, it can display the standard terms in close proximity to the description of the computer information (or the instructions for acquiring such information).
- Second, it can disclose the standard terms in a prominent place on the website where the licensor offers the computer information; it must also provide a copy of those terms upon request prior to the sale or license of such information.

Such a provision is necessary to protect consumers in a click-wrap transaction. Without such a provision, a licensor would be obligated to make the terms available in the shrink-wrap context, but would be permitted not to make the terms available in the click-wrap context.

If the consumer enters a retail store (or visits a website that sells the same or similar information), under the provisions discussed above, she can contract with the licensor with the knowledge that the licensor must provide the terms of the agreement before the contract can become effective. Once the contract becomes binding, certain issues that arise will be governed by any warranties that the licensor gave to the user.

5.2.2 Warranties

Recall that the Act will apply to computer information transactions unless parties agree to opt out. Warranties are an important component of the Act because they provide protections to licensee (especially to consumers in the mass-market licensing context) and impose requirements upon the licensor. These warranty sections control in the absence of contract terms to the contrary. Express warranties and the three implied warranties of merchantability of computer program, informational content, and licensee's purpose/system integration—and the disclaimers of those warranties—are important obligations about which the developer should be aware and the consumer should not permit to be disclaimed (UCITA §§402–406).[23]

5.2.2.1 Express Warranty

The easiest of all warranties to extend—and perhaps the most dangerous—is the express warranty because it can arise in so many instances during the marketing and sales process. Anyone who has the opportunity to discuss software with a potential customer must be aware of aspects of the express warranty; ignorance may lead to the extension of a warranty that was never intended. A licensor (or his employees) can create an express warranty in several ways (UCITA §402(a)):

- An affirmation of fact or promise made by the licensor to its licensee in any manner, including in a medium for communication to the public such as advertising, which relates to the information and becomes part of the basis of the bargain creates an express warranty that the information to be furnished under the agreement must conform to the affirmation or promise.
- Any description of the information which is made part of the basis of the bargain creates an express warranty that the information must conform to the description.
- Any sample, model, or demonstration of a final product which is made part of the basis of the bargain creates an express warranty that the performance of the information must reasonably conform to the performance of the sample, model, or demonstration, taking into account such differences as would appear to a reasonable person in the position of the licensee between the sample, model, or demonstration and the information as it will be used.

---

[23] The Act imposes an additional warranty concerning quiet enjoyment and noninfringement in §401. This warranty basically guarantees the licensor delivers the information free of any third party claims.

The Reporter's Notes indicate that express warranties focus on "dickered" aspects of a particular bargain. Therefore, a licensor could make separate and distinct express warranties to various licensees. These express warranties would be unique to each respective licensee; one could not, upon talking with the other, assert an express warranty intended for the other.

The requirements of an express warranty state that the warranty must become the basis of the bargain. The "basis of the bargain" concept is one found in the UCC and implemented in the Act. In its most basic form, if an express affirmation, promise, or similar statement is part of the package that constitutes the basis of the contract, such statements form the basis of the bargain (UCITA §402, Note 2). It is not important for a licensee to rely on a particular statement. However, in her decision to enter into the contract with the licensor, the statements merely need to play a role in the licensee's decision-making (UCITA §402, Note 2). There is no requirement that a licensor have specific intent or use words like "guaranty" or "warrant" to create an express warranty (UCITA §402(b)). If a licensor merely expresses a prediction of the value of the informational rights or his opinion, or uses a display or description of a part of the information as illustrative of market appeal or similar concepts, the licensor does not create an express warranty(UCITA §402(b)). Such expressions will not become the basis of the bargain.

The Act's drafters also borrow another concept from the UCC—*puffing*. Puffing, which is simply a statement of opinion, does not create an express warranty and does not form the basis of the bargain. A court will decide on a case by case basis whether puffing has occurred because it is a fact-specific inquiry. A continuum exists on which a court could judge whether puffing occurred. At one end, in a computer information transaction, the more a statement describes technical specifications, technical performance, or information description, the more likely it will form an express warranty. Conversely, the more a statement relates to predictions regarding expected benefits that might result from the use of the information, the more likely a court will consider it puffing.

Disclaiming this warranty is a difficult task because general language of disclaimer is ineffective to avoid express warranties. Section 406(a) instructs a court that

> [w]ords or conduct relevant to the creation of an express warranty and words or conduct tending to disclaim or modify an express warranty must be construed wherever reasonable as consistent with each other.

When inconsistency between contract terms of disclaimer and language of express warranty occurs, the language of express warranty controls, which provides an inherent benefit to the consumer. In theory, express warranties can be disclaimed; in practice, they cannot be disclaimed (UCITA §406, Note 2). Often, a licensor will attempt to rely on language in a contract that the alleged warranty did not form a basis of the bargain and therefore cannot constitute an express warranty. Courts usually do not accept such assertions. One excellent example is an attempt to disclaim an express warranty regarding the description of the information itself. Express product descriptions are important because, despite any disclaimer, computer information must conform to its description. For example, an accounting program still must operate as an accounting program, irrespective of any attempt to disclaim express warranties to the contrary.

5.2.2.2 Implied Warranty: Merchantability of Computer Program

Implied warranties are distinct from express warranties and "rest on inferences from a common factual situation or set of conditions so that no particular language is necessary to create them" (UCITA §402, Note 1). Implied warranties operate differently from express warranties because an implied warranty exists unless the merchant or licensor affirmatively disclaims or modifies the warranty.

Under the implied warranty of merchantability, a merchant licensor of a computer program, whether delivered electronically or in tangible form, is obligated in three separate ways:[24]

- First, the merchant warrants to an end user "that the computer program is fit for the ordinary purpose for which such computer programs are used" (UCITA §403(a)(1)). "Ordinary purposes" mean the type of uses to which the program was marketed, or that it conforms to expected user applications. The computer program that the licensee selects need not be the one that is best suited or optimal for the intended use; it need only perform within the range of expected uses. Such a requirement removes the burden from the licensee to have specific knowledge in the area of computer information. The protections, however, do not strictly assist the consumer because merchantability does not translate into "perfection." The expectation is not that the program is flawless but rather that it will perform within

---

[24] This warranty does not apply to informational content, including aesthetics (UCITA §403(c)). The Reporter's Notes give some guidance on the aesthetic aspect of this section, construing aesthetics as involving matters of personal taste. For merchantability to apply, a complaint must stem from the failure of the program to be what it purports to be and whether it is useable. Aesthetics comes into play when a user does not like artistic character, tastefulness, beauty or pleasing nature of the informational content (UCITA §403, Note 5).

the average standards applicable in the commercial setting for information of a similar type. (UCITA §403, Note 3(a)). The drafters recognize the difficulty of producing defect-free software, as discussed above.

- Second, a merchant licensor guarantees the distributor that the program is both adequately packaged and labeled and in conformity with what the agreement or circumstances require, and that multiple copies are within the range of variations that the agreement permits (of even kind, quality, and quantity, both within every unit and among all units in the transaction) (UCITA §403(2)). For this portion of the warranty to apply, the program must be truly resellable by a person who is acquiring the program for redistribution.

- Third, a merchant licensor warrants that "the program conforms to the promises or affirmations of fact made on the container or label, if any" (UCITA §403(3)). Therefore, a merchant is bound to conform to any descriptions of fact (but not opinion) on the label or container; a licensee can be assured that he will receive what is promised (UCITA §403, Note 3(c)).

A licensor may disclaim an implied warranty of merchantability by using "merchantability," "quality" or words of similar import, as long as the alternative words indicate the disclaimer (UCITA §406(b)(1)(a)). The Reporter's Notes specify that "[o]ther language suffices only if it reasonably achieves the purpose of clearly indicating that the warranty is not given in the particular case" (UCITA §406, Note 4. Although it may seem unfair to the consumer to disclaim such a warranty, the consumer is none the less protected in the mass-market license context because he must have the benefit of reviewing the license prior to being bound by its terms. Therefore, the consumer will have the opportunity to review the license and if he is uncomfortable with the disclaimer of the warranty, he may choose not to enter into the license agreement.

5.2.2.3 Implied Warranty: Informational Content
If a special relationship between the merchant and the licensee exists in which the licensee relies on the merchant to collect, compile, process, provide, or transmit informational content, the merchant "warrants to its licensee that there is no inaccuracy in the informational content caused by the merchant's failure to perform with reasonable care" (UCITA §404(a)). Two specific exemptions are made to this warranty, which will not arise with respect to published informational content or to a person who provides collection, compilation or distribution services as a conduit or in an editorial capacity (UCITA §404(b)). This provision does not place

undue burden on the merchant because it does not create absolute liability, nor does it mandate absolute accuracy; reasonable results are the goal (UCITA §404, Note 2).[25] Rather, it provides assurance that inaccuracies are not caused by a failure to exercise reasonable care. Once again, the drafters recognize the almost certain impossibility of developing a defect-free program. In lieu of demanding perfection, the Act requires reasonable care. The circumstances dictate whether a merchant has exercised reasonable care.

According to the Reporter's Notes, "[i]nformational content is accurate if, within applicable understandings of the level of permitted errors, the informational content correctly portrays the objective facts to which it relates" (UCITA §404, Note 2(a)). If a licensee expects greater accuracy, he must contract for that level and make it express in the agreement. In addition, this warranty will not arise simply because a licensee relies on the licensor to compile or collect information. The merchant must personally tailor the information to the licensee's specific needs; if the information is generally available in the same standardized form to other licensees, the warranty will not arise (UCITA §404, Note 3(a)). This warranty, although protecting the licensee who has relied on the licensor, does not give absolute protection. Instead, the licensor will only be obligated if it is performing a function that is not generally available.

To disclaim this warranty that arises under this section, the licensor must mention "accuracy" or words of similar import (UCITA §406(b)(1)(B)). Like the disclaimer for the warranty of merchantability, if a licensor is using other language, that language must clearly indicate that the licensor is not extending the warranty in that particular case. However, since this warranty will not arise in a mass-market license because, by its nature, it is specific to the licensee, this will likely be a bargained-for provision. A savvy licensee will read the entire contract and object to the disclaimer of this warranty.

5.2.2.4 Implied Warranty: Licensee's Purpose and System Integration

A licensor extends this implied warranty, if "at the time of contracting [he] has reason to know any particular purpose for which the information is required and that the licensee is relying on the licensor's skill or judgement to select, develop, or furnish suitable information" (UCITA

---

[25] Furthermore, this warranty balances the protection of client expectations against excessive liability risk for informational content providers by the imposition of a special relationship of reliance. Such a relationship is "characterized by the provider's knowledge that the particular licensee plans to rely on the data in its own business and expects that the provider will tailor the information to its needs."

§405(a)).[26] For example, a licensee that requests a particular brand of software does not rely on the skill or judgement of the licensor; the licensee has used their own skill and judgement in selecting the software.

This warranty provision delineates two rules.

- First, an implied warranty that the information is fit for the particular purpose arises, subject to certain limitations (UCITA §405(a)(1)). A particular purpose means that the licensee will employ it in a specific way peculiar to the nature of that business. The warranty will only arise when the licensee has particularized his needs and the licensor has implicitly undertaken to fulfill those needs.

- Second, based on the circumstances, if the licensor would receive payment for his time and/or effort regardless of the fitness of the resulting information, an implied warranty arises that "the information will not fail to achieve the licensee's particular purpose as a result of the licensor's lack of reasonable effort" (UCITA §405(a)(2)).

A skilled licensor must expressly agree to guaranty a result suitable to the licensee to be held to such a standard in these types of contracts (UCITA §405, Note 3). Despite the particular purpose articulated, however, a warranty will not arise under this provision in relation to aesthetics, market appeal, subjective quality of informational content, or published informational content (UCITA §405(b)).[27]

The warranty can also arise in a situation in which a licensor provides or selects a system of computer programs and goods under his agreement with the licensee. In that situation, if the

> licensor has reason to know that the license is relying on the skill or judgement of the licensor to select the components of the system, there is an implied warranty that the components provided or selected will function together as a system (UCITA §405(c)).

In a system integration contract, a licensee is offered greater protection under this new warranty than it enjoys under current law. The protection is not unlimited, though. Various selected components must function as a system under this warranty, but the warranty does not assure anything other than the functional operation of those components.

A proper disclaimer of this warranty must be in a record. A statement such as "There is no warranty that this information or efforts will fulfill any of your particular purposes or needs" is sufficient to disclaim the warranty

---

[26] Note that this warranty can apply to both merchant and nonmerchant licensors.

[27] A warranty regarding published informational content may, however, arise from the licensor's selection of such content from various providers.

(UCITA §406(b)(1)(B)(2)). Specific language is unnecessary as long as the licensor communicates his intent to disclaim the warranty. Once again, the licensee should be careful when entering into a license agreement and should not permit disclaimers to be a part of the license.

5.2.2.5 More About Disclaiming Implied Warranties For any disclaimer, it will apply to all performances in a contract of ongoing performance or a series of performances rather than solely the first performance (UCITA §406(b)(3)). In addition to the information provided above, the Act sets out several key principles that are applicable to the disclaimer of the warranties discussed above. The licensor can further protect himself by doing the following.

- First, a licensor can sufficiently disclaim the three implied warranties discussed above by individually disclaiming each warranty with a statement like "Except for express warranties stated in this contract, if any, this [information] [computer program] is provided with all faults, and the entire risk as to satisfactory quality, performance, accuracy, and effort is with the user" (UCITA §406(b)(3)). Such language must be in a record for all transactions; for mass-market transactions, the disclaimer must be conspicuous (UCITA §406(5)).[28]

- Second, the implied warranties discussed above can be disclaimed by language like "as is" or "with all faults" or "other language that in common understanding calls the licensee's attention to the disclaimer of warranties and makes plain that there are no implied warranties" (UCITA §406(c)). The import of a statement to this effect is that the licensee bears the entire risk regarding the quality of information he will receive. Unfortunately, a consumer licensee may unfairly bear the burden if he is not savvy in computer information, but this standard is not unlike UCC Article 2 that permits the merchant to disclaim all implied warranties and sell the items "as is."

- Third, a licensee who either has the opportunity to examine the information or sample or model as fully as he would like or has refused to examine the information will lose the benefit of an implied warranty—even if not disclaimed—if the defects were of such a nature that the licensee's examinations should have revealed the defects under the circumstances (UCITA §406(d)). Therefore, a licensee who discovers the defect and still uses the information, or a licensee who unreasonably fails to examine information prior to using it, does not

---

[28] This additional hurdle aims to prevent undue surprise. However, despite the disclaimer, the licensor may not avoid the applicability of unconscionability, fundamental public policy, or good faith.

get the benefit of an implied warranty. The law sees the damage as resulting from the licensee's own action. However, the Act does not confer the entire benefit on the licensor. A licensor must make a demand or offer that the licensee examine the information, thus putting the licensee on notice that he assumes the risk of a defect that a reasonable inspection should reveal (UCITA §406, Note 4(b)). For example, "failure to notice defects which are obvious cannot excuse the licensee, [but] an examination made under circumstances which do not permit extensive testing would not exclude defects that could be ascertained only by such testing" (UCITA §406, Note 4(b)). To further carve out a protection for the consumer, this section imposes different standards on merchant and non-merchant licensees. "A merchant licensee examining a product in its own field is held to have assumed the risk as to all defects which a merchant in the field ought to observe, while a non-merchant licensee is held to have assumed the risk only for such defects as an ordinary person might be expected to observe" (UCITA §406, Note 4(b)). This additional protection for the consumer can assist her in seeking the benefits of this warranty when she, like any ordinary person, does not have the sophistication to discover defects in a complicated system.

5.3   UCITA's Future

The 50 states of the US, the District of Columbia, Puerto Rico and the US Virgin Islands now have the option to adopt UCITA, and California is currently reviewing the Act. In addition to the provisions discussed above, UCITA addresses many other issues, including reverse engineering, nondisclosure, transfer restrictions and self-help. Consumer groups attack these issues as pro-vendor because the Act [31]:

- makes presumptively enforceable clauses in mass-market software licenses that ban reverse engineering and publication of benchmarks or critical reviews
- permits mass-market software publishers to prohibit their customers from either selling or donating the software
- allows the vendor, upon cancellation of its software license, to shut down its software.

If any of the jurisdictions mentioned above adopt the Act, courts and consumers alike will wrestle with these arguably pro-vendor provisions.

6. Technical Protections

This chapter has discussed the legal remedies that a licensee could pursue against a developer for defective software. The remainder of this chapter focuses on what licensees can do to reduce the negative consequences of acquiring defective software. The goal in this section is to discuss technical actions that a licensee can take to reduce its exposure. After all, it is the law that places the consumer, not the vendor, in the vulnerable position. Fortunately, there are technologies that can partially mitigate that vulnerability. Developers can also apply several of the technologies that will be needed to build a case that they did "above and beyond" what a "reasonable" developer would do to ensure quality. While the law may not require developers to go above and beyond the reasonable standard, their reputations will.

6.1 Licensee Responsibility

Neither users nor system integrators can rely solely on laws for protection from defective software. It is up to the software licensees to protect themselves when they deem the consequences of failure severe enough.

To developers, it is intuitive that persons and organizations that license software must accept some level of responsibility for the software that they acquire. For example, if a shopper observes a piece of meat for sale in a supermarket that is green with rot but opts to purchase and eat it, is it fully the fault of the store that they are sick? Developers do not want to assume such a burden.

Software licensees should consider creating, either on paper or in their minds, a set of acquisition policies for determining what software to license (as well as when not to license software). Today, many large corporations (and even the US Department of Defense) are in the process of creating enterprise-wide acquisition policies for commercial software. The reasons are numerous but essentially, the costs to qualify a single acquired software package can be enormous, and re-qualifying that same package over and over for each project that employs it is impractical. Admittedly, some amount of re-qualification may be necessary for the nuances of specific projects. Nevertheless, the goal of these acquisition procedures and standards is to create a database of commercial software packages from which a company's sub-organizations can select. Once such a database is created, re-testing for specific needs on a per project basis is prudent and not redundant.

If the fear of a catastrophic outcome from licensing software is too great, consumers should not license it. Consumers always have the option, although it is usually impractical, to write their own software instead of licensing it.[29] If enough consumers were sufficiently worried, they could band together and write their own code. The Linux operating system is a prime example of how resourceful users can be when they work together to build an alternative product to those on the marketplace. Linux is a competitor to commercial UNIX operating systems that is free. In fact, Linux is considered a reasonable alternative to Microsoft's operating system for personal computers. Linux is delivered with open source code, and a "Windows-like" GUI is being built for the operating system such that Linux will appeal to users that demand the look and feel of a Windows GUI. If this occurs, it is possible that this free operating system will take "operating system" market share away from Microsoft.

There is another key impediment for a consumer to writing its own software, however: "time-to-market." Even if the consumer has the resources to "build" versus "buy," the amount of time required to do so could impede its ability to market products quickly enough. This limits its ability to compete, which nullifies any gains made by building its own software.

Because of the pro-vendor stance of UCITA, the onus ultimately falls on users and system integrators to take proactive steps to defend themselves from defective commercial software. It may seem strange to say that system integrators need protection since they could also employ shrink-wrapped licenses or stand behind future laws such as UCITA as their way to thwart liability. This may be true, but the more serious problem is "reputation." Integrators must be concerned whether their reputations will suffer because of a bad decision to license an inferior product. Huge shrink-wrap companies can get away with "poor" reputations simply because the quality of their products is marginally good enough for the majority of their consumer base. Smaller organizations that compete fiercely for market presence are not so lucky.

The reality is that the amount of software quality offered is market driven. The top suppliers of reusable commercial software have determined how to maximize profit with minimal acceptable quality. There is no intent to slight the software "giants" by saying this. It is simply a fact. Also, the giants frequently enjoy the additional advantage of being the only supplier in the marketplace. Such a position furthers their ability to trade between quality and profitability.

Because of the risk to integrators (based on the assumption that their customers will not absolve them of blame when an information system fails

---

[29] In this section, the term "consumer" is used in a larger sense than in the prior sections on legal remedies. In this section, the term encompasses any software user, including licensees, and can include corporations and other commercial entities.

and the acquired software was the root cause), it is prudent for system integrators and users to take one or more of the following steps in order to deploy acquired software with greater confidence. Note that not all of these processes provide assurances about the product. Some tasks only provide assurances about the processes that the software publisher used. This is clearly a "fallback" position, but it is still better than nothing at all.

1. Go to the vendor site and do a product/process audit.
2. Ask for an independent, third party product certification.
3. Perform "stand-alone" testing on the acquired software.
4. Perform system-level testing on the acquired software with it embedded in the system.
5. Determine the robustness of the system if the COTS functionality were to fail and then build appropriate wrappers ("middleware").

The remainder of this chapter will discuss each of these alternatives in greater detail.

6.2 Assumptions

A discussion about the defensive steps that system integrators and users can employ is based on several assumptions. These assumptions underlie the justifications for the recommendations that this section provides.

- The first assumption is that the acquired software does not come with source code access, test plans, test cases, etc. Such information is likely to exist at the vendor's site, but it may be difficult for outsiders to gain access to it. Access may be provided if the licensee is either willing to pay an additional fee or is a large enough consumer that it has the economic clout to demand source code access without paying additional costs.

- The second assumption is that the software is so important that any failure has economic or life-threatening consequences. If the software is games software and it fails, there are no life-threatening ramifications. Successful litigation is nearly impossible when no damages accrue. However, as stated earlier, the supplier of the game may wake up one day to find themselves out of business if their products become notorious for failing. Therefore, if software failure carries no economic or life-damaging consequences, the recommendations made in this section will be unwarranted.

6.2.1 Vendor Site Visit

Visiting a vendor's site is the only way to get a 360° view into the organization, its people, and its processes. The benefit of a site visit cannot be underestimated. From as little as a couple of hours, a quick assessment can be made for issues such as whether:

- the vendor will be in business a year from now
- the developers know about the latest technologies and standards for building maintainable code
- the organization operates in "fire mode" or uses reasonable project scheduling and staffing models
- the vendor has a reasonable process for bug fixes and upgrades.

Positive answers to these questions should encourage a consumer about the vendor's offer.

The main reason for visiting a vendor's site is to do an audit of how its software is developed. Visit expecting access to internal documentation about the product and/or source code. Visiting and only getting the "marketing pitch" will not serve the critical goal of trying to weed out unscrupulous vendors. If the vendor is cooperative, Table I provides a list of tasks that a consumer should attempt to perform. Note that many software vendors may not have this information documented and organized. If they do not, that should be a warning that their software development processes are suspicious.

Another piece of information that the consumer can request without going to the vendor's site is customer "testimonials." These are simply statements or client references that the consumer can pursue by contacting their reference list. This is particularly useful when dealing with a small development organization that has few clients.

6.2.2 Independent Product Certifiers

Independent product certification involves contracting a separate organization (that is not affiliated with the developer) to test and warranty that the software satisfies a set of required behaviors. For example, suppose the consumer system mandates that the acquired software exhibits behavior Z when an input value of 0 or 1 is used. The consumer could test this themselves, or hire a testing laboratory to do it. The beauty of using an independent testing laboratory is that it assumes the responsibility for making the assessments. Further, the laboratory can likely do it at a lower cost if it is a full-service testing laboratory with the appropriate tools and environments.

TABLE I

ON-SITE TASKS TO PERFORM

1	Review the test plans to determine what assumptions were made when test scenarios were created. Here, the consumer should ask to see what scripts were used, whether the test cases were for unit testing, integration testing, and whether system-level testing was performed. Whether the vendor used a coverage tool and what levels of coverage were achieved is a question that the consumer must ask. Did the vendor simply generate meaningless test cases (in terms of what the unit would normally execute) simply to achieve a level of coverage, or did the vendor use reasonable test cases during unit testing? The consumer should also ask whether the system-level test cases are traceable back to the specification. Who in the organization does the testing? Determine whether developers do their own testing or if there is a separate test organization is a key question. It is prudent for developers to do some testing on smaller units, but it is better if an independent organization within the organization does the system and integration testing. Learning when testers get involved in a project is the final piece of the puzzle. When an organization gets the test team involved at an earlier time (as opposed to the end of the cycle), such early involvement is a sign of a much more mature development organization.
2	Ask to see logs of known (patent) and unfixed defects. Finding out the severity ratings of these defects is important. How long does it typically takes to "close a bug" in their defect tracking system? If the organization does not employ a defect tracking system and simply sends out e-mail messages when bugs are reported from customers, it is a sign of a chaotic development organization. The sign of a good development organization is one that has quick turnaround on defects and low "incorrect fix" rates. A good development organization never releases software with known bugs of high severity.
3	Obtain upgrade and patch release schedules from the vendor. How does the organization handle feature requests from customers? Not getting patches in a timely manner is problematic, but it is equally problematic to get too many releases in a short period of time. What constitutes a major upgrade, minor upgrade, and periodic upgrades?
4	Make a "spot check" assessment of the maturity of the development organization. Doing a formal process assessment is not necessary, but request the results if the vendor has had one done recently. (In fact, hiring a consultant to make his/her own assessment is an option if process maturity is an important issue.) If the vendor has never done a self-assessment or hired a consultant to do one, that almost certainly suggests that the vendor is not compliant with any of the major standards (ISO, CMM, SPICE). It also suggests that the software publisher does not care to be in compliance. All process maturity ranking schemes have problems and it is understandable why some organizations dispute the value of those schemes, but larger development organizations that pay no attention to them are likely to suffer from high levels of disorganization and chaos. Both will lead to expensive software and, in extreme cases, may eventually destroy the ability of the organization to stay in business. This theory raises an interesting issue. This chapter focuses mainly on legal remedies for defective software and how a consumer should protect itself against defective acquired code. However, another real concern is that the consumer must take the appropriate steps to protect itself against liability if it loses support from its supplier, whether due to business foreclosure or due to their opting to drop a particular product. Such events could lead to the consumer's demise, and that must be factored into its decision as to whether to license their code.

TABLE I

CONTINUED

5	Spot-check the test cases used that best mimic how the consumer plans to use the product. For example, if there is a particular feature that the consumer is more inclined to use, it should review how that feature was tested. The goal here is to find out whether the consumer's way of using the product was ever considered by the test team. If it was not, then the testing done on the product is not relevant to it, which is concerning. If this is the case, the consumer should find out who the developers consider the typical user to be and why the consumer is an "off nominal" user. They may well be correct, and the consumer should possibly be labeled that way. By predetermining this information, what the consumer may find is that the developers have no idea who represents their average user, and thus have not customized their system level testing to the largest base of their customers.
6	Ask for the right to test the software in their test harness (using test cases that the consumer brings along that reflect how it plans to use the product). This will not always be possible from the vendor's perspective. In fact, in some cases, the consumer might not know what test cases are likely in its environment.
7	Ask for access to the source code. It is not uncommon for organizations to allow the consumer to view the source code on their site. The consumer will have to sign non-disclosure agreements and will not be allowed to take the code with it. Reading their code will be difficult, but the goal should be to see how the code is organized and structured, not precisely what the code says.

By hiring a testing laboratory, the consumer reduces its liability. Why? The consumer has contracted out the task of determining the quality of the software. If the consumer then were to err on the side of deciding the software would operate properly and it did not, consumer will suffer the consequences of that error. By contracting out this work, the onus is placed on the third-party laboratory to make this determination. And if the laboratory makes a mistake (i.e., false positives or false negatives), they are accountable [32].

Although the number of independent third-party certification laboratories is still quite limited, it is interesting to note that Underwriter's Laboratory appears poised to make a substantial splash into this market. According to Councill [33], Underwriter's Laboratory is seriously considering extending its standard, *UL Standard 1998 for Software in Programmable Components*, to "general purpose" software components.

6.2.2.1 *Standalone testing*

Although independent certifiers may be able to increase the consumer's confidence in a product, its greatest increase in confidence will come when the consumer sees the product operate successfully. This section addresses standalone testing of the product and the subsequent sections addresses system-level testing. The consumer can apply both approaches.

Standalone testing involves testing the candidate software in isolation. The reason for performing standalone testing is to first verify that the acquired software operates properly by itself before it is tested in the context of system with which it will operate. By first evaluating whether the COTS offering executes as expected, a licensee can free themselves from most concerns about whether other parts of the system are causing interference. Such a determination becomes a more difficult concern during system-level testing.

Several issues must be addressed before standalone testing can begin. The hardest problems of testing acquired software in isolation come from:

- no access to source code
- hidden or unknown interfaces
- unrealistic standalone test cases or the total inability to generate any standalone test cases
- no access to test drivers
- calls to other software functions, that if absent, render standalone testing ineffective.

The ramifications of each of the above issues are discussed in more detail below.

When source code is absent, white-box test case generation and coverage analysis is not possible. Thus, the consumer cannot determine how much of the code has been exercised. Worse, all code-based analysis techniques (e.g., formal verification) are useless. This is a serious concern since more defects can be flushed out of code at this point (per dollar spent) than after the software enters into integration or system-level testing.

Interfaces carry information in and out of software components. When the interfaces to a piece of software are unknown (i.e., undocumented), generating appropriate test cases and accurate oracles are difficult. Undocumented interfaces in acquired software are possibly the greatest fear of system administrators; they are very difficult to detect without source code. The fear stems from the possibility that the acquired software will make requests to the operating system that have malicious intent via undocumented interfaces. Such requests include reading files or writing to files that the software should not have access to.

Naturally, a publisher will rarely document malicious intent. Such undocumented functionality is difficult enough to detect with access to source code, let alone without it. It is even harder to detect if the behavior is context-sensitive, which means that the same requests made by the acquired software to the operating system are nonmalicious in some cases and malicious in others. Such an outcome suggests that if the application is security-critical, the consumer must be able to assess what communications are occurring between the acquired software and the operating system. How to accomplish this is an open issue when source is unavailable.

Another difficulty, one that goes hand-in-hand with the problem of the user building an oracle for the acquired software, will be to build the test harnesses (or what is sometimes referred to as the "driver"). The driver is the software that will send the input into the acquired software and receive the output from the acquired software. Drivers will have to be created in order to perform standalone testing.

Finally, in order to standalone test the acquired software, the consumer must be prepared for the software under test to make calls to:

- other acquired software utilities
- code that it has written.

When true, the "called" software will have to exist (or, in the worst case, be emulated). Although that may not seem problematic, the problem manifests itself when the standalone component fails because a determination must be made as to why the standalone software failed. Is it because the acquired function under test is defective and causing the problem? Or is it a result of the interaction with the other software components that calls are being made to?

This brings up a difficult problem known as the *integration testing problem*, which is not unique to licensees who are trying to make a "license" or "no license" decision. The integration testing problem is the situation where software components test satisfactorily but start failing when joined with other components. Many software projects face this hurdle; some never get out of this phase of test and are ultimately scrapped. The problem stems from nonspecified behaviors of components that cause semantic interference. This problem ultimately results in difficulty assigning blame to the culprit component or components that are causing the composite failures. When there is no source code access for the components, debugging the problem is nearly impossible.

Note also that this problem increases in magnitude as a system scales upwards. It is hard enough when a component undergoing standalone testing makes a few calls to other components. The problem becomes magnified during the system-level testing phase when there could literally be hundreds of acquired components communicating. For distributed systems, determining the correct ordering and timing of events makes this problem nearly impossible to rectify.

6.2.2.2 *System-level testing*

Although the tasks of auditing vendor processes, seeking independent certification, and standalone testing are beneficial, those efforts are unlikely to provide precise information concerning how acquired components will interact with other system components. In addition, sound evidence that the acquired software will behave properly in the context of the other components of the system and the system's operational environment is mandatory.

System-level testing can provide such evidence. This is testing the entire software system. When possible, it is preferable to perform system-level testing according to the environment that the system exists in. System-level testing should be performed after stand-alone testing is completed. This type of testing is the consumer's best opportunity to "test drive" the acquired software in the proper environment.

System-level testing suffers from the same "integration" problem as standalone testing can. Successfully tracing the cause of any system failure to the culprit component is not trivial. Is the culprit the component under consideration? Or is it the rest of the system? Or is the component interfering with the system or the system interfering with the component? Recall that the biggest challenge here will be to determine:

- whether there are unspecified behaviors occurring in the different subsystems that do not manifest themselves until they are linked
- where those unspecified behaviors are originating from.

As an example, suppose that a licensee discovers that the candidate component is causing behaviors that the system cannot tolerate. The options here are clear:

- avoid the component and find an alternative
- discuss with the vendor the possibility of getting a customized component that does not exhibit those behaviors
- build a "wrapper" around the component to limit its interactions with the system.

Probably the greatest problem with system-level testing as a means for testing the acceptability of a component to the system is for highly reliable components. Such components will rarely fail during system-level testing, which, although desirable from a pragmatic viewpoint, does not provide insight as to whether the component can be tolerated when indeed it does fail. Fortunately, robustness testing (see below) can forcefully simulate the failure of a component, and hence allow a consumer to determine how the component behaves when it fails.

In summary, the following sections discuss robustness testing and wrapper creation. These two technologies provide an excellent means for protecting a system from defective acquired software. Wrappers are also well suited for protecting a system from acquired software with unspecified semantic behaviors. These technologies provide the best opportunity to thwart defective acquired software if forced to accept it.

6.2.2.3 *Robustness Testing*

6.2.2.3 Robustness Testing One of the greatest problems in assigning blame for system failure occurs when the system's software has components that were acquired from a variety of vendors. Such systems are increasingly commonplace today. For instance, modern satellite communication systems can contain off-the-shelf (OTS) software from over 100 different vendors. This creates enormous system-level testing problems as well as maintenance problems. The key maintenance problem is knowing when to accept an upgrade from an OTS vendor.

When a system's software is written by a single vendor, assigning blame for logical defects is straightforward (ignoring the possibility that the client for the software gave incorrect or ambiguous requirements to the vendor). For system integrators, such root cause analysis is nontrivial when multiple-vendor acquisitions have been made. Therefore, ideas about how the user or system integrator can protect themselves from expected component failures that may have not been observed during system-level testing are provided here.

This requires a change in emphasis. Rather than trying to test a system and contacting the vendor when problems arise in attempts to get more reliable versions, the new position is to expect component failures and build the fault tolerance into the consumer system itself. Although expensive, this is the best way to reduce the consumer's exposure to the failure of acquired software (assuming your system is critical enough to warrant such actions).

First, the assumption is that all acquired software is logically defective, i.e., there are one or more faults in the software that will lead to failure for one or more input vectors. Technically speaking, if there is no input on which the software will fail even though the code is logically defective, the software is actually correct. The reason for this is simple: to assert that a program is defective, there must be at least one input that:

- exercises a logical fault

- causes the software's state to become corrupted

- propagates that corrupt state through the software (in such a way that the software fails).

Further, even if a piece of acquired software is correct with respect to its specification, the possibility still exists that the commercial software will exhibit non-specified behaviors. Because of this possibility, the consumer must consider non-specified behaviors of acquired software as failure modes (even though the acquired software, as a standalone entity, is correct) of the acquired software.

The question then becomes, what can be done to limit the problems caused by component failure modes? There are different approaches that study how failures in one component propagate and cause problems elsewhere. Useful techniques include: failure mode, effect, and criticality analysis (FMECA) [34], program slicing [35], fault tree analysis [36], and software fault injection [37]. The first three techniques are static causal analysis techniques that do not execute the code. The fourth technique is dynamic (i.e., the software is executed to determine the impact). This technique is a means for testing a system to determine its robustness to component failures.

Both causal analysis and robustness testing predict how failure modes can propagate between system components and thus are valuable tools for building robust systems. For brevity, an in-depth discussion of the causal analysis techniques is not provided since those techniques are described in most software engineering or systems safety texts. However, the next section briefly addresses software fault injection since it is a less well-known procedure. The caveat to this discussion is that each of these four techniques only help isolate how serious a problem might be. Defensive measures such as wrappers or negotiations with the vendor to get a customized version are still needed in order to reduce the severity of those problems.

6.3   Software Fault Injection

Software fault injection is a dynamic technique that can simulate the failure of acquired software in order to see how the system reacts or how other components of the system react [37]. Fault injection can be used to simulate [38]:

- the failure of some computation or component of the system
- incorrect data being fed into the system or a component of the system
- various types of human operator errors (for systems that involve manual control, such an airplane pilot).

The process of applying fault injection involves first hypothesizing that something gets corrupted in the state of the software and then observing how badly the software behaves from that event forward. Because the assumption is that all acquired software will fail at some point, fault injection provides an opportunity to see how the system will react when that occurs. This analysis can occur long before a component is actually licensed and embedded; such testing may present economic or physical harm, depending on the type of system.

Further, fault injection can be customized to simulate only those failure modes observed when standalone testing was performed. Typically, system-level fault injection is based on random failure modes, but that does not have to be the case [37]. Fault injection can be customized to only those failure modes that were observed when standalone testing occurred. This will provide a highly accurate view of how the system will tolerate such problems. However, this is essentially no different than system-level testing, except that here each system-level test is forced to be a case where the component fails. In practice, it may be very difficult to select system-level test cases that actually trigger components to fail.

Software fault injection allows system integrators to gain a more precise understanding (before licensing) as to whether they can tolerate a software offering. This is one step in the battle to reduce the impact of software failure from licensed software. The next and final step is to build the wrappers.

6.4 Building Wrappers from the Results of System-level and Robustness Testing

Previous sections have demonstrated how system-level and robustness testing can help determine the impact of "acquired" software failures. Once it is deemed that either:

- any software failure from the acquired software cannot be tolerated, or
- that only certain failure modes from the acquired software cannot be tolerated,

then the user or system integrator needs to take defensive actions against those failures.

Clearly, the first and easiest thing to do is to negotiate with the software publisher to provide guarantees or a different version of the software that cannot output those unacceptable states. Although most practical, this alternative is likely not to occur in a timely manner unless the consumer is a highly-valued client to that developer.

The next alternative is to build wrappers around the acquired software. Wrappers are simply software functions (sometimes referred to as *middleware*) that control what input is fed into the acquired software from the system and what outputs are returned to the system from the acquired software. Wrappers can be thought of as software that sits between the interfaces of a component and whatever else it communicates with. They inspect and mediate the information that different components produce.

For example, suppose that a call to a component returns a pointer. It is prudent to check to see that the pointer is not null. This can be done outside of the system and outside of the component by writing a middleware utility that checks to see what the component is returning to the system. If the pointer is null, then the wrapper could return a non-null pointer or throw an exception. Neither alternative is particularly desirable, but both options are preferable to the system crashing because it received a null pointer.

Wrappers can also be used to reduce the functionality offered by the software publisher. For example, most software packages contain much more functionality than a user needs. By disallowing calls to that extra functionality, the system integrator pares down the amount of acquired software that is actually active in the system. This reduces the amount of acquired software to be concerned about during standalone testing as well as reduces costs. Recognize that the desired ultimate end result is the least amount of software functionality that serves the specific needs. By cutting down the amount of potentially active acquired software in a system, the amount of software that must be protected against is reduced as well.

7. Summary

Admittedly, the future may someday provide consumers with laws that are geared toward consumer protection instead of being geared toward software publishers avoiding liability. However, as this chapter demonstrates, uniform legislation such as UCITA is not as consumer-friendly as it could be. Until legislators create greater protections for consumers, publishers will be able to continue to use either shrink-wrapped (or click-wrapped) licensing schemes or UCITA to mitigate their liability. This is unfortunate but it is a reality in the USA today.

This chapter has explained the current state of a uniform software liability law in the USA and provided proactive ideas from which licensees can protect themselves in the absence of legal remedies. One thing not addressed is *why* software failure is so easily accepted by society. It is because of this acceptance that legislation such as UCITA is possible. To emphasize the point, a comparison between the software industry and the automotive industry is illustrative. Would failure of a car's braking system be as easily tolerated? Would consumers tolerate rebooting their televisions several times a day? Clearly not. But with software, consumers seem to have a mindset that software fails, and therefore expect it to.

There is also a technical justification for this mindset: software is hard to write correctly. Everyone who has written software knows that. Further, no "silver bullet" for how to write defect-free software has been produced, nor is one likely to be found. And even if writing correct software someday becomes trivial, the problem of ambiguous or incomplete specifications will always haunt the software engineering process. That problem alone can result in software that is no less dangerous than if it were incorrect. After all, software that is semantically correct with respect to an incorrect specification is worthless and possibly dangerous.

Because of the combination of consumer tolerance and widespread acceptance of the difficulty to produce defect-free software, the legal system, and politicians seem more willing than ever to hold software publishers to fairly low standards of professionalism. Little case law is available to guide consumers and software developers. Instead, intense competition and market forces have forced developers who have sold programs with flaws to make concessions to the users before the issues have been presented in court.[30] One article notes that that

> [i]ncreases in the demand for a diversity of applications by both commercial and retail markets have changed the legal environment of development organizations from the comfortable world of *caveat emptor* toward the high accountability of *caveat venditor* [2 at 26].

Although the pendulum has not yet traveled quite that far, recent developments indicate that a shift, albeit slight, is occurring in the legal landscape that may eventually catch up with the pace of technology and adequately protect consumers without imposing undue burdens on developers.

REFERENCES

[1] Cisco Company (1999). Internet economy tied to internet ecosystem of networked businesses and customer. Press release, 10 June.
[2] Sipior, J. *et al.* (1998). The increasing threat of legal liability for software developers. *Information Resources Management Journal,* **11**(4), 26.
[3] Marciniak, J. (ed.) (1994). *Encyclopedia of Software Engineering.* John Wiley and Sons, 2 volume set, 1994, New York, NY.

[30] For example, when Intuit's TurboTax program displayed errors a few weeks before the 1995 tax deadline, market forces prompted the company to revise and replace the software at no charge to the users. In addition, Intuit agreed to pay any penalties that the Internal Revenue Service assessed as a result of errors in the software [39].

[4] Moskun, J. (1996). Viewpoint: improving software quality requires a "check early, check often" approach. *IEEE Spectrum*, **33**(1), 63.
[5] Black's Law Dictionary (1990). 6th edn., 322.
[6] Vergari, J. and V. Shue, (1991). *Fundamentals of Computer–High Technology Law*.
[7] *Chatlos Sys. v. National Cash Register Corp.*, 479 F. Supp. 738 (D.N.J. 1979).
[8] *RKB Enterp. Inc. v. Ernst & Young*, 182 A. D.2d 971 (N.Y.S.2d 1992).
[9] Restatement (Second) of Torts § 282.
[10] Keeton, W. *et al.* (1984). *Prosser & Keeton on Torts*, 4th edn.
[11] Sherman, P. (1981). *Products liability for the general practitioner*, 4.
[12] *Knight v. United States*, 498 F. Supp 315 (E. D. Mich. 1980).
[13] *Diversified Graphics, Lts. v. Groves*, 868 F.2d 293 (8th Cir. 1989).
[14] *LeSueur Creamery, Inc. v. Haskon, Inc.*, 660 F.2d 342 (8th Cir. 1981).
[15] Restatement (Second) of Torts § 525.
[16] Nimmer, R. T. (1997). *The Law of Computer Technology*, 3rd edn.
[17] *Scala v. Sequor Group, Inc.*, 1995 WL 225625 (S. D. N. Y. April 14, 1995).
[18] *Ritchie Enterp. v. Honeywell Bull, Inc.*, 730 F. Supp. 1041, 1051 (D. Kan. 1990), quoting *Ford Motor Credit Co. v. Suburban Ford*, 699 P.2d 992, cert. denied, 474 U.S. 995 (1985).
[19] *Sparacino v. Andover Controls Corp.*, 592 N. E.2d 431 (Ill. App. 3d 1992).
[20] Boss and Woodward, (1988). Scope of the Uniform Commercial Code: survey of computer law cases. *Business Law*, **43**, 1513.
[21] Rodau, (1986). Computer software: does article 2 of the Uniform Commercial Code apply? *Emory Law Journal*, **35**, 853.
[22] Holmes, (1982). Application of article two of the Uniform Commercial Code to computer system acquisitions. *Rutgers Computer and Technical Law Journal*, **1**, 9.
[23] *Advent Sys., Ltd. v. Unisys Corp.*, 925 F.2d 670 (3d Cir. 1991).
[24] 13 Pa. Const. Stat. Ann. § 1102, comment 1 (Purdon 1984).
[25] *RRX Indus. Inc. v. LabCon, Inc.*, 772 F.2d 543 (9th Cir. 1985).
[26] *Triangle Underwriters, Inc. v. Honeywell, Inc.*, 604 F.2d 737 (2d. Cir. 1979).
[27] NCCUSL (1999). NCCUSL to promulgate freestanding Uniform Computer Information Transactions Act: ALI and NCCUSL announce that legal rules for computer information will not be part of UCC (*www.nccusl.org/pressrel/2brel.html*). Press release, 7 April, 1999
[28] Ring, C. *et al.* (1999). Uniform law for computer info transactions is offered. *National Law Journal*, 30 August.
[29] Miller, F. and Ring, C. (1999). Article 2B's new uniform: a free-standing Computer Information Transactions Act (*www.2bguide.com/docs/nuaa.html*). Downloaded 30 April.
[30] Kaner, C. and Pels, D. (1998). Bad Software 312
[31] Kaner, C. (1999). Closing notes on UCITA. *UCC Bulletin*, October.
[32] Miller, K. and Voas, J. (1999). An Ethical Can of Worms for Software Certifiers, *ITPro Magazine*, **1**(5), 18–20.
[33] Councill, W. T. (1999). Third party testing and the quality of software components. *IEEE Software*, July.
[34] Lawson, D. L. (1983). Failure model, effect, and criticality analysis. In *Electronic Systems Effectiveness and Life Cycle Costing*, ed. J. K. Skwirzynski, NATO ASI Series F3, Springer-Verlag, Heidelberg.
[35] Weiser, M. (1984). *Program slicing. IEEE Transactions on Software Engineering*, **10**(4), 352–357.
[36] Barlow, R. B., Fussell, J. B., and Singpurwalla, N. D. (1975). *Reliability and Fault Tree Analysis: Theoretical and Applied Aspects of System Reliability and Safety Assessment*. Society for Industrial and Applied Mathematics, Philadelphia, PA.

[37] Voas, J. and McGraw, G. (1998). *Software fault injection: inoculating programs against errors.* John Wiley and Sons, New York, NY.

[38] Voas, J. (1998). Analyzing software sensitivity to human error. *Journal of Failure and Lessons Learned in Information Technology Management,* **2**(4), 201–206.

[39] Lewis, P. (1999). The inevitable: death, taxes, bugs. *New York Times,* C1, 24 March.

Author Index

Note – Page numbers in *italics* indicate where a reference is given in full.

Subject Index

Wrappers, results, 493–4
Write–invalidate cache coherence
   mechanism, 24

X

Xerox, 214, 219, 230

XML (eXtensible Markup Language), 248,
   254–6

Y

Yahoo, 214, 250

Contents of Volumes in This Series

ISBN 0-12-012153-0

9 780120 121533

Printed and bound by CPI Group (UK) Ltd, Croydon, CR0 4YY

03/10/2024

01040418-0011